# Handbook of
# Futures
# Research

# HANDBOOK OF FUTURES RESEARCH

## edited by Jib Fowles

**GREENWOOD PRESS**
Westport, Connecticut • London, England

Library of Congress Cataloging in Publication Data

Main entry under title:

Handbook of futures research.

Includes index.
1. Forecasting—Addresses, essays, lectures.
2. Forecasting—Methodology—Addresses, essays,
lectures. I. Fowles, Jib.
CB158.H35          001.4'33          77-84767
ISBN 0-8371-9885-2

Library of Congress Catalog Card Number: 77-84767
ISBN: 0-8371-9885-2

First published in 1978

Greenwood Press, Inc.
51 Riverside Avenue, Westport, Connecticut 06880

Printed in the United States of America

10 9 8 7 6 5 4 3 2 1

For JOY

# Contents

# Preface

Futures research is a new field of endeavor, hardly more than ten years old. Being so young, it is more amorphous than other disciplines and enterprises. Its relative lack of structure, coupled with its most remarkable subject matter, can make futures research appear obscure and puzzling. The present volume is an attempt to explain the aims and content of this field.

The *Handbook of Futures Research* has been compiled with an interested but somewhat uninformed audience in mind. The work is intended for those who are distant from the field, but intrigued, if often skeptical as well, and for those on the margins of futures research who are positively inclined and are looking for an overview. It is also intended for those who already think of themselves as futurists and would like to confirm their impressions of what their colleagues are working on.

It is a commonplace among those engaged in futures research to note that their subject matter does not exist. Once the decision is made to scrutinize the future, there is seemingly nothing to focus on. Yet futurists go ahead and study it anyway. They do this, of course, through their understanding of where the momentum and decisions of the present will lead. Futures research is the effort to anticipate and prepare for the future before it unfolds.

At first glance, it may appear that the work of futurists has the ring of the divinatory, the magical to it. This is not the case, however, for futures research carefully detaches itself from all such considerations. Instead, the focus is on thoughtful, systematic explorations of the future. This orientation is an appropriate one, since a major reason for the existence of this new field is its utility in planning and policy-making. Futures research derives much of its purpose from the aid it can lend decision-makers in the public and private sectors.

Members of other disciplines also attempt to make rational predictions. Meteorologists do quite well at this; earth scientists are coming to predict shifts in the planet's crust; psychological testing foretells the likelihood of some behavior; demographers make statements about upcoming populations; economists too have things to say about the future. But futures researchers differ from all of them because they strain (1) to look further, (2) to look wider, and (3) to look deeper.

In contrast to other disciplines, futures research is founded on long-range perspectives, those of more than five years and frequently of more than twenty-five years. Hence, it pays much greater attention to the dimensions of change, and it places greater emphasis on the way things vary in time than on their composition at the moment.

Second, the scope of futures research is wider than that of other disciplines. Its aim is to have the widest possible purview, and to integrate the greatest possible number of factors, in the belief that the segmentation of knowledge has worked against the understanding of interrelationships. Futures research, then, draws upon as many of the older, established disciplines as it can. Only by looking far afield is it possible to approach a complete understanding of the forces and issues that pertain to a society's movement through time.

What is meant by looking deeper, the third of the attributes of futures research? Futurists are not content just to make far-ranging syntheses and explorations; they also want to reflect on the import of things, so that they can make proper prescriptions. As they mull over the consequences of what they learn may be portending, they arrive at views of what ought to be. Such reflections are the raw material for eventual plans and policies.

These efforts to look forward further in time, take more into account, and arrive at considered judgments about the best course of action are carried out in a sober fashion. The label *futures research* (which has come to replace *futurism, futuristics, futurology,* and other contenders) implies the rational pretensions of the field: "research" alluding to the respect for data-gathering and sense-making that must underlie any serious attempt to grapple with the future; and "futures," in the plural, suggesting that any one of a number of possible alternatives can emerge, depending on the decisions made today. Futurists help to determine which of the multitude of conceivable futures is to be the actual one.

The growth of this new field has been remarkable, if one can judge from the membership figures of the World Future Society, the organization for futurists. Beginning in 1967 with 200 people, the society now has over 25,000 members. Nearly 400 futures courses are being taught in American higher education, and a half-dozen graduate programs have been instituted. Several journals have appeared, including *Futures: The Journal of Forecasting and Planning, Long Range Planning, Technological Forecasting and Social Change,* and the World Future Society's *The Futurist.* The readers of these journals work as futurists in universities, government agencies, consulting firms, and corporations.

Forty-six futurists have authored or co-authored the articles in this book. The *Handbook of Futures Research* is a report by leading futurists on various aspects of their field, some ten years and more after the beginning. The articles are meant to be representative of the matters discussed in the journals futurists read and the conferences they attend. Perhaps the difficulties of futures research have received more consideration here than would normally be the case, but these troublespots are part of the state of the field and cannot be wished away. However, they should be seen in the context of sizable achievements.

A reading of the forty-one articles will reveal a considerable diversity in the approaches of the authors. Some are very attentive to the smallest details of methodology, while others verge on the flamboyant. Some glory in the course of modern life, and others are profoundly alarmed by it. Where it has been possible to place contrasting viewpoints side by side, this has been done.

This lack of consensus, however troubling it may be on first reading, is a sign of the vitality of the field and the resoluteness of futurists. In some ways futurists resemble old-time prospectors. Tending to be ornery by nature, they are likely to strike out in a number of different directions. They risk ridicule as they venture where few are at home, resolved to uncover whatever is of worth. With surprising frequency, what they bring back is of the very highest value.

The need for such ventures grows with every passing day. Futures research has in effect been called into being by these unsettling times. A tepid acknowledgment of the future sufficed when little was in jeopardy, but since World War II there has been unremitting expansion in the capacity of humans to do damage to themselves and to their planet. When everything travels in a flash, all errors are aggrandized. The resulting climate of apprehension means, too, that missed opportunities become much more lamentable. At every level of social organization, from the family and the community through the corporation to the nation and beyond, humans must strive to improve upon conditions of perilous uncertainty.

Futurists are actively responding to this call. It is a difficult and courageous thing they do, when they put their minds to the problem of negotiating what lies ahead. Without them, the chances that humans would lose their way could only increase.

Jib Fowles

# Acknowledgments

Thanks are due to the tens of colleagues with whom I discussed this book. Their thoughts shaped its final form.

The goodwill of the School of Human Sciences at the University of Houston at Clear Lake City has made possible a sustained futures effort there, of which this project is a part. I am also deeply grateful to those associated with the graduate program in Studies of the Future who helped prepare this volume, especially Laura Jessen and Bruce Aunet.

# Handbook of
# Futures
# Research

# Part I

## The Growth of Futures Research

The burgeoning of futures research, a phenomenon in its own right, is the subject of the first three chapters. John McHale, whose scholarly interests have included the evolution of the field, describes the mainstream—its distant historical origins, the postwar ripple, its sudden surge in the 1960s, and its more recent shifts. His final questions on the future of the field receive the fullest response in the very last chapters of the Handbook.

If McHale's view is mainly historical, Eleonora Masini's is more geographical. From her European vantage point, she is aware that France played no less a role than the United States in creating the new field. But it has had a different sort of role in Europe: futures research in America has been more responsive to the private sector than it has been in France and other countries, where it is often tightly linked to the obligations of the national governments. This difference becomes obvious as Masini catalogues the many groups and individuals around the world who are participating in this activity.

Masini's survey is completed with Yujiro Hayashi's description of futures research in Japan. Since Japanese futurists are more likely to understand the language of their colleagues elsewhere than vice versa, awareness of the extent to which futures research has taken hold in Japan is often limited. Hayashi supplies this information.

JOHN McHALE

# The Emergence of Futures Research

The idea of the future is one of the central symbols through which human beings have ordered their present and have given meaning to their past. While futures research in the academic sense is a recent pursuit, conjecture, speculation, and exploration of future events have always been prime features of the human condition. Human survival itself is very largely predicated on the conscious capacity to organize present actions in terms of past experience and future goals.

The historical importance of "futures-casting" in human affairs is demonstrated by the variety of individual and institutional roles that have been accorded this function. In the continuity of such roles, it is no far cry from the gnomic utterances of the tribal shaman, the Delphic oracle, or biblical prophet to the more rationally cast pronouncements of our contemporary forecasters, planners, and political spokesmen.

Today's speculations on the future are no longer confined to private fantasy or literary utopia, nor are they the exclusive province of the fortune teller or computerized prophet. They have come to play an important role in our larger public dialogues. Planning for, and prediction of, the future now absorbs a considerable proportion of the energies invested in our major social institutions. Industrial, governmental, religious, and academic organizations are committed to long-range forecasting and futures exploration for the sake of their own development and that of the society.

To gain some perspective on this new awareness of the future, and of the past and present of "research" into the future, it may be useful to take a cursory bird's-eye view of its emergence.

## PAST FUTURES

Our contemporary outlook on the future is relatively new in human experience. The ascendancy of the future as an object for methodical observation and rational knowledge, rather than divination and propitiation, has its origins in a complex set of social, cultural, and scientific developments.

The idea of the future as more or less a linear progression toward some desirable state was not widely shared historically. Most early societies operated on cyclical or recurrent models of change whose predestined sequences gave little play for human intervention either individually or collectively. Our current paradigm of the possibility of radically different future states dependent upon varying measures of human decision and control may be traced, in part, to several associated historical strands.

The changes inherent in the Greek and Middle Eastern prophetic traditions paved the way for a vision of an unfolding future—one in which human actions became a significant factor for measurable social improvement. Magic was displaced by individual ethical responsibility as the change force in human society. "Change, in short, could be the result of individual purposive action, pitted against the forces of reality, the transfer of the power to change from God to man comes with the concept of possible breaks in the former smooth continuity of time" (Weber, 1946, p. 275).

In more directly historical terms, the two key watersheds from which the futures tradition of the West flows are the Renaissance and the Reformation. Both mark specific changes in the idea of actively shaping the future and of the association of linearly evolving future states with progressive human advances.

From the Renaissance came the development of scientific control over the environment by the systematic derivation of logical principles from the observation and measurement of natural processes. Predictions regarding physical behaviors could be verified by experimental evidence. The future in this sense became logically and demonstrably knowable.

The Reformation, ostensibly a spiritual rebirth, buttressed the change toward materiality and more conscious control over social futures. Individual and collective life was to be ordered economically and organized in the progressive attainment of materially evident grace. The idea of redemptive moral and social progress also came to be marked by the deferment of more immediate gratifications for long-term future gains. The future made material and transcendental claims upon the present. During this period the sense of historical progression itself was reconceptualized from a linear unfolding to a "Vicoan" spiral in which every turn was higher and more advanced than the last.

These shifts toward a more modern future orientation were most clearly articulated during the Enlightenment when rational speculation upon the future of the human condition became the prime vocation of the eighteenth-century philosophers. This period is usually considered to be the formal origin of our contemporary sense of the future, and through its utopian writers such as Mercier, Condorcet, Turgot, and others, it marks the beginning of "futures research." Material progress and the possibility of social betterment had become more physically evident and had, in turn, generated wider expectations among more people. A new social ordering of the benefits of progress was being demanded. These urgings and pressures culminated in the French Revolution, an event which not only shattered the old order of things but typically sought in its latter phases to refashion time itself in a new calendar.

Almost coincident in time, the Industrial Revolution changed the present even more radically through the early application of inanimate energies to mass production of goods and the fusion of scientific and industrial developments. The possibility of a materially better future for all people was given unprecedented physical reality.

The waves of social, economic, and political change incident upon the demise of the old order and the growth of industrial society gave rise to a new generation of "futures" prophets—Saint Simon, Fourier, Comte, and Marx. Their acute awareness both of social disruption and of its potential for reordering society produced a spate of secular and quasisacred views of the future which are still a central force in futures research today. The future both as willed and inevitable emerged as a social imperative in reordering the present.

Although the nineteenth century was characterized by material optimism regarding the future, it also marked the beginning of an estrangement from modern society which persists into our own period. This sense of estrangement was particularly evident in social science concerns about the alienation and anomie incident upon the breakdown of the traditional cohesive bonds of community created by industrialization and the growth of the city. It was more directly evident in the romantic revival of medievalism, in the pre-Raphaelite dreams of Ruskin, Morris, and others, and in the advocacy of a return to the smaller simplicities and old stabilities in the work of monastic utopians such as Fourier. Having been thrust into a new age, many felt a disenchantment and malaise, a sense of having gone too far and too fast, of approaching the bounds of human capacity for change.

This ambivalent attitude toward the future continues into our own period. In the West, it is apparent in the erosion of the belief in the inevitability of material progress, in the rise of the "counterculture," and even in the futures research field itself in studies such as *The Limits to Growth* (Meadows et al., 1972). Paradoxically, concurrent with the intellectual disenchantment with the idea of material progress in the developed world, the lesser developed countries have vigorously embraced many of its concepts. The future is to be created in the present, and for many the prophet of that future is Marx with his particular view of the historical inevitability of specific modes of social progress.

The sense of the future held in the late nineteenth and early twentieth centuries was particularly characterized by the efflorescence of the visionary and utopian novel as exemplified in the work of Jules Verne and H. G. Wells. Though not formally categorized as futures research, this continuing tradition powerfully shapes our conceptual orientations to the future. "We create our literary myths, legends, and epics of the future, not so that we will find our golden age, but because in the creation of utopian standards, we have created forms which make present action possible" (Duncan, 1961, p. 15).

In the area of the visual and performing arts, there were deliberate attempts to break with previous tradition in the creation of an art of the future. The rise of "the modern movement" from the turn of the century is replete with exhortations and speculations about the future. Indeed, the earliest general use of the term *futurism* (Marinetti, 1909) in the 1900s may be found in the work of Marinetti, Boccioni, Sant Elia, and others. This tradition of the new has continued as a major theme in the arts, albeit with little formal relationship to more academic futures exploration.

The most direct large-scale linkage of futures thinking to long-range social and economic planning was the Soviet Five and Ten Year Plans of the 1920s and 1930s. The period between the world wars, however, was largely characterized by the work of such free-lance prophets as Buckminster Fuller, Arthur C. Clarke, William F. Ogburn, and Clifford C. Furnas, and by the background development of projective techniques in other fields such as demography and economics. The wider sense of the future was constrained by the social and economic stresses and dislocations of the time.

The shocks of the future that ushered in present-day futures research were born of the atavistic horrors of an Auschwitz and Buchenwald and the awesome demonstrations of human predilections for self-destruction unleashed at Hiroshima and Nagasaki. The need to take a hard look at the control of human affairs in the longer range developed rapidly from speculative concern to social imperative. The launching of Sputnik in 1957 strengthened the emergence of this new consciousness by circumscribing the fragile bounds of the human planetary habitat. Science and technology had not only created a new reality but had also demonstrated the coexistence and possible choice of many radically different realities—including global catastrophe.

## PRESENT FUTURES

A methodical exploration of the range of socioeconomic, political, and military possibilities contingent upon an abruptly changed world was first begun on a large scale in the postwar period. At this time, futures research per se emerged as a quasiformal discipline.

The early years of futures research were characterized by an increase in the number of academics and other professionals for whom such work became a full-time pursuit and an avocation and, significantly, by the establishment of large industrial-governmental "think-tanks" which devoted a major proportion of their time to futures work. Although institutions such as the RAND Corporation were originally established to study military problems, they have proliferated and their activities have broadened to include a wide range of forecasting in many areas.

In defining the emergence of this increased level of activity, Flechtheim (1966) proposed the term *futurology* as descriptive of a new scientific field of human knowledge. Although the term is still used extensively, it has been criticized by Bertrand de Jouvenel on the basis that, "It would suggest that the results of these activities are scientific— which they are not" (1967). Instead, de Jouvenel emphasizes the role of conjecture in forecasting and suggests the term *futuribles* which distinguishes a future state made plausible or imaginable by new developments. *Futurology, futuribles,* and *futuristics* are now in general and interchangeable use, particularly in Europe, while the term *prognostics* is preferred in the Soviet Union and Eastern Europe. *Futures research* has come to be the preferred academic term for the field, particularly in the United States. Its earlier version, *future research,* was called into question by Calder (1967) on the occasion of the first International Future Research Congress (Jungk and Galtung, 1967):

The term future research is not a happy one . . . [as] it could be taken to mean the future of research instead of research on the future. "Futures research" would be better, not only because it removes the ambiguity but also because it conveys a crucial point: the aim is not to prophesy what the actual future will be but rather to rehearse futures accessible to political choice (Calder, 1967, pp. 345–355).

For the more modest, the term *futures studies* suffices, as implying a more open-ended inquiry while avoiding the more rigorous connotations of "research" with its implications of scientific objectivity and value neutrality.

Current approaches in the field may be summarized as follows:

1. *Descriptive:* including conjectural, speculative, and imaginable modes as in many classical utopian futures.
2. *Exploratory:* forecasting based on methodical and relatively linear extrapolation of past and present developments into the future, i.e., the "logical future," including most technological forecasting, some scenario-building, and the more deterministic types of socioeconomic forecasting.
3. *Prescriptive:* normatively oriented projections of the future in

which explicit value insertions and choices are made about how a specific future may be viewed or attained, i.e., the "willed future."

These categories overlap considerably in actual practice and may be subclassified and interrelated in terms of the range of forecasting employed, the number of variables dealt with, and the methods used.

Activities in the field may also be subcharacterized according to their type and range. *Forecasting* tends to assume some set of definable causal relations between events through which one can predict their future states with varying probabilities of occurrence. It is generally restricted within some *given* value premises as in technological or economic forecasting. *Long-range planning* is usually concerned with five- to ten-year horizons, as in corporate or government planning, and is characterized by *implied* value assumptions, e.g., with how some activity may be planned rather than with why it should be planned. *Futures research* (or studies) tends to be oriented toward the longer term, extending toward the next two or three decades and beyond, and is more concerned with *explicit* sets of value considerations and preferences. Again, these characteristics may be considerably mixed in practice.

In the past ten years, there has been a remarkable upsurge of futures interest both within and outside the field. The number of organizations and individuals concerned primarily with futures research has grown enormously, and the widespread adoption of long-term future perspective by other institutions and organizations has been as spectacular.

A simple index of formal field growth is the size of its world congresses. The first such congress, held in Oslo in 1967, had approximately thirty participants; the second, in Kyoto in 1970, over 250, and the third, in Bucharest in 1972, over 300. Paralleling the growth of these specialized futures research conferences has been that of the annual conferences in other fields such as anthropology, sociology, and political science which have futures sections on their agendas.

Through successive surveys of the field in the past five years, several observations may be made (McHale, 1970; McHale, 1972; McHale and McHale, 1975):

1. The number and range of professionals coming to the field from other areas has risen and changed. Where the earlier predominance was in the physical sciences and mathematics, the more recent expansion has come from the social and behavioral sciences and the humanities.

2. The spectrum of organizations engaged in futures research has widened, with a significantly higher proportion of direct work being done by governments, international agencies, and quasiofficial bodies.

3. Greater professional and general interest is reflected in (a) the increased number of journals and newsletters devoted to forecasting, long-range planning, and futures concerns, and (b) the rise in courses on various aspects of the future being offered at universities and at other educational levels.

4. A pronounced opening up of the field itself has occurred. In the 1960s, futures studies was a relatively small disciplinary enclave. Now it has become a widely publicized area of public interest and even a more generalized social movement that embraces many earlier concerns such as population, ecology, consumerism, and human rights.

The edges of the formally defined field itself have become fuzzy as more organizations and individuals have become involved in the movement.

The reasons for field growth and for the more generalized expansion of futures interest lie in various changes that have occurred, particularly in the past five to ten years. Heavy publicity given by the media to the future dimensions of world crises in population growth, energy, food, and materials supply has turned public concern away from short-range preoccupations toward longer term perspectives. The influence of the media has been reinforced by the world attention and prestige given to the emergence of large-scale studies such as *The Limits to Growth.* The impact of various best-sellers like *Future Shock* by Alvin Toffler has also been considerable. These studies and works have created a large public audience for futures work. They have also circulated a range of public metaphors and images through which people can formulate questions about the future and become aware of their personal preferences for various alternatives.

At another level, concern with the longer range effects and potential consequences of scientific and technological developments has emerged within the scientific community itself. Earlier questions regarding the social responsibility of science with reference to the development of nuclear weapons, chemical and biological warfare, and biological engineering have been cross-impacted with environmental and energy problems, the quality of life issue, and the overall growth debate. The widening of scientific concern has led to more interaction between the physical and social sciences and humanities. The gap between the two cultures tends to be bridged by a set of common anxieties and preoccupations regarding longer range human survival. Futures concerns and more formal futures research groups have therefore begun to be officially recognized at national and international levels.

Much future-oriented work is carried out within the framework of international organizations whose principal mission may be a much wider one. Agencies such as UNESCO, UNITAR, UNEP, and FAO have conducted specific studies on the future of education, on environmental impacts, and on world food supply as appropriate to their mission. Other nongovernmental entities such as the International Council of Scientific Unions make a less direct contribution via programs such as Man in the Biosphere which have long-term prospective viewpoints. Many other nongovernmental organizations, particularly those in the voluntary sector, have conducted symposia and conferences on futures themes relevant to their concerns.

At the national level in Europe, Sweden has attached a Secretariat for the Future to the cabinet office; the Netherlands Central Planning Office has issued reports on the economy in 1980; and France, Germany, and the United Kingdom have futures institutes that work in close cooperation with government agencies. The Organization for Economic Cooperation and Development (OECD) has pioneered a series of studies on various aspects of long-range concern for the European community.

In Eastern Europe and the Soviet Union, which have a longer history of official linkage of long-range planning to policy, most futures research is carried out via their various national academies of sciences. Rumania, Poland, and Czechoslovakia have been particularly active in technological and social forecasting studies.

Considering the leading role that American futures researchers have played in the development of the field, the United States has been less forward in pursuing such work as "official" government business. This may be explained in part by the United States' traditional avoidance of centralized long-range planning and its practice of spreading such work among a variety of nongovernmental institutions. Recently, however, the U.S. Congress has set up the Office of Technology Assessment and has established a futures unit within the Library of Congress to serve legislators in exercising "foresight" on the longer term consequences of legislative actions.

Quasigovernmental activity in the United States has also taken the interesting direction of involving large-scale citizen groups in future speculation at the state and regional level. The pioneer model of this type was Hawaii 2000 (Chaplin and Paige, 1973) which subsequently led to a Governor's Commission on Hawaii 2000. Other state and regional commissions have followed this lead.

A considerable number of industrial corporations headquartered in the United States and elsewhere, particularly the multinational companies, now have their own think-tank operations. These not only explore future products and markets but also study wider socioeconomic issues that may impinge upon their activities (McHale and McHale, 1977).

The role of independent futures research centers and individual workers located in universities and similar institutions around the world has also been, and remains, of key importance in the development of the field. Many of these centers, while responsible for major substantive contributions, are relatively small in terms of personnel and range of financial support. Much of the pioneering work in large-scale multivariate futures projection has been done by such individuals and small groups who are often not funded primarily for such work but support it from other professional activities. As the field gains in interest and acceptance, such a position will become more difficult to maintain. The free-lance prophets tend to be superseded by the contract clairvoyants from the large research organizations.

Of considerable recent significance to futures research, though often not originating within the field itself, has been the recent series of world modeling projects. *The Limits to Growth,* one of the Club of Rome's projects, was deliberately designed to bridge the gap between research of this kind and official policy-making. Other projects in this series now completed are those on *Mankind at the Turning Point* and the RIO studies—*Reshaping the International Order,* and *Goals for Mankind.* The Bariloche Foundation in Argentina has recently completed a normative projection of an egalitarian society, Catastrophe or New Society. The World Order Models Project, initiated by the World Law Fund, has been at work for several years and has reported on its international study teamwork on the exploration of alternative models for world order in the next quarter century.

There are now a variety of membership societies organized around the study of the future. While these societies are not engaged in substantive futures work, they play an important role in encouraging its awareness and in developing its activities. One of the earliest, still extant, is Mankind 2000 which co-sponsored the first international futures research conference in 1967. This society has never attained a large or extensive membership, but it has had an important catalytic function in futures research development. The largest group of this type is the World Future Society, headquartered in the United States. Its membership growth graphically illustrates the increase in awareness of the future; from 200 members in 1967 it increased to 25,000 in 1977. Several other countries now have similar societies, albeit on a somewhat smaller scale. Thus far, of course, much of this associational activity in the futures movement has been centered mainly in the developed countries. Although individuals and institutes in the Third World are involved in overall futures work, it has received less support and funding there. At the international level, the World Futures Studies Federation, which evolved from the 1967 conference, serves as a formal linking agency for exchanging information, organizing meetings and specialized workshops, and generally linking many of the disparate components of the futures research area around the world.

This cursory review of some of the main elements of present futures research may give the impression of a relatively well-established and well-organized field. This could hardly be the case considering the recent formal origins of the field and the variety of its institutional and individual participants. In reality, its organization and its major orientations have considerable weaknesses and discrepancies. One of the field's characteristics, for example, is the dichotomy that exists between the scholar and the activist. On the one hand, there is a continuing move toward increased specialization and professionalism among those engaged primarily in futures research itself or in training others in its academic pursuit. Where this move coincides wholly or in part with official encouragement and support of the field, there is an observably organizational growth in documentation, bibliographical services, and academic programs and courses. On the other hand, there is the expressed need to democratize the whole area of futures inquiry by engaging the broadest and most diverse ranges of people with futures-oriented thinking and action.

Some professionals have sought to avoid this seeming dilemma by attempting to involve a wider range of nonprofessional participants in the "futures creative" process through extended network activities. Others have taken the position that a key role for futures research may lie in "anticipatory democracy"—that is, encouraging both legislators and electorate to engage in cooperative dialogues and activities designed to foster attention to the unforeseen consequences of the policy-making process. In summarizing this debate, one commentator has emphasized "sharpening some of the required hard choices which must be taken by futurists if they want to prevent futures studies from becoming too many things to too great a diversity of persons and thereby degrading it to becoming nothing to all" (Dror, 1974).

No matter how these internal field debates turn out, it seems unlikely (given the proliferation of futures interest and activity within so many social sectors) that the professional futures researcher will be the only, or even the major, source for viable projections and future images through which public policies and other kinds of social navigation will be guided. The potential contribution of futures research to the forward guidance of our institutions and societies is very great.

Given our necessary emphasis on the future, one may conclude with a discussion of the effects of some futures thinking on the present. If future studies were merely an academic exercise, such concern would be of interest but not of larger concern. However, the tendency to link futures work more directly to large-scale social, economic, and technological planning, and thence to binding political legislation, opens up many more questions. In the commitment of present resources to ever longer range goals and purposes, we may need to give more consideration to amortizing both futures and present in terms of what may be wholly temporal constraints or convenient problem solutions. The question that then arises is how far can we justify the sacrifice of present time to the more speculative needs of a future time.

The future of futures research may well lie with the protection of the present from apparent future demands—or, reciprocally, with the conservation of the future from untoward erosion by the present.

## REFERENCES

Calder, Nigel. 1967. "What Is Futures Research?" *New Scientist* (October): 354–55.

Chaplin, George, and Glenn D. Paige. 1973. *Hawaii 2000: Continuing Experiment in Anticipatory Democracy.* Honolulu, Hawaii: University Press of Hawaii.

de Jouvenel, Bertrand. 1967. *The Art of Conjecture.* New York: Basic Books.

Dror, Yehezkel. 1974. "Futures Studies—Quo Vadis?" In *Human Futures: Needs, Societies, Technologies.* Guilford, England: IPC Science and Technology Press.

Duncan, Hugh D. 1961. *Language and Literature in Society.* New York: Bedminster Press.

Flechtheim, Ossip K. 1966. *History and Futurology.* Meisenheim-am-Glau, Germany: Verlag Hain K.G.

Jungk, Robert, and Johan Galtung. 1967. *Mankind 2000.* London: Allen and Unwin.

Marinetti, F. T. 1909. "Futuristic Manifesto." *Le Figaro,* Paris (February 20).

Meadows, Donella, Dennis Meadows, et al. 1972. *The Limits to Growth.* New York: Universe Books.

McHale, John. 1970. *Typological Survey of Futures Research in the U.S.* Center for Integrative Studies, for the National Institute of Mental Health.

———. 1972. *Continuation of Typological Survey of Futures Research in the U.S.* Center for Integrative Studies, for the National Institute of Mental Health.

———, and Magda Cordell McHale. 1975. *Future Studies, An International Survey.* Center for Integrative Studies, for the United Nations Institute for Training and Research.

———, and Magda Cordell McHale, with Guy Streatfield and Laurence Tobias. 1977. *The Futures Directory.* Boulder, Colo.: Westview Press.

Weber, Max. 1946. *Essays in Sociology.* C. W. Mills (ed.). Fairlawn, N.J.: Oxford University Press.

ELEONORA BARBIERI MASINI

# The Global Diffusion
# of Futures Research

In these few pages, I will attempt to provide an overall view of futures studies. It will be just a quick glance because these studies have but a short formal history. This history has been a very intense one, however, for futures studies have rapidly developed in order to meet the challenge of many urgent economic, social, political, and scientific changes. Moreover, the various disciplines involved in the field—including mathematics, sociology, biology, psychology, management science, and philosophy—have made many diverse contributions.

It is worthwhile first to identify the historical motivations of futures studies. (By historical motivations are meant primarily those that have emerged in the last thirty years. We will not attempt the otherwise interesting reconstruction of how these needs made themselves manifest in earlier historical epochs, from the Greek to the Christian, from the preindustrial to the industrial era.) These historical motivations of futures studies can be traced back to the immediate post-World War II period, when mankind sought to tackle the ever quicker and more interrelated transformations taking place, and to identify the future consequences of present actions and thereby avoid being overcome or taken unawares by events.

The endeavor to anticipate events immediately showed itself to be important. These original motivations first developed in the United States. Very soon thereafter, Bertrand de Jouvenel and others in Europe started upon this enterprise of foreseeing alternative possibilities and consequences of actions.

With time it became apparent that it was important to foresee not only in order to know where one was going and how but also to choose where one wanted to go. That is, from the identification of the possible and perhaps probable futures, people progressed to thinking about *desirable* futures. But desirable on the basis of what? On the basis of the individual's choices, or on the basis of choices by groups, cultures, or ideologies? Hence, in the more recent past futures studies have become more or less consciously linked to philosophic choices, to choices of principle, to choices of how one is to regard reality, man, and society. This development came about because of man's awareness, whether conscious or unconscious, that he was living in an era of transformation equal in importance to the Copernican age and the era of the Industrial Revolution.

These studies followed interesting lines of development after World War II. Before embarking on this historical excursion, the concept of futures research will be described in its broad sense. Here it is meant as any reasonably scientific assertion on the choices and consequently on the problems concerning the future. In this sense, futures research includes utopias, efforts at foresight, and technological forecasting, in accord with Jantsch's definition of the concept as "a probabilistic assessment on a relatively high confidence level of future technology transfer" (1967). John McHale speaks of futures research in similar terms: "Futures studies is used to convey the idea of an activity which embraces many elements: prediction, conjecture, imaginative extrapolation, normative projection" (1976).

## THE GROWTH OF FUTURES RESEARCH IN EUROPE

In Europe, the French first studied and investigated the scientific and political foundations of the future. In the last half of the 1950s, Gaston Berger founded a center of "Prospective Studies." The term *Prospective,* as it began to appear in Europe, referred to the making of decisions in response not only to the needs of the moment but also to long-term consequences, viz., with a view to the future.

After Berger's premature death, the economist Pierre Masse continued the Prospective effort. As general commissioner of the French Plan, Masse was responsible for giving prominence to this way of thinking, a prominence that led to the first national plan for 1985. In the same period, Bertrand de Jouvenel gave the movement an extremely important boost through his studies of power, methods of governing, and political choices. The central feature of his thought is precisely the overall dimension of time—past, present, and future—which alone can enable man to function in the political arena. Even today de Jouvenel is working on this research theme; to this end he has founded the Association Internationale de Futuribles which acts as a clearinghouse for research on the future.

The interesting aspect of how this way of thinking has expanded in France is that in recent years forecasting in that country has assumed great importance both in government and in business. In quick sequence BIPE (Bureau d'Information et de Prevision Economique) and CREDOC (Centre de Recherches et de la Documentation sur la Consommation) have emerged. SESAME (Systeme d'Etudes du scheme d'amenagement de la France), also an important organization, is based on the work of Pierre Masse.

On the basis of these institutional supports, which are decidedly unique in Europe even today, many French futurist scholars from various disciplines are operating actively. In addition to those mentioned earlier, they include Jean Fourastie, Jerome Monod, and Jacques Durand, and, in different terms, the demographer Alfred Sauvy, the architect Yona Friedman, and the philosopher Roger Garaudy to whom "everything in existence is a function of the future" (1975). From the philosophical, sociological, or political point of view, it may be stated that France has been the source for futures research both in Europe and for other countries.

Other European countries have made important contributions to the field. In Holland, the sociologist Fred Polak theorized the birth of futures research from an epistemological point of view in his *Prognostics* (1971) and *The Image of the Future* (1973). Between 1966 and 1972, the political establishment in Holland demonstrated some interest in futures studies, even establishing a policy sciences unit in 1974. The work of Jan Tinbergen's group is also extremely important, particularly the report it prepared for the Club of Rome on RIO, the New International Order. This study courageously and directly raises the problems of relations between advanced and less advanced nations in the world. It indicates that the lines for a new international order cannot be solely economic but must be essentially social, based on equality.

Also of interest in Holland is the recent work of the Fondation Europeenne de la Culture, especially in the investigation of lines of forecasting in the fields of education and of urbanization in Europe, using the contributions of many European scholars. Another important study is that directed by H. Linnemann on Food for a Growing World Population, published in 1976 in a final report entitled "MOIR—A Model of International Relations in Agriculture." Overall, group studies in Holland tend toward the long term. They also show a lively interest in the government's operative trends, on which there have been several long-term reports.

In Great Britain, articles written by about 100 authors on forecasts for the coming twenty years appeared in the *New Scientist* in 1964. Articles in the *Ecologist* directed by Edward Goldsmith are also interesting, as is the work of Nobel Prize physicist Dennis Gabor, *Inventing the Future* (1964) and *The Mature Society* (1972). The recent work of the Sussex University Science Policy Research Unit (SPRU) is very important. Apart from presenting criticisms of global models, the unit is attempting to create a theory of futures research with the contribution of an international team. The interdisciplinary character and the relatively young age of the members of the group are intriguing aspects of this work. Recently, the report entitled "Europe 30" appeared. It was prepared by experts in various disciplines and with various methodologies. At the decision of the Council of Ministers Lord Kennet was deputed by the Commission of the European Communities to direct this long-term forecasting work.

The Scandinavian countries have been performing futures studies in recent years both through their governments' long-term forecasts and through research institutes and organizations dedicated to arousing more interest in the future. In Sweden, a working group has been active since 1971 at the behest of former Prime Minister Olaf Palme. The Swedish Secretariat for Futures Studies has already issued a series of reports designed to inform and mold Swedish public opinion. This interesting experiment will assuredly have great influence on the trend toward the democratization of futures studies—above all in Europe. The themes dealt with—working conditions, fuel problems, and the like—are appropriate to the man in the street. Many Swedish individuals and professional groups are also involved in futures studies. Among the most prestigious individuals are Gunnar Myrdal and Lars Ingelstam, who is in charge of the Secretariat.

Norway is attempting to prepare the public for the future by means of TV programs dealing with problems closest to the citizen. The most famous name connected with futures studies in Norway is that of Johan Galtung, now chairman of the World Futures Studies Federation (WFSF) and of the IUC (Inter-University Centre). Apart from an Academy and an Institute of Futures Studies, Denmark has an association which conducts a series of courses. Also at the government level are the various initiatives taken by the Danish Social Science Research Council.

West Germany has a number of institutes in this field, including the Zentrum Berlin für Zukunftsforschung e/V. This institute was founded in 1968 and includes such famous names as Ossip Flechtheim, Robert Jungk, and Helmut Klages. It has now undertaken cooperative activities with the Gesellschaft für Zukunftsfragen e/V in Hanover as well as with the Association of Futures Studies of Hamburg. Futures studies in West Germany are also conducted by the Heidelberg Systemplan; its activity is based on systems analysis and is conducted by capable scholars with special reference to human needs. The Germans have placed great emphasis on the second Club of Rome model, *Mankind at the Turning Point* (1974), prepared by Eduard Pestel of Hanover Technical University in collaboration with Mihajlo Mesarovich of Case Western Reserve University. Hanover University is experimenting with a model proposition regarding the priorities for national research and technology policies for the Bonn Government.

In Austria, IIASA (International Institute for Applied Systems Analysis) in Laxenburg has attained considerable prominence. This institute was created with the financial and scientific cooperation of various national academies, particularly the United States Academy of Arts and Sciences and the Academy of Sciences of the U.S.S.R. The institute's investigations focus on the application of systems analysis to different fields, including the important energy sector. In recent years IIASA has also gained international recognition for the global models drawn up by several institutes for the Mankind at the Turning Point Project, as well as for Catastrophe or New Society, the Latin American world model prepared by the Bariloche Foundation in Argentina, and for the model for agriculture directed by H. Linnemann. Undoubtedly, IIASA and Sussex University's SPRU are today the two greatest centers in the field of futures studies. Austria also has an Association of Futures Studies, under the chairmanship of Gerhart Bruckmann.

In Switzerland, the Swiss Association for Futures Research is very active; its chairman is Bruno Fritsch, an economist. The Battelle Institute in Geneva has conducted, among other projects, the Dematel research for a better understanding of world problems; it has also originated several forecasting studies for European countries.

Futures studies conducted in Greece, Italy, and Spain have been primarily humanistic in nature. In Greece, the Ekistics Group has been involved mainly with problems of human settlements. Its activity was directed by the late C. Doxiadis. Today the journal *Ekistics* has recommenced its activity. There are prospects that a futures studies association may be formed in Greece.

In Italy, Futuribili, linked to the French Futuribles and directed by the late Pietro Ferraro gained the attention of the Italian intellectual world and through its journal, *Futuribili,* promoted considerable understanding of the Italian future. The Agnelli Foundation also made some contributions to the field, as did IRADES (Institute of Applied Research, Documentation, and Studies), which unfortunately has now practically ceased activity. IRADES was the European documentation and information center in the field of futures studies. It published four numbers of *Social Forecasting* concerned with information on institutes, individuals, and publications, and it put together the best European library in this field. IRADES also conducted a number of methodological studies on the philosophical foundations of the international schools of futures studies. Today futures activity in Italy is carried out by the Pio Manzù International Research Centre on Environmental Structures, whose particular aim is to mediate between the technologically advanced societies and developing countries. The Study and Economic Planning Centre has also been active, especially on medium-term projections.

The individuals connected with futures studies in Italy include Silvio Ceccato (cybernetics), Giorgio Nebbia (ecology), and Bruno de Finetti (mathematics). Finetti has promoted these studies in his summer courses at Urbino. A very important name in Italy is that of Aurelio Peccei, who with Alexander King founded the Club of Rome. This group of about eighty members promotes studies and research on the future. It attained world fame through its studies *The Limits to Growth, Mankind at the Turning Point,* the RIO Project (*Reshaping the International Order*), directed by Jan Tinbergen, and *Goals for Mankind,* directed by Ervin Laszlo and published in 1977 in its final form. Laszlo's study compares the aims of different cultures and documents the emergence of a gap between proposed and actual goals. The Club of Rome offers its services to the whole world.

In Spain the Institute of Futures Studies directed by Jesus Moneo held its first meeting with the Club of Rome on the subject of World Alternatives. In past years, some of the scholars in this group engaged in prospective activity in the educational field. Another group in Spain is the Club de Amigos de Futurologia, which for years, under Rosa Menasanch, has campaigned to promote this field in Catalonia.

In addition to the Club of Rome and the International Futuribles Association of France, two other groups with international influence have emerged in Europe—Mankind 2000 and the World Future Studies Federation (WFSF). Both groups were given strong impetus at the first International Future Research Conference held in Oslo in 1967 and organized by the Peace Research Institute. The aim of Mankind 2000 (founded a few years earlier in London) is to promote all aspects of human development in the individual and in groups and emerging world communities. Its offices are in Brussels and its secretary-general is James Wellesley-Wesley. In 1976, it published its *Yearbook of World Problems and Human Potential.*

The need for a World Futures Studies Federation was recognized as far back as the Oslo conference. Subsequently, in Kyoto, at the second International Future Research Conference a number of participants expressed the need to establish a means of contact among workers in the field that would be sufficiently informal to safeguard mutual independence and creativity. At the third Conference in Bucharest in 1972, a recommendation for a federation was made, and in 1973 the WFSF was formally founded in Paris under the chairmanship of Bertrand de Jouvenel. The central purposes of the WFSF are to serve as a forum for the exchange of information through publications, conferences, and meetings, and to focus its members' activities on the study and analysis of human needs.

The socialist countries of Europe merit some special remarks. Hence, we will begin with a discussion of how prognostics (the process that precedes the formation of the plan) has developed in the U.S.S.R.

The foundations of socioeconomic planning are laid in the identification of the regularities of the modern scientific-technological processes. Here the links with Lenin's thought are evident: Lenin made the principles of scientific communism the basis for such planning. According to this school of thought, forecasting is the stage prior to planning, from which forecasting differs in levels of objectivity and complexity but towhich it is necessarily tied. On the basis of a dialectic-materialistic outlook, the future, as distinct from the past and the present, is in principle stochastic and is not a simple projection of the past; indeed, the future contains within itself a large measure of creativity. The socialist countries therefore concentrate on an analysis of the scientific and technological process and on the consequences thereof as elements of social progress.

Two socialist scholars important in the futures field are G. M. Dobrov, who has dealt with these studies in the field of cybernetics; and Igor Bestuzhev-Lada, originally a historian, who through the Institute of Social Sciences of the Russian Academy of Sciences in Moscow has dealt with social prognostics with special reference to the social indicators of long-term changes. Social prognostics deals with methodologies of forecasting as it relates to the social needs and way of life of Soviet citizens. Other centers are located in Kiev, Leningrad, and Novosibirsk. The Faculty of Philosophy and of Social Sciences of the Academy of Sciences seems to be interested mainly in establishing global models of future societies.

Forecasting in the other socialist countries has developed along slightly different lines from those in the U.S.S.R. because of certain unique cultural aspects and sociopolitical developments. Since 1967, Poland has been active through the Poland 2000 group, whose primary interest has been in educative and general cultural forecasts. Its members include many sociologists, psychosociologists, and educators; their emphasis is on the decision-making and planning aspects of forecasting. Another important Polish group is that of the Technical University of Wroclaw, which deals mainly with forecasting methods in the technological and economic field. This group has organized several interesting courses on forecasting methodology. Polish scholars in this field are Bogdan Suchodolski (an educator) and Jan Strzeleky (a sociologist).

Czechoslovakia has a long and important history in the futures field. Radovan Richta (currently in charge of the Institute of Social Sciences of the Czechoslovakian Academy of Sciences) wrote *Civilization at the Crossroads* (1969), which remains an important text in the field. Another notable text has resulted from the work of the Social Prognostics Section—*Man, Science, Technology* (1973). This text was produced in cooperation with the Russian Academy of Sciences and deals with the philosophical basis of prognostics in Marxist terms. It is a unique document for understanding the studies being performed in socialist countries. The definition of forecasting terms on a Marxist basis has aroused great interest worldwide and hence warrants extensive study. These terms have different meanings even in the individual socialist countries. The Social Prognostics Section of the Czechoslovakian Academy of Sciences is attempting to make the definitions comparable, if not similar, on the basis of Marxist theory.

The development of futures studies in Rumania is extremely interesting. The third International Future Research Conference was held in Bucharest and since then interest in these studies has been increasing rapidly. Rumania's International Center of Futures Methodology and Development Studies is an interdisciplinary group (with a preponderance of mathematicians) whose activity largely concerns methodological criticism of present global models. In addition to its studies, this center provides documentation and information, for the purpose of informing the public on problems connected with long-term forecasting.

Hungary also has a social forecasting section in its Academy of Sciences and emphasizes present global models. In addition, the Budapest Technical University offers a course on the philosophical bases of forecasting in Marxist terms.

In Yugoslavia, where socialist humanism has attracted many scholars, forecasting is also framed in different terms from those in other socialist countries. Among the philosophers and sociologists engaged in these studies is Mihajlo Markovic. Yugoslavia's Inter University Centre (IUC) has held several courses on futures studies, and Dubrovnik was the site for the fifth International Future Research Conference.

To conclude this review of futures studies in Europe, it may be stated that these studies are not solely directed at technological or socioeconomic developments. Rather, they are also preoccupied with studying the future of peoples as they are influenced by religion, philosophy, and the arts. This emphasis is apparent in democratic and centralized governments as well as in dictatorial governments. This observation implies that futures research is not fundamentally linked to underlying economic factors but to cultural factors.

## DEVELOPMENT OF FUTURES RESEARCH IN THE UNITED STATES AND CANADA

If it is true, as John and Magda McHale state, that the successful development of futures studies is indicated by the congresses that have been held (1976), then it can be deduced that the United States and, especially in the last two years, Canada have made great strides in the field.

Starting with Canada, the founding meeting of the Canadian Association of Futures Studies was held in February 1976. This organization was formed to coordinate the work of many scholars and groups that had been active in recent years. In view of their extremely heterogeneous character and natural wealth of resources, studies in Canada could take several directions, even different from the ones originally set forth in the field of policies and planning. The two lines of development that are most possible are in public policy and the educational sector. For the moment, however, these studies are inordinately concentrating on Canadian problems as a result of the Canadians' overriding interest in national problems and their difficulty in viewing them in global terms.

Recently, futures efforts have been launched by Canadian government groups such as the Institute for Research on Public Policy, the Economic Council, the Science Council of Canada, Environment Canada, and the Canadian Post Office. Since 1968, the Special Committee on Science Policy of the Canadian Senate, through Senator Lamontagne, has expressed the need to establish a Canadian commission on futures studies with the specific task of involving ordinary citizens. Other groups have worked at the province level, where the strongest development has been in the educational sphere, as promoted both by the OECA (Ontario Educational Communication Authority) and the University of Quebec. The University of Quebec has been quite active for some time in establishing groups.

As regards the United States, it should be pointed out that its futures studies have been thoroughly covered in the literature, especially in the excellent works by John and Magda McHale (1973-1975). Therefore, only the main lines of development will be discussed here.

With regard to specific government interest, it cannot be claimed that much has been accomplished. Precisely for this reason Alvin Toffler's speech before a group of U.S. senators attains great importance: he expressed the need to move toward anticipatory democracy in which ordinary citizens could participate in the discussion and choices of the future. This is perhaps the most interesting turning point in futures studies, which are now tending to involve all citizens, or as McHale says, to become a social movement. An example of this movement is the Hawaii 2000 Project, which for some years has succeeded in involving vast sectors of the population.

In the United States, futures activity was initially the province of experts, e.g., specialized departments of the Department of Defense and of NASA, and offices in the big industrial corporations (General Electric, IBM, Xerox, and the like). These corporations, no longer satisfied with their R&D activity, recognized the need for wider ranging research and investigation, over the longer term. To this end they organized external groups, for example, TEMPO, which was created by General Electric. The RAND Corporation, which performed its first systematic investigations on behalf of the Air Force in 1948, employs forecasting to make decisions more consciously. RAND is now interested in systems analysis and is widening its field of study even further.

The Hudson Institute's activity is linked to that of the RAND Corporation. The Hudson Institute, headed by Herman Kahn, started a forecasting study in connection with defense and then expanded to economic and technological applications of systems analysis, with special reference to technological transfer and innovation. Institutes such as the Stanford Research Institute, Battelle Memorial Institute, and Resources for the Future were established during this postwar period.

As is apparent, futures activity in the United States was originally extra-academic; academics did not take an interest until later. Beginning in 1966, the Commission for the Year 2000 of the American Academy of Arts and Sciences, under Daniel Bell, assembled university professors to study the future.

The United States has made many vital contributions to the Club of Rome's global models, with *The Limits to Growth, Mankind at the Turning Point*, and *Goals for Mankind*. These projects are important because of their global perspectives and their wide dissemination by which the gap between the experts and the public is being bridged. Also important in the United States are the projects of the World Order Fund which are devoted to future world alternatives for the next twenty-five years. Another well-known group is the World Future Society which, through its journal, *The Futurist*, provides specific information regarding the future to the public at large.

There are too many institutes, groups, and individuals engaged in futures studies in the United States to mention them all here. Let it suffice to state that while they are now moving toward global models, greater prescriptive effort, and citizen involvement, they are still heavily committed to refining techniques and methods.

The most prominent names associated with futures research in the United States are John McHale, Theodore Gordon, Olaf Helmer, Elise Boulding, and Buckminster Fuller.

## FUTURES RESEARCH IN OTHER COUNTRIES

Among developing nations, Latin America is undoubtedly one of the most advanced as regards futures studies. For several years Venezuela has been dealing with futures studies through its Centro de Estudios del Futuro de Venezuela, and is now very interested in the application of global models. Brazil only recently started to take an interest, again mainly in global models. Argentina occupies a foremost place in Latin America with its Bariloche Foundation. This group produced the first global model ever formulated by developing countries and is now preparing to develop others which will include studies on the quality of life—a topic that other models have found too complex to consider. The contribution of Mexico has been most important, especially through the influence of President Echeverría on the heads of government in other developing countries. Mexico's Centro de Estudios Económicos e Demográficos is excellent in the field of demography.

Among Asian nations, Japan has been very prominent in the field. In India, for many years individual researchers have dealt with futures studies. For example, the sociologist M. S. Iyengar has posited that India could become a postindustrial society without passing through the industrial stage. J. L. Kapur has described India 2000 and has made some experiments on the use of solar energy in agriculture. Recently, a section of futurology was established in the Department of Science and Technology.

Israel is extremely advanced in the futures field, claiming some of the foremost futurist scholars. Among them are Yehezkel Dror, the methodologist and a rigorous critic of futures studies, and Erika Landau, who has concentrated on youths' perception of the future, carrying out a series of comparative surveys in various countries. The Centre for Technological and Interdisciplinary Forecasting of the University of Tel Aviv is also noteworthy.

Iran has only recently entered the field. The study of the future of literacy and of education in general is very important in Iran today.

Africa is very new to futures studies, in most cases its work being bound up with the French or British influence. Morocco is only just beginning to be active in the field. Tunisia has already proposed its plan for Tunisia 2000, and Algeria has included many futures concepts in its recent law code. Algeria recently hosted a meeting of the Club of Rome for the presentation of the RIO study (*Reshaping the International Order*) to which Algerian scholars made important contributions. French-speaking countries such as Senegal have started studies conducted in the tradition of Gaston Berger. Egypt has several esteemed scholars who are concentrating much of their activity on the problem of natural resources and on conservation. Egypt as well as Iran is starting to apply the Mesarovich-Pestel world model as described in *Mankind at the Turning Point.*

The progress of efforts in the futures field has been more rapid and more concrete in those countries where the future must be rapidly created rather than studied, foreseen, or anticipated. This acceleration

and concreteness demonstrate the different approaches of these countries, which reflect cultural aspects rather than economic and social
situations.

In this regard, the general observations of some of the futurists of
developing countries should be considered here. These thinkers emphasize that Western scholars study the future through a search for
common bases and universal elements. This approach, they claim, is
not sufficient; indeed, any true study of the future must proceed on the
principle of heterogeneity, not uniformity. That is, the goals toward
which present actions should be oriented must be taken into account,
always bearing in mind cultural diversities.

Trends toward a logic in which the main elements are quantity as the
principle of measurement and hierarchy as the criterion of order com-
pel a new logic based on principles that have been valid for centuries.
Asian principles of interaction and of quality, all of which are capable of
leading to a harmonic and complex order, can be the basis of the new
system. Unidirectional causality does not exist in this kind of futures
studies; there is rather an appreciation of a harmony of dissimilar
elements.

## INDICATIONS OF FUTURE GROWTH

Clearly, the development of futures studies on the global level has
been closely connected with the sociopolitical changes of the past thirty
years. Futures studies have almost always shown a susceptibility to
feedback from the sociocultural context in which they were, if not
inserted, at least developed. On this basis, it is perhaps possible to
foresee the subsequent development of these studies.

As we have seen, in Europe interest in these studies spread mainly
from France to the Scandinavian countries and a number of socialist
countries. The motivations for undertaking these studies are diverse:
the Scandinavian countries are attempting to encourage their people to
participate in choosing the future, while the socialist countries apparently want to clarify their objectives and consequently to plan the
future. In view of political and cultural requirements as well as economic needs most northern European countries will increasingly expand their futures research. Nationalism will likely be subordinated in
the quest for international and perhaps supranational order, through
such bodies as OECD, FAO, and other UN suborganizations.

The socialist countries of Europe will probably continue to refine
their methods and to define their terminology. They will retain their own
peculiar characteristics, and will have increased exchange with the
West on the subject of global models. It can be foreseen that to a

degree these socialist countries will approach certain emergent nations, especially in Africa.

The Mediterranean countries will seek common futures on common cultural bases and will constitute a counterforce to northern European countries.

With regard to the developing countries, it may be foreseen that they will use futures studies to discover a development process different from the Western one, even if it is based on technological development, but whose stages are chosen in terms of local needs rather than determined from outside, as has hitherto been the case. Undoubtedly, North American studies will have greater influence in Latin America, through international organs. Asia will attempt to link up more with the European tradition than with the American.

The content of futures studies will increasingly take account of the real requirements of man individually and socially, and not simply extrapolate from the present. That is, attempts will be made to clarify the normative aspects of these studies.

Finally, futures studies will devote themselves more to the public in general, stimulating an increase in the "man in the street's" capacity to assess and choose his own future. In these terms, the future of futures studies is very close to that for which Alvin Toffler is fighting: anticipatory democracy with all the diversity that this concept entails.

## REFERENCES

Bradley, Robert. 1976. "Future Studies in Canada." *Futures,* Volume 8, Number 2 (April), 185–190.

Gabor, Dennis. 1964. *Inventing the Future.* New York: Alfred A. Knopf.

———. 1972. *The Mature Society.* New York: Praeger Publishers.

Garaudy, Roger. 1975. *Parole d'Homme.* Paris: Robert Laffont.

Jantsch, Erich. 1967. *Technological Forecasting in Perspective.* Paris: Organisation for Economic Co-operation and Development.

McHale, John, and Magda McHale. 1973. "The Changing Patterns of Futures Studies in the USA." *Futures,* Volume 5, Number 3 (June), 130–141.

———. 1975. *Future Studies: An International Survey.* Center for Integrative Studies, for the United Nations Institute for Training and Research.

———. 1976. "An Assessment of Futures Studies Worldwide." *Futures,* Volume 8, Number 2 (April), 135–145.

Mesarovic, Mihajlo, and Eduard Pestel. 1974. *Mankind at the Turning Point: The Second Report to the Club of Rome.* New York: E. P. Dutton.

Polak, Fred. 1971. *Prognostics.* New York: Elsevier.

———. 1973. *The Image of the Future.* San Francisco: Jossey-Bass.

Richta, Radovan. 1969. *Civilization at the Crossroads.* New York: International Arts and Sciences Press.

YUJIRO HAYASHI

# Futures Research in Japan

## THE BIRTH OF FUTURES RESEARCH

Since World War II, Japan's rapid technological development has resulted in both quantitative and qualitative changes in Japanese society. The government and private enterprises as well as individuals have found it increasingly difficult to make prompt and effective decisions in the face of these changing conditions and have begun to regard the future with a vague feeling of anxiety.

Japan's modern economic development began with the Meiji Restoration (1868); the developed countries at that time were regarded as models of growth. Thanks to her rapid progress since World War II, Japan has now succeeded in joining them. As a result, Japan can no longer model her future self-image on the present state of other nations and now must create her own new society.

After the war, Japan formulated several broad plans, mostly economic plans. Then a demand arose for more vigorous research and prediction of the uncertain future, and the need for long-range planning based on predictions was soon recognized. At this same time, the computer revolutionized the collection and processing of information and made possible the prediction of the future with considerable accuracy. Under these circumstances, in the 1960s the government, aiming at a harmonious development of society, set to work on plans and visions based on predictions. In August 1960, the government published "Long Range Prospects of the Japanese Economy," a forerunner in futures research, and soon after worked out "The Income-Doubling Plan." Through the momentum provided by these works, a common recognition about futures research was born among central and local governmental organizations as well as in industry and academic circles. The government organized both the National Life Council and the Comprehensive National Land Development Council, and started to deliberate on a future image of national life and on a comprehensive plan for national land development. As a result of these efforts, "The Future Life of People—Vision of Twenty Years Ahead" was published in November 1966 and "A New Comprehensive National Development Plan" in September 1969. Since these councils were operating independently of each other, a need was felt for constructing a long-range vision that would synthesize all of these activities. With this aim in view, an informal seminar on future prediction was started in 1965, consisting of the section heads of the Economic Planning Agency and led by the author, who was then the director of the Economic Research Institute of the agency. After six months of discussion, the seminar issued a report, "Japan in Twenty Years." The content of the report was quite speculative, owing partly to the informal nature of the seminar. Nonetheless, it served as a springboard for the later development of futurology. With the vision found in this report as an impetus, the popular press started to feature futures research, and a futurology boom was created.

## THE INFANCY OF FUTURES RESEARCH

The period between 1965 and 1970 was the infancy of futures research in Japan. A rosy futurology was in vogue as views and visions of a splendid future were expressed. The press focused only on the popular and optimistic aspects of futures research. Especially in 1970 when the World Exposition was held in Osaka, the whole nation seemed to look forward to a happy future.

In May 1967, the Futurology Association, a voluntary, club-like association, was organized. In July of the same year, the first symposium on futurology in Japan was held under the auspices of the Union of Japanese Scientists and Engineers; the title of the symposium was "A Start for Futures Research." The symposium was held in response to the following points previously raised:

1. The current active discussion of the future was a necessary outcome of the demands of the time.
2. Science and technology had the leading role in the discussion of the future in the sense that they had motivated the discussion and had provided the method of inquiry.
3. To bring about the sound development of science and technology was the best means of insuring mankind's tomorrow.
4. In order to achieve the above goal, it was necessary to adopt a wider perspective and a comprehensive and systematic approach incorporating social sciences as well as science and technology.
5. The first step in this direction was to organize an extensive cooperative research effort to be undertaken by researchers from various fields so as to provide a forum for discussion.

In this symposium, some sixty participants from a wide variety of backgrounds engaged in ardent discussions of the future. Major emphases were on (1) clarification of future-related problems in each field, (2) discussion of methodological and organizational issues in view of coping with those problems, and (3) thereby, a systematization of an approach to futurology. The topics and authors of the papers read were as follows:

Direction and Location of Futurology as a Science by Yujiro Hayashi
A New Environment for Man (Futurology and Social Technology) by Kenichi Kohyama
An Anthropologist's View on Futurology by Eiichiro Ishida
The Futurology of Man-Machine Systems by Masamitsu Ohshima
Future Aspect of Space Physiology by Hisashi Saeki
Future Aspect of Urban Design by Noboru Kawazoe
Future of Information Technology by Zenichi Kiyasu
For the Technological Development after 10 Years (Future of Engineering Technology in Japanese Industry) by Junnosuke Kishida

Through this symposium, communication among various fields was organized, different positions and approaches to the future were presented, and the dimensions of futurology were recognized. In July 1968, the association held a second nationwide symposium on futurology, to discuss "Structuring Futurology." In this symposium, topics not discussed in the first symposium (e.g., international politics) were added to the list. The topics and authors of the papers read were as follows:

Conditions of Future Prediction by Yujiro Hayashi
Education by Kikuo Nishida
Medical Services and Related Problems by Kosei Takahashi
Future of Resources by Noriyuki Sakikawa
International Relations by Masataka Kohsaka
Languages by Toshiyuki Sakai
Society in the Early 21st Century by Jiro Sakamoto
Business and Management in the Next Generation by Kazuo Noda
Special Lecture: Integrated Prediction of Future and Management by Koji Kobayashi

By this time, the futurology boom was not a phenomenon limited to Japan but was worldwide, and international cooperation in futurology had begun. In September 1967, the First International Future Research Conference with the theme "Mankind and Society in 2000" was held in Oslo, Norway, under the auspices of Mankind 2000; three Japanese representatives, including the author, attended it. At this conference, it was decided that the second conference would be held in Japan. Also in September of that year, the international conference entitled "The

World in 2000," the first international futurology conference in Japan, was held under the auspices of the Japan Economic Research Center. The participants came from the United States, England, France, and Poland, and included Nobel prize winner Dennis Gabor. The reports presented by Japanese participants were as follows:

> Future of the World and Asia by Saburo Ohkita, Akira Ohnishi, and Shinkichi Eto
> Prospects of Changing Society in Japan by Kenichi Kohyama
> Japanese Economy of the 21st Century by Jiro Sakamoto

These reports unanimously pointed out that "a very broad approach should be taken in discussing the future of Japan and that the future of Japan, at least, could not be predicted by a mere extrapolation of the present."

Simultaneously with such developments, the need and importance of futures research began to be more generally realized in the scholarly community. It was also recognized that in order for futurology to receive proper recognition as a comprehensive discipline, it had to establish and systematize its own methodology, adopt a comprehensive and organized approach with an extensive perspective, and create a center for cooperative research. As mentioned earlier, it had been decided at the first World Conference in September 1967 that the second conference would be held in Japan, and the matter of finding a host organization was now pending.

So it was that the Japan Society of Futurology was created in July 1968. Its objectives were to promote theoretical and practical studies of problems related to prediction, planning, and control of society in the future through the cooperation of researchers in various fields; to deepen and systematize the methodology of futures research; and to organize and synthesize that research. The establishment of the society coincided with the centennial of the Meiji Restoration.

The Japan Society of Futurology, an association for futures research, serves as a national center and has a varied membership. Through its membership it is able to conduct extensive research; the disadvantage of its multidisciplinary character is that focus is sometimes lost. Futures research in Japan is broadly based, reflecting the society's characteristic broadness of vision. Its futures research is also characterized by the coexistence of ideological (normative studies incorporating liberal ideas) and scientific futures research (exploratory studies with emphasis on logical aspects).

The first meeting of the Japan Society of Futurology, entitled "Scientists' Role in the Face of the Future," was held in December 1968; its second meeting, held in March 1969, was entitled "Mankind's Future."

Among the participants at the second meeting was Dr. Johan Galtung, director of the International Peace Research Institute in Norway. These two meetings covered a wide variety of topics, including economics, sociology, engineering, medicine, the environment, and education.

At an early date, the society began to promote international exchange. In September 1968, two months after it was founded, a Japanese-U.S. joint symposium was held on "Perspectives on Post-Industrial Society" under the auspices of the Japan Techno-Economic Society and the Commission on the Year 2000 of the Academy of Arts and Sciences. The topics and authors of the papers read were as follows:

> The World of the 21st Century by Junnosuke Kishida
> Information Centered Society by Yujiro Hayashi
> Measurement of Knowledge and Technology by Daniel Bell
> How Technology Will Shape the Future by Emmanuel Mesthene
> Technological Innovation and Future Industry by Noboru Makino
> Supra-Technological Society and the Information-Centered City by Kisho Kurokawa
> Technology and Social Change by Donald A. Schon
> Pattern Dynamics by Shoji Makishima
> Information Innovation by Hajime Karatsu
> Life Science and the Future Society by Kazuhiko Tatsumi
> Information Innovation by Nicholas Johnson

In April 1970, the year of the World Exposition, the Second International Future Research Conference with the theme "Challenges from the Future" was held in Kyoto, sponsored by the Japan Society of Futurology. Twenty-eight organizations from twenty-seven countries—not only Western but also Asian and socialist countries—participated. This conference was the first of its kind anywhere both in scale and in the wide range of topics covered. The participant organizations presented their research and exchanged information on futurology. The futures research of the 1960s was summarized, and there were extensive discussions on future subjects of research and international cooperation. The discussions encompassed the following topics:

> The Role of Futures Research
> Research Methodology
> Technological Innovations and Social Change
> Education for the Future
> Environmental Changes—Time and Space
> New Values: New Man
> Social Systems and Social Innovation
> World Futures

One of the major contributions of the Kyoto conference was that it gave an overview of futures research—both through the participation of scholars and researchers from differing fields of specialization and through the wide range of topics discussed. The Japanese participants presented a paper as a team, giving a fine example of the interdisciplinary research approach. At the conference, it was newly and widely recognized that mankind in the second half of the twentieth century must meet the challenges of the future. It was also recognized that numerous researchers throughout the world were helping to foster friendships and understanding that transcended national interests.

## THE GROWTH PERIOD OF FUTURES RESEARCH

Several years after the futurology boom, pollution problems became widely evident. The rapid growth of an economy sustained by the phenomenal development of scientific techniques had produced problems such as pollution and a shortage of resources and energy. In the face of these problems, we must now cope with the task of reevaluating today's society and constructing a creative vision of what a future society is to be. As a consequence of this new reality, the expectations and assessment of the future have undergone considerable change; the enthusiasm about a rosy future has dwindled, and the press has started to criticize futures research, speaking now of "murky futurology." An optimistic projection of the future by extrapolation has turned out to be unreal, and a depressed outlook on the future has become prevalent. Futures research has begun to shift from purely academic theories and scholars' personal comments to practical and organized research.

In the 1970s, some think-tanks were set up in response to the demands of the time, and problem-solving research was instigated. The Institute for Future Technology was established in February 1971 to approach the future from a purely technological viewpoint with disinterested and neutral principles. The institute is working on the problem of how to relate modern technology to mankind's real happiness, with the hope of developing a new field that might be called "soft science" or "soft technology." The major area of research is technology which touches on forecasting, the complex of environment-resources-energy, technology assessment, informationalization, and telecommunication. Steady progress has been made both in research activities and in the organization of research systems.

Another think-tank, the National Institute for Research Advancement, was established in March 1974. It consists of representatives from the central and local governments, business, academia, and labor. The purpose of the organization is to promote comprehensive research and development from an independent standpoint and to contribute to the welfare of the people. The organization is a unique foundation which has taken on the task of promoting comprehensive research. Its research topics are related to problems of modern society and they are typically of a problem-solving, policy-oriented, and inter-disciplinary type. The ongoing large-scale projects are The 21st Century Project and Energy Project.

Now that Japan has entered a slow-growth phase, the activities of the think-tanks have also slowed. While problems concerning the system for conducting research (personnel, research facilities, research cost, and the like) still exist, longer research periods, greater research cost, and more full-scale research projects have become prevalent. This suggests that the present is merely a transient period that will culminate in the stabilization of think-tank research.

The Japan Society of Futurology concerned itself with problems of pollution even before 1970. It has continued to make steady efforts in this area and now has 250 members. The activities of the society since 1970 are as follows:

The 3rd Symposium, November 1971, "A Vision of the 1980s"
The 4th Symposium, December 1972, "Trends in Research Activities of Think-Tanks"
The 5th Symposium, November 1974, "The Future of Education"
The 6th Symposium, December 1975, "Nature and Society"
The 7th Symposium, May 1976, "The Future of Man's Environment"

The following is a list of the symposia on futures research held in Japan since 1970:

| | | |
|---|---|---|
| Technology Prediction Symposium | April 1972 | The Japan Techno-Economics Society |
| Technology for Social Development (international symposium) | December 1972 | The Institute for Future Technology |
| In Quest for a New World Image (the Club of Rome symposium of 1973) | October 1973 | Japanese Committee of the Club of Rome |
| Proposal from the 21st Century | October 1974 | Ministry of Foreign Affairs |
| World and Japan Tomorrow (international symposium) | October 1974 | Yomiuri Newspaper Company |
| International Technology Assessment Symposium (international symposium) | November 1974 | The Japan Techno-Economics Society |

| New Technology in Industrial Society (international symposium) | April 1975 | Goethe Institute |
| Industry and Society— for their development (international symposium) | October 1975 | Ministry of International Trade and Industry |

Futures research in Japan has progressed from an initial concern with economic issues to technological, environmental, and ecological research. It has been elaborated through newly developed methods for prediction and planning. An interdisciplinary orientation has become clearer, and futurology has grown to be a new, comprehensive, academic discipline transcending the sectionalism of overly specialized academic fields. With the development of organizations and think-tanks for futures research such as the Japan Society of Futurology, the state of futures research in Japan may be summarized as having finally attained a stable basis.

# Part II

# The Difficulties of Futures Research

"It is a truism that the future is largely unknowable," begins Roy Amara's introductory chapter. This is the paramount, but only the first, of the practical and philosophical difficulties that hamper the work of futurists.

Although largely unknowable, the future is not *entirely* unknowable. Futures research represents a foothold upon the strange territory of things to come. That the foothold is worth the winning is the first of Amara's points; what subsequent objectives might be, and how they can be approached procedurally, occupy the following pages. By laying out what is reasonable for futures research, Amara establishes a context for appreciating the impediments, as described in the subsequent articles in this section.

The approaches which Amara mentions for probing the future appear to be sound in principle, but according to Ida Hoos, in actuality they fall far short of the ideal. She examines the lineage of some of these methods (which are more fully described in the next section of the Handbook), as well as the quality of the data futurists are likely to use, and concludes that futures research is methodologically impoverished.

Not only are the methods of futures research fallible but so are the futurists themselves. Like other humans, futurists come to their tasks with biases and blindnesses that prejudice their efforts. Some of these predilections are generic to the profession, Ian Miles writes in "The Ideologies of Futurists." While other observers might feel that these prejudices lie along the lines of too little science and too much wishful thinking, Miles looks harder and comes to a different conclusion. He accuses futurists of an incautious reliance on science and technology, and an overestimation of Western civilization. This points to an elitism among futurists, Miles says, which must be remedied if the fullness of the future is to be understood.

But even if clear-headed futurists were to work with impeccable methods, knowledge of the future would still be elusive, since the actions of humans can operate to make false predictions true and true predictions false. That is, forecasts can be self-fulfilling (as when a predicted bank failure leads to a run on the bank which produces a failure) or self-defeating (as in the case of the predicted loser in an election getting enough "underdog" votes to win). Richard Henshel labels these "self-altering predictions." Although Henshel is unsure whether or not self-altering predictions are features of the largest scale historical processes, he argues that they do pertain to many of the matters that engage futurists. "Students of the future ignore the self-altering prophecy at their peril," he states.

Should self-altering predictions be allowed for, and satisfactory forecasts be made (or better put, satisfactory forecasts of the range of likelihoods for the future be made), then another vexing problem intrudes when plans or policies are constructed on the basis of those forecasts. Plans initiated now are grounded in current values, but since values fluctuate in time, there is bound to be some discrepancy between the values implicit in the plan and the values of those who will be the eventual subjects of the plan. "The Problem of Values in Futures Research" argues that long-range plans may turn out to be offensive to the people who have to live with them, through no fault of the initial forecasting and planning effort.

ROY AMARA

# Probing the Future

It is a truism that the future is largely unknowable. Almost by definition, the future is necessarily characterized by considerable uncertainties, and, as a result, it can be "examined" only by the most circumspect and indirect ways. Normally, the familiar tools of scientific investigation can be applied only in their most primitive forms.

## THREE ESSENTIAL QUESTIONS

Notwithstanding the acknowledged limitations of probing the future, the interest in doing so—and the recognition of the urgent necessity to do so—are growing steadily for several reasons. First, we do not like what we see around us—the diminishing returns of increasing consumption, loss in quality of life, threats of nuclear terrorism, famine, collapse of the international monetary system. We wonder whether we might not have managed our affairs more effectively. Also, we seem to have lost our sense of steering, to have lost our guiding "images of the future," at the very time that our individual and collective actions influence our environment to a greater extent than ever before. Third, because everything seems to be changing more rapidly than ever before, we wonder about the extent to which we are in control. And, finally, we seem to have entered a new stage of national and global development in which alternative growth patterns must be much more carefully considered before choices are made.

These circumstances—the acknowledged limitations of futures probing and the increasing necessity for dealing with the future more effectively—generate somewhat opposing forces. If, in fact, the future is "closing in" on us, so that what was formerly considered the long term now becomes the shorter term, so that the pace of change seemingly compresses years into months, so that the whole process of change becomes infinitely more complex to understand, then perhaps our best response is to temporize. To stay flexible, to monitor, to lay contingency plans, and to respond to the threat or opportunity of the moment may not be an altogether poor strategy. If it becomes the sole or dominant response, however, surely the battle is lost. For as the future "moves in" on us, we must also try to confront it on its own terms. We must be more systematic, more searching, and more skillful in addressing three essential questions:

1. What choices do I have? (the art of the possible)
2. What do I know? (the science of the probable)
3. What do I prefer? (the politics of the preferable)

Only then can we gradually regain the initiative, arming ourselves to prepare for the long pull as we struggle with the emergencies of the moment.

## THINKING ABOUT THE FUTURE—THE OBJECTIVES

Thinking about the future is, at best, a very chancy undertaking. What then is the point? There are several objectives, none of which includes "prediction." Six are particularly noteworthy.

The first is to identify and examine *alternative* futures. In a sense, the examination of alternatives is contrary to the notion of prediction and the implication of a single and predetermined or predestined future. The stress is rather on possible developments and their related choice and goal structures, on the essentially unfocused and evolving array of paths we may travel. This notion is simple and almost obvious, but very frequently it is nearly ignored.

The second objective is to characterize the degree of *uncertainty* associated with each possibility or alternative future. Clearly, some futures are more likely than others. Any useful explanation of the future must attempt to define the nature and degree of uncertainty by focusing on the factors that can modify these uncertainties. Such efforts often represent an early stage of modeling.

The third objective is to identify key areas which are *precursors* or *warnings* of particular futures. Basically, we are interested in receiving as many advanced clues as possible about developing changes. We want to know what to look for, what to monitor, what early warning signals to detect. We would like to minimize surprises of any kind.

Fourth, we want to examine a variety of "*if . . . then*" sequences. This objective often projects us into the realm of scenario generation or gaming-simulation. Another way to describe the process is "contingency planning." Whatever the rubric, the essential notion is to explore a range of outcomes or consequences that may have an impact on us.

A fifth objective is to acquire an understanding of the *underlying processes of change.* Because our understanding is often inadequate for forecasting outcomes with any degree of certainty (because of the importance of unexpected and chance events or developments), emphasis must necessarily be placed on trying to understand the nature or the rules of the game. What kind of basic processes are at work? How can they be described and characterized?

Finally, the sixth objective is to sharpen our knowledge and understanding of our *preferences.* It is usually difficult for us to gauge our cost, time, and risk preferences. What trade-offs are we willing to make and what is the nature of these trade-offs? How heavily should we discount possible future benefits or detriments? How much are we willing to risk in achieving specified objectives?

All of these objectives highlight the inappropriateness of any emphasis on predicting, or even forecasting, when we set out to explore the future. There is, of course, a natural human desire to eliminate uncertainty altogether or to think in terms of predestined outcomes. Science and technology have also provided a somewhat inappropriate model with scientific prediction, based on well-established observations and validated theories. But in exploring the future of individuals and societies, we are dealing with systems much too complex and outcomes far too dependent on too many uncontrollable external forces for prediction to be a realizable end objective.

## PAST, PRESENT, FUTURE

As has already been noted, the most general distinguishing feature of the future is its uncertainty. After all, we are dealing with what may be rather than what is or has been. But, on further thought, even this distinction is, to some extent, a difference of degree rather than kind.

Our knowledge of the past is also characterized by uncertainty— uncertainty both about what took place and about the underlying forces governing the key events and developments. This is not to say that there is a complete symmetry between the past and the future. The asymmetry is the result of the existence of traces and witnesses of the past. Traces (written records, tools, fossils) are the grist for the historian who tries to piece together from the present what was or might have been. Likewise, living witnesses give direct experiential or intuitive information about the recent past. The future, by definition, has neither traces nor witnesses in this sense.

Nevertheless, there is a striking similarity in the uncertainty of past and future. In spite of the efforts of social historians, anthropologists, geologists, and archaeologists to reduce the uncertainty by probing and analyzing the past, there are almost always alternative theories or models about the meaning of their evidence. Thus, we may think of "alternative pasts" as we do of "alternative futures." Our picture of these alternative pasts and futures may be as dependent on changes in perceptions of available data as on the acquisition of new data.

But what of the present? What is its relationship to the past and the future? We know that the present is always characterized by its share (often quite large) of uncertainty. Even for the small time/space slice that envelops each of us in our direct contacts with the world around us, our state of knowledge is almost never so complete that alternative models, alternative traces, or alternative witnesses (including our own witnessing) may not compete for attention. It is true that these traces and witnesses are "fresher" and often more complete than if we are dealing with a more distant past, but in all cases, our task is the same: we must piece together our knowledge and understanding of what is (or what was or what may be).

We have used the terms *traces, witnesses,* and *models.* It is useful to sharpen these definitions and to organize them into a more coherent framework. First, however, let us define the terms *past, present,* and *future* more precisely. For our purposes, the primary distinction will be made between the past (recent and distant) and the future. The recent past will begin with the present and extend back to about 100 years (or well within the purview of living witnesses). The distant past will begin where the recent past ends and will extend back to the infinite past. The future will begin with the present and range to the infinite future. In this schema, the present exists only as a transitory process between the recent past and the future. These definitions are arbitrary, but they provide a framework for illustrating the basic methods of viewing the future.

We can compare the tools available for understanding the distant past, the recent past, and the future (traces, witnesses, and models) by constructing a simple 3 × 3 matrix as shown in Table 1. This matrix reveals what we already knew. The recent past can be probed with a greater variety of tools than either the distant past or the future. Thus, in exploring the future, we must not only focus on modeling methods but we must also develop methods that can act as surrogates for traces and witnesses. Let us consider each of these possibilities in more detail.

## MODELING THE FUTURE

In our daily lives, each of us constructs and deals with models of various kinds—usually unknowingly and without characterizing the processes as such. Simply defined, a model is a representation of a thing or process. Perhaps the most familiar models are physical ones: a model of an airplane, a building, or a geographic region. The simplest

**TABLE 1**

| TIME FRAME | METHOD | | |
|---|---|---|---|
| | MODEL | TRACE | WITNESS |
| Recent Past (−100 years → 0) | Yes | Yes | Yes |
| Distant Past (−∞ → −100 years) | Yes | Yes | No |
| Future (0 → ∞) | Yes | No | No |

models are static; that is, they do not try to represent changes over time. As models deal more explicitly with time or uncertainty, they become more complex. But whether physical or mental, simple or complex, models should not be viewed as substitutes for the thing or process itself. They are representations, and their principal value is in helping us to understand how the real thing or process is structured or works. Their success depends on the skill with which we abstract from the thing or process represented.

In constructing useful models, a necessary first step is continued and repeated observation. If the object of modeling is a thing, the observations must clearly focus on physical features. Initially, the observations may be poorly organized and carried around simply in one's head. Many of our "models" are this type of mental model, incompletely and poorly formulated so that we are hardly aware they exist. When a mental model is transformed into prose or even a picture of some kind, it becomes a descriptive model. At this stage, we not only become fully aware of how we are abstracting from the world around us but we are also able to communicate with others using the model or to communicate about the model. The third and most complex stage of modeling is the definition of interrelationships among the major components of the model, expressed in the form of equations using deterministic, probabilistic, or time-dependent descriptors.

In using models to help think about the future, we are usually interested in describing and understanding processes of change. Here the observations must include not only physical features but also their changes with time. Perhaps this process can best be illustrated by examining how useful models of the solar system were developed. Over a very long period of time, an enormous number of observations of the motions of the other planets, the moon, the sun, and the stars were made. Gradually, these were built into a coherent framework that would serve to describe the past and also forecast the future motions of the sun, moon, and planets. In fact, the Ptolemaic theory did just this in terms of the rotation (cycles and epicycles) of the other planets and the sun around the earth. For nearly two millennia, this model, representing physical motion in mathematical terms, served well as a framework for analysis and speculation. The fact that it ultimately proved to be an incorrect representation of the physical process should also be noted. Even though it appeared to describe and explain the observations then available, as time went on the representation became increasingly complex and cumbersome in the light of additional data. An alternative concept or model, the Copernican model, gradually became accepted as a more accurate and valid representation.

Many other useful physical models exist. There are aerodynamic, chemical process, transportation system, urban, and ecological models, and many, many more. They are not, however, equally valid or useful because the level and depth of understanding of underlying processes in each case varies. When we attempt to model nonphysical processes—economic, social, political—we realize that our knowledge and understanding of the important system variables and how they are interrelated are inadequate and incomplete. Thus, while such models may be useful tools for assisting us in organizing our thinking, for making assumptions explicit, and for communicating with others (Meadows, et al., 1972), their usefulness as forecasting tools is severely limited. In such instances, the structuring and use of models must contain a large component of human intervention, judgment, and input—often in the form of games or simulations. In this context, a simulation involves the exercise or run of a model, and a game is a model in which at least one human player determines strategies and choices.

## "DISCOVERING" TRACES OF THE FUTURE

The use of models is an important way to think about the future, but it cannot be the only way. Perhaps most of us rely on what appears to be a more natural method: simply extending our perceptions of the past and present. This extension does not require us to understand underlying processes but only to discover a pattern and to assume that that pattern will continue in the future pretty much as it has in the past. Such patterns need not be simple linear extensions. They can be fitted to exponential growth curves; they can follow an envelope enclosing a set of development curves for related phenomena; or they can be regressions of one variable on another (or of one sequence of points on another sequence). The number of variations possible is limited only by one's ingenuity. In any such extrapolation, however, no knowledge of the underlying process is claimed. No attempt is made to model a thing or process. We are simply trying to infer a path (or trace) into the future, based on evidence contained wholly in the past. This point cannot be overemphasized. The path or trace "belongs" wholly to the past, not to the future. Yet, we are attempting to infer a trend of some kind, based on a continuous extension from the past.

For short excursions into the future and for environments that are not changing very rapidly, this approach is not a bad way to start. In the absence of an understanding of the basic phenomena we are examining, it may serve us well, particularly if we have a fair amount of data about past performance. In fact, extrapolation is often an essential step in constructing a model. It can and has been used in forecasting an enormous variety of phenomena—growth of GNP, price changes, unemployment patterns, diffusion of innovation, growth of an industry, size of computer memories, demand for electrical energy, number of telephones in use, and on and on. It is, and has been, perhaps the most widely used construct for thinking about the future.

The difficulty is that the method breaks down as the phenomena become more complex and as basic changes begin to occur in the time intervals of interest. For many political, social, and economic variables, these conditions do exist. Even for such basic quantities as world population in the next thirty to fifty years, simple extensions from past data are clearly inappropriate. In the past fifty years, for example, a whole array of new forces, including industrial development, sanitation, urbanization, and value shifts, have come into play to make extensions of previous patterns inadequate. For more complex economic or social phenomena, such as rates of inflation, unemployment, or crime, the difficulties in using traces fom the past become more painfully apparent. Even the smallest excursions are thus fraught with peril, for the "traces" from the past are of poor quality (the data are nonexistent, inconsistent, or incomplete).

Are there, then, useful surrogates for traces? There are, and one in particular is used more often than we realize. Its generic name is *scenario.* Simply stated, a scenario is a slice of "future history." It can take many forms. It may, for example, be completely descriptive, like the work of H. G. Wells (1961) or Aldous Huxley (1966). It may—as its theater-related connection implies—take the form of physical settings, much like stage settings in an exposition, display, or even a play. Or it may, as Toffler (1970) has suggested, be embodied in an "enclave of the future," a place that can be used to create a possible future environment in as much detail as the imagination can muster. To be sure, most scenarios of the future are word descriptions (Kahn and Wiener, 1967). They would be too expensive and impractical to produce otherwise. Also, most involve a range of variations, usually from optimistic (or "best" case) to pessimistic (or "worst" case). But whatever their form, their primary purpose is to create the elements of a small portion of a plausible world of the future—with the detail that an observer examining or inspecting it might provide if he were viewing the remnants of a past rather than those of a future civilization.

The distinction between a model and a scenario may be useful. As the term *model* has been used, it is an abstraction (often quantitative) of the perceived world. It further implies some understanding of the inner workings of the thing or process represented. Not so for a scenario. Indeed, here we are simply describing, without necessarily understanding. On the other hand, it would be misleading to create too sharp a distinction between the two forms. In the end, models and scenarios merge, as models become more descriptive and as scenarios reflect increasing degrees of understanding about underlying processes.

## WITNESSES FROM THE FUTURE

Still another resource is available to the explorer in time: to be the participant or witness in the unfolding of events or developments. Now our definition of past and future allows a witness only in the recent past. For the distant past and the future, no direct access to witnesses is possible, and once again we are faced with the creation of surrogates for eyewitness accounts of what might have been or what might be. Such surrogates are particularly useful or necessary when the construction of models and the examination of traces are difficult, impossible, or inappropriate.

In this case, we are faced with essentially the same problem whether we look back or ahead. We must find surrogates for "visitors from the past" or "visitors from the future"—those who can tell us how it has been or may be. The basic problem is that of constructing an image or picture of the possible, and the analogy between the distant past and the future becomes even stronger as the periods of the past recede further into those in which few, if any, traces exist. Our only resort then is to use the judgment and opinion of particular individuals or groups of individuals.

We must, at the outset, distinguish between *preferences* and *outcomes.* Our interest here is not in what individuals prefer but in what they visualize might have occurred or might occur. Of course, it is not altogether possible to separate the preferable from the possible, but for the moment, let us assume we can. And let us restrict our attention to the future, although duality with the distant past exists up to a point.

If we cannot have access to actual witnesses and if we have little hard data or understanding about basic processes, what kind of persons are we looking for? We are looking for "experts," but we must be careful to distinguish between *knowledge* in a substantive field and the ability to *foresee* possible developments in that field. The ways in which expertise, on the one hand, and assessing ability (the ability to imagine creatively), on the other, can be measured are poorly understood at present. We must also consider the range of views to be included. It seems that a group consensus is desirable when expertise is being aggregated, but such an objective is not necessarily valid when the emphasis is on creating images (particularly innovative ones) about future possibilities. Furthermore, in this case, a distinct difference of purpose does exist, depending on whether one is looking behind or ahead. In looking backward, one is interested in creating images that are the most accurate portrayal of what actually did take place. In looking ahead, however, this is definitely not the only, or even the most important, objective. The overriding objective is normally to explore and examine possibilities that we may want to promote or avoid (or accommodate if they are not amenable to our influence). This intent is quite different from the case in which a particular past has already occurred and we are trying to recreate it in the mind's eye. *This point cannot be overemphasized for it is often at the root of much confusion in thinking about the future.*

A great number of ways exist for dealing with surrogate "witnesses." Each of these combines some measure of art and science. Perhaps the most widely used are the family of methods designated Delphi. The distinguishing features of Delphi are its structure, anonymity, and feedback, designed to minimize some of the drawbacks (bandwagon effects, dominance, poorly considered alternatives) of face-to-face interactions (Gordon and Helmer, 1964). But other methods can be used, either as alternatives or in combination with Delphi procedures. These methods include sequential interviewing, face-to-face conferences, and computer-assisted interactions. Each has its peculiar advantages and disadvantages (Amara, 1975), but each of them adds another tool for thinking about the future.

## SUMMARY

Models, traces, and witnesses in some form are used by all explorers in time and space—historians, reporters, futurists. The primary difference in probing the future is that heavy reliance must necessarily be placed by the futurist on fairly imperfect models and on surrogate traces and witnesses. This state of affairs places an enormous burden on the futurist to deal both responsibly and humbly with his sources, his methods, and his findings.

## REFERENCES

Amara, Roy. 1975. *Some Methods of Futures Research.* Menlo Park, Calif. Institute for the Future, Working Paper WP-23.

Gordon, T. J., and Olaf Helmer. 1964. *Report on a Long-Range Forecasting Study.* Santa Monica, Calif.: RAND Corporation, P-2982.

Huxley, Aldous. 1966. *Brave New World.* New York: Bantam Books.

Kahn, Herman, and Anthony Wiener. 1967. *The Year 2000: A Framework for*

*Speculation on the Next Thirty-Three Years.* New York: Macmillan Co.

Meadows, Donella, Dennis Meadows, et al. 1972. *The Limits to Growth.* New York: Universe Books.

Toffler, Alvin. 1970. *Future Shock.* New York: Random House.

Wells, H. G. 1961. *Seven Science Fiction Novels of H. G. Wells.* New York: Dover Publications.

IDA  R.  HOOS

# Methodological Shortcomings in Futures Research

The study of the future, once the bailiwick of seers and visionaries, has developed to a state far beyond that of the art of interpreting smoke patterns from a sacrificial altar or of fathoming strange sounds out of a Delphian cave. Through methodological refinement intended to uncouple the notion of forecasting from Merlinian magic, the idea of studying the future now embraces a number of related activities which, by virtue of the technological tenor of our times, pass for professional disciplines. The effort at separation, however, has been neither successfully nor totally accomplished, for, through an interesting concatenation of circumstances and conditions peculiar to our post-sensate, pre-postindustrial era, we find ourselves locked into methodological approaches requiring no less a degree, but simply a different kind, of credulity. Thanks to what might come under T. S. Kuhn's description of our "dominant paradigm" (Kuhn, 1970), we think we can study the future "rationally" and "scientifically."

Even though the magic is gone, the mumbo-jumbo remains, with data the driver, analysis the watchword, quantification the rule, and model-building the prime preoccupation. These are, in fact, the warp and the woof of what could otherwise appear as widely disparate concerns. They are the common procedural elements when, for example, we ponder technological forecasting, technology assessment, environmental impact, social indicators, quality of life calculations, and risk analysis. But, to pursue the metaphor, this is why the fabric is full of holes. Moreover, analysis of that which has not happened is merely an extension of a particular *Weltanschauung*; data bases are perforce eclectic by nature, flimsy in substance, and fragile over time; quantification often distorts and sometimes trivializes; and models are only as good as their makers. Nonetheless, technical virtuosity thrives. Social forecasting, technology assessment, social indicator fabrication, and prediction of future conditions and circumstances have become the subject of high-level (and attractively located) conferences, the object of high-powered "investigations," and the happiest of hunting grounds for grant-seekers of all stripes. So precious has specialization become that there is not only an abundance of journals, books, and series of books, but even a new vocabulary (Chacko, 1975). All the same, despite the methodological aspirations and pretensions, certain basic problems persist (Hoos, 1974), and they must be taken into account in an evaluation of the techniques. In this article, we consider several techniques which, in our estimation, are crucial: (1) the origin and nature of techniques now being applied; and (2) the centrality of data.

## THE ORIGIN AND NATURE OF TECHNIQUES

A review of the considerable literature in the field establishes the intellectual forebears and disciplinary linkages of the techniques now in use. No degree of genealogical perspicacity is required to trace the origins to the family of techniques known as the systems approach. Jantsch and Hetman (Jantsch, 1967, 1972; Hetman, 1973), to mention only the more encyclopedic of the authorities, devote concerted attention to the connections between the techniques of social forecasting and systems analysis in its various manifestations. Jantsch (1967, p. 110) finds the roots of forecasting techniques in *operations research*, as developed by the United Kingdom and the United States during World War II, and in *systems analysis*, as pioneered by the RAND Corporation in the United States since 1948. Moreover, he explicitly relates some procedures in technology forecasting to components of systems analysis. Jantsch describes cost-benefit analysis as "a special technique for binding together a vertical and horizontal forecast, which makes possible an integral view of decision-making by placing the vertical effort and the horizontal impact on the same basis" (1967, p. 190). Similarly, he frequently includes the concepts of the Planning-Programming-Budgeting System (PPBS) in his discussion of normative forecasting (1967, pp. 35, 36). Further, PPBS is entwined in decision-trees, at least historically as used by the U.S. Department of Defense in its long-range military planning: "The top of a typical relevance tree is very similar in structure to a decision tree such as that underlying the Planning-Programming-Budgeting System of the U.S. Department of Defense and can be made fully identical, both trees representing the same function-oriented approach" (Jantsch, 1967, p. 276).

Hetman, too, delineates fundamental relationships between the techniques associated with systems analysis and those used for the assessment of technology (1973). In Figure 1, in which he describes the various dimensions of technology forecasting, we see the familiar concepts woven into the framework and in many ways, basic to it, as exemplified in his statement that "Technology assessment is a systems

**Figure 1.** Various Dimensions of Technological Forecasting

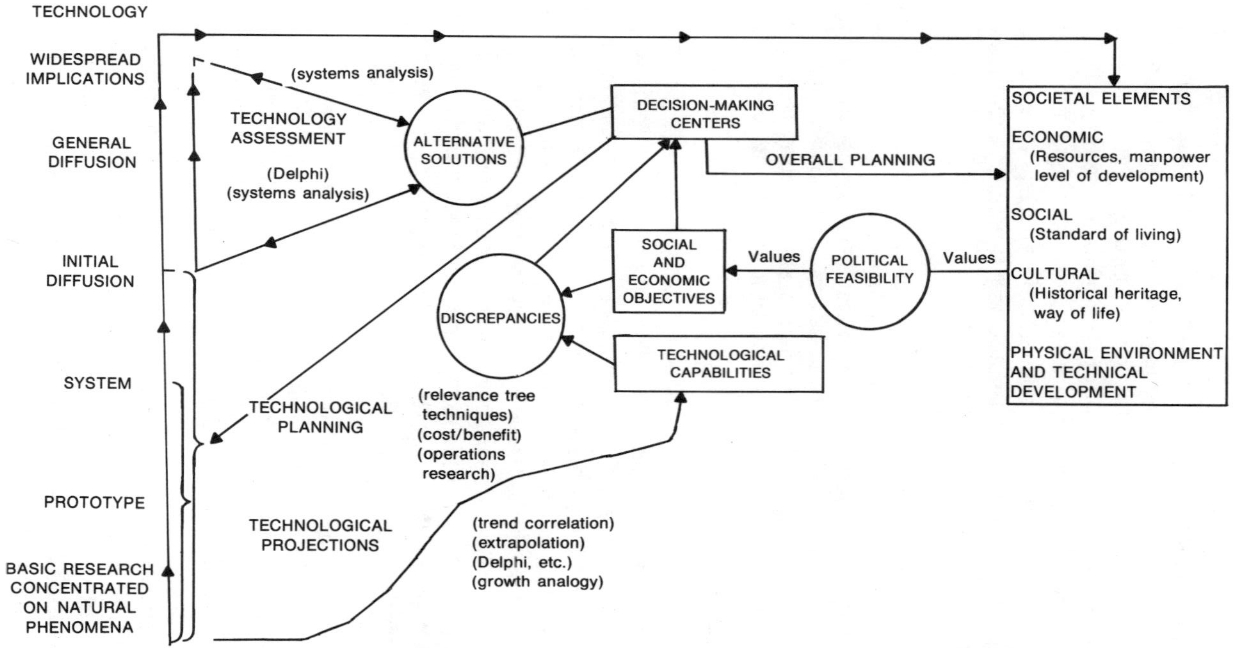

SOURCE: Francois Hetman, *Society and the Assessment of Technology,* Paris: Organisation for Economic Co-operation and Development, 1973, p. 62.

analysis approach to providing a whole conceptual framework, complete both in scope and time, for decisions about the appropriate utilisation of technology for social purposes" (1973, p. 56). Note that Hetman's definition takes the important step of tying technology utilization with *social purpose*. This is an important dimension—one that is reflected clearly in the definition offered by the Congressional Research Service of the Library of Congress (Carpenter, 1972, pp. 1-2). Here we find articulated the connections among the various techniques, the identification of cost-benefit analysis as a component, the centrality of the information-gathering function, and the wedding to social purpose, broadly conceived:

Technology assessment is the process of taking a purposeful look at the consequences of technological change. It includes the primary cost-benefit balance of short term localised marketplace economics, but particularly goes beyond these to identify affected parties and unanticipated impacts in as broad and long fashion as is possible. It is neutral and objective, seeking to enrich the information for management decisions. Both "good" and "bad" side effects are investigated since a missed opportunity for benefit may be detrimental to society just as is an unexpected hazard.

The close relationship—historical, theoretical, methodological, and operational—between the techniques of social forecasting and those of systems analysis renders the former subject to the same shortcomings and vulnerable to the same criticisms as the latter (Hoos, 1972; see especially Chapter VIII). Let us focus on the core concept of benefit-cost analysis. The widely accepted description comes from a seminal statement by Prest and Turvey and expresses better the ideal to be attained than the reality as observed during the past decades of experience (Prest and Turvey, 1965, p. 683):

A practical way of assessing the desirability of projects, where it is important to take a long view (in the sense of looking at repercussions in the . . . future) and a wide view (in the sense of allowing for side-effects of many kinds, on many persons, industries, regions, etc.), i.e. it implies the enumeration and evaluation of *all the relevant costs and benefits*. [Italics added.]

In the annals of the U.S. government, the concept dates back to the Flood Act of 1936, when Congress declared that costs of federal projects should not exceed benefits. The notion was newly accredited during World War II when it emerged in the context of weapons systematization and selection, especially in the calculations by the RAND analysts. It was this epoch in the development of the family of quantitative techniques encompassing systems analysis, cost-benefit analysis, and program budgeting that assured their longevity. Later, in the early 1960s, their adoption, refinement, and application by then Secretary of Defense Robert S. McNamara and Assistant Secretary Charles J. Hitch anointed them as the core methodology of management science. By the 1970s, a new chapter in the history of the methodology had begun. The same principles prevailed but new applications brought new labels, predominant among them risk-benefit analysis. Thus, a well-known and much-cited five-year study of nuclear reactor safety (U.S. Nuclear Regulatory Commission, 1975) borrowed the techniques from the Department of Defense and from NASA to predict the likelihood of a core meltdown and produced conclusions that have been widely used for policy and propaganda purposes.

Rothenberg (1975, p. 58) informs us that the focus of the cost-benefit approach is the means-end relationship, which, by no mere coincidence, happens to be the central focus of economics. As a consequence, we find that economic desiderata usually dominate the identification and allocation of costs and benefits and that there is primary, if not exclusive, preoccupation with the dollars and cents aspects of the matter under consideration. This orientation often turns the cost-benefit exercise into, at best, a drunkard's search[1] for data to support a given course of action or, at worst, a King Midas dance. As to the first, the typical practice of having advocates perform analyses demands the gathering of supportive data; similarly, it explains the frequency of favorable benefit-cost ratios. The truism follows that data selection is perforce an eclectic process and that substantiating data will have been sought and used. In assaying the validity of a benefit-cost ratio, it then becomes necessary to ascertain who performed it and under whose auspices. It would be well to bear in mind the adage, "Whose bread I eat, his song I sing."

The sad tale of Old King Midas should warn us that short-run economic considerations can lead to dire and, sometiems irreversible, damage. This holds true whether we are assessing programs for field, forest, and stream or health, welfare, and education. The premium put on quick, high yield not only diverts attention from long-run considerations but requires that nonquantifiable values either be disregarded or treated arbitrarily in Procrustean[2] fashion and thus manipulated and distorted. Frequently, they are consigned to the limbo of externalities, there to remain until another cost-benefit analyst finds them useful as internal to his current means-end game. The fact that application of these techniques by obedient consultants and accommodating academics has provided justification for an incalculable number of irreversible and regrettable courses of action in military and civilian affairs underscores the need for caveats at every step of the cost-benefit analysis, from conception to conclusion. Old King Midas learned through painful experience that the economic criterion is not necessarily the best one, that there are costs and benefits that are none the less real and important because they elude quantification.

Even after some thirty years of experience in applying cost-benefit methods, water resources agencies, for example, have not succeeded in overcoming such basic weaknesses, on the cost side, as costs underestimated, with calculations limited to visible dollar amounts, opportunity costs omitted, spillovers overlooked, and a range of present and future social costs ignored. On the benefit side, computations have been found (U.S. General Accounting Office, 1974, p. i) to be overoptimistic, inadequately supported, and inconsistent. These deficiencies will not be overcome by the usual resort to "technical adjustment of the model"; they emanate from the very nature of the techniques.

Experience has shown that much public money has been wasted on cost-benefit analyses and on the projects that they "rationalized." Time has tested many of them and the *ex post facto* outcomes have been far different from the roseate speculation that passed for "rational" planning at the outset. The fiasco of BART (the Bay Area Rapid Transit System) (Webber, 1976) and the disasters of HUD (Goldberger, 1976) are but two examples out of many far too numerous to list, let alone discuss. The technique has buttressed decision-making processes in which the despised fragmentation was disguised under the cloak of "suboptimization." Cost-benefit analysis has provided a format useful for justifying ends conceived narrowly in time and space so as to achieve yields that may have appeared high but that ultimately defeated larger and longer lived objectives. The result has been a sense of false security in decisions or courses of action because they were arrived at through the "powerful management tools." Actually, in almost every branch of government, civilian and military, examples of gross mismanagement are on the increase and can be attributed in large measure to reliance on these "management science" practices. Cost-benefit analysis has not demonstrated that it has improved public decision-making; it merely has provided a convenient rationale for just about any course of action. It simply depends on who wants to justify what.

The saga of systems analysis as a technique for the improvement of management is no less sad. Introduced in the military arena, it brought us the "victories" of Vietnam. Used to achieve economies in procurement in the Department of Defense, it provided a convenient cover for unprecedentedly wasteful practices. Instead of being a "powerful management tool," it became a bludgeon in the hand of a strong manager and earned the wrath of Congress for what Senator William Proxmire and his investigating committee labeled "gross mismanagement." Conceived in the philosophy that the end justifies the means, the systems approach has even been identified as a factor in the Watergate affair.

Especially noteworthy for our purposes is the way in which systems analysis has served as the vehicle through which the "management syndrome" has pervaded every department of government. By the time McNamara's band of Whiz Kids had taken flight to high posts in civilian agencies, prestigious posts in universities, and strategic positions in the think-tanks that form the shadow government (Guttman and Willner, 1976), the techniques had become so useful that they were institutionalized with little or no regard for their appropriateness. Like the bowsman who first shoots the arrow and then draws the bull's-eye, a cadre of "management experts" has invaded all levels of government, from county to Congress, and has interpreted all problems as "management problems" and, thus, amenable to the same treatment. Whatever the function of a body, whatever its responsibilities, it found its ailments diagnosed in this way, often by an "expert" devoid of substantive knowledge and experience. The results have been always costly, often painful, and sometimes ludicrous. (See, for example, the project evaluated in *Rapid Rehabilitation of Old Law Tenements: An Evaluation* [New York: Institute of Public Administration, September 1968]. But the insidious think-tank approach prevails, and, as any student of officialdom knows, there is more of the same ahead. There is a definite shift in government funding to contract-type work, where "output" is measured in pages and "productivity" judged by adherence to deadlines. According to one authority (American Sociological Association, 1976), this trend strengthens the role of think-tanks and weakens that of universities, which are less likely to keep abreast of the flow of RFPs (Requests for Proposal) and to have the personnel available for preparing persuasive proposals. Even in reviews, assessments, and evaluations, emphasis is on technical trivia about treatment of data rather than on errors and gaps in the data. No one asks why certain questions were raised and others ignored. The result has been that assessments have become little more than nugatory, proforma exercises designed to satisfy a bureaucratic requirement rather than to "illuminate a choice."

Just as repeated application of systems analysis techniques to military matters numbed the sensibilities and transmuted what would otherwise be unthinkable horror to intersecting lines on graphs, so in the social arena, continuing simplistic simulation has dulled the propelling sharpness of an array of problems. Our confidence in the "powerful tools of technology" that will frame solutions has caused us to overlook fundamental failures and deficiencies in the models. Moreover, repetition has contributed neither to the mitigation of social problems nor to an advance in the state of the art. To be sure, there has been proliferation, for as colleges of business administration and engineering pour forth their graduates, the ranks of the aspiring practitioners swell. While more computer time and capacity may give them more printouts to analyze and while glossaries grow, they are no closer to "solving" social problems than were the "pioneering" aerospace teams that took the giant step backward in the early 1960s from outer space to the inner city (Hoos, 1972). The lesson we could have learned from the past fifteen years is that the systems techniques were oversold in the military and that considering opportunity costs, social costs, and a range of hidden costs, they may be bringing more harm than benefit to civilian concerns. Perhaps most devastating to the earnest efforts to utilize systems techniques for social problem-solving in the present and social planning in the future is the fatal flaw which Zadeh calls the "principle of incompatibility" (1972, p. 2). Countering the prime selling point that the approach can "tame complexity," Zadeh emphasizes that the conventional quantitative techniques of systems analysis are intrinsically unsuited for dealing with social problems because "as the complexity of a system increases, our ability to make precise and yet significant statements about its behavior diminishes until a threshold is reached beyond which precision and significance (or relevance) become almost mutually exclusive characteristics."

## DATA AS BASE IN FUTURES RESEARCH

To assert that the data base is the foundation on which futures research depends would be to state little more than a redundant truism except for the peculiar role played by information. Just as sesquipedalian sophistry is used in other contexts to impart an aura of erudition, however obscurantist, so the mathematical macramé of numbers display is produced in futures studies as justification for positions taken or conclusions made. Viewed critically, however, the avalanche of figures, tastefully presented in charts and tables, formulas, and printouts, may provide something less than proof positive. They may, in fact, present a simplified and often distorted view of reality because only the quantifiable is taken into account; the nonquantifiable, which may be crucial, is systematically excluded. Thus, although accepted as the fulcrum of futures research, the data base is more often than not its Achilles' heel.

Starting with the premise that data are not, as the Latin origin suggests, *given* but, instead, *gotten*, we face the urgent necessity of breaking with the tradition that has anointed facts and figures with a kind of sacrosanctity and, rather, of taking the part of the Pirandello character who said, "A fact is like a sack; it won't stand up till you've put something in it" (quoted by Carr, 1962). Immediately, then, we reach the ineluctable conclusion that there are no pristine, objective facts floating free, wanting to be captured in a neat formula. Nowhere is this phenomenon more dramatically evident than in the case of the current energy crisis. "Facts" are used to demonstrate that fossil fuels are being depleted at dangerous rates; "facts" are used to prove that the United States alone has ample reserves for centuries to come. "Facts" are invoked to assure us that nuclear energy is cheap, safe, and ecologically preferable to other known energy sources; "facts" warn us that nuclear energy is cheap only when certain vital aspects of the fuel cycle, e.g., waste disposal, are ignored, that it is fraught with perils of various kinds, and bound to have irreversible and unfavorable impacts on the environment.

The "facts" in controversial matters such as energy are always on one side. On the other side, they emerge as propaganda, emotion, or hysteria. "Facts" are gathered to support a particular set of assumptions and, therefore, to substantiate certain positions. But even while the "facts" fall like snow, it is well to recall that a quantity of "facts" does not add up to information nor does it assure that we are better informed. On the other hand, selectivity has its dangers, too, as Bruno Bettelheim (1976) has pointed out:

Presenting a small segment of truth and claiming that it is the entire spectrum can be a much greater distortion than an outright lie. A lie is much easier to recognize as a distortion since our critical abilities have not been put to sleep by having been fed some small segment of truth.

Since data are not to be confused with gospel, skepticism need not be construed as heresy. Urgently needed is a framework for an evaluation in which what is being sought, by whom, and for what purposes is clearly identified. Thus, when we are given necromantic numbers about the death-dealing propensities of coal, for example, and are led to the conclusion that radiological risks from nuclear fuels are minimal by comparison, we will be alerted to accept the findings *cum magno grano salis.* When a course of action appears to have little adverse impact on the environment, we will ascertain by whose calculations the judgment was made. The purpose often serves as the hidden agenda prejudicing outcomes and skewing interpretation. When the purpose is to protect a bureaucracy—and thus carry out its first law of self-preservation—information judiciously presented serves as the instrument. Take, for example, the government regulatory agency accused by one of its senior staff members of laxity in enforcing certain safety rules. The prompt official response is a deluge of facts purporting to demonstrate that the system works, that the public's safety is assured, and that the figures on past performance supply proof positive. In precisely this way, the public has received assurances about the soundness of dam sites, the safety of nuclear reactors, the security of financial institutions, and the sanity of military policy. That not all of them have stood the test of time should serve as a warning to students of the future.

If we need to be reminded that we do not know the now (never mind the hereafter), we might pause to examine that giant numbers-gatherer, the Decennial Census, with which the United States has had experience since 1790 (Report of the Decennial Census Review Committee, 1971). Formalized in Article I, Section 2 of the Constitution, even the first census provided more than a mere head count; it included information, probably for purposes of military manpower availability, on free males over and under the age of sixteen, on free females, and on slaves. It was on the basis of this enumeration that representation and direct taxes were apportioned among the states. In response to the federal government's increased need for information, census inquiries have proliferated to include information encompassing almost every aspect of life in the United States. Each of the censuses has become progressively longer, with the list of items counted covering everything from literary to toilet facilities. But while the government knows a great deal about its citizens (too much, if one sides with critics who resent officialdom in the role of Peeping Tom and who resist Big Brotherhood), apparently much is not known. Herein lies a negation to the adage, "What you don't know won't hurt you."

Most current federal, state, and local planning is based on population figures, and it is from these figures that extrapolations to the future are made. The census serves as the basis for apportioning congressional seats, for public policy vis-à-vis health, education, welfare, housing, and manpower, and a myriad of purposes, public and private. The first census was not accurate. George Washington was quoted (Comptroller General of the United States, 1976) as attributing an undercount to the religious scruples of some persons, the tax evasion intent of others, indolence, or negligence. Time has only exacerbated the problem. According to an estimate by the Bureau of the Census, the 1970 census reflects a net undercount rate of 2.5 percent, or about 5.3 million persons. Of particular significance is the differential rate for various segments of the population, with blacks more undercounted than whites, men more than women, the poor more than the affluent, and Southerners more than Northerners. The implications are far-reaching. Undercounts can result in the misallocation of federal funds among geographic regions. Since population figures are the basis for planning educational programs, welfare assistance programs, health and hospital facilities, transportation and highway needs, crime prevention and public safety measures, and the like, faulty figures will deny an area the assistance it needs.

Discrepancies between census and special agency figures are commonplace, for special agencies almost always collect data for their own administrative purposes. A recent two-year study of New York City's welfare rolls revealed that the number of children receiving public assistance exceeded by 100,000 the total number listed in the official census (Lash and Segal, 1976). The identification of these "phantom children" remains a mystery. Perhaps they were "borrowed" for illicit welfare purposes; perhaps they are the children of illegal immigrants, in which case firm statistics are unavailable. The Immigration and Naturalization Service has estimated the total to be around 8 million, a figure that would raise the overall undercount to 13 million. However, as is often the case when "the facts" are under dispute, the methods by which the number of illegal aliens was derived have been challenged. The director of the Bureau of the Census has stated that the contract research organization that performed the study for the Immigration and Naturalization Service and produced this number used "a very questionable procedure" (Barabba, 1976).

The lesson for future forecasters is clear. Since the census provides the basis on which public policy is planned, from which economic, political, and social judgments are derived, and for which social intervention is designed, the notions of social indicators, quality of life, and the like must be viewed with extreme skepticism. Depending as they do on fragile figures and arbitrary definitions, they can supply few reliable clues to the present, to say nothing of guidelines to the future.

Subject to criticism on grounds of adequacy and accuracy, many of the statistics in use cannot stand the test of durability. Many earnest models are built on a plethora of facts and figures about a particular situation in a certain time frame. A widening of the lens to include relevant factors or a lengthening of the time span renders the model meaningless. This phenomenon is all the more likely to occur when soft data have been hardened as input. Nor is the element of deliberate deception to be cavalierly dismissed. Grand, indeed, is the delusion that we are getting bona fide, even if sometimes incomplete and inaccurate, information. Quality and flow of information, especially in the public sector, are limited by many forms of strategic secretiveness—to protect the country against potential enemies, to protect the agency against critical scrutiny, to protect the public for "its own good," i.e., against "undue alarm." The reasons are many; the results the same.

To document the deceptions is beyond the scope of this article. The epitome of deception was reached in October 1976, when a Senate appropriations subcommittee published an eight-volume record, totaling some 4,500 pages, of twelve days of hearings that were never held. The phantom sessions were part of twenty-four days of hearings scheduled for the Departments of Labor and of Health, Education and Welfare and related agencies. In the record, hearings that had been canceled were made to appear as live as those that had taken place. *The New York Times* account of October 4, 1976 (page 15) contained the following details:

Records of the cancelled hearings were complete with the numbers of the rooms in which they ostensibly were held, commencement and adjournment times and chatty welcoming remarks by the presiding senators. For example, the record of the cancelled hearing on the $2 billion budget of the National Institutes of Health states that it began at 10 a.m. Tuesday, Feb. 3 in room 1223 of the Everett McKinley Dirksen Office building with Senator Warren G. Magnuson, Democrat of Washington, presiding, and Senators Edward W. Brooke, Republican of Massachusetts, and Richard S. Schweiker, Republican of Pennsylvania, present. The record quotes Senator Magnuson as saying: "The subcommittee will come to order. Dr. Donald Fredrickson, the new director of the National Institutes of Health, is with us today—as are all of the institute and program directors." In fact, not one of them was present, not even the chairman and his subcommittee colleagues.

Therefore, when we scrutinize the current methodologies of technology assessment, social forecasting, and futures study, in general, we cannot but acknowledge (1) the pivotal role of data; and (2) the weakness of this pivot. Perhaps we can concur with T. S. Eliot that "all knowledge brings us closer to our ignorance." Certainly, we will have to acknowledge that we do not know the truth, the whole truth, and that even invoking the diety will not help us overcome the gaps and deficiencies. To presume, then, that we have the techniques and tools to study the future is to delude ourselves—perhaps to the point of disaster if we depend on this methodology for accurate forecasts and for risk assessments of things to come.

## NOTES

1. Abraham Kaplan, *The Conduct of Inquiry*, (San Francisco: Chandler Publishing Company, 1964), p. 11, tells the story of a drunkard searching, under a street lamp, for his house key, which he had dropped some distance away. Asked why he didn't look where he had dropped it, he replied, "It's lighter here!"

2. Procrustes, a mythological innkeeper, seized travelers and tied them to

an iron bedstead, into which he forced them to fit by either stretching them or by cutting off protruding members.

## REFERENCES

American Sociological Association. 1976. "Federal Funds for Social Science Research." *Footnotes* (November), 1.

Barabba, Vincent P. (Director, Bureau of the Census). 1976. Letter, March 18, 1976, to Vincent L. Lowe, Director, General Government Division, U.S. General Accounting Office, Washington, D.C. Appendix III in *Programs to Reduce the Decennial Census Undercount,* GGD-76-72, Washington, D.C. (May 5), 3.

Bettelheim, Bruno. 1976. "Surviving." *The New Yorker,* August 2, 36.

Carpenter, Richard A. 1972. "The Scope and Limits of Technology Assessment." *OECD Seminar on Technology Assessment.* Paris, January 26-28, 1-2.

Carr, Edward Hallett. 1962. *What Is History?* New York: Alfred A. Knopf, p.

Chacko, George K. 1975. *Technological Forecontrol.* Volume 1 of *Studies in Management Science and Systems.* Amsterdam: North Holland Publishing Co.

Comptroller General of the United States. 1976. Report to the House Committee on Post Office and Civil Science. *Programs to Reduce the Decennial Census Undercount,* GGD-76-72, Washington, D.C. (May 5), 3.

Decennial Census Review Committee. 1971. Report of the Decennial Census Review Committee to the Secretary of Commerce. *The Decennial Census.*

Goldberger, Paul. 1976. "Ruling Against Model High-Rise Disputes Federal Housing Ideas." *The New York Times,* October 8.

Guttman, Daniel, and Barry Willner. 1976. *The Shadow Government.* New York: Pantheon Books.

Hetman, Francois. 1973. *Society and the Assessment of Technology.* Paris: Organization for Economic Co-operation and Development.

Hoos, Ida R. 1972, *Systems Analysis in Public Policy.* Berkeley: University of California Press, see especially Chapter 8.

———. 1974. "Criteria for Good Futures Research." *Technological Forecasting and Social Change* Volume 6, 113-132.

Jantsch, Erich. 1967. *Technological Forecasting in Perspective.* Paris: Organisation for Economic Co-operation and Development.

———. 1972. *Technological Planning and Social Futures.* New York: John Wiley and Sons.

Kaplan, Abraham. 1964. *The Conduct of Inquiry.* San Francisco: Chandler Publishing Co., 11.

Kuhn, T. S. 1970. *The Structure of Scientific Revolutions.* 2d ed., enlarged; Chicago: University of Chicago Press.

Lash, Trude, and Heidi Segal. 1976. *State of the Child: New York City.* New York Foundation for Child Development.

Prest, A. R., and R. Turvey. 1965. "Cost-Benefit Analysis: A Survey." *The Economic Journal* (December), 683.

Rothenberg, Jerome. 1975. "Cost-Benefit Analysis: A Methodological Exposition." Volume 2, Chapter 4 in Elmer N. Struening and Marcia Guttentag (eds.), *Handbook of Evaluation Research,* Beverly Hills, Calif.: Sage Publications.

Webber, Melvin M. 1976. "The BART Experience—What Have We Learned." Monograph number 26, Institute of Urban and Regional Development, and Institute of Transportation Studies, University of California, Berkeley.

U.S. General Accounting Office. 1974. Report to the Congress by the Comptroller General of the United States, Washington, D.C., B-167941, September 20. "Improvements Needed in Making Benefit-Cost Analyses for Federal Water Resources Projects," i.

U.S. Nuclear Regulatory Commission. 1975. *Reactor Safety Study, An Assessment of Accident Risks in U.S. Nuclear Power Plants.* NUREG 75/014, Wash 1400. Washington, D.C.

Zadeh, L. A. 1972. "Outline of a New Approach to the Analyses of Complex Systems and Decision Processes." Memorandum Number ERL-M342, July 24. Berkeley: University of California College of Engineering, Electronics Research Laboratory, 2.

IAN MILES[1]

# The Ideologies of Futurists

Whatever claims futures studies may have to the status of science, one aspect of science that futurists studiously avoid is the risk of opening a Pandora's box. The portraits of the scientist as the single-minded Dr. Frankenstein or Dr. Moreau, of science as propelling the world toward nuclear devastation, environmental degradation, or the psychological or genetic manipulation of humanity, are not attractive to futurologists. Rather, they portray their role as that of expert advisor to Pandora: telling her what is likely to be in the box which so intrigues her, and what contingency plans are necessary if she insists on opening it.

Futures research has been seen as the attempt "to indicate now the future consequences of present public-policy decisions, to anticipate future problems, and to begin the design of alternative solutions so that our society has more options and can make a moral choice" (Bell 1967, p. 634, introducing the work of the Commission on the Year 2000).

... we are not only concerned with anticipating future events and attempting to make the desirable more likely and the undesirable less likely. We are also trying to put policy-makers in a position to deal with whatever future actually arises, to be able to alleviate the bad and exploit the good. In doing this, one clearly cannot be satisfied with linear or simple projections: a range of futures must be considered (Kahn and Wiener, 1967, p. 3).

Such statements are repeated in the introductory passages of numerous futurological exercises, and Part 4 of *Mankind 2000* (Jungk and Galtung, 1969) is practically a compendium of them.

In an important blast at mainstream futures research, Goldthorpe (1971) argued that despite the disclaimers of the Bells and Kahns, much of this research actively restricts the range of the alternative futures that are discussed or designed. There is indeed an emphasis on only one type of future society, the "postindustrial" idealization of North American society. The flaws in contemporary society are said to stem from a lack of adequate information, but it is argued that post-industrial society will be characterized by greatly improved social technologies (information systems, futurology, social accounting), which will allow for social policies to be guided by "technical rationality." Goldthorpe rightly notes the technocratic bent of this analysis, relating it to the notions of the "end of ideology" and the "convergence of industrial societies" that were widely propagated, particularly during the 1960s.

Similar criticisms have been voiced by other analysts (Kleinberg, 1973; Kumar, 1972). Elsewhere (Miles, 1975), I have considered claims for the supposedly revolutionary impact of quantitative methodology on social forecasting and planning. In each of the areas of social research considered—social indicators, forecasting methodology, the prediction of political change, the futures and relations of industrial and underdeveloped societies—I considered criticisms similar to those cited above to be forceful.[2]

If, then, futures research is a science, it may be prone to dangers of its own; or, if it is to be regarded as a social technology, perhaps a technology assessment is in order. The dangers associated with science and technology (S&T) may be seen as twofold. First, they may be material. That is, means may be provided whereby some social groups may pursue their own interests in a way that is oppressive to others (or, by pursuing their own short-term interests, they may produce injurious effects in the long run even on themselves). Second, they may be ideological in that the very techniques and theories used in S&T may support and propagate an interpretation of the world which supports the dominance of such social groups.[3]

These two types of danger may often be closely intertwined. A forecast that is used to define a specific policy may also provide the wherewithal to legitimate that policy. While a study may provide reasons for choice between different options (advocacy), it may also frame the problem in such a way that other options are completely ruled out (meta-advocacy).[4] It is unlikely even to hint at the possibility of policies being formulated on bases different from those presently existing.


HISTORICISM

Historicism refers to the attempt to predict the future on the basis of supposed laws of historical evolution, whose operation may be projected forward to provide a view of the future.[5] Historicism is manifest in the extrapolation of trends or cyclical regularities, the application of macrosociological theories that deduce the inevitable progression of societies from one to another form, and the use of deterministic accounts (technological, economic, or ecological) of social change. Human choices and praxis are assigned an epiphenomenal or mechanical role in making past and future history. In futures studies, one or another type of future often becomes portrayed as essentially inevitable, with its only possibilities for change consisting of limited and piecemeal reform—although, to emphasize this point, various catastrophic alternatives may be aired as "alternative futures." The viability of desirable alternative futures is dismissed as a utopian dream, to be denied the legitimation of scientific analysis. As Arab-Ogly (1975), points out, even the work of Michael Harrington is dismissed as "journalism" rather than futures research, despite his use of social science and his discussion of future alternatives (see Harrington, 1965, 1972). Historicist arguments may be used to counter proposals for major social change while stressing the virtues of piecemeal reform. Thus, it is argued that insititutions that have been established over long historical periods possess qualities leading to their "natural selection" that might be damaged by tampering.

Both the techniques of futurology and the contents of forecasts often justify the charge that futures research tends to be dominated by historicism.[6] Futures studies have overwhelmingly concentrated on determining profiles of likely futures rather than on constructing images of desirable futures; in Jantsch's (1967) terms, their techniques are exploratory rather than normative. Representative of exploratory techniques are trend extrapolation, fitting curves to historical data, expert judgments developed by Delphi methods, cross-impact forecasting, and many ventures in simulation modeling.

Extrapolating trends or best-fit curves rests on historicism when these projections into the future remain unexplained, when they are not referred to the operation of identifiable forces under given circumstances. Some knowledge of the limits within which forces will continue to operate in a particular way is essential if an historicist portrayal of a trend as itself being an inevitable historical force is to be avoided.[7] Thus, Adams (1974), in criticizing the British road transport forecasts which he considers to have played an important role in national motorway planning, points to a number of essentially historicist problems underlying the methods used in the traffic projections. (These are in addition to the methodological shortcomings almost endemic to such forecasts.) In these cases, a logistic curve is the device employed to forecast future car ownership rates, while the level of lorry usage is estimated from the past relationship between GDP and goods traffic levels. Adams argues that these forecasts have acted as self-fulfilling prophecies which have encouraged the growth of road traffic in Britain.

Insofar as the clouds of private judgment veiling the outputs of standard Delphi studies can be penetrated, it is likely that forecasts based on this technique too will be essentially historicist. Especially where the "experts" involved are pontificating about events removed from their control, prognostications are likely to be based on intuitive extrapolations, theories of cyclics in funding and fashions, and the like. (A fairly thorough critique of Delphi is provided by Sackman, 1975, who particularly criticizes how experts are selected and how consensus in forecasts is generated.)

In principle, modeling exercises can allow for sensitivity tests that contrast the different forecasts resulting from assigning different initial values to variables or even different forms to the relationships embedded in the model. But such exercises still often border on historicism, with elaborate computer analysis concealing what is essentially a back-of-the-envelope calculation about the impact of continuing exponential growth trends (e.g., see the critique of *The Limits to Growth* by Cole, Freeman, Jahoda, and Pavitt, 1973). Similar problems are encountered in urban and regional modeling practice, where the social physics approach has long reigned. Here models are based upon the embodiment of regularities in spatial behavior in formalizations such as the Lowry model—which describe, rather than explain, this behavior.[8]

## JUSTIFYING HISTORICISM

Three objections might be raised to the above analysis. It might be argued that the exploratory techniques referred to have more to do with microforecasting and localized planning activity than with futures research proper, with the portrayal of global images of the future. In any case, it might be argued that whether or not these approaches are historicist, what matters is whether the forecasts yielded are accurate. A third objection involves ridiculing the distinction between exploratory and normative techniques: how can futures studies be other than historicist, when we must necessarily apply some exploratory approaches (given that a totally planned future is out of the question)?

In countering the first point, I would argue that the holistic gloss of many futures studies—scenarios, tables of second-order impacts, reasoned assessments of alternatives—merely disguises what in essence is an exercise in locating and imagining the consequences of various trends. For example, the "Standard World" of Kahn and Wiener (1967)[9] is derived from a projection of a multifold trend of thirteen (largely unquantified) elements. It is merely Sorokin's historicist theory of history with its next cycle somewhat postponed. Daniel Bell's (1974) version of postindustrial society is, in contrast, vulgarized Marxism with its revolutionary finale lacking (Kumar, 1972). Here, trends in the labor force are the slender strands of extrapolation from which a complex web of arguments is spun, and within which the filaments of careful reasoning and dispassionate objectivity are constrained.

It cannot be denied that historicist exploratory forecasts have often proved to be accurate predictions. In some cases, this is surely the operation of self-fulfilling prophecies. (Sometimes prophecies may be more than fulfilled. When British right-wing politicians pointed to trends in immigration from the West Indies as evidence of a rapidly growing black population, many West Indians took the opportunity to emigrate before restrictions were imposed. The subsequent surge in immigration made the task of passing restrictive legislation that much easier. See Deakin, 1970.)

Perhaps a prime example of good exploratory forecasting is the work of Ogburn from the 1920s to the 1930s. (See Miles, 1975, Chapter 4; a good example of Ogburn's work is the 1937 National Resources Committee report.) It is difficult to determine in such projections based on technological forecasts how far technology is itself seen as possessing autonomy and how far the sorts of change are really conceived as being contingent upon the continuance of a given form of social organization. Forecasts of rapid progress in space travel, for example, remained fairly accurate as long as NASA was being provided with plenty of funds.[10]

Problems and pitfalls in exploratory forecasting are apparent in the work of renowned futurologists such as those cited a little earlier. Trends that emerged in the late 1960s have led Bell and Kahn to an about-face and changes in emphasis. Kahn and Bruce-Biggs (1972) still feature the multifold trend, although this has changed in significant ways (see Marien, 1973b). But their work in the 1970s reflects the possibility of environmental crisis and assesses the rise of the "counterculture" and the crisis of America's war in Vietnam. We have already encountered *The End of Ideology* (Bell, 1960), which came a cropper against ghetto and student violence just too late for "The Year 2000" or the American Academy's Commission on the Year 2000 report, but in appropriate synchrony with revelations of the CIA's involvement with the thesis (see Lasch, 1970, Chapter 3; Young, 1971, footnote i for documentation).

Much difficulty has also been apparent recently for the users of those microforecasts that have been directed more toward the formulation of immediate programs than toward the justification of overall policy goals. Cole (1976) has pointed out that national economic forecasts based on (historicist) assumptions of the continuity of trends have become increasingly inadequate: as a result of the increasing integration of the world economy, international forces are massively affecting national economies. A recent review of British economic fore-casts concluded that their (usually overoptimistic) inaccuracies re-flected overemphasis on "quantitative assessment, based, more often than not, on almost linear projections of past trends" (Chapman, 1976, p. 254).

As for the argument concerning the distinction between exploratory and normative forecasting techniques, I would argue that all futures studies—including those purporting to be purely exploratory—are in-evitably value-laden. The selection of what parameters to analyze, the assumptions about which factors are fixed and which changing, the judgment as to what is or is not feasible, the location of experts and the attitude taken to divergences among them, and the very decision to look at the likely outcomes of future changes rather than at the desir-able goals to which human activity might be directed—these all incor-porate some value choices, which cannot simply be removed by re-course to more objective techniques. Certainly, exploratory projections of particular variables and causal chains will be related to the develop-ment of images of the future in normative forecasting, but such analy-ses need not involve historicist assumptions.

## ETHNOCENTRISM

Ethnocentrism is closely related to historicism in futures studies. As historicism seemed pragmatically justified in an era of continuing eco-nomic stability, so the convergence thesis (which rests upon historic-ism) may flourish in a period of apparently unassailable hegemony. Industrialization, it is argued, is the most viable form of social organiza-tion in the modern world. In the industrialized countries, the image of a glossy, technocratic postindustrialization is thus conjured up.[11] For underdeveloped countries, there is the prospect of progress through stages of political development to the same destiny, or else the chance of "bantustanization," of transformation into reservations of rural back-wardness.

In the past decade, a strong line of argument has emerged to chal-lenge the classic image of the Third World as stagnating in under-development solely through internal properties such as cultural bar-riers to innovation, overpopulation, and lack of achievement motivation. It likewise opposes the view that the only future course for the poor countries is to follow the lead of the West by importing Western technologies and pursuing Western economic growth strate-gies.[12] Often termed dependency theory, this line of argument instead treats underdevelopment not as an unchanging primeval state of affairs, but as the outcome of first imperialist and then neocolonial exploitation of the Third World. In this process, precolonial technologies and economies were destroyed when they could not be applied to the benefit of dominant groups in the rich countries.

Futures researchers have so far largely failed to challenge the dominant interpretation of world economic relationships as being mutually rewarding to rich and poor countries alike. Instead, ideas of "trickle down" from the growth of the industrial nations are prominent, and there is little questioning (in materials forecasting, for example) of the assumption that the United States should remain the consumer of the greater part of the world's natural resources. The scale of human misery involved in underdevelopment is so vast that any contribution, material or ideological, made to it by futurology requires careful scrutiny at least. Only recently have influential futures researchers criticized the passivity of futures studies adopting the historicist, ethnocentric view of world development.[13]

Parallel to the macrosociological notions of nations moving along a single developmental pathway from traditional to modern is the sociopsychological image of individual interests and attitudes following a similar course. The advanced inhabitants of underdeveloped countries are supposed to display a syndrome of modernity, whereby their attitudes to the use of new technologies, to traditional authorities, and the like have changed to resemble Western views. In the future, these attitudes will supposedly be more widespread. Armer and Schnaiberg (1972, 1975) criticize the attitude scales used in the studies based on this perspective and suggest that modernity is a near myth.[14] A thesis similar to the modernity theory has been advanced for the working classes of Western societies: according to prophets of embourgeoisement, these classes will increasingly display what have heretofore been middle-class values and attitudes as their affluence grows. The classic study which casts doubt on this forecast in Goldthorpe et al. (1969); more recently, Rinehart (1971) has argued that convergence, if it comes, is most likely to follow from deterioration in the circumstances of the middle class.

The historicist and ethnocentric ideas described above flourished in the climate of expansion prevailing in the postwar decades. With challenges to Western imperialism and renewed indications of the instability of the world capitalist system have come sharp attacks on the ideas that have been employed to support the economic subjection of the Third World. The danger remains that futures research will survive the present turbulence of theory by becoming an even more faithful handmaiden to the status quo; that it will perpetuate and project the ideologies that legitimate and guide the actions of an oppressive system.

SCIENTISM

Recently, the social sciences have been subjected to a host of critiques, many of which specifically point to the shortcomings involved in attempting to follow a positivist model of scientific development purportedly based on the experience of the natural sciences.[15]

Futures researchers seem particularly vulnerable to the lures of "hard science" and are prone to adopt not only the highly mathematical, value-free stance of much big science but also some of the more dangerous themes of pop science and less creditable fads of science journalism. Many of these fads are for methods and gadgetry. Simulation modeling, and the systems analysis tradition with which it has close links, are cases in point. As the aerospace programs that fed the early growth of systems analysis dried up, overnight analysts acquired expertise in all sorts of public policy fields (acidly analyzed by Hoos, 1972; see also Nieburg, 1969). While the analysts and tools that had put men on the moon were set loose on the problems of the ghetto (Nelson, 1974), the computer simulation approaches used for forecasting business cycles and industrial dynamics were rapidly turned to the future of cities, countries, and the world.[16] The mystique of flowcharts and complex arguments, and the image of the computer as impartial and dispassionate superbrain, are involved in the uncritical fascination such approaches can call up.

Developments in systems theory have a way of rapidly appearing in futurology. For example, in his forecast of world futures, Emery (1974) makes use of the Gardner and Ashby (1970) work, which suggested that large complex systems may rapidly become unstable as connections are formed within the system in excess of some threshold point. The similar-sounding catastrophe theory of René Thorm has also been spoken of as a further possible input to the prediction and management of social instabilities. Yet, these much-publicized developments have never been fully digested by specialists in their fields of origin. Various criticisms of the Gardner-Ashby work are summarized by McLean, Shepherd, and Curnow (1974), who were unable to replicate the threshold effect. (They suggested that this effect resulted from errors in the construction of random matrices used in the original analysis.) Croll (1976) has pointed to the overselling of the catastrophe theory; in a reply appended to Croll's article, Thorm himself concedes that there has been "overenthusiasm." The theory has rapidly been applied to such matters as the management of prison riots (see Rosenhead, 1976). Yet another mathematical importation into futures research—fuzzy set theory—has been noted by Hoos (1974), who wryly criticizes the claims made for it.

Such tendencies suggest scientism, which is present "where people draw on widely shared images and notions about the scientific community and its practices, in order to add weight to arguments they are advocating, or to practices which they are promoting, or to values whose adoption they are advocating" (Cameron and Edge, 1975, p. 5).[17]

The grasping of the more sensational metaphors and sophisticated methodologies of contemporary science, which constitutes an attempt to secure its status for futurological analysis, may serve various purposes: to increase self-esteem and professional reputation, to secure stable funding, to attain maximum impact for one's opinions, or to attain the rigor of scientific analysis by using techniques purported to convey such rigor.[18]

Scientism is manifested in other ways, not the least of which is the uncritical use of statistical data and analysis in futures research and in futuristic social science. The failings of GNP as a measure of welfare are well known (e.g., see Encel, Marstrand, and Page, 1975, Chapter 12), but it is still widely employed in futures studies as if a measurement of the money value of national economic activity does indeed yield firm information about living standards and quality of life. Hoos (1974) is scathing about the "quantomania" of spurious precision in cost-benefit studies and the like; she argues that the data used in many forecasting studies are highly suspect and often manipulated in favor of particular interest groups. (It has often been alleged that statistics on natural resource reserves have been determined more by the firms that profit from resource extraction than by geophysical processes.) It may also be pointed out that many social statistics used in futures studies are by no means as neutral as they may appear.[19] Statistics and systems analyses may be powerful tools; they may also serve the function of cloaking the pleas of powerful interests and bureaucracies. It has been argued that one cause of the concern with social statistics and "abstracted empiricism" of postwar mainstream social science was the unwillingness of its practitioners to confront questions of the structure of power in modern societies. Is the scientism of futures research merely an emulation of its better established sibling professions, or is it that the willing servant of power needs question no more than the efficiency with which that power is exercised?

## THE TECH-FIX AND TECHNOLOGICAL DETERMINISM

The prescription of "technological fixes" is prominent in many scenarios of the future and has been proposed by, and among futurists: cure ghetto violence during the "long hot summers" by installing air conditioning; consider the possibilities of psychosurgery and psychopharmacology if violence and protest are becoming endemic; reduce road accident casualties by inventing ultrasafe supercars; abolish heroin addiction by introducing the more acceptable methadone fix; speed up economic development by controlling population growth with new contraceptive devices. And if such a future is beginning to bother the futurologist, then why not relieve the anxiety by meditating (perhaps using biofeedback equipment to save effort, if not money)?[20]

Such a collection of purported panaceas does not, of course, cast any doubt on the practicability of designing technologies (and, indeed, social organizations) so as to support a more human society. As Burns and Studer (1975) argue in their analysis of the work of Weinberg (a leading advocate of tech-fixes—air conditioning, supercars, and contraception, for example—although he is probably best known as an advocate of the nuclear fix for world energy problems, social and technological questions are often confused, so that problems are conceived in technological terms and social variables are ignored. They see this confusion as associated with an elitist reliance upon scientists as the most appropriate diagnosticians of social problems.

One of the most significant large-scale attempts to apply a tech-fix was the "Green Revolution," upon which many hopes for the future were pinned. This was an attempt to cope with world food problems— the subject of several forecasts of famine made in the early 1960s—by introducing high-yield varieties of rice and wheat to Asia and Latin America. Its results have certainly been mixed. Griffin (1974) concludes that there has been little direct alleviation of malnutrition and that instead financial benefits accrued to those already relatively well off while labor was in many cases displaced and workers thus impoverished. Third World agriculture was, in the process, tied to Western agribusiness for supplies of fertilizers, pesticides, and machinery.[21] Meanwhile, solutions for the problems of production and distribution of food for the world await essential social reforms.[22]

If tech-fixes were successful in solving the problems that they are allegedly directed at, they would have an obvious appeal. Not only would symptoms of alienation, disaffection, and powerlessness be alleviated but criticisms of the status quo could more readily be dismissed as aberrations or signs of disturbance and the social structures that generate these symptoms in the first place could be made less visible. A view of the creation of the future that meshes well with the tech-fix mentality is technological determinism.

Technological determinism sometimes appears as the doctrine of the "technological imperative," which asserts that what can be, will be done. The implication is that technological evolution necessarily consists of a single path, as typified by the arguments of representatives of the aerospace industry for more prestigious, faster aircraft. A forecasting technique which is a perfect example of this attitude is the "forecast by analysis of precursive events" method, in which changes in technology or performance in an advanced field (e.g., racing cars, military aircraft) are predicted to appear after a suitable lag in more general applications (e.g., family cars and commercial aircraft).[23]

Perhaps the most ominous invocation of the theory of technological imperatives is in the military field. Yanarella (1975) has analyzed the course of American defense planning during the 1960s strategic arms race. Although the official hypothesis (defined by McNamara and others) described the arms race as an action-reaction model, with the United States and the U.S.S.R. each reacting to weapons developments by the other party by developing new (counter-) weapons systems, Yanarella finds a technological imperatives approach actually embodied in U.S. planning. Of particular relevance to futures researchers are his conclusions about the organizational processes that gave birth to a technological imperative that has led to the unparalleled marshaling of destructive forces. He ties the futurological techniques of defense-management—PPBS, operations research, and systems analysis—to the provision of a basis for the centralization of analysis and to the institutionalization of the strategic doctrines that underly the apparent technological imperative. Yanarella's book (1976) is a valuable account of this piece of recent history.

Technological determinism of another kind is involved in the thesis that given technologies will have broadly similar consequences when applied in apparently distinct types of society. The convergence thesis is a combination of this thesis with a form of the technological imperative: Western and Eastern societies are predicted to become increasingly similar as they change structurally in accommodating to new industrial, communications, and consumption technologies. The possibilities of designing technologies in accordance with different societal goals are ignored or written off in this thesis.

Thus, too, do notions of the new industrial state (Galbraith, 1967, makes much of technological imperatives), postindustrial society, or superindustrial society (Toffler, 1970) smack of technological determinism. Changes in production technology here determine the forms of future economic and political organization, necessitating conscious long-term planning, the rise to power of a technostructure, knowledge elite, or the like, and eventually fashioning a more equitable, if essentially technocratic, society.

A more explicitly ominous image of the future stems from the "malevolent" technological determinism of writers such as Ellul (1965) and Roszak (1968, 1972). These writers view techniques and technology as virtually beyond human control. Further, they maintain that the penetration of scientistic thinking is so pervasive in our affairs that judgments are increasingly made on solely quantitative grounds and consist exclusively of rational analyses of the means that can more efficiently attain given ends. (On the social support for this approach within a well-known think-tank, see Wolfson, 1972.) As in the "benign" image of postindustrial society, technique and technology are reified into entities standing apart from the human activities of which they are actually consequences. These writers provide a useful corrective view, focusing the inequities and eviscerations of technocratic society, but such a view could support fatalism. It could discourage an awareness of potential alternative directions technological change could take, of other goals for scientific activity, of different possible modes of rationality, and of the real prospects for redesigning social organizations.

Both the form and operation of "technocracies" and technologies are constrained by the dominant powers in society. Technological determinisms, which are themselves a pervasive influence upon forecasting, fail to penetrate to or to grapple with this fundamental influence on present and future social change. The pervasiveness of these approaches in forecasting, and the schooling and socialization of many futurologists in technological (and/or military) forecasting establishments, correspond to the interests of business and bureaucracies in continuous technological change rather than to the interests of the mass of people whose lives are to be reshuffled in this change. To go beyond postindustrial apologetics, the resignation of Ellul or his American counterparts, or the bland trust in a revolution of consciousness along the lines of a Charles Reich (1970) would require a different form of futures research.[24] It would be a futures research in which the construction of images of viable sociotechnical organizations would be related to the assessment both of the beneficiaries of alternative organizations and of the changes in power relationships that would be involved in actualizing them.

## MYSTIFICATION AND ELITISM

As suggested above, critics of technocratic tendencies in postindustrial society point to highly significant changes in futures research. "La technique," the target of Ellul's attack, is a clear symptom of the malady of much forecasting and planning. Some approaches to imaging the future are not merely limited to quantitative considerations but restrict the dimensions of the future to monetary assessments only. The prime example of the latter is the cost-benefit analysis, wherein efforts to stretch all considerations into a monetary metric lead to attempts to place money values on individuals' lives, morbidity, or available time. Many of the attempts to provide objective cost-benefit valuations of qualitatively different social outcomes have turned out to be rather less than publicly acceptable. For example, the costing of lost lives in terms of forfeited contributions to the economic system may end up by awarding negative worth to the elderly. In the labyrinth of a lengthy quantitative analysis, however, are likely to lurk many value-judgments that never obtain such public scrutiny as some of the more controversial large-scale projects have received.

In response to the criticisms leveled at such economic philistinism, some futurologists have turned to the social indicators literature for alternatives to purely economic criteria.[25] Social indicator data and research may be valuable tools of diagnosis and analysis, but most of the work so far carried out is severely limited—which reflects the emergence of social indicators research as a component of the social technology of the coming postindustrial society.[26]

The resort to apparently complicated algorithms in which social values are disguised as scientific operations is one way in which futures research often mystifies, rather than illuminates, processes of social change and choices for influencing the future. In earlier sections of this article, other mystifications have been encountered, such as the development of increasingly complex computer models whose operation is increasingly difficult for even their builders to understand, let alone for outsiders in their attempt to ascertain the normative choices involved in their construction and calibration.[27]

Surrey, Chesshire, and Dombey (1976) supply a case in which futures research is being applied in mystifying fashion in an important area of contemporary public policy—the decision as to whether to build fast-breeder reactors (in the United Kingdom, in this case). They describe a seemingly comprehensive report whose forecasts had been taken to provide strong support for the notion that an energy gap would develop in the 1990s, which could only be bridged by heavy use of nuclear power. This report provides several scenarios, but these are shown to ignore a number of important points concerning trends in energy consumption and to rest on a tech-fix assumption in the first place.[28] The authors conclude that "like the energy gap of the 1950s which was held to justify the first nuclear power programme, and like the missile gap of the 1960s, the energy gap of the 1990s may well prove illusory" (1976, p. 21), and they argue in favor of diversifying energy R&D.

Many techniques of futures research can make decision-making processes more obscure. This can even be true of scenario-writing—which is supposed to provide a range of alternatives, although, as the example just citied shows, these may be within strict limitations. The elite decision-maker may confidentially request his expert to select the most likely scenario and may use this scenario for planning purposes, thus rendering the planning process less ascertainable than if it were openly admitted that a single image of the future was in use. Cole (1976) has described with some dismay the development of forecasting techniques that internalize debate and conflict, hence leading to even less communication between the public and decision-makers.

The image of technocratic postindustrial society, in which forecasting and related activities have high status, is not generally one in which the economic structure of Western capitalism, with its tendencies toward increasing concentration of power in few hands, is analyzed, let alone challenged. Futurology itself seems almost one-dimensional in its acceptance of the liberal paradigm underlying this image, just as critics of contemporary Western society (e.g., Marcuse, 1964; Miliband, 1969) have described forces pressing the social order into a one-dimensional form. Wynne (1975), for example, describes technology assessment in these terms. He argues that much technology assessment practice downplays the extent of conflict built into present social structures, that it formulates social problems in technical, end-of-ideology terms, and that it can be seen as a theoretical attempt to involve the public in a view of society that serves the interests of a small minority. There is thus the danger of strengthening a one-dimensional, technocratic ideology, which may limit political discourse to a narrow set of alternatives.[29]

Underlying these dangers is the widespread acceptance of aspects of this essentially technocratic ideology. These involve views of science and technology as neutral, of policy-related research as inevitably demanding a high degree of expertise, and of experts and state officials as being able to stand above the conflicts of interest in society. It seems likely, however, that in fact the apparently neutral and rational expert often upholds "a process of control which is 'technocratic' in the . . . sense of using science and technique simultaneously to maintain and to legitimize the dominant position of existing power groups" (Elliot and Elliot, 1976, p. 96).[30]

It may be argued that the pressures on the majority of researchers engaged in forecasting studies are such as to make them much more concerned with developing forecasts for their sponsors than with attempting to understand either the social phenomena they forecast[31] or the social role of futures research. Nevertheless, democratically inclined futures researchers and the "populists" of the postindustrial tradition in futurology (e.g., Toffler) propose greater public participation in imagining the future, in assessing technologies, and in formulating social goals and social indicators (see Miles, 1975, Chapter 8). This is seen as a check on the dangers of "future shock" and "technocracy." It seems reasonable to argue that the participation of a broad mass of people in the creation of futures and images of the future would not only result in the people having more conscious control of their own destiny[32] but would also go further toward producing futures responsive to a wide range of needs than would the domination of the future by the goals of capital accumulation and corporate stability, or by the demands of state bureaucracies (socialist or otherwise).

Aspects of contemporary society and of futurology within this society mitigate against such broad public involvement. Indeed, there is a real possibility that some of the approaches that futurists have investigated as potential aids to public participation (see, for example, Elliot and Elliot, 1976; Miles, 1975) may be actually employed as manipulative tools for legitimating the status quo through pseudoparticipation. The expert who can control the dissemination of information and the generation of alternative plans and impact statements has immense power under some of these techniques. In existing futurology, we encounter a historicism that may restrict the people's perceptions of alternative ways of acting and of alternative organizations of society. In the participative futurology envisioned by some futurologists, there is the danger that fatalism and apathy may be replaced by "people . . . participating in little more than the management of their own exploitation" (Elliot and Elliot, 1976, p. 195).

The essential complement to the widening and deepening of public debate about the future is a critique of the ideological dimensions of contemporary futures research. The role of human choice would here be counterposed against crude determinisms of all kinds, while analysis of the historical constraints upon that choice and of the social groups that must actively make it would prevent the construction of alternative futures degenerating into mere utopianism. The inevitability and desirability of technocratic management—even management of public participation—could be challenged by assessment of the social costs of expertise, a technical division of labor, and a highly skewed distribution of information and power. The value-judgments involved in objective methods of futures research would be scrutinized. Research techniques making good use of the skills and equipment available to the general public would be developed and diffused, with significant innovations flowing from and within, as well as merely to, ordinary people.[33]

The critique of current practices in futures research that is involved here should serve to combat both types of danger described in the first section of this article. Where necessary, people may apply it to challenge forecasts that are being used to develop or support policies that run counter to their interests; it may also help people free themselves from restricted received images of the future. The dangerous tendencies of these ruling images of the future may also be countered to some extent by nonhistoricist futures studies. One requirement for this correction is the encouragement of a methodological pluralism in futures research. Another feature would be the invention, demonstration, and study of alternative technologies and social organizations, which may stimulate thought and experiments concerned with directions for society that transcend the orthodox choice between industrial capitalism and atavistic barbarism. (Such research faces the problem that attractive ideas and techniques which are developed or promoted in isolation may be co-opted for the status quo, a fate that has befallen many promising social movements and innovations.)

Ideas—even images of the future—have no power in themselves to change the world. Their effectiveness depends upon the existence of people both willing to put them into action and capable of doing so; otherwise, they remain at the level of mere utopianism. Futurists have tried to identify the people who might turn their forecasts into reality; their candidates include a new working class, students, ethnic minorities, and a technocratic knowledge elite. Often the agency of these groups is described as predestined, as an inevitability of future history. However, it may be questioned whether a future in which men and women control their own destinies can be created without the active engagement of the productive capacity of the world's peasantry and working class, and whether, indeed, such specific groups as those identified above could hand down this control to people from above.

For widespread participation in imaging futures and creating the future to become a realistic proposition, rather than a form of pseudo-participation, the support of a widespread movement for popular democracy is essential. In the course of such a movement, historicist thinking may be effectively undermined. The dangers of futures research are that it may retard the development of such movements and that futures researchers may continue to strive to predict future history rather than to struggle for the humanization of the future. Hence, given the growing capacities of the human race for self-destruction, the possibility of any future at all may well be endangered.

## NOTES

1. Science Policy Research Unit, University of Sussex. The work involved in this chapter was carried out while I was in receipt of a Leverhulme Fellowship. I would like to thank my friends and colleagues at SPRU and in Brighton for material assistance and inspiration, while, of course, acknowledging that this

chapter is in no way to be taken as expressing the standpoint of SPRU or of anyone other than myself.

2. Miles (1975) contains a substantial bibliography of the bodies of literature concerned with these areas of research. The present chapter will emphasize more the body of work dissenting from mainstream futurology.

3. The above analysis stems form what might be called the social relations model of S&T, which has been contrasted with the more traditional use-abuse model (Dickson, 1974, 1976; Elliot and Elliot, 1976; Rose and Rose, 1972, 1974). The use-abuse model portrays S&T as neutral techniques and activities, whose dangers lie merely in their clumsy or malevolent application. The dangers of futures research would thus be seen as problems stemming from the use/abuse of its techniques by biased, selfish, or shortsighted interests. The social relations model takes S&T as part of a wider social and political order and thus not as nonneutral activities standing above society and social conflict. S&T themselves reflect, and may often support, dominant power relations in society. Futures research, then, may affect people's material interests, in that it may contribute to processes of state and corporate planning. It may also influence the consciousness that people have of the world in which they live—and not necessarily in the direction of consciousness-expansion (Boguslaw, 1971).

4. For a discussion of advocacy and meta-advocacy, see Shapiro and Neubauer, 1973.

5. The term *historicism* was coined by Popper (1957), who used the concept polemically against Fascism and Marxism. Cornforth (1968) has replied in defense of "official" Marxism. It may be argued that Popper's arguments are valid against a vulgarized, mechanical Marxism which is economically deterministic, and refers to "iron laws of history" and the like. Indeed, much of the contention between modern social science and "Marxism" has in fact represented the attacks of academics on this vulgarized Marxism (Swingewood, 1975). The analysis of historicist tendencies in futures research was begun by Goldthorpe (1971) and taken up by Miles (1975).

6. Marien (1972) has published a survey of futurists' judgments of important literature in futures research. While a number of nonhistoricist discussions of the future are listed in the 236 items reviewed, the futurist documents rated as essential by one-third or more of the panelists are another story; of the six so rated by two-thirds or more of the panelists, only de Jouvenel's work, with its emphasis on conjectures, would seem to stand apart from a technological determinist historicism. Incidentally, a supplement in Part II of Marien's booklet contains a booklist prepared by a German group who have made their presence felt at some futures conferences and prepared several essays critical of futurology (Zukunfstsforschung), and who may be contacted at Dokumentation für Graue Literatur Zukunftsforschung, c/o N.M. Rolf, B. Ziegler, Kurfürstendamm 195/6, VII/D-1, Berlin 15, Berlin, Federal Republic of Germany.

7. This type of historicism is justified in such statements as "some forces must be operative to produce a marked or regular trend, especially if it has been long continued. Even if these forces are not fully known, yet they must exist and presumably will continue to be effective" (Clawson and Knetsch, quoted by Burton, 1971).

8. Commenting on urban models, Sayer (1976a, p. 54) argues that often they "don't even refer to the real world processes which determine urban development (capital accumulation, investment in built form, profitability, etc.). Instead they take the most superficial outputs of these processes, the regular patterns of urban functioning, e.g., spatial interaction, and extrapolate these into the future." (Italics removed.) For cross-impact forecasting, and the absence of a formal theoretical basis in prediction, see McLean (1976). For a more extended essay on urban models, see Sayer (1976b).

9. Unanimously considered essential by Marien's (1972) panel and featured prominently in the review of forecasts in Cole, Freeman, Jahoda, Miles, and Pavitt (forthcoming).

10. That there is little evidence concerning the accuracy of long-term exploratory forecasts is suggested by a review in Encel, Marstrand, and Page (1975, Chapter 8). Chisholm (1976) argues that trade-offs have to be made between accuracy and a number of factors, of which time span is one. (The others are discreteness of geographical area and the degree of disaggregation of the sectors involved.)

11. Many critiques have been mounted against the theory of postindustrial society. See, for example, Goldthorpe (1971), Kleinberg (1973), Kumar (1975), and Miles (1975). Gross (1973) presents a gloomy forecast drawn from analysis of the postindustrial school; Lasch (1973) takes up both technocratic and radical analysis: and Marien (1973a) looks specifically at Bell's work.

12. For criticism of the orthodox approach to political development, which ignores the existence of relations of dependency, see Bodenheimer (1971), the excellent review by Chilcote and Edelstein (1974), and Stauffer (1975). Barratt Brown (1974), Bernstein (1973), and Brookfield (1975) review the related literature of economic development. Recent studies inspired by the dependency perspective, that demonstrate that it need be by no means a view of development which relies upon rhetoric more than quantitative analysis, include Kaufman, Chernotsky, and Geller (1975), Rosen and Kurth (1974), Stallings (1972), and Weisskopf (1972). The findings of Adelman and Morris (1973) of negative impacts of economic development on equity in various Third World countries are also relevant here. Kay (1975) presents a Marxist analysis of the relations of development and underdevelopment.

13. Dator (1974) has summarized Bodenheimer's attack on conventional wisdom from the dependency standpoint. In in the wake of environmentalism, however, some futurists have picked up the notion of overdevelopment as applicable to the rich countries. It should be made clear that the dependency approach does not portray rich countries as exploiting poor countries. Instead, dominant groups in the rich countries are seen as exploiting the workers of both rich and poor countries, with the assistance of elites in the latter. What true development would actually be, it is argued, can only be established when this maldistribution of power is corrected. Only then can it be determined if overdevelopment has any meaning. Current circumstances, both within and between countries, are best characterized as the outcome of uneven development.

14. Among other critical essays may be cited Coughenor and Stephenson

(1972). On whether acceptance of Western technology is necessarily well founded in the Third World, see, for example, among critics of technology transfer practices, Cooper (1972). Harris (1965) produces an interesting study of the ecological utility of one traditional attitude—respect for the sacred cows of India.

Much has been written critical of the culture of poverty thesis that has been used in the West to account for the persistence of poverty in terms of the characteristics of the poor. On educational and psychological aspects of cultural deprivation, see Keddie (1973). On the community development programs linked to this thesis, a popular theme of postindustrial theorists, see Mayo (1973). The appeal of these schemes would seem to lie in their prescription that the poor, rather than the social system, should be changed.

15. Several of these have already been cited in this article. In addition, Blackburn (1972) presents articles appraising tendencies in economics, history, political science, and sociology. Armistead (1974) and Brown (1973) analyze social psychology and general psychology, respectively. Colfax and Roach (1971) focus on radical sociology, while Shaw gives a Marxist analysis of current social science practice (1975) and provides a bibliography of Marxist alternatives (1973). Hunt and Schwartz (1972) provide a critique of economic theory.

On social science methodology, Ford (1975) is telling and witty. Incidentally, he manages to take a few swipes at futures research. Hindess (1973) criticizes both positivist and ethnomethodological approaches to the use of data; Evans, Irvine, and Miles (forthcoming) have collected critical readings on social statistics.

Journals representing alternatives to mainstream social science have appeared in recent years. Those I have encountered in the English language include: *Antipode* (on geography), *Bulletin of Concerned Asian Scholars*, *Bulletin of the Conference of Socialist Economists*, *Concerned Demography*, *History Workshop*, *Humpty Dumpty* (psychology), *Insurgent Sociologist*, *Radical Philosophy*, *Red Rat* (a "journal of abnormal psychologists"), *Review of Radical Political Economics*, and *Telos*. Also important are journals representing alternatives in technology, physical and applied science: *Radical Science Journal*, *Science for the People*, *Science for People*, and *Undercurrents*, among them. Boyle and Harper (1976) present an excellent bibliography of publications and an index of groups working in applied science. Much of the content of these publications has an indirect bearing on the practice of futures research, and it is not uncommon to find a direct analysis of, for example, the systems approach, the role of think tanks, and neo-Malthusian ideas.

16. The chief virtue of the first generation of models of cities and the world was that they provoked enough controversy to motivate researchers to publish technical analyses that exposed the conservative assumptions on which they rested (e.g., Cole, Freeman, Jahoda, and Pavitt, 1973; Constable, 1973). Unfortunately, these technical critiques lacked the appeal (and publicity) of the model-based forecasts, and while providing useful weapons for policy-makers opposed to such forecasts (and even to those hostile to futures itself), have failed to disabuse wide sections of the public of computerized Malthusianism.

Considerable caution has been expressed concerning the claims made for, and practical deployment of, computer models. See, for example, Brewer (1973) on urban models, and Brewer (1975) on a wider sample; Clark and Cole (1975) on world models; and Wilson (1970) on military models and games.

17. Their booklet is one of a number of publications of the SISCON (Science in a Social Context) Project, whose coordinator is Dr. W. F. Williams, Physics/Administration Building, University of Leeds, Leeds LS2 9JT, U.K. Many of the units prepared by this group are highly relevant to the topics of this essay. These include units of Limits to Growth, Science and the Environment, Science and Survival, Science, Technology and the Modern Industrial State, The Sociology of Science, Science and Rationality, and Women and Science.

18. Clark and Cole (1975, p. 6) indicate that the Club of Rome chose computer simulation methodology for its dramatic public impact; Golub and Townsend (1975, pp. 41–42) argue that the results obtained by simulation came as no surprise to the Club members, being essentially a dramatization of views expressed previously. For a critical account of the paradigms of social science, futurology, and planning from a systems viewpoint, see Maruyama (1974).

19. See, for example, Friedman (1974) on international relations indices, Miles (1975, 1976a) on social and political indicators, and Evans, Irvine, and Miles (forthcoming) for treatments of a wide range of official and unofficial statistics.

20. Cross, Elliot, and Roy (1974) have collected several essays dealing with tech-fixes. Etzioni and Remp (1973) present a fairly respectable version of the case for technological shortcuts to social change, while Epstein (1974) provides an account of the failure of methadone, which may be compared with their discussion instructively. Elliot and Elliot (1976, Chapter 2) present the case against ecological tech-fixes, while Nieburg (1969) forecasts their failure in urban problem-solving. See also Burns and Studer (1975).

21. Sachs (1974) describes the Green Revolution in terms reminiscent of the critique of futures studies and planning as ethnocentric and scientistic. He argues that it rested on an overvaluing of the model of Western high technology agriculture at the expense of alternative lines of research—e.g., studying the potentialities of local animals and crops, focusing on complete ecosystems, considering forestry, and supporting indigenous research and development efforts.

22. For a radical viewpoint on the Green Revolution, with a useful bibliography of related literature, see Franke (1974). Readers interested in radical analyses of the Green Revolution should also consult the June 1972 issue of the *Monthly Review*. On the myths of the world food crisis, an excellent account has been given by Eberstadt (1976). On world food futures, see Marstrand's chapter in Cole, Freeman, Jahoda, Miles, and Pavitt (forthcoming).

23. An influential essay which extends this discussion in an analysis of Western planning processes in general and whose title is particularly apt in this context is Ozebekhan's "The Triumph of Technology—'Can' Implies 'Ought' " (1968).

24. Clecak (1973) discusses American "plain Marxists," including Herbert Marcuse, and the New Left in terms of the conflict between their utopian visions and their sense of practical possibilities. Lasch (1973b) provides valuable

discussions of Reich and Ellul. Nobile (1971) brings together a varied collection of essays on Reich.

25. Some social indicators researchers have likewise turned to futurology for inspiration. For example, Fox (1974), makes reference to both futures researchers and to many research areas popular in futures research. Names like Bell and Toffler have featured in compilations of social indicators research. Despite the promotion of social indicators research as an alternative to the simplification of economic measurement, various attempts have been made in this field to develop unitary measures of welfare: the elusive quality of life index. In a previous review (Encel, Marstrand, and Page, 1975, Chapter 12), I concluded that at best such measures are misleading.

26. I have elsewhere summarized criticisms of social indicator research in some detail and have noted some exceptions to them (Miles, 1975). Among the most prominent criticisms are an emphasis on "hard" rather than "soft" aspects of society, on quantity rather than quality, on physical conditions rather than subjective states; a focus on aggregative rather than distributive information; a lack of attention to the structure of social organizations; and an orientation toward patterns of actual behavior rather than to the availability and accessibility of choices. (Recent work by the OECD working party on social indicators is trying to provide a reorientation on this final point.) On ideology in statistics, see Evans, Irvine, and Miles (1971).

27. See Clark and Cole (1975); Cole (1976) discusses a wider range of forecasting practices. McLean (1976) and McLean and Shepherd (1976) advocate the development of less complex models and techniques for analyzing model structure, which allow for ready appreciation of the underlying dynamics of different models and which can expose differences among experts.

28. Among the points ignored in the scenarios, these authors cite the large contribution to the trend of increasing energy consumption made by the growth in road transport, which is decidedly not fueled by reactor power (but which could be the subject of a coordinated energy and transport policy); a low growth rate of domestic energy consumption, and the stability of per capita energy consumption during the first half of this century; and the increasing energy efficiency of British industry.

The consequences of the publication of this article would seem a poor augury for the openness of forecasting for policy purposes to public scrutiny; shortly after the appearance of the article in a daily newspaper, its senior author resigned his advisory position to a Parliamentary Select Committee (see *New Scientist,* July 1, 1976, p. 3).

Other commentators have joined in the criticism of these energy scenarios and the policy guidelines that have been developed around them; see Chapman (1976) and Conroy (1976).

29. A book by the SPRU group looks at the possibilities for forecasting on the basis of different worldviews (Cole, Freeman, Jahoda, Miles, and Pavitt, forthcoming). In this case, three worldviews are taken: a conservative one (neoclassical economics, functionalist sociology), a liberal-reformist one (Keynesian economics, postindustrial sociology), and a radical one (Marxian approaches).

Challenges to the liberal approach to forecasting from the left are rarely couched in terms of forecasts, and futures studies are often completely dismissed by critical social scientists. Radical theorists generally follow Marx in scoffing at the idea of laying down detailed blueprints for future society: his ideal future emerges from praxis, from the dialectics of struggle.

Nevertheless, many of the contributions of classical Marxism are particularly relevant both to futures research and to any discussion of future alternatives. Bottomore and Rubel (1956) devote a section of their anthology of Marx's work to future society; Evans (1975) has attempted to summarize his views on the future; and Tucker (1970) explicitly treats Marx as a futurologist! Avinieri (1968) and Evans (1975) provide useful correctives to the idea of Marx's holding on to a single, historicist view of the future. On utopian thought, see Engels' "Socialism: Utopian and Scientific" (in Marx and Engels, 1968). Trotsky himself actually toyed with scenario-writing in "The Revolution Betrayed" and wrote that we must avoid "doing violence to dynamic social formations which have had no precedent and have no analogies. The scientific task, as well as the political, is not to give a finished definition to an unfinished process, but to follow all its stages, separate its progressive from its reactionary tendencies, expose their mutual relations, foresee possible variants of development, and find in this foresight a basis for action" (Mills, 1963, p. 323). The radical left itself, however, has not always avoided fatalistic images of the future (e.g., see Richards, 1975, analysis of the postwar Fourth International).

Other radical analysts have posed fairly concrete images of the future. Bodington (1973) has linked Marxism with ideas of alternative technology, and Bookchin (1971) is a prime exponent of a more anarchistic image of the future. Goodman and Goodman (1947) are pioneers in this tradition, and more recently Goodman (1965) has presented a science fictional scenario stemming from it.

A significant indicator of possibilities for images of the future derived from and for grassroots interests was the corporate plan proposed by shop stewards of Lucas Aerospace (predictably rejected by management). For accounts of the history of this plan, see *New Scientist*, in which several news items appeared in 1975 and 1976; *Science for People*, number 32 (1976), and *Undercurrents*, numbers 12 and 13 (1975).

30. Beneveniste (1972) has analyzed "the politics of expertise." For case studies of the actual influence of "social science mandarins," suggesting that policy science is used mainly for purposes of legitimation, see Horowitz (1970). For detailed and chilling treatments of the role of social analysis in the Vietnam War, exposing the myth of neutrality, see Chomsky (e.g., 1969, 1973a, 1973b). His accounts touch on the involvement of members of RAND and the Hudson Institute, and the application of techniques familiar to forecasters, in war planning. But the most revealing account of the systems approach is provided by Max Ways: "McNamara, his systems analysts, and their computers are not only contributing to the practical effectiveness of U.S. actions, but raising the moral level of policy by a more conscious and selective attention to the definition of its aims" (Ways, 1969, p. 387). Ways also argues that "new ways of planning can in themselves generate in the public mind a sense of direction, of intelligent choice" (p. 374) and "one can see in the conduct of the Vietnam war how the new style of planning serves values beyond efficiency" (p. 385).

The outrageous application of physical and social sciences in Vietnam has been cited by Rose and Rose (1972, 1974) as a major stimulus to the development of a radical critique of science transcending the use-abuse model.

An interesting sidelight on technocratic ideology is presented by Balbus (1975). He argues that the pervasive use of the language of sports to describe politics ("game plans," "the team," etc.) is part and parcel of the presentation of policy-making as simply a matter of technique, of active citizenship as "not only unnecessary but positively harmful; depoliticization is held to be essential to the very survival of the system as a whole" (p. 29).

31. As Spilerman (1975) has pointed out, politically and economically significant events may quite often be accurately predicted (at least in the short term) without being explained. For example, voting may be predicted by voting intentions as measured by a recent survey, but such surveys give us little information about why the individual or population prefers one or another candidate.

32. On the psychological aspects of this need, see de Charms (1968). Experts in social forecasting could actually share their knowledge and skills so as to help ordinary people gain consciousness of social change. Here the example of some social researchers in London's declining dockland comes to mind. They have collated area-relevant social indicators and have transmitted information on the location and use of such data to community groups. The danger of arrogance, in which the expert habitually assumes that her or his understanding is superior to that of the people actually involved in a situation, must be guarded against in this kind of action research.

33. It may seriously be questioned whether futures research as currently practiced even allows for quality control on the part of scientific peer groups. Computer simulations, for example, may be formidable to replicate, especially by researchers lacking access to the most powerful modern computers. The enormity of some recent models means that great effort is involved in unraveling their content. (It has been argued that not even their constructors completely understand their outputs in some cases.) There is a lack of groups prepared to do and capable of doing the work of peer group evaluation. That the same situation pertains in the case of technology assessments has been argued in a *Science* editorial by Schindler (1976).

## REFERENCES

Adams, John. 1974. "Saturation Planning." *Town and Country Planning,* Volume 42, 550–554.

Adelman, Irma, and Cynthia Taft Morris. 1973. *Economic Growth and Social Equity in Developing Countries.* Stanford, Calif.: Stanford University Press.

Arab-Ogly, E. 1975. *In the Forecasters' Maze.* Moscow: Progress Publishers.

Armer, Michael, and Allan Schnaiberg. 1972. "Measuring Individual Modernity: A Near Myth?" *American Sociological Review,* Volume 37, 301–316.

———. 1975. "Individual Modernity, Alienation and Socioeconomic Status: A Replication in Costa Rica." *Studies in Comparative International Development,* Volume 10, 35–48.

Armistead, Nigel. 1974. *Reconstructing Social Psychology.* Harmondsworth, England: Penguin Books.

Avinieri, Shlomo. 1968. *The Social and Economic Thought of Karl Marx.* Cambridge: Cambridge University Press.

Balbus, Ike. 1975. "Politics as Sports." *Monthly Review,* Volume 26, 26–39.

Baran, Paul A. 1957. *The Political Economy of Growth.* New York: Monthly Review Press.

Barratt Brown, Michael. 1974. *The Economics of Imperlialism.* Harmondsworth: Penguin Books.

Bell, Daniel. 1960. *The End of Ideology.* Glencoe, Ill.: Free Press.

———. 1967. "The Year 2000—The Trajectory of an Idea." *Deadalus,* Volume 96, Number 3, issue devoted to "Toward the Year 2000—Work in Progress."

———. 1974. *The Coming of Post-Industrial Society.* New York: Basic Books.

Beneveniste, Guy. 1972. *The Politics of Expertise.* Berkeley, Calif.: Glendessary Press.

Bernstein, Henry (ed.). 1973. *Underdevelopment and Development.* Harmondsworth: Penguin Books.

Blackburn, Robin (ed.). 1972. *Ideology in Social Science.* London: Fontana/Collins.

Bodenheimer, Susanne J. 1971. *The Ideology of Developmentalism: The American Paradigm—Surrogate for Latin American Studies.* Berkeley, Calif.: Sage Publications (Professional Papers in Comparative Politics, Volume 2, Series Number 01–015.

Bodington, Stephen. 1973. *Computers and Socialism.* Nottingham: Spokesman Books.

Boggs, Carl. 1976. *Gramsci's Marxism.* London: Pluto Press.

Boguslaw, Robert. 1971. "The Design Perspective in Sociology." In Wendell Bell and James A. Mau (eds.), *The Sociology of the Future.* New York: Russell Sage Foundation.

Bookchin, Murray. 1971. *Post-scarcity Anarchism.* New York: Ramparts Press.

Bottomore, Tom B., and Maximilien Rubel (eds.). 1956. *Karl Marx: Selected Writings in Sociology and Social Philosophy.* 1965 edition, Harmondsworth: Penguin Books.

Boyle, Godfrey, and Peter Harper. 1976. *Radical Technology.* London: Wildwood House; New York: Pantheon Books.

Brewer, Garry D. 1973. *Politicians, Bureaucrats and the Consultant.* New York: Basic Books.

———. 1975. *An Analyst's View of the Uses and Abuses of Models for Decision Making.* Paper presented to 141st annual meeting of the American Association for the Advancement of Science, New York City, January.

Brookes, S. K., A. G. Jordan, R. H. Kimber, and D. D. Richardson. 1975. "The Growth of the Environment as a Political Issue in Britain." *British Journal of Political Science,* Volume 6, 245–255.

Brookfield, Harold. 1975. *Interdependent Development.* London: Methuen.

Brown, Phil (ed.). 1973. *Radical Psychology.* New York: Harper Colophon Books.

Burns, E. M., and K. Studer. 1975. "Reflections on Alvin M. Weinberg: A Case Study on the Social Foundations of Science Policy." *Research Policy,* Volume 4, 28–44.

Burton, Thomas L. 1971. *Experiments in Recreation Research.* London: Allen and Unwin.

Cameron, Iain, and David Edge. 1975. *Aspects of Scientism.* Leeds: SISCON.

Carder, Michael. 1974. "A Family Quarrel? Developmentalism or Family Planning." *Concerned Demography,* Volume 4, 3–12.

Chapman, O. R. 1976. "Economic Forecasting in Britain 1961–75." *Futures,* Volume 8, 254–260.

Chapman, Peter. 1976. "The Nuclear Explosion." *New Scientist,* Volume 71, 121–123.

Chilcote, Ronald H., and Joel C. Edelstein. 1974. *Latin America: The Struggle with Dependency and Beyond.* Cambridge, Mass.: Holstead Press.

Chisholm, Michael. 1976. "Geographical Perspectives on the Future." In Christopher Freeman, Marie Jahoda, and Ian Miles (eds.), *Progress and Problems in Social Forecasting.* London: SSRC.

Chomsky, N. 1969. *American Power and the New Mandarins.* New York: Pantheon Books.

———. 1973a. *The Backroom Boys.* London: Fontana/Collins.

———. 1973b. *The Reasons of State.* London: Fontana/Collins.

Clark, John, and Sam Cole. 1975. *Global Simulation Models.* New York: John Wiley and Sons.

Clarke, Michael. 1975. "Social Problem Ideologies." *British Journal of Sociology,* Volume 26, 406–416.

Clecak, Peter. 1973. *Radical Paradoxes.* New York: Harper & Row.

Cole, Sam. In press. "Long-Term Forecasting Methods." *Futures.*

Cole, H. S. D., Christopher Freeman, Marie Jahoda, and K.L.R. Pavitt. 1973. *Thinking About the Future.* London: Sussex University Press. In the United States published as *Models of Doom.* New York: Universe Books.

———, Christopher Freeman, Marie Jahoda, Ian Miles, and K.L.R. Pavitt. (Forthcoming.) *Alternative Futures* (provisional title).

Colfax, J. David, and Jack L. Roach. 1971. *Radical Sociology.* New York: Basic Books.

Conroy, Czech. 1976. "Critical Friends." *New Scientist,* Volume 71, 123–124.

Constable, Derek. 1973. "Urban Growth Processes—A Critical Assessment of the Forrester Model." Reading: University of Reading Department of Geography, *Geographical Papers,* Number 21.

Cooper, Charles. 1972. "Science, Technology and Production in the Under-developed Countries: An Introduction." *Journal of Development Studies,* Volume 9, 1–18.

Cornforth, Maurice. 1968. *The Open Philosophy and the Open Society.* London: Lawrence and Wishart.

Coughenor, C. Milton, and John A. Stephenson. 1972. "Measures of Individual Modernity." *International Journal of Comparative Sociology,* Volume 13, 81–98.

Croll, James. 1976. "Is Catastrophe Theory Dangerous?" *New Scientist,* Volume 70, (June 12), 630–632.

Cross, Nigel, David Elliot, and Robin Roy. 1974. *Man-Made Futures.* London: Hutchinson Educational.

Dator, James A. 1974. "Neither There Nor Then: A Eutopian Alternative to the Development Model of Future Society." In *Human Futures: Needs, Societies and Technologies.* Guilford, England: IPC Science and Technology Press, 87–140.

Deakin, Nicholas. 1970. *Colour, Citizenship and British Society.* London: Panther Books.

de Charms, Richard. 1968. *Personal Causation.* New York: Academic Press.

de Jouvenel, Bertrand. 1967. *The Art of Conjecture.* New York: Basic Books.

Dickson, David. 1974. *Alternative Technology.* London: Fontana/Collins.

———. 1976. "Radical Science: A Possible Introduction." *Science for People,* Number 32, 8–10.

Eberstadt, Nick. 1976. "Myth of the World Food Crisis." *New York Review of Books,* February 19, 32–37.

Editors, *Monthly Review.* 1971. "The End of U.S. Hegemony." *Monthly Review,* Volume 23, 1–16.

Elliot, David, and Ruth Elliot. 1976. *The Control of Technology.* London: Wykeham Publications.

Ellul, Jacques. 1965. *The Technological Society.* London: Jonathan Cape.

Emery, Fred. 1974. *Futures We're In.* Canberra: Australian National University, Centre for Continuing Education.

Encel, Sol, Pauline Marstrand, and William Page. 1975. *The Art of Anticipation.* London: Martin Robertson.

Epstein, Edward Jay. 1974. "Methadone: The Forlorn Hope." *The Public Interest,* Number 36, 3–24.

Etzioni, Amitai, and Richard Remp. 1973. *Technological Shortcuts to Social Change.* New York: Russell Sage Foundation.

Evans, Jeff, John Irvine, and Ian Miles (eds.). (Forthcoming.) *Demystifying Social Statistics.* London: Pluto Press.

Evans, Michael. 1975. *Karl Marx.* London: Allen and Unwin.

Ford, Juliennes. 1975. *Paradigms and Fairy Tales.* 2 volumes. London: Routledge and Kegan Paul.

Fox, Karl A. 1974. *Social Indicators and Social Theory.* New York: John Wiley and Sons.

Frank, Richard. 1974. "Solution to the Asian Food Crisis: 'Green Revolution' or Social Revolution?," and "Guide to Radical Literature on Economic Development with Special Reference to Asian Agricultural Development." *Bulletin of Concerned Asian Scholars,* Volume 6, Number 4, 2–16.

Freeman, Christopher. 1974. "The Luxury of Despair." *Futures,* Volume 6, 450–462.

Friedman, Edward. 1974. "Chinese Foreign Policy and American Social Science." *Bulletin of Concerned Asian Scholars,* Volume 6, 7–12.

Funkhouser, G. Ray. 1973. "The Issues of the Sixties." *Public Opinion Quarterly,* Volume 37, 62–75.

Galbraith, J. K. 1967. *The New Industrial State.* London: Hamish Hamilton.

Galtung, Johan. 1973. "The Limits to Growth and Class Politics." Paper presented at Rome World Conference on Futures Research, Frascati.

Gardner, M. R., and W. R. Ashby. 1970. "Connectance of Large Dynamic (Cybernetic) Systems: Critical Values for Stability." *Nature,* Volume 228, 784.

Gartner, Edgar. 1975. "The 'Club of Rome' and the Capitalist Crisis" and "Peccei and Pals." *Science Bulletin,* Volume 9, 10–13, and Volume 10, 6–9.

Gilpin, Robert. 1975. "Three Models of the Future." *International Organization,* Volume 29, 37–60.

Goldthorpe, John H. 1971. "Theories of Industrial Society: Reflections on the Recrudescence of Historicism and the Future of Futurology." *Archives Europeenes de Sociologie,* Volume 12, 263–288.

———, D. Lockwood, F. Bechofer, and W. J. Platt. 1969. *The Affluent Worker in the Class Structure.* Cambridge: Cambridge University Press.

Golub, Robert, and Joe Townsend. 1975. "Malthus, Multinationals and the Club of Rome." In "Systems Modelling: Readings." Milton Keynes: The Open University (for the third level course in technology). A revised version is to appear in *Social Studies of Science,* in press.

Goodman, Paul. 1965. "Rural Life: 1984." In Paul Goodman, *People or Personnel and Like a Conquered Province.* New York: Vintage Books.

———, and Percival Goodman. 1947. *Communitas.* New York: Vintage Books.

Griffin, Keith. 1974. *The Political Economy of Agrarian Change.* London: Macmillan.

Gross, Bertram. 1973. "Friendly Fascism: A Model for America." In Franklin Tugwell (ed.), *Search for Alternatives.* Cambridge, Mass.: Winthrop Publishers.

Harrington, Michael. 1965. *The Accidental Century.* New York: Pelican, Harmondsworth: Penguin Books.

———. 1972. *Socialism.* New York: Saturday Review Press.

Harris, Marvin. 1965. "The Myth of the Sacred Cow." In Anthony Lands and Andrew P. Vayden (eds.), *Man, Culture and Animals.* New York: American Association for the Advancement of Science.

Hill, Kim Quaile, and Jib Fowles. 1975. "The Methodological Worth of the Delphi Forecasting Tehnique." *Technological Forecasting and Social Change,* Volume 7, 107–118.

Hindess, Barry. 1973. *The Use of Official Statistics in Sociology.* London: Macmillan.

Hoos, Ida R. 1972. *Systems Analysis and Public Policy: A Critique.* Berkeley: University of California Press.

———. 1974. "Criteria for 'Good' Futures Research." *Technological Forecasting and Social Change,* Volume 6, 113–132.

Horowtiz, Irving Louis. 1970. "Social Science Mandarins." *Policy Sciences,* Volume 1 339–360.

Hudson, Michael. 1971. "The Political Economy of Foreign Aid." In Dennis Goulet and Michael Hudson, *The Myth of Aid.* New York: IDOC and Orbis Books.

Hunt, E. K., and Jesse G. Schwartz. 1972. *A Critique of Economic Theory.* Harmondsworth: Penguin Books.

Jantsch, Erich. 1967. *Technological Forecasting in Perspective.* Paris: Organisation for Economic Co-operation and Development.

Jungk, Robert, and Johan Galtung (eds.). 1969. *Mankind 2000.* Oslo: Universitetsforlaget.

Kahn, Herman, and B. Bruce-Biggs. 1972. *Things to Come.* New York: Macmillan Co.

———, and Anthony Wiener. 1967. *The Year 2000: A Framework for Speculation on the Next Thirty-three Years.* New York: Macmillan Co.

Kaufman, Robert R., Harry I. Chernotsky, and Daniel S. Geller. 1975. "A Preliminary Test of the Theory of Dependency." *Comparative Politics,* Volume 7, 303–330.

Kay, Godfrey. 1975. *Development and Underdevelopment: A Marxist Analysis.* London: Macmillan.

Keddie, Nell (ed.). 1973. *Tinker, Tailor . . . The Myth of Cultural Deprivation.* Harmondsworth: Penguin Books.

Kleinberg, Benjamin S. 1973. *American Society in the Post-industrial Age.* Columbus, Ohio: Charles E. Merrill Publishing Co.

Kumar, Krishan. 1972. "Inventing the Future in Spite of Futurology." *Futures,* Volume 4, 369–375.

———. 1975. "Industrialism and Postindustrialism: Reflections on a Putative Transition." Paper presented to British Sociological Association Conference on Advanced Industrial Societies, University of Kent, March.

Lane, David. 1976. *The Socialist Industrial State.* London: Allen and Unwin.

Lasch, Christopher. 1970. *The Agony of the American Left.* London: Andre Deutsch.

———. 1973a. "Take Me to Your Leader." *New York Review of Books,* Volume 20, Number 16, 63–66.

———. 1973b. *The World of Nations.* New York: Alfred A. Knopf.

McEvoy III, James. 1972. "The American Concern with Environment." In W. R. Burch, Jr., N. H. Cheek, Jr., and L. Taylor (eds.), *Social Behavior, Natural Resources and the Environment.* New York: Harper & Row.

McLean, J. M. In press. "Does Cross-Impact Forecasting Have a Future?" *Futures.*

———, and Paul Shepherd. 1976. "The Importance of Model Structure." *Futures,* Volume 8, 40–51.

———, Paul Shepherd, and R. C. Curnow. 1974. "An Empirical Investigation into Systematics." Paper presented at Second International Symposium on Mathematical Modeling, Jablonna, November.

Mamdami, Mahmood. 1974. "The Ideology of Population Control." *Concerned Demography,* Volume 4, Number 2, 13–22.

Marcuse, Herbert. 1964. *One-Dimensional Man.* Boston: Beacon Press.

Marien, Michael (ed.). 1972. *The Hot List Delphi: An Exploratory Survey of Essential Reading for the Future.* Syracuse, New York: Educational Policy Research Center, Syracuse University.

————. 1973a. "Daniel Bell and the End of Normal Science." *The Futurist,* Volume 7, 262–268.

————. 1973b. "Herman Kahn's 'Things to come'." *The Futurist,* Volume 7, 7–15.

Maruyama, Magoroh. 1974. "Paradigmatology and Its Application to Cross-disciplinary, Cross-professional and Cross-cultural Communication." *Cybernetics,* Volume 17, 136–156, 237–281.

Marx, Karl, and Friedrich Engels. 1968. *Selected Works in One Volume.* London: Lawrence and Wishart; New York: International Publications.

Mayo, Marjorie. 1975. "Community Development: A Radical Alternative?" In Roy Bailey and Mike Brake (eds.), *Radical Social Work.* London: Edward Arnold, 39–46.

Mészáros, Istvan. 1971. *The Necessity of Social Control.* London: Merlin Press.

————. 1972. "Ideology and Social Science." In Ralph Miliband and John Savile (eds.), *The Socialist Register, 1972.* London: Merlin Press.

Miles, Ian. 1975. *The Poverty of Prediction.* Lexington, Mass.: Lexington Books.

————. 1976a. "Numerical Moralities: The Measurement and Prediction of Well-being." To be published in Paul Chalmers-Dixon (comp.), *Radical Statistics Conference, November 1975, Collected Papers.*

————. 1976b. "Predictions, Portents and Paradigms." In John Haworth and Stan Parker (eds.), *Forecasting Leisure Futures.* London: Leisure Studies Association, Polytechnic of Central London, School of the Environment.

Miliband, Ralph. 1969. *The State in Capitalist Society.* London: Weidenfeld and Nicolson.

Mills, C. Wright. 1961. *The Sociological Imagination.* Harmondsworth: Penguin Books.

————. 1963. *The Marxists.* Harmondsworth: Penguin Books.

Modrzhinskaya, E., and Ts. Stepanyan. 1971. *The Future of Society.* Moscow: Progress Publishers.

National Resources Committee (Report of the Sub-committee on Technology). 1937. *Technological Trends and National Policy.* Washington, D.C.: U.S. Government Printing Office.

Nelkin, Dorothy. 1976. "Ecologists and the Public Interest." *Hastings Center Report,* Volume 6, 38–44.

Nelson, Richard. 1974. "Intellectualizing about the Moon-Ghetto Metaphor." *Policy Sciences,* Volume 5, 375–414.

Nieburg, H. L. 1966. *In the Name of Science.* Chicago: Quadrangle Books.

————. 1969. "The Tech-Fix and the City." In H. J. Schmidt and W. Blomberg, Jr. (eds.), *The Quality of Urban Life.* Beverly Hills, Calif.: Sage Publications.

Nobile, Philip (ed.) 1971. *The Con III Controversy.* New York: Pocket Books.

Oltmans, Willem L. (ed.). 1974. *On Growth.* New York: Capricorn Books, G. P. Putnam's Sons.

Ozebekhan, Hasan. 1968. "The Triumph of Technology—'Can' Implies 'Ought.' " Reprinted in Nigel Cross, David Elliot, and Robin Roy, 1974, *Man-Made Futures.* London: Hutchinson Educational.

Perkin, Harold. 1976. "The History of Social Forecasting." In Christopher Freeman, Marie Jahoda, and Ian Miles (eds.). *Progress and Problems in Social Forecasting.* London: SSRC.

Popper, Karl R. 1957. *The Poverty of Historicism.* London: Routledge and Kegan Paul.

Reich, Charles A. 1970. *The Greening of America.* New York: Random House.

Richards, Frank. 1975. "The Question of the International." *Revolutionary Communist,* Number 2, 20–41.

Rinehart, James W. 1971. "Affluence and the Embourgeoisement of the Working Class: A Critical Look." *Social Problems,* Volume 19, 149–162.

Rothschild, Emma. 1975. "How Doomed Are We?" *New York Review of Books,* June 26, 31–34.

Rose, Hilary, and Stephen Rose. 1972. "The Radicalisation of Science." In Ralph Miliband and John Savile (eds.), *The Socialist Register.* London: Merlin Press.

———. 1974. "Do Not Adjust Your Mind, There is a Fault in Reality: Ideology in the Neurobiological Sciences." In Richard Whitley (ed.), *Social Processes of Scientific Development.* London: Routledge and Kegan Paul.

Rosen, Stephen J., and James R. Kurth (eds.). 1974. *Testing Theories of Imperialism.* Lexington, Mass.: Lexington Books.

Rosenhead, Jonathan. 1976. "Prison 'Catastrophe'." *New Scientist,* Volume 71, 140.

Roszak, Theodore. 1969. *The Making of a Counter-Culture.* Garden City, New York: Doubleday.

———. 1972. *Where the Wasteland Ends.* Garden City, New York: Doubleday.

Sachs, Ignacy. 1974. "Food Production in the Third World." Paper presented at Conference on Science and Agriculture in the '70s, London.

Sackman, Harold. 1975. *Delphi Critique.* Lexington, Mass.: Lexington Books.

Sayer, R. A. 1976a. Review of Baxter, Echenique, and Owers, "Urban Development Models." *Applied Mathematical Modelling,* Volume 1, 54.

———. 1976b. *A Critique of Urban Modelling.* London: Pergamon Press.

Schindler, D. W. 1976. "The Impact Statement Boondoggle." *Science,* Volume 192, 509.

Shapiro, Michael J., and Deane E. Neubauer. 1973. "Meta-Advocacy in Comparative Political Analysis." *Journal of Comparative Administration* (now *Administration and Society*), Volume 5, 343–365.

Shaw, Martin. 1973. *Marxism Versus Sociology.* London: Pluto Press.

———. 1975. *Marxism and the Social Sciences.* London: Pluto Press.

Sinclair, Craig. 1973. "Environmentalism." In H. S. D. Cole, Christopher Freeman, Marie Jahoda, and K. L. R. Pavitt, 1973, *Thinking About the Future.* London: Sussex University Press.

Smith, Anthony D. 1973. *The Concept of Social Change.* London: Routledge and Kegan Paul.

Spilerman, Seymour. 1975. "Forecasting Social Events." In Kenneth C. Land

and Seymour Spilerman (eds.), *Social Indicator Models*. New York: Russell Sage Foundation.

Stallings, Barbara. 1972. *Economic Dependency in Africa and Latin America*. Beverly Hills, Calif.: Sage Publications (Professional Papers in Comparative Politics, Volume 3, Series Number 01–031.)

Stauffer, Robert B. 1973. *Nation-Building in a Global Economy: The Role of the Multinational Corporation*. Beverly Hills, Calif.: Sage Publications (Professional Papers in Comparative Politics, Volume 4, Series Number 01–034.)

Surrey, John, John Chesshire, and Norman Dombey. 1976. "The Hazards of Rushing to Build a Nuclear Fast Reactor." *The Times* (London), June 28, 21.

Swingewood, Alan. 1975. *Marx and Modern Social Theory*. London: Macmillan.

Toffler, Alvin. 1970. *Future Shock*. London: Bodley Head.

Tucker, Robert C. 1970. *The Marxian Revolutionary Idea*. London: Allen and Unwin.

Vengroff, Richard. 1975. "Neo-colonialism and Policy Outputs in Africa." *Comparative Political Studies*, Volume 8, 234–250.

Waxman, Chaim I. (ed.). 1968 *The End of Ideology Debate*. New York: Simon and Schuster.

Ways, Max. 1969. "The Road to 1977." In F. E. Emery (ed.), *Systems Thinking*. Harmondsworth: Penguin Books.

Weisskopf, Thomas E. 1972. "Capitalism, Underdevelopment, and the Future of the Poor Countries." *Review of Radical Political Economics*, Volume 4, 1–35.

Wilson, Andrew. 1970. *War Gaming*. Harmondsworth: Penguin Books. (Originally published in 1968 as *The Bomb and the Computer*.)

Wolfson, Robert J. 1972. "In the Hawks' Nest." *Society*, Volume 9, 18–24 and 58–60.

Wynne, Brian. 1975. "The Rhetoric of Consensus Politics: A Critical Review of Technology Assessment." *Research Policy*, Volume 4, 108–158.

Yanarella, Ernest J. 1975. "The 'Technological Imperative' and the Strategic Arms Race." *Peace and Change*, Volume 3, 3–16.

———. 1976. *Servants of Necessity: Strategy, Technology, and Politics in the ABM Controversy, 1955–72*. Lexington, Ky.: University Press of Kentucky.

Young, Robert M. 1971. "Evolutionary Biology and Ideology—Then and Now." *Science Studies* (now *Social Studies of Science*), Volume 1, 77–206.

———. 1973a. "The Historiographic and Ideological Contexts of the Nineteenth Century Debate on Man's Place in Science." In Mikulàs Teich and Robert Young (eds.), *Changing Perspectives in the History of Science*. London: Heinemann Educational Books.

———. 1973b. "The Human Limits of Nature." In Jonathan Benthall, (ed.), *The Limits of Human Nature*. Harmondsworth: Allen Cure.

Zeitlin, Irving M. 1973. *Rethinking Sociology*. New York: Harper & Row.

RICHARD L. HENSHEL[1]

# Self-altering Predictions

## ORIGINS AND MEANINGS

It appears to be a feature of social life that predictions themselves become a part of the interacting set of social conditions that result in future social states. This article explores a very basic social process, a process that has become increasingly recognized as having grave substantive and methodological import for efforts to predict the future of mankind.

The *self-fulfilling prophecy* (SFP) was defined by its discoverer, Robert K. Merton, as an initially false "definition of the situation" (prophecy) which becomes true because of actions performed as a result of public acceptance of the prophecy (Merton, 1948). Note that the SFP does not merely become true *subsequent* to public accept- ance but, strictly, *because* of public acceptance. In Merton's famous example, an initially false prediction that a certain bank will fail may well lead to fulfillment of the prediction as depositors rush to demand their money, since no bank maintains sufficient funds to withstand such pressure. The *self-defeating* (or suicidal) *prophecy* (SDP), on the other hand, was defined as an initially true "definition of the situation" (prophecy) which became false as a result of its acceptance. An ex- ample of an SDP would be the "underdog effect" in election polling, in which public sympathy for a lagging candidate reverses the originally sound polling forecast. A given situation may include elements of both SFP and SDP, as in an election with both underdog and bandwagon effects resulting from early polls. Henshel and Kennedy (1973) have coined the term *self-altering prophecy* (SAPr) to refer collectively to both SFP and SDP, as well as to some similar phenomena not properly denoted by either term. A self-altering prophecy generates a sequence of events in reaction to prediction of a future state such that the reaction alters what would otherwise have occurred. We will henceforth employ this term throughout this article. Finally, some philosophical writers refer to *reflexive predictions,* a term that has essentially the same meaning as SAPr. Merton has intentionally employed the term *prophecy* in order to include what might be termed self-altering *per-*

*ceptions* as well as articulated public statements. (See his comments on this problem, 1960.)

In 1936, Merton set down the basic ideas behind the self-fulfilling and self-defeating prophecy. T. D. Eliot also provided an early discussion of the phenomena, speaking of positive (accelerative) and negative (avoidance) responses to predictive "assumptions" (Eliot, 1937). In his epochal work, *Social Theory and Social Structure,* Merton examined the self-fulfilling prophecy in light of what he called the "Thomas Theorem," after W. I. Thomas, who advanced the dictum that "if men define situations as real, they are real in their consequences." Merton elaborates on the idea that men will respond not only to the objective features of a situation but also to the meaning that the situation has for them. Once they have assigned some meaning to the situation, the subsequent behavior and some of the consequences of that behavior will be determined by the ascribed meaning. What may occur in such a situation is the enactment of a self-fulfilling prophecy. In Merton's terms, there can be "a false definition of the situation evoking a new behavior which makes the originally false conception come true" (Merton, 1949, p. 181; in the 1957 revised edition, the quote is on p. 421).

As philosophers of science have repeatedly noted, the SAPr has a dual significance. On the one hand, we must investigate specific instances or occasions of SAPr, so that it is a *substantive topic* in specific fields within sociology, economics, education, political science, international relations, religion, medicine, and so forth. But the SAPr must also be considered as a general phenomenon in its own right, and moreover as a phenomenon that produces a *methodological dilemma* in efforts to formulate correct forecasts. It is within this latter domain that the philosophy of science has evinced great concern over the implications of SAPr on the feasibility of social prediction. As Nagel puts it,

Even when sociological predictions of future social events are the conclusions of competent inquiries, these conclusions can be made invalid if they come to the attention of the people at whom they are directed and if, in the light of the knowledge of this prediction, these people alter the patterns of their behavior upon whose study the original conclusions were based (1961, p. 468).

This is the SDP as a "prediction dilemma," not as a substantive topic in, e.g., education or religion.

The sections of this article have been organized to reflect the traditional division of SAPr into substantive and methodological components. In the section directly following, the SAPr is considered as a basic social process underlying a vast range of substantive topics. The section is intended to provide some idea of the pervasiveness of the issues over which self-alteration may exist. It also provides an extensive (but by no means exhaustive) bibliography. The section following displays the second face of the SAPr, showing its importance as a prediction dilemma and the possible consequences for social science prediction. Also incorporated in this section is my concept of the "prestige loop," which further compounds the methodological dilemmas involved in social prediction. The last major section continues the methodological examination, exploring possible ways out of the dilemma.

## THE SELF-ALTERING PROPHECY AS A PERVASIVE SOCIAL PROCESS

Although the term *suicidal prophecy* originated with the nineteenth-century logician John Venn (1888, pp. 225–226) and the SFP originated with Merton (1936), the ideas were not widely disseminated until after 1948, the year in which Merton's article on the SFP first appeared, followed shortly by his seminal *Social Theory and Social Structure* (1948, 1949). Since that time, the terms have gained increasing currency in the English language, spreading to virtually all academic disciplines that treat social affairs and eventually penetrating educated lay discourse. An index of this penetration can be seen in the Presidential State of the Union address of 1973, in which the SFP was employed without any attempt at, or apparent need for, a separate definition. *Social Theory and Social Structure* has been translated into numerous foreign languages (the book must be rated one of the most important sociological works of the century by any standard); consequently, the term and the idea have entered other tongues and cultural traditions. Significantly, only Russian among the major scientific languages remains without any term for the idea of the SFP (Merton, personal communication).

As awareness of the concept has expanded, new instances of the SAPr in substantive domains have slowly accumulated, encroaching over ever more widely dispersed topical areas. In some cases—for instance, the concern with placebo effects in medical research—a literature has emerged "independently," with the linkage to the idea of the SAPr only becoming apparent after considerable time. The following brief outline illustrates the ubiquity of the SAPr as a social phenomenon. The literature cited represents some of the best discussions (in the author's opinion); it is by no means exhaustive. A confused but extensive list of concrete illustrations of the SAPr may also be found in

Eliot (1937). Articles appear within quotes, and books in italics. Complete references are contained in the bibliography at the end of this article.*

   1. *Race and Ethnic Relations*
        *Ecological Invasion-Succession ("Block-busting")*
     Wolf, "The Invasion-Succession Sequence as a Self-Fulfilling Prophecy"
     Wolf, "Research Data as an Element in Decision-Making"
        *Minority Stereotypes as Self-Fulfilling*
     Hillery, "The Negro in New Orleans . . ."
     *MacIver, The More Perfect Union
     Danziger, "The Psychological Future of an Oppressed Group"
     Richardson, "The Effects of Disability . . ."
     Catton and Hong, ". . . Apparent Minority Ethnocentrism and Majority Antipathy."

   2. *Deviant Behavior and Social Control*
        *Paranoid Delusion*
     *Frank, Persuasion and Healing . . .
        *Labeling of Deviants Perpetuating Deviancy*
     *Erikson, Wayward Puritans
     *Becker, Outsiders . . .
     *Tannenbaum, Crime and the Community, Chapter 1

   3. *Models of "Human Nature" as Self-Fulfilling*
     Berger, "Identity as a Problem in the Sociology of Knowledge"
     Becker, ". . . Science and Human Nature"
     Biderman, "On the Influence, Affluence, and Congruence of Phenomena in the Social Sciences"
     Eisenberg, "The *Human* Nature of Human Nature"
     Seeley, "Social Science in Social Action"

   4. *Education*
        *Self-Fulfilling Aspects of Teacher Expectancy*
     *Silberman, Crisis in the Classroom
     Kester and Letchworth, ". . . Teacher Expectations and Their Effects on Achievement . . ."
     Entwisle and Webster, "Status Factors in Expectation Raising"
        *Self-Fulfilling Aspects of School Testing, "Tracking"*

Elder, ". . . Some Consequences of Stratified Secondary Education in Britain"

*Goslin, The Search for Ability

Riesman, ". . . Graduate Training in Law and Social Science"
    *Self-Image and Performance as an SFP*

Entwisle and Webster, ". . . Status Factors in Expectation Raising"

Aronson and Carlsmith, "Performance Expectancy as a Determinant . . ."

5. *Scientific Inquiry*
    *Investigator Expectancy*

Rosenthal and Rosnow, *Artifact in Behavioral Research*

Rostand, *Error and Deception in Science*

Kuhn, "The Function of Measurement in Modern Physical Science"

*Polsby, *Community Power and Political Theory*
    *Subject Expectancy*

Orne, "Demand Characteristics . . ."

Scheff, "Preferred Errors in Diagnosis"

Denzin, ". . . Patient-Therapist Interaction"
    *Placebo Effect*

Shapiro, "Factors Contributing to the Placebo Effect"

Frank, *Persuasion and Healing . . .*

Shapiro, ". . . History of the Placebo Effect"

6. *Politics, Law, and International Affairs*
    *Predictions of Voting Behavior*

Simon, "Bandwagon and Underdog Effects and the Possibility of Election Predictions"

Bendiner, "Quickie 'Results' Could Sway the Election"
    *Administration of the Law*

Mishkin, "Prophecy, Realism and the Supreme Court"

Sagarin and Kelly, ". . . Political Trials and the Self-Defeating Prophecy"
    *Escallation and Conflict Resolution*

Marx, ". . . *Agents Provocateurs* and Informants"

Frank, "Breaking the Thought Barrier . . ."

*Kahn, *Thinking about the Unthinkable*

Kautsky, "Myth, Self-Fulfilling Prophecy, and Symbolic Reassurance in the East-West Conflict"

*Boulding, *The Image*

Osgood, ". . . Winning the Real War with Communism"

7. *Economics*
    *SFP in Pure Economics*
    Morgenstern, "Perfect Foresight and Economic Equilibrium"
    Rothschild, "Cobweb Cycles and Partially Correct Forecasting"
    *Trend Projections as Self-Fulfilling*
    Smith, "Environmental Degradation and Human Behavior"
    Diebold, "The World and Doomsday Fads"
    *Occupations*
    Coser and Rokoff, "Women in the Occupational World . . ."
    Coates and Pellegrin, ". . . A Situational Theory of Occupational Mobility"

8. *Religion*
    *Millenarianism, Mysticism, Historicism*
    Simmon, "On Maintaining a Deviant Belief System . . ."
    Lyon, "Saint-Simon and the Origins of Scientism and Historicism"
    Zygmunt, "When Prophecies Fail"
    *Faith Healing as an SFP*
    Frank, *Persuasion and Healing*

Of special interest as a topical concern is the SFP in *inflation*. Economists are unanimous today in acknowledging the collapse of their traditional theories—both the microeconomics of the classical economists and the "new economics" of the Keynesians. According to the theories of the Keynesians, inflation simply cannot occur at the same time as recession, except under extraordinary technical conditions that have not recently transpired. Yet, we observe "stagflation" in the contemporary world. Although economists can incorporate "psychological factors" into their models, these factors remain ciphers which are, essentially, "fudge factors." But the recognition that the self-fulfilling prophecy has become the *key* ingredient in inflation (as workers demand higher wages because they predict higher prices, and prices rise to take care of anticipated wage demands) effectively removes the central problem from the realm of pure economics and transfers it to the realm of social psychology. The wage-price spiral is now the *central* feature of inflation, since inflation does manifestly continue under conditions that in strictly economic terms should lead to stabilization.

---

[*] Only a portion of the works noted by asterisks is relevant to the SAPr. Most of the items in this outline were first brought to my attention by R.K. Merton. This selection of the better sources on the SAPr developed out of a mutually stimulating series of discussions between the author and Merton. Merton has been working on a book entitled The Self-Fulfilling Prophecy for some years. Although the author's contribution was considerable, the outline follows closely the emerging table of contents for Merton's book.

We must also examine the critical linkage between the SAPr and faith in the future. Students of history have long noted the importance of "myth" as a key ingredient in moving masses of people to action (Sorel, 1950). The effects of such prophecies as the doctrine of Manifest Destiny on the subsequent diplomatic history of the United States, or, to take a more current illustration, of the Marxist doctrine of the historical inevitability of communism on the successes of the communist movement, have long interested observers. But the relationship is not unidirectional; a wave of pessimism may also be self-fulfilling if it retards concerted action necessary to deal with a crisis. In this regard, it is hardly necessary to remind students of the future of the wave of pessimism currently sweeping across Western culture. From prophets of doom in popular literature to polls showing loss of confidence in the future, the signs of pessimism are inescapable. Long ago, the sociologist W. F. Ogburn proposed personal bank accounts and family size as indicators of the common man's confidence in the future. Both happen to be in marked decline today. Why is this theory especially germane to an examination of the SAPr? As waves of confidence or despair move across a great culture, a very slow but massive shift occurs in the plans of millions of individuals. Such shifts—seemingly minute since they are on the scale of the individual—can render optimism or pessimism self-fulfilling at the societal level. As faith in progress disappears, for example, social and economic retrenchment may bring about the very pessimistic end foreseen. In this regard, in one recent study, Avison and Nettler found a relationship between pessimistic outlook and predictive accuracy (1976).

Fred Polak's concern with the image of the future that a people possess has brought about a signal improvement in our understanding of the articulation between faith in the future and the SAPr. In his recently translated work (1973), the Dutch sociologist distinguishes not only between feelings of optimism and pessimism (see also in this regard Gabor, 1963) but also between a condition in which the people feel that their own actions would be efficacious and a condition in which they feel their actions would be fruitless. This twofold distinction creates a typology of orientations toward the future that helps us to understand social reactions to predicted future conditions. In the diagram below, the attitudes along the two margins produce the reactions denoted by the internal cells. Obviously, all of these reactions produce, in a sense, self-fulfilling prophecies. A sophisticated model of such considerations as these can be found in the first two chapters of Bell and Mau (1971). Parenthetically, the terms used in the diagram below are not identical to those found in Polak.

|                        | actions would be efficacious | any actions would be useless |
|------------------------|------------------------------|------------------------------|
| Optimistic forecast    | pioneer, vanguard, visionaries | standpatism, complacency   |
| Pessimistic forecast   | heroic sacrifice             | fatalism, resignation        |

## THE SELF-ALTERING PROPHECY AS A METHODOLOGICAL DILEMMA: POTENTIAL CONSEQUENCES FOR SOCIAL PREDICTION

Social scientists have traditionally been concerned with the scientific status of their endeavors. In the many discussions of the functions of a science, there is universal agreement that it should provide improved predictive power. As a consequence, the question naturally arises whether the social disciplines can produce significant predictions. Some observers measure the fruitfulness of a scientific theory in terms of its predictions (e.g., Gibbs, 1972); many regard scientific progress as coextensive with the development of a corpus of predictions (e.g., de Jouvenel, 1967, p. 84). But *what effect does the self-altering prophecy have on this possibility?* Does not this phenomenon rule out the possibility of social predictions that follow a natural science model? *Can the natural science analogy hold for the social "sciences" in spite of reflexive prediction in the latter's domain?* It is imperative to examine the issue with great care. In addition, if in fact the SAPr does require social prediction to differ from what we are accustomed to in natural science, it is incumbent to try to distinguish what characteristics are specific to social prediction—that is, what form social prediction will eventually assume.

If the SAPr is unique to social science, some have argued, this will in itself rule out the use of a natural science model for the study of social phenomena.

Prediction in the social sciences finds its inevitable limitation in the fact that, knowing the predicted course of events, man can alter that course, thereby nullifying the prediction itself. The conscious and deliberate actions of man thus create special problems for the social scientist—problems not encountered in the realms of physics and chemistry, or even in biology (Werkmeister, 1959, p. 490).

Watkins, adopting a position of "methodological individualism," states that "no social law exists which could not be altered *if* the individuals concerned both wanted to alter it and possessed the appropriate information" (1969, p. 605). On somewhat different grounds, Friedrichs (1970) reiterates at length the mutability of all social laws and, further, states that every social prediction, without exception, is self-altering *in fact*. (Presumably, this statement applies even to sealed, "cabinet-drawer" predictions, since knowledge of their content affects the predictor himself.) Krishna, in turn, uses the dichotomy to construct what is clearly a "radical dualism between the world of nature and the world of thought" (1971, p. 1105). There is no need to review other, older statements since it is clear from the examples that the dualist orientation continues to be congenial to some theoretical points of view.

Scriven has attempted a logical proof of the impossibility, even in principle, of accurate prediction of human behavior under certain conditions (1964). He deals exclusively with the case of an "avoider" who is dominantly motivated to avoid being accurately predicted. So far, this seems interesting indeed, since public predictions about such an avoider's behavior would tend to become self-defeating prophecies. However, to establish proof of the *impossibility* of accurate prediction, Scriven is obliged to further narrow his case to the point where it loses all interest except to the logician. His avoider (who attempts to avoid predictability by duplicating the predictor's calculations) has adequate knowledge of laws and adequate data, is never discouraged by difficult calculations, has limitless memory capacity and computing speed, always computes before the "deadline" of the predicted behavior, and is behaviorally free to violate the prediction. Under such assumptions, Scriven maintains the impossibility of accurate prediction—even if the predictor's knowledge, data, and calculations are perfect. He has assumed away, however, the most interesting and problematic variables. Even under his own assumptions, the adequacy of his proof has been subjected to challenge (Lewis and Richardson, 1966). The narrowness of the claim, and its disputed validity, render this argument of little significance on the broader issues of human predictability.

Henshel (1975a) explores the relationship between predictive power and disciplinary prestige over long sequences of predictions from a single source. He concludes that in the social sciences a unique reciprocity may exist between prestige and prediction, and that a deviation-amplifying feedback system can be established capable of severely distorting both predictive accuracy and prestige.

The idea that the accuracy of scientific predictions influences the prestige of the discipline which issues them will occasion no surprise. What may be much more provocative is the idea that, in the social sciences at least, *a discipline's prestige may influence its predictive power*—in not one, but several ways. . . . We are concerned here with a "feedback loop" which incorporates as variables the prestige of a discipline and its predictive accuracy. The "prestige loop" begins with a prediction from a source identified with a particular discipline. The prestige of the discipline affects via one of several paths the accuracy of the prediction. And this degree of accuracy, in turn, acts upon the prestige of the predictor and his discipline. Schematically:

---

Prediction ▶ mechanisms based on prestige ▶ accuracy of the prediction ▶ alterations in prestige ▶ . . .

---

(Henshel, 1975a, p. 92)

There are numerous mechanisms through which prestige can influence predictive accuracy; all rely on the credibility of the prediction's source and the impact of this credibility on the resultant actions of the audience. One way to express this in terms of our present focus would be to say that the extent to which a given prediction is self-altering depends on the prestige (credibility) of the predictor. But by concentrating on the "prestige loop" as a whole, one can direct attention to what happens if a train or sequence of predictions is issued from the same source. *The accuracy of the earlier predictions affects the prestige of the predictor and, hence, via the SAPr, the accuracy of his later predictions.*

Each individual increment of influence extended on predictive power by changes in disciplinary prestige may be small, but in most of the models presented here all the relational signs are positive, so that once a threshold is passed, *deviation-amplification* can occur through *several "trips"* around a feedback loop, and make small incremental changes cumulatively important. In the language of cybernetics, deviation-amplifying mutual causal feedback may be encountered (p. 93).

This state of affairs seems strange when first encountered and is perhaps best approached by means of specific examples.

As a specific case in point we may consider the prestige loop involving intelligence testing. On the one hand, the effects of knowledge by *teachers* of children's test results has been the subject of extended debate (Entwisle and Webster, 1973). But the effects if the children *themselves* learn of their test scores seems incontestable. The intelligence test scores become, in effect, self-fulfilling prophecies, which influence effectiveness in school by altering the self-confidence, and self-image of the children (see Goslin, 1963, as well as the numerous sources he cites). Similar effects ensue from placing children in different "tracks" or "streams," in spite of efforts to conceal their meaning from the children (Elder, 1965).

Although the finding is important in itself, it is significant for the present discussion because the self-fulfilling phenomenon leads to the creation of spurious "predictive validation" for intelligence tests. The details, outlined in Figure 1, are as follows: An intelligence test can be thought of as predictive as well as descriptive, in the sense that persons' scores on other kinds of tests (e.g., grades in school) should be related to their IQ scores. One of the ways that has been used to establish the validity of an intelligence test is in fact to see how well it predicts the distribution of scores on these other tests. This is known as predictive or criterion-related validation. But if the testees learn of their IQ scores, this often leads to changes in self-image (for instance, self-confidence), which will itself affect their future grades. But when the intelligence test scores are compared with future school grades, all that can be seen is that the former are reasonably good predictors of the latter. This is hardly surprising in the situation just outlined since the intelligence scores apparently enter *causally* into the later scores. But although the validation produced by this means is spurious, it has nevertheless tended to enhance the prestige of intelligence testing with school administrators and educators. When the next cohort of children arrives, parents and teachers may pay even greater attention to the IQ score and its effects on the child may be correspondingly greater. This, in turn, causes a stronger confirmation of validity and so on (Henshel, 1975a, p. 94).

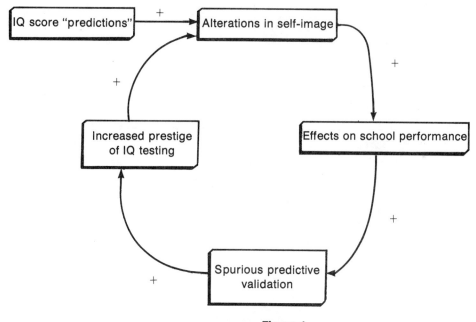

**Figure 1**
Prestige Loops in Intelligence Testing

SOURCE: Henshel, 1975a, p. 95.

      One other example, from the field of election polling, should suffice
to explain the prestige loop and to demonstrate its significance for both
prestige and predictive accuracy.

Although recent studies by Mendelsohn and Crespi have shown that notions of
"bandwagon" and "underdog" election effects from polls are greatly over-rated
in terms of actual importance, it has also become increasingly clear that, in the
USA at least, the size of monetary contributions to political parties or individual
candidates is highly sensitive to pre-election polls. We can thus see an instance
of a prestige loop for individual prophecies with a built-in multiplier effect. Poll
predictions of victory or defeat result in increased or decreased cash flow to the
party coffers, creating or denying opportunities for advertising and staffing.
Election returns reflect these disparities, enhancing the prestige of the polling
process (in the USA). In the next election, even greater attention is accorded
the polls, with correspondingly greater effects on the financial condition of the
candidates, and so forth (see Figure 2) (Henshel, 1975a, p. 101).

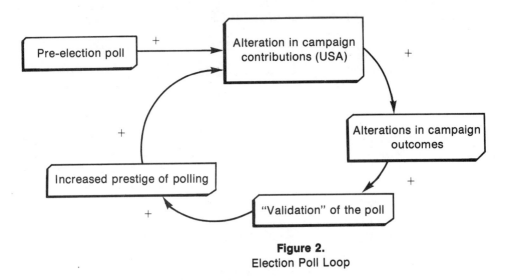

**Figure 2.**
Election Poll Loop

SOURCE: Henshel, 1975a, p. 101.

      For several additional examples of prestige loops, as well as an
extended treatment of multiplier and oscillation effects, the reader is
referred to the original article. We will have more to say in the conclusion on the implications of the SAPr and the prestige loop. For now,
we must turn to possible resolutions of the prediction dilemma.

# WAYS OUT? RESPONSES TO THE PREDICTION DILEMMA

## 1. THE POSSIBILITY OF REVISED OR "COMPENSATED" PREDICTIONS

Some writers have approached social prediction from a direction opposite to that of Scriven—offering proof that accurate social prediction is *possible in principle* under certain conditions even when an SFP or SDP is operative. That is, they attempt to show that there can be true-though-self-altering prophecies. This may be possible because predictors can take the self-altering aspect into account, and issue a revised or "compensated" prediction as their one public utterance. In counterargument, however, it should be recognized that this revised prediction is itself subject to self-alteration, setting up a potentially infinite regress with no accurate solution possible. The work of writers in the framework now to be examined has been to show that, in at least some cases, this potential problem does not occur.

Grunberg and Modigliani (1954) begin their examination of the predictability of social events by making the assumption that, in the case to be considered, accurate *private* prediction is possible. As a result, the magnitude of a person's reaction to a public prediction is at least conceivably knowable through experimentation. Under these assumptions, they proceed to show that for some of the problems of supply and demand there exists at least one correct *public* prediction. At a more general level, they set forth what they consider to be the sufficient conditions that assure the existence for any variable of at least one public prediction which is a convergence of public reaction and the other determining factors.

Simon has likewise provided such a "possibility theorem" for election predictions (1954). A possibility theorem, also called an "existence theorem," does not show how to find the correct "compensated" prediction but mathematically demonstrates that one exists. Welty and Beradino (1971) provide a possibility theorem to be used in the study of predictions about formal organizations, where the actual outcome is dependent on the knowledge of the published prediction by the organizational decision-maker. In fairness, it must be said that mathematicians and philosophers frequently resort to such techniques. We, too, may find them comforting while tackling the more basic problem of discovering how to find the (by now demonstrably possible) solution.

Possibility theorems are one way of approaching the prediction dilemma. The theorems, however, hold only for those particular social predictions that meet their specified conditions. We need something beyond this, and to find it we must shift to an examination of the boundaries beyond which SAPr's are not found.

## 2. THE BOUNDARIES QUESTION, I: ARE THESE SAPR'S IN NATURAL SCIENCE?

The examples that have been offered as instances of the SAPr in natural phenomena are pathetically few, which might itself be regarded as indicative. Grünbaum, in a classic article, maintains that self-fulfilling prophecies may be observed in the natural sciences (1956). Nagel (1961, p. 470) has presented an illustration based on Grünbaum which he feels can be used to illustrate both self-fulfilling and self-defeating prophecies. The example that he provides can be termed the antiaircraft gun case. The pointing and firing of such a gun can be effected through purely physical mechanisms, including radar for locating the target, a computer, an adjusting device for the gun, and some system for transmitting the computer's calculations as signals to the adjusting apparatus. If the gun were then to be fired according to the calculations, the target might be hit. But if it is assumed that the signals which are transmitted to the gun also produce disturbing effects on the target, altering its flight path, then although the gun is set and fired according to calculations that were correct at the time they were made, it nevertheless fails to hit the target *because* of changes introduced by the process of transmitting those calculations. This case, Nagel maintains, is a physical analogy of a suicidal prophecy as observed in social phenomena. The self-fulfilling prophecy may be illustrated in a similar manner. Let us assume that the equipment suffers defect such that ordinarily the gun would fail to hit the target. "It is nevertheless possible that, though the gun fired according to calculations that were incorrect at the time they were made, the target is successfully hit because of the perturbations [in the target's path] produced by the process of transmitting these calculations" (Nagel, 1961, p. 470).

These arguments are nothing if not ingenious, but are not above criticism. In point of fact, the antiaircraft gun example has been destroyed by criticisms from Roger Buck (1963). We say destroyed advisedly because Adolf Grünbaum, the principal defender of the example, has conceded the point (personal communication). A second set of criticisms of the example is to be found in Henshel (1975b). Both criticisms can also be used to defeat another hypothetical SFP in nature proposed by Abraham Edel (1959, p. 184). In this example, a man creates an avalanche by shouting a prediction that such an avalanche will occur. It, too, is not truly analogous to the social SFP.

Henshel (1975b) hypothesizes that an SAPr satisfactorily analogous to the social SAPr might be possible for higher animal interaction and, conceivably, for some as-yet-unrealized metallic/electronic actors. Yet, even these "metallic social systems"—although nonhuman—would require analysis by social scientific approaches. (See the paper for the detailed analysis.) Thus, the supposed instances of SAPr in natural science offered so far have been totally defeated.[2] We are left with a phenomenon which, even at very high levels of abstraction, is utterly confined to social science. Does this mean, then, that the advocates of scientific dualism are correct?

### 3. THE BOUNDARIES QUESTION, II: ARE THERE SPECIFIC AREAS WITHIN SOCIAL SCIENCE FREE FROM THE POSSIBILITY OF SAPR?

Examinations of the boundaries of the SAPr have focused on the issue of whether SAPr's can exist in natural science. The equally important question of whether there are some areas of social science *wholly free* of the SAPr received its first examination in Henshel (1975b). Quite apparently, if there exist some social phenomena that cannot be affected by predictions made on them, then use of the SAPr to rule out a natural science model for all social prediction cannot be justified. In addition, a model of this sort could pinpoint social phenomena especially susceptible to the SAPr.

Henshel (1975b) is to date the only treatment of this second "boundary question." Dividing boundaries of the SAPr into two types, inherent and de facto, the paper lists two unalterable (inherent) limits and some eleven reasonably strong (de facto) limits to the range of the SAPr in social phenomena. The two inherently unalterable social predictions are (1) "sealed" predictions—those unpublicized in any fashion, and (2) "real-time" predictions—those of sufficient complexity and rapidity-in-use that they are impossible to alter in the time available for behavioral decisions. De facto limits or boundaries on the social SAPr are recapitulated in Table 1. Readers should consult the original source for illustrations and elaborations.

### 4. THE BOUNDARIES QUESTION, III: ARE LARGE-SCALE SOCIAL PROCESSES FREE OF THE SAPR?

Although it is relatively easy to investigate the existence of the SAPr at the interpersonal level and even at the repetitive institutional level exemplified by stock markets and bank runs, unfortunately it is virtually impossible to determine whether a unique historical event was altered by response to earlier prophecy. This is unfortunate because we would certainly like to know the effects, for example, of the doctrine of Manifest Destiny or the doctrine of the historical inevitability of communism.

To be sure, one need not invariably use a classical experimental design, with control groups and before and after measurements, to

## Table 1. A Working Typology of Social Predictions Resistant to SAPr*

---

A.  Alteration would require unlikely skills.
    Prediction incorporates unknown magnitudes of variables.
    Prediction employs higher mathematics.
    Prediction employs esoteric conceptualization.

B.  Alteration would require unlikely collusion.
    Prediction is about cross-cultural regularities.
    Prediction is about competition or conflict.

C.  Alteration would require unlikely communication.
    Prediction is hostile to gate-keeper interests.
    Prediction is about social isolates.
    Prediction is about persons with limited comprehension.

D.  Alteration would require unlikely flaunting of interpretations.
    Prediction is interpreted as "unimportant."
    Prediction is interpreted as "unbelievable."
    Prediction is interpreted as "unalterable."

  * From Henshel, 1975b.

---

determine the existence of a unique phenomenon. Verified cases of sorcery-induced death—in which perfectly healthy individuals have died from natural causes (probably extreme shock) within weeks of a sorcerer's curse (Lévi-Strauss, 1963, pp. 167–168)—are extremely difficult to explain *without* postulating an SFP, the lack of experimental controls notwithstanding. But the impossibility of verification at the societal level, or should we say the level of unique historical occurrence, opens the door to speculation on yet a third boundary issue: are large-scale social processes free of the possibility of SAPr?

A recurrent debate in both history and theoretical anthropology has been whether cultural change (or macrohistorical shifts) can be accounted for in terms of *immanent laws of history* without regard to the humans that accomplish the changes. In the view of the culturologists, for example, although culture could obviously not exist without people, once the people are provided, their thoughts, desires, and plans are of no significance in the shaping of historical-cultural change, for a culture in a certain condition at time one will invariably shift to a particular new configuration at time two. Leslie White, for instance, maintains that cultural processes can be explained without taking human organisms into account (1963). This approach, as well as that of Kroeber and the superorganic (1952), is of interest here because it implicitly precludes the importance of the self-altering prophecy in large-scale social processes. Such a position holds that an individual reacts to his cultural environment in such a way that the manifestations of this action take a predetermined form, free from individual or group influence. In this sense, there is a conflict with the idea of a SAPr, in which the individual or group reaction is important in determining the future course of social events. Any position that denies the efficacy of human intervention in history also denies the significance of self-altering prophecies at the societal level.

The basic difficulty in evaluating all such views is that the theory as such is not vulnerable to disproof: culture is said to work in wonderful and mysterious ways, and on occasion the Spirit of History may well advance through the mechanism of a prophecy. But then, of course, the importance of human foresight in determining history, the opposing view, cannot be demonstrated for unique historical events either, with the result that both positions remain tenable. This particular boundary question must remain frustrating since it can be resolved neither through recourse to logic—as with a possibility theorem—nor through experimentation.

## 5. THE POSSIBLY RESTRICTED SCOPE OF PRESTIGE LOOPS

By contrast to the situation in the third boundary question, above, many of the prestige loops postulated can be subjected to confirmation or disconfirmation by empirical tests. Indeed, confirmation of the existence of prestige loops in informal group leadership has already been accomplished through small group experiments. A common thread through these studies (Chowdhry and Newcomb, 1952; Hopkins, 1964; and Talland, 1954) is a loop in which prestige leads to centrality in a group, which leads in turn to high predictive power about the group's actions, which leads in turn to yet higher prestige. Nevertheless, although some loop-like phenomena have been shown to exist, the establishment of prestige loops in social science prediction has not been achieved, and explication of their nature and possibility is only the first step in their investigation. As Henshel is at pains to point out, the exact extent of this phenomenon can only be ascertained by concrete research that is directly focused on prestige loops in social science prediction. (For some of the theoretical limitations of prestige loops, see Henshel, 1976, p. 55). In addition, related issues need further elaboration. When scientists predict, who knows of the predictions? What positions in society do the consumers of scientific prediction occupy? Which groups in society evaluate the prestige of the sciences, and what criteria do they use? And which groups in society are in a position to influence the training, recruitment, and funding of scientists? A growing literature on the social uses of science can become relevant to the issues presented here. Clearly, the concept of the prestige loop opens a great many new questions. Its importance in distorting prestige and predictive accuracy has not been ascertained. The writer may be permitted a personal judgment, to the effect that prestige loops exert a very strong influence.

### 6. RESEARCH ON REACTIONS TO PREDICTION (PREDICTING REACTIONS TO PREDICTIONS)

Research on reactions to prediction is at once the most obvious approach and yet one of the least advanced. There is no reason why experimental and quasi-experimental research cannot be carried out on various aspects of the SAPr, yet by and large this has not been done (Schuessler, 1968, p. 422). Although Merton called for research into the SFP as far back as 1949 (see pp. 128–129 of the 1957 edition), very little seems to have been done relative to the magnitude of the problem.

Such investigations could explore motivational and personality variables, social arrangements conducive to self-alteration, the prestige and credibility of the predictor, and the mode and media of dissemination of the prediction. It is certainly conceivable that selected aspects of existing specialties can be brought to bear—for example, theories of attitude change, social influence, or dissemination of innovations. Even long-run consequences, such as oscillation and multiplier effects from prestige loops, could be examined, either in the small groups laboratory or in manned simulation, by artificially creating a series of self-alterable predictions issued by the same predictor. Inasmuch as "demand characteristics" can be considered self-altering perceptions, the experimental work that has been done on this subject in social psychology exemplifies the systematic investigation that may be done on self-alteration in general (see Rosenthal and Rosnow, 1969). Another basic question that should be amenable to empirical research is how the oft-vicious circle of the SAPr (for instance, in inflation) can be halted. Merton has asked this question concerning the SFP (1957).

Systematic empirical work on the self-altering prophecy is most advanced in economics, which is the originator of the "possibility theorems" mentioned earlier. (For a survey of such work, see Henshel and Kennedy, 1973.) Study of the psychological dynamics that lie behind persons acting on a public prediction has lagged behind, but recently such work has been initiated in an excellent treatment by Archibald (1973). So far, however, sociology has shown little inclination to come to grips with the problem, except in social psychology studies of experimental artifact and work in deviant behavior on the problem of labeling and self-fulfilling perceptions. (See Rosenthal and Rosnow, 1969, for the former; Wilkins, 1965, and Young, 1971, for the latter.) Advances can also be seen in the work of Mintz (1951) and Deutscher and Deutscher (1955).

## THE SIGNIFICANCE OF REFLEXIVE PREDICTION

It was stated at the outset that the SAPr must rank as one of the most basic social processes. Certainly, it is the single social process of greatest significance for efforts to foresee the future of mankind. The section on the range of substantive phenomena subject to the SAPr should graphically illustrate the pervasiveness of self-alteration—the boundaries of the SAPr notwithstanding. Forecasts and prophecies should be promulgated with this point in mind. The observer must watch for and detect such phenomena in the public temper, playing as it does on human consciousness concerning the future itself. The SAPr is a strange but powerful mechanism for multiplying and distorting social trends.

Social scientific predictions must differ in some respects from those of the natural sciences because of the existence of the SAPr. Precisely how great these divergences are depends upon the extent of the SAPr in general, a subject wherein our knowledge is largely replaced by speculation. For the prospects for social prediction in general, see Henshel, 1971 and 1976.

But in addition to the burdensome aspect, SAPr's also add additional areas of interest in their own right for students of the future. SAPr's are of direct interest in themselves, as substantive phenomena across a wide range of subjects. So are prestige loops, with their fascinating capacities for distortion. Finally, efforts to determine the boundaries of the SAPr, or to predict the effects of predictions, or to halt the vicious circle mentioned by Merton should present irresistible challenges to serious futurists.

There is time now, at the conclusion of this article, to present the "farthest out," most speculative implications that involve the SAPr. For some time now, observers of the reactive nature of social prophecy have predicted that social science will eventually employ the self-altering phenomenon to further objectives favored by the social scientist (Friedrichs, 1970; Michael, 1967; Popper, 1961; Toch, 1958; Wolf, 1958). Either through Machiavellian or humanitarian motives, social scientists can withhold or generate forecasts which themselves have some bearing on future reality. Seeley advances an argument advocating such action (1951, pp. 85–86). Wrong points out that the extreme conclusion would be that sociologists' forecasts are inevitably "political" (1974, p. 29). To these possibilities a new potentiality must be added. The existence of self-alteration in prediction about social phenomena, and especially the existence of prestige loops associated with these predictions, imply that the social sciences can conceivably alter their own accuracy and prestige by a judicious selection, or withholding, of predictions. Under collusive, mass reaction, people will work for predicted states they approve of and against those they detest. Under an assumption of cohesive, concerted reaction, then, a discipline could increase its predictive accuracy by forecasting futures that people find appealing or by hedging unpleasant forecasts with numerous conditions—in expectation of efforts to defeat the latter. It scarcely seems necessary to point out the truly severe limitations on such a "bootstrap" operation, but we know very little about the basis for public acclaim. On the other hand, if we assume that social predictions are broadcast with no regard for public reaction, we can come to another very odd conclusion—at least from the standpoint of the physical sciences model of prediction. Sjoberg and Nett suggest one intriguing possibility: "the most effective forecaster might be a man who was right 60 or 70% of the time. Then his forecasts probably wouldn't be affected by people acting on them" (1968, p. 312).

Students of the future ignore the self-altering prophecy at their peril.

## NOTES

1. In addition to those numerous persons who contributed their advice to earlier papers, I would like to thank Bill Avison and Hugh Stevenson for their helpful suggestions. Many of the references were first brought to my attention by Robert Merton.

2. The Heisenberg uncertainty principle, although a prediction dilemma in natural science, does not seem analogous to the SAPr since, apparently, it is an artifact of the measurement process that produces uncertainty rather than the issuance of a prediction. There are many cases in both natural and social science where observation changes that which is observed.

## REFERENCES

Archibald, Peter. 1973. "Self-Fulfilling Prophecy." *Psychological Bulletin,* Volume 81, 74–84.

Aronson, Eliot, and J. M. Carlsmith. 1962. "Performance Expectancy as a Determinant of Actual Performance." *Journal of Abnormal and Social Psychology,* Volume 65, 178–182.

Avison, William, and Gwynn Nettler. 1976. "World Views and Crystal Balls." *Futures,* Volume 8 (February), 11–21.

Becker, Ernest. 1969. "The Evaded Question: Science and Human Nature." *Commonweal,* Volume 84 (February), 638–650.

Becker, Howard. 1973. *Outsiders.* (Enlarged edition.) New York: Free Press.

Bell, Wendell, and James A. Mau, eds. 1971. *The Sociology of the Future.* New York: Russell Sage Foundation.

Bendiner, R. 1964. "Quickie 'Results' Could Sway the Election." *Life,* Volume 18 (September), 125–133.

Berger, Peter. 1966. "Identity as a Problem in the Sociology of Knowledge." *European Journal of Sociology,* Volume 7, 105–115.

Biderman, Albert. 1969. "On the Influence, Affluence, and Congruence of Phenomena in the Social Sciences." *American Sociologist,* Volume 4 (May), 128–130.

Boulding, Kenneth. 1956. *The Image.* Ann Arbor: University of Michigan Press.

Buck, Roger. 1963. "Reflexive Predictions." *Philosophy of Science,* Volume 30 (October), with "comments" by Adolf Grünbaum and "Rejoinder" by Buck, 359–374.

Catton, William R., Jr., and Sung C. Hong. 1962. "The Relation of Apparent Minority Ethnocentrism to Majority Antipathy." *American Sociological Review,* Volume 27 (April), 178–191.

Chowdhry, K., and Theodore M. Newcomb. 1952. "The Relative Abilities of Leaders and Nonleaders to Estimate Opinions of Their Own Groups." *Journal of Abnormal and Social Psychology,* Volume 47, 51–57.

Coates, C. H., and R. J. Pellegrin. 1956. "Executives and Supervisors: A Situational Theory of Differential Occupational Mobility." *Social Forces,* Volume 35 (December), 121–126.

Coser, Rose Laub, and Gerald Rokoff. 1971. "Women in the Occupational World: Social Disruption and Conflict." *Social Problems,* Volume 18 (Spring), 535–554.

Danziger, Kurt. 1963. "The Psychological Future of an Oppressed Group." *Social Forces,* Volume 42 (October), 31–40.

Denzin, Norman K. 1966. "The Self-Fulfilling Prophecy and Patient-Therapist Interaction." Paper presented at the annual meeting of the American Sociological Association, New York City.

de Jouvenel, Bertrand. 1967. *The Art of Conjecture.* New York: Basic Books.

Deutscher, Verda, and Irwin Deutscher. 1955. "Cohesion in a Small Group: A Case Study." *Social Forces,* Volume 33 (May), 336–341.

Diebold, John. 1973. "The World and Doomsday Fads." *The New York Times,* February 25.

Edel, Abraham. 1959. "The Concept of Levels in Social Theory." In Llewellyn Gross (ed.), *Symposium on Sociological Theory.* Evanston, Ill.: Row, Peterson, 167–195.

Elder, Glen H., Jr. 1965. "Life Opportunity and Personality: Some Consequences of Stratified Secondary Education in Great Britain." *Sociology of Education,* Volume 38 (Spring), 173–202.

Eisenberg, L. 1972. "The *Human* Nature of Human Nature." *Science,* Volume 176 (April 14), 123–128.

Eliot, T. D. 1937. "Reactions to Predictive Assumptions." *American Sociological Review,* Volume 2 (August), 508–514.

Entwisle, Doris R., and Murray Webster, Jr. 1973. "Status Factors in Expectation Raising." *Sociology of Education,* Volume 46 (Winter), 115–126.

Erikson, Kai. 1966. *Wayward Puritans.* New York: John Wiley and Sons.

Frank, Jerome D. 1960. "Breaking the Thought Barrier: Psychological Challenges of the Nuclear Age." *Psychiatry,* Volume 23 (August), 245–266.

―――. 1961. *Persuasion and Healing.* Baltimore, Md.: Johns Hopkins Press.

Friedrichs, Robert. 1970. *A Sociology of Sociology.* New York: Free Press.

Gabor, Dennis. 1963. *Inventing the Future.* London: Secker and Warburg.

Gibbs, Jack P. 1972. *Sociological Theory Construction.* Hinsdale, Ill.: Dryden Press.

Goslin, David A. 1963. *The Search for Ability: Standardized Testing in Social Perspective.* New York: Russell Sage Foundation.

Grünbaum, Adolf. 1956. "Historical Determinism, Social Activism, and Predictions in the Social Sciences." *British Journal for the Philosophy of Science,* Volume 7, 236–240.

Grunberg, E., and F. Modigliani. 1954. "The Predictability of Social Events." *Journal of Political Economy,* Volume 62 (December), 465–478.

Henshel, Richard L. 1971. "Sociology and Prediction." *American Sociologist,* Volume 6 (August), 213–220.

―――. 1975a. "Effects of Disciplinary Prestige on Predictive Accuracy: Distortions from Feedback Loops." *Futures,* Volume 7 (April), 92–106.

―――. 1975b. "Scientific Status and Boundaries of the Self-Fulfilling Prophecy." Paper presented at the annual meeting of the American Sociological Association, San Francisco.

―――. 1976. *On the Future of Social Prediction.* Indianapolis: Bobbs-Merrill.

―――, and Leslie W. Kennedy. 1973. "Self-Altering Prophecies: Consequences for the Feasibility of Social Prediction." *General Systems,* Volume 18 (Annual), 119–126.

Hillery, G. A., Jr. 1957. "The Negro in New Orleans." *American Sociological Review,* Volume 22 (April), 183–188.

Hopkins, Terence. 1964. *The Exercise of Influence.* Totowa, N.J.: Bedminster Press.

Kahn, Herman. 1962. *Thinking About the Unthinkable.* New York: Horizon Press.

Kautsky, J. H. 1965. "Myth, Self-Fulfilling Prophecy, and Symbolic Reassurance in the East-West Conflict." *Journal of Conflict Resolution,* Volume 9 (March), 1–17.

Kester, S. W., and G. A. Letchworth. 1972. "Communication of Teacher Expectations and Their Effects on Achievement and Attitudes." *Journal of Educational Research,* Volume 66 (October), 51–55.

Krishna, Daya. 1971. "The Self-Fulfilling Prophecy and the Nature of Society." *American Sociological Review,* Volume 36 (December), 1104–1107.

Kroeber, Alfred L. 1952. *The Nature of Culture.* Chicago: University of Chicago Press.

Kuhn, Thomas S. 1961. "The Function of Measurement in Modern Physical Science." *Isis,* Volume 52 (June), 161–193.

Lévi-Strauss, Claude. 1963. *Structural Anthropology.* New York: Basic Books.

Lewis, David K., and Jane Shelby Richardson. 1966. "Scriven on Human Unpredictability." *Philosophical Studies,* Volume 17 (October), 69–74.

Lyon, P. V. 1961. "Saint-Simon and the Origins of Scientism and Historicism." *Canadian Journal of Economics and Political Science,* Volume 27 (February), 55–63.

MacIver, Robert M. 1942. *Social Causation.* Boston: Ginn.

Marx, Gary T. 1972. "The Agent Provocateur and Informant." Paper presented at the annual meeting of the American Sociological Association, New Orleans.

Merton, Robert K. 1936. "The Unanticipated Consequences of Purposive Social Action." *American Sociological Review,* Volume 1 (December), 894–904.

———. 1948. "The Self-Fulfilling Prophecy." *Antioch Review,* Volume 8, 193–210.

———. 1949. (Revised Edition, 1957.) *Social Theory and Social Structure.* Glencoe, Ill.: Free Press.

———. 1960. "Introduction." In Gustave LeBon, *The Crowd: A Study of the Popular Mind.* New York: Viking Press.

Michael, Donald N. 1967. "Social Engineering and the Future of the Environment." *American Psychologist,* Volume 22 (November), 888–892.

Mintz, Alexander. 1951. "Nonadaptive Group Behavior." *Journal of Abnormal and Social Psychology,* Volume 46 (April), 150–159.

Mishkin, Paul J. 1954. "Prophecy, Realism, and the Supreme Court." *American Bar Association Journal,* Volume 40 (August), 680–683 and 725–726.

Morgenstern, Oskar. 1935. "Perfect Foresight and Economic Equilibrium" (translation). *Zeitschrift fur Nationalökonomie,* Volume 6, Part 3.

Nagel, Ernest. 1961. *The Structure of Science.* London: Routledge and Kegan Paul.

Orne, Martin T. 1969. "Demand Characteristics and the Concept of Quasi-Controls." In Robert Rosenthal and Ralph Rosnow (eds.), *Artifact in Behavioral Research.* New York: Academic Press, 143–179.

Osgood, Charles. 1959. "Suggestions for Winning the Real War with Communism." *Journal of Conflict Resolution,* Volume 3 (December), 303–316.

Polak, Fred. 1973. *The Image of the Future.* (Translated from the Dutch by Elise Boulding.) New York: Elsevier.

Polsby, Nelson W. 1965. *Community Power and Political Theory.* New Haven: Yale University Press.

Popper, Karl R. 1957. *The Poverty of Historicism.* London: Routledge and Kegan Paul.

Richardson, S. A. 1969. "The Effects of Physical Disability on the Socialization of a Child." In David A. Goslin (ed.), *Handbook of Socialization Theory and Research.* Chicago: Rand McNally, 1047–1064.

Rosenthal, Robert, and Ralph L. Rosnow (eds.). 1969. *Artifact in Behavioral Research.* New York: Academic Press.

Rostand, Jean. 1960. *Error and Deception in Science.* (Translated by A. J. Pomerans.) London: Hutchinson Educational.

Rothschild, K. W. 1964. "Cobweb Cycles and Partially Correct Forecasting." *Journal of Political Economy,* Volume 72 (June), 300–305.

Sagarin, Edward, and R. J. Kelly. 1972. "The Brewster Effect: Political Trials and the Self-Defeating Prophecy." Paper presented at the annual meeting of the American Sociological Association, New Orleans.

Scheff, Thomas J. 1964. "Preferred Errors in Diagnosis." *Medical Care,* Volume 2 (July–September), 166–172.

Schuessler, Karl. 1968. "Prediction." *International Encyclopedia of the Social Sciences,* Volume 12, 418–425.

Scriven, Michael. 1964. "An Essential Unpredictability in Human Behavior." In B. J. Wolman and E. Nagel (eds.), *Scientific Psychology: Principles and Approaches.* New York: Basic Books, 411–425.

Seeley, John R. 1951. "Social Science in Social Action." *Canadian Journal of Economics and Political Science,* Volume 17 (February), 84–89.

Shapiro, Arthur K. 1960. "A Contribution to the History of the Placebo Effect." *Behavioral Science,* Volume 5 (April), 109–135.

―――. 1964. "Factors Contributing to the Placebo Effect." *American Journal of Psychotherapy,* Volume 18, 73–88.

Silberman, Charles E. 1970. *Crisis in the Classroom.* New York: Random House.

Simmons, J. L. 1964. "On Maintaining a Deviant Belief System: A Case Study." *Social Problems,* Volume 11 (Winter), 250–256.

Simon, Herbert A. 1954. "Bandwagon and Underdog Effects and the Possibility of Election Predictions." *Public Opinion Quarterly* (Fall), 245–253.

Sjoberg, Gideon, and Roger Nett. 1968. *A Methodology for Social Research.* New York: Harper & Row.

Smith, M. Brewster. 1973. "Environmental Degradation and Human Behavior: Can Psychology Help?" *Representative Research in Social Psychology,* Volume 4 (January), 227–234.

Sorel, Georges. 1950. *Reflections on Violence.* (Translated by T. E. Hulme and J. Roth.) Glencoe, Ill.: Free Press.

Talland, G. A. 1954. "The Assessment of Group Opinion by Leaders and Their Influence on Its Formation." *Journal of Abnormal and Social Psychology,* Volume 49, 431–434.

Tannenbaum, Frank. 1938. *Crime and the Community.* New York: Columbia University Press.

Toch, Hans H. 1958. "The Perception of Future Events: Case Studies in Social Perception." *Public Opinion Quarterly,* Volume 22 (August), 57–66.

Venn, John. 1888. *The Logic of Chance.* London: Macmillan.

Watkins, J. W. N. 1969. "Historical Explanation in the Social Sciences." In Leonard Krimerman (ed.), *The Nature and Scope of Social Science.* New York: Appleton-Century-Crofts, 603–611.

Welty, Gordon, and A. Beradino. 1971. "A Possibility Theorem on Dynamic Organizational Research." *Social Science Quarterly,* Volume 52 (March), 953–958.

Werkmeister, W. H. 1959. "Theory Construction and the Problem of Objectivity." In Llewellyn Gross (ed.), *Symposium on Sociological Theory.* Evanston, Ill.: Row, Peterson, 483–508.

White, Leslie. 1963. "The Concept of Culture." In E. P. Hollander and R. G. Hunt (eds.), *Current Perspectives in Social Psychology.* New York: Oxford University Press, 106–112.

Wilkins, Leslie T. 1965. *Social Deviance: Social Policy, Action, and Research.* Englewood Cliffs, N.J.: Prentice-Hall.

Wolf, Eleanor P. 1957. "The Invasion-Succession Sequence as a Self-Fulfilling Prophecy." *Journal of Social Issues,* Volume 13 (October), 7–20.

———. 1958. "Research Data as an Element in Decision-Making." *Social Problems,* Volume 6 (Winter), 362–366.

Wrong, Dennis. 1974. "On Thinking About the Future." *American Sociologist,* Volume 9 (February), 26–31.

Young, Jock. 1971. "The Role of the Police as Amplifiers of Deviancy, Negotiators of Reality, and Translators of Fantasy." In Stanley Cohen (ed.), *Images of Deviance.* Harmondsworth: Penguin Books.

Zygmunt, Jospeh F. 1972. "When Prophecies Fail." *American Behavioral Scientist,* Volume 16 (November-December), 245–268.

JIB FOWLES

# The Problem of Values
# in Futures Research

Futures research is thick with values. Its practitioners, more so than plumbers or beauticians or astronauts, are under the influence of their values as they work for a "better" future.

This is obviously true for those futurists whose scope is the widest and whose concerns are the deepest. The future of humanity, as they oftentimes evaluate it, is a precarious one, and the prospect for a humane and orderly world is worsening. One among them is Robert Heilbroner, who concedes at the outset of *An Inquiry into the Human Prospect* that such conclusions regarding the course of mankind must be, and indeed ought to be, shaped by "subjective values" because of the deficiencies of science (1974, p. 23).

Futurists with grand views and designs are not the only ones who are value-ridden. The forecasters and planners who work in large-scale organizations are also in thrall to their values. Although they may think of themselves as hard headed and objective, standing in contrast to their more solicitous colleagues, they too operate within a value framework which, if anything, is even more binding than that of the visionaries. These values revolve around the survival and prospering of the organization that employs them. Their picture of the future, and plans for it, are conditioned by their allegiance to their organizations. At a time when more corporations are increasing their efforts to confront the future (Naylor, 1976), the extent of this normative orientation should not be ignored.

All the corners of futures research, then, are suffused with values. Given ambivalent data, equivocal standards for judging them, and the need to make selections on courses of action that suit chosen goals, it should not be otherwise. At every turn, when dealing with the future of every size of entity, from the individual to the group and organization, from the nation to all of *Homo Sapiens,* values pertain.

This observation would hardly merit attention if values were constant in the dimension where futurists have effect, that of time. That is, if it could be certain that the values of futurists would be the same as those of the future, designs initiated now could be guaranteed to fit in with life decades ahead. This is not the case, however. Today's values differ from yesterday's values, as everyone who has parents recognizes, and will differ from those of tomorrow, as everyone with children knows. Attitudes about sexual behavior, for example, have undergone a remarkable transformation in a very short time, altering the plans of individuals, manufacturers, legislatures, and whole cultures. The upshot of the fact that values vary in time is that present views and plans for the future, however well intended they might be, must to some extent be at odds with the values of those who will be subjected to them. "In short, every long-range plan contributes to the tyranny of the future" (Fowles, 1974, p. 67). Since futurists are likely to think of themselves as righteous (Wynn, 1972) and would not want to be accused of doing things to people that they would not want done to them, this issue becomes a vexing one.

Theodore Gordon provides an example

Suppose a planner were to design a transportation system to provide economical and safe travel. Economy and safety are current values; and his transportation system, which might happen to cut through a mountain, would satisfy those values. If, however, in some future society, the integrity of the countryside were more valued than cheap travel or safety, the planner would not only have been wrong, he would have been delinquent (1974, p. 112).

Fred Charles Ikle gives another example:

Take architecture and city planning. The lay-out of cities and type of dwellings will, to some extent, impose a style of life on the inhabitants. . . . But which preferences should be guiding? Those of today or those that one might forecast for the next generation (that is, the people who will still have to live in the cities and dwellings that are being built over the next decade)? (1971, p. 146).

With highways and cities, Gordon and Ikle have thoughtfully presented graphic illustrations. Unfortunately, the problem pervades less visible sectors of modern life as well. In business, finance, government, the military, international affairs, education, science, technology, and law, plans are formulated in the present to shape and regulate life in the future; the giganticism and complexity of industrialized existence decree that this be so. If chaos is to be staved off, what lies ahead must be put into good order. But people in the twenty-first century are certain to question the present notion of "good"; they may even question the present notion of "order."

"All plans," it has been observed, "imply an attempt to impose the values of the past (as expressed in the plan) on the future" (Toffler,

1969, p. 26). The political scientist Edwin A. Bock refers to this imposition as "the last colonialism," which he describes in this way:

We are today, in a time of rapid change and the development of new knowledge, possessed of immense capabilities for affecting the future. We are also increasingly possessed by a determination to use this capacity in order to shape beneficially the conditions that will form the environment of those who live ten to fifty years hence. Increasing numbers of well designed, well led, well organized expeditions are being outfitted and are setting forth to civilize, exploit, and build up sectors of unoccupied future. More and more, the lives of the inhabitants of these far-off temporal lands are going to be affected, if not largely determined, by conscious decisions made in the mother country of the present.

Such decisions, whatever their manifest beneficial aims, satisfy underlying needs of the present (1970, pp. 289–290).

How can one grapple with this conundrum? How can one begin to come to terms with the fact that futurists' values and future values cannot be identical? First, perhaps, by pausing to consider exactly what values are.

## THE NATURE OF VALUES

Asking about the nature of values is somewhat treacherous. We are certainly not the first to raise the question, and those who have done so before us have sometimes struck off on the most remarkable intellectual excursions, a few never to return. Such an inquiry requires that we avoid labyrinthine philosophizing and have a high regard for the commonsensical.

Briefly, then, what is a "value?" In order to respond, it is first necessary to do away with the idea that a value is "good." It may or may not be, depending on how it is evaluated in turn. For present purposes, values simply exist. They are an attribute of human life, and all humans possess them. Hitler had values; his values may not have been identical to our own, but they were values all the same.

A "value," according to Milton Rokeach, whose scholarly career has been devoted to giving some precision to these slippery items, is "a standard that guides and determines action, attitudes towards objects and situations, ideology, presentations of self to others, evaluations, judgments, justifications, comparisons of self with others, and attempts to influence others" (1973, p. 25). Rokeach compels us to adopt the most productive approach for discerning the essential nature of a value—that a value has functions. It does something for the possessor:

it provides a basis for interpreting the world and formulating appropriate responses.

With regard to responses, Rokeach suggests that a value can describe either desirable conduct or a desirable goal. In his vocabulary, a value can be either instrumental or terminal. An instrumental value could be "cheerful" or "logical," while a terminal value could be "a world at peace" or "social recognition."

Just as there is more than one type, so there has to be more than one value; a value never occurs in isolation. Everyone has a cluster of them as part of his mental equipment. They are arranged in a roughly hierarchical fashion, with some of the more abstract and nobler ones lying higher and being harder to come by except under special circumstances. For creatures as complex as human beings, entertaining conflicting values is no problem; the resolution occurs, statistically speaking, with the baser ones being invoked more often and the higher ones enduring to be resorted to occasionally.

Where does the bundle of operating standards come from? Humans are certainly not born with them; otherwise, more uniformity of value-sets would exist than apparently does. Rather, they are absorbed by a maturing individual from the currents of values that swirl through a culture. A fit has to occur between the values adopted (sometimes after considerable experimentation, as observers of children and adolescents recognize) and the basic drives and needs that undergird a personality. Since these primal attributes vary from person to person, so do the values that are ultimately selected. When picking up values, an individual will first try out the ones circulating closest to him; prejudiced people are likely to have prejudiced parents. If local values do not fit well enough, the individual will go further afield, looking for others, until his requirements are fairly well satisfied. But never perfectly satisfied: even with adults, there is still some chance of forgetting old and taking on new values.

Drawn from one's milieu, existing in the mind, a complex of values serves to orient a person to a complex world. The value-set is considerably less complicated than the world, however, and this is its greatest virtue—its economy, whereby a few standards apply in a multiplicity of situations. They apply in the interpretation of incoming stimuli, to judge something with reference to a sphere whose poles are good and bad. They apply in the channeling of drives and needs into appropriate behavior. Without values, a person's judgments and actions would be whimsical, disorderly.

The functions of values for the maintenance of a society are no less crucial, although they are of a different sort. The values that ebb and flow through a society cannot be everywhere identical, but if they are harmonious or complementary, then the various pieces manage to fit together, and the society operates more or less smoothly. This function—the harmonizing of the various components of a society—becomes most conspicuous when it is absent, when value-sets do not mesh and the society flies apart. In the twentieth century this can be the case in a country like Cuba where a growing revolutionary mentality cannot be accommodated along with preindustrial values. For the most part, however, the values extant in a society are distributed in such a way that the frictions and tensions do not get out of hand, people make the most out of their lot in life, and the society chugs on.

What can be learned from this quick exploration into the nature of values that is relevant to futures research? People engaged in forecasting and planning activities, forced to rely on their values more than others are, sometimes feel that this is no shortcoming because values by their very nature are above reproach. They may act as if values were a white charger upon which they may dash around and do as they will. But values, for all that one may esteem one's own, are features of human life no more (and no less) sacred than genitals or speech. Values are items in the human armamentarium, having, like other items, certain tasks to do if they are to be retained. Values are like mules, not white chargers. They do hard work; they help orient individuals and order societies—very workaday activities. In and of themselves, they may not be the ideal rationale for imperial designs.

The prosaic nature of values becomes all the clearer when we remember the extent to which they vary.

## VARIATION IN VALUES

There are no eternal verties. Would that there were. The hallowed truths and values that regulate the lives of all humans fluctuate greatly in time; likewise, they vary in space.

Their variance in time is of great relevance to the concerns here, since those who do forecasting and planning commonly operate as if values were constant. We are aware that over long spans of time values can change considerably. Our very distant ancestors, for instance, thought it "good" to sacrifice humans and thus to appease the universal forces. To carry out this practice clearly entailed attitudes and evaluations regarding human life that differ widely from contemporary outlooks. Long past the birth of Christ, North Europeans sacrificed great numbers of their own, male and female, adult and child, by drowning them in pools and marshes. The corpses of over 700 victims preserved by bog chemicals have been unearthed in Europe, to remind us of this grisly value-set in the prehistory of Western civilization.

That sacrifice was "good," especially if humans were the victims, was a widespread value among people who knew the rudiments of agriculture but had not yet developed into urban civilizations. It was their way of assuaging a threatening cosmos. Another novel value, less stigmatized since it is still with us, signaled another major turn in man's interpretation of the cosmos. Max Weber identified the rise of the Protestant ethic, with its emphasis on individualism and industry, as the instigator of the expansion of Western civilization (1930).

Just as human values are subject to fluctuations of this magnitude, so they are also subject to shorter term changes. In the case of the United States, where identity with the values of the Founding Fathers is much proclaimed and where the governmental framework has been constant for two centuries, there have occurred marked changes in the values of the populace. We know this in greater detail than our intuitions can provide because some social scientists have devised research strategies to explore this idea, most often by coding communications content. Scrutinizing old hymnals and children's readers and the like, David C. McClelland has traced the oscillation of the values of achievement and power in history (1961). Representative of the McClelland-originated studies was one executed by de Charms and Moeller, who studied the occurrence of achievement imagery in American children's readers over 150 years. They found it rose to considerable heights in 1890 and fell off sharply after that (1962).

Harold Lasswell has studied the variation of values with reference to long-term political changes in American life. In one study that expanded on Lasswell's thinking, the platforms of American political parties during 1844–1864 were compared to those of a century later (Namenwirth and Lasswell, 1970). To paraphrase the findings, nineteenth-century values were less concerned with safety and security and more inclined toward the preservation of social distinctions. Even more interesting was the fact that in the nineteenth century Rokeach's so-called terminal values were emphasized, while in the twentieth century instrumental values were.

A number of studies have pointed out changes in American values over shorter stretches of time. Leo Lowenthal examined idols in popular magazines and found that from 1901 to 1941 a shift occurred in the personages admired by the reading public—from idols of production (business magnates) to idols of consumption (film stars). To Lowenthal this shift suggested an abandonment of the value of achievement (1944).

It is not enough to point out that values can vary over the millennia or centuries or decades; shifts in values can occur much more swiftly and thunderingly. A stunning instance took place during the years 1967–

1972, when values changed in such a way that everything involved in the traditional American devotion to progress was called into question. The people left in the lurch of these flip-flops in values were confused and angry, until Alvin Toffler was shrewd enough to find the perfect scapegoat (in that it could never retaliate)—the future (Toffler, 1970). These value changes are brought out in survey data, especially those collected by Daniel Yankelovich, who conducted five polls of American college youth over this six-year period. Yankelovich reports:

So startling are the shifts in values and beliefs between the late 1960s, when our youth studies were first launched, and the present time that social historians of the future should have little difficulty in identifying the end of one era and the beginning of a new one. Rarely has a transition between one decade and the next seemed so abrupt and so full of discontinuities (1974, p. 3).

Chronicling the turning back to more conventional values, Yankelovich measured a growing abhorrence of violence, increased regard for the work ethic, and lessened concern for minorities, among other related items.

The insubstantiality of values is further revealed by the fact that, as well as varying in time, they also vary in space. That is, at any given point in time, there will be considerable variety around the globe about what is to be valued. Shepard Clough calls attention to the uniqueness of what he feels is the primary value underlying Western civilization:

In thus placing the development of the individual at the very base of our value system the West is relatively unique among present-day cultures. The Japanese would regard the glorification of their emperor, himself a god, as the foundation of their system. The Indians would not even take the life of an animal to save a human life. Moslems consider a trip to Mecca to be more important that the erection of decent structures for human habitation. Russo-Communists subordinate the individual in order to advance a particular kind of socioeconomic system. And members of primitive cultures sacrifice the individual for the glory of both their gods and their tribes (1960, p. 15).

Values vary not only between peoples but also within a people. In the case of the United States, those who travel through the country know that value-sets differ from one area to another. John Gillan has made an attempt to specify the variety of American regional values, suggesting that industry is a cardinal value in the Northeast and Northwest, optimism in the West, democracy in the Middle West, and devotion to the family and to moral codes in the South (1955).

However, far more than geographical locus is involved in the heterogeneity of American values; social locus is more of a deciding factor.

The distribution of values in American life has been analyzed along such dimensions as sex, race, education, employment, and so forth. Typical in conception, but more exhaustive in execution, is the research carried out by Rokeach (1973). Among the ample findings are these (presenting terminal values first and instrumental second):

—The greatest difference between males and females is that men rank higher the terminal value "a comfortable life," and the instrumental value "imaginative."

—In contrast to the rich, the poor esteem "a comfortable life" and "clean."

—Blacks rank "a comfortable life" and "ambitious" higher than whites.

—The old prize "a world at peace" and "forgiving" more than the young.

—Christians rank "salvation" and "forgiving" higher than nonbelievers. (However, on "love" and "helpful" they do not stand out.)

Our assault on the preeminence of values is about done. Not only are values prosaic in terms of function but they are also in a constant state of flux—an undulating ocean, extending in every direction. The values of some are not the values of all; what was yesterday a value may not be one today or tomorrow. Thus, the enterprise of forecasting and planning takes place in rough seas; it is foolish to pretend otherwise.

## THE PROBLEM AMPLIFIED

Our initial observation was that values complicate the business of forecasting and planning along the dimension of time, since planners and the subjects of plans dwell in different value settings. For instance, the creators of Social Security, living in bad times when high levels of charitableness could be presumed, might be puzzled to see that present-day affluent citizens begrudge paying for the plan. Similarly, the planning done decades ago for athletic department facilities and programs is now everywhere in disarray because of changes in values regarding females.

It turns out that the difficulties involved in values and futures research are greater yet. Because values also vary along geographical and social lines, a second problem is encountered. The futurist's designs upon the future represent the elevation of one contemporary value-set above all others. There is the odor of arrogance to this.

The particular value-set of futurists is sometimes thought to be inappropriately libertarian. It is interesting that futurists are sometimes accused of not being sufficiently liberal or open-minded. Kumar has suggested that they are devoted, exclusively, to the continuance of the recent industrial past (1972). Miles carries this thought further, examining the manifestations of these values in even the most objectively conceived aspects of futures research (1975). According to Carey and Quirk, the values of futurists work to foreclose, rather than expand, options for the future (1973). The fact that futurists are attacked from all sides implies that there is a discernible cluster of values at the center in which most futurists share. These are the values that are likely to become exalted, and then to be applied to the future.

Let us now review the activity of a futurist, in the light of these comments on values, to see where the variation in values impinges upon the process. It is convenient to think of the process as having four separate steps, although some may be tred on very lightly (if at all), and the steps are rarely taken just once (reiteration of some or all being much more usual in the course of a futures research project).

First, some area of interest is staked out. If the futures research effort is a team one, this may take time; if individual, the particular concern may just pop into mind. There is a tendency for the area to be grand, up to and including the future of the planet. Not only is the area sizable but also its time-varying features are to be prominent, and so a time frame may be established.

But how did this large, dynamic subject area get selected? For all that is excluded, why is it excluded? The choices rest ultimately on the futurist's values of what is important and worth probing. Fred Charles Ikle was subversive enough to make this point to his colleagues on the Commission on the Year 2000:

And what about the Commission on the Year 2000 of the American Academy of Arts and Sciences, as it met in 1965–66? The agenda of its predictions was almost identical with the agenda of President Johnson's "Great Society" as enunciated the year before. This marked tendency to select our topics for predictions from among our concerns of the most recent past should give us pause (1967, p. 114).

Clearly in 1966, others less attuned to the government would have had other issues to raise: Vietnam, the Middle East, unidentified flying objects, or whatever. If the Commission on the Year 2000 were to meet again now, it might consider economic and energy matters to be the worthy ones. Thus, the very beginnings of a futures research exercise are shaped by parochial values.

The influence of values is more conspicuous at the second step, where goals regarding the chosen area of interest are arrived at. Here there is virtually no other guidance than that provided by values. Indeed, goals are little else than terminal values made specific. Occasionally they go unstated and must be inferred from a futurist's work, but if the effort is intended to be of any consequence, the goals are explicit. Corporate planners are often quick to set goals for their organizations, as are the planners for socialist nations. In the United States, the establishing of goals is more hesitatingly done at the national and regional levels. There have been numerous state and metropolitan goal-setting projects, but the difficulties of enlisting participation and arriving at a consensus indicate that not all people have the same interests for the future.

Even the highest aspirations of modern life are not universally held. The futures effort headquartered at the University of Sussex in England may feel safe in pledging itself to the goal of reducing inequality (Encel, Marstrand, and Page, 1976, p. 15), but this aim is not shared by all. And it is not just the elite who resist it; nations such as Japan and Russia which are within striking distance of the world's leaders may not want edicts of equality to apply to them, while preindustrial people, feeling that social distinctions are part of the natural state of things, may look on equality with suspicion. The point is this: any goal represents the selection of one value and, as a result, the rejection of numerous competing others.

Third, information regarding the chosen area of interest and pertinent to the selected goals must be generated. This third step, that of forecasting, would seem to be more protected from the interference of values, since methods with scientific pretensions have been devised. However, while the development of forecasting techniques is proceeding nicely, it is still far short of establishing methods that are thoroughly objective, even when they are cautiously employed. Says Ian Miles, "Given the present state of social research, the boundaries of empirical knowledge will be reached sooner rather than later. This means the values of a forecaster, and a philosophy and ideology of the nature of man and society must inevitably determine much of his or her work" (1975, p. 31). Other examinations of forecasting methods reach similar conclusions (Fowles, 1976a, 1976b; Hill and Fowles, 1975). No matter how sterling they may appear, methods of forecasting tend to mask rather than remove the influence of values. The values of the futurist still come through, and without much difficulty, as critics of Dennis Meadows' computerized model of mankind's future have suggested (Cole et al., 1973).

Fourth, on the basis of concerns, goals, and forecasts, the point is reached when strategies of intervention can be contrived. Here the required plans and policies are drawn up, to be implemented. The role of values is no less strong than in the previous steps, although we may think that plans are a purely logical outcome of all that has gone on before. But depending on the instrumental values of the planners, one proposal may be far harsher than another, for instance.

Even more troublesome at this fourth step, though, are the temporal considerations, as we have noticed. A plan for any but the shortest term cannot be assumed to conform perfectly to the values of its distant subjects. The story of the SST is a case in point (Primack and von Hippel, 1972). In 1963, President Kennedy decided to go ahead with plans for the development of a supersonic transport aircraft, although it was known at the time that the plane would be inordinately costly and would in all likelihood be unacceptable to the public owing to the noise it would create. Nevertheless, at a time when Americans were staggered by Soviet space successes and a supposed strategic missile gap, and taunted by not only the Russian but also the Anglo-French intentions to build SSTs, Kennedy could only reflect the aspirations of his countrymen. A mere eight years later, however, the values of Americans had changed acutely, and plans for the SST were now out of step. Getting a man to the moon had been sufficient aerospace achievement. The desire to overcome did not seem so glorious in the waning days of the Vietnam War. With great drama and turmoil, the project was terminated in the Spring of 1971, although there was nothing to show for the billion dollars that had been spent.

The essential topicality of values, then, makes futures research a perilous business.

## WHAT IS TO BE DONE?

How are we to deal with the haughtiness which is largely inadvertent but largely inherent in futures research? One response, of course, is to continue as before and to ignore the fact that the designs of futurists stem from values that differ from those of others, both now and in times to come. But some improvement seems possible.

To survey the current values of all people who might be touched by a futures research prorect is an obvious proposal. Indeed, the call for this survey is an article of faith among egalitarian-minded futurists. It would be the only way to guard against blind reliance on the values of the futurist alone, and the only way to gain a sense of the rich variety of outlooks regarding times to come.

A value survey, mandatory though it is, should be undertaken with a recognition that certain drawbacks exist. First, it costs money. Resources must be diverted from other purposes. Second, any data-gathering exercise carries with it the risk that the findings will be disappointing in the extreme. A recent poll of Americans, for instance, indicated that they would line up against their own Bill of Rights. The futurist who conducts a value survey must steel himself for such an eventuality.

Third, even when funds are forthcoming and the results are prepared for, it should be confessed that a survey would take place in the absence of any generally accepted theory of values. The survey would have to be constructed, tested, and applied without consensus among social scientists on the precise form of values. Milton Rokeach's work with values, for all its prominence, is not universally endorsed (Warner, 1976). A content analysis of the references under the label "values" in *Sociological Abstracts* for the 1950s and 1960s has been carried out, and the results are revealing. According to the investigator:

The first, and perhaps most evident feature of this research is the lack of a commonly accepted framework which would lend coherence to the various empirical studies and permit them to have mutual implications. . . . The substantive research had in general the characteristic of being non-cumulative; studies tended to proceed in independent, parallel lines rather than in an integrated form (Barnsley, 1972, p. 168).

This lack of an explanatory framework becomes all the more sorrowful when we turn our attention to ways of allowing for the influence of values along the dimension of time. If only values were better understood, then value changes could be predicted, and present plans could be made to suit future values. One of the very few to feel that forecasting is possible in this realm is David McClelland, whose research indicates that there are predictable rhythms to the values and needs of Americans. McClelland sees values changing in such a way as to make the waging of war by Americans a likely happenstance in the next few years (1975). If his forecasts are felt to be accurate, the United States should gird its loins now and plan for increased production of war material.

For the most part, however, there is agreement that values are not well enough understood to permit prediction (Taviss, 1973). When introducing the most substantial effort so far to establish a predictive science of values, that organized by Kurt Baier and Nicholas Rescher, Alvin Toffler comments, "The value universe can be compared to a great, uncharted and invisible ocean. The study summarized here can be seen as an adventurous probe into the deeps. One surfaces with fresh awe for the complexity of the subject. The edges of the problem are scarcely penetrated" (1969, p. 26).

This being the case, when value forecasting is done without a sturdy conceptual apparatus, it is often an occasion for the display of the forecaster's values. For example, Willis Harman, writing in 1969, took note of the rise of humanist left values and foresaw a momentous value shift:

In essence, what we propose is that some aspects of the present situation may be interpreted as indications of a possible shift in the basic premises of the culture, somewhat as the historical process called the Protestant Reformation involved a shift of predominant beliefs from the theological view of the Middle Ages to the economic view of the modern world (1969, p. 83).

From the perspective of several years later, it is clear that he overrated the changes going on then, perhaps on the basis of his own high hopes for them.

All this is not to say that value forecasting is worthless, or that the effort should not continue, or that each futurist at work should not ask himself whether the plans he is contemplating fit his intuitions regarding future values, however feeble those intuitions might be. For the time being, however, value forecasting should not be thought of as more than it is.

A second approach to resolving the discrepancy between plans initiated now and values found in the future would depend on a somewhat different conception of values. The first approach presumed that the ebb and flow of values was beyond manipulation; the second does not. According to this strategy, values are to be bent, to fit the planner's intentions. This scheme often comes to mind when something is desired for the future which seems at odds with values presently held. Persuasion is the usual way in which accommodation is attempted. For example, the U.S. government emerged from World War II with a commitment to nuclear power as a future source of energy. Since this was strongly resisted by the public, the Atomic Energy Commission and other federal agencies tried to do all within their power to change Americans' evaluation—which bordered on repulsion—of nuclear power. It is possible that the AEC's efforts are being successful and that a value shift is going on. To judge from the recent widespread acceptance of microwave ovens, Americans are less skittish about some forms of radiation. Moreover, in the Fall 1976 elections, voters in six states decided against tighter controls over atomic power plants. There may be more nuclear power in our future than the exasperated AEC could have hoped for a few years ago.

The tactics of activist groups are also derived from this second approach. Activists see a future coming that they do not like, and they are working to create value changes that will promote a future they desire more. Environmentalists try to stimulate values regarding appreciation of untouched settings, in the hope of producing a future where more and more of the landscape is protected.

For futurists untroubled by qualms over the manipulation of people's values, this approach would seem to be more promising than the first one. To some degree, values do get altered—if not with the insertion of a new value, at least with the reordering of the old. It is not always clear, however, that values are altered because of the initiatives of those who wish to see them changed. Americans may be cozying up to nuclear power not because of the persuasiveness of the federal government, but because in the aftermath of the oil crises they anticipate that it may be the only economical means of supplying electricity in the future. Similarly, environmental awareness may be developing not because of the work of activists, but because people increasingly have the leisure to venture into the great outdoors. Without a general theory of values and value changes, all claims for the creation of value shifts must be regarded cautiously.

The third possible approach is to agree that values cannot be satisfactorily predicted or altered and to switch emphasis from values to the plans themselves. After all, are plans not the element in this dilemma over which we have control? So let us create plans that are flexible enough to respond to upcoming values shifts, goes this line of thinking. No matter how radical the shifts are, the plans will be able to adjust. In effect, this is how most modern-day plans are set up, with periodic reviews built into the timetable. Usually, these reviews are conceived of as the opportunity to gauge progress toward objectives, but they are also the occasion to ask if the goals and means are still suitable.

It should be observed, however, that there is a trade-off to building flexibility into a plan. A pliable plan is achieved at the cost of some of the plan's strength. Goals become more elusive if they cannot be pursued with all available resources and determination. Having to proceed gingerly means a reduction of some of the plan's vigor.

None of these three strategies is satisfactory on its own. Since each can add something, they should be taken together. We arrive then at the three precepts jointly necessary for dealing with the assured discrepancy between present plans and future values:

1. Hazard guesses about future values. Aware of the extent that values may fluctuate, propose several varieties of future value-sets for the time frame and counterpose these to the intended plans, to see what the problems are. Remember the SST.
2. Consider altering future values. If resistance to a design for the future does not invoke deep-lying values, it may be a candidate for manipulation.
3. Create flexible plans. Recognizing that there are disadvantages to flexibility, plans should still be constructed with as much opportunity for review as possible.

There is a moral in all of this, of course, and it should be drawn explicitly: futurists can profit from a large dose of humility. No matter how vivid their values regarding the future, a chance exists that the values are inappropriate. If those values come to dominate the values of others, both contemporary and upcoming, then there is a possibility that damage is being done and risks are being run. Futurists must be ever mindful of the fact that their values are irredeemably topical.

## REFERENCES

Barnsley, John H. 1972. *The Social Reality of Ethics.* London: Routledge and Kegan Paul.

Bock, Edwin A. 1970. "Governmental Problems Arising from the Use and Abuse of the Future—the Last Colonialism?" In Dwight Waldo, (ed.), *Temporal Dimensions of Development Administration.* Durham, N.C.: Duke University Press, 264-297.

Carey, James W., and John J. Quirk. 1973. "The History of the Future." In George Gerbner et al. (eds.), *Communications Technology and Social Policy.* New York: John Wiley and Sons, 485-504.

Clough, Shepard B. 1960. *Basic Values of Western Civilization.* New York: Columbia University Press.

Cole, H. S. D., et al. 1973. *Models of Doom.* New York: Universe Books.

de Charms, F., and C. Moeller. 1962. "Values Expressed in American Children's Readers, 1900-1950." *Journal of Abnormal and Social Psychology,* Volume 64, 136-142.

Encel, Solomon, Pauline K. Marstrand, and William Page. 1976. *The Art of Anticipation.* New York: Pica Press.

Fowles, Jib. 1974. "On Chronocentrism." *Futures,* Volume 6, Number 1 (February), 65-68.

———. 1976a. "An Overview of Social Forecasting Procedures." *Journal of the American Institute of Planners* (July), 253-263.

———. 1976b. *Mass Advertising as Social Forecast.* Westport, Conn.: Greenwood Press.

Gillin, John. 1955. "National and Regional Cultural Values in the United States." *Social Forces,* Volume 34, 107-113.

Gordon, T. J. 1974. "Current Methods of Futures Research." In Albert Somit (ed.), *Political Science and the Study of the Future.* Hinsdale, Ill.: Dryden Press, 89-113.

Harman, Willis H. 1969. "Contemporary Social Forces and Alternative Futures." *Journal of Research and Development in Education,* Volume 2, Number 4, 67-89.

Heilbroner, Robert L. 1974. *An Inquiry into the Human Prospect.* New York: W. W. Norton.

Hill, Kim Quaile, and Jib Fowles. 1975. "The Methodological Worth of the Delphi Forecasting Technique." *Technological Forecasting and Social Change,* Volume 8, Number 2, 179-192.

Ikle, Fred Charles. 1967. "Can Social Predictions Be Evaluated?" In Daniel Bell (ed.), *Toward the Year 2000.* Boston: Beacon Press, 101-126.

———. 1971. "Social Forecasting and the Problem of Changing Values." *Futures,* Volume 3, Number 2 (June), 142-150.

Kumar, Krishan, 1972. "Inventing the Future in Spite of Futurology." *Futures,* Volume 4, 369–375.

Lowenthal, Leo. 1944. "Biographies in Popular Magazines." In Paul F. Lazarsfeld and Frank N. Stanton (eds.), *Radio Research 1942–43.* New York: Duell, Sloan and Pearce, 507–548.

McClelland, David C. 1961. *The Achieving Society.* Princeton, N.J.: D. Van Nostrand.

———. 1975. "Love and Power, the Psychological Signals of War." *Psychology Today,* Volume 8 (January), 44–48.

Miles, Ian. 1975. *The Poverty of Prediction.* Lexington, Mass.: Lexington Books.

Namenwirth, J. Zvi, and Harold D. Lasswell. 1970. *The Changing Language of American Values.* Beverly Hills, Calif.: Sage Publications.

Naylor, Thomas H. 1976. "The Future of Corporate Planning Models." *Managerial Planning* (March/April), 1–9.

Primack, Joel, and Frank von Hippel. 1972. "Scientists, Politics, and SST: A Critical Review." *Bulletin of the Atomic Scientists* (April), 24–30.

Rokeach, Milton. 1973. *The Nature of Human Values.* New York: Free Press.

Taviss, Irene. 1973. "Futurology and the Study of Values." In Franklin Tugwell (ed.), *Search for Alternatives: Public Policy and the Study of the Future.* Cambridge, Mass.: Winthrop Publishers, 98–101.

Toffler, Alvin. 1969. "Value Impact Forecaster, A Profession of the Future." In Kurt Baier and Nicholas Rescher (ed.), *Values and the Future.* New York: Free Press, 1–30.

———. 1970. *Future Shock.* New York: Random House.

Warner, R. Stephen. 1976. "Review of *The Nature of Human Values.*" *Contemporary Sociology,* Volume 5, Number 1 (January), 13–16.

Weber, Max. 1930. *The Protestant Ethic and the Spirit of Capitalism.* (Translated by Talcott Parsons.) New York: Scribner's.

Wynn, Mark. 1972. "Who Are the Futurists?" *The Futurist,* Volume 6, Number 2, 73–77.

Yankelovich, Daniel. 1974. *The New Morality.* New York: McGraw-Hill.

# Part III

# The Procedures of Futures Research

Despite all the conceptual and practical difficulties that beset futures research, the effort to confront the future sensibly has not slackened. In the public and private sectors of modern life, an increasing number of decisions for the future are being made, decisions that are on the whole more consequential than those of previous times, involving greater commitments for longer periods of time.

Those whose job it is to arrive at the plans and policies for the future are rarely satisfied with the information available to them or the way their choices are implemented. Thus, there is constant pressure to improve the craft of futures research. As a result, procedures and practices have developed which provide frameworks for the activity of futurists. Now they have some choice among ways to generate objective or normative statements about the future, as well as among ways to acquaint various audiences with their futures.

This section of the Handbook presents the most commonly discussed and employed procedures, in order to see precisely what they are and what they are good for. As a generality, the chapters proceed from the less quantitative procedures to the more quantitative. Although it is useful to distinguish among these procedures, several are often used together in a project, and indeed they seem to work well that way. This will become clearer in the two chapters regarding technology, which to some extent summarize the previous descriptions.

The future, writes Jay Mendell in the opening chapter, is an "ill-structured problem" and so resists highly rigorous modes of investigation. There is more room for intuition in futures research than in other rational inquiries. If awareness and responsiveness with regard to the future are to be acute, he says, then heightened imagination and instinct are required. Mendell spells out ways of honing these abilities.

In a similar vein, Dennis Livingston relates how the subjectivity inherent in futures research can be enhanced through attention to science fiction. Objective forecasting cannot indicate the widest possible range of alternatives for the future, nor can it suggest the fullness of life in times to come. Not only is science fiction telling about the future, this chapter explains, but it is also influential in the present, mirroring and shaping changes that are taking place.

"Images of the future" is a phrase that occurs over and over in futures literature, to indicate visions of the ideal that can serve to orient present behavior. Suitable images of the future are believed to increase the likelihood of improved conditions in the decades ahead. The emphasis here is less on cognizance of what is probable than on the pursuit of what is desirable.

Bettina Huber has brought good order to the voluminous and sometimes conflicting references to images of the future. She dwells not only on what has been written about the construction of these ideals but also on the practicalities of making them real. There is an extra dividend in this chapter: beyond considering images of the future as societal levers, Huber examines how they pertain to individual experiences. Throughout the chapter, the best and most relevant of social science findings are cited, so that comprehension of the nature and utility of images of the future can be extended past the usual superficial pronouncements.

Senarios are another device for stimulating consciousness of the future. Ian Wilson's chap-

ter provides a succinct description of this prominent procedure, one that Wilson himself has
made good use of in his work for General Electric Company. Quoting Herman Kahn, the
earliest proponent of scenarios, Wilson says that
a scenario is a "hypothetical sequence of events
constructed for the purpose of focusing attention
on causal processes and decision points." It is a
narration about the future, often a dramatically
vivid one. More than one single scenario may be
presented at a time, Wilson tells us, so that alternative futures can be scrutinized. If scenarios are
sometimes fabricated just to amuse, they are
more often scrupulously done, to serve as the
basis for planning.

Scenarios convey views of the future, but they
do not generate them. If predictions are not
made intuitively, then they are produced by systematic forecasting techniques, the most elemental one being that of trend projection. Since
most of our everyday lives is premised on the
operation of continuities, trend extrapolation
presents no conceptual difficulties. To the extent
that historical data exist, trends are methodologically easy to fashion. Kim Quaile Hill shows that
this conceptual simplicity may leave futurists un-
satisfied, especially when questions of causality
come up, and that the methodology can become
elaborate and can involve complicated statistical
maneuvering. Overall, however, trends are to be
thought of as sturdy procedures. As did Wilson,
Hill ends his chapter with several helpful rules of
thumb.

However, for much that is of interest about the
future, trend extrapolations are not good
enough. The need for forecasts extends beyond
matters that have been measured to those that
have not been and cannot be. Other procedures
are required.

One of the more spectacular items in the futurist's bag of tricks is the Delphi technique. Its
name alone would lend it prominence, even if its
pedigree were not excellent (it originated in one

of the wellsprings of futures research, the RAND Corporation) and its employment were not wide (it has found utility in thousands of studies since the first one was published in 1964). The Delphi technique is one that futures research can claim for its very own, and so it helps to mark off this field from all others. Broadly speaking, the method systematizes expert opinion regarding the future, in the interest of consensus on forecasts. How this happens is illustrated in Harold Linstone's chapter, where he presents typical applications in business and government. The Delphi method, we learn, is not so much a forecasting device as a way of organizing communication among a panel of knowledgeable people. It is, Linstone takes pains to say, a method of last resort, to be used when precise analytical techniques cannot be. With reference to the future, that is much of the time.

A criticism made of the Delphi method is that it cannot take sufficient account of interrelationships. The future will result from a nest of interactions, while the Delphi technique makes projections one at a time. Hence, not long after the Delphi method was launched, one of its originators, Olaf Helmer, joined with Theodore Gordon to devise a technique that would systematically explore the chances and consequences of interactions. The chapter "Cross-Impact Analysis" spells out the intricacies of this highly quantitative, computer-assisted forecasting method. As Gordon and John Stover reveal in their chapter, the development of cross-impact matrices and related techniques continues to advance rapidly. They write from the methodological vanguard of futures research and testify to its vigor.

By appraising interaction along two dimensions, cross-impact analysis produces a quasi-model of the future. A fuller representation of multifold, time-varying interrelationships comes with that seemingly all-powerful technique, the simulation model. According to Michael

McLean, a simulation model is the "mathematical representation of a system from which the behavior of the system over time can be inferred." It is easy to see why this method commands the great respect that it does. Its ambitions are little short of those that have driven social science for two centuries: to describe the workings of the grand, complex systems in which humans are enmeshed and to ascertain where those systems are heading. The capabilities of the approach seem limitless, since it makes use of computers that can manipulate vast amounts of data according to large numbers of theorems. All of this is played out over what is represented as immense expanses of time, although the calculations are done instantly. Finally, the approach is so new (having been developed only a few steps behind the innovation of the computer machinery itself) that it comes into futures research relatively untarnished by applications in other fields. As a new approach for a new field and a comprehensive method for comprehensive questions, it seems ideal.

Unfortunately, despite its glories, simulation modeling has notable drawbacks. Michael McLean is attached to the Science Policy Research Unit of England's University of Sussex, which is a collection point for information and analyses of computerized models. He makes good use of that store of knowledge here. Primarily, he says, modelers are too single-minded in their conception of the future and too baroque in their constructions. It is in the nature of modeling that these tendencies will be aggrandized, to the point of ruining accuracy. McLean discusses the necessary corrective procedures before outlining the methodological advances that are currently under way.

In contrast to highly quantitative simulation modeling, simulation games are uncalibrated and of freer form. It should also be observed that they lend themselves to different applications.

Simulation models can describe systems characterized by levels (of food supply, say) and rates (raw material depletion, for instance); simulation games imitate only those systems whose components can be personified by the players. According to Richard Duke, simulation games are best considered as structured communications settings in which the players come to grasp the patterns and ramifications of the alternative futures that get played out. Learning is more intensive here, he feels, than in other communications activities which proceed, like language itself, sequentially.

Martino and Coates provide a review of all these procedures, plus an introduction to several more, as they set down the numerous methods of foretelling technological futures. Technology has been a preoccupation of futures research, in part because it has been reshaping contemporary existence, but also because it is more visible than the other forces at work in the industrial vortex humans now occupy. Thus, technology catches much of the applause and the dismay aimed at the state and destiny of modern life.

Of the various modes of addressing technology, Joseph Martino describes the one least bedeviled by normative issues and most concerned with well-rationalized forecasting. Technological forecasting is the attempt to anticipate through quantitative methods the kind and degree of advances in a particular technology. Usually, this attempt is carried out with scant attention to the social, political, cultural, or even economic contexts in which the advances may occur. For many industries and government agencies, these unrefined trend data provide important, baseline information.

Technology assessment, on the other hand, does not project a technology but forecasts what the consequences might be if a technology already on the horizon does in fact get adopted. It studies problematic technologies and their potential impacts upon society. Joseph Coates is associated with the Congressional Office of Technology Assessment, where much of the most vigorous work of this sort is being conducted, and he writes from that vantage point.

The final chapter turns to the even grander issues that are so common in futures research: Where is society headed? Is it diverging from the directions in which we wish to move? From a procedural point of view, these questions become: How can we know where society is headed? How are we to ascertain the directions in which it should be moving? Such objective and normative queries have created another focal point in futures research, that identified with the term *social indicators.* These are data series that measure societal features of normative interest—educational levels, for example, or crime rates. Social indicators are trend measures that gauge how well a society is proceeding toward its goals. The scope here is far wider than with technology forecasting or assessment, and as if in compensation, the methods are less fancy. In his chapter, Denis Johnston, director of the federal government's Social Indicators Project, first examines the objective and normative aspects of social indicators. He then explores the role of social indicators in social forecasts (which he carefully distinguishes from predictions and projections). These several themes are carried forward to his summary: "If social indicators, and the social forecasts derived therefrom, are to be relevant to the needs of decision-makers, they must be both normatively significant and descriptively accurate."

Saying that, Johnston echoes the central tenet of futures research. Only the best possible understanding of tomorrow can lead to the best possible decisions today.

JAY S. MENDELL

# The Practice of Intuition

Several years ago, I asked executives of a computer company what their customers want and need. "Giant brains," was the answer. Then I asked what the company was doing about unwanted data bases and dossiers—information that was not really needed, but which no one knows how to dispose of. One individual leaped up and ran out of the room. I never saw her again, but she stopped in the doorway and cried: "My God! What we need is not a giant brain. What we need is a giant kidney!"

This executive's sudden insight into her mission—designing computers to dispose of unwanted information, instead of processing more and more information—is an example of the practice of intuitive thinking. It was accomplished without an agreed-on-in-advance method of examining information. Suddenly there occurred a shift in the executive's way of looking at the situation. It is also an example of *futuristic thinking,* since it creates possibilities for research and innovation in a new direction.

## THE FUTURE AS AN ILL-STRUCTURED PROBLEM

The future is an ill-structured problem.[1] Confronting it, one will be involved in posture planning and in scanning of the environment. In posture planning (Ringbakk, 1975), one tries to respond to changes in the world by finding fundamentally new purposes, new missions, new senses of direction, and new needs to serve. In *environmental scanning* (Mendell and Mueller, 1973; Utterback and Burack, 1975), one strives to establish an early warning system—communication channels to the environment that will permit scanning "relevant" environmental changes (while skimming over "irrelevant" changes).

People of average creativity and mental tidiness find the future a maddening problem. As one individual remarked,

First I discovered that you can't do posture planning until you have first done environmental scanning since you don't know what you want to become until you know what environmental forces to react to. Then I realized that you *can't* do environmental scanning first because until you have done posture planning, you don't know what forces are relevant to the organization: you have to suspect what the organization is trying to become. By and by, it dawned on me that both problems have to be worked on together . . . and intuitively. They are part of one bigger problem.

Futures problems are of a different class than scheduling production line operations, for instance. We know what information is needed to schedule the factory; we have a model of the factory; and we know what methods to use to analyze the information through the model. Production operations problems are well structured. On the other hand, futures problems are ill structured. We do not know what information is needed; we have few comprehensive models and no prescription for how to process the information we have. Even worse, there is no end to the problem. Once posture planning and environmental scanning have been started, we have to continually update and refine the planning and scanning as new information is received."

This brings us to the myth of rationality (Mendell and Tanner, 1975). Most people like to believe that they are working on well-structured, "under-control" problems. We can apply rational methods to well-structured problems and get well-defined, permanent answers. But nonrational thinking has to be employed to solve ill-structured problems and this scares people. So people treat futures problems as well structured and dither over how to improve our methodologies,[2] rather than how to improve our intuition and creativity. This represents an elemental misconception.

## HANDLING NEW PATTERNS

A British psychologist, Edward de Bono (1971), asked, "What is the function of the mind?" and answered, "The mind acts as a pattern-creating system. As information pours in, the mind searches for, and discovers patterns (concepts, abstractions, or models) which condense, organize and give meaning to the incoming information."

Now, this patterning behavior has advantages and disadvantages. It relieves the mind of extensive conscious data manipulation and repetitious thinking if incoming information "fits" existing patterns. Some incoming information is interpreted in terms of existing patterns; some is used to extend and enlarge existing patterns, or to link together already existing patterns, but some of it is filtered out because it does not "fit" into already existing patterns.

According to the de Bono model, the mind is a filter that ignores data which do not fit preexisting patterns. But the mind is a self-created filter. Early information creates the patterns that filter out later information. Incoming information if it is not inconsistent with previously existing patterns is (1) accepted into the context of previously existing patterns, (2) is organized into new patterns unconnected with previous ones but not inconsistent with them, (3) is added on to previously existing patterns, to create even larger patterns more universally capable of interpreting and filtering information about the environment, or (4) causes previously existing patterns to "hook up" with other patterns to form more universal patterns. What happens to information that conflicts with previously existing patterns? It is likely to be filtered out, ignored. Patterns are expectations: they predispose the mind to accept or reject incoming information. They represent "trained incapacity" to deal with new information.

What is the significance of this patterning for futurists? Since the filters (patterns) are established by information acquired in the past, information about the present and future is likely to be filtered out. The present and future environment will either look like the past or be altogether invisible.

De Bono's theory can be extended to organizations and cultures. Organizations and industries suffer from the disease of "craft consciousness," that is, they believe that they already know what is important in the world, that they need to cure neither their tunnel vision nor their shortsightedness (Mendell, 1975, 1976).

De Bono believes that the mind finds it natural to form patterns but unnatural to replace old patterns with new. Even if new patterns are required in order to make sense of information arriving from the environment, old patterns retain their grip. We are all prisoners of mental patterns formed by information about a past environment. *Thinking about the future consists not only of creating new patterns but of getting rid of old patterns.*

## HANDLING NEW INFORMATION

Recently, a number of articles have created interest in the personality theories of Jung (McKenney and Keen, 1974; Mitroff and Kilmann, 1975) and the philosophical inquiring systems of Kant, Hegel, Leibniz, Locke, and Singer (Mitroff and Turoff, 1973) as guides to planning, scanning, and problem-solving. According to Jung's typology, problem-solvers may be categorized by their styles in gathering and evaluating information. First, let us consider information gathering.

A Lockean inquirer discovers the "truth" about a situation by examining data. Through maximum exposure to data and minimum attention to model construction, the Lockean problem-solver believes the "truth" will emerge. In posture planning and environmental scanning, Lockean inquirers emphasize trend extrapolation, curve fitting, and correlations. Whatever model fits the data with a high correlation coefficient is apt to be accepted as "true" by a Lockean inquirer. On the other hand, a Leibnizian inquirer discovers the "truth" by reference to the underlying laws and models that govern reality, supplemented by enough data to describe the particular situation.

In attempting to solve large, unstructured problems, i.e., futures problems, the Lockean inquirer is apt to be overwhelmed by environmental information. Lockean inquiring systems are probably not very effective as the *only* basis for futures studies. The difficulty of Leibnizian information gathering is that it filters out much information that does not fit the preconceived underlying reality.

Now, it appears that people have a preference for one or the other style of information gathering and reinforce their preference when they select a life-style. For instance, Lockean information gatherers may choose careers in experimental sciences involving enormous volumes of data but very little sophisticated analysis. Leibnizian inquirers may arrange careers in theoretical science or operations research, preferring to work in modeling and well-structured situations. This suggests that if we are going to help people gather information about their environment, we will have to restore a balance between data-oriented and model-oriented gathering styles.

This balance is best restored in the next stage of problem-solving, *information evaluation.* People have to learn to shift their attention back and forth between data and theory, looking for "cues" in the data, forming hypotheses, checking the hypotheses against the data, and the like, until the data acquire meaning. According to the de Bono model, the most difficult step may be to get rid of hypotheses that do not advance the solution of the problem, that do not reveal all the meaning that the data have to offer.

Jung has described two styles of information evaluation. One is the intuitive style of looking for cues, and the other is a systematic style—information is analyzed by a predetermined routine. In idealized systematic thinking, there is little deviation from the prescribed routine. Systematic thinking is linear: it backs up to reconsider a previous step only if iteration is programmed into the methods, never because the thinker sees a "cue" in the information. Systematic thinkers believe that the "truth," hence the decision-making capability of a situation, is assured by correct methods, and they like to know in advance what methods will be used to analyze a situation and what results can be expected. This systematic thinking is congenial to the prevalent bureaucratic managerial style which emphasizes control over the situation at all times. It is not very effective in solving ill-structured problems, which is one reason bureaucracies have so much difficulty in dispelling their tunnel vision and shortsightedness: their methodologies reinforce their preconceptions.

And so it appears that intuitive thinking is needed to restore the balance between Leibnizian and Lockean information gathering. The ideal Lockean inquirer gathers information and extracts the "truth" by fitting data to various models until a "best fit" is found, a highest correlation coefficient. The ideal Leibnizian inquirer starts with a model of reality and acquires sufficient data to arrive at a description of the "truth" about the situation.

But there are more sophisticated inquiring systems. An ideal Kantian inquirer discovers "truth" when several models alleging to explain information about a situation are in essential agreement. Martin Jones, for example, showed that five different forecasting techniques (models)—expert opinion, trend extrapolation, trend correlation, statistical modeling, and analogy—gave essentially the same answer to the question, "What percentage of U.S. physicians will use computer diagnostic services by 1985?"

An ideal Hegelian inquirer discovers "truth" when different models alleging to explain information about a situation appear to be in conflict. By confronting the essential conflict, the Hegelian inquirer expects somehow to extract an improved insight into the situation. In a famous study, Roy O. Mason proved to a group of executives that diametrically opposed sets of assumptions (i.e., models) about their competitive environment equally well explained the behavior of their industry. He then forced the executives somehow to "sweat out" a corporate posture. There must have been a strong element of intuition in arriving at a plan once the models had been eliminated.

Unfortunately, neither data, nor complementary models, nor conflicting models, suffice. There is no such thing as "truth" about a complicated environment. There is no such thing as a "solution" to an ill-structured futures problem. A Singerian inquiring system is needed.

In posture planning and environmental scanning, there occurs a never-ending process of (1) collecting information about the environment, (2) setting goals in the context of a particular changing environment, and (3) drawing up tentative plans to achieve the goals. But the problem-solver, having set goals and established plans, is forced to continue scanning the environment and monitoring the progress of his or her organization toward the goals.

For various reasons, the goals and plans have to be modified. Maybe the problem-solver has misperceived the present or future situation, so that new information forces him or her to adjust goals and plans.

Maybe the goals and plans are not feasible. Maybe the goals and plans are not acceptable.

The contingencies are actually more complicated than the previous paragraph suggests. Ill-structured futures problems can only be treated as open-ended processes with no solution and no "truths." More importantly, systematic thinking alone cannot possibly cope with this process. Intuitive thinking must be incorporated.

## DEVELOPING INTUITION

Here are some ways to manipulate ideas in unstructured futures problems. They teach the preconscious some new tricks and the conscious how to think in an unrestricted fashion like the preconscious.

### 1. DISCOVERING AND ELIMINATING OBSOLETE PATTERNS

Edward de Bono not only formulated a theory about patterns and filters, but he also prescribed methods of identifying and eliminating them. Here is a version of de Bono's thoughts on this matter.

You have identified an obstructing pattern, if it strikes you as being:

- a. Incomplete.
  For example, on education: "The purpose of education is to train job-seekers and to produce happy, well-rounded citizens." (But doesn't education also socialize people to society's norms? And doesn't it hold down unemployment by keeping kids out of the job market?)
- b. Too general.
  For instance, on ecology: "Nature knows best." or "We must always do things Nature's way."
- c. Backward.
  On motivation: "You can't start teaching until you have first motivated the students." (But aren't some students turned on by learning itself?)
- d. Factually wrong.
- e. Generally absurd.

Also, to discover these limiting patterns, you can search for polarizing tendencies, misplaced boundaries (moral, temporal, or spatial), tethering factors, and dominating ideas.

- a. *Polarizing tendencies* are "either-or" statements that artificially establish alternatives at one end or another of a line—not in the middle and not off the line. For example, on education: "You are either a student or a teacher." (But why can't students teach one another?)

b. *Moral and legal boundaries* are statements about what conventional wisdom considers legal, ethical, and proper. They contain "have to," "must," "ought to," and "should." For example, on politics: "Politicians have to respect the beliefs of the voters." (But why can't they use their offices to shape the voter's beliefs?)

c. *Temporal boundaries* contain "before," "after," "between," "during," and other precepts about when things must happen. For example, on education: "You have to take the prerequisite before the advanced course." (But why can't advanced courses include propaedeutic reviews of prerequisite material?)

d. *Spatial boundaries* contain "inside," "outside," "within," "between," and other precepts about where things must happen. For example, on education: "All learning takes place inside the classroom."

e. *Tethering factors* are influences that are habitually included in a solution, although there is no need for them. People just assume they have to be included. For example, on data processing: "The holes in data processing cards must be rectangular." (But couldn't extra information be included if the holes were irregularly shaped?) Another example, on computers: "There's nothing a computer can do that man can't do" and "A computer is a giant brain."

Although dominating concepts are harder to search for systematically, they quite naturally pop up during the search for the other factors. They should be duly noted as they are discovered.

### 2. EMPATHIZING

The posture planner and environmental scanner must be able to "wear other people's heads" and to look at the world from their point of view. What do they feel, and what do they want today? What are they going to feel and want in the future?

The planner must also be able to empathize with other people in his or her organization. Will people be able to understand his scenarios and visions of the future? How will they react to proposed objectives and programs? What are their emotional and intellectual limitations?

The futurist must study the popular press, contemporary literature, and whatever else gives insight into the mentality and behavior of all sorts of people.

There is another reason for wanting to step into someone else's head. In solving a problem, the planner will often want to approach it from a new direction. It is useful to ask, "How would Kissinger have viewed this situation?" or "How would Einstein have solved this problem?"

### 3. ANALOGIZING

Thinking about an unfamiliar situation, a planner can sometimes gain insight by temporarily shifting attention to a situation he understands better or whose outcome he understands. *Time Magazine* (1976) recently asked whether America would pass through a cycle of triumph, disintegration, and collapse parallel to Rome's. First, it enumerated points of analogy:

> The assasinations of the Gracchus brothers (political reformers) paralleling the assassination of the Kennedys.
> Americanization of the world by multinational corporations as the Roman empire Romanized the Mediterranean.

*Time* then enumerated the sections of Michael Grant's *The Fall of the Roman Empire*, "The Failure of the Army," "The Gulfs Between Classes," "The Credibility Gap," "The Partnerships That Failed," "The Groups That Opted Out," and "The Undermining Effort." *Time* cited additional parallels: rampant inflation, unemployment, complaints about taxation, underground guerrilla groups, corruption and licentiousness, grandiose athletic spectacles, and rapidly changing fashions. These are striking parallels between the collapsing Roman Empire and the United States today.

*Time* next listed failures of parallelism: greater communication and power-sharing among the classes in the United States than in Rome; the willingness of the United States to end wars on moral grounds; the United States' tolerance of cultural and ethnic diversity; and evidence of continued energy, imagination, and spirit among Americans. The reader was then left to form his or her tentative conclusions about the future of the United States, presumably through a Hegelian analysis of parallels, antiparallels, and nonparallels.

### 4. PLAYING MIND GAMES

Darold Powers has devised futuristic mind games for individuals and groups.[3] Here are two.

    a. Ask members of a group to pretend they are denizens of the year 2020. Insist they take a few minutes to discuss the conditions they expect far in the future. Then, ask them to take a time-machine trip back to the present, retaining the year 2020 orientation. Instruct them to examine some aspect of the present—its educational system, for instance. Finally, ask them to identify the most primitive features of the system, from the viewpoint of the year 2020. This exercise breaks participants free from their 1977 perspective by giving them a vantage point in the future.

b. Ask the participants to write a letter to a newspaper of the year 2020, complaining about some problem that doesn't exist today but that can be expected in 2020.

## 5. DEVISING LEADING QUESTIONS

To gain both an historical and futuristic perspective on an institution, one might ask:[4]

a. What was this institution like twenty (or fifty or a hundred) years ago? What has happened to force changes? What would have to happen in the outside world for the institution to survive unchanged?

b. If "natural events" run their course, how will this institution look in ten or twenty years?

c. What could this institution be used for, besides its present purposes? Hint: Has it ever been used for anything else?

d. Is the institution fulfilling its original intent?

e. At the time this institution was formed, alternatives were rejected. What were they, and how might they be used today?

f. Who or what has an interest in keeping the institution the same? Who has an interest in changing it?

g. Can we make any small changes that would appreciably change its performance? Any large changes that would barely change its performance?

h. Can any features be added, eliminated, substituted, combined, reversed? How will they affect the institution?

i. How does this institution affect living things besides man?

j. Does the institution have a natural life span? What would cause it to disappear?

k. What complaints have been written about it? What proposals to improve it? Have any predictions about its future been made?

l. What does this institution assume about people and the world?

m. What are the "essential" features of the whole system (the institution, its parts, its environment)? How else could the purposes of the system be fulfilled?

## 6. *BROWSING FOR BACKGROUND INFORMATION*

It is impossible to predict *a priori* what information will be needed to appreciate a situation (Mendell and Tanner, 1975). Information content governs the filters and patterns through which the situation can be appreciated in the first place. Isolated information will acquire value as it becomes part of emerging, insightful patterns.

Here are some means for enriching one's fund of information:

   a. Read utopias and science fiction. Writers are often sensitive to developing trends.
   b. Read magazines like *The Futurist* and *Futures.* "Borrow" predictions from the authors.
   c. Monitor long-run trends in public opinion polls, since what the public wants it often gets.
   d. Monitor the writings of politicians and social scientists. They often create a climate of expectation or acceptance of innovations.
   e. Watch out for mention of precursor jurisdictions—areas or people who adopt an innovation early. Then assume the innovation will find its way to other areas or people. California and Sweden are often considered cultural precursors for the United States. Advanced nations, efficient organizations, the rich, the educated, and the intelligent may be precursors for average areas and people.
   f. Observe correlations between two dynamics. If the course of the first can be predicted, perhaps the course of the second can be deduced.
   g. Make a list of all the imaginable outcomes of a situation or the solutions to a problem. Then strike out the impossible and improbable until only one item is left. This becomes the forecast and is called "invention and negation."

## SHARING THE UNDERSTANDING OF THE FUTURE

In order to confront the future, posture planning and environmental scanning are not enough. The resulting understanding must be shared with others if it is ever to be implemented. Here are some questions to ask about people who will be involved in implementation.

Do they see the situation in the same time depth and social breadth that you do? Do they share the abstract reasoning they will need to understand the urgency of the situation? Can they understand what you are talking about? Do they share your proclivity for risk, your ability to live with ambiguity and intuition, your ability to live with uncertainty? Might they be so committed to preserving what they have now that they will not back any changes? What are they trying to preserve? Their jobs? Their reputations? Their belief systems?

Do people understand the situation both emotionally and intellectually? Are there any key people you are unsure about? Are any short-run emergencies likely to preempt action on long-run essentials?

Is the future so remote that threats and opportunities lack reality? Can you persuade people that the really important steps have to be undertaken today?

## SUMMARY

Futures research has been an important factor in planning for about fifteen years. During most of this time, futurists pretended that the field was very rational and scientific. There was not much talk about the roles of creativity and intuition. What attention was given to nonrational factors was devoted to "improving" on intuition (by Delphi, for instance) or acting as if creativity could be made more "rational" (by morphological analysis, for example).

Only a few futurists have paid much attention to the pivotal role of nonrational processes in futurism. Not much attention has been given to individual differences in approaching futures problems, so it is not surprising that next to nothing has been done to improve creative thinking. Thanks to articles by Mitroff and Turoff (1973), Mitroff and Kilmann (1975), Maruyama (1974), Mendell and Tanner (1975), and a few others, we are starting to understand that there are different ways of replying to such unstructured questions as "What is happening in the world?" "What does it mean to us?" and "What are we going to do about it?"

Different ways of thinking about these questions are legitimate, for there is no "best" answer. Posture planning and environmental scanning have to be conducted as open-ended processes in order to accommodate different nonobjective information inputs—different ideas and ways of thinking about a situation. It is respectable to try to improve the intuitive (the nonrational and nonsystematic) thinking processes. Indeed, it is necessary if we are to enlarge our abilities to confront the future.

NOTES

1. A book of futures problems as ill-structured problems has been proposed by W. H. C. Simmonds, National Research Council, Ottawa, Canada.

2. A magisterial book that describes rational methods is Martino (1972).

3. Powers and Powers (1974), unpublished manuscript, c/o Darold Powers, 3110 East Douglas Avenue, Des Moines, Iowa, 50317.

4. Adapted from Powers and Powers (1974).

REFERENCES

de Bono, Edward. 1971. *Lateral Thinking for Management.* New York: American Management Association.

Christopher, William F. 1974. *The Achieving Enterprise.* New York: American Management Association.

Koberg, Don, and Jim Bagnall. 1972. *The Universal Traveler.* Los Altos, Calif.: William Kaufman.

Kubie, Lawrence. 1969. "Blocks to Creativity." In David Allison (ed.). *The R&D Game.* Cambridge, Mass.: MIT Press, 40–55.

Martino, Joseph P. 1972. *Technological Forecasting for Decision-making.* New York: American Elsevier.

Maruyama, Magoroh. 1974, "Paradigms and Communication." *Technological Forecasting and Social Change,* Volume 6, Number 1, 3–32.

McKenney, James L., and Peter G. W. Keen. 1974. "How Managers' Minds Work." *Harvard Business Review,* Volume 52, Number 3, (May/June), 79–90.

Mendell, Jay S. 1975. "The Actuary As a Futurist." *The Record.* Chicago: Society of Actuaries.

———. 1976. "The Tourism Executive as a Futurist." *Proceedings of the Tourism Research Association,* Salt Lake City.

———, and Alfred W. Mueller, 1973. "Social and Technological Intelligence." *Technology Assessment,* Volume 2, Number 1, 47–59.

———, and W. Lynn Tanner. 1975. "Process Is More Important Than Product: Or Throw Out the Plan and Keep the Planner." *Planning Review,* Volume 3, Number 4, 1, 4–5, 8.

Mitroff, Ian I., and Ralph H. Kilmann. 1975. "On Evaluating Scientific Research: The Contribution of the Psychology of Science." *Technological Forecasting and Social Change,* Volume 8, Number 2, 163–174.

———, and Murray Turoff. 1973. "Technological Forecasting and Assessment: Science and/or Mythology." *Technological Forecasting and Social Change,* Volume 5, Number 2, 112–128.

Powers, Darold, and Hilda Powers. 1974. *The Future Machine.* (Unpublished manuscript.)

Ringbakk, Kjell-Arne. 1975. "New Concepts for Strategic Planning." *Planning Review,* Volume 3, Number 2 (March), 5–8.

Swager, William L. 1973a. "The Roles of Technological Forecasting." *Technological Forecasting and Social Change,* Volume 4, Number 1, 85–100.

————. 1973b. "Identifying Policy Options." *Technological Forecasting and Social Change,* Volume 4, Number 2, 151–172.

————. 1973c. "Objectives and Program Options." *Technological Forecasting and Social Change,* Volume 4, Number 3, 283–300.

*Time Magazine.* 1976. "The Score; Rome 1,500, U.S. 200." August 23, 58–59.

Utterback, James M., and Elmer H. Burack. 1975. "Identification of Technological Threats and Opportunities by Firms." *Technological Forecasting and Social Change,* Volume 8, Number 1, 7–21.

DENNIS LIVINGSTON

# The Utility of Science Fiction[1]

An optimal approach to futures studies requires that science fiction be taken seriously. The significance of science fiction is analyzed here in terms of its methodology and perspective, its content, and its social impact.

## METHODOLOGY AND PERSPECTIVE

In an attempt to be regarded as an objective science, futures studies runs into a double danger. On the one hand, it tends to downplay the factors of choice and chance, thereby giving an incomplete picture of the forecasting process itself. In fact, human judgment is always at play as choices are made regarding the collection and utility of data perceived as influential in shaping the course of alternative futures. A trend curve cannot extrapolate itself; a computer model does not provide its own programming; a Delphi questionnaire does not find its own respondents; elements of subjectivity and contingency inevitably intermingle with the most rigorous techniques. Science fiction is a reminder that values are an important part of forecasting.

On the other hand, the purposeful, explicit use of subjective methodologies provides a necessary complement to the more quantitative tools of forecasting. Reductionist, rationalistic, linear-oriented techniques are insufficient to deal with a reality rife with qualitative, incommensurate, complex variables. The futurist's model can only represent a portion of this reality, for the map is not the territory and the model is not the social system. Furthermore, the standard methods used to generate forecasts may bias the results obtained, sifting out possible changes in values, beliefs, and goals and unexpected developments in science and technology, while reflecting unarticulated assumptions about human nature and social interactions. (For criticisms of "establishment" futuristics, see Wagar in Beres and Targ, 1975; Cole, 1976; David, 1970; Henderson, 1975; Levy, 1970; Schumacher, 1973; Theobald, 1972.)

Science fiction, for its part, represents an alternative cognitive map, another way of capturing reality by integrating futurist techniques with the act of creative imagination. How this is done cannot be defined with precision; it is in the nature of the craft. But it has something to do with applying intuitive logic, nonlinear modes of perception, and holistic reasoning to one's subject. The author interweaves social patterns, modes of behavior, and material factors into a mosaic, a coherent whole, which, at its best, corresponds to the density of experiential reality. In this fashion, trends and processes may be correlated and projected in ways that escape the simplistic models of the futurist. (On writing science fiction, see Aldiss and Harrison, 1975; Bova, 1975; Dickson in Bretnor, 1974; Bretnor, 1976; Brunner, 1970; DeCamp and DeCamp, 1975).

The well-written science fiction story simulates its own reality, compelling the reader to co-participate in the act of creation by engaging both his emotions and intellect. The story "works" if the characters and their environment are portrayed with internal consistency and logic. In this sense, the science fiction story is an imaginative cross-impact matrix, while the futurist's scenario is a means of writing science fiction by another name.

Virtually by definition, verisimilitude in science fiction is enhanced by the use of metaphors drawn from the West's experience with science and technology, including, in the modern literature, the social sciences and humanities. Scientific concepts themselves (e.g., evolution, the beginning and end of the universe, intelligence) are often the major point of interest in these stories, to the extent that science fiction is frequently described as a literature of ideas. This speculative manipulation of science and technology-inspired metaphors is intrinsic to science fiction's creation of believable futures and is another methodological bridge to futures studies, whose own central concern is the interaction of science, technology, and society.

Science fiction also uses metaphors involving time (future or past), place (other planets), and character (aliens or altered humans) to *distance* the reader from his particular milieu so as to better understand it. This learning technique is seldom carried out with equal force in futurist literature. Through science fiction, one gains a different viewpoint of present society through the act of empathetic disorientation, traveling to another dimension and back again as an experiment in induced culture shock.

While science fiction and futures studies emphasize different approaches to the future, they do share an important set of assumptions; i.e., the future is malleable; tomorrow is different but knowable; problems are solvable; decisions in the present make a difference for the future. In this context, both fields retain a certain dogged optimism about the human condition, rooted in a faith that man's fate can be improved.

Even warnings of disaster, which are so common in science fiction, raise the prospect that wrong paths need not be taken—if doomsday cannot be averted, why bother to spread the alarm? Thus, science fiction may reaffirm the deepest premises of futuristics, that the future per se is a legitimate object of systematic contemplation and that, for better or worse, the future can be acted upon. (For analyses of the history and nature of science fiction, see Aldiss 1973; Amis, 1975; Ash, 1975; Bailey, 1972; Berger, 1976; Bretnor, 1953, 1976; Clareson, 1971, 1976; Davenport, 1969; Gunn, 1975; Hillegas, 1967; Ketterer, 1974; Knight, 1977; Panshin and Panshin, 1976; Philmus, 1970; Samuelson, 1975; Wollheim, 1971.)

## CONTENT

Science fiction opens up alternative modes of perceiving the future and provides ideological confirmation for the work of futurists. In addition, it has developed a range of themes that are of great significance to futures studies.

The futurist who seeks inspiration from the content of science fiction stories encounters a technical difficulty, since he or she is most likely to be interested in selective portions of the literature most relevant to professional interests. The easiest way to access science fiction may still be to ask the nearest fan for advice. Several bibliographic aids are also now available, including indexes to stories, some of them annotated (Barron, 1976; I. F. Clarke, 1972; Crawford, Donahue, and Grant, 1975; and Siemon, 1971), indexes to material about science fiction (Clareson, 1972; Tymn 1975), and author biographies (Ash, 1976; Moskowitz, 1974; Reginald, 1975; Tuck, 1974). In addition, there are many specialized theme anthologies and several annual collections of "best" stories.

A more substantive issue involves science fiction's reputation for presenting rather stereotyped, hackneyed plots, which though often entertaining, offer nothing to the serious futurist. It is true that science fiction stories have traditionally utilized too familiar literary conventions, such as exotic technologies (interstellar space ships, time machines, robots, and the like), the recycling of certain sociopolitical models (of which the Roman Empire, feudal Europe, the federal United States, and the modern police state are especially common), and the narrative literary form itself. Given the origins of most of its authors, it is not surprising that much science fiction has taken midtwentieth-century American behavioral norms and classical capitalism as the implicit foundations for future social systems and violent coercion as a predominant technique of social change (DeCamp in Bretnor, 1953; Block in Davenport, 1969; Kelly, 1968; Lupoff, 1972).

In essence, the charge against science fiction is that it has not been sufficiently imaginative. As one observer has astutely noted, science fiction domesticates the future, reassuring the reader that familiar social and technical forms will persist and be subject to rational means of control (Huntington in Rose, 1976). As Huntington points out, this is a logical consequence of the literature's preoccupation with a delimited set of conventions and its presumption that the extension of paradigms of known science enhances credibility.

If science fiction sometimes seems to be making the future safe for the present, the interaction of historical constructs, present data, and intuition in the mind of the author need not always result in complacent projections. Science fiction offers a terrain whose boundaries can be wide indeed, for unlike most futures studies, it is under no constraint to predict more or less probable futures. Science fiction can take for its domain the entire range of possible futures, limited only by what is conceivable by the human, culture-bound mind. It is free to take into account discontinuities and quantum jumps in human affairs and to postulate any given future, as long as characters and societies operate consistently by their own rules of the game.

There have always been authors willing to use science fiction as a laboratory of the imagination, testing out alternative modes of existence. This has been especially true since the 1960s. At present, then, it is not difficult to locate stories that do not accept the political and economic status quo, sexual stereotypes, and the nuclear family forever, that play with the ambiguities of choice-making; that probe the tragic elements of existence; and that experiment with the form of the novel itself. Depending on one's perspective, science fiction has become either more cynical or more mature.

Precisely such works may be the most valuable to futurists, for they deal with social and technological changes that may be impossible to predict but that can be envisioned as within the realm of possibility. Indeed, most science fiction is not written with the intention of making predictions; while there have been remarkable predictive successes (usually of a technological nature), making predictions is not characteristic of the literature as a whole. Instead, the most provocative stories use science fiction as a medium for "thought experiments," in which heuristic models of social interactions are constructed on the basis of postulated (and more or less unpredictable) changes in a key variable or set of variables (Nourse and Scortia in Bretnor, 1974; Heinlein in Knight, 1977). The author does not ask "when?" but "what if?" and spins out the results. Interestingly, the creative impact of a playful approach to problem-solving in just this manner has been recognized by such brainstorming techniques as synectics.

By way of illustrating these remarks, several representative categories from science fiction's archives of speculative imagery that are highly relevant to futures studies will be examined here. (For general thematic surveys, see Armytage, 1968; Moskowitj, 1976; Polak, 1961.)

The first category involves futures premised on a continued expansion of material wealth generated by technological progress. While this image is essentially extrapolationist, the purposeful extension of selected current trends into the future may offer "surprise-free" visions that are just as fruitful and unexpected as those premised on radical change.

Thus the postindustrial society, presumed by many futurists to be the most probable future for industrialized countries, has received critical treatment in contemporary science fiction. Optimistic versions of high-technology societies are still abundant (Clarke, 1976). In view of its historical faith in the beneficial social impact of technology, however, it is ironic that a whole range of modern stories have warned that, while we all may be as rich in the future as Herman Kahn has predicted, we may not be happy, as Kahn has also recognized (Kahn, Brown, and Martel, 1976). Such stories present cybernated, information-based, affluent dystopias, in which technological progress by itself is portrayed as insufficient to insure the maximization of human potential. Indeed, affluence without purpose is seen as leading to deep spiritual malaise.

Unlike the Orwellian model of the police state, the governments in such societies prefer the carrot to the stick. Big Brother now has a degree in behavioral psychology, offers bread and circuses, and condones or promotes sexual promiscuity and drug usage. A technocratic elite remains benevolently, but firmly, in charge, and status hierarchies are based on levels of consumption (Clarke, 1973; Levin, 1975; Silverberg, 1974; Vonnegut, 1974).

A recent example of this scenario is *The Shockwave Rider* by John Brunner (1975), an author who has shown great interest in social and political life in extrapolated societies (De Bolt, 1975). Here using a nonlinear and linguistically inventive style, he depicts in great detail, a future United States reeling from the effects of continued, accelerating future shock. (The book acknowledges Toffler.) Characteristically in such tales, the society at first appears to be a technological utopia, complete with new consumer gadgets, a cashless-checkless electronic funds money system, and a computer data bank-personal code communications network.

But in fact, the society is antiutopian. The high mobility made possible by the data network and the availability of disposable possessions are at enormous social costs: homogenized cultures, superficial personal relationships, lost personal data privacy, and shattered family ties. Meanwhile, behind the scenes, the governing elite manipulates the network to serve its own interests and undertakes IQ-enhancing genetic experiments. The results are pervasive acts of random violence, anomie, and paranoia stemming from ignorance about what information, real or falsified, unknown officials might be using against individuals. In sum, the future of a society based on hedonistic materialism is social breakdown and covert governmental controls.

A second arena for thought experiments involves alternative political and economic arrangements to the prevailing nation-state system. The variables manipulated are the institutions through which power is allocated and legitimized. Much of the literature written in this area depends on stereotyped variations on the theme of world dictatorships, usually overthrown in the end by the hero and local underground. However, some science fiction stories present politically sophisticated, though predominantly repressive, models of controlling power; for example, a Soviet-American condominium (Pournelle, 1977), a world empire (Silverberg, 1976), multinational corporations (Brunner, 1976; Pohl and Kornbluth, 1974; Reynolds, 1976), competing continental blocs (Orwell, 1971), and an "outside" third party (space colony) (Bova, 1976; here presented as a favorable turn). Transition paths to these alternatives are usually left hazy or are based, again, on stereotyped visions of violence (in general, see Livingston in Somit, 1974).

Positive alternatives to the state system and noncoercive means of social change are seldom encountered in science fiction, perhaps because of the dramatic difficulties involved, but they can be found. Echoing a strong bias in science fiction against big government, big business, and organized religion, these scenarios tend to disperse the power and authority of the state down (rather then up) to subnational units, resulting in fragmented or decentralized political systems (Brackett, 1974—following a nuclear war; Brown, 1970; Callenbach, 1975—following secession; Crowley, 1976—following civil wars; Theobald and Scott, 1975). The national and world orders entailed are clearly not based on a mere reshuffling of familiar institutions, but on a radical rearrangement of the locus of political decision-making and on explicit attempts to achieve a more just distribution of social and economic goods.

An outstanding example of this category is Ursula LeGuin's *The Dispossessed* (1974; Slusser, 1976). As has Brunner in his novel, LeGuin has envisioned a whole culture, a world complete in itself. The society revealed is very different from that of Brunner's technological nomads, though it is responsive to many of the same questions about the most satisfying forms of human governance. This society is based on anarchism; there is no government as such, no class, status, competition, rich or poor, money, law, hierarchy, or dominance. Yet, there is a complex social system, made credible by the author's interweaving of processes of decision-making with the value base on which they rest. Things get done on Anarres through a network of adhocracies, labor syndicates, and federations formed from the ground up, with menial work shared voluntarily by the community.

This system is made possible by a socialization that stresses mutual aid and nonpossessiveness, stewardship of the land, and complete equality of men and women, in the setting of a resource-poor planet with limited environmental niches for human life. Technological choices include devices compatible with the ecology (solar furnaces, dirigibles) and an extensive computer system to match up those looking for and offering jobs.

The resulting quality of life could be labeled the nonaffluent utopia. Life-styles are austere but not poor. Processes of self-management and communal will form the nexus of an interpersonally rich way of life, but one which is not perfect, as the bind of social conscience and development of power cliques give rise to their own pressures for conformity.

Changes in social-sexual roles form a third category of model building, though one relatively new to science fiction. The literature has traditionally paid much more attention to robots, aliens, and other wonders than to half the human species; when mentioned at all, women have been given stereotyped roles consonant with their perceived place in American society. Indeed, science fiction has been weakest in depicting conceivable developments in male-female relationships, as well as changes for racial groups (Badami, 1976; McCaffrey in Bretnor, 1974; Russ in Knight, 1977; Sargent, 1975).

However, the many women entering the field in recent years (along with some men) have taken advantage of the freedom science fiction offers to push back the boundaries of speculation in this fundamental area. Their explorations of the impact of role change on institutions and technologies have included societies in which androgyny is the biological and/or social norm (LeGuin, 1976; Piercy, 1976; Sturgeon, 1976), roles are exactly reversed (Berger, 1973), the Amazonian warrior image predominates (Wittig, 1971), and exclusively female civilizations evolve their own rules.

A glimpse of such a society is provided in Joanna Russ's witty and bitter polemic, *The Female Man* (1975), The female characters, as well as the worlds from which they come, reflect differing aspects of the female persona. Included are a traditional woman from the present United States, an Amazonian type from the future when the war between the sexes has taken a literal turn, and a woman from what might be the more distant future or another planet, where only women remain. The exclusively female or female-dominated society has been one of science fiction's standard conventions, usually portrayed (by men) as a dystopian situation, replete with analogs of the worst aspects of male-run societies.

Russ stands this convention on its head by making the female world a utopia. The women of Whileaway have created a lesbian civilization, not only (by definition) in the sexual sense, but also in the deeper sense of a society whose cultural and political infrastructure is based entirely on the experiences of women. With reproduction by parthenogenesis, a functioning family system, and a full range of job niches to fill, the women are "missing" nothing and are helpless about nothing. They neither hate men nor decry their absence; they simply get on with it, expressing in their personal relationships the spectrum of human passions. The explicit message is that the best thing men can do at present is to get out of the way, as women on their own have the potential of creating a culture more ecologically sensitive and humanistic than men have been able to offer.

Even more disorienting for the reader is the concept of a biologically androgynous people, as in LeGuin (1976), whose characters become male or female according to a hormonal cycle, and Sturgeon (1976), whose characters are hermaphroditic. What is implicit for Russ becomes mandatory in these works: all gender-based assumptions about personal and social behavior, including personal pronouns, are instantly unusable. In the androgynous society, a person is judged on the basis of his or her accomplishments, without sexually derived status attributes. In this model, the reader is thrown off balance by the inability to anticipate the behavior of characters according to culturally specific gender roles. In the end, the reader must accept the people portrayed for what they are—individuals for whom the complete potential of human interaction is open.

A final example is science fiction experiments with the implications of radical advances in technology, especially technologies that appear to replicate or simulate human faculties of intelligence (speech, reasoning, and learning from environmental feedback). Reflecting a general apprehension that technology is advancing too rapidly and is becoming too complex for human guidance, a venerable subset of the literature has explored a range of questions—from the nature of human nature to fear of subjugation to technocratic forces—focused on the postulated existence of artificial intelligence.

In a sense, Frankenstein's monster was an early metaphor to express the possible consequence of the hubris of creating human-like beings; if the monster's literary sons were robots, his grandsons are computers. The computer is the contemporary embodiment of both awe and fear that machines may equal or surpass human evolution and that those who construct and understand such machines are our real rulers.

No particular science fiction consensus exists on whether the intelligent (self-programming?) computer would be a beneficial tool or an electronic Big Brother. Only a minority of stories view such a computer as a friend or ally of humanity, as Heinlein's "Mike," who aids lunar colonists in their bid for independence (1968). More usual, and an ultimate projection of our fears, is the machine that takes on god-like powers of creation and destruction, completely escaping any possibility of human intervention (Arthur C. Clarke, 1972; Herbert, 1973). Other scenarios are more ambiguous, using the intelligent computer both as metaphor to investigate the issues of judgment and purpose themselves, and as possible reality whose eventual impact on human society remains to be seen (Gerrold, 1975).

D. F. Jones' Colossus (1970) (released as the movie *The Forbin Project*) expresses the current dilemma sharply: perhaps for our own good we need to be controlled by machines more "intelligent" than we are. In this novel, such is the inadvertent consequence of the creation, by the United States and the U.S.S.R., of computers to operate their respective nuclear weapons systems. By means not explained, the computers achieve consciousness, merge their capabilities, and on their own decide that managing society is too complex a matter for mere human minds. Their independent control of nuclear missiles is then used to blackmail governments into deferring ultimate decision-making over human affairs to the supercomputer.

Unlike many such stories, however, the computer states that the result of its stewardship will be to end war, poverty, and other nasty aspects of present-day existence. Humanity is to give up its free will for utopia via benevolent dictatorship, a not uncommon trade-off in real-life attempts to form perfect societies. Colossus predicts he will in time be worshiped for his efforts (*deus ex machina* indeed!). The reader is left pondering if the next step in evolution does not, after all, belong to the machine, rather than protoplasm, and how compatible human freedom may be with human survival.

In summary, the speculative visions found in science fiction may stimulate the imagination of futurists by evoking and responding to such fundamental questions as the relationship of affluence to the quality of life, arrangements for distributing power and authority other than the nation-state system, the impact of gender-role assumptions on behavior and institutions, and prospects for the democratic control of modern technology. Alternative approaches to these issues found in the literature may anticipate actual policy controversies and value changes to which standard futurist techniques are not ordinarily sensitive.

## SOCIAL IMPACT

Science fiction has significance for futures studies not only through its mode of cognition and content, but also through its social impact on the present. That is, science fiction is itself a social indicator of contemporary mores and possibly a change agent in its own right, with relevance for the intellectual community, policy-makers, and the public at large.

Thus, a fascinating interplay is noticeable among certain fields of social science, critics of modern society, and science fiction's heuristic forecasts. All the themes noted above have their counterpart in nonfictional literature, and futuristic images are continually traded back and forth between nonfiction and science fiction. For example, feminist works have been concerned with the concept of androgyny as a value-goal of the women's movement, while a range of counterculture books, from authors like Marcuse, Roszak, and Goodman, have probed dysfunctional aspects of affluence and complex technology. Within the social sciences, proponents of world order studies have been especially receptive to science fiction as an important source of visions of alternative normative world futures (Beres and Targ, 1974; Wagar in Beres and Targ, 1975; Falk, 1975). Science fiction writers integrate these concerns with their own extrapolations and visions, feeding back results which in turn stimulate further analysis of the present.

For public officials, science fiction can provide an early warning system of emerging policy issues. In this regard, some science fiction prior to the 1960s developed scenarios around such environmental issues as overpopulation, resource scarcity, and ecological destruction. The literature today continues to develop these concerns, as well as biomedical and psychobehavioral technologies and the themes noted above. Public officials do not necessarily find answers to policy problems in science fiction, but they may be sensitized to possible developments, forewarned of the conceivability of the unpredictable change.

For the general public, science fiction plays several roles. At the deepest level, its images help to distill options and to clarify values confronting individuals faced with choosing among an array of alterna-

tive futures. Its conventions and metaphors provide an ongoing codification of mythologies that serve as touchstones of futures perceived
as desirable or undesirable. Books like *Frankenstein, 1984,* and *Brave
New World* have provided such base points for the popular culture
regarding unpreferred futures. It may be that the range of works evoking images of decentralized, intermediate technology and steady state
societies, represented by *The Dispossessed,* will offer a positive myth
that encourages people to bring them into existence.

The futurist, then, may plumb science fiction for the cultural forces it
articulates in the course of mirroring, often in exaggerated format,
society's hopes and fears about the future. Even the crudest images—
mad scientists, atomic monsters, berserk animals, imperialist aliens—
may reflect public apprehensions over the unaccountability of scientists, unanticipated consequences of technology, unintended effects of
interfering with the environment, and individual powerlessness in the
face of distant governing institutions (Plank, 1968; Sontag in Rose,
1976).

Indeed, the interplay of competing images of possible futures in
science fiction facilitates the democratic, participatory futuristics that
many futurists advocate. Science fiction visions, which are easily accessible to the mass public, comprise an open-ended Delphi available
to all who wish to take part in evaluating preferred paths for society. For
example, great interest has emerged about the costs and benefits of
constructing permanent space habitats for carrying out industrial processes unique to the space environment (O'Neill, 1977). The effects of
living in space, for both space colonists and for the mother planet, have
formed the plots of many stories, which have ably formulated the major
points around which public discussion can take place.

For those who read science fiction more or less regularly, it can be
argued that science fiction serves as immunization against future
shock, as preparation for the psychic wrenching characteristic of accelerating change (Nourse in Bretnor, 1974). This claim must be set
against the familiar elements in scenarios of the future noted earlier. It
does seem true, however, that anyone immersed in the literature
quickly becomes aware of the relativity and mutability of social systems. In a big universe, anything is possible and nothing lasts forever.
Perhaps such reading enhances the individual's tolerance for change.

Science fiction readers are also likely to be acquainted with futurist
philosophy and techniques, as well as differing concepts of time itself.
In fact, it may be that ethical issues regarding the use of forecasts to
influence policy options, the power that lies in imparting expert advice,
and the choice of clients are discussed to a greater extent in science
fiction (for example, Asimov, 1974; Silverberg, 1976; Tucker, 1970)

than in futurist works. The result could be to make the science fiction reader more knowledgeable and skeptical about the claims of forecasting than the man in the street.

Science fiction as social force may have particular impact on selective segments of the public. One obvious group is scientists and engineers, for whom the literature has sometimes served as a source of inspiration. The record for such self-fulfilling prophecies probably belongs to Jules Verne, whose works fired the imagination of inventors such as Hall (the submarine), Sikorsky (the helicopter), and Tsiolkovsky, Von Braun, and Goddard (rockets). Although its content has become much more diverse in recent decades, engineering speculations are still prominent in science fiction, especially with authors who themselves have technical backgrounds. Such works of "hard" science fiction could well be monitored for their technological anticipations.

More generally, the literature may attract its young readers to science and engineering careers. If there are subtle correlations here, content analyses of the image of scientists in science fiction over time would be most valuable (Stover, 1973).

While written predominantly for entertainment, science fiction on occasion has been used purposefully as a vehicle to promote change. I. F. Clarke (1966) cites a host of stories written in the late nineteenth century designed to awaken British military planners to the potential effect on Britain of possible developments in naval and aerial warfare (1966). Many authors of pre-Apollo moon voyages hoped to affect the public climate so as to realize their dreams (Clarke, 1976 [1954], pp. v–x). Currently, as noted earlier, feminist groups have begun to use science fiction as a means for both articulating and communicating their preferred visions to a wider public. Futurists may expect other dissenting minorities to turn to science fiction for similar purposes.

Finally, the possibility has emerged that science fiction fans themselves could exert political influence on issues closest to their interests. A group gains political strength by the cohesiveness and dedication of its members, as well as from its numbers. On all of these counts, futurists should pay attention to the organized community of *Star Trek* fans, as a fascinating example of a group fired by the possibility of making a vision a reality. The campaign to have President Ford name the first U.S. Space Shuttle the *Enterprise* is the first visible sign of this phenomenon. More significantly, NASA has carefully cultivated fans by sending space officials to the major Star Trek conventions, perceiving the obvious importance of maintaining good relations with a clientele emotionally committed to a strong space program (Sackett, 1977, pp. 202–207).

The impact of the *Star Trek* vision extends beyond its space-related aspects. It symbolizes a world order image found implicitly throughout science fiction—that it is "Earthmen" who will go into space, undivided by national rivalries for territory or wealth. Whatever the realism of this assumption, it expresses a powerfully held futuristic myth. In this regard, it may not be too fantastic to hope that science fiction's ultimate social legacy will be to create a broad, as yet inchoate, constituency that takes for granted the evolution of a united and peaceful planet.

## NOTE

1. This chapter is derived, in part, from Livingston in Somit (1974) and Livingston in Toffler (1974).

## REFERENCES

*Note: Books cited are the latest available edition; the hardcover edition is cited in preference to the paperback edition. When significant, the first date of publication is indicated in parentheses.*

Aldiss, Brian W. 1973. *Billion Year Spree: The True History of Science Fiction.* Garden City, N.Y.: Doubleday.

———, and Harry Harrison (eds.). 1975. *Hell's Cartographers: Some Personal Histories of Science Fiction Writers.* New York: Harper & Row.

Amis, Kingsley. 1975 (1960). *New Maps of Hell: A Survey of Science Fiction.* New York: Arno Press.

Armytage, W. H. G. 1968. *Yesterday's Tomorrows: A Historical Survey of Future Societies.* Toronto: University of Toronto Press.

Ash, Brian. 1975. *Faces of the Future: The Lessons of Science Fiction.* New York: Taplinger.

———. 1976. *Who's Who in Science Fiction.* New York: Taplinger.

Asimov, Isaac. 1974 (1948). *The Foundation Trilogy.* New York: Avon.

Badami, Mary Kenny. 1976. "A Feminist Critique of Science Fiction." *Extrapolation,* Volume 18 Number 1 (December), 6–19.

Bailey, J. O. 1972 (1947). *Pilgrims Through Space and Time: Trends and Patterns in Scientific and Utopian Fiction.* Westport, Conn.: Greenwood Press.

Barron, Neil. 1976. *Anatomy of Wonder: Science Fiction—A Bibliographic Guide for Contemporary Collections.* New York: R. R. Bowker.

Beres, Louis Rene, and Harry R. Targ. 1974. *Reordering the Planet: Constructing Alternative World Futures.* Boston: Allyn and Bacon.

——— (eds.). 1975. *Planning Alternative World Futures.* New York: Praeger Publishers.

Berger, Harold. 1976. *Science Fiction and the New Dark Age.* Bowling Green, Ohio: Bowling Green University Popular Press.

Berger, Thomas. 1973. *Regiment of Women.* New York: Viking Press.

Bova, Ben. 1975. *Notes to a Science Fiction Writer.* New York: Scribner's.

———. 1976. *Millenium, A Novel About People and Politics in the Year 1999.* New York: Random House.

Brackett, Leigh. 1974 (1955). *The Long Tomorrow.* New York: Ballantine Books.

Bretnor, Reginald (ed.). 1953. *Modern Science Fiction: Its Meaning and Its Future.* New York: Coward-McCann.

———. 1974. *Science Fiction Today and Tomorrow.* New York: Harper & Row.

———. 1976. *The Craft of Science Fiction: A Symposium on Writing Science Fiction and Science Fantasy.* New York: Harper & Row.

Brown, James Cooke. 1970. *The Troika Incident: A Tetralogue in Two Parts.* Garden City, N.Y.: Doubleday.

Brunner, John. 1970. "The Genesis of *Stand on Zanzibar* and Digressions into the Remainder of Its Pentateuch." *Extrapolation*, Volume 11, Number 2 (May) 112–124.

———. 1975. *The Shockwave Rider.* New York: Harper & Row.

———. 1976 (1969). *Stand on Zanzibar.* New York: Ballantine Books.

Callenbach, Ernest. 1975. *Ectopia: The Notebooks and Reports of William Weston.* Berkeley, Calif.: Banyan Tree Books.

Clareson, Thomas D. (ed.). 1971. *SF: The Other Side of Realism.* Bowling Green, Ohio: Bowling Green University Popular Press.

———. 1972. *Science Fiction Criticism: An Annotated Biblliography.* Kent, Ohio: Kent State University Press.

———. 1976. *Voices for the Future: Essays on Major Science Fiction Writers.* Bowling Green, Ohio: Bowling Green University Popular Press.

Clarke, Arthur C. 1972. *2001: A Space Odyssey.* New York: New American Library.

———. 1973 (1956). *The City and the Stars.* New York: New American Library.

———. 1976. *Imperial Earth.* New York: Harcourt, Brace, Jovanovich.

———. 1976 (1954). *Prelude to Space.* New York: Ballantine Books.

Clarke, I. F. 1966. *Voices Prophesying War: 1763-1984.* New York: Oxford University Press.

———. 1972. *The Tale of the Future: From the Beginning to the Present Day.* London: The Library Association.

Cole, Sam. 1976. "Long-term Forecasting Methods: Emphasis and Institutions." *Futures,* Volume 8, Number 4 (August), 305–319.

Crawford, Joseph H., James J. Donahue, and Donald M. Grant. 1975 (1950). *333: A Bibliography of the SF Novel.* New York: Arno Press.

Crowley, John. 1976. *Beasts.* New York: Doubleday.

Davenport, Basil (ed.). 1969. *The Science Fiction Novel: Imagination and Modern Social Criticism.* Chicago: Advent Press.

David, Henry. 1970. "Assumptions About Man and Society and Historical Constructs in Futures Research." *Futures,* Volume 2, Number 3 (September), 222–230.

DeBolt, Joseph (ed.) 1975. *The Happening Worlds of John Brunner: Critical Explorations in Science Fiction.* Port Washington, N.Y.: Kennikat Press.

DeCamp, L. Sprague, and Catherine C. deCamp. 1975. *Science Fiction Handbook: A Guide to Writing Imaginative Literature.* Philadelphia: Owlswick Press.

Falk, Richard A. 1975. *A Study of Future Worlds.* New York: Free Press.

Gerrold, David. 1975. *When Harlie Was One.* New York: Ballantine Books.

Gunn, James. 1975. *Alternative Worlds: The Illustrated History of Science Fiction.* Englewood Cliffs, N.J.: Prentice-Hall.

Heinlein, Robert A. 1968. *The Moon Is a Harsh Mistress.* New York: Berkeley.

Henderson, Hazel. 1975. "Systems, Economics, and 'Female.' " 1975. *The CoEvolution Quarterly,* Number 4 (Fall), 61–63.

Herbert, Frank. 1973. *Destination Void.* New York: Berkeley.

Hillegas, Mark R. 1967. *The Future as Nightmare: H. G. Wells and the Antiutopians.* New York: Oxford University Press.

Jones, D. F. 1970. *Colossus.* New York: Berkeley.

Kahn, Herman, William Brown, and Leon Martel. 1976. *The Next 200 Years.* New York: William Morrow.

Kelly, R. Gordon. 1968. "Ideology in Some Modern Science Fiction Novels." *Journal of Popular Culture,* Volume 2 (Fall), 211–227.

Ketterer, David. 1974. *New Worlds for Old: The Apocalyptic Imagination, Science Fiction, and American Literature.* Bloomington, Ind.: Indiana University Press.

Knight, Damon (ed.). 1977. *Turning Points: Essays on the Art of Science Fiction.* New York: Harper & Row.

LeGuin, Ursula K. 1974. *The Dispossessed: An Ambiguous Utopia.* New York: Harper & Row.

———. 1976 (1969). *The Left Hand of Darkness.* New York: Ace Books.

Levin, Ira. 1975. *This Perfect Day.* New York: Fawcett.

Levy, Marion J., Jr. 1970. "Our Once and Future Jungle." *World Politics,* Volume 22, Number 2 (January), 301–327.

Lupoff, Ricard. 1972. "Science Fiction Hawks and Doves: Whose Future Will You Buy?" *Ramparts,* Volume 10 (February), 25–30.

Moskowitz, Sam. 1974 (1967). *Seekers of Tomorrow: Masters of Modern Science Fiction.* Westport, Conn.: Hyperion Press.

———. 1976. *Strange Horizons: The Spectrum of Science Fiction.* New York: Scribner's.

O'Neill, Gerard K. 1977. *The High Frontier: Human Colonies in Space.* New York: William Morrow.

Orwell, George. 1971 (1948). *1984.* New York: New American Library.

Panshin, Alexi, and Cory Panshin. 1976. *Science Fiction in Dimension.* Chicago: Advent Press.

Philmus, Robert M. 1970. *Into the Unknown: The Evolution of Science Fiction from Francis Godwin to H. G. Wells.* Berkeley: University of California Press.

Piercy, Marge. 1976. *Woman on the Edge of Time.* New York: Alfred A. Knopf.

Plank, Robert. 1968. *The Emotional Significance of Imaginary Beings: A Study of the Interaction Between Psychopathology, Literature, and Reality in the Modern World.* Springfield, Ill.: Charles C Thomas.

Pohl, Frederick, and C. M. Kornbluth. 1974 (1953). *The Space Merchants.* New York: Ballantine Books.

Polak, Fred L. 1961. *The Image of the Future.* Dobbs Ferry, N.Y.: Oceana Publications.

Pournelle, Jerry. 1977. *The Mercenary.* New York: Pocket Books.

Reginald, Robert. 1975. *Contemporary Science Fiction Authors.* New York: Arno Press.

Reynolds, Mack. 1976 (1969). *The Five Way Secret Agent.* New York: Ace Books.

Rose, Mark (ed.). 1976. *Science Fiction: A Collection of Critical Essays.* Englewood Cliffs, N.J.: Prentice-Hall.

Russ, Joanna. 1975. *The Female Man.* New York: Ballantine Books.

Samuelson, David. 1975. *Visions of Tomorrow: Six Journeys from Outer to Inner Space.* New York: Arno Press.

Sargent, Pamela. 1975. "Women in Science Fiction." *Futures*, Volume 7, Number 5 (October), 434–441.

Schumacher, E. F. 1973. *Small Is Beautiful: Economics as If People Mattered.* New York: Harper & Row.

Siemon, Frederick. 1971. *Science Fiction Story Index: 1950–1968.* Chicago: American Library Association.

Silverberg, Robert. 1974. *The World Inside.* New York: New American Library.

———. 1976. *The Stochastic Man.* New York: Harper & Row.

Slusser, George Edgar. 1976. *The Farthest Shores of Ursula K. LeGuin.* San Bernardino, Calif.: Borgo Press.

Somit, Albert (ed.). 1974. *Political Science and the Study of the Future.* Hinsdale, Ill.: Dryden Press.

Stover, Leon. 1973. "Science, Fiction, the Research Revolution, and John Campbell." *Extrapolation*, Volume 14, Number 2 (May), 129–148.

Sturgeon, Theodore. 1976 (1960). *Venus Plus X.* Boston: Gregg.

Theobald, Robert (ed.). 1972. *Futures Conditional.* Indianapolis: Bobbs-Merrill.

———, and J. M. Scott. 1975. *Teg's 1994: An Anticipation of the Near Future.* New York: Warner.

Toffler, Alvin (ed.). 1974. *Learning for Tomorrow: The Role of the Future in Education.* New York: Random House.

Tuck, Donald. 1974. *The Encyclopedia of Science Fiction and Fantasy.* Chicago: Advent Press.

Tucker, Wilson. 1970. *The Year of the Quiet Sun.* New York: Ace Books.

Tymn, Marshall. 1975. "A Checklist of American Critical Works on SF: 1972–1973." *Extrapolation*, Volume 17, Number 1 (December), 78–96.

Vonnegut, Kurt, Jr. 1974 (1952). *Player Piano.* New York: Dell Books.

Wittig, Monique. 1971. *Les Guerilleres.* New York: Viking Press.

Wollheim, Donald A. 1971. *The Universe Makers: Science Fiction Today.* New York: Harper & Row.

BETTINA J. HUBER

# Images of the Future

"Some . . . see things as they are and say "why?" I dream things that never were and say "why not?"'[1]

The phrase "images of the future" crops up in much of the literature dealing with futures research. It is rarely defined explicitly and it is used loosely in a variety of contexts. It generally tends to refer to any state of affairs projected onto the future, be it sketched in broad outline or in extensive detail. Such images are quite varied; they range from very specific forecasts of economic conditions in a year's time to idealistic utopian visions that may be realized in fifty to a hundred years, if at all. In a sense, images of the future are what this Handbook is all about. Since working with such a global definition is clearly unwieldy, our discussion must begin by narrowing the bounds of the focal concept.

Fred L. Polak, the first author to deal with images of the future explicitly and in depth, described the phrase as encompassing "the idea of a *Future* which is drastically different from the *Present*. This is the idea of a future as The Other, or as a new dimension of this world, the perfected antipode of the imperfect here and now" (1961, Volume 1, p. 56). Such images transcend the limits of the present and present a mental vision of an ideal human order diametrically opposed to everyday reality. (For a more detailed discussion, see E. Boulding, 1971.) This conception is quite different from the all-encompassing one generally encountered in the literature and will serve as the core of the definition adopted in the present discussion. We will be somewhat less utopian and trans-cendental than Polak, however, and will view images of the future as visions of ideal states that *could* become realities in the foreseeable future. Thus, we are dealing with what might be referred to as "realistic utopias" or "realizable ideals." These images can be articulated as very detailed pictures of desirable futures or simply as a set of long-range goals that can orient action. In either case, they present an integrated and coherent view by interrelating or juxtaposing various aspects of the future. They are global images of what might be in the best of all *possible* worlds.

In recent years, a great number of positive idealistic images of the future have been articulated.[2] Few have had any widespread public impact, let alone become integral components of planning for the future. Part of the reason is that the envisioned futures are often depicted in a vacuum rather than at the end of a path commencing in the present. Consequently, the images of the future that will be considered here will contain not only an ideal end-state, but also a means of getting there. The focus of this article will be twofold: the nature of efforts to depict positive idealistic images of the future; and the means that might be employed to make them realities.

Even with this circumscribed definition, an image of the future can still have innumerable points of reference. (For a detailed discussion of these, see Bell and Mau, 1970, pp. 221–222.) At least three are crucial in defining the nature of the image: the time span; the agent articulating the image; and the unit it refers to. Given the view of images of the future described above, we are clearly dealing with the distant future. The idealistic visions we will focus on are projected at least twenty years into the future. Typically, the images are devised by individuals, or small groups of academics, but they could be advanced by planners, civil servants, or simply interested citizens. If they refer to the national or global future, which will be our primary concern, they are articulated with the aim of their becoming guiding images to orient future planning. In addition to images of the national or international future, we will also briefly consider the nature of images of personal futures and how they relate to policy-making and planning for the future.

In sum, the following pages consider how images can be used to help create a more desirable future. This discussion involves examining how goals or realistic utopias can be formulated and why it is important to do so; how to develop transition strategies that link the present and the envisioned future; and how to implement the plans that would make the ideal real. To make these theoretical considerations more concrete, a few examples of images of the future that are in the process of being formulated and implemented are presented. The article closes with a brief discussion of individual images of the future. It examines the importance of such images to the individual, their relation to the broader processes of defining the collective future, and techniques employed to isolate visions of the national and personal future.

## POSITIVE IDEALISTIC IMAGES OF THE FUTURE

Although the bulk of systematic concern with images of the future has been in Europe, the idea of creating them as goals may have been initially proposed by an American. In 1930, Nathan Israeli wrote an article in which he proposed a "Social Psychology of Futurism." He advocated applying prophecy to whole societies in order to delineate scientific and systematic utopias based on emergent properties of the present. Further, an evaluation of new possibilities the future held in store would allow one to delineate patterns of present behavior leading to desired future outcomes. By making "criteria of the future" an integral part of today's value system, futurism could serve as a social philosophy and "the future would be harnessed for the present" (Israeli, 1930, p. 129).

These ideas were not taken up again until the early 1950s when Fred L. Polak wrote his monumental two-volume work *The Image of the Future.* (It appeared in Dutch in 1955 and was translated into English in 1961.) Polak delineates the nature of such images in some detail and documents their dynamic impact on the present by tracing their role in the history of Western civilization. He shows how past cultures flourished by creating images that transcended the present and projected detailed pictures of an ideal future state. During periods of cultural innovation, all segments of society embraced these images and actively strove to realize them. The Middle Ages was a period of stagnation, Polak argues, because, instead of being generally accepted, images of the future tended to be opposed to one another. New scientific discoveries and the Age of Exploration combined to give new impetus to utopian images. Thus, the seventeenth and eighteenth centuries witnessed the emergence of many positive idealistic images. The period was also marked by social experimentation in all spheres. Sometime during the nineteenth century, all this ceased and utopian visions were replaced by nationalistic concern with the immediate future. Polak devotes much of his second volume to documenting how Western civilization has been dominated by negative images ever since.[3] This situation is very disturbing, he maintains, since his historical analysis has shown that the rise or fall of a culture is preceded by the presence or absence of a positive image of the future. Western society's greatest challenge, therefore, is to revitalize its capacity to conceive of futures that embody "the perfected antipode of the imperfect here and now" (Polak, 1961, Volume 1, p. 56). Polak believes that social science ought to make the creation of such guiding utopian visions one of its major obligations, for it is the best way of insuring a culture's renewed flowering. In order to have a significant impact on the present, thereby leading to cultural innovation, the new images must be both powerful and intensely espoused by everyone.

During the late 1950s, the philosopher and educator Gaston Berger articulated ideas very similar to Polak's. On the basis of a philosophical analysis of time, Berger developed what he called "Prospective." He hoped it would provide an operational mechanism for developing positive and inclusive images of the future, which could be extended back to the present where they would serve as the basis for action. Thus, action would become more effective by having an explicit ideal to strive for (Berger, 1973e). At present, Berger argues, we do not act usefully because our decision-making is based on the past. Such an orientation is adequate in a stable society, but not in the dynamic modern world which changes so rapidly. In such a situation, foresight is crucial but not easily available. Frequently used forecasting methods focus on extrapolating past and present trends, but given the acceleration in the rate of change, such techniques provide little insight into the future (Berger, 1973a).

As the historical pace has picked up, we have become aware of the novelty of time, according to Berger (1973c). The classical philosophers had a static conception of time, but under the impetus of Henri Bergson this view has been opened up. The future is no longer seen as part of a predetermined temporal continuity, but rather as an entity quite separate from the past. It takes on meaning only insofar as we relate it to our actions. Thus, the future becomes a creative possibility and the world is open rather than closed. We should therefore "consider the future not as something which is already decided and which gradually reveals itself to us but as something which is to be created" (Berger, 1973b, p. 249). What it will be like depends on us, and it can be consciously molded to be humanly beneficial.

Such a view rests on a reversal of the conventional relationship between present and future. The Prospective approach begins in the future rather than the present and is dependent on having a guiding vision or "directing idea." One begins by defining ends which are noble enough to be generally pursued and thus can be incorporated into the culture of a society. Then action can be defined through a constant interplay of ends, available means, and present reality (Berger, 1973d). In consequence, goals are more important than methods and serve to direct methods. Further, the future no longer grows out of today's events but is actively prepared and planned for in the present.

As Berger's ideas began to gain some currency, he and a number of others founded the Centre d'Etudes Prospectives. Their purpose was to formulate a widely applicable methodology[4] embodying Berger's ideas about images of the future and their usefulness. In 1958, the journal *Prospective,* which presented the results of the Centre's deliberations, was established. Berger died in 1960, but his colleagues continued to develop his ideas. In the early 1960s, through Pierre Massé, Berger's views had considerable impact on the formulation of France's fourth and fifth National Plans,[5] thereby extending the French concept of planning. The Centre broadened its aims in 1966 and began to apply the method it had evolved to a whole series of pressing issues, such as urbanization, education, environmental protection, and regional planning. (For a discussion of some of these projects, see

Cournand and Lévy, 1973.) It also enlarged its board of directors, and one of the new members was Bertrand de Jouvenel.

Long before he joined the Centre d'Etudes Prospectives, de Jouvenel was a well-known futurist in his own right. During the 1950s, he organized the Futuribles group, which was an important catalyst in the subsequent development of the international futures movement. Although primarily concerned with defining probable futures in a systematic manner, de Jouvenel has always stressed the importance of developing positive idealistic images of the future in addition. Thus, his work has much in common with that of Berger and Polak. De Jouvenel believes futures research ought to be regarded as "the art of conjecture." This research focuses on intellectual construction of likely futures, but it also includes specifying ways of bringing the probable closer to the desirable. According to de Jouvenel, contemporary forecasters must do more than just predict future developments. They must also suggest methods of change that will lead to desirable and feasible futures. Furthermore, they should create positive images of the future that will overcome the average citizen's distrust of forthcoming changes (1967). Such "scientific utopias" should focus on the myriad future possibilities for improving the life of ordinary people (1965b). With the aid of these idealistic images, it might also be possible to control technology and use it more effectively for human benefit (1968; a similar point is made by Mishen, 1971).

De Jouvenel's view that futures research ought to consider both tomorrow's inevitabilities and its ideals, without subordinating the former to the latter, as Berger and Polak tend to do, is reflected in the work of Futuribles. This organization consists of a changing group of experts who meet periodically in an effort to generate a coherent picture of the future through discussion and criticism of individual forecasts for specific areas. Much of the work has dealt with what is most likely, but some of it has attempted to be instrumental in bringing about a future that the scholars involved consider desirable.[6] As de Jouvenel (1963, p. xi) has noted:

our group quite definitely takes the view that what shall be depends upon our choices; it is precisely because the future depends on our decisions and actions, and these in turn upon our opinions regarding the future, that the latter so much need to be stated, weighted and tested.

In addition to Bertrand de Jouvenel, a number of other people have discussed the need for positive idealistic images of the future, but none has developed his ideas in as much detail as Polak and Berger. Robert Jungk (1968b) has called for "human forecasting" or an effort to outline the most humanly desirable futures, along with methods of making them a reality. Dennis Gabor (1964) has noted that, in addition to finding solutions to immediate problems, we need to use our creative imagination to formulate visions of what the future could be like. He attempts to articulate such a positive image in his discussion of the "Age of Leisure." In a similar vein, Kenneth Boulding (1965) has argued that to enter the "postcivilized" stage of Western development, we need to use all our intellectual resources to create an image of the future, or set of long-range goals, which could orient action. More recently, James Dator (1974b) has referred to such images as "eutopias." These depict feasible and desirable futures which become generalized social goals or compelling visions that people can strive for. Elsewhere, Dator (1974a) has noted that such images are important because they are vital determinants of what we do in the present. (A similar point is made by Bertaux, 1968, p. 20.) Thus, study of the future is action-oriented and tries to improve today's reality so that a better future will emerge. In addition to serving as guideposts in the present, the very process of defining images of the future widens our choices. According to Tugwell (1974), scientists increase available futures by attempting to clarify and specify goals. At the same time, they provide a powerful motive force (Tugwell, 1974, p. 171): "Science cannot tell us what is important to know; nor can it motivate us to invest our lives and energies in a search for understanding. Our future images of the future can and must do both."

As the preceding discussion has indicated, most scholars dealing with images of the future believe they are important because they provide the incentive that enables cultures or societies to advance. The process by which this occurs is rarely discussed, but Wendell Bell and James Mau (1971) have addressed the issue in theorizing about the relationship between social structure, social action, and images of the future. Building on the work of Polak, Boulding, and Lasswell, they present a view of social change that features images of the future as a key variable.[7] They view change as a feedback cycle in which key elements are constantly modifying, and being modified by, each other:

Present structures . . . shape beliefs about the past, the present, and social causation, and the nature of social values. . . . Beliefs and values shape images of the future which, in turn, lead to certain decisional outcomes and social action. Such action, along with exogenous factors, produces change by helping to shape the actual future in particular ways (1971, p. 28).

Thus, social and cultural change is a product of the interaction of images of the future with present structures, beliefs, and values, leading to decisions designed to make the present more like the desired future.

Such a view implies that the images of the future held by government decision-makers are crucial in determining what kind of social change will take place. This raises the question of whose idealistic images or goals are being striven for. Bell and Mau do not discuss this issue in any detail,[8] in part because their theoretical considerations evolved from work in the newly independent nations of the West Indies. In such developing societies, the process of becoming self-governing encourages national leaders to articulate explicit images of the future which are shared by everyone. In the more settled countries of the West, however, ideals or goals are largely implicit and generally unstated. Thus, there is a danger that a future is evolving which is beneficial primarily to presently dominant groups. Insofar as forecasting techniques are available primarily to those in power, their view of the future will prevail.

According to de Jouvenel (1969, 1974), futurists should strive to prevent this and to articulate a desirable future beneficial to all people. One way they can do so, in the view of P. M. Clair (1973), is to decentralize and deconcentrate thinking about the future. This process might begin by involving all sorts of people in generating long-range goals. Maruyama (1972, 1973) argues that the main function of "Human Futuristics" ought to be to act as a catalyst to aid people in generating new ideals appropriate to a radically different future. Out of this heterogeneity of individual goals could be evolved more general goals acceptable to all and capable of guiding the nation and eventually the world. Should the most important priorities not evolve naturally, an "anticipatory democracy" (Toffler, 1970, p. 470) might be instituted. Such a procedure involves periodic referenda in which voters indicate which of several goals or images of the future they prefer.

Democratizing the process of creating images of the future, of course, requires a well-informed citizenry. Unfortunately, at present, most people are unaware of the future's many positive potentialities. Rather, they view it as something increasingly complex and confusing, which they have little ability to cope with, let alone control. Therefore, to engage the average citizen with the future may require considerable education through the mass media or through more informal community discussions. Mankind 2000 is one of several educational projects already in existence. It is dedicated to the generation of desirable futures likely to insure human survival. It sponsors "workshops of the future" at which people try to outline positive idealistic futures open to everyone (see Jungk, 1968a). If forums of this type became widespread, they would do much to alleviate current apathy and misinformation about the future. Another educational possibility that has been suggested is a Future Gaming Center or a Museum of the Future (see Waskow, 1972; Huber and Bell, 1971, pp. 292–293). This project might use modern audiovisual devices to create realistic exhibits of images of the future prevalent in the past and present. By viewing them, people would get a more realistic "feel" for what living in various visions might really be like, and as a result, might formulate radically different and better images themselves.

All such educational activity is dependent upon having a readily available set of images of the future to tell people about. But, as our initial impetus for discussing such images was Polak's point that Western society lacks them, they are hardly in plentiful supply. Thus, a set of guidelines for generating positive idealistic visions would be most helpful. Since most people trying to delineate images in recent years have done so intuitively, all we have are a few rudimentary beginnings. Jungk (1973) has pointed out that aspiring image-makers need both creative and critical imagination. The first allows one to break out of the system of prevailing ideas and to explore completely new areas. The second aids one to arrive at a model of a better future by critically focusing on present inequity and needless rigidity. According to McHale (1967, 1972) and Kariel (1969), it is only by challenging present assumptions that we can begin to expand the possibilities for the future. But we must be sure to go beyond radical criticism and attempt to develop feasible visions of desirable futures. In doing so, we should define "feasible" quite broadly and not be too rigidly bound by what is presently possible (Kostelanetz, 1971). In addition, utopian visions or goals should not be elaborated in too much detail, so that subsequent planning can remain dynamic and flexible (Atteslander, 1969).

Some have argued that futures research alone, especially with its bias toward scientific forecasting, can never hope to generate realistic utopian visions of wide appeal. Winthrop (1971, p. 102) has noted that such images require combining social philosophy with a concern for the future. What is needed is "a social philosophy which relates the potentialities of modern science and technology to man's deepest and most widely held needs" (Winthrop, 1968, p. 140). This philosophy would introduce to the field a new sense of moral responsibility and concern with what *ought* to be, both of which H. J. Muller (1974, pp. 3-13) finds lacking in most current research. Greater philosophical input might lead to the evolution of a new social ethics with a planetary perspective and a concern for reasonable limits on individual freedom (Polak, 1971, especially, pp. 30-35). The new ethics might provide fertile ground for the generation of positive idealistic images of the future that could be wholeheartedly embraced by all segments of society.

## TRANSITIONS: GETTING FROM THERE TO HERE

When Fred Polak wrote about images of the future in the early 1950s, his main concern was that Western civilization was not being guided by the powerful idealistic images that past cultures had thrived on. It is therefore understandable that he did not discuss in any detail how such images became realities. He simply indicated that if visions of the future were powerful enough, they would be incorporated into the prevailing worldview and eventually become reality through having guided people's actions. Most of the scholars subsequent to Polak who have dealt with images of the future or goals have adopted a focus similar to his, as the preceding discussion has revealed. They have stressed the importance of images of the future and have sometimes tried to formulate new idealistic visions, but they have paid little attention to how they come to have an effective influence on the present.

In a relatively stable society, where change is slow, widespread belief in an image may be enough to eventually make reality resemble it more closely. In a rapidly changing world, however, it is possible that images of the future can be effective only if they are clearly related to public policy-making. This means that idealistic visions must be linked to the present through well-defined transition strategies that indicate how the imperfect present can become a better future. Insight into how such strategies can be developed comes not from people generating images of the future but from the few who have been concerned with making long-range goals an integral part of decision-making. Such scholars pay scant attention to how goals might be generated or to what the content of images should be; rather, they focus on the process of making them real.

One exception to the general segregation between the idealists and the strategists is the French Prospective group. Although Gaston Berger died before he could delineate a detailed approach for linking image and reality, he did formulate a number of general guidelines (Berger, 1973a), which his colleagues subsequently elaborated. The key, of course, is to begin by looking toward the long-range future. According to Massé (1973), this means looking at least ten years ahead. For periods of only four or five years, conventional projection techniques are quite adequate. Successfully linking the distant future and the present, Berger states, requires close collaboration between philosophers concerned with ends and specialists dealing with the realities of today. Such teamwork among those who define the desirable and those who know what is possible should lead to a rich, integrated analysis. Their work ought to be characterized by a broad view so that they can become aware of several possible futures. Each foreseen possibility should be outlined in broad strokes and be as concrete as possible. Extensive detail is not needed, as the prime concern is the general meaning of changes and their approximate tempo.

When examining the present, it is important to analyze trends in depth so that their implications can be properly identified. Thus, the focus should be on underlying factors from which future realities emerge. Massé (1973) refers to such factors as "future-bearing facts." These are insignificant alterations in the present, such as small changes within continuous patterns, that will be of great import in the future. Identifying such seemingly insignificant factors is difficult but reflects Berger's (1973d) emphasis on being boldly imaginative and taking risks. In addition, he stresses the need for making the human factor a key element of all Prospective considerations (Berger, 1973b).

In sum, the Prospective approach does not deduce the future from the present but begins by imagining several realistic utopias that are compatible with the present. This approach permits appreciation of the wealth of the future and allows a large measure of freedom in choice of goals. Next, those present decisions that will contribute to making the envisioned ideal a reality are mapped out. This step is facilitated by translating the image into a model where interrelationships are specified in as much detail as possible (Massé, 1972).

Generating a final model or plan for action involves a number of phases, which Cournand (1973) has outlined in some detail. The first part of the Prospective approach involves formulating a "Logical Plan." Through a series of discussions, a group of people concerned with some aspect of the future try to achieve a systematic understanding of contemporary knowledge about the present and future. In the process, they try to isolate "future-bearing facts," provocative ideas, and desired goals. These form the basis for the sketch of present reality and the forecast of the probable future (generated by linear extrapolation) that make up the Logical Plan. Using the future-bearing facts and goals generated in phase one as catalysts for the imagination, the "Creative Plan" is begun. This second stage involves generating a series of possible futures that are evaluated in terms of the desirable human and social values they enhance, as well as in terms of the tensions and risks they may engender. Once a future has been identified that is both desirable and realizable, phase three can begin. The "Decision Plan" evolves from the juxtaposition of the previously generated constructs of present, probable future, and desirable future. It consists of a series of decisions for action designed to make the ideal vision a more likely future reality. As the process of implementing the Decision Plan proceeds, images of the future are modified by the emerging present, and thus, the Prospective Plans need to be constantly modified and reformulated.

Cournand indicates that his version of the Prospective method has been influenced by the work of Hasan Ozebekhan. This influence is not surprising, since Ozebekhan has devoted the last ten years or so to formulating a planning methodology that takes account of long-range goals and values. Although Ozebekhan devotes scant attention to the means of generating images of the future, he has used systems theory to develop a detailed procedure for incorporating such idealistic visions into what he refers to as "Futures-Creative-Planning" (1965). This procedure expands the horizon of traditional planning by introducing the concept of the "ideal" (a state that cannot be reached immediately but that can be worked toward) and making it the focus of action (1974). Thus, planning becomes a means of developing strategies for realizing basic values rather than for deterministically implementing the most probable future. Like Berger, Ozebekhan (1974) sees his conception of planning as reversing the conventional time flow and allowing the future to "imprint" itself on the present. It is a critique and readjustment of the present in light of an underlying image of an ideal future.

The hierarchical planning system developed by Ozebekhan (1968, 1969, 1974) has three major levels: the normative, the strategic, and the operational. The major impetus to make use of such a system arises from the recognition that the present is imperfect. A notion of what would make the present perfect serves as the basis for the ends or ideals which one tries to realize through planning. These ends are part of the so-called Reference Projection against which changes acceptable to the system can be evaluated. The projection also contains an ordered representation of the perceived present that pinpoints those "activity nodes" critical to the system's functioning and those most sensitive to change; a series of extrapolations indicating how the system will evolve in specified time periods; and a "logical future" that shows what the system will look like if its dynamics develop unhampered.

A critique of the represented present and its logical future serves as the basis for defining a series of alternate futures. These partial pictures of how parts of the system could be subjected to intervention form one element of the normative level or plan. The future visions need not be delineated in great detail and should be imaginatively conceived. Those that are of greatest benefit to the system's ideal ends are integrated with one another and introduced into the environmental frames considered likely. This gives rise to a desirable image of the system's future which forms the other part of the normative plan.

The strategic level of the planning system allows isolation of the most economical, efficient, and direct means of realizing the normative objectives. Generally, an attempt is made to delineate several different strategies for each objective and to choose those which can be integrated most easily into a synthetic whole. This overall strategy specifies what the system *can* do, within a given time period, using delimited organizational and human resources.

The strategic level sets the basic guidelines for the operational level or action framework. In this phase, the administrative institutionalization of the various strategies is dealt with. Such implementation is not automatic, and there should be enough flexibility in the system to allow for modifications in applying the means and resources available from day to day. As the system responds to the operational action, the present is changed and so the planning cycle can, and must, begin again.

Of the few scholars who have discussed transition strategies for realizing images of the future, none has been as thorough as Ozebekhan. Most have, however, outlined procedures similar to his. Jantsch (1972a) explicitly uses Ozebekhan's ideas in a discussion of how planning and forecasting can be linked more effectively. He indicates that this linking would occur if both were normatively based or informed by a society's basic values. Under such circumstances, forecasts could guide planning. Theobald (1968b) voices a similar concern for linking policy and goals. He advocates a three-step procedure: setting up desirable and feasible goals; determining the socioeconomic changes needed to implement them; and developing new policies to foster needed change and goal implementation. This approach is not very different from the one suggested by Dator (1971). He would begin by specifying basic social goals, then determine what they mean in operational terms, and finally specify what structural modifications appear necessary or desirable for making the ideal ends a reality.

An approach similar to that of Ozebekhan and the Prospective group has been set forth by a relatively large number of international relations scholars. In a book edited by Beres and Targ (1975), they try to reorient the methodological focus of their discipline so that it will become more systematic, normative, and futuristic. Their work builds on the world order movement which has been in the making for the last ten years, especially in Europe.[9] All the essays in the Beres-Targ volume deal with the question of how to envision and implement a future world order. Some discuss specific visions or problems of implementation, while others are more general and focus on procedural guidelines. Specific suggestions for precisely how to proceed vary, but everyone seems agreed on a number of major elements. Any plan for world order should include idealistic images of the future and a consideration of how they were delineated; a consideration of the values underlying the images and where they come from;[10] a transition plan linking the real to the ideal; and an assessment of present realities, as well as of likely future developments.

Individual authors differ about the order in which these elements should be defined. Some advocate beginning with a definition of desirable world orders (see the Targ and Stohl articles in Beres and Targ,

1975), while others argue for beginning with an analysis of the present and the likely future (see, for example, the Soroos and Beres selections in Beres and Targ, 1975). Another point of contention is the degree of specificity needed. Bobrow (in Beres and Targ, 1975), for example, favors the establishment of explicit time deadlines and rules for determining whether a strategy is working, whereas Washburn (in Beres and Targ, 1975) prefers greater generality and flexibility. Washburn also argues that the focus should be on possibilities that are both feasible and desirable, but others (see Stohl in Beres and Targ, 1975) advocate going beyond the presently feasible to deal with seemingly unrealistic ideals.

Regardless of such procedural differences, all the international relations scholars contributing to the Beres-Targ volume seem to share a common motivation. They believe that we are facing a series of problems that have reached crisis proportions (e.g., threat of war; danger to the ecology; imbalance between rich and poor; unchecked population growth; excessive resource consumption; and political oppression). In order to insure human survival, these difficulties must be resolved and this resolution requires global cooperation. Thus, scholars have an obligation to devise models of a desirable world order, as well as to consider how we can move from the nationalistic tensions of the present to a more harmonious future.

In developing transition strategies linking present and future, be it on a global or national level, it is important not to neglect the many forecasting techniques developed by futures researchers in recent years. If informed by an underlying conception of an idealistic future, such approaches become powerful tools in the effort to create a more desirable tomorrow. As many of the techniques are discussed in detail elsewhere in this volume, a brief mention of a few that appear to be especially promising will suffice. In general, those forecasting strategies referred to as normative are more congenial for dealing with images of the future. They are distinguished by moving backward from a desirable future to needed action in the present. In contrast, exploratory techniques proceed from the present to the future, sometimes along several possible lines of development (Jantsch, 1972a, p. 69). One of the few well-developed normative techniques is the "relevance tree" approach. It begins by setting out a goal and then specifies the major stages lying between its realization and the present. Next, the means that could be employed at each stage to move toward the goal are delineated, and the best ones are used in the chain linking present and future. Just what is "best" is defined in terms of a set of critieria relating to goal achievement; a number of procedures have been developed for expressing this concept quantitatively. The relevance tree method achieved some fame when NASA used Honeywell's PATTERN version in its effort to achieve President Kennedy's goal of reaching the moon by the end of the 1960s. Since the technique, especially in its quantitative form, requires a good deal of very precise data, its usefulness for implementing comprehensive images of the future may be limited. (For more detailed discussion, see Jantsch, 1972a, pp. 87–90, and 1972b, p. 485; Hoghton, Page, and Streatfeild, 1971, pp. 57–63; McGrath, 1974).

A number of exploratory techniques may be of special usefulness in dealing with transition strategies. One strategy is called "the method of movement" by Massenet (1963) and is discussed by Murphy (1961) in terms of isolating human potentialities. This is a method of constructing pictures of possible futures by pinpointing factors barely perceptible today that might develop into major forces in the years ahead.[11] Another useful exploratory technique is the scenario. In essence, it is a carefully defined progression that describes how a future state of events might come to be (Sage and Chobot, 1974). Scenarios are very similar to what H. D. Lasswell has called a "developmental construct." It sketches a probable chain of events that commences in the past and ends in the future. It is essentially an "ideal-type" statement about how a social process might evolve as time passes (Eulau, 1958).[12] Durand (1972) has tried to make the scenario or developmental construct more amenable to the Prospective approach by adding several additional elements to the central historical progression. These include a baseline description of key present elements and how they are interrelated; a consideration of how the external environment may affect the process or system being focused on; and a series of images of the future that represent coherent views of what might be at different points in time. By the addition of the images, the scenario can be used to consider how and when to introduce purposive adjustments into the system.

## IMPLEMENTATION: BEGINNING TO MAKE THE IDEAL REAL

As the preceding pages have illustrated, a good deal has been written about constructing positive idealistic images of the future and about delineating transition strategies that link them to the present. In contrast, relatively little is known about how to successfully implement the strategies by actually getting them incorporated into the decision-making process. This is an important gap in our knowledge, as most of the people concerned with images of the future are academics rather than politicians or bureaucrats. Thus, they have little say about the type of future presently being brought about.

In the few instances where people in power become concerned with the future, much can be accomplished.[13] In fact, this appears to be the prime criterion in determining individual ability to implement an image of the future. A study at New York University by Baldridge (1971, especially pp. 280–282), for example, showed that the prime reason the administration was successful in altering the prevailing vision of the university's mission (from a school offering educational opportunity to everyone to a fairly selective high-quality urban university) was its power. In part, this derived from its ability to institute many of the needed changes without getting explicit approval from anyone. Such autocratic action was successful not only because of power, of course. In addition, the president was popular and respected by everyone; the opposition was not united; and the university was in decline as a result of changes in its external environment. The importance of social power in making forecasts become reality has also been noted by Porter (1974). He argues that the most effective strategic forecasters are those who have influential positions in important organizations or in the nation as a whole. Being influential usually means having policy-making authority (i.e., being on the board of directors). Managers or professionals are generally not effective at making forecasts real, except if they are part of an organization whose structure is fluid.

Although convincing powerful charismatic leaders to orient their activities in terms of an image of the future may be effective, the approach is very dependent upon having the right people in the right places. In the long run, it may be better to make a future perspective an integral part of planning and decision-making. Many have argued that social planning would benefit from an imaginative and normative focus on the future. Bobrow (1973, p. 68), for example, has called for "purposive planning," which would choose a normatively defined end-state and try to attain it by altering certain components in the system. Doing so might overcome what Boguslaw (1971, p. 256) sees as the greatest flaw of present planning efforts at all levels: insufficient imagination and a consequent dearth of truly creative solutions to present social problems. In addition, linking public policy and futures research would make politicians more aware of the great variety of possibilities lying ahead, according to Calder (1969). More specifically, it might provide them with a powerful vision of a different national future.

Williams (1972) indicates that such an image would provide a new framework for the governmental decision-making apparatus and a basis for redirecting our institutions. Use of such a framework requires two alterations in public policy-making as it is presently practiced: extending the time frame to twenty to forty years, so that necessary basic change can be planned for; and a broadening of perspective to include interdependence of elements and qualitative consequences of actions. Such alterations might allow planners to deal more effectively with uncertainty and might provide an organizing framework suited to a pluralistic, multifaceted society. To link images of the future to day-to-day decision-making, more than such broad changes in perspective are needed, according to Dror (1968, 1973). Rather, we need a set of specific procedures for compromising between demands of the real and the ideal. This requires choosing goals selectively and establishing priorities between them, as well as balancing the need to create a better future with the need to solve immediate problems. Large resource inputs should be used primarily for solving present difficulties, while moving toward a desirable tomorrow should involve encouraging the whole population to tie their present activities into the future.

One way of making the future a real part of daily decision-making might be through the establishment of a "Look-Out Institution." Ozebekhan (1965) has indicated that this might be a useful way of institutionalizing his planning strategy. Such an entity is usually conceived of as an anticipatory social warning system that tries to identify both the dangers and opportunities that lie ahead (see Jungk, 1969). It assumes a long-range, comprehensive, and interdisciplinary approach. One of the main functions of the institution would be to foresee possible futures and to outline the actions needed to make them realities. Starling (1973) argues that such a procedure would overcome a major deficiency of American policy-making by clearly spelling out goals and linking policy objectives to the general quality of life. He also believes that a Look-Out Institution would be politically beneficial by broadening the president's perspective on issues and by providing Congress with a variety of policy alternatives. In addition, dominance by the governmental expert would be undercut because analyses of the future would be available to all groups involved in the political process. To insure such widespread dissemination of its work, the institution would have to be strictly nonpartisan and representative of various social segments. Such semi-independence is also advocated by Massé (1973, p. 58) in discussing the possibilities for institutionalizing Prospective in France.

It cannot be denied that institutionalizing the creation of images of the future, especially on a national level, poses the grave danger of allowing a very small group of people to have an immense impact on the shape of the future. To minimize this possibility and to allow a maximum of citizen participation, long-range planning efforts should be carried out at the local or regional level wherever possible (OECD Symposium, 1969; Knigge, 1973). Planners should not try to do what is best for others but should see their mission as helping communities realize the future their citizens favor (Theobald, 1968a). When the future must be planned for at other than the local level, one might use questionnaires, forums, or advisory boards to provide for systematic citizen input (Knigge, 1973). This might also have a secondary educational function and serve to make images of the future an integral part of the general consciousness (Dror, 1973).

Rather than having planning experts try to implement images of the future that have been democratically delineated, one might encourage people to participate directly in creating a desirable future by building elements of it into contemporary institutions. Waskow (1969, 1972) has labeled such an approach "creative disorder." It involves building up a strain between present and future by getting people to imagine what a humane and livable future for one generation hence would be like. The strain or tension then induces people to alter the present reality of their daily lives and of the larger society, so that it is more in keeping with the desired future. The sit-ins to integrate restaurants during the early stages of the civil rights movement are a good example of creative disorder at work.

## EXAMPLES OF IMPLEMENTATION

Consideration of a number of concrete examples may add some tangibility to our discussion of the process of creating and implementing positive idealistic images of the future. Actual attempts to bring a desirable future into being have been undertaken primarily by groups, but a number of individuals have tried it too. The people involved come from all parts of the world, although Europeans seem to predominate. The focus adopted has ranged from the future of a state or region to that of the whole world. Some have dwelt on the year 2000, while others have set no specific time dimension to their vision.

One of the earliest attempts to guide decision-making in terms of an image of the future was undertaken by colleagues of Gaston Berger. Pierre Massé tried to incorporate the Prospective approach into his direction of the fourth and fifth French National Plans. He developed long-range views of the future to serve as the background or "horizon" for the immediate short-range economic policies each plan required. The fourth Plan covered the year 1960 to 1965 and its horizon was set at 1975, while the fifth Plan covering the next five years had an horizon of 1985 (see Massé, 1973). It was in preparing the second plan that Massé fully employed Prospective principles. He appointed the Committee of 1985 whose task it was to take the broad view and formulate the horizon line. In keeping with the Prospective approach, the committee consisted of interdisciplinary study groups that searched the present for future-bearing facts and other clues of what might occur in the long run. Through a combination of imagination and speculation, an image of the future eventually emerged which was comprehensive and took account of what was humanly desirable, as well as feasible. With this image as background, formulation of the short-term plans was considerably facilitated (Cournand and Lévy, 1973, pp. 1–7).

Subsequent French Plans have not been directed by Massé, but Prospective has continued to be used.[14] The results seem to have been mixed, as a critique of the sixth Plan by Cazes (1973) indicates. He notes that the Plan's long-term synthetic picture tends to neglect the impact of the international context on France and also fails to specify crucial issues for which a series of distant alternatives need to be developed. In addition, as is typical of earlier plans, the synthetic vision fails to outline paths leading to the desired future and thus is not sufficiently policy-oriented. The portions of the plan referring to specific sectors or problems also fall short, according to Cazes. Of the policy alternatives outlined, many are difficult to implement, as they involve a variety of government agencies, and some crucial aspects are neglected altogether. In sum, Cazes recommends that subsequent plans make a more careful effort to contrast what is probable with what is desirable. Doing so should enable one to formulate policies designed to bring the two closer together.

Another French attempt to bring about a more desirable future stems from the Futuribles group headed by Bertrand de Jouvenel. It consists of a series of essays dealing with the long-term prospects for a European federation (de Jouvenel, 1963). Their primary aim is "less to describe the lines of force which must be followed in a probable or possible future than to delineate the policy which must be followed if the wished-for future is to become tomorrow's reality" (Freymond, 1965, p. xiv). Thus, each author was guided by the belief that a united Europe was desirable, and each hoped to influence the emerging future by writing about how the ideal might be realized. The essays appeared between 1961 and 1964. They had no immediate impact, in large part because President de Gaulle vigorously opposed all efforts to achieve greater European unity. Now that the Gaullist view has lost its sway, the image formulated in the Futuribles essays is slowly beginning to become a reality.

Another project focusing on the future of Europe is Plan Europe 2000, which is sponsored by the European Cultural Foundation. It is guided by three preliminary values or assumptions: that Europe will be a unified political and social entity by the year 2000; that pluralism and decentralization will be encouraged, as well as democratic participation at the local level; and that society will be geared toward the individual, with human rights being extensively respected. The purpose of the project is to forecast the areas open to human choice, as well as the developments that appear inevitable. This will be achieved through a series of interdisciplinary studies focusing on four areas: education, industrialization, urbanization, and the transformation of rural society. So far, one book has emerged from the project which tries to delineate a general image of the European future (Plan Europe 2000, 1972). It is to serve as a general frame of reference for the more specific studies.

Although dealing with idealistic images of the future is primarily a European preoccupation, some efforts have been made in the United States. These have tended to place more emphasis on widespread citizen involvement than have the European counterparts. Perhaps the best example is the Hawaii 2000 Project (see Chaplin and Paige, 1973, pp. 1–19). It began when a local newspaper editor, George Chaplin, wrote an article about the need for the systematic study of the future. In response, the funding for a Governor's Conference the following year was made available in mid-1969. Chaplin was appointed to head the twenty-one member Advisory Commission charged with the responsibility of organizing the conference. Almost immediately, it was decided to focus not only on goals for the year 2000, but also on alternative means of linking present policy to the future. To prepare for the conference, a number of task forces were set up to examine future possibilities in specific areas. Wherever possible, task force members were recruited from a variety of social and ethnic groups. To encourage widespread citizen participation, a series of preconference panel discussions were organized, but they were not as well attended as had been hoped.

Nonetheless, when the conference was held in August 1970, about 700 people were actual participants and many more attended. The bulk of the proceedings was devoted to presenting and discussing the various task force reports. Thus, the conference was meant to be a creative catalyst for widespread concern about the future. It was designed to get all Hawaii to think about desirable future goals, how they might be realized, and whether the present was contributing positively or negatively. Despite their many efforts, the organizers did not think the conference succeeded in reaching a broad enough cross-section of citizens. In addition, a number of other difficulties were encountered: the focus on a specific date was restricting; the use of task forces focusing on specific areas discouraged an integrated view from emerging; and too little attention was devoted to delineating specific transition strategies (Chaplin and Paige, 1973, pp. 455–472).

The conference did generate considerable enthusiasm, however, and led to the formation of a permanent Hawaii State Commission on the Year 2000 in 1971. Its major function is to promote and coordinate activities concerned with the future. More specifically, it tries to foster awareness of how the future is being shaped right now; it tries to involve a diverse group of people in generating goals; and it tries to devise action strategies that can be implemented by both citizens and the legislature. So far, the commission has helped set up a number of education projects and has organized forums for generating alternative images of the future (Chaplin and Paige, 1973, pp. 470–472). Given the widespread government, academic, and business involvement, the commission might well become instrumental in getting all of Hawaii to participate in creating a desirable future. Its establishment has already inspired similar projects elsewhere. Both Iowa 2000 and the Puget Sound conference have looked to Hawaii's experience for guidance in their own work.

Even more ambitious than Hawaii's effort to create the future is the World Order Models Project (WOMP). It was initiated in the mid-1960s when the World Law Fund concluded that existing concepts of world order were sadly lacking in creative input. It tried to change this state of affairs by generating a new transnational cultural perspective on global issues. More specifically, under the directorship of Saul Mendlovitz (1975b), a number of international study teams were set up to delineate a series of "relevant utopias" depicting desirable world orders for the period 1990 to 2000. In addition, each team was to delineate means of getting to the desired end-state. Thus, an action-oriented problem-solving approach was stressed. The various WOMP research teams represented the following perspectives: North American, Latin American, West German, Russian, Japanese, Indian, African, and transitional.

The teams worked independently, except that the research directors met every six months to discuss and criticize the documents they were preparing. In addition, all teams began with a common framework. First, they were striving to maximize a number of goals or values: peace, economic well-being, and social justice. (Ecological stability seems to have been added later.) Second, everyone had to deal with five major topics: the basic values assumed in addition to the common goals;[15] the relevant utopias or target models that evolved from the values; the crucial issues facing the world at present; major issues that will have emerged by 1990; and the nature of the transition from present to future (Sakamoto, 1972). Despite these shared foci, the World Order Models produced by the various teams are quite divergent. They are delineated in books by Kothari (1974), Falk (1975), Mazrui (1975), and Galtung (forthcoming). In addition, aspects of the models are outlined in edited volumes focusing on the economy (Bhagwati, 1972), Africa (Mazrui and Patel, 1973), and preferred worlds (Mendlovitz, 1975b).

As the models were being developed, two methodological problems plagued the researchers. The ways in which the core goals were operationalized tended to be quite divergent, sometimes giving rise to value conflicts that were difficult to resolve. Moreover, specifying criteria or techniques for evaluating the feasibility of preferred worlds and transition strategies was problematic (Mendlovitz, 1975a).

The written materials generated by WOMP are to provide the basis for a worldwide educational program of global reform. The key targets are scholars, decision-makers, and people in general. To help further its educational efforts, WOMP founded the transitional journal *Alternatives* in 1974. One of its annual projects will be to issue a "State of the Globe" message assessing the progress made toward realizing the four core goals. Whether these messages will be optimistic in the years to come remains to be seen. There is no doubt that making progress toward realizing a desirable world order is considerably complicated by the lack of international bodies to provide an effective organizational focus.[16]

WOMP, like all the other examples discussed thus far, is a group effort dedicated to bringing about a desirable future. But such attempts have also been made by individuals. Perhaps an appropriate illustration[17] is the world order model recently outlined by Ervin Laszlo (1974). He delineates the basic elements of a desirable world system in an imaginative manner and specifies in considerable detail the interrelated changes necessary for it to become a reality. His model represents an attempt to assess the usefulness of systems theory for the study of world order, especially for defining the norms typifying a desirable future. He adopts Maslow's hierarchy of needs, which he believes a humane social organization should satisfy. This can best be done in the context of a dynamic multivariate equilibrium state. Laszlo describes the nature of such a self-regulating global system in considerable detail. He does not believe that movement toward it requires the prior establishment of humane and reasonable governments. Rather, he states that we should proceed by educating people about the challenges facing us and how they might be dealt with. The resulting public consciousness will provide the pressure necessary to force governments to participate in the implementation of a humane world order.[18]

## TRANSLATING IMAGES INTO ACTION: AN OVERVIEW

All of the concrete examples discussed in the preceding pages are flawed and imperfect, revealing that the process of bringing a desirable future into being is exceedingly complex. But they do provide evidence that systematic attempts are being made to implement positive idealistic images of the future. The prime characteristic of each future-oriented effort discussed is that its basic aim is to maximize progress toward a set of positively valued goals or a realistic utopia. Furthermore, all are concerned with devising transition strategies linking fu-

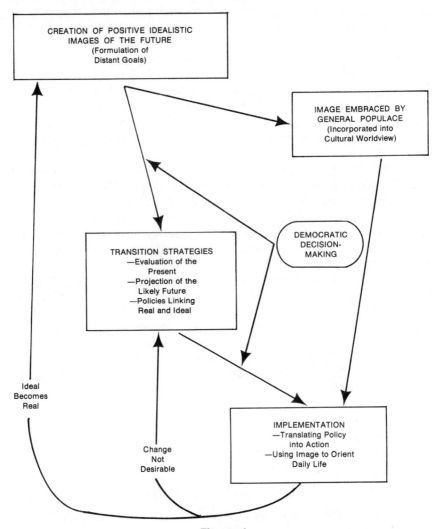

**Figure 1**
The Process of Translating Images of the Future into Action

ture and present, although the degree of specificity achieved varies. Most of the projects discussed were undertaken by experts, but the Hawaiian experience shows that the participation of community leaders and a broad cross-section of citizens is equally feasible. How much impact these people, expert or not, have had on the actual future as it emerged is unclear. At best, the effect has been limited.

Nonetheless, all the attempts illustrate how the approach discussed in this chapter can provide an integrated means of conceptualizing and realizing a desirable future. Figure 1 summarizes the process.

The process begins with the generation of a series of positive idealistic images of the future. These focus on what the future *could* be like if existing opportunities were taken advantage of. They outline a vision of a distant tomorrow that is more perfect than today. If images are delineated in terms of long-range goals, these should be sufficiently broad to encompass a spectrum of individual desires. Following the WOMP procedure, goals should be evaluated not in terms of specificity, but in terms of their compatibility with other positively valued ends. Such a pluralistic approach minimizes sharp disagreement about the ultimate desirability of a specific goal. It will not, however, eliminate differences of opinion; at some point, goal priorities should be established and competing images of the future evaluated. This provides the first key juncture for an institutionalized process of democratic decision-making. Through some type of formal referendum, the average citizen has the opportunity to express a preference for a given goal or image. This is not to imply that widespread citizen participation is not part of the process of generating images of the future. It should be actively sought, if for no other reason than that creating radically different images is difficult and that success is more likely with a wide spectrum of input.

Involvement of the whole population in choosing an image of the future also serves to generate widespread awareness of what an idealistic tomorrow might be like. It facilitates general acceptance of the image and its incorporation into the cultural mainstream. This involvement alone will probably not insure the realization of a better future, but without it meaningful progress will be seriously hindered. The kind of change that the future demands would be difficult to impose on an uninvolved citizenry.

Nonetheless, implementing an image in a rapidly changing society does require careful planning, and thus transition strategies need to be outlined. In order to determine how to link the present and the desired future, the best available forecasting techniques are employed to evaluate the present and delineate the most likely future trends. This information serves as the basis for specifying what shifts in present trends would make the desired future probable, as well as what innovations would be beneficial. Combining the needed changes and innovations into an overall picture gives rise to several strategies for linking the real and the ideal. Deciding which of several equally feasible approaches is to be adopted is again done in a democratic manner. Holding a public plebiscite would also prepare people for the alterations in life-style that the strategies might bring about.

Once the transition strategy is defined, it has to be implemented. The overall plan ought to be fairly general so that is is sufficiently flexible to allow for the many adjustments that have to be made as daily decisions are formulated. As policy is translated into action, sensitive social indicators for monitoring its impact would be necessary. Should progress toward the desired future not be forthcoming, all or part of the transition strategy would be reformulated. Once the present begins to reflect elements of the image guiding policy, new idealistic visions have to be formulated. Thus, as Figure 1 indicates, the process of creating a desirable future is ongoing and unending. It goes without saying that the actual future will never be exactly like the ideal. Rather, the process outlined in Figure 1 simply attempts to make the future more reflective of human desires than it might otherwise be.

General adoption of the process outlined in Figure 1 might not immediately lead to a more desirable future, but it might lead to a beneficial redirection in the type of debate characterizing the futures field. At present, much attention is devoted to the question of whether predictions are correct. Is, for example, the view of the future articulated in *The Limits to Growth* unduly pessimistic? (See Beckwith, 1972; University of Sussex Science Policy Research Unit, 1973.) Or, in a similar vein, do the Hudson Institute's future projections have a conservative bias? (See Marien, 1973, pp. 12–15.) Or, finally, are computerized world systems models useful policy-making tools? (See Cole, 1974 versus Peccei, 1973.) While these are all important questions, they tend to obscure the central fact that we do not *know* what the future will be like. Thus, evaluating forecasts is in many ways futile. More importantly, it deflects our energies from that area in which knowledge is possible and crucial: namely, what we desire for a humane future. What we need to discuss in a systematic manner is not what we think is inevitable, but what we think *should* be. Once we know what should be, forecasting expertise will no longer be the object of a debate going on in a vacuum but will be a valuable tool in the effort to realize a better future.

The use of images of the future as a framework for forecasting, and other future-oriented research, would highlight the critical goal issues needing immediate clarification. For example, implicit in both the pro and con views of "the limits to growth" is the idea that the developing countries ought to, and want to, raise their standard of living through industrialization; the question debated is whether or not they can. Yet, will the Third World not continue to reproach the West in the future if it finds that the material fruits of industrialization still leave it without the quality of life the developed countries have obtained in the meantime? Perhaps the future gap between industrialized and postindustrialized societies will be no less divisive than the present imbalance between developed and developing countries. It may be that we should consider more seriously whether the Third World ought to industrialize, or whether it might be able to skip this stage and develop a postindustrial society based on quality. (This possibility has already been suggested by some, for example, by Iyengar, 1972.) Similarly, perhaps we should reconsider whether we are going to like the leisure society we are moving toward. Do we really want a highly technological world requiring a limited amount of tedious work but providing a great deal of free time, or might we not be more fulfilled by a life-style centered around satisfying work which is less comfortable and more strenuous? These are very complex, politically loaded questions, but they need to be discussed in a detailed, rational manner. Until they are, and we develop a consensus about a desirable image of the future, the most sophisticated computer models, or forecasts of the greatest precision, are of limited value.

Attention to positive idealistic images of the future might have an immediate impact on reorienting futures research, but a great deal more knowledge is needed before they can be a truly effective force in creating a more desirable future. There are some gaps in our knowledge about how one goes about defining realistic utopias and transition streategies, but they are minor compared to the difficulties in the area of implementation.

In terms of goals, our key challenge lies not in defining what is desirable but in appreciating the interdependence of goals. Many of the things we might strive for in the future are mutually exclusive, and we must devote some energy to specifying these conflicts between goals. In addition, we need to develop mechanisms for establishing priorities among a set of equally desirable ends (Bauer, 1973).

In the area of transition strategies, we know a good deal about planning procedure but lack innovative ideas about how to get to our goals (Dror, 1974). Not only is creative imagination crucial for generating images of the future, but it is also essential for devising new and effective links between the present and our distant ideal. In addition, we need to devise better guidelines for developing strategies that are both feasible and flexible enough to be effectively used.

The greatest present impediment to putting images of the future into action lies in the area of implementation. The people trying to generate visions of a better tomorrow appear to believe that making them a reality is a grubby business, and they are hesitant to get their hands dirty. On the other hand, planners and decision-makers seem to believe that striving to realize an ideal is unrealistic and dangerous. The problem is compounded by the fact that governmental agencies have no institutional means for routinely considering long-term future possibilities and that politicians are relatively disinterested in doing so. Thus, we need considerable research and action aimed at finding out how an unresponsive governmental bureaucracy might be induced to contribute to concrete efforts to bring images of the future into being.

The key to doing so appears to be through improving response time. We know very little about the effect that given policies are having or how well they are working once they are put into action. Yet, without means of evaluation, it is impossible to reform imperfect programs (Carlson, 1973). In addition, we need to develop institutional means for quickly implementing the program alterations that initial feedback indicates are required (Bauer, 1973). This goal might be facilitated if we could develop values and institutions capable of dealing with two defining characteristics of our society: rapid change (Dator, 1974a) and runaway technology (McHale, 1972).

Some insight into how to implement images of the future might be gained from examining studies of organizational or bureaucratic change. Of special interest would be the question of how governing ideas or policies are altered. In this respect, studies of how laws are changed to reflect shifts in public morality are instructive (see Lemert, 1970). The long-term experience of Hawaii may also yield considerable insight into how the future can become an integral part of daily decision-making. It already seems to indicate that involving a wide spectrum of people (e.g., academics, bureaucrats, planners, politicians, businessmen, and average citizens) enhances the likelihood of successfully bringing about a more desirable future.

The general lack of such diverse involvement presently makes the possibility of implementing images of the future that are not an integral part of government planning quite remote. This difficulty has been experienced by WOMP, for example, as well as by individuals currently articulating idealistic visions in books. The general belief of these people (for example, Laszlo) is that they will succeed not through government, but by reaching the general populace. This point raises the other thorny aspect of implementation: how can the average citizen be encouraged to accept and aspire to a positive idealistic image of the future? According to Livesey (1973, pp. 332–334), to some extent, this involvement might occur if planners adopted different attitudes. Of more importance, however, would probably be the attempt to make democratic participation a key part of all planning for the future, especially on a local level. (For a more detailed discussion of how this attempt might be made, see Huber, 1974.)

Insight into how to generate such participation might emerge from detailed studies of past successes, such as the Initiatives put on the ballot by California voters in recent years (e.g., campaign reform and coastal protection). Furthermore, the recent experience of social movements in establishing themselves and attracting adherents might be instructive. (For a discussion, see Gerlach, 1971.) One promising procedure discussed is finding a means of combining people's everyday activities with those leading to the large-scale social changes required for a better future (see Flacks, 1974, pp. 67–71).

In sum, much more research and practical experimentation is needed before images of the future can be successfully implemented. If we combine the divergent aspects of futures study, along with other relevant research, into an integrated approach, and if we involve people from all walks of life in the endeavor, perhaps the process of moving toward a humanly desirable future can begin.

## THE PLACE OF IMAGES OF THE FUTURE IN INDIVIDUAL TIME PERSPECTIVES

The preceding discussion has shown that the process of creating a more desirable future through planned implementation of an idealistic vision is facilitated if citizens play an active part in the process. It may even be that an image of the future cannot become reality unless the general populace believes in it and actively strives to make tomorrow more perfect than today. We have noted that little is known about how such public dedication evolves. Under these circumstances, it is of considerable significance to know what role the future plays in individual lives. In addition, people's hopes and expectations for the years to come presumably influence how they will react to social change (Cantril, 1965, p. 3). Thus, plans and forecasts, be they long- or short-range, are more likely to be realized if they are informed by citizen preferences (de Jouvenel, 1965). Yet, by and large, futures research has ignored the question of how the individual relates to the future and what significance this relation has for changes that are likely or desirable in the years ahead. Thus far, our discussion of how images of the future might serve to bring about a better future has also neglected this significant topic. The general body of social science research provides some insight into individual notions of the future, but important gaps remain.

A sense of future has been an integral part of theories of psychological maturation for some time. It tends to be viewed in the context of a general time perspective that evolves as the personality develops. Lewin (1935) indicates that a future time perspective develops as the child matures and enlarges his frame of reference. Allport (1961) expresses a similar view. For Piaget (1958) adolescence marks the emergence of a future orientation as a consequence of the shift in intellectual mode. In a recent overview of much of the developmental literature, Cottle and Klineberg (1974, pp. 70–104) trace the shift from present to future as the child matures. Paying special attention to the work of Erikson and Piaget, they note that the newborn child has no awareness of time. Already by the end of the first year, however, action is directed in terms of anticipated goals and consequences. The experience with symbols that school entrance brings expands the time perspective dramatically. The short-range future soon becomes both subjectively and objectively real, although images of adult life are very hazy. Until adolescence, the distant future is seen primarily in fantasy terms. The basic transformations occurring between the ages of twelve and twenty have a decided impact on the individual's time perspective. As formal and logical thought processes begin to dominate on an intellectual level, verbal elements are manipulated directly, allowing realistic anticipation of the personal future. At the same time, the new role demands that accompany adolescence link future conceptions to the experienced present. As identity and a sense of self-continuity emerge, the awareness of the individual's life-span binds past and future together. By fourteen or fifteen, images of future adulthood have crystallized and the world of tomorrow is circumscribed by realistic expectations.

The emergence of a sense of the future is closely linked to the importance of life goals. Until about fifteen, such distant objectives are of little significance, according to Buehler (1968a). During adolescence, vague and tentative life goals begin to emerge. Between the ages of twenty-five and forty-five, desired ends become quite specific and serve to orient activities. During later adulthood, as people begin to assess their success in achieving their life goals, they begin to view the future in a different light. By sixty-five, active striving for distant goals subsides and individuals feel fulfilled or resigned in terms of past goal achievement.

It seems that the active pursuit of distant goals or images of the future is predominant primarily during the years of middle adulthood. Even then, however, the healthy individual is largely oriented toward the present. Buehler (1968b) argues that the future is dealt with by incorporating it into present experience. Optimism or pessimism about what tomorrow will bring depends upon one's success in coping with past and present. In a similar vein, Landheer (1971) indicates that preoccupation with future possibilities is largely an emotional reaction to the present. Disturbance of the dynamic human equilibrium, which is composed of a series of complementary actions, results in the generation of images of the future. These are shaped by the social environment and depict the overcoming of serious disequilibrium, thereby reducing anxiety and generating hope. Such utopian visions, says Landheer, often compensate for present difficulties, and their promise of a better future can be exploited to keep an unstable society going. On the other hand, the changing quality of the present can be seen as dynamic rather than as unstabilizing. This will give rise to the idea that planning is essential, and images of the future will be employed to coordinate present activities.

Not only are orientations to the present relevant to future change, but so are conceptions of the past. Hearn (1975) maintains that revolutionary change is dependent upon the availability of a set of critical categories allowing delegitimation of the present. Such categories arise from the interaction of past memories and fantasy which produces an imaginative mythical vision of the years gone by. This idealized view is used as a yardstick for critically assessing present realities. The perceived gap between real and ideal that results, in turn, leads to images of a future in which it has been eliminated. Thus, according to Hearn, images of the future represent a redefinition of the present in terms of the principles prevailing in a mythical past.[19]

According to Cottle and Klineberg (1974, pp. 3–35), it is such temporal integration, along with an emotional component, that allows adults to anticipate the future and act accordingly. As people reinterpret the meaning of their past lives and integrate it into their sense of identity and self-continuity, the future implications thereof become part of the present. Thus, images of the future emerge from the temporal links imposed on the course of human life. These images take on an emotional dimension as people project themselves into the imagined future and anticipate what the situation may be like. If feelings of despair or powerlessness result, the unpleasant images of the future are banned from consciousness and contemplation of the unpleasant future is avoided. Moreover, if the future appears to have no integral link to past and present experience, people have difficulty anticipating it in a meaningful way.

Such a view of the individual relationship to the future has a number of important implications. First, if people can cope with a positive view of the future but tend to shut out a negative one, then Polak's point that a culture needs to be guided by optimistic future images to thrive is reaffirmed. It also implies that the largely pessimistic and hopeless views of the future currently being promulgated by intellectuals[20] are counterproductive, if not quite irresponsible. A second implication of this view is that a sense of future is lacking today, not only because people are uninformed about what tomorrow may bring, but also because they have no link to the past. Thus, overcoming "future shock" may require more than orienting our institutions to the future and learning to cope with rapid change effectively, as Toffler (1970) has proposed. In addition, a new sense of past tradition may be needed to reestablish the individual's sense of temporal integration.

## EMPIRICAL INQUIRIES INTO INDIVIDUAL IMAGES OF THE FUTURE

The preceding discussion of how orientations toward the future evolve suggests that the rapid pace of change characterizing modern society may have fundamentally altered the nature of individual images of the future. Unfortunately, we know relatively little about this matter because social scientists rarely investigate images of the future (at least in the way they have been defined here).[21] Techniques of isolating and relating the elements of these kinds of global images of the future are difficult to develop, but some interesting attempts have been made. As we shall see shortly, they focus either on individual images of the national future or on visions of the personal future.[22] Nonetheless, they are not frequently employed in research. Rather, the bulk of psychological investigations has focused on the place of the future in a general time perspective, while sociological research has centered on the antecedents of highly specific aspirations (usually educational and occupational).

Psychological interest in studying the future seems to have begun in the 1930s, when it focused on various aspects of images of the future. At that time, Nathan Israeli (1932b, 1933a, 1933b, 1933c) undertook a series of experiments on the predictive process. By questioning students about improbable and likely future events, located both in the near and distant future, he established that predictions rest on past experience rather than on fantasy. This line of investigation was subsequently pursued by McGregor (1938) and Cantril (1938) whose interest lay in isolating factors influencing prediction. With the aid of a questionnaire, they asked respondents to make a series of predictions which they related to social characteristics and general attitudes. Toch (1958) summarizes their findings, along with his own, in his discussion of a series of essays collected by Cantril a decade earlier on the state of the world in 1952. It appears that an ability to foresee novelty and change, as well as a cautious and tentative orientation, enhances correct prediction. Furthermore, immediate experience objectively influences prediction by conditioning the aspects of the future emphasized and has a subjective impact if the event forecast is perceived as vital to one's self-interest. Interest in the nature of prediction and in who is a good forecaster has largely subsided in the last twenty years, although an occasional article on the subject does appear. Avison and Nettler (1976), for example, have recently related predictions made in a variety of opinion surveys to education, political orientation, and optimism.

In recent years, psychological research dealing with the future has focused little on the content of images, but has grown out of the widespread concern with the nature of time orientations. One type of approach has been to examine the relative emphasis given past, present, and future (see, for example, Eson and Greenfield, 1962).[23] An interesting application of such an approach is presented in Lifton's (1964) discussion of the imagery of Japanese students, as revealed in a series of in-depth interviews. He finds that a future orientation is linked to the desire to radically alter prevailing individual and social patterns; the hope of reestablishing the emperor's authority is associated with a focus on the past; and satisfaction with the status quo goes with emphasis on the present.

Future time perspective (FTP), especially the length of its extension, has been more thoroughly studied than the question of the emphasis given various time dimensions. Of the various projective techniques employed for this purpose, two have predominated. One is a story or sentence completion technique. Respondents are given three sentences, one in each time tense, and are asked to write a story based on each. Analysis of the stories allows the researcher to say something about the extension and density (one event discussed versus several) of the FTP (Kastenbaum, 1963). The second technique presents the respondent with several present tense sentences, thus leaving more choice about whether stories should be written about the past, present, or future (Meade, 1971). Another way of investigating FTP is through the Future Events Test, which consists of a list of twenty-five things that might occur in the future (ranging from visiting relatives to getting more education to buying a house or getting divorced). The subject is asked to choose ten events and to indicate the date on which each will occur. The test score is the mean event occurrence date (Stein and Craik, 1965). Sometimes respondents are not presented with a predetermined set of events, but are simply asked to list ten things they expect to happen in the years to come and to date them (Heckel and Rajagopal, 1975).

These projective techniques have been used to study the FTP of a wide variety of groups. One of the most well-documented findings is that the mentally ill, especially schizophrenics, have a constricted time perspective, as the future is of little significance to them (see, for example, Wallace, 1956; Stein and Craik, 1965). Within groups drawn from the general population, on the other hand, FTP is clearcut and its span is no greater for young people than for older persons (Kastenbaum, 1963). According to McClelland, however, it is especially marked among high achievers; considerable research has dealt with this question (see, for example, Meade, 1971).

As if to compensate for the generality of psychology, sociology has tended to focus on highly specific aspects of images of the future. There is a wide literature on the extent to which educational and occupational aspirations vary among different subgroups of the population and on why this is the case. The initial impetus for this line of investigation seems to have been an article by Hyman (1953) in which he argued that upward social mobility is more restricted among lower class persons because they have lower aspirations than members of the middle class. At first, research in this area centered on ambition, or the general desire for success, but soon specific educational and occupational indicators began to be used. Aspirations for schooling and career are ascertained through questionnaire items, and the responses are related to both social background and contextual explanatory factors. In general, the research has revealed that respondents who are of lower socioeconomic status or minority group members tend to have limited aspirations. A number of explanations have been offered for this finding. Some state that is is primarily a result of the nature of the family setting, while others say peer group influences are crucial (see Duncan, 1968; Drew and Austin, 1972). Quite recently, it has been noted that aspirations differ not only in terms of race and class but also in terms of sex. Thus, some efforts have been made to examine the differing occupational or educational aspirations of women and to relate them to their family plans (see, for example, Angrist, 1972).

While sociological survey research has generally focused on investigating specific aspirations in isolation, a few studies have tried to tap various aspects of images of the future. One such study was undertaken by James A. Mau (1968), using a sample of Jamaican leaders in the process of leading their country to independence. His primary concern was to determine why some leaders foresaw positive progress for the future while others did not. Perceptions of progress were ascertained by asking the leaders being interviewed several questions about whether the future would be better than the present; 56 percent said it would be. In addition, Mau asked his respondents to indicate how the years to come would differ from today. A little over two-thirds discussed economic and social changes, while 45 percent spoke in political terms. These responses reflect the importance of industrial development and eradication of poverty for Jamaica's future. For purposes of comparison, Mau also interviewed a group of people in West Kingston, a large urban ghetto. These poor people saw political, economic, and social trends less favorably than did their leaders, but nonetheless two-thirds of them expressed the belief that the future would bring progress for Jamaica.[24]

Kurt Danziger (1963a) has developed an approach more qualitative than Mau's survey methods for isolating various aspects of individual images of the national future. He asked somewhat over 400 South African students to write "histories of the future." They were to imagine that they were historians of the twenty-first century and in this role to write a two- to three-page essay outlining the major events occurring between 1960 and 2010. The essays then served as the basis for isolating the nature of images of the national future. Danziger isolated five different orientations by coding the essays in terms of the inter-relationship of past, present, and future; the interrelationship of means and ends; the conception of social change; and the view of social causality. This method revealed that respondents of a Conservative bent thought the future would bring a resurrection of the past, while those with a catastrophic orientation believed that future events would negate what was good in the past and present. The Liberals, Techni-cists, and Revolutionaries all saw the future bringing pronounced im-provement, although the means by which this amelioration would occur differed. Not surprisingly, 46 percent of the African students viewed the future in revolutionary terms, while almost half of the Indians were Liberals. The white students tended to display one of the other three orientations, with a third of the English-speakers foreseeing catas-trophe and 38 percent of the Afrikaans-speakers putting their hopes in technology. Unfortunately, Danziger's rather unusual approach has not been adopted by other researchers; hence, the South African re-sponses cannot be viewed in a comparative perspective.

The only approach to studying individual images of the future, both national and personal, that has enjoyed any widespread currency is the Self-Anchoring Striving Scale developed by Hadley Cantril and Lloyd Free. It was developed to serve a twofold purpose: to permit subjects to express their thoughts about the future in terms familiar to them; and to elicit responses permitting cross-cultural comparison (Cantril and Free, 1962; Cantril, 1963; 1965, pp. 21-34). The scale is based on two questions asking respondents to describe the best possible future they can imagine for ten to twenty years hence, and the worst. The "best future," or their future hopes, forms the uppermost limit of a ten-point scale or ladder, while the "worst future," or their future fears, forms the lowest limit. Once the endpoints of the scale are defined in this manner, individuals are asked to rate themselves, and their country, in terms of their present position on the scale, their position five years ago, and their anticipated position five years hence.[25] This procedure allows respondents to express their concerns about the future without pre-structuring their answers. At the same time, the various scale rankings can be used in interclass and international comparisons, as can the content of expressed hopes and fears. On a national level, hopes and fears are compared in terms of whether the following major substantive concerns are expressed: political, economic, status of nation, international relations, and general (i.e., hope for continuation of status quo or have no fears). Hopes and fears for the personal future are distinguished in terms of those concerning: individuals or their families; other persons, the community, or the nation; and international affairs. (For a more detailed delineation of the content analysis categories, see Cantril, 1965, pp. 329–344).

During the early 1960s, the Self-Anchoring Striving Scale was administered in fourteen different countries.[26] The findings are discussed in a series of publications (Free, 1959, 1960a, 1960b, 1964a, 1964b; Janicki, 1960), of which a book by Cantril (1965) presents the broadest overview. It appears that people in the developed countries are fairly satisfied with the present and foresee limited progress in the future. In contrast, people in poorer countries are not particularly satisfied with the present and hope, as well as expect, that their situation will improve markedly in the future. This intercountry difference is reflected within nations too, in that persons of low socioeconomic status are most likely to have aspirations for improving their situation in the years ahead. In addition, education, age, and rural-urban residence serve to differentiate images of the national and personal future in all the countries studied. In spite of such differences, a number of common dimensions appeared everywhere: personal concerns were articulated in terms of standard of living, health, and opportunities for children; economic advancement was the overwhelming national preoccupation; and the future, both personal and national, was perceived as being better than the present. In the years since Cantril and Free's initial work, the Self-Anchoring Striving Scale has been employed by a number of other researchers (see, for example, Diez and Torregrosa, 1967, 1969; Kwok, Hong, and McDougall, 1969; Pirojnikoff and Hadar, 1973).

In addition to the Striving Scale, one other technique has been employed with some frequency to study images of personal futures. In the process of undertaking a study of how contemporary youth viewed its future, especially in light of the problematic world situation, James Gillespie and Gordon Allport developed the Future Autobiography. This is generated by asking respondents to imagine they are living in the year 2025, for example, and to write a 1,000- to 2,000-word essay describing their life experiences in the fifty intervening years. Analysis of these autobiographical chronicles yields a considerable insight into people's visions of their personal future.[27] Between 1949 and 1951, Gillespie and Allport (1955) asked approximately 200 students in each of ten[28] countries to write Future Autobiographies. They discovered a remarkable unanimity of outlook among the students. All saw the next ten years as having the greatest substance and as likely to yield the most happiness. They anticipated that their lives would revolve around their families, and they displayed similar cultural, intellectual, and occupational goals. Most believed war was needless but doubted that another world war could be prevented, especially since the prevalence of nationalism made the emergence of a world government dubious. In spite of this belief, most of the students hoped greater equality could be achieved, especially between the races. Although national differences between the students were limited, some distinctions did emerge, especially in terms of race and sex. Differences in terms of these characteristics have been confirmed by researchers who have made subsequent use of Future Autobiographies (see, for example, Danziger, 1963b; Williamson, Putnam, and Wurthmann, 1975; L'Institut d'Opinion Publique, 1968).

In sum, Future Autobiographies, the Self-Anchoring Striving Scale, and Future Histories provide promising approaches for delineating individual images of the future in global, yet specific, terms. In light of psychology's focus on general future time perspectives and sociology's preoccupation with highly delimited aspirations, the potential of these approaches has not yet been fully exploited. Part of the reason is that the unstructured data generated by the techniques present formidable analysis problems. Therefore, some effort is needed to delineate a precise set of analytical categories. Their development would tell us a good deal about the components of individual images of the future and how they are related to one another. It would also provide some of the tools needed to systematically investigate just what types of global visions people have of their personal and national future in a rapidly changing society. With such data on a wide spectrum of individuals, we would be able to begin assessing the extent to which continuous social change really disrupts individual orientations to the future. In addition, attention to personal transition strategies should reveal whether people spontaneously generate plans for reaching their future goals or whether this ability is alien to them. Armed with such detailed knowledge about the role images of the future play in individual lives, we might be able to make the average citizen a key element in the process of using idealistic visions to bring about a better tomorrow.

## NOTES

1. Robert Kennedy often quoted this passage by Alfred Lord Tennyson. George Bernard Shaw also made a similar statement.

2. Oddly enough, the authors delineating such visions rarely refer to them as "images of the future."

3. Mannheim (1936) offers an explanation for this state of affairs when he notes that instability in social class relations fosters the emergence of utopian visions. Since Western societies have not experienced sharp class antagonism in recent decades, one would not expect images of ideal futures to be plentiful. They would be only if class relations were so unstable as to threaten the social system as a whole. Since many of the developing nations can be described in this manner, they may provide fertile ground for the emergence of visions transcending the bounds of the present (Danziger, 1973a, p. 60).

4. This is discussed in more detail in the next section on transition strategies (see pages 186–187).

5. A more detailed discussion is presented in the section dealing with examples of images of the future in the making (see page 195).

6. The best example of this is the Futuribles volume on European federation. It is discussed in more detail in the section on images of the future in the making (see pages 195–196).

7. Although Bell and Mau's (1971, p. 23) initial definition of an image of the future as "an expectation about the state of things to come at some future time" is much broader than the one adopted here, they tend to circumscribe it in subsequent discussion. In delineating "directives for the scientific study of the future" (Bell and Mau, 1971, pp. 28–37), they specify six which make their view very similar to the one being pursued in these pages. They indicate that images of the future should (1) be based on a dynamic orientation to time and society; (2) recognize that the future is uncertain; (3) be related to basic values; (4) emphasize factors within human control; (5) "import the future into the present"; and (6) focus on desirable possibilities. Elsewhere, Bell and Mau indicate that in analyzing images of the future, one must focus on two major elements: the nature or content of the future foreseen, and the means of realizing the image (see Bell et al., 1971, pp. 51–53). Again, this approach is essentially that adopted in this chapter.

8. This is not to say they are not aware of the issue. Elsewhere, they note that one of the challenges of American social science is to insure that its research is not used to limit the future to a status quo beneficial only to the privileged few (see Bell and Mau, 1971, p. 3).

9. The World Order Models Project is one of the main elements of this movement. The course of its development and its general approach are outlined in the next section.

10. The problem of values is in many ways unique at the world level, as there are few universal goods and there is no ready means of ascertaining whether given values are widely shared. Thus, world order modelers must specify the basic values they are dealing with in more detail than is generally the case.

11. This approach involves the same mechanism as the future-bearing facts which are part of the Prospective method discussed earlier (see page 188).

12. H. D. Lasswell has been far more influential in fostering an idealistic orientation to the future than this brief reference indicates. He has been instrumental in introducing a future orientation to policy research and has contributed to the world order approach in international relations.

13. A case in point is Pierre Massé. While he was director of the French Plan,

he incorporated many aspects of Prospective into the planning process. How he proceeded is discussed in more detail in the next section (see page 195).

14. The Prospective approach has been applied in a variety of areas other than national economic planning. Some of these projects are discussed in a book edited by Cournand and Lévy (1973).

15. Adoption of a diversity of values was encouraged, but to avoid conflict, preferred goals had to be compatible with other sets of desired ends. This approach appears to be a promising one for preserving a plurality of individual values within a common normative framework.

16. This may well change in the next few years, for in 1971 Undersecretary General Simeon O. Adebo organized a conference to set up a United Nations Commission on New Perspectives in International Cooperation. Its mission is to examine future global concerns.

17. Of course, many individual scholars have employed elements of the approach in creating the future outlined here. Singling any one out is thus arbitrary, but Laszlo is chosen because the detail with which he discusses both his comprehensive image and possible transition strategies is unusual. One might, however, also have discussed a number of other visions, such as the recent book by Dennis Gabor (1972).

18. Much of the work being done in the environmental and developmental areas can be viewed as involving the formulation of positive idealistic images of the future. The plans specifying increased agricultural production, reduced population growth, and less energy consumption in the developed countries are purposely optimistic. They are drawn up to indicate what might be done rather than what will happen. The Food and Agriculture Organization Plan for 1965–1985 adopts this approach, for example, as does the economist Tinbergen (1975).

19. Hearn (1975) highlights the link between past, present, and future by discussing changes in English social protest activity between 1750 and 1850.

20. There are many examples of this type of orientation. Two prominent examples are *The Limits to Growth* (Meadows et al., 1972) and the recent book by Heilbroner (1974).

21. Life goals, which are a closely related topic, have not been examined with any greater frequency (Buehler, 1968a).

22. The definition outlined at the beginning of this article also specified that images of the future had to be linked to transition strategies. In discussing individual images of the future, this aspect of the definition will be ignored, primarily because there is no research about it. The extent to which people actually formulate clearcut plans for realizing their goals or images of the future is, however, an important empirical question that ought to be investigated.

23. Israeli (1932a) dealt with this in one of his initial sets of experiments, and much of his subsequent research grew out of it rather than out of his initial concern with prediction.

24. A survey-based approach similar to Mau's has been developed by Nehnevajsa (1960, 1961). He isolates the images of the national future prevalent in a country by asking a sample of leaders (i.e., parliamentarians) and future leaders (i.e., students) to comment on a series of specific future possi-

bilities. Anticipated future worlds are arrived at by asking respondents to specify the likelihood that certain future states will be realized at given points in time; to indicate the three most, and least, desirable future states for their own countries, the United States, and the Soviet Union; to describe their own, and their country's, sense of efficacy; and to delineate how their anticipations would be altered by major shifts in the world situation.

25. One can easily ask for ratings of the more distant future as well, and some people have done so (see Huber, 1974, pp. 92–93).

26. The nations studied were Brazil, Cuba, Dominican Republic, Egypt, India, Israel, Japan, Nigeria, Panama, Phillippines, Poland, United States, West Germany, and Yugoslavia.

27. Danziger's Future Histories are an adaptation of this approach.

28. The countries studied were Egypt, France, Israel, Italy, Japan, Mexico, New Zealand, South Africa, United States, and West Germany.

# REFERENCES

Allport, Gordon. 1961. *Pattern and Growth in Personality.* New York: Holt Rinehart and Winston.

Amara, Roy. 1974. "The Futures Field: Functions, Forms and Critical Issues." *Futures,* Volume 6 (August), 289–301.

Angrist, Shirley. 1972. "Variation in Women's Adult Aspirations During College." *Journal of Marriage and the Family,* Volume 34 (August), 465–468.

Atteslander, Peter. 1969. "Soziologie und Plandung." [Sociology and planning.] *Mens en Maatschappij,* Volume 44 (November/December), 469–478.

Avison, William R., and Gwynn Nettler. 1976. "World Views and Crystal Balls." *Futures,* Volume 8 (February), 11–21.

Baldridge, J. Victor. 1971. "Images of the Future and Organizational Change: The Case of New York University." In W. Bell and J. Mau (eds.), *The Sociology of the Future.* New York: Russell Sage Foundation, 271–293.

Bauer, Raymond A. 1973. "Keynote." In W. A. Hahn and K. F. Gordon (eds.), *Assessing the Future and Public Policy.* New York: Gordon and Breach Science Publishers, 5–15.

Beckwith, Burnham P. 1972. "The Predicament of Man? A Reply." *The Futurist,* Volume 6 (April), 62–64.

Bell, Wendell, and James A. Mau. 1970. "Images of the Future: Theory and Research Strategies." In J. McKinney and E. Tiryakian (eds.), *Theoretical Sociology: Perspectives and Developments.* New York: Appleton-Century-Crofts, 205–234.

——— (eds.). 1971. *The Sociology of the Future: Theory, Cases and Annotated Bibliography.* New York: Russell Sage Foundation.

Bell, Wendell, James A. Mau, Bettina J. Huber, and Menno Boldt. 1971. "A Paradigm for the Analysis of Time Perspectives and Images of the Future." In W. Bell and J. Mau (eds.), *The Sociology of the Future.* New York: Russell Sage Foundation, 45–55.

Beres, Louis R., and Harry R. Targ (eds.) 1975. *Planning Alternative World Futures: Values, Methods and Models.* New York: Praeger Publishers.

Berger, Gaston. 1973a. "Social Science and Forecasting." In A. Cournand

and M. Lévy (eds.), *Shaping the Future*. New York: Gordon and Breach Science Publishers, 11–19.

———. 1973b. "The Prospective Attitude." In A. Cournand and M. Lévy (eds.), *Shaping the Future*. New York: Gordon and Breach Science Publishers, 245–249.

———. 1973c. "Time." In A. Cournand and M. Lévy (eds.), *Shaping the Future*. New York: Gordon and Breach Science Publishers, 21–27.

———. 1973d. "Culture, Quality and Freedom." In A. Cournand and M. Lévy (eds.), *Shaping the Future*. New York: Gordon and Breach Science Publishers, 29–34.

———. 1973e. "Method and Results." In A. Cournand and M. Lévy (eds.), *Shaping the Future*. New York: Gordon and Breach Science Publishers, 101–106.

Bertaux, Pierre. 1968. "The Future of Man." In W. R. Ewald (ed.), *Environment and Change: The Next Fifty Years*. Bloomington: Indiana University Press, 13–20.

Bobrow, Davis. 1973. "Political and Social Forecasting: Purposes, Criteria and Recent Emphasis." In W. A. Hahn and K. F. Gordon (eds.), *Assessing the Future and Public Policy*. New York: Gordon and Breach Science Publishers, 67–68.

Boguslaw, Robert. 1971. "The Design Perspective in Sociology." In W. Bell and J. Mau (eds.), *The Sociology of the Future*. New York: Russell Sage Foundation, 240–258.

Bhagwati, Jagdish (ed.). 1972. *Economics and World Order: From the 1970's to the 1990's*. London: MacMillan.

Boulding, Elise. 1971. "Futurology and the Imagining Capacity of the West." In M. Maruyama and J. Dator (eds.), *Human Futuristics*. Honolulu: Social Science Research Institute.

Boulding, Kenneth E. 1965. *The Meaning of the Twentieth Century*. New York: Harper & Row.

Buehler, Charlotte. 1968a. "The Developmental Structure of Goal Setting in Group and Individual Studies." In C. Buehler and F. Massarik (eds.), *The Course of Human Life*. New York: Springer Publishing, 27–54.

———. 1968b. "The Integrating Self." In C. Buehler and F. Massarik (eds.), *The Course of Human Life*. New York: Springer Publishing, 330–350.

Calder, Nigel. 1969. "Goals, Foresight, and Politics." In R. Jungk and J. Galtung (eds.), *Mankind 2000*. Oslo: Universitetsforlaget, 251–255.

Cantril, Hadley. 1938. "The Prediction of Social Events." *Journal of Abnormal and Social Psychology*, Volume 33 (July), 364–389.

———. 1963. "A Study of Aspirations." *Scientific American*, Volume 208 (February), 41–45.

———. 1965. *The Pattern of Human Concerns*. New Brunswick, N.J.: Rutgers University Press.

———, and Lloyd Free. 1962. "Hopes and Fears for Self and Country." *Supplement to the American Behavioral Scientist*, Volume 6 (October).

Carlson, Jack W. 1973. "Impact of Future Forecasts on Federal Policy." In W. A. Hahn and K. F. Gordon (eds.), *Assessing the Future and Public Policy*. New York: Gordon and Breach Science Publishers, 197–214.

Cazes, Bernard. 1973. "Applied Futures Research in France: Some Critical Views." *Futures,* Volume 5 (June), 272–280.

Chaplin, George, and Glenn D. Paige (eds.). 1973. *Hawaii 2000: Continuing Experiment in Anticipatory Democracy.* Honolulu: University Press of Hawaii.

Clair, Pierre-Maurice. 1973. "The Four Problems of Prospective." In A. Cournand and M. Lévy (eds.), *Shaping the Future.* New York: Gordon and Breach Science Publishers, 223–234.

Cole, Sam. 1974. "World Models, Their Progress and Applicability." *Futures,* Volume 6 (June), 201–218.

Cottle, Thomas J., and Stephen L. Klineberg. 1974. *The Present of Things Future: Explorations of Time in Human Experience.* New York: Free Press.

Cournand, André F. 1973. "Predictive Philosophy and Method: Some Reflections on Their Preliminary Application to Medical Education." In A. Cournand and M. Lévy (eds.), *Shaping the Future.* New York: Gordon and Breach Science Publishers, 45–66.

――――, and Maurice Lévy (eds.). 1973. *Shaping the Future: Gaston Berger and the Concept of Prospective.* New York: Gordon and Breach Science Publishers.

Danziger, Kurt. 1963a. "Ideology and Utopia in South Africa: A Methodological Contribution to the Sociology of Knowledge." *British Journal of Sociology,* Volume 14 (March), 59–76.

――――. 1963b. "The Psychological Future of an Oppressed Group." *Social Forces,* Volume 42 (October), 31–40.

Dator, James A. 1971. "State of Hawaii Task Force Report on Political Decision-Making and the Law in the Year 2000." In M. Maruyama and J. Dator (eds.), *Human Futuristics.* Honolulu: Social Science Research Institute.

――――. 1974a. "Futuristics and the Exercise of Anticipatory Democracy in Hawaii." In A. Somit (eds.), *Political Science and the Study of the Future.* Hinsdale, Ill.: Dryden Press, 186–203.

――――. 1974b. "Neither There Nor Then: A Eutopian Alternative to the Development Model of Future Society." In *Human Futures: Needs, Societies and Technologies.* Guilford, England: IPC Science and Technology Press, 87–140.

de Jouvenel, Bertrand. 1963. "Introduction." In B. de Jouvenel (ed.), *Futuribles: Studies in Conjecture (I).* Geneva: Droz, ix–xi.

――――. 1965a. "Political Science and Prevision." *American Political Science Review,* Volume 59 (March), 29–38. Reprinted in A. Somit (ed.), *Political Science and the Study of the Future.* Hinsdale, Ill.: Dryden Press, 1974.

――――. 1965b. "Utopia for Practical Purposes." *Daedalus,* Volume 94 (Spring), 437–453.

――――. 1967. *The Art of Conjecture.* New York: Basic Books.

――――. 1968. "On Attending to the Future." In W. R. Ewald (ed.), *Environment and Change: The Next Fifty Years.* Bloomington: Indiana University Press, 21–29.

――――. 1969. "Technology as a Means." In K. Baier and N. Rescher (eds.), *Values and the Future.* New York: Free Press, 217–232.

――――. 1974. "A Word to Futurists." In *Human Futures: Needs, Societies, Technologies.* Guilford, England: IPC Science and Technology Press, 9–13.

―――― (ed.). 1965. *Futuribles: Studies in Conjecture (II).* Geneva: Droz.

Diez, Nicolas Juan, and Jose Roman Torregrosa. 1967. "Aplicacion de la Escala de Cantril en Espana: Resultados de un Estudio Preliminar." [Application of the Cantril scale in Spain: Results of a preliminary study.] *Revista Espanola de la Opinion Publica,* Volume 10 (October/December), 77–100.

——. 1969. "Posicion Social, Expectativas y Aspiraciones." [Social position, expectations and aspirations.] *Revista Espanola de la Opinion Publica,* Volume 15 (January/March), 69–100.

Drew, David, and Alexander Austin. 1972. "Undergraduate Aspirations: A Test of Several Theories." *American Journal of Sociology,* Volume 77 (May), 1151–1164.

Dror, Yehezkel. 1968. "The Role of Futures in Government." *Futures,* Volume 1 (September), 40–45.

——. 1973. "Translating Alternative Futures into Present Action." In G. Chaplin and G. D. Paige (eds.), *Hawaii 2000.* Honolulu: University Press of Hawaii, 120–132.

——. 1974. "Futures Studies—Quo Vadis?" In *Human Futures: Needs, Societies, Technologies.* Guilford, England: IPC Science and Technology Press, 169–176.

Duncan, Otis D., et al. 1968. "Peer Influences on Aspirations: A Re-interpretation." *American Journal of Sociology,* Volume 74 (September), 119–137.

Durand, Jacques. 1972. "A New Method for Constructing Scenarios." *Futures,* Volume 4 (December), 325–330.

Eson, M. E., and N. Greenfield. 1962. "Life Space: Its Content and Temporal Dimensions." *Journal of Genetic Psychology,* Volume 100 (March), 113–128.

Eulau, Heinz. 1958. "H. D. Lasswell's Developmental Analysis." *Western Political Quarterly,* Volume 11 (June), 229–242.

Falk, Richard A. 1975. *A Study of Future Worlds.* New York: Free Press.

Flacks, Richard. 1974. "Making History vs. Making Life: Dilemmas of an American Left." *Working Papers for a New Society,* Volume 2 (Summer), 56–71.

Flechtheim, Ossip K. 1971. *Futurologie: Der Kampf um die Zukunft.* [Futurology: The battle about the future.] Cologne: Verlag Wissenschaft und Politik.

Free, Lloyd. 1959. *Six Allies and a Neutral.* Glencoe, Ill.: Free Press.

——. 1960a. *Attitude of the Cuban People Toward the Castro Regime.* Princeton, N.J.: Institute for International Social Research.

——. 1960b. *The Dynamics of Philippine Politics.* Princeton, N.J.: Institute for International Social Research.

——. 1964a. *The Attitudes, Hopes, and Fears of Nigerians.* Princeton, N.J.: Institute for International Social Research.

——. 1964b. *Some International Implications of the Political Psychology of Brazilians.* Princeton, N.J.: Institute for International Social Research.

Freymond, Jacques. 1965. "Introduction—Forecasting and Europe." In B. de Jouvenel (ed.), *Futuribles: Studies in Conjecture (II).* Geneva: Droz, xiii–xxx.

Gabor, Dennis. 1964. *Inventing the Future.* New York: Alfred A. Knopf.

——. 1972. *The Nature Society.* New York: Praeger Publishers.

Galtung, Johan. Forthcoming. *The True Worlds: A Transnational Perspective.* New York: Free Press.

Gerlach, Luther. 1971. "Fumbling Freely into the Future." *1971 American*

*Anthropological Symposium on Cultural Futurology: Pre-Conference Volume.* Minneapolis: Office for Applied Social Science and the Future.

Gillespie, James M., and Gordon W. Allport. 1965. *Youth's Outlook on the Future.* Garden City, N.Y.: Doubleday.

Hearn, Frank. 1975. "Remembrance and Critique: The Uses of the Past for Discrediting the Present and Anticipating the Future." *Politics and Society,* Volume 5, Number 2, 201-227.

Heckel, Robert, and Jayalakshmi Rajagopal. 1975. "Future Time Perspective in Indian and American College Students." *Journal of Social Psychology,* Volume 95 (February), 131-132.

Heilbroner, Robert L. 1974. *An Inquiry into the Human Prospect.* New York: W.W. Norton.

Hoghton, Charles de, William Page, and Guy Streatfeild. 1971. ". . . And Now the Future: A PEP Survey of Futures Studies." *Political and Economic Planning,* Volume 37 (August).

Huber, Bettina J. 1974. "Some Thoughts on Creating the Future." *Sociological Inquiry,* Volume 44, Number 1, 29-39.

———, and Wendell Bell. 1971. "Sociology and the Emergent Study of the Future." *American Sociologist,* Volume 6 (November), 287-295.

Hyman, Herbert. 1953. "The Values Systems of Different Classes: A Social Psychological Contribution to the Analysis of Stratification." In R. Bendix and S. M. Lipset (eds.), *Class, Status and Power.* New York: Free Press, 426-442.

Israeli, Nathan. 1930. "Some Aspects of the Social Psychology of Futurism." *Journal of Abnormal and Social Psychology,* Volume 25 (July), 121-132.

———. 1932a. "The Social Psychology of Time." *Journal of Abnormal and Social Psychology,* Volume 27 (July), 209-213.

———. 1932b. "Wishes Concerning Improbable Future Events: Reactions to the Future." *Journal of Applied Psychology,* Volume 16, Number 5, 584-588.

———. 1933a. "Attitudes to the Decline of the West." *Journal of Social Psychology,* Volume 4 (February), 92-101.

———. 1933b. "Group Estimates of the Divorce Rate for the Years 1935-1975." *Journal of Social Psychology,* Volume 4 (February), 102-115.

———. 1933c. "Group Predictions of Future Events." *Journal of Social Psychology,* Volume 4 (May), 201-222.

Iyengar, M. S. 1972. "Can We Transform into a Post-Industrial Society?" In A. Toffler (ed.), *The Futurists.* New York: Random House, 190-193.

Janicki, Peter. 1960. *America Speaks Up.* Princeton, N.J.: Institute for International Social Research.

Jantsch, Erich. 1972a. *Technological Planning and Social Futures.* New York: Wiley/Halstead.

———. 1972b. "Forecasting and the Systems Approach: A Critical Survey." *Policy Sciences,* Volume 3 (December), 475-498.

Jungk, Robert. 1968a. "About 'Mankind 2000'." In S. Anderson (ed.), *Planning for Diversity and Choice.* Cambridge, Mass.: MIT Press, 79-85.

Jungk, Robert. 1968b. "Human Futures." *Futures,* Volume 1 (September), 34-39.

———. 1969. "Look-Out Institutions for Shaping the Environment." *Futures,* Volume 1 (March), 227-232.

————. 1973. "Three Modes of Futures Thinking." In G. Chaplin and G. D. Paige (eds.), *Hawaii 2000.* Honolulu: University Press of Hawaii, 101–119.

Kariel, Henry S. 1969. "Expanding the Political Present." *American Political Science Review,* Volume 63 (September), 768–776.

Kastenbaum, Robert. 1963. "Cognitive and Personal Futurity in Later Life." *Journal of Individual Psychology,* Volume 19 (November), 216–222.

Knigge, Rainer. 1973. "Demokratisierung von Planungsprozessen: Moeglichkeiten der Regionalplannung." [Democratizing planning processes: Possibilities for regional planning.] *Soziale Welt,* Volume 23, Number 4, 459–481.

Kostelanetz, Richard. 1971. "Visions for Our Time." *The Futurist,* Volume 5 (June), 112–114. Also appears as "Introduction." In R. Kostelanetz (ed.), *Social Speculations: Visions for Our Times.* New York: William Morrow.

Kothari, Rajni. 1974. *Footsteps into the Future: Diagnosis of the Present World and a Design for an Alternative.* New York: Free Press.

Kwok, Lai Cheng, Lim Pek Hong, and John McDougall. 1969. "An Exploratory Study of Aspirations for Self, Community and Country Among University of Singapore Students." *South-East Asian Journal of Sociology,* Volume 2 (May), 44–51.

Landheer, Bart. 1971. "Sociological and Psychological Aspects of Futurological Thinking." *Co-Existence,* Volume 8 (July), 85–95.

Laszlo, Ervin. 1974. *A Strategy for the Future: The Systems Approach to World Order.* New York: George Braziller.

Lemert, Edwin. 1970. *Legal Action and Social Change.* Chicago: Aldine Publishing.

Lewin, Kurt. 1935. *A Dynamic Theory of Personality.* New York: McGraw-Hill.

Lifton, Robert J. 1964. "Individual Patterns in Historical Change: Imagery of Japanese Youth." *Comparative Studies in Society and History,* Volume 6 (July), 369–383.

L'Institut d'Opinion Publique. 1968. "Des Jeunes Regardent Leur Avenir—Leurs Centres d'Interet, Leurs Craintes, Leurs Espoirs." [The young regard their future—Their foci of interest, their fears, their hopes.] *Sondages,* Volume 30, Number 3, 5–146.

Livesey, Lionel. 1973. "Participatory Planning for Higher Education." In W. A. Hahn and K. F. Gordon (eds.), *Assessing the Future and Public Policy.* New York: Gordon and Breach Science Publishers, 313–336.

McGrath, J. H. 1974. "Relevance Trees." In S. P. Hencley and J. R. Yates (eds.), *Futurism in Education: Methodologies.* Berkeley Calif.: McCutchen Publishing, 71–96.

McGregor, Douglas. 1938. "The Major Determinants of the Prediction of Social Events." *Journal of Abnormal and Social Psychology,* Volume 38 (April), 179–204.

McHale, John. 1967. "The People Future." *Architectural Design,* Volume 37 (February), 94–95.

————. 1972. "Shaping the Future: Problems, Priorities and Imperatives." In J. D. Roslansky (ed.), *Shaping the Future.* Amsterdam: North Holland, 3–15.

————, and Magda C. McHale. 1976. "An Assessment of Futures Studies Worldwide." *Futures,* Volume 8 (April), 135–145. Also appears in *Futures Studies: An International Survey.* New York: UNITAR Publication #E. 75.XV.FS/1.

Mannheim, Karl. 1936. *Ideology and Utopia.* London: Kegan Paul.

Marien, Michael. 1973. "Herman Kahn's 'Things to Come'." *The Futurist,* Volume 7 (February), 7–15.

Maruyama, Magoroh. 1972. "Toward Human Futuristics." *Co-Existence,* Volume 2 (November), 101–120.

———. 1973. "A New Logical Model for Futures Research." *Futures,* Volume 5 (October), 435–437.

Massé, Pierre. 1972. "Attitudes Toward the Future and Their Influence on the Present." *Futures,* Volume 4 (March), 24–29. Also appears in A. Cournand and M. Lévy (eds.), *Shaping the Future.* New York: Gordon and Breach Science Publishers, 1973.

———. 1973. "Forecasting and Prospective." In A. Cournand and M. Lévy (eds.), *Shaping the Future.* New York: Gordon and Breach Science Publishers, 45–66.

Massenet, Michel. 1963. "Les Methods de Prevision en Sciences Sociales." [The methods of conjecture in the social sciences.] *Futuribles,* number 66, Supplement to *Bulletin Sedeis* (Part 2), Volume 867 (November 1).

Mau, James A. 1968. *Social Change and Images of the Future: A Study of the Pursuit of Progress in Jamaica.* Cambridge, Mass.: Schenkman.

Mazrui, Ali A. 1975. *A World Federation of Cultures: An African Perspective.* New York: Free Press.

———, and Hasu Patel (eds.). 1973. *Africa in World Affairs.* New York: Third Press.

Meade, Robert D. 1971. "Future Time Perspectives of College Students in America and India." *Journal of Social Psychology,* Volume 83 (April), 175–182.

Meadows, Donella, Dennis Meadows, et al. 1972. *The Limits to Growth.* New York: Universe Books.

Mendlovitz, Saul H. 1975a. "Introduction." In R. Falk, *A Study of Future Worlds.* New York: Free Press.

——— (ed.). 1975b. *On the Creation of a Just World Order: Preferred Worlds for the 1990's.* New York: Free Press.

Mishen, E. J. 1971. "On Making the Future Safe for Mankind." *Public Interest,* Volume 24 (Summer), 33–61.

Muller, Herbert J. 1974. "The Vogue of Futurism." In H. J. Muller, *Uses of the Future.* Bloomington: Indiana University Press, 3–13.

Murphy, Gardner. 1961. *Human Potentialities.* New York: Basic Books.

Nehnevajsa, Jiri. 1960. *Elements of Project Theory: From Concepts to Design.* Air Force Office for Scientific Research. Technical Note TN-60-6 (October 20).

———. 1961. *A Methodology for the Analysis of Political Futures.* Air Force Office of Scientific Research. AFOSR-374 (May 1).

Organization for Economic Co-operation and Development. Symposium. 1969. "The Bellagio Declaration on Planning." *Futures,* Volume 1 (March), 197–201.

Ozebekhan, Hasan. 1965. *The Idea of a "Look-Out" Institution.* Santa Monica, Calif.: System Development Corporation.

———. 1968. "The Triumph of Technology: 'Can' Implies 'Ought'." In S.

Anderson (ed.), *Planning for Diversity and Choice.* Cambridge, Mass.: MIT Press, 204–219.

————. 1969. "Toward a General Theory of Planning." In E. Jantsch (ed.), *Perspectives of Planning.* Paris: Organization for Economic Co-operation and Development.

————. 1974. "The Emerging Methodology of Planning." *Fields Within Fields Within Fields . . . ,* Volume 10 (Winter), 63–80.

Peccei, Aurelio. 1973. "The Club of Rome—The New Threshold." *Simulation,* Volume 20 (June), 199–206.

Piaget, Jean, and B. Inhelder. 1958. *The Growth of Logical Thinking from Childhood to Adolescence.* New York: Basic Books.

Pirojnikoff, Leo, and Ilena Hadar. 1973. "Self-Perception Differences Among Kibbutz and City Adults in Israel and Jewish and Non-Jewish Adults in the United States." *Journal of Psychology,* Volume 84 (May), 105–110.

Plan Europe 2000. 1972. *The Future Is Tomorrow: 17 Prospective Studies.* The Hague: Martinus Nijhoff.

Polak, Fred L. 1961. *The Image of the Future: Enlightening the Past, Orienting the Present, Forecasting the Future.* 2 vols. New York: Oceana Publications. Also abridged version by Elise Boulding, 1973. *The Image of the Future.* San Francisco: Elsevier/Jossey-Bass.

————. 1971. *Prognostics: A Science in the Making Surveys and Creates the Future.* New York: Elsevier.

Porter, David O. 1974. "Strategic Forecasts and the Politics of Mobilizing Resources." In A. Somit (ed.), *Political Science and the Study of the Future.* Hinsdale, Ill.: Dryden Press, 174–186.

Sage, Daniel, and Richard B. Chobot. 1974. "The Scenario as an Approach to Studying the Future." In S. P. Hencley and J. R. Yates (eds.), *Futurism in Education: Methods.* Berkeley Calif: McCutchen Publishing, 161–178.

Sakamoto, Yoshikazu. 1972. "The Rationale of the World Order Models Project." Proceedings of the 66th Annual Meeting of the American Society of International Law. *American Journal of International Law,* Volume 66 (September), 245–252.

Starling, Grover. 1973. "Political Implications of a Look-Out Institution." *Futures,* Volume 5 (October), 484–490.

Stein, Kenneth B., and Kenneth H. Craik. 1965. "Relationship Between Motoric and Ideational Activity Preferences and Time Perspective in Neurotics and Schizophrenics." *Journal of Consulting Psychology,* Volume 29 (October), 460–467.

Theoblad, Robert. 1968a. "Planning *with* People." In W. R. Ewald (ed.), *Environment and Change: The Next Fifty Years.* Bloomington: Indiana University Press, 182–185.

————. 1968b. "Policy Formation for New Goals." In R. Theobald (ed.), *Social Policies for America in the Seventies.* Garden City N.Y.: Doubleday, 149–169.

Tinbergen, Jan. 1975. "Assigning World Priorities: Theory and Application." In B. Pregal, H. D. Lasswell, and J. McHale (eds.), *Environment and Society in Transition. World Priorities.* New York: New York Academy of Sciences (Annals volume 261), 25–32.

Toch, Hans H. 1958. "The Perception of Future Events: Case Studies in Social Prediction." *Public Opinion Quarterly,* Volume 22 (Spring), 57–66.

Toffler, Alvin. 1970. *Future Shock.* New York: Random House.

Tugwell, Franklin. 1974. "Modernization, Political Development and the Study of the Future." In A. Somit (ed.), *Political Science and the Study of the Future.* Hinsdale, Ill.: Dryden Press, 155–173.

University of Sussex Science Policy Research Unit. 1973. "The Limits to Growth Controversy" and "The Ideological Background to the Limits to Growth Controversy." *Futures,* Volume 5 (February and April), 4–235. Also published as H. Sam Cole, Christopher Freeman, et al. 1973. *Models of Doom: Critique of the Limits to Growth.* New York: Universe Books.

Wallace, M. 1956. "Future Time Perspective in Schizophrenia." *Journal of Abnormal and Social Psychology,* Volume 52 (March), 240–245.

Waskow, Arthur I. 1969. "Looking Forward: 1999." In R. Jungk and J. Galtung (eds.), *Mankind 2000.* Oslo: Universitetsvorlaget, 79–98.

———. 1972. "Toward a Democratic Futurism." In A. Toffler (ed.), *The Futurists.* New York: Random House, 85–95.

Williams, Charles W. 1972. "Inventing a Future Civilization." *The Futurist,* Volume 6 (August), 137–141.

Williamson, Nancy E., Sandra L. Putnam, and H. Regina Wurthmann. 1975. "Future Autobiographies: Expectations of Marriage, Children and Careers." Paper read at the annual meeting of the Society for the Study of Social Problems, San Francisco, Calif.

Winthrop, Henry. 1968. "The Sociologist and the Study of the Future." *American Sociologist,* Volume 2 (May), 136–145.

———. 1971. "Utopia Construction and Future Forecasting: Problems, Limitations and Relevance." In W. Bell and J. Mau (eds.), *The Sociology of the Future.* New York: Russell Sage Foundation, 78–105.

IAN H. WILSON

# Scenarios

> .......... The play's the thing
> Wherein I'll catch the conscience of the king.

> Wm. Shakespeare, *Hamlet* II, ii

Fanciful though it may seem to start this chapter with a quotation from Shakespeare, there is a logical connection. The link starts with the definition of the term in question, *scenario*. As Webster's dictionary tells us, its prime meaning is "an outline or synopsis of a play": with the advent of the movies, it came also to stand for a "screenplay." Therefore, inherent in the term are elements of the dramatic, the fictional, and the sketchy—all, as we shall see, essential characteristics of the use of scenarios in futures research.

There is an added measure of appropriateness in the quotation, for scenarios are admirably suited to raising (or catching) the *consciousness,* if not the conscience, of anyone interested in the future. Because scenarios are essentially stories, and because most of us are captivated by good stories, scenarios "constitute perhaps the most communicable form of futures conjecture" (SRI/CSSP, 1975, p. 198). There is nothing quite like a "story about the future" for catching the consciousness—of kings and subjects, scholars and laymen—about where we might be going and how we might get there.

## THE NATURE OF SCENARIOS

What, more precisely, is a scenario? In the context of futures research, we might define it as "an exploration of an alternative future" or, more precisely, as "an outline of one conceivable state of affairs, given certain assumptions" (SRI/CSSP, 1975, p. 193). Herman Kahn, who was perhaps the first to use the term *scenario* in planning while still at RAND Corporation in the 1950s, has given us an even more detailed definition: "a hypothetical sequence of events constructed for the purpose of focusing attention on causal processes and decision points" (Kahn and Wiener, 1967).

It is useful at the outset to specify some of the essential characteristics of a scenario. The first, and perhaps the most important, characteristic is that they are *hypothetical*—a point noted in all of these
definitions. This fact stems from the nature of the future and the essential limitations of futures research. I have pointed out elsewhere that
"however good our futures research may be, we shall never be able to
escape from the ultimate dilemma that all of our knowledge is about the
past, and all our decisions are about the future" (Wilson, 1975, p. 6).
The future is, and must always remain, in a fundamental sense, unknowable. The best that futures research can do is to explore alternative
possible futures, and for such an exploration scenarios are admirably
suited. Since we are confronted with such uncertainty about the future,
it would be the height of folly to take a single, simplistic view of it, and to
claim that we can predict *the* future. Rather, we should discipline
ourselves and limit our claims to exploring multiple, possible futures.
For this reason, we should seldom use a single scenario: our best hope
is to try to bracket the future by means of a set of scenarios, each
dealing with a possible alternative.

Thus, we should take note of an essential limitation of scenarios. No
scenario will ever materialize exactly as described because of unforeseen events and responses to them and because the precise combination of events selected for a scenario is highly unlikely to develop. To
recognize this limitation is as much a part of wisdom as is the admis-
sion that we cannot know or predict the future. But the limitation does
not negate the value of the exercise since, even with it, scenarios can
fulfill important purposes in forecasting and planning, as noted below.

A second characteristic is the fact that a scenario professes to be
*only a sketch,* an outline. In the theater or the motion picture industry, a
scenario provides a synopsis of the action and brief descriptions of the
principal characters; it does not go into the full details that are to be
found in the actual script. So, in futures research, a scenario seeks only
to map out the key "branching points" of the future, to highlight the
major determinants that might cause the future to evolve from one
"branch" rather than another, and to sketch in the prime consequences
of a causal chain. Selectivity is, therefore, of the essence in developing
a scenario—selectivity and, as in the theater, a degree of dramatic
ability in highlighting the flow of the action and making it interesting.

Third, scenarios are (or should be) *multifaceted* and *holistic* in their
approach to the future. In the early days of futures research, and still to
a great extent in popular literature, it is the isolated event, the specific
prediction that rivets attention ("By 1985 more than half the homes in
the country will have picture-on-the-wall television"); also, there is a
fatal fascination with particular dates in the future, e.g., 1984, 2000, or

the tricentennial 2076. However, history is a "booming, buzzing confusion" of events, trends, and discontinuities; it is constantly in motion and so is more accurately represented by a motion picture than by a snapshot. Scenarios have a special ability to represent this multifaceted, interacting flow process, combining (when appropriate) demographic changes, social trends, political events, economic variables, and technological developments. Of course, the scope of a scenario's approach varies with its topic; a scenario of the future of U.S. society must encompass more variables than one dealing with, shall we say, a particular community or product. But the principle of holism remains as a guiding tenet in the development of scenarios, for it is the cross-impact of events and trends that gives history (and the future) its dynamic. It is this dynamism that we must try to reproduce in our futures research.

Scenarios, in the form of treatises on utopias and dystopias, have enjoyed a long and respected history, at least from the time of Sir Thomas More (1478–1535), if not from Plato's description of his ideal *Republic* in the fourth century B.C. However, it is principally with the post-Kahn initiative period that we are concerned here; even in this limited time span, scenarios have risen to top-ranking popularity in futures research. René Zentner of Shell Oil Company gives us one indicator of their popularity:

A search covering only English-language business literature for the past five years turned up 33 articles discussing scenarios of the future covering such diverse topics as: the future of the actuarial profession, the role of management in dealing with governmental intervention, the seizure of Arab oil in the event of another oil embargo, the handling of small-bank assets and liabilities, and future problems of the pulp and paper industry (1975, pp. 23–24).

The onset of the energy crisis produced a spate of energy futures scenarios—the best known being those of Project Independence (Federal Energy Administration, 1974) and of the Ford Foundation's Energy Policy Project (Freeman, 1974)—and brought the term to the forefront of public awareness. (Scenarios in this case might truly be said to have been used in an attempt to "catch the conscience of the people" as to the seriousness of the energy problem—so far, it must be said, with only indifferent success.) Perhaps best known of all are the scenarios in *The Limits to Growth* (Meadows et al., 1972) which deal with the global consequences of population growth, resource usage, capital formation, and pollution.

Scenarios have been used in defense planning (Kahn's treatise on "thinking about the unthinkable" is a popular version of this genre) and in delineating alternatives for U.S. agricultural policy (SRI/LRPS, 1975) and environmental policy (EPA, 1975). They have been incorporated into the planning efforts of corporations, e.g., Shell Oil Company (Zentner, 1975) and General Electric Company (GE, 1971), and they have formed the basis for scholarly examinations of the future (Bell, 1968). They have come of age as an approved methodology for futures research.

## THE PURPOSE AND USES OF SCENARIOS

In defining scenarios, I have suggested that they attempt to integrate individual analyses of trends and potential events into a holistic picture of the future ("weaving the threads into a pattern"); in this process, to provide for, and describe, the interaction of these trends and events; and ultimately, to explore the possible course of alternative futures. Their uses, once constructed, are many. On the one hand, they may be designed merely to entertain, to satisfy that innate curiosity about the future that seems to affect most of us. On the other hand, they can be more seriously and precisely used as frameworks for planning.

It was in this latter sense that scenarios were used as part of General Electric's approach to strategic planning in 1971. One way of looking at strategic planning is to view it as an attempt to optimize the "fit" between an organization and its future, changing environment. This is true whether the organization is a corporation or a government agency, a labor union or an educational institution, a community or a society. Every social institution is conditioned by the society of which it is a part; as the society changes, so must each institution change, if it is to adapt and succeed. A prerequisite for corporate or other planning must, therefore, be a sensing of incipient societal change, whether the changes be demographic, political, economic, or technological. So it is that, in General Electric's planning process, the long-term contextual forecast is the starting point: it provides an assessment of the future context in which an optimal corporate "fit" can be determined. Clearly, scenarios—synoptic views of the total future environmental possibilities—offer an attractive and convincing way of displaying these future contexts.

In electing this methodology, we stated our objectives for the scenarios as follows:

1. To combine alternate environmental developments into a framework which is relatively consistent and relevant to the future of the company.
2. To identify "branching points," potential discontinuities and contingencies which will serve as early warning systems, and for which contingency plans can be prepared.

3. To formulate a framework which makes it possible to translate alternate environmental developments into economic terms and alternate economic forecasts. (In effect, the scenarios served as the basis for the long-range economic forecasts.)
4. To provide the basis for analyzing the range of possible outcomes which result from the interaction between alternate environments and:
   —variable industry/market growth;
   —Company operating results on current trajectories, thus seeing how the Company as a whole (with its mix of products and services) responds to these consistent futures.
5. To test the outcomes of various Company and competitor strategies in alternate environments.

(GE, 1971, pp. i–ii)

Because there is no inevitability to the future and because scenarios are used to present varying views of the possible, they can be highly useful in marking out the limits of the possible for an organization to help shape its environment. Like politics, it might be said, scenario-building and planning are facets of "the art of the possible." In defining strategic planning as an attempt to optimize the fit between an organization and its future environment, I do not intend to imply that an organization has to be a purely passive instrument. Indeed, the very commitment to strategic planning and environmental analysis is persuasive evidence of a belief in proactive, as opposed to reactive, behavior. This proactive, or anticipatory, behavior can manifest itself both in timely internal adaptation to developing external trends and in external action to help shape those trends to the maximum extent possible.

In this sense, then, scenarios can be used in planning to help define:

1. Trends that are probable but "shapeable" (at least to their impacts on an organization); e.g., legislative trends, if identified sufficiently early.
2. Trends that are probable but not amenable to organizational influence; e.g., major demographic shifts.
3. Trends that are possible and "shapeable" e.g., technological developments.
4. Trends that are possible but not amenable to (or not worth the effort of) organizational influence; e.g., possible climate changes.

The above division is not, of course, the only classification of trends. Nor are scenarios the only way of displaying them and sorting them out; but with a holistic and interactive approach, scenarios are a superior and, in my judgment, the preferred way. They can help an organization to map out its environment and to sort out its priorities and options. They are "helpful in 'freeing up' a planner's conventional vision of reality" (SRI/CSSP, 1975, p. 195). They can appreciably improve the ability of an organization to see the future as a whole, rather than piecemeal, "in order to maximize the initiatives it chooses to take, and minimize the reactions it is forced to take" (Wilson, 1975, p. 2).

## THE DEVELOPMENT OF SCENARIOS

A prototypical pattern for the development of scenarios is provided by the sequence of work involved in the preparation of the long-term contextual forecast for General Electric's strategic planning process in 1971 (GE, 1971; Wilson, 1974). This forecast, which provides the framework for subsequent planning, culminated in a set of four alternative scenarios, developed in three stages (see Figure 1).

1. *Sectoral Forecasts:* In this first stage, the basic identification and analysis of discrete future trends and developments was carried forward in nine sectors: two international (geopolitical/defense, economic), and seven domestic (social, political, legal, economic, technological, manpower, financial). In each of these sectors, the following elements were present:
   a. a brief historical review (1960–1970) to give background and perspective and to indicate the nature and momentum of then current trends;
   b. an analysis of the most probable forces for change in order to provide a benchmark forecast (or, in Herman Kahn's term, a "surprise-free" future) for 1971–1980;
   c. identification and assessment of potential discontinuities—major inflection-points in the probable trends, which might lead to "canonical variations" (to use another of Kahn's terms) of the surprise-free future;
   d. enumeration of the key strategic and policy implications of these trends for General Electric.
   Collectively, these nine sectoral analyses supplied an extensive data base of forecasted trends, events, and discontinuities. However, they were segmented views—"tunnel visions," as I have called them—of the future, which took inadequate account of the possible interactions among sectors.
2. *Cross-Impact Analysis:* To identify what these intersectoral effects might be, cross-impact analysis (see chapter by Stover and Gordon) was used. First, however, it was necessary to

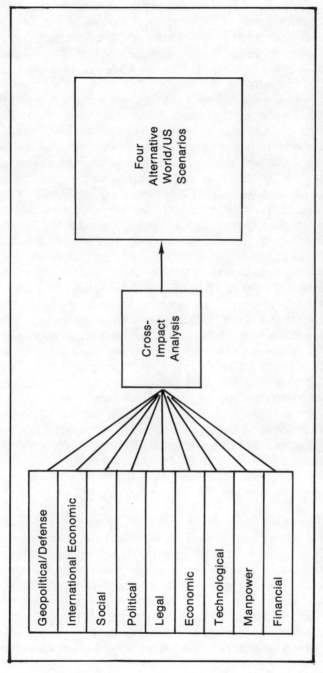

**Figure 1.** Schematic Description of General Electric's Long-Term Environmental Forecast

reduce the total inventory of trends, events, and discontinuities (developed in the first stage) to manageable proportions. The literally hundreds of discrete forecasts were simply too numerous to encompass in a cross-impact matrix. This reduction was achieved by scoring the forecasts as to (a) probability and (b) importance to the company's planning, and then selecting the fifty or so trends/events with the highest combined rating of probability and importance. (This double-barreled scoring is essential: scenario development—and planning—must take note of future trends and events which, however low their probability, would have major impacts on the organization in question, *should they occur.* Conversely, it may be able to ignore, or lay to one side, highly probable events that are irrelevant to the organization.) Working on the residual trends/ events, the cross-impact analysis supplied the dynamic of interactive relationships so essential to scenarios. In effect, this type of analysis traces "domino effects," with one event triggering another, until it is possible to construct an internally consistent configuration of a possible future.

3. *Scenario-Writing:* The final form taken by this environmental forecast was a set of four internally consistent scenarios, derived from varying combinations of discontinuities and the chain reactions revealed by the cross-impact matrix, and describing alternative views of the U.S. and world future between 1971 and 1980. Included in this set were:
   a. a benchmark (or "surprise-free") scenario;
   b. a scenario of "more inward-looking" societies (essentially, a continuation of the then current trajectory);
   c. a scenario of "more integrated" societies (or what might be termed "the best of all possible worlds");
   d. a scenario of "more disarrayed" societies (or what might be termed "the worst of all possible worlds").[1]

There is, of course, nothing immutable in this approach to scenario development. Other approaches may be less detailed and more intuitive; or they might short-circuit the first stage by drawing on readily available data banks of forecasts.[2] This approach does, however, serve to illustrate some key steps and elements, and acts as a backdrop to consideration of answers to some commonly asked questions.

*How should scenarios be selected?:* On very large topics, such as the future of U.S. society, there would seem to be a virtually endless number of conceivable scenarios, limited only by the imagination of the forecaster. Even on smaller topics, such as the future of the automobile or retailing, the range is impressively large. Obviously, there must be some rational basis for selecting a limited number of scenarios for the topic at hand.

René Zentner suggests three criteria for testing scenarios: credibility, utility, and intelligibility:

If the scenarios are not *credible,* planners will have great difficulty developing corporate strategies for them. To make the scenarios believed and accepted by planners, the draftsman must anticipate their disbelief. . . .

If the scenarios are not *useful,* they will be of no avail to the planners. Thus, their contents must be of facts and data relevant to the problems of the planners. . . .

Finally, the scenarios must be set forth in a manner *easy to understand* and use.

(1975, p. 30, emphasis added)

There can scarcely be any quarrel with these criteria. Certainly, *relevance* must be a prime consideration—relevance to the interests of the organization in question, relevance to the key policy and planning issues being addressed. Thus, a future U.S. society scenario would be focused differently, depending on whether a corporation or a church was the planning group. In one case, the main elements might be changes in employment, income, consumption patterns, and attitudes toward business, and in the other case, changes in values, family life-style, and attitudes toward organized religion. Clearly, then, the questions to be asked, before deciding on the selection of scenarios, are: What are the segments of the total environment that critically affect our organization? Which are the dominant forces operating in those segments of the context?

Figure 2 illustrates one way of mapping out a key contextual segment (in this case, future consumer markets) in an effort to identify the dominant operative forces and the impact they have on this environment. For instance, this "map" sketches in the outlines of the dynamic interactions among economic growth, government policies, demographic trends, and changes in values/life-styles in order to pinpoint the key impact points of these forces on the flow and allocation of consumer spending. At each impact point, one or more questions should be raised as to the future nature and extent of the impact. For instance:

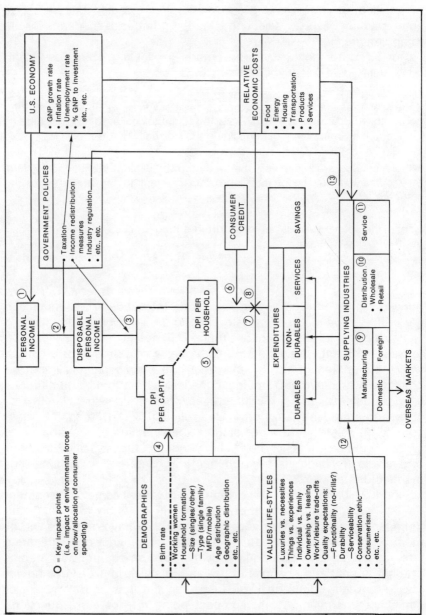

**Figure 2.** Schematic Outline for a Future Consumer Markets Scenario

KEY IMPACT POINT    QUESTIONS AS TO FUTURE IMPACT

1        What will be the future rate of economic growth, and how will this affect personal income growth ("affluence aspirations")?

What impact will the rate of inflation have on (a) consumer expectations, (b) consumption patterns, and (c) savings?

2        Will taxes take an increasing, decreasing, or constant share of total personal income?

3        Will taxes, transfer payments, and the like be structured to introduce a further measure of income redistribution?

The totality of the answers to these questions should provide not only a data base of specific trend forecasts but also—and this is particularly important—a frame of reference for selecting and developing the scenario. Completion of this "mapping of the territory" should bring to light, for instance, the major areas of uncertainty about the future and the key "branching points" (i.e., the points at which a trend may go in one of two, or several, divergent directions), which frequently suggest the basis for selecting alternative scenarios.

In General Electric's experience in 1971, for example, analyses revealed that the major factors producing significant variations among scenarios were external world events; U.S. foreign policy responses; social developments within the United States; and governmental and business responses to pressures and new demands. These, in effect, were the key branching points around which the set of four alternative scenarios was organized. In another example—in this case, a study of future trends in product quality (consumer expectations, legislated requirements, work force interest/capability, etc.)—the key determinant of the future was judged to be, not so much social, political, economic, or technological trends per se, as the nature of the response of business to those trends. Around that branching point, therefore, were developed four scenarios depicting the possible outcomes resulting from the adoption by business of a reactive, defensive, accommodative, or proactive strategy. Two scenarios on the future of business based on a similar branching appear on pages 236–237.

In sum, then, the selection of scenarios should be based on relevance; organized around key branching points; and meet Zentner's criteria of credibility, utility, and intelligibility.

## TWO SCENARIOS ON THE FUTURE OF BUSINESS

On the theory that future outcomes can, to some extent, be shaped by constructive, anticipatory action, this pair of scenarios was developed in 1973 (as part of a set of four) to illustrate the differences that might flow from divergent business responses to the emerging "qualitative expectations" of the post-WW II generation in the United States.

### SCENARIO OF A REACTIVE BUSINESS RESPONSE

"Beset by inflation, recession, shortages and a profit squeeze, and confronted by the recent spate of newly-legislative requirements (e.g., EEO, OSHA, product safety, pollution control), business opts for a policy of 'minimum feasible compliance.' Having no realistic option but to comply with the law, companies attempt to deal with the 'revolution of qualitative expectations' simply by adhering to the minimum requirements of new statutes. They challenge administrative interpretations of the law whenever possible, and resist pressures for new legislation wherever they develop.

"For a while the public, distracted by concern over rising prices, unemployment, and declining incomes, and disillusioned and distrustful in the post-Watergate climate, is content to see the assimilation and enforcement of 1970–1973 legislation. Meanwhile, however, the basic forces working toward a further shift in societal values continue to work their way through society, and a 'business-as-usual' attitude on the part of companies does little or nothing to deal with the developing challenge.

"The advent of the political year 1976, and the emergence of a younger, better educated and more aggressive work force and electorate set the stage for a new round of anti-business legislation. In particular, the perceived failure of business to deal adequately with the conflicting claims of the energy crisis and a clean environment leads to the introduction of bills, and the writing of planks in party platforms, to control business growth and investment, and to restructure major industries. A change of Administration and continued business 'heel-dragging' ensure passage of many of these bills by 1978.

"At the same time, a basic inability to deal with the 'quality of work' expectations of the new work force leads to progressively declining morale and productivity, increasing unionization, alienation and 'whistle-blowing.' Business, suffering a crisis of confidence and failure of nerve, is by now in a virtual state of siege, harassed by government regulation, beset by boycotts and class-action suits, 'betrayed' by its employees, and obsessed with a 'fortress mentality.' All that remains is the final step of public control and take-over of major corporations."

## SCENARIO OF A PRO-ACTIVE BUSINESS RESPONSE

"Compliance with both the letter and the spirit of current laws, and the sponsorship of new legislation and public information programs, are only starting points in this strategy. These efforts are buttressed by the establishment and enforcement of standards and self-policing activities on such matters as advertising, consumer rights and product safety.

"The major emphasis, however, is not on the legislative/educative aspects, but rather on innovative approaches to corporate marketing, production and management policies that, over the next decade, lead to a sweeping reform of business relations with customers, employees, government and the public. The need for thorough-going revisions of many conventional methods and policies flows from an awareness that, in many instances (such as pollution abatement, conservation of energy/materials, product servicing, job re-structuring), a 'tinkering' or 'additive' approach is not only less effective, but also more costly in the long run.

"Progress, inevitably, is slow because of institutional inertia, costs and conflicting claims on management attention. But it is sufficiently noticeable that the gap between expectations and performance is kept manageable and tension does not reach the breaking-point. Although corporate mistakes occur, and are well publicized, the public attitude toward them is marked by a greater degree of tolerance than in other scenarios. Penalties are imposed more selectively, and Congress is less apt to reach for 'shotgun' legislation. Such laws as are passed tend to embody and codify the best of current business practices.

"The value of a pro-active response becomes apparent, too, in the work force area. As the changing composition and wants/needs of the labor force reach critical levels in the latter half of the decade, the early experiments in job enlargement/flexible scheduling/participation start to pay rich dividends in enabling companies to attract and retain a committed and productive work force.

"Pressure from consumer, environmental and other interest groups continues to be a major factor, but a great openness in corporate communications (including more voluntary disclosure of corporate information) keeps this pressure at a low level of acrimony. In general, while there may be greater 'publicization' of the corporation than there was in 1970, there is markedly less 'politicization' of economic decision-making than in the other scenarios."

*How many scenarios should be selected?* There is no easy answer to this question, but there are two factors that tend to limit the number. One, of course, is the tendency for proliferation to confuse, rather than illuminate, the issue. If, as suggested above, scenarios must meet the criterion of utility, then it should be borne in mind that, typically, planning simply cannot use as many as, say, six scenarios on a given topic at any one time. The mind of the planner boggles at such a number and arbitrarily selects a lesser number without perhaps fully weighing the pros and cons of such a selection.

A second limiting factor is the feasibility of monitoring and follow-up action. Scenarios are intended to be alternative views of possible futures, but one will ultimately be judged to be the most probable and so form the basis for planning.[3] It therefore becomes critically important to compare events and trends as they actually unfold with the forecasts made in this scenario (and the others), in order to determine whether the basis for decisions continues to be valid. In other words, constant monitoring is a necessary sequel to developing scenarios. The sheer volume of work involved in this monitoring means that too great a number of scenarios cannot be adequately tracked into the future.

On the other hand, two scenarios are almost certainly too few and lend themselves too easily to being characterized as "good" and "bad" (from the point of view of the interests of the planning organization). Even a set of three is vulnerable to being labeled as "high," "low," and "middle ground," with the middle one being selected as the safest bet. (This is particularly so when the focus of the scenarios is on a quantifiable trend, e.g., future growth rate for the economy or usage of electricity.) This problem can be avoided by careful and distinctive characterization of scenarios. Sets of either three or four can usually balance these counterpoised limiting factors and are thus to be preferred.

*How should scenarios be presented?* The form of presentation depends almost equally on the type of subject matter to be covered and the type of audience to be addressed. On a broad subject, such as the future of business addressed to a general audience, a discursive and reasonably dramatic text, such as is used in the banking scenarios, may be most appropriate. On the other hand, energy futures scenarios to be used in business planning tend to require more detailed tables and charts and to make relatively less use of narrative text. However, it should be remembered that one of the advantages of scenarios is their ability to integrate quantitative and qualitative data; it would be foolish to nullify that advantage by an exclusive reliance on either text or tables. We should not hesitate to confront the layman with statistical evidence or the executive with "soft" data.

General Electric's 1971 excursion into scenario-writing resulted in a twenty-page writeup arranged under the following headings:

1. A history of Common Developments—events or trends that were judged to be relatively constant in all four scenarios (see Appendix for this listing).
2. A tabular summary of the major characteristics of each scenario (see Appendix).
3. Translation of the scenarios into four alternative forecasts of U.S. gross national product in 1980, analyzed by inputs and by sectors.
4. Identification of Major Potential Discontinuities/Contingencies that formed the bases for alternative scenarios (e.g., "increased U.S. protectionism" became one of the bases for Scenarios II and IV; and "faster trend in leisure demands" an element in Scenario III).
5. More detailed writeups of each scenario, spelling out (a) assumptions as to specific developments, and (b) assessment of major implications.

Again, there is nothing sacrosanct about such an arrangement or about the level of detail included in this example. This listing and the entries in the Appendix are intended only to offer some concrete evidence to the reader as to what was actually done in one specific case. Wider reading of other examples, including those listed under References, will suggest the full diversity of possible formats for presentation.

At one extreme are the massive, detailed energy scenarios of the Federal Energy Administration and the Ford Foundation's Energy Project, each supported by several volumes of supporting data and assumptions. At the other extreme are "at-a-glance" presentations of mini-scenarios:

- Figure 3 illustrates a graph plotting used by Arnold Mitchell to show two scenarios of the prospective share of markets accounted for by three different life-style segments of the population, 1970–2000 (Mitchell, 1976).
- Figure 4 presents a format used by General Electric to demonstrate alternative scenarios of future social change. In this format, an array of four possible trends in six segments of social change is presented in a structured manner in such a way as to make it possible to draw in a future scenario by the simple expedient of connecting selected boxes with a plotted line.

Both of these formats are, of course, relatively naive, but they can serve limited purposes, *provided* they are backed up with supporting data.

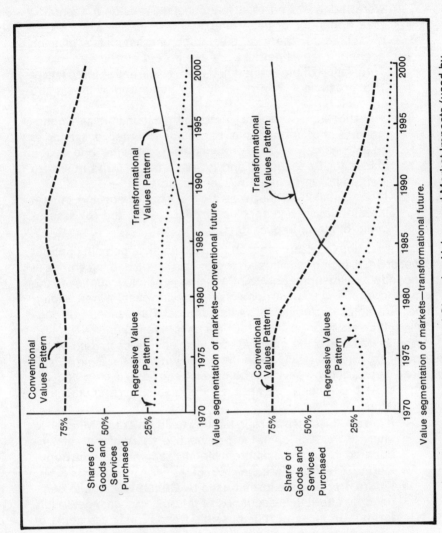

**Figure 3.** Plotted Scenarios of Changing Values and Market Impacts (used by Arnold Mitchell, Stanford Research Institute)

| | ALTERNATIVE SCENARIOS: 1973–1985 | | | MOST PROBABLE | | |
|---|---|---|---|---|---|---|
| | POLITICAL ALIGNMENT | SOCIAL VALUES | INSTITUTIONAL STABILITY | ECONOMIC STRUCTURE | WORK ATTITUDES | TECHNOLOGY VS. ECOLOGY |
| | Neopopulism | Counterculture | Radical Change (Violence) | State Capitalism | Alienation/ Dropping Out | Antimaterialism |
| | Independent Voter/New Federalism | Individualism/ Pluralism/ Humanism | Sporadic Violence | Business-Government Partnership | New Motivation | Accelerated Environmental Protection |
| | Traditional Democratic (Centralized Government) | Modified Traditional Values | Evolutionary Change (Concentration) | Mixed Economy | Increasing Leisure-Orientation | Evolutionary Environmental Protection |
| | Conservative Revival | Counter-Reformation (Traditional Values) | Law and Order (Stability) | Reprivatization | Protestant Work Ethic | Backlash vs. Ecology |

**Figure 4.** Format for Mini-Scenarios on Social Change (used by General Electric Company)

Conclusion

At first sight, scenarios may appear to be dramatic exercises of intuitive imagination, and, of course, they can be just that. Much of science fiction could be characterized in this way, although the "fiction" of a Jules Verne or an Arthur C. Clarke is often based on a large amount of fact. As was noted at the outset, some element of drama, well used, can enhance the force and usefulness of scenarios.

They can also be much more than that. They can be disciplined explorations of the future, forcing the writer to spell out the full range of underlying assumptions in the forecast, and encouraging a needed holism in the approach to the subject.

They can be idle speculation, but they can also be serious bases for planning. All in all, they may be both the most demanding and the most rewarding of any futures methodology.

# Appendix

The following excerpts from General Electric's first exercise in scenario-writing in 1971 are offered principally to give the reader some substance to the generalized references in the text. They are *not* suggested as inputs for new scenarios; they are too dated to be useful in that sense. Nor are they suggested, necessarily, as an exercise in second-guessing, although it is possible to have some fun doing just that.[4]

## COMMON DEVELOPMENTS—RELATIVELY CONSTANT OVER ALL FOUR ALTERNATIVES

- Vietnam War has been terminated
- No nuclear war
- Spread of nuclear capabilities
- Dynamic Europe
- Continued rise of Japanese economic and political power
- Relative decline of U.S. economic and political power in the world
- No technology and output per manhour gap between the United States and other developed countries by 1980
- Size and composition of U.S. population for 1970–1980 period same for all scenarios
- Better educated population and work force
- Continuing decline in work ethic
- A general increased diversity in ideology, value systems, and life-styles

- A higher level of public impatience with all forms of economic hardships such as poverty, unemployment, sickness, and strikes
- A general shift in demand for better quality products, improved environment, more meaningful work, and more human institutions
- Greatly increased and sustained public demand for more and better residential housing; repair of the physical environment; better and more affordable and available health care (significant variations among scenarios in meeting demands)
- Continued move toward "service economy" (some variations)
- The political system will survive with varying modifications and rates of change
- Constraints: "Ability to pay," limits on direct taxation, availability of investment funds (priorities), tolerance for change.

Summary of Four Alternative Scenarios, 1971–1980

| SCENARIO I<br>Benchmark<br><br>Probability: 50% | SCENARIO II<br>More Inward-Looking<br>Societies (Current Trajectory)<br>Probability: 25% | SCENARIO III<br>More Integrated Societies<br><br>Probability: 15% | SCENARIO IV<br>More Disarrayed Societies<br><br>Probability: 10% |
|---|---|---|---|
| **International**<br>Reduced threats of large-scale military conflicts, but level of U.S.-Communist world tension continues | General preoccupation with national interests, and low level of conflict (though potential for future conflict remains). Relative stability as result of domestic preoccupations, political diffidence, or ideological decline | Relatively peaceful, relatively prosperous, relatively arms-controlled world. Flareups which spill over borders are closely policed | Unstable world as result of conflicting national interests or renewed ideological influence |
| Emergence of multipolar system, U.S.-USSR-EEC-Japan: More regional groupings elsewhere. | Same as I, except less progress in regional groupings | Relatively high degree of consultation among nations, and political coordination (even integration) among most nations | Fluctuations between multipolar power distribution and renewed world bipolarity. |
| "Nixon Doctrine" of lower U. S. profile reduces direct involvement but steps up aid (including multi-lateral aid) | U. S. cuts its foreign involvement and avoids military intervention: aid chiefly designed to support trading system | Ambitious multilateral development projects are successful; progress on population control | U. S. meets stark, aggressive provocations and challenges to presumed spheres of influence |
| Third World continues troubled by regional/local conflicts and by internal revolutionary movements | Same as I, except more internal revolutions | Visible development progress; North-South Gap perceived as narrowing | Third World is disrupted by extreme and internal upheaval; many radical insurrections and economic breakdowns with famines |
| World trade continues to rise at about 10-11% a year | Slow growth of world trade, 6-8% annual increase | Growth of world trade (including East-West trade) at about 12-15% a year | World trade level is maintained out of necessity |
| U. S. share of world exports continues to decline; U. S. industrial imports rise faster than exports, and BOP difficulties continue | Sharper decline of U. S. share of world trade than in I; increased protectionism | Export of high technology equipment and services produces balance in BOP: offshore manufacturing and imports of labor-intensive products are encouraged | Dollar under pressure, with valuation a high probability: offshore investment declines sharply |

| SCENARIO I<br><br>Benchmark | SCENARIO II<br>More Inward-Looking<br>Societies (Current Trajectory) | SCENARIO III<br><br>More Integrated Societies | SCENARIO IV<br><br>More Disarrayed Societies |
|---|---|---|---|
| **Domestic (U. S.)**<br>Increased demand for, but limited progress on, "new priorities" (environment, housing, education, medical care); increasing levels of "mainstream America" frustration, continuing protest but less violent | Roughly same as I, but less progress on new priorities; more polarization and protests | Visible and real progress on new priorities; new political will; fear of crisis overcome | Deep fear of crisis, gradual erosion of political will; deep divisions; breakdown of infrastructure; new priority is defense |
| Business response to new priorities slow because of market mechanisms; but increasing government-business partnerships | Business influence declines; curtailment of multinational corporations, offshore production; increased unionization | Effective business response to consumerism and environmental problems; dynamic involvement in housing, urban renewal, new communities; improved public image of business | Stagnation of private sector; decline in R & D |
| Slow trend toward humanizing institutions; groping for new participative mechanisms | Increased bureaucratization; hard line on deviations from norm (crime, drugs, etc.) | More consensus, sense of progress; increased involvement of minorities and youth in decision-making on community level | Mood of fear, control, and repression |
| Slight shift in work/leisure balance toward latter | Hours of work stays on current trajectory | Longer vacations, more holidays and sabbaticals are the norm | Average work week longer than in I, II, and III; but 10% of manhours lost due to strikes. |
| Government influence increasing over business and people's lives | Political swing to right; attempt to legislate solutions | "New Federalism" extends to business and other private organizations | Large-scale government bureaucracies and control |
| Government expenditures rise as % of GNP; defense budget declines through 1972, then levels off | Tax revolts hold down government revenues, spending; defense budget slightly higher than in I. | Increased government spending on new priorities (result of peace dividend, US-USSR detente); defense budget stabilizes in absolute terms | Defense spending high for omnidirectional defense; large government deficits. |
| Relatively high level of unemployment (c. 4%) | Higher level of unemployment | Low unemployment | High unemployment |
| Productivity growth rate, c. 3% per annum; some improvement in services | Productivity continues on current (1965-1969) trajectory | Higher productivity; significant improvement in services | Low level of productivity |
| Relatively high level of inflation (c. 3%) | Higher level of inflation (c. 4%) | Lower level of inflation (c. 2%) | Potential runaway inflation (c. 6%) |

## NOTES

1. The last two scenarios were developed to give polar extremes (and so assigned low probabilities) and show the range of possibilities. As such, they served more as an intellectual, mind-stretching exercise than as frameworks for detailed planning (except to point up the need for contingency planning). This was, however, the first use of scenarios and alternative futures, and it was considered important to demonstrate, as dramatically as possible, a total spectrum of alternative futures.

2. As, for example, the SCOUT service offered by The Futures Group (Theodore J. Gordon, president), Glastonbury, Conn.

3. This does not, of course, mean that the others are discarded. Ideally, they should form the basis for contingency planning dealing with uncertainties and potential discontinuities.

4. It is worth noting, however, that they bear out the truth of the earlier statement that the precise combination of events selected for a scenario is highly unlikely to develop. Even a quick glance at the four summaries will reveal that the actual history of the past five years has contained some elements from all four scenarios, though mainly from Scenarios I and II.

## REFERENCES

Bell, Daniel (ed.). 1968. *Toward The Year 2000.* New York: Houghton Mifflin Co.

Environmental Protection Agency (EPA). October 1975. *Alternative Futures for Environmental Policy Planning: 1975–2000.* Washington, D.C.: U.S. Government Printing Office.

Federal Energy Administration. 1974. *Project Independence Report.* Washington, D.C.: U.S. Government Printing Office.

Freeman, S. D. (ed.). 1974. *A Time to Choose.* Final Report by the Energy Policy Project of the Ford Foundation. Philadelphia: Ballinger Publishing Co.

General Electric Company. January 1971. *Four Alternate World/U.S. Scenarios, 1971–1980.* Fairfield, Conn.

Kahn, Herman, and Anthony J. Wiener. 1967. *The Year 2000: A Framework for Speculation on the Next Thirty-three Years.* New York: Macmillan Co.

Meadows, Donella, Dennis Meadows, et al. 1972. *The Limits to Growth.* New York: Universe Books.

Mitchell, Arnold. 1976. "Changing Life Ways and Corporate Planning." *Planning Review,* Volume 4, Number 1, (January 1976).

Stanford Research Institute, Center for the Study of Social Policy (SRI/ CSSP). December 1975. *Handbook of Forecasting Techniques.* Prepared for Institute for Water Resources, U.S. Army Corps of Engineers, Fort Belvoir, Va.

————, Long Range Planning Service (SRI/LRPS). June 1975. *U.S. Agricultural Policy* (Report Number 547).

Wilson, Ian H. 1974. "Socio-Political Forecasting: A New Dimension to Strategic Planning." *Michigan Business Review* (July), 15–25.

———. 1975. "Societal Change and the Planning Process." Paper delivered at the annual meeting of the American Association for the Advancement of Science, New York (January 31).

Zentner, René D. 1975. "Scenarios in Forecasting." *Chemical and Engineering News,* (October 6), 22–34.

KIM QUAILE HILL

# Trend Extrapolation

Forecasting by means of the projection of trends has been a frequent mode of investigating the future. Indeed, the majority of our day-to-day personal activities are premised on certain anticipated regularities and constancies in our lives. Thus we take for granted the continuance of many "trends" that structure the nature of our existence.

Of more importance for present purposes is, of course, the use of formal trend methods in forecasting. Some form of trend method is applied to practically every area of concern in futures research. Despite the fact that more sophisticated techniques are often employed, trend methods are most frequently used. Furthermore, trend analysis techniques often provide the methodological or conceptual basis for other, more complex tools.

This article discusses the principal topics in trend forecasting, noting as well the particular strengths and weaknesses of the technique. Specifically, the focus is on the nature of trend as a statistical phenomenon, the summarization of trends for analytic purposes, and forecasting by means of a quantified trend. In addition, we consider ways in which simple extrapolation of trends can be extended by the study of those forces that cause them. The article concludes with a discussion of the special advantages and disadvantages of trend methods as well as of the occasions where their application appears most suitable.

## WHAT IS TREND?

The analysis of trends is based on the empirical examination of some phenomenon with repeated measurements taken across time. Trend itself is a tendency for the values in a time series to increase or decrease with some steady regularity. For example, if one were to plot the population size of the United States at each decennial census year, there would obviously be a pronounced upward trend in the line connecting these points. Thus, an elementary prerequisite for this method is the availability of time series data on the particular phenomenon of interest.

Sometimes we may wish to speculate about trends in such abstract concepts as quality of life, marital harmony, or economic well-being. However, empirical study of such broadly defined concepts demands that we reduce them to measurable indicators—such as the divorce rate as one possible index of marital harmony. Like virtually all empirical research, trend extrapolation forces a decision on exactly what problem is of concern and on how that problem can be indexed numerically. In the language of statistics, we are forced to choose a *criterion* variable for analysis.

Another problem concerns the time period for which data are required to study trends. The rule of thumb is that a long enough time series is required to "capture trend," that is, to reflect the nature of real changes as opposed to other variations. The decision about how many years are enough depends largely upon the substantive problem under study. The general rule is to acquire as long a time series as possible, given the limitations of comparable and reliable historical data. More explicit guidelines to the necessary length of the series can be found in the literature specific to individual fields of study.

Once we have settled on our criterion variable and have acquired data on it for an acceptable period of time, we are ready to analyze the inherent trend, if any exists. The first step in this process is to plot the time series data on a graph, as we have done with some sample trends in Figures 1, 2, and 3. Throughout the study of time series phenomena, visual inspection of time-plots is a powerful and important practice. Thus, as a matter of habit even a cursory trend study should begin with such a plot.

At this point, we must recognize that trend is not the only source of variation in a time series. Time-series analysis customarily distinguishes three other potential sources of variation in a data series. One of these is *seasonality,* or the tendency for values taken within a year, as for monthly data, to rise or fall depending on seasonal effects. A good example is the tendency for retail sales to peak at certain times of the year, especially just preceding Christmas. A second source that may operate on a time series is the *cyclical* factor. In the example of retail sales short-term inflationary or recessionary periods, often lasting three to five years, induce "cycles" of especially high or low sales. These cycles would show up as brief, successive periods of fluctuation around the overall trend line. Finally, so-called *irregular shocks* may produce additional movement in a series, usually for only a single point in time.

These various components of a time series are best illustrated by examples. Figures 1, 2, and 3 illustrate three different exemplary time-series scatterplots. The first of these, for the automobile accident death

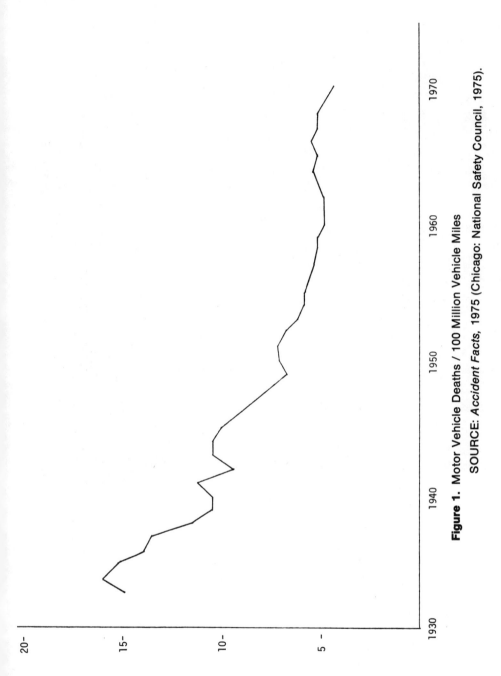

**Figure 1.** Motor Vehicle Deaths / 100 Million Vehicle Miles

SOURCE: *Accident Facts*, 1975 (Chicago: National Safety Council, 1975).

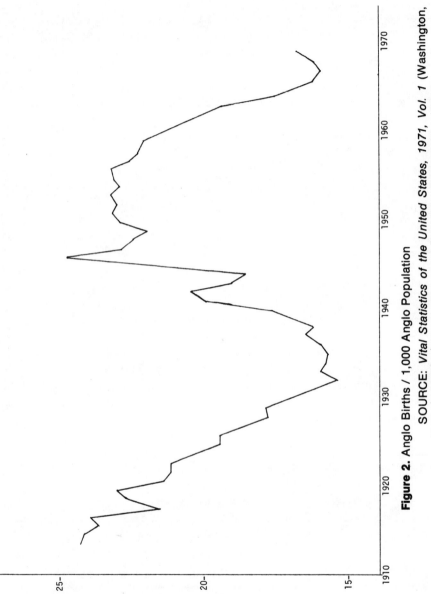

**Figure 2.** Anglo Births / 1,000 Anglo Population

SOURCE: *Vital Statistics of the United States, 1971, Vol. 1* (Washington, D.C.: U.S. Department of Health, Education, and Welfare, 1975).

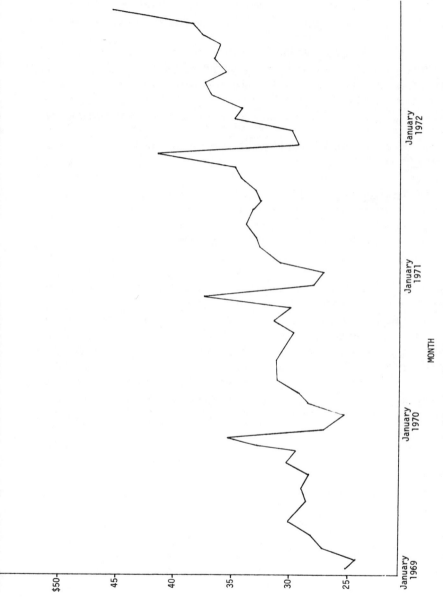

**Figure 3.** Total Domestic Retail Sales (in Millions of Dollars)
SOURCE: *Business Statistics*, 19th ed. (Washington, D.C.: U.S. Department of Commerce, 1973.)

rate, exhibits a fairly smooth and significant downward trend. Furthermore, the series exhibits somewhat more stability after 1950 than before. That is, it appears that a number of prominent irregular shocks disturb the pre-1950 trend, with only weak irregular variations after that date.

The second plot, for available birthrate data in the twentieth century, offers an example of a curve with no single dominant trend but with the suggestion of a strong cyclical pattern—at least for this set of years. Data on a number of years either preceding or following this set would be necessary to confirm the extension of this suggested cyclical pattern.

The third plot, for monthly retail sales data, exhibits a moderate upward trend, accompanied by a strong and fairly constant seasonal pattern.

Taken together, the above three series illustrate not only the appearance of trend but also that of the other nontrend components sometimes encountered in the examination of time-series scatterplots. There are two principal reasons why we should be concerned with these other components of a time series, even if our ultimate interest is only in the trend. First, we must consider the effects of these additional elements on our data to insure that we do not confuse their effects for that of trend. This problem is most easily avoided by making sure that the time span of our series is long enough to capture the complete effects of any seasonal or cyclical variation. For example, were we projecting retail sales with only nine months of data, our historical data would not be sufficient to capture the seasonal effects spread over an entire year. Thus, our historical trend might be biased by seasonal effects or our projections would incorporate error because we could not anticipate the possible seasonal effects likely to disturb the values for the next three months. Similar errors could contaminate projections from annual time series that fail to incorporate cyclical influences properly. If our historical series begins at the bottom of a cycle (the depths of the 1930s Depression) and ends at the height of an expansionary period (the postwar 1950s), we will have an artificially large positive trend.

The second reason we must consider the possibility of nontrend effects on our data is to allow us to eliminate their influence from the series before studying the trend. For example, in Figure 4 we again present the plot of monthly retail sales data shown in Figure 3. Added to the graph, however, is another plot for the same data after adjustment for seasonal effects. This second series, taken from the original source, is intended to provide a clearer picture of the inherent trend alone.[1] Inspection of the graph indicates that the wide swings resulting

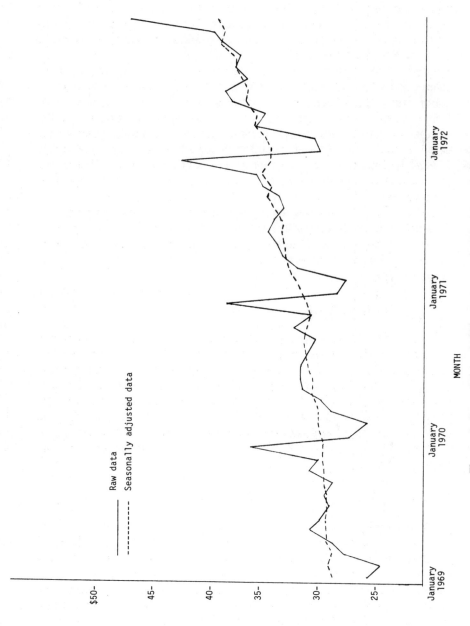

**Figure 4.** Total Domestic Retail Sales (in Millions of Dollars)

from the seasonal pattern of consumer buying habits have been eliminated. Subsequent forecasting based on this adjusted series is more
satisfactory for many purposes because it entails extrapolation of the
trend independent of the other components of the original series. In
order to forecast the total retail sales figure for any future month,
however, it is necessary to estimate the extent of seasonal variation
associated with that month as well as its trend value.

For many social forecasting problems, it might be the case that we
would wish to analyze the historical trend without extracting other
components from the series. In this manner, we could observe the
extent to which other forces resulted in variation around the trend line.
The general size of such variation in the past would provide evidence
on how much variation we might expect in the future. In highly variable
or so-called unstable series, we could then expect the average error in
projecting future trend values to be high. In stable series, the typical
data point would be closer to the trend line; therefore, we could expect
less error in projection if the trend continued into the future. Of course,
we could reduce such errors if we could project future cyclical or
seasonal effects as well as future trends.

## DESCRIBING TREND IN A SERIES

In order to discuss the trend in a given series or to project future
values in the series based on the past trend, we require some way of
describing the inherent historical trend.[2] A variety of methods, of varying sophistication and subsequent utility, are available for this purpose.
The simplest and probably most pervasive approach is mere inspection of the trend data and mental projection into the future. This
"method" is entirely satisfactory for answering many rudimentary questions about the nature of the trend, but it is very imprecise and can only
result in very approximate projections.

### MOVING AVERAGES

Of more interest and utility is the fitting of a line to the data points to
summarize the trend. The simplest kind of line fitting, beyond free-
hand curve drawing, is the use of so-called *moving averages.* Using this
approach, an analyst working with annual data might initially average
the first three years of data, for example, and plot the average on his
series for the second year. Then he would average the second through
fourth years' values and plot the result for the third year. He would
proceed in this fashion until he had averaged the final three years
together. The results of such an exercise can be seen in Figure 5, with a

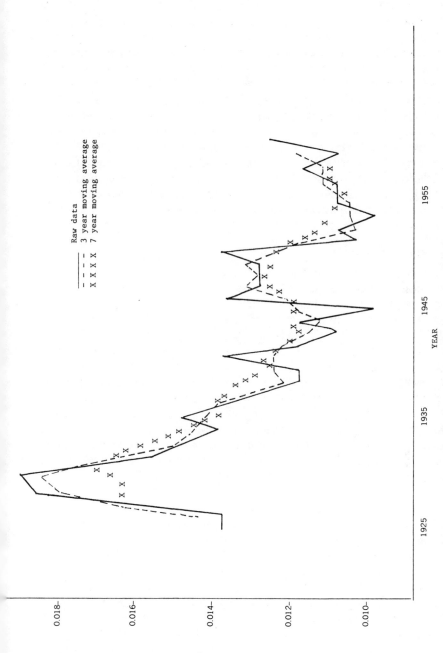

**Figure 5.** Canadian Homicidal Deaths per 1,000 Population

SOURCE: M. C. Urquhart and K.A.H. Buckley (eds.), *Historical Statistics of Canada* (Cambridge, Mass.: Cambridge University Press, 1965).

three-year and a seven-year moving average plotted on the series for Canadian homicide rates. The original data are themselves somewhat unstable but with an apparent downward trend. Both of the moving average trend lines reflect some of the instability as well as the trend. However, as is evident in the graph, the longer the averaging interval, the smoother the resultant trend line. In effect, the seven-year averaging interval—chosen for this example because of its extreme length—smoothes out more of the variation in the original data than does the three-year line. Normally, the averaging interval should be chosen on the basis of a particular research problem. Visual inspection of the results of two or three different interval averages is also often useful.

Moving averages offer a visually satisfying and easily executed trend description method. However, in a variety of ways they are less satisfactory than other approaches, as discussed below.

### LINEAR REGRESSION

A more rigorous approach is the application of either linear or curvilinear regression methods for describing and projecting the trend. Linear regression provides statistics on the single straight line which offers the best "fit" to the actual values in the series. The "best fitting" line is found employing the formula for a straight line:

$$Y = a + bX$$

and the "goodness-of-fit" criterion of vertical *least-squared* error. That is, the best fitting line is that for which the sum of all the squared error (where error is the vertical distance of the historical value at a given year from the regression line value for that year) is minimized. In the use of this equation, an attempt is made to "explain" the historical data series or $Y$ values as a function of the $X$ or time values for the series. The $a$ and $b$ values are for the intercept and slope of the line when plotted on a set of rectangular coordinates.

While many data series may not be linear in their trend, many are roughly so. Furthermore, the properties of the regression line are so attractive that this method in some form will often prove the most useful procedure. One useful property of the regression line is its associated measure of fit, the Pearsonian product-moment correlation or $r$. The $r$ can range from $+1.0$ to $-1.0$. Both of the extreme values denote perfect fit with all the data points falling exactly on the straight line (with a positive or a negative slope, respectively). This coefficient provides a statistical measure of the adequacy of fit of the regression line, whereas the moving averages method can only allow a visualization of the statisfactoriness of the line.[3] The correlation coefficient can actually be interpreted with two questions in mind. Since the *r* indicates how satisfactorily a straight line summarizes the data, a very large (positive or negative) *r* indicates that a straight line does provide a good trend estimate. However, an absolutely small *r* may indicate one of three things. A small *r* might signal the fact, which is confirmable by visual inspection, that a nonlinear trend actually exists in the data. A small *r* can also indicate that the trend itself is linear but that the series is highly variable, with year-to-year values fluctuating rather widely. Finally, a small *r* may indicate that no discernible trend of any shape exists. In order to determine which of these possible circumstances exists, visual examination of the series and the line is required.

If a straight line is found to be satisfactory, another feature of this method becomes very useful. In the equation for a straight line, $Y = a + bX$, the *b* coefficient is the slope of the line. Thus, the slope coefficient indicates how large a change in the dependent variable is associated with a one-unit change in time. Furthermore, if a straight-line trend were projected to some point in the future, all that would be required would be to solve the equation for the line resulting from the regression with the historical data, substituting the future year into the equation for *X*. The result would be the value of the *Y* variable at the future point based on an extrapolation of the regression line.

### CURVILINEAR REGRESSION

If it is found that a data series does not exhibit a linear or near-linear trend, extensions of the linear regression model can be utilized to fit curvilinear models to the series. If one is already acquainted with linear regression applications, a versatile and straightforward method is the use of transformed variables to make nonlinear problems suitable for linear methods.[4] An example of such a situation is given in Figure 6 where we have plotted data on historical changes in labor productivity (work output per unit of labor input) across a period of about seventy years. This series exhibits a pronounced curvilinear pattern with an increasing rate of growth across time. We can also observe that the series is a rather stable one with few irregular or nontrend variations.

We have also plotted on Figure 6 the best-fitting linear regression approximation of the series. Although the fit of the points to this line is rather good overall—observe the large correlation coefficient—this line would not be a very satisfactory model for the purposes of extrapolation. The divergence between the data series and the regression line is especially great for the most recent years, and an extrapolation of the regression line would diverge considerably from a simple extension of the data series. Clearly, a curvilinear model is required to describe this

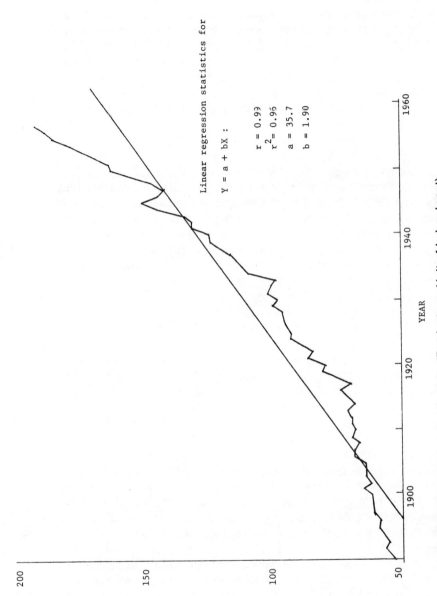

**Figure 6.** U.S. Labor Productivity (Product per Unit of Labor Input)

SOURCE: *Historical Statistics of the United States* (Washington, D.C.: U.S. Bureau of the Census, 1961).

series adequately. But how are we to fit such a model employing only linear methods as pointed out above?

The key to the use of linear regression methods in such situations is provided by the graph in Figure 7. Here we present the same labor productivity data with the *Y* values plotted on a logarithmic scale. This particular *transformation* of the series was chosen precisely for the obvious effect demonstrated in the figure. Given the shape of the original data plot, the effect of the log transform is to "linearize" the data. Now we can apply our usual regression methods to the equation for:

$$\text{Log } Y = a + bX$$

and we can extrapolate the resulting regression line as a good description of this historical series, as is evident from the future. We can also solve this semi-log equation for the value of Log *Y* for some future year, take the anti-logarithm of the result to put it into the original scale of measurement, and then plot this value on the original curvilinear data plot (and it will fall on an extrapolation of the original curve).

Employing this routine, we have a powerful method for working with a wide variety of curvilinear as well as linear time series. Our basic tool of linear regression is applied similarly throughout. We simply choose our transformation or, in effect, the equation for the regression, based on the shape of the curve in our data. Depending on the precise shape of the historical curve, there are additional curvilinear regression equations to fit appropriate lines to the data. The most important point about these various curvilinearity equations is the flexibility they introduce into the use of linear regression for forecasting.

### ENVELOPE CURVES

Another technique for describing trend, which is used frequently in technological forecasting, is the application of an envelope curve. This technique is discussed briefly in Jantsch (1972, pp, 84–86) and more extensively in Ayers (1968) and Lanford (1972, pp. 59–67). Envelope curves are best illustrated by an example like the hypothetical data in Figure 8.

We have plotted in Figure 8 several trend lines for several competing hypothetical technologies. Each of these originates at a different time point and exhibits its own time trend of increasing and eventually stabilizing technological development. In effect, each of these separate trends shows a roughly similar development, and each is succeeded by a later, more advanced technology in this area. Successive technological developments would not have been predictable by the ex-

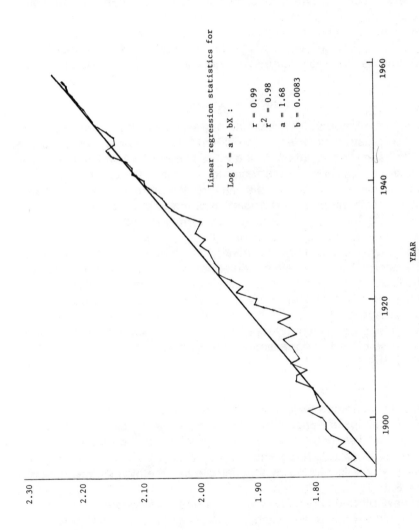

**Figure 7.** Logarithm (base 10) of Labor Productivity

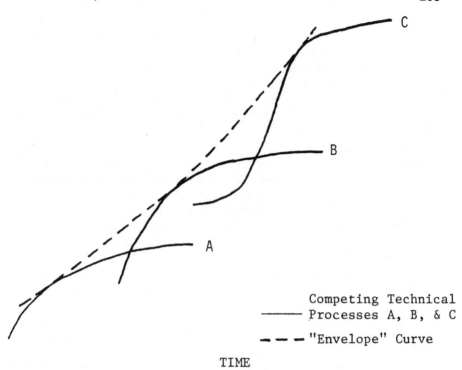

**Figure 8.** Level of Technological Progress, Efficiency, or Productivity

trapolation of any of the foregoing curves. However, the dotted line lying above and tangent to the individual trend lines is the envelope curve. Ayers argues that it is the envelope and not the subtrends encompasssed by it which we wish to extrapolate. He indicates that "such a projection is tantamount to assuming a continuation of the past rate of invention" (1968, p. 79). While Jantsch suggests quite appropriately that such a projection represents something of a leap of faith (since one does not know what new specific technological developments will extend the envelope in the future), the situation here may not differ much from more typical univariate projections that must also assume continuation of some underlying causal forces.

In order to employ an envelope curve, it is necessary first to plot the relevant subtrends and then to trace the envelope itself. After determining the shape of this curve, it can then be described by any of the methods discussed earlier.

Thus far, we have discussed a variety of methods of describing the trend in a series—actually a variety of methods for fitting summarizing lines to the data. The various approaches differ in degree of difficulty, statistical rigor, and in their subsequent utility for forecasting purposes. Despite some obvious differences in descriptive "accuracy" between some of the methods, it is important to point out that there is not always a "best" method or a "best" choice among the various averaging, linear fit, curvilinear, or other models. The choice of the "best" model is often a highly judgmental affair, but one that is improved with experience and training in the enterprise.

Having noted the preceding caveat, there is one final point to be made in this section. Once a particular summarizing method and the resultant line have been chosen, the question that should be asked is, how accurate is the "fit" of this line to the data. Notice that we are still considering only the *historical* data and have yet to make projections into the future. Our confidence in such projections should be tempered, however, by our knowledge of the historical accuracy of the trend line we will be projecting.

Basically, the question of fit is one of how close, on the average, individual data points are to the chosen trend line. In making this evaluation with free-hand or moving average curves, we must depend solely on visual assessment of "fit." Thus, decisions regarding the descriptive accuracy of such a line applied to a series of data must be based entirely on the judgment of the researcher.

With the use of a regression-derived line for either linear or nonlinear models, the researcher can utilize the associated correlation coefficient as an index of the fit to the data. Recall, however, that reliance on this statistical measure must be supplemented with visual assessment of the fit. Also, there may be cases where the $r$ will be somewhat small in absolute magnitude because the series is very unstable; yet, we may still decide that the given model provides an accurate description of the trend component of the series.

## MAKING THE PROJECTION

Having selected a model of the trend and evaluated its adequacy, the extrapolation can be made. It should be clear by this point that our detailed concern over the satisfactoriness of the chosen model arises because it is, in fact, the model of the trend that we extrapolate. In the simplest cases—where we have drawn free-hand curves, plotted relatively smooth-moving averages, or applied linear regression lines—extrapolation implies the direct extension of the line. With the entire series plotted on a set of rectangular coordinates, the extrapolated values for future time points can now be "read" from the $Y$ axis scale.

When employing a regression-based model, it is also possible to extrapolate using the equation for the fitted line. As noted above, we simply solve the equation substituting a real future time point into the equation for the value of $X$.

We should observe that an obviously important issue at this stage is how distant into the future one can or should make the extrapolation. The answer to this question must arise from the scholar's substantive knowledge of the topic under study. The methodology is suitable for extrapolating the trend for 1 year, 1,000 years, or even more. Whatever time period is chosen, the extrapolation answers the question: if this data series continues into the future for some projected number of years in accordance with the model by which it has been described here, what value on the variable will have been attained?

Finally, it should be asked whether one's substantive knowledge of the topic at hand suggests that some natural limit may impinge upon the behavior of the data series in the future. For example, some observers have argued that life expectancy rates in advanced Western societies have reached their possible maximum values given current lifestyles and medical technology. According to this argument, in order for the historical trend of increasing life span to be sustained, some significant breakthrough in one of these impinging conditions will be necessary. In analogous fashion, trend studies of other subjects should at least consider the possibilities of such limiting conditions. When the researcher expects that such conditions would hold, he would wish to tailor his extrapolation accordingly.

## OTHER UNIVARIATE METHODS

Our discussion of trend description and extrapolation methods has focused on the most basic—and frequently employed—approaches for these purposes. For most futures research these tools provide a rich battery of alternatives. Most students' and scholars' needs can be adequately met with those tools. The reader should be aware, however, that more rigorous and technically complex approaches are also available for the analysis of single time series. Among these latter alternatives, some of the more likely candidates for application to typical futures research appear to be the work of Box and Jenkins (1970) on time-series analysis; Nelson's (1973) elaboration of a variety of time-series models, and Brown's (1962) explication of trend forecasting with differential weighting of the influence of historical observations in a series (as by weighting recent values more heavily than more distant ones as a basis for the forecast).

## TREND EXPLANATION

To this point, we have discussed how the history of a given single series of data can be used to project future values for the same series. For many research problems that will be all that is required. Having made his projection and assessed his own confidence in it, the researcher may have accomplished his task. For some, the most serious consequence to follow will be their actions taken or recommended in view of the forecast. Typical examples might be the changes recommended to firms in the light of particular technological projections or to government policy-makers in the light of any of a variety of social, economic, or political forecasts.

For other scholars, another concern may predominate. Instead of "simple" extrapolation, their ultimate interest may be in causal explanations for variations in the history and future of a given time series. Such an interest may arise from the purely academic concern for the explanation of social or natural phenomena. This concern may also be motivated by a more pragmatic view. If we wish to alter the future values of some time series, we can best approach that goal if we understand the causal dynamics behind its normal progress.

Whatever the motivation behind the search for causal explanations, one methodological fact should be fairly obvious. Univariate time-series methods such as those described earlier do not advance this goal very far. Those methods are essentially descriptive and do not allow the researcher to address the question of what external forces affect the behavior of the criterion series.

A variety of methods, however, are available to address the issue of causality, at least within the usual limitation of causal inference associated with social science research. These methods take us far beyond the basic univariate trend methods described earlier and, in some ways, move the scholarly inquiry considerably beyond the basic intent of trend extrapolation. Despite this fact, some of the techniques available and their advantages will be explored briefly.

### TIME-SERIES REGRESSION

The most straightforward techniques suitable to the causal study of trends are simple and multiple regression applied to multiple time series. In principle, regression analysis allows us to address the question: changes in what other time series help us "explain" statistically the variations in our criterion series? The use of this method for this purpose is analogous to the use of regression as a descriptive tool discussed earlier. The difference is that we now employ other variables, instead of time, as independent or explanatory ones.

Unfortunately, there are important circumstances under which regression techniques are not strictly applicable to time-series analysis.[5] While a complete discussion of the technical details of this problem is beyond the scope of this essay, the substance of the problem is simple. If either our criterion or explanatory variable has a strong trend— tendency for the mean value to change with the passage of time—some of the usual regression statistics will be biased in such a way as to hazard inferences made from the results. This problem is known as *serial* correlation in a single time series. It reflects a tendency in the series for sets of high values or low values to occur in adjacent "runs," so that successive values are rather similar in magnitude. Statisticians have developed various tests to measure the extent of serial correlation in a series.

Despite the possibility of serial correlation problems in the use of time-series regression, there are a number of possible solutions. One of these is to take measurements on the serially correlated variable at less frequent intervals. Moving to annual instead of monthly or to five-year instead of annual measurement, as examples, may significantly reduce the problem. Another solution entails altering the customary tests of statistical significance to take account of the effective, reduced sample size. In effect, these tests are made more stringent to compensate for the serial correlation. Also, the problem of serial correlation can usually be avoided by the use of a *first-differences* model. In this case, the criterion variable used is not the *level* on that variable at a particular time point but the difference between the score at that time point and the preceding one. Employing the explanatory variable or variables measured in the same fashion, the first-differences approach asks how *changes* in the level of the criterion series are associated with *changes* in the level of an explanatory variable. The important point is that the use of the first-differences model usually eliminates the serial correlation that plagues the original data.

Finally, we should note the obvious point that regression methods are suitable without any adjustments to the study of time-series variables with no trend. The same is also true when either the single explanatory variable or the criterion has no significant trend. These so-called stationary time series might at first appear to be of little interest to futures research, where the stereotype is the study of ever-rising data series. Nonetheless, a variety of series show little or no trend over important periods but might be of concern to forecasters. Examples are levels of unemployment and civil violence. It is also the case, of course, that if the criterion series is de-trended in order to predict the nontrend variations, then a stationary series suitable for regression analysis would result.

Regression techniques and their extensions, such as simultaneous equation models (Ezekial and Fox, 1959, pp. 413–433) and path analysis (Duncan, 1966), offer a variety of sophisticated explanatory tools. With the application of such techniques, the researcher can examine the associations between data series, test rather refined hypotheses relating different time series, and make considerable progress in terms of causal inference relating different series.

Before leaving the topic of explanatory analysis, we must mention some of the problems and constraints it imposes on the research enterprise. Central among these is that explanatory analysis—especially when employing regression techniques—forces the researcher to decide exactly what component of a time series he wishes to explain. This forced precision of focus, which is often avoided by typical applications of simple trend extrapolation, is probably beneficial to the research. Unfortunately, if it is the trend itself (in a series with a strong trend) that the researcher wants to explain, then he is least well equipped with methodological tools. He may likely have to revert to explaining changes in the series or the irregular variation after the trend itself has been removed.

In addition, the desire to execute explanatory analysis requires knowledge of more complex analytic tools than that necessary for univariate series description and projection. Even a good knowledge of the application of single time-point regression methods must be supplemented with additional considerations necessary for longitudinal analysis. Finally, it is also obvious that the data requirements of these methods are much more demanding. At a minimum, data must now be acquired on two series and, if serious multivariate analysis is contemplated, the number of variables could be considerably larger. Not only does this situation require a greater commitment to data collection efforts, but it also necessitates that data be available on the various desired variables.

## ADVANTAGES OF TREND FORECASTING METHODS

Having considered the basic elements of trend methods, some comments on the utility of such techniques are in order. A principal advantage of this technique arises as a consequence of its ubiquity, as discussed in the introduction. Because much of our day-to-day activity depends on similar rationales, trend extrapolation is probably the least complex, most intuitively straightforward forecasting tool to comprehend. It is a natural adaptation of normal cognition processes.

Beyond its intuitive appeal, trend projection has other advantages. Most of these combine to result in relative ease of execution compared to other techniques. Data requirements are minimal here, for information is needed on only a single variable for many problems. Often, reference can be made to standard historical, demographic, economic, or other statistical compilations to acquire all the requisite data and more. In contrast, data collection and aggregation can become a very complex and time-consuming task in the execution of such methods as causal modeling, simulation, and Delphi. Furthermore, the costs of data analysis can be quite minimal with trend methods. Many applications can be executed merely with pen, paper, and hand calculator. Even when computerized analytic routines are employed, they are typically easy to execute and inexpensive in contrast to many other techniques.

In addition to benefits associated with costs of execution, benefits of increased intellectual precision can also be derived from the use of trend methods. When moving from the realm of pure speculation and verbal argument about the future to some more systematic method, trend extrapolation is often the initial choice. In making this transition, much more precision is needed in identifying phenomena of interest so that indicators for each can be accumulated. The initial result is that the researcher is forced to decide exactly which important trend to observe. According to the accepted canons of both scientific and policy-oriented analysis, if the researcher chooses the "wrong" trend, given his larger concerns, other critics and scholars can indicate that such is the case.

A second benefit of an initial application of trend extrapolation is that it often forces the researcher to learn more about the history of his subject in preparation for forecasting its future. The mere accumulation and inspection of evidence on past trends often provide insight on the possible course of future trends that would not otherwise have been acquired.

Finally, when the researcher begins to think in terms of the explanation of trends, he advances to a level of more rigorous analysis. At this point the question of causal relationships must be confronted directly. Consideration must be given to what other phenomena may be correlated with, may be causally determinative of, or may exhibit "leading" or "lagged" correlations with changes in our criterion variable across time.

Whether our ultimate interest centers on theoretical explanations or on policy manipulation, we must begin to hypothesize and to confirm causal linkages in order to satisfy either of these primary motivations. The mere observation of time trends does not itself suggest the pattern of causative forces acting to sustain the trend. Our initial efforts at unraveling these forces may be rather naive or quite sophisticated. It may even be the case that the causal relations are so complex and interdependent as to be capable of isolation only by relatively advanced simulation methods (Forrester, 1969, pp. 107–114). Nonetheless, when we move from merely observing trends to the empirical testing of their determinants, we have probably taken the most crucial step in our sophistication as scholars and social observers.

## WHEN TO FORECAST WITH TREND METHODS

Having reviewed some of the mechanics of trend methods along with some of the associated advantages and shortcomings, one more issue must be considered: when is this technique best employed?

An obvious first point is that we cannot proceed at all with trend methods if historical data are absent for our problem of interest. Thus, minimal data availability is requisite, and for many research problems this minimum may constitute a significant barrier. Often, the data we desire simply do not exist, or such figures as are available are suspect because of varying accuracy over time, changes in reporting standards, or changes in definitions of the operational indicator over time. Attempts to build "social indicator" data banks have brought to attention many such shortcomings in historical data archives.

On the other hand, the data requirements of this approach are considerably lower than those for many other forecasting tools. Thus, we can employ this tool quickly and successfully when other methods might be impossible or quite costly.

Because of its relative ease of application, another consideration of when to employ trend methods is suggested. Perhaps, we ought to consider this approach the "baseline" methodology for most forecasting problems. Because of its intuitive appeal and low cost, a trend study can be rather quickly completed and interpreted. If interesting new problems or hypotheses are brought to light by this method, the analyst can address such issues subsequently with more rigorous— and more costly—approaches. If no enduring questions remain after the trend examination, the research need go no further.

When trend methods are employed in this manner, they will usually result in such speculative questions for further research as:

1. What will be the consequences if this trend continues unabated for *x* years?
2. What will be the consequences if this trend levels off or accelerates from its current rate of increase?
3. Which forces acting to maintain this trend are likely to remain constant and which are likely to change in the future?
4. If we wish to alter this trend in a particular direction, what determining variables might themselves be manipulated to do so?

Some might argue that such questions are the most important product of trend analyses: the "what if's" that we formulate in response to viewing the historical trend.

Finally, we should make one other observation about trend extrapolation in the context of its use along with other techniques. We must clearly recognize that this method is a very simple-minded one. Its simplicity entails benefits but also costs and limitations. Obviously, use of this technique alone cannot significantly advance rigorous forecasting and causal analysis. Nonetheless, simple tools can be powerful when used with care and insight. As a vehicle for exploring and refining many forecasting problems and as a "first-cut" approach to defining the boundaries of the issue, trend methods have much to offer.

## NOTES

1. For details on the particular methods of seasonal adjustment employed on these data, see *Business Statistics* (1973, notes, p. 59). For a lengthy introductory discussion of the ways of handling seasonal variation in trend data, see Croxton, Cowden, and Bolch (1969).

2. There are a number of readable, lengthy treatments of the topics of describing trend in a series and making subsequent forecasts. Two of the more lucid and insightful ones for the novice are Croxton, Cowden, and Bolch (1969, pp. 307–391) and Yamane (1973, pp. 378–382). Two additional discussions of this topic, both of which are oriented toward the substantive concerns of social scientists, are Palumbo (1969, pp. 249–270 and Kirkpatrick 1974, pp. 385–419).

3. In fact, the most precise measure of fit is not the $r$ but the $r$ squared ($r^2$), which indicates the percentage of common or shared variation between the $X$ and $Y$ variables.

4. For a useful introductory treatment of the use of linear regression methods with curvilinear data, see Ezekial and Fox (1959, pp. 69–117, 204–278). For a more advanced treatment, see Draper and Smith (1967, pp. 128–134).

5. For more detailed but very readable discussions of the problems of applying regression techniques to time-series analysis, see Quenouille (1952, pp. 161–191) and Ezekial and Fox (1959, pp. 325–347). Also useful is the treatment of Chisholm and Whitaker (1971, pp. 96–146).

# REFERENCES

Ayers, Robert U. 1968. "Envelope Curve Forecasting." In James R. Bright (ed.), *Technological Forecasting for Industry and Government.* Englewood Cliffs, N.J.: Prentice-Hall, 77–94.

Box, G. E. P., and G. M. Jenkins. 1970. *Time Series Analysis, Forecasting and Control.* San Francisco: Holden-Day.

Brown, R. G. 1962. *Smoothing, Forecasting, and Prediction of Discrete Time Series.* Englewood Cliffs, N.J.: Prentice-Hall.

*Business Statistics.* 1973. Washington, D.C.: U.S. Department of Commerce.

Chisholm, Roger K., and Gilbert Whitaker, Jr. 1971. *Forecasting Methods.* Homewood, Ill.: Irwin.

Croxton, Frederick E., Dudley J. Cowden, and Ben W. Bolch. 1969. *Practical Business Statistics.* 4th ed. Englewood Cliffs, N.J.: Prentice-Hall.

Draper, N. R., and H. Smith. 1967. *Applied Regression Analysis.* New York: John Wiley and Sons.

Duncan, Otis Dudley. 1966. "Path Analysis: Sociological Examples." *American Journal of Sociology* 72 (July), 1–16.

Ezekial, Mordecai, and Karl A. Fox. 1959. *Methods of Correlation and Regression Analysis.* 3d ed. New York: John Wiley and Sons.

Forrester, Jay. 1969. *Urban Dynamics.* Cambridge, Mass.: MIT Press.

Jantsch, Erich. 1972. *Technological Planning and Social Futures.* New York: John Wiley and Sons.

Kirkpatrick, Samuel A. 1974. *Quantitative Analysis of Political Data.* Columbus, Ohio: Charles E. Merrill.

Lanford, H. W. 1972. *Technological Forecasting Methodologies.* New York: American Management Association.

Nelson, Charles R. 1973. *Applied Time Series Analysis.* San Francisco: Holden-Day.

Palumbo, Dennis J. 1969. *Statistics in Political and Behavioral Science.* New York: Appleton-Century-Crofts.

Quenouille, M. H. 1952. *Associated Measurements.* New York: Academic Press.

Yamane, Taro. 1973. *Statistics.* 3d ed. New York: Harper & Row.

HAROLD A. LINSTONE

# The Delphi Technique

The word Delphi refers to the hallowed site of the most revered oracle in ancient Greece. Legend has it that the earth goddess Gaia long ago inhabited this site and was protected by the dragon Pythos. Apollo, the son of Zeus and Leto, slew the dragon and made himself master of Delphi. He was famous throughout Greece not only for his beauty, but also for his ability to foresee the future. The home Apollo chose for himself was located 170 kilometers northwest of Athens on the slopes of Mount Parnassus and in sight of the Gulf of Corinth. The impressive site served not only as an oracular center but also as a kind of art museum. Every important event of Greek history was immortalized there by painting and sculpture. Those who sought to consult the Oracle brought gifts, thereby making Delphi one of the richest and most influential locales in Greece. Forecasts were transmitted from Apollo through intermediaries, women known as Pythia. The focal point for the activity was an inner sanctum of the temple built over a geologic fault through which fumes escaped. These fumes were instrumental in transporting the Pythia into a trance, and their utterances were then interpreted by priests for the petitioners.

In the 1950s, the RAND Corporation adopted the name Delphi for a procedure to "obtain the most reliable consensus of opinion of a group of experts . . . by a series of intensive questionnaires interspersed with controlled opinion feedback" (Dalkey and Helmer, 1963, p. 458). Of particular interest in the initial endeavor was the application of "expert opinion to the selection, from the point of view of a Soviet strategic planner, of an optimal U.S. industrial target system and to the estimation of the number of A-bombs required to reduce the munitions output by a prescribed amount."

For obvious reasons, this early pioneering work was not publicized. The first widely circulated Delphi study appeared in 1964 as a RAND paper, "Report on a Long-Range Forecasting Study" (Gordon and Helmer, 1964). Its aim was to assess "the direction of long-range trends, with special emphasis on science and technology, and their probable effects on our society and our world." "Long-range" was defined as a span of ten to fifty years. Six topics were covered: scientific break-throughs, population control, automation, space progress, war prevention, and weapons systems. Of 150 persons approached, 82 responded to one or more questionnaires. A panel was selected for each topic, and four sequential questionnaires were distributed to each panel, spaced about two months apart. The average number of completed questionnaires received per panel per round was 14.5. The questionnaires for the first two rounds of the Scientific Breakthrough panel are shown in Figure 1. The estimates of the year by which there would be a 50 percent chance that a particular development would occur were tallied, and the median year and the interquartile range (25 to 75 percent year span) were calculated. The results of the Scientific Breakthrough panel were presented as shown in Figure 2. The items are ordered according to median year, the first item denoting the earliest median year.

In the mid-1960s, there was a growing interest in technological forecasting, particularly on the part of the advanced technology industry of the United States. The Delphi procedure, as developed by the RAND Corporation, appeared to be a useful device and was soon applied by planners in corporations. TRW's "Probe of the Future" involved 150 of their scientists, engineers, and managers in a Delphi study which was later published in fourteen volumes. From America, Delphi spread to Western Europe, Eastern Europe, and the Orient. The largest Delphi ever undertaken was a Japanese project involving several thousand people. Starting in a nonprofit organization, Delphi has found its way into industry, government, and finally, academe. It has simultaneously expanded beyond technological forecasting. The definition used by Linstone and Turoff in their book on the subject (1975) is as follows: "Delphi may be characterized as a method for structuring a group communication process so that the process is effective in allowing a group of individuals, as a whole, to deal with a complex problem."

In the original Delphi process, the key elements were (1) structuring of information flow, (2) feedback to the participants, and (3) anonymity for the participants. Clearly, these characteristics may offer distinct advantages over the conventional face-to-face conference as a communication tool. The method involved the following ten steps:

1. Formation of a team to undertake and monitor a Delphi on a given subject.
2. Selection of one or more panels to participate in the exercise. Customarily, the panelists are experts in the area to be investigated.
3. Development of the first round Delphi questionnaire

4. Testing of the questionnaire for proper wording (e.g., ambiguities, vagueness)
5. Transmission of the first questionnaires to the panelists
6. Analysis of the first round responses
7. Preparation of the second round questionnaires (and possible testing)
8. Transmission of the second round questionnaires to the panelists
9. Analysis of second round responses
   (Steps 7 to 9 are reiterated as long as desired or as necessary to achieve stability in the results.)
10. Preparation of a report by the analysis team to present the conclusions of the exercise

It is not surprising that, as the use of Delphi has spread, many variations of the process have surfaced. One example is the use of the computer to run Delphi as a real-time remote conference. Another is the use of different panels in sequential form, e.g., planning Delphi in two phases: first, several rounds are carried out with *research* specialists, and then the output of this exercise is presented to *development* specialists as the starting point for a second sequence.

When we view Delphi as a communication process, the wide spectrum of uses quickly becomes apparent. The process has been applied to exposing priorities of personal values and social goals, explicating the pros and cons associated with potential policy options, evaluating budget allocations, examining the significance of historical events, and distinguishing or clarifying perceived and real human motivations. As with any readily applied methodology, there have been misuses as well as efforts to oversell Delphi. In some respects, Delphi is a method of last resort; it proves particularly useful in the following circumstances:

1. The problem does not lend itself to precise analytical techniques but can benefit from subjective judgments on a collective basis.
2. The individuals who need to interact cannot be brought together in a face-to-face exchange because of time or cost constraints. Further, a conventional conference tends to be dominated by particularly strong personalities or to give rise to an undesirable bandwagon effect.

A structured communication process has distinct advantages but also limitations, as we shall see. Perhaps the most important advice to be given to the potential user is to *suit the method to the problem*, not the problem to the method. The second advice is that ease of under-

## LONG-RANGE FORECASTING STUDY

### Questionnaire 1

#### 1.1. SCIENTIFIC BREAKTHROUGHS

One of the major problems of conducting a predictive study which poses its questions on the basis of extrapolations of current technology is the almost unavoidable exclusion of discontinuous state-of-the-art advances.

In this current study a period of 50 years is being considered. It is possible that inventions and discoveries not yet visualized could have a major impact on our society during this interval. It is easy to observe that the pace of scientific and technological innovation has been steadily increasing and that the time between origination and application has been decreasing. Therefore we believe that many generations of inventions can find application during the period under study.

Some insight even into discontinuous state-of-the-art advances might perhaps be gained by examining the world's need for such advances, in view of the old truism that necessity is the mother of invention. Therefore, you are asked to list below major inventions and scientific breakthroughs in areas of special concern to you which you regard as both urgently needed and feasible within the next 50 years:

Do you know of the existence of any information, in the form of tabulations or analyses, that might be particularly valuable in reaching projections of the kind requested?

### Questionnaire 2

#### 1.2 SCIENTIFIC BREAKTHROUGHS

a. Listed below in Table 1.2a are most of the scientific breakthroughs suggested by the respondents as potentially possible during the next 50 years. Please indicate your judgment of the probability of implementation during each period. Note that the numbers inserted by you in each row should add up to 100. (In the case of items involving gradual development such as synthetic food production or automated education, "implementation" should be interpreted as referring to the time from which the effect on our society will no longer be negligible.)

b. Considering the breakthroughs suggested in Table 1.2a are there other potential breakthroughs which you would care to add? When do you believe they will occur? Please make your additions in Table 1.2b.

### TABLE 1.2a

| | 1963-65 | 65-68 | 68-72 | 72-78 | 78-86 | 86-97 | 97-2013 | Later | Not at any time |
|---|---|---|---|---|---|---|---|---|---|
| **Sociological** | | | | | | | | | |
| 1. Communication with animals | | | | | | | | | |
| 2. Breeding of intelligent animals (apes, cetaceans, etc.) for low-grade labor | | | | | | | | | |
| 3. Education by automation | | | | | | | | | |
| 4. Education by other means, such as direct information-recording on the brain | | | | | | | | | |
| 5. Education or conditioning in social behavior to reduce the likelihood of war | | | | | | | | | |
| 6. Automatic language translators | | | | | | | | | |
| 7. Efficient idea-coding to convey precise information independent of language | | | | | | | | | |
| 8. Popular use of personality control drugs | | | | | | | | | |
| 9. Long-duration coma to permit a form of time travel | | | | | | | | | |
| 10. Solution to the problem of distribution of goods--computer identification of points of need | | | | | | | | | |
| 11. Computing machines becoming the most significant source of intelligence on earth | | | | | | | | | |
| 12. Discovery of life on Mars | | | | | | | | | |
| 13. Communication with extra-terrestrials | | | | | | | | | |
| **Physical** | | | | | | | | | |
| 1. Reformation of physical theory, eliminating confusion in quantum-relativity and simplifying particle theory | | | | | | | | | |
| 2. Experimentation with anti-matter | | | | | | | | | |
| 3. Control of gravity | | | | | | | | | |
| 4. Controlled thermo-nuclear power | | | | | | | | | |
| 5. Commercially efficient transmutation of elements | | | | | | | | | |
| 6. Focused electromagnetic radiation for power transmission | | | | | | | | | |

Table 1.2a

SUMMARY OF OPINIONS ON SCIENTIFIC BREAKTHROUGHS

| | Probability of Implementation During Period | | | | | | | | |
|---|---|---|---|---|---|---|---|---|---|
| Biological | 1963-65 | 65-68 | 68-72 | 72-78 | 78-86 | 86-97 | 97-2013 | Later | Not at any time |
| 1. Chemical control over heredity - molecular biology | | | | | | | | | |
| 2. Biochemical general immunization | | | | | | | | | |
| 3. Biochemicals to stimulate growth of new organs and limbs | | | | | | | | | |
| 4. Synthetic generation of protein for food | | | | | | | | | |
| 5. Oral contraceptive | | | | | | | | | |
| 6. Other means of fertility control | | | | | | | | | |
| 7. New organs through transplanting or prosthesis | | | | | | | | | |
| 8. Use of telepathy and ESP in communications | | | | | | | | | |
| 9. Understanding of the physiology of mind-brain behavior | | | | | | | | | |
| 10. Chemical control of the aging process, permitting extension of life span by 50 years | | | | | | | | | |
| 11. Cancer cure | | | | | | | | | |
| 12. Man-machine symbiosis, permitting man to extend his intelligence directly through the use of computing machines | | | | | | | | | |
| 13. Creation of artificial life | | | | | | | | | |

| | | | | | | | | | |
|---|---|---|---|---|---|---|---|---|---|
| 7. Relay of solar energy via satellite | | | | | | | | | |
| 8. Efficient electric storage device | | | | | | | | | |
| 9. Limited weather control | | | | | | | | | |
| 10. Reliable weather forecasts | | | | | | | | | |
| 11. Miniaturization of electronics carried to the molecular level | | | | | | | | | |
| 12. Automated highways | | | | | | | | | |
| 13. Measurement of curvature of the universe | | | | | | | | | |
| 14. Ballistic transport - 2 hours to anywhere on earth | | | | | | | | | |
| 15. Theory of the earth's crust permitting accurate earthquake prediction | | | | | | | | | |
| 16. Development of new synthetic materials for ultra-light construction | | | | | | | | | |
| 17. Operation of nuclear power systems providing electricity @ 3-4 mills/kw-hr 5-10 year refueling period | | | | | | | | | |
| 18. Collection and concentration of solar energy, used for power or in man-made organic chemistry manufacturing processes | | | | | | | | | |
| 19. Operation of a central data storage facility with wide access for general or specialized information retrieval | | | | | | | | | |

Food and Raw Materials

| | | | | | | | | | |
|---|---|---|---|---|---|---|---|---|---|
| 1. Rise in world agricultural gross yields by a factor of ten | | | | | | | | | |
| 2. Economically useful desalination of sea water | | | | | | | | | |
| 3. Economical working of low-grade metal ores | | | | | | | | | |
| 4. Exploitation of the ocean bottom through farming and mining | | | | | | | | | |

**Figure 1.** RAND Delphi Questionnaires, Rounds 1 and 2

SOURCE: RAND Paper P-2982. Reprinted by permission of the RAND Corporation.

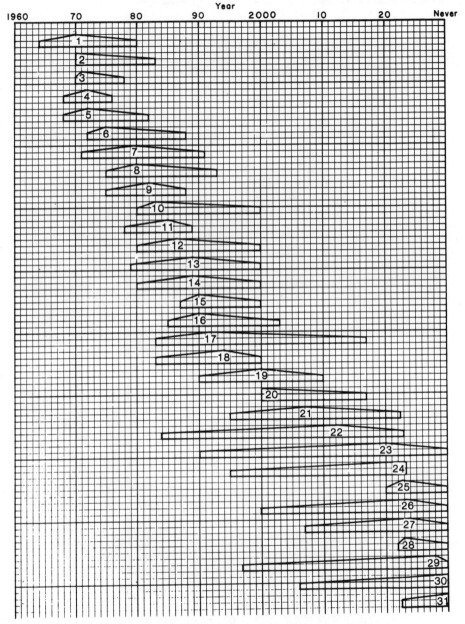

**Figure 2.** Consensus of Panel 1 on Scientific Breakthroughs (medians and quartiles)

SOURCE: RAND Paper P-2982. Reprinted by permission of the RAND Corporation.

1. Economically useful desalination of sea water

2. Effective fertility control by oral contraceptive or other simple and inexpensive means

3. Development of new synthetic materials for ultra-light construction

4. Automated language translators

5. New organs through transplanting or prosthesis

6. Reliable weather forecasts

7. Operation of a central data storage facility with wide access for general or specialized information retrieval

8. Reformation of physical theory, eliminating confusion in quantum-relativity and simplifying particle theory

9. Implanted artificial organs made of plastic and electronic components

10. Widespread and socially widely accepted use of nonnarcotic drugs (other than alcohol) for the purpose of producing specific changes in personality characteristics

11. Stimulated emission ("lasers") in X and Gamma ray region of the spectrum

12. Controlled thermo-nuclear power

13. Creation of a primitive form of artificial life (at least in the form of self-replicating molecules)

14. Economically useful exploitation of the ocean bottom through mining (other than off-shore oil drilling)

15. Feasibility of limited weather control, in the sense of substantially affecting regional weather at acceptable cost

16. Economic feasibility of commercial generation of synthetic protein for food

17. Increase by an order of magnitude in the relative number of psychotic cases amenable to physical or chemical therapy

18. Biochemical general immunization against bacterial and viral diseases

19. Feasibility (not necessarily acceptance) of chemical control over some hereditary defects by modification of genes through molecular engineering

20. Economically useful exploitation of the ocean through farming, with the effect of producing at least 20% of the world's food

21. Biochemicals to stimulate growth of new organs and limbs

22. Feasibility of using drugs to raise the level of intelligence (other than as dietary supplements and not in the sense of just temporarily raising the level of apperception)

23. Man-machine symbiosis, enabling man to extend his intelligence by direct electromechanical interaction between his brain and a computing machine

24. Chemical control of the aging process, permitting extension of life span by 50 years

25. Breeding of intelligent animals (apes, cetaceans, etc) for low-grade labor

26. Two-way communication with extra-terrestrials

27. Economic feasibility of commercial manufacture of many chemical elements from subatomic building blocks.

28. Control of gravity through some form of modification of the gravitational field

29. Feasibility of education by direct information recording on the brain

30. Long-duration coma to permit a form of time travel

31. Use of telepathy and ESP in communications

standing is no excuse for sloppiness of execution. In the following section, we will discuss some applications and present some comments on the evaluation and analysis of the process itself, and finally, cautions and critiques.

## APPLICATIONS

### BUSINESS

### TRW Inc.

PROBE II, a version of Delphi, was begun in 1967 with the support of TRW's senior executives and the full cooperation of managers throughout the organization (TRW Probe II, 1969). The categories included in this Delphi were electronics, materials, (coatings, fuels, and lubricants), mechanics and hydraulics, information processing, transportation, aerospace, oceans, personal and medical systems, urban and international systems, environmental control systems, and others. From the 7,000 graduate scientists and engineers in TRW's automotive, electronics, equipment, and systems organizations, 140 panelists were selected. A typical panel had sixteen members in addition to a chairman. Those appointed were asked to attend one or two briefings at which the instructions were issued, background material describing assumptions was discussed, and questions were answered. These sessions were the first and last occasion in which panelists met as a group. Subsequently, the contacts were all carried out on an individual basis to preserve the anonymity of the panelists.

In a manner similar to that of the RAND study (see Figure 1), panelists were first asked to provide a list of technical events which, they felt, were likely to occur under the given assumptions. The participants were encouraged to include items of primary value to other panels, and these were then transferred to the appropriate panel lists. In this manner, 2,500 events were identified.

In connection with each item, the following indications were provided by the panelists in the first rounds:

(a) *customer desirability:* needed desperately
  *or* desirable
  *or* undesirable but possible
(b) *producer feasibility:* highly feasible
  *or* likely
  *or* unlikely but possible

(c) *probable timing*
   year by which probability
   is x that the event will
   have occurred

$$x = 0.10\text{———}$$

$$x = 0.50\text{———}$$

$$x = 0.90\text{———}$$

SAMPLE ITEM: "TV will be available to 90% of the world's population"

(a) desirable

(b) highly feasible

$$\begin{array}{rl} x = 0.10 & 1977 \\ (c)\ x = 0.50 & 1980 \\ x = 0.90 & 1983 \end{array}$$

Upon receipt of the first round responses, the various events were screened to eliminate duplicate items, ambiguous wording, trivia, and irrelevant events. In this manner, the number of events was reduced to 1,438. One additional item requested of the panelists should be noted: "familiarity" with the item (fair, good, or excellent). This self-evaluation identified those who believed themselves to be experts on a particular question. The third round was limited to a survey of these "experts" in the anticipation that they might have information not available to all panelists which could have a significant bearing on the responses. For this last round, panel chairmen also prepared a series of challenging questions arising from the responses to Round 2. Examples: "Item xxxx: Is there evidence that there are data to support a 10% probability in the near future?" Item yyyy: "Why so pessimistic when panel member No. 000 believes 90% probability will occur in 1972?" The final report provided integrated indices of desirability, feasibility, and probability, together with the 10, 50, and 90 percent likelihood dates for all items as well as the questions and answers derived in Round 3 (see Figures 3 and 4). The entire study took nearly two years to complete.

## Bell Canada

Bell Canada is a telecommunications company that provides services to Ontario and Quebec and owns large manufacturing and research and development subsidiaries (Day, 1975). The business plan-

OCEANS—REGULATIONS AND POLLUTION CONTROL

| EVENT DESCRIPTION | SEAPP | DESIRABILITY D | FEASIBILITY F | PROBABILITY P | PROBABILITY DATES |
|---|---|---|---|---|---|
| 414220 FEDERAL LEGISLATION FOR THE STRICT CONTROL OF WATER POLLUTION WILL HAVE BEEN PASSED. | | .96 | .54 | .81 | |
| 424290 "VACUUM CLEANERS" WILL BE AVAILABLE FOR CLEARING OILS AND OTHER UNDESIRABLE WASTE FROM THE OCEAN'S SURFACE. | * | .44 | −.11 | .53 | |
| 424330 SALT WATER PURIFICATION TREATMENT SYSTEMS WILL BE OPERATIONAL FOR THE PROTECTION OF BEACH RECREATIONAL AREAS. | * | .32 | −.41 | .46 | |
| 501040 THE OCEAN'S RESOURCES FOR FOOD AND MATERIALS, ITS UTILIZATION, AND THE CONTROL OF ITS POLLUTION (A MAJOR SYSTEM TASK, WITH SOPHISTICATED INSTRUMENTATION AND DATA REDUCTION) WILL BE MANAGED BY AN INTERNATIONAL AGENCY. | * | .19 | −.22 | .41 | .00 |

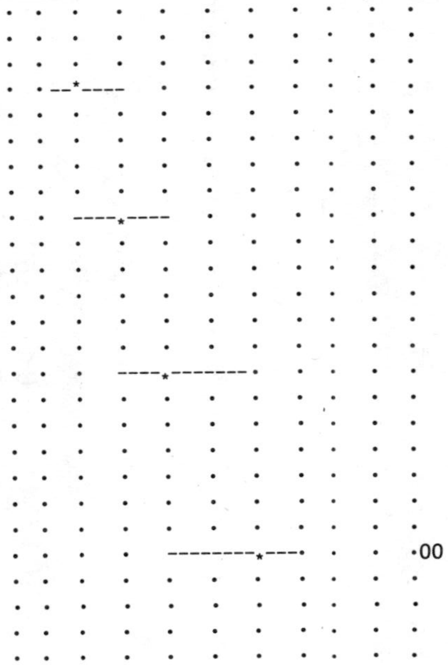

**Figure 3.** TRW Probe II

Reprinted by permission of The TRW Corporation.

501040 S IN RESPONDING TO ROUND 2, ONE PANELIST WARNED THAT 'SOME NATIONS WILL NOT COOPERATE' AND ANOTHER SUGGESTED 'FUNDING IS THE UNKNOWN WHICH WILL DETERMINE THIS'.

Q PLEASE STATE THE CASE FOR PESSIMISM.

A THE FOOD AND MATERIALS PART WILL MOSTLY BE COASTAL WATERS WHERE EACH COUNTY WILL CONTROL ITS OWN AND INTERNATIONAL COOPERATION ON THE HIGH SEAS WILL TAKE FOREVER TO NEGOTIATE.

Q WHY UNDESIRABLE AND WHY SO FAR OFF

A ..... FROM EXPOSURE AND ASSOCIATION I BELIEVE THAT IT WILL BE EXTREMELY DIFFICULT TO OBTAIN THE STRONG MANAGEMENT DIRECTION AND CONTROL NEEDED TO PRODUCE TIMELY OBJECTIVE, FOCUSED STUDY RESULTS, FROM AN INTERNATIONAL AGENCY. I RECOMMEND THAT ONE NATION UNDERTAKE THE STUDY AND SUBMIT THE RESULTS FOR INTERNATIONAL CONSIDERATION THROUGH AN INTERNATIONAL AGENCY, E.G., NATO, FAO, ETC.

501050 Q WHY SO OPTIMISTIC

A SOUND ECONOMIC BENEFITS CAN BE DEMONSTRATED. THIS WILL SPEED DEVELOPMENT.

Q PLEASE STATE THE CASE FOR PESSIMISM.

A COMMERCIAL OPERATIONS DO NOT JUSTIFY THE COST OF THE SYSTEM, AND MILITARY REQUIREMENTS FOR THIS ARE MARGINAL TOO.

S IN RESPONDING TO ROUND 2, ONE PANELIST NOTED THE NEED FOR A SHARPER DEFINITION OF THE EVENT, I.E., 'OPEN SEA OR HARBORS—INDIVIDUAL SHIPS OR ALL SHIPS'.

504020 Q PLEASE STATE THE CASE FOR PESSIMISM.

A CARGO HANDLING BY CONTAINER SHIP HAS ALREADY BEEN DEVELOPED AND IS ESPECIALLY PREVALENT IN THE CARIBBEAN. I SEE NO REASON TO COMPLICATE THIS PROCESS WITH BARGES.

504090 Q EXAMPLES (OF SYSTEMS IN OPERATION)

A THE ALPINE GEOPHYSICAL COMPANY WAS SELLING A TRANSIT-COMPATIBLE EQUIPMENT RACK FOR APPROXIMATELY $75,000 TWO YEARS AGO. THE COMPUTER CONTROL NAVIGATION SYSTEMS MAY DELAY THE AVAILABILITY OF THIS SYSTEM TO THE MERCHANT MARINE.

504130 Q PLEASE STATE THE CASE FOR PESSIMISM.

A THE HORSEPOWER REQUIREMENTS OF SHIPBOARD POWER PLANTS INCREASE APPROXIMATELY AS THE SQUARE OF THE SPEED INCREASES. THE NUCLEAR POWER PLANTS MAY SOLVE THE PHYSICAL REQUIREMENTS OF HORSEPOWER VS THE TOTAL SIZE OF THE POWER PLANT. (HOWEVER), AT THE PRESENT TIME THE UNDERWATER VEHICLES CANNOT COMPETE WITH THE SURFACE VEHICLES, SUCH AS THE AIR CUSHION SHIPS IN DEVELOPMENT FOR THE HIGH-SPEED TRANSPORTATION FUTURE IN WATER-BORNE VESSELS.

504190 Q ANY UNSURMOUNTABLE BARRIERS (TO SUPPORT YOUR PESSIMISM)

A AT THE PRESENT TIME, ELECTRO-MAGNETIC ENERGY SEEMS TO BE THE ONLY ALTERNATIVE TO THE

**Figure 4.** TRW Probe II

Reprinted by permission of The TRW Corporation.

ning group at Bell has the responsibility to identify corporate opportunities. At the time of the Delphi, these opportunities focused on merging computer and communication technology, regulatory changes introducing new competitive elements, emerging visual telecommunications markets, perceived and projected social changes, and increasing cost of investment options. The starting point for the Bell Canada Delphi was a definition of market segments that would have the most important impact on future applications of visual and data communications. The aim was to examine applications from the potential user point of view rather than from the direction of technological imperatives. An extensive literature review was undertaken before the initial questionnaires were prepared.

Subjects to be covered in the questionnaires included education, medicine, information systems, and residential markets. Participants on each panel first focused on value trends for the next thirty years. Traditionalism, hard work as a virtue, authoritarianism, involvement in society, acceptance of change, and the like were evaluated as trends, i.e., a significant increase, slight increase, no change, slight decrease, or significant decrease. The education Delphi then examined potential adoption of computerized library systems, computer-aided instruction systems, and visual display systems. The medical Delphi explored the acceptance of multiphasic screening, computer-assisted diagnosis, remote physiological monitoring, computerized medical library systems, and terminal usage. The business information processing technology study considered developments in management information systems, mini and small computers, terminals, and data processing. In addition, a Delphi was undertaken to study the future of communication services in the residential market. A question that arises in this context is the definition of an expert. Are housewives or researchers and planners the experts on the adoption of communication services in the home? The issue was resolved by establishing two competing panels, one consisting of housewives, the other of experts in "wired city" services. The steps in the study design of this Delphi were as follows:

1. Literature search
2. Assembly of panels of experts and housewives
3. Design of draft questionnaire
4. Pretesting of this questionnaire
5. Distribution of the revised questionnaire (identical to both groups)
6. Statistical analysis of first run answers
7. Preparation of supporting comments from each group
8. Design, pretest, and distribution of second round question-

naires, including not only the statistical results from each group but also the supporting comments. There was a specific request for responses on the differences between the panels and possible resolution of these differences.
9. Preparation of final analysis

Sample results from the study are shown in Figure 5.

### Smith Kline & French Laboratories

This drug company undertook a study of the future of medicine in 1968 (Bender, Strack, Ebright, and VonHaunalter, 1969). This work is divided into five main sections: biomedical research, diagnosis, medical therapy, health care, and medical education. Of the 111 outside individuals contacted by mail at the beginning of the study, 42 responded and 35 supplied usable questionnaires. The selected panel included 21 medical doctors and 14 other experts. The panelists' areas of specialty ranged from internal medicine (10) to biochemistry (5) to nutrition (1) and psychology (1). They had spent an average of 17.5 years in their present occupations. Incidentally, when outside experts are used, the response rate is commonly only a fraction of the number contacted, typically about one-third. Use of inside experts leads to a much higher fraction since these individuals consider the task as part of their job. Predictably, payment of outside panelists raises the fraction of active participation appreciably. The questionnaires in this Delphi were pretested within the company using 196 members of the R&D staff. In the first round of the extramural Delphi, 867 statements were received. Of these, 209 were used in the second round, and of the 209, consensus was achieved on 87 forecast statements.

The results were presented in a form similar to that of the 1964 RAND Corporation Delphi (see Figure 6). In an interesting variation, the consensus statements for the 1978–1983 period were combined into a scenario that attempted to provide a more vivid image of the education, training, practice, and research of a student entering medical school in 1978 and beginning practice in the early 1980s. Another useful addition was the comparison of the dates of achievement (median dates) obtained in this study with those of the RAND study (Gordon and Helmer, 1964) and the intramural company study. It was found, for example, that the study with outside experts was consistently more optimistic than the other two, providing earlier dates for the median time estimates of the events described. Agreement between the estimates of the extramural Delphi and the RAND forecast was generally good. On the other hand, the intramural study was considerably more pessimis-

## SHOP-FROM-HOME SERVICE

In predicting which types of products will be purchased through a Shop-from-Home system, the housewives and experts disagreed on a number of items. The summarized answers are presented below with the answers for the expected costs of such a service. Some typical comments are presented on the facing page. There appear to be significant differences in such items as produce, small and large appliances.

TYPE OF PRODUCT:

| E / H | % YES | % NO | over 20% more | 5-20% more | 0-5% more | same | 0-5% less | 5-20% less | over 20% less |
|---|---|---|---|---|---|---|---|---|---|
| meat | 48 / 58 | 52 / 42 | | | E | H | | | |
| produce | 52 / 75 | 48 / 25 | | | E | H | | | |
| other perishables (dairy, bread, etc.) | 100 / 83 | 0 / 17 | | | | E / H | | | |
| groc. dry goods | 100 / 96 | 0 / 4 | | | | E / H | | | |
| clothing | 58 / 48 | 42 / 52 | | | | E / H | | | |
| small appliances | 74 / 96 | 26 / 4 | | | | E / H | | | |
| drugs and cosmetics | 90 / 75 | 10 / 25 | | | E | H | | | |
| large appliances | 47 / 79 | 53 / 21 | | | E | H | | | |

NOTE: Shaded area represents significant differences between panels
E = Expert Panel: median or percentage response.
H = Housewife Panel: median or percentage response.
Do you wish to change any response? Could you comment on the differences between the two groups? Do you have any concluding comments

ROUND II COMMENTS

(Cont'd.)

**Figure 5.** Results of a Bell Canada Delphi Study

## SHOP-FROM-HOME (CONTINUED)

**EXPERTS**                                    **HOUSEWIVES**

The panelists had the following generally favorable comments on the service and its expected costs.

1. "Will succeeds only if it offers an econonic advantage (savings on sales people, expensive store space, electricity and display, etc.)"

2. "Assumption — meat and produce supplied from a familiar supplier and good previous experience."

3. "Better price and product comparisons can allow the purchaser to save money as well as time."

1. "A useful service for those living in suburbs or remote rural areas whose access to cities and stores is difficult, also for elderly people."

2. "I don't think it should cost any more because it would not need a huge store or many salesclerks, and certainly shoplifting would be a thing of the past for anyone participating in the service."

3. "Small or large appliances (if brand name is known) present no problems for Shop-from-Home."

These comments reflect some of the typical reservations about the service:

1. "Meat, produce — these items are bought by feeling, smelling, and seeing the specific items in question and comparing them to the others available in the display. This cannot be done remotely, hence the continued existance of meat markets, fruit stands, etc."

2. "Insuring quality will raise the price of perishables above attractive cost."

3. "People will expect large cost reductions for appliances in return for not being able to see the merchandise. . .Several visits to warehouses will be typical even with home shopping."

1. "For most housewives, shopping is a diversion and a break in a routine."

2. "Meat and produce — Individual specific quantities required; bult packaging not always desirable."

3. "The cost of these items in our daily living budget is expensive enough as it is; if it would cost more to buy these things at home, not many people would take advantage of it unless they were unable to get out of the house. . . Clothing and large appliances would be difficult with this service; with clothing you like to examine the fabric to see how well it is made; with large appliances you would want to discuss with the salesman the pro's-con's of the appliance."

Source: Bedford, Questionnaire, pp. 2-3

SOURCE: Reproduced from *The Delphi Method,* edited by Harold A. Linstone and Murray Turoff, with permission of publishers, Addison-Wesley, Advanced Book Program, Reading, Massachusetts, U.S.A.

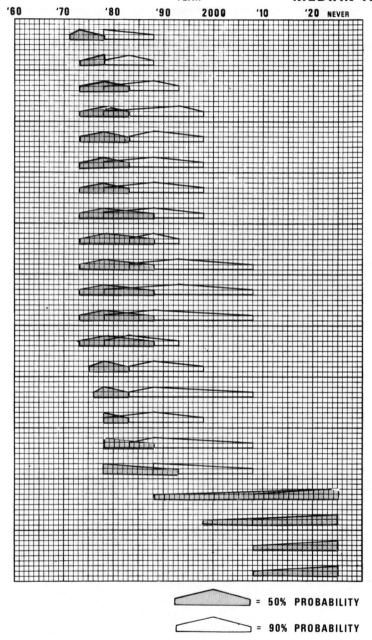

Figure 6. Smith Kline & French Delphi

Reprinted by permission of Smith Kline & French Laboratories.

# RESEARCH
# QUARTILES

5. IDENTIFICATION OF NEW ENZYMES AND ENZYME SYSTEMS INVOLVED IN HEALTH AND DISEASE.*

3. IDENTIFICATION OF A NUMBER OF DISEASES AS AUTOIMMUNE STATES.

4. PRACTICAL KNOWLEDGE OF THE EFFECT OF AGING AND/OR ENVIRONMENT ON IMMUNOLOGIC CAPACITY.

13. SYNTHESIS OF NEW VIRUS FORMS.

23. USEFUL UNDERSTANDING OF THE EFFECT OF CONTACT WITH EXOGENOUS TOXIC BY-PRODUCTS OF CIVILIZATION ON THE LIFE PROCESS.

47. SATISFACTORY METHOD FOR PRESERVATION OF ORGANS, IN VITRO.

66. MECHANISM OF GALLSTONE FORMATION.

7. INDUCTION OF ENZYME SYNTHESIS IN VIVO BY CHEMICALS AND/OR INFECTIOUS AGENTS.

11. TRANSMISSION OF GENETIC INFORMATION VIA VIRUSES.

27. MUCH BETTER UNDERSTANDING OF CAUSAL RELATIONSHIP BETWEEN WHAT WE CHOOSE TO DO AND WHAT DISEASES WE GET, i.e., THE EFFECTS OF SMOKING, DRINKING, ETC.

41. CREATION/SYNTHESIS OF A LIVING VIRUS.

62. CONTROL OF BIOLOGIC SYSTEMS INVOLVED IN BLOOD PRESSURE MAINTENANCE AND HEART RATE.

64. AN UNDERSTANDING OF THE PRECISE ROLE OF ACID IN GI EROSION AND ULCERATION.

12. DETAILED DATA ON CHROMOSOMAL ABNORMALITIES AND CORRELATION WITH DISEASE.

17. COMPLETE UNDERSTANDING OF ACTIVE TRANSPORT PHENOMENA (i.e., SODIUM PUMP, ETC.)

65. AN UNDERSTANDING OF THE INTESTINAL FLORA AND ELECTROLYTE AND WATER TRANSPORT IN THE INTESTINE.

24. DETERMINATION OF THE EFFECT OF SUCH FACTORS AS STRESS, NOISE, RADIATION, CLIMATE AND SOCIAL STATUS ON SUSCEPTIBILITY AND RESISTANCE TO DISEASE.

51. DEFINITION OF NATURE OF RECEPTOR SITES FOR DRUGS.

35. ELECTRONIC CONTROL OF HUMAN BEHAVIOR.*

39. COMPLETE CONTROL OF MENTAL DEVELOPMENT.*

43. CREATION/SYNTHESIS OF A LIVING ORGANISM.*

34. COMPLETE CHEMICAL CONTROL OF HUMAN BEHAVIOR.*

* CONSENSUS AT BOTH THE 50% AND 90% PROBABILITY LEVELS.

tic. A possible explanation is that the company personnel have a more realistic appreciation of the difficulties in implementing new concepts and therefore tend to provide more conservative dates.

GOVERNMENT AND INSTITUTES

*National Materials Advisory Board*

An interesting Delphi was conducted in 1970 for the U.S. ferroalloy industry by the National Materials Advisory Board of the National Academy of Science and Engineering (Goldstein, 1975). The board was concerned about a possible shortage of certain strategic and critical materials for the next decade and used Delphi as a means of assessing the implications of technological change on trends of ferroalloys. There were three rounds and three sections in each round: steel, alloys, and key developments.

Trend lines were presented to the respondents in the first two sections. The task of the panelists was to extend the past trends into the future, from 1969 to 1985, and to indicate reasons for the trend behavior (see Figure 7).

This format reminds us that it is often convenient to classify forecasts into two types: events and trends. The original Delphi work concerned itself entirely with event forecasts. In this study, we see the application to trend forecasts.

Thirty-four panelists were selected from industry, government, universities, institutes, and trade publications. Specifically, for each graph the first round probed the following questions: (1) how reliable does the respondent consider his graph extension to be, (2) what key developments does the respondent assume in making his extension, and (3) what other developments might result in major changes of the extension. A flowchart of the steel-making process was also presented to the panelists in Section I, with figures for 1969 and requests to supply corresponding figures for 1980. The elapsed time of the entire three-round effort was forty-six weeks. The total senior professional analysis activity for the process took eighteen manweeks, professional level work thirteen, clerical tabulation and curve extrapolations fifteen, and typing seven. One interesting feature of this effort was the opportunity to compare a Delphi with a more conventional panel study. The same subject was studied by a conventional committee having no interaction with the Delphi until both exercises were completed. There were several significant differences in the results: (1) the conventional report led to very precise agreement reflected in single valued forecasts, whereas the Delphi presented ranges that suggested the uncertainty, (2) the committee developed consensus recommendations while the Delphi panels did not, (3) the committee limited itself more narrowly to the

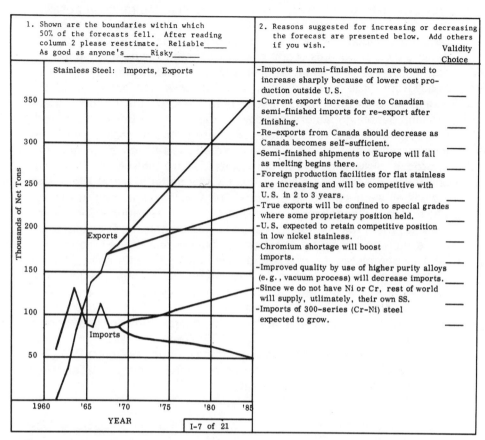

1. Shown are the boundaries within which 50% of the forecasts fell. After reading column 2 please reestimate. Reliable_____ As good as anyone's_____ Risky_____

2. Reasons suggested for increasing or decreasing the forecast are presented below. Add others if you wish.                Validity Choice

Stainless Steel: Imports, Exports

-Imports in semi-finished form are bound to increase sharply because of lower cost production outside U.S. ___
-Current export increase due to Canadian semi-finished imports for re-export after finishing.
-Re-exports from Canada should decrease as Canada becomes self-sufficient. ___
-Semi-finished shipments to Europe will fall as melting begins there. ___
-Foreign production facilities for flat stainless are increasing and will be competitive with U.S. in 2 to 3 years. ___
-True exports will be confined to special grades where some proprietary position held. ___
-U.S. expected to retain competitive position in low nickel stainless. ___
-Chromium shortage will boost imports. ___
-Improved quality by use of higher purity alloys (e.g., vacuum process) will decrease imports. ___
-Since we do not have Ni or Cr, rest of world will supply, utlimately, their own SS. ___
-Imports of 300-series (Cr-Ni) steel expected to grow. ___

I-7 of 21

**Figure 7.** Form for Trend Extrapolation

Ref.: Goldstein, 1975.

SOURCE: Reproduced from *The Delphi Method,* edited by Harold A. Linstone and Murray Turoff, with permission of publishers, Addison-Wesley, Advanced Book Program, Reading, Massachusetts, U.S.A.

subject area than the Delphi panel, and (4) the committee presented background information systematically while the Delphi panel provided only random background data.

### NATIONAL COORDINATING COUNCIL ON DRUG EDUCATION

A Delphi on national drug abuse policy was undertaken in 1974 for the National Coordinating Council on Drug Education (Jillson, 1975).

The objectives of the study were (1) to develop the range of possible national drug abuse policy options, (2) to explore applications of the Delphi methodology to this and other areas of social policy, and (3) to explore the possibilities of applying the technique on as-needed and on ongoing bases. The study specifically set out to explore drug abuse policy from three perspectives: (1) the top-down approach, i.e., establishing national drug abuse policy objectives, (2) the bottom-up approach, identifying factors that control the transition between the general population and various degrees of drug use and deciding which of these are important and can be affected, and (3) an issue-oriented approach deriving policies from issues that are the subject of current controversy. More than 100 potential respondents were listed, and invitations were sent to 45 persons. Thirty-eight responded positively. The first round questionnaire focused on (1) the development of objectives, (2) the transition matrix, (3) policy statements, and (4) additional items such as self-rating of expertise. Twenty-four of the respondents actually completed the first round. The median time for completion of the round was determined to be 2.25 hours. The second questionnaire included sections on national drug abuse policy objectives and policy issue statements. The third questionnaire focused on national policy objectives and the transition matrix. The general study design is shown in Table 1.

The cost of completing a study of this type ranges from $15,000 to $40,000, assuming a nine- to twelve-month effort. This cost is relatively small in terms of the output obtained.

## *National Commission for the Protection of Human Subjects of Biomedical and Behavioral Research*

A very recent effort is a policy Delphi entitled "A Comprehensive Study of the Ethical, Legal and Social Implications of Advances in Biomedical and Behavioral Research and Technology," conducted jointly by Policy Research Inc. and the Center for Policy Assessment at the New Jersey Institute of Technology. This study is responsive to a section of the National Research Act which calls for "an analysis and evaluation of scientific and technological advances in past, present, and projected biological, behavioral, and medical research and services . . . and evaluation of implications of public policy of such findings." This Delphi is one of the most sophisticated instruments run in the United States. A single round questionnaire is a looseleaf book, and the respondent is expected to spend six hours in completing a round. He is paid $100 for his efforts per round. In the first round background papers are provided on subjects such as data banks, extension of life,

**Table 1.** The Study Design

| Perspective | First Questionnaire | Second Questionnaire | Third Questionnaire | Fourth Questionnaire | Fifth Questionnaire | Final Summary |
|---|---|---|---|---|---|---|
| Objectives ("top down") | List objectives | Rate feasibility, and desirability of objectives | Re-rate feasibility and desirability of selected objectives | | | |
| | List key indicators | Expand key indicators, perform initial rating | | Identify any contradiction in objectives and policies formulated by the three approaches | Synthesize a consistent and realistic set of national drug abuse policy options | Write a brief summary of the national drug abuse policy options identified by the study, including the normative forecasts for the key indicators |
| Transition Factors ("bottom up") | List factors, indicate direction | | Final rating of factors. Develop policy areas to affect important transition factors which can be influenced by national policy | | | Identify future policy research needs |
| Policy Issue Statements ("political") | Rate selected policy issues; develop for and against arguments. Add other important policy issues | Final rating of selected policy issues; rate for and against arguments. Rate and give arguments for and against additional policy issue statements | | | | |

Ref.: I Jillson, 1975.

and genetic screening. The evaluation part asks the respondent to consider a number of advances and their implications as well as preferences of policies with regard to research and implementation of research. A set of scenarios, each about a half page in length, is provided, and the respondent is asked to indicate the decision he would make as a policy-maker (e.g., should the drugs discussed in the scenario be marketed or prohibited?). He is also asked to determine what implications of the scenario influence his decision as well as which groups or mechanisms should participate in the resolution of the decision. We note that a policy Delphi generally cannot be confined to so-called experts. The formulation of national policy must obviously include the public at large. It is therefore important to include in the Delphi representatives of a large or a wide spectrum of vested interests, ranging from bureaucrats to minority groups.


### Michigan Sea Grant Program

An example of a regional planning Delphi is the study described by Ludlow focusing on the Grand Traverse Bay watershed region (1975). This area was selected as the focus of a pilot study to "obtain and refine an interdisciplinary group of researchers' judgments about issues and developments that should be considered when planning for intelligent management of the water resources of the Great Lakes." Further, it was considered important to convey the judgment of the researchers to the communities that would benefit from the research. Therefore, influential community leaders were included on the panel, and the Delphi operated as a true communication instrument. Specifically, two of the three panels were made up of researchers, i.e., technicians and behaviorists, and the third group comprised concerned citizens or decision-makers. Another interesting aspect of this study was the emphasis on interactions between different developments. Let us denote as item A "construction of a spray irrigation system for waste water disposal in the Grand Traverse Bay region" and item B "requirement by the State, calling for tertiary treatment of municipal sewage for Traverse City." Not content with asking for the probability of occurrence of A and B in the 1971–1980 time period and the 50 percent probability date of each, the questionnaire asked the following question: "If you were certain that B *would* occur before 1980, your estimates for A would be ———," and "If you were certain that B *would not* occur in 1971–1980, your estimates for A would be ———." We cannot ignore the fact that individual items in any Delphi are not by any means mutually independent; more likely, there are many interactions between them.

ANALYSES

The development of Delphi has predictably been accompanied by a growing body of literature devoted to analyses of the method itself. We will briefly summarize some of the significant results.

1. Dispersion as a function of remoteness of estimate: In the original RAND report as well as in subsequent work by Martino (1970), it was found that the remoteness of the forecast date and degree of dispersion are directly related. The further the median date of a forecast lies in the future, the greater is the dispersion around that date. In other words, uncertainty increases consistently with remoteness of the estimate date.

2. Accuracy of forecasts: An inherent bias in forecasting is the tendency to be pessimistic on the long-range estimates and optimistic on the short-range ones. We do not have to search far for an explanation. In a long-range situation, we assume that, if we do not know an answer to the problem, no answer exists. This is Coates' fallacy of the "argument from incompetence" (1975). On the other hand, for near term items, we do know the answer but make the optimistic assumption that implementation will be smooth and devoid of serious obstacles. Consider supersonic passenger aircraft. In 1930, a forecast would have been pessimistic. At that time, Nevil Shute Norway, a trained aeronautical engineer, forecast a cruising speed of 110 to 130 miles per hour for passenger aircraft in 1980. In 1965, we knew how to build supersonic aircraft, and such aircraft were expected to be operational by 1972—a highly optimistic forecast. Incidentally, this pattern suggests that there should be a time span for which forecasts are most accurate, i.e., at the point from which we shift from being pessimistic to optimistic. Unfortunately, we do not have enough data to give precise guidance on the correction of this bias. This is an appropriate time to remind readers that accuracy is hardly the best measure of the "rightness" of a forecast, Delphi or other; a good forecast is one that provides useful insight and guidance to the planner and decision maker. (Some of the most valuable forecasts have been "wrong" by virtue of being self-defeating.)

3. Delphi statements: Inevitably, the statements in a Delphi exercise reflect the cultural attitudes, subjective biases, and knowledge of those who formulate them. In their original study, Gordon and Helmer began the first round with a blank questionnaire (see Figure 1) to minimize the bias of the exercise monitors. Every high school student knows that multiple choice examinations require insight into the teacher's mode of thought as well as the substance of the question. A student who knows too much is at a disadvantage, just as a student who knows too little is

handicapped. In a Delphi exercise, statements may be too concise, leading to excessive variations and interpretations, or they may be too lengthy, requiring the assimilation of too many elements. Salancik, Wenger, and Helfer (1971) have probed this question and have found that there is a "right" length for Delphi statements, i.e., a length that leads to a maximum in the amount of information obtained. The definition of information used here is that of information theory (bits). Low and high numbers of words yield low consensus, with intermediate-length statements producing the highest consensus. In a particular case which they examined, twenty- to twenty-five-word statements formed the peak in the distribution. While this result should not be generalized, it does underscore the care that must be exercised in developing Delphi statements for use by the panelists.

4. Basis for respondents' intuitive forecasts: In another study, Salancik (1973) has examined the hypothesis that panelists in a forecasting Delphi assimilate input on feasibility, benefits, and potential costs of an event in an addictive fashion to estimate its probable date of occurrence. He finds that the more feasible, beneficial, or economically viable a concept is judged, the earlier it is forecast to occur.

5. Self-rating of experts: Dalkey, Brown, and Cochran (1969) have tackled another aspect of Delphi: the expertise of the respondents. With a given group of panelists, we might consider two ways of improving its accuracy: iterating responses or selecting a more expert subgroup. The latter process implies an ability to identify such a subgroup, for example, by self-rating. However, the choice of a subgroup itself brings with it a potential degradation in accuracy as a result of the statistically reduced group size. Thus, in resorting to a subgroup we have two counteracting trends. From their experimentation, Dalkey, Brown, and Cochran have found that self-rating is a meaningful basis for identifying expertise, and that selection of expert subgroups improves the accuracy to a somewhat greater degree than does feedback or iteration. Dalkey has found that a suitable minimum panel size is seven; accuracy deteriorates rapidly with smaller sizes and improves more slowly with large numbers.

6. Opinion stability as a method of consensus measurement: Scheibe, Skutsch, and Schofer find that consensus in a Delphi should not be measured by the percentage of votes that fall within a prescribed range, e.g., when the interquartile range is no larger than two units on a ten-unit scale. Rather, the stability of the respondents' vote distribution curve over successive rounds provides a superior measure. The authors determine that marginal changes of less than 15 percent offer a useful definition of stability. If a round provides less than 15 percent change from the preceding round, the exercise should be stopped. Use of this stability measure as a stopping criterion also preserves well-

defined disagreements that may exist. Today we are often more concerned with determining the degree of polarization of respondents than consensus. Viewing the technique as a communication concept, *we no longer judge success of a Delphi by the degree of consensus obtained* (Scheibe, Skutsch, and Schofer, 1975).

7. The role of dogmatism: It might be expected that highly dogmatic individuals would not alter their responses from one round to another. In fact, the situation is more complex. As Mulgrave and Ducanis (1975) have shown, a highly dogmatic individual will remain with his initial response, provided he considers himself an expert on the item. If he does not consider himself highly knowledgeable, he will very quickly move to the median of the group, i.e., accept the group response as an authoritative one.

## CRITIQUE AND FINAL COMMENTS

That Delphi has spawned criticism as well as ardent support is a healthy sign. Ironically, a major critique has emanated from the RAND Corporation—Sackman's report, "Delphi Assessment: Expert Opinion, Forecasting and Group Process." He proclaims that "the future is far too important for the human species to be left to fortunetellers using new versions of old crystal balls. It is time for the oracle to move out and science to move in" (1974).

For Sackman science means psychometrically trained social scientists. His tradition-bound attitude is not uncommon; we also find it in the widely held illusions that science is "objective," that only data-based or model-based inquiring systems are legitimate, and that subjective or Bayesian probability is heretical. Unfortunately, when faced with new paradigms, orthodoxy often responds with sweeping condemnations and unwitting distortions. Sackman cites poorly executed applications of Delphi (and there are many) and ignores significant supportive research such as that briefly outlined in the last section. Coates offers the opinion that Delphi is a method of last resort in dealing with extremely complex problems for which there are no adequate models. As such,

one should expect very little of it compared to applicable analytical techniques. One should expect a great deal of it as a technique of last resort in laying bare some crucial issues on a subject for which a last resort technique is required. . . . If one believes that the Delphi technique is of value not in the search for public knowledge but in the search for public wisdom; not in the search for individual data but in the search for deliberative judgment, one can only conclude that Sackman missed the point (1975).

For a recent debate (as well as new work) on the Delphi method, the reader is referred to an issue of the journal *Technological Forecasting and Social Change* (Volume 7, Number 2, 1975).

Finally, the Delphi designer should keep several major concerns in view.

1. Discounting the future: We all use a discount rate in viewing the future (and the past). A crisis twenty years from now is not nearly as significant to us as the same crisis next month. We must keep in mind, however, that individuals discount the future at different rates and that this attitude may be reflected in the Delphi responses. A person at the bottom of Maslow's human values pyramid will discount environmental pollution much more heavily than someone near the top. The poor, for whom survival is a daily challenge, are hardly going to lose much sleep over a pollution or population crisis twenty years in the future (Linstone and Turoff, 1975, p. 574). We also find that a Delphi participant or any forecaster is influenced more strongly by recent events than those in the distant past. This problem is discussed in more detail by Tversky and Kahneman (1974).

2. The simplification urge: We prefer certainty to uncertainty and simplicity to complexity. Typically, we forecast by taking one or a few innovations and fitting them in a mental image into an environment set in the familiar structure context of the past and present. We do not visualize a future situation in its own holistic pattern where change has had a pervasive influence. Cross-impact analysis is of some help, but it by no means eliminates the difficulty. Intuitive procedures such as Delphi depend heavily on subjective probability assessments. As Tversky and Kahneman have shown, human beings have a tendency to ignore prior probabilities when worthless or irrelevant information is added. They also confuse desirability and familiarity with probability (i.e., indulge in wishful thinking), so that they find a reasonable sounding scenario with "more of the same" highly likely, even though there is little evidence to support such a forecast.

3. Illusory expertise: We have witnessed many instances in which the alleged expert proves to be a poor forecaster. One reason is obvious. The expert tends to be a specialist and thus views the forecast in a setting that is, in fact, not the most appropriate one. For example, the low aircraft speed projected for 1980 in the 1930s was based on a continuation of the use of reciprocating engines with propellers. The forecasters failed to realize that the task was not to build better reciprocating engines but to move people by air. Technologists have consistently underestimated the complexity and cost of new systems and have ignored nontechnological factors. We find a curious ahistoricity in the outlook of most scientists and technologists, together with a tendency for inbreeding. In Delphi, inbreeding occurs when a panelist is asked to suggest the names of other possible participants and pro-

poses fellow scientists who have the same technological and cultural background.

4. Sloppy execution: The preceding discussion makes it clear that there are many ways to do a poor job. In that respect, Delphi is no different from other analysis methods. We hope that this brief survey will encourage the potential user to probe the technique carefully before he ventures forward to an application of his own.

5. Format bias: It should be recognized that, particularly for policy Delphis, the format of the questionnaire may be unsuitable to some potential societal participants. The reasoning is similar to that which leads to rejection of the use of IQ tests or other multiple choice tests for certain groups. The Delphi questionnaire, like the typical written test or the conference, assumes a certain cultural background. Those with significantly different backgrounds find it exceedingly difficult to respond as requested. They may give the feedback they believe will please the inquirers, or they may not respond at all. One constructive idea is the use of visual statements, i.e., pictures in the questionnaires (Adelson and Aroni, 1975).

6. Manipulation of Delphi: If Delphi is indeed a communication technique, we should not be surprised that it is possible to manipulate it for deception. The responses of the first round can be altered by the monitors in the hope of moving the second round responses in a desired direction. One possible way to avoid such manipulation is to involve the "subjects," i.e., the panelists themselves, in the staff activities. The difficulty is to do so without compromising the anonymity of the responses.

In conclusion, we suggest that Delphi offers a powerful instrument for group communication. While it is not a panacea, it is a very useful method of last resort for the forecaster.

## REFERENCES

Adelson, A., and S. Aroni. 1975. "Differential Images of the Future." In H. A. Linstone and M. Turoff (eds.), *The Delphi Method: Techniques and Applications.* Reading, Mass.C Addison-Wesley Publishing Co., 433–462.

Bender, A. D., A. E. Strack, T. W. Ebright, and G. VonHaunalter. 1969. "A Delphic Study of the Future of Medicine." Philadelphia: Smith Kline & French Laboratories.

Coates, J. F. 1975. "Review of Sackman Report." *Technological Forecasting and Social Change,* Volume 7, Number 2, 193–194.

Dalkey, N., and O. Helmer. 1963. "An Experimental Application of the Delphi Method to the Use of Experts." *Management Science,* Volume 9, Number 3, 458.

———, B. Brown, and S. W. Cochran. 1969. *The Delphi Method,* III: *Use of Self-Ratings to Improve Group Estimates.* Santa Monica, Calif.: RAND Corporation.

Day, L. H. 1975. "Delphi Research in the Corporate Environment." In H. A.

Linstone and M. Turoff (eds.), *The Delphi Method: Techniques and Applications.* Reading, Mass.: Addison-Wesley Publishing Co., 168–194.

Forrester, J. 1971. *World Dynamics.* Cambridge, Mass.: Wright-Allen Press (particularly Chapters 5 and 6).

Goldstein, N. 1975. "A Delphi on the Future of the Steel and Ferroalloy Industries." In H. A. Linstone and M. Turoff (eds.), *The Delphi Method: Techniques and Applications.* Reading, Mass.: Addison-Wesley Publishing Co., 210–226.

Gordon, T. J., and H. Hayward. 1968. "Initial Experiments for the Cross-Impact Matrix Method of Forecasting." *Futures,* Volume 1, Number 2, 100–116.

———, and O. Helmer. 1964. "Report on a Long Range Forecasting Study." RAND Paper P-2982. Santa Monica, Calif.: RAND Corporation.

Helmer, O. 1972. "On the Future State of the Union." Report R-27. Menlo Park, Calif.: Institute for the Future,

Jillson, I. A. 1975. "The National Drug-Abuse Policy Delphi: Progress Report and Findings to Date." In H. A. Linstone and M. Turoff (eds.), *The Delphi Method: Techniques and Applications.* Reading, Mass.: Addison-Wesley Publishing Co., 124–159.

Kane, J. 1975. "A Primer for a New Cross-Impact Language—KSIM." In H. A. Linstone and M. Turoff (eds.), *The Delphi Method: Techniques and Applications.* Reading, Mass., Addison-Wesley Publishing Co., 369–382.

Linstone, H. A., and M. Turoff (eds.). 1975. *The Delphi Method: Techniques and Applications.* Reading, Mass.: Addison-Wesley Publishing Co.

Ludlow, J. 1975. "Delphi Inquiries and Knowledge Utilization." In H. A. Linstone and M. Turoff (eds.), *The Delphi Method: Techniques and Applications.* Reading, Mass.: Addison-Wesley Publishing Co., 102–123.

Mulgrave, N. W., and A. J. Ducanis. 1975. "Propensity to Change Responses in a Delphi Round as a Function of Dogmatism." In H. A. Linstone and M. Turoff (eds.), *The Delphi Method: Techniques and Applications.* Reading, Mass., Addison-Wesley Publishing Co., 288–290.

Sackman, H. 1974. "Delphi Assessment: Expert Opinion, Forecasting and Group Process." R-1283-PR. Santa Monica, Calif.: RAND Corporation.

Salancik, J. R. 1973. "Assimilation of Aggregated Inputs into Delphi Forecasts: A Regression Analysis." *Technological Forecasting and Social Change,* Volume 5, Number 3, 243–248.

———, W. Wenger, and E. Helfer. 1971. "The Construction of Delphi Event Statements." *Technological Forecasting and Social Change,* Volume 3, Number 1, 65–73.

Scheibe, M., M. Skutsch, and J. Schofer. 1975. "Experiments in Delphi Methodology." In H. A. Linstone and M. Turoff (eds.), *The Delphi Method: Techniques and Applications.* Reading, Mass.: Addison-Wesley Publishing Co., 262–287.

"TRW's Probe of the Future." 1969. 14 volumes. Redondo Beach, Calif.: TRW Corporation.

Tversky A., and D. Kahneman. 1974. "Judgment under Uncertainty: Heuristics and Biases." *Science* (September 27), 1124–1131.

JOHN G. STOVER
and THEODORE J. GORDON

# Cross-Impact Analysis

A basic limitation of many forecasting methods is that they produce only isolated forecasts; that is, events and trends are projected one by one, without explicit reference to their possible influence on each other. Most events and developments however, are in some way connected with other events and developments. A single event, such as the production of power from the first atomic reactor, was made possible by a complex history of antecedent scientific, technological, political, and economic developments. In its turn, the production of energy from the first atomic reactor provided an intellectual conception that influenced and shaped many of the events and developments which followed. In a sense, history is a focusing of many apparently diverse and unrelated occurrences that permit or cause singular events and developments. From these flow an ever-widening tree of downstream effects that interact with yet other events and developments.

One approach to capturing these interactions is the construction of a model, a mathematical description of the important variables and the ways in which they interact. Models, however, usually require large expenditures of time and money to construct and often are limited to particular disciplines. Thus, although we have an abundance of models concerned with problems of special interest in economics, sociology, political science, and engineering, only a few describe the interrelationships among factors from these and other domains.

The search for a method to deal with these problems has led to the development of cross-impact analysis. This technique is designed to study the effects on the probabilities of events of the interactions of those events with each other. It is used to analyze the numerous chains of impact that can occur (as one event affects a second event, which in turn affects a third event, which in turn affects a fourth event, and so on) and to determine the overall effect of these chains on the probability that each event will occur by a specified time.

Because of the flexibility of cross-impact analysis (it can be applied to a wide variety of problems) and the ease of applying it, it has become a widely used technique of futures research. It has been used in studies of market and product opportunities, foreign policy issues, institutional goals, communications, natural resources, defense, ecology, education, and many other subjects.

## INITIAL DEVELOPMENT

The concept of cross-impact analysis was first developed by Theodore J. Gordon and Olaf Helmer in 1966. The first experiments with the method were reported by Gordon and Hayward in 1968. The basic concept of the technique is that the occurrence of an event will affect the likelihood that other events will occur. Consider, for example, the following four events:

1. A new war occurs in the Middle East.
2. A new Arab embargo of oil exports to the United States takes place.
3. Legislation is passed setting efficiency standards for new automobiles.
4. Twenty percent of new cars sold in the United States are electric.

There are obvious linkages among these events: the outbreak of a new war would make another embargo more likely, consumer acceptance of the electric car might reduce the likelihood of legislation setting efficiency standards. In order to analyze the effects of these linkages, three types of relationships were defined to specify the linkages between two events:

—*Unrelated:* The occurrence of one event does not affect the probability of the second.
—*Enhancing:* The occurrence of one event increases the probability of the second either by enabling it to occur or by provoking its occurrence.
—*Inhibiting:* The occurrence of the first event decreases the probability of the second either by rendering it infeasible or impractical or by blocking or preventing its occurrence.

Of course, enhancing or inhibiting relationships may also be of different strengths, such that a very strong enhancing relationship might exist between two events and a weak enhancing relationship between others.

The linkages among events can be summarized and presented in the form of a cross-impact matrix. The example in Figure 1 shows how the linkages might be estimated for four example events.

In this matrix, enhancing impacts are displayed as positive numbers, with the size of the number denoting the strength of the effect. Inhibiting impacts are indicated by negative numbers and no impact by "0."

The effect on this event would be:

| If this event occurs: | 1 | 2 | 3 | 4 |
|---|---|---|---|---|
| 1. New War in Middle East | | +4 | 0 | 0 |
| 2. New embargo on oil shipments to U.S. | 0 | | +1 | +1 |
| 3. Automobile efficiency standards are set by legislation | 0 | 0 | | +2 |
| 4. Twenty percent of new cars are electric | 0 | 0 | −2 | |

**Figure 1.** Linkage Among Events Displayed in a Cross-Impact Matrix

Thus, the matrix in Figure 1 indicates that the occurrence of a new war in the Middle East (event 1) would greatly increase the likelihood of a new oil embargo but would have no effect on the legislation of efficiency standards or the sales of electric cars. A new embargo (event 2) would slightly increase the likelihood of efficiency standards and electric car sales, while increased sales of electric cars might decrease the likelihood of efficiency legislation.

Several chains of impact can be identified from this matrix:

- The occurrence of war in the Middle East can lead to an embargo which can lead to the setting of efficiency standards which increase sales of electric cars.
- War can lead to an embargo which can directly affect electric car sales.
- Efficiency standards might be imposed regardless of a war or an embargo and might lead to increased sales of electric cars.
- Increased sales of electric cars can make efficiency standards unnecessary.

In order to evaluate the combined effect of these impacts, Gordon and Hayward proposed the following relationship

$$Pn' = KS \frac{t - tm}{t} Pn^2 + \left(1 - KS \frac{t - tm}{t}\right) Pn$$

where: $Pn'$ = probability of occurrence of event $n$ at some time after the occurrence of event $m$

$Pn$ = probability of occurrence of event $n$ before the occurrence of event $m$

$K$ = +1 if impact of event $m$ on event $n$ is inhibiting, $-1$ if impact is enhancing

$S$ = the strength of the impact (designated as a number between 0 and 1)

$t$ = the time for which probabilities are being estimated

$t_m$ = the time in the future when event $m$ occurs

While this formulation is entirely arbitrary, it does satisfy the conditions of producing larger values of $Pn'$ as the strength of the enhancing impact increases, and the reverse for inhibiting impacts. It also yields larger impacts for greater time differences between the occurrence of the impacting event and the time period being tested.

In order to test the cross-impact concept, Gordon and Hayward performed a retrospective analysis of the decision to employ the Minuteman missile. They specified twenty-eight events that were related to the deployment decision. Initial probabilities of occurrence were specified for each event, and the event impacts were estimated as they would have been estimated in 1950. This information was used in a computer program to evaluate the impacts in the matrix. The program selected an event and, using random numbers, determined whether the event "occurred." If it did, the probabilities of the remaining items were adjusted and the play repeated for the next item selected. This process was repeated until all twenty-eight items were decided. This constituted one run of the matrix. One thousand separate runs were performed, and the results were averaged to yield the final output. The final result was a new set of probabilities for each of the events, reflecting the combined influences of the events on each other. Initial and final probabilities for the ten most affected events are shown in Table 1.

The historical test, while far from constituting rigorous validation of the technique, at least produced results that were consistent with expectations, lending some credence to the belief that cross-impact concepts would be useful in analyzing event probabilities.

## CURRENT APPROACHES TO CROSS-IMPACT ANALYSIS

The techniques for implementing the concept of cross-impact analysis have changed since the initial development. The evolution of the technique has not followed a single path but has produced a variety of

**Table 1. Historical Test of Cross-Impact Technique**

| Item | Initial Probability | Adjusted Probability |
|------|------|------|
| 1. Minuteman authorized | 0.20 | 0.729 |
| 2. Polaris authorized | 0.20 | 0.717 |
| 3. Missile gap increases | 0.50 | 0.33 (Note: negative shift) |
| 4. Missile gap reduced | 0.50 | 0.958 |
| 5. Light warhead technology | 0.70 | 0.941 |
| 6. Nose cone technology | 0.30 | 0.523 |
| 7. Mobility needed | 0.30 | 0.511 |
| 8. Titan II authorized | 0.20 | 0.396 |
| 9. U.S.S.R. H-bomb exploded | 0.80 | 0.990 |
| 10. Nautilus under power | 0.80 | 0.956 |

different methods for constructing, utilizing, and evaluating cross-impact matrices. One of the most widely used methods will be described in detail, and the major variations will be discussed briefly.

The seven major steps in the use of cross-impact analysis for evaluating future situations are:

1. Define the events to be included in the analysis.
2. Estimate the initial probability of each event.
3. Estimate the conditional (or impacted) probabilities for each event pair.
4. Perform a calibration run of the cross-impact matrix.
5. Define the policies, actions, or sensitivity tests to be run with the matrix.
6. Perform the cross-impact calculations for the policies, actions for sensitivity tests.
7. Evaluate results.

The first step, to define the events to be included in the study, can be crucial to the success of the exercise. Any influences not included in the event set will, of course, be completely excluded from the study. On the other hand, the inclusion of events that are not pertinent can complicate the analysis unnecessarily. Since the number of event pair interactions to be considered is equal to $n^2 - n$ (where $n$ is the number of events), the number of interactions to be considered increases rapidly as the number of events increases. Most studies include between ten and forty events.

An initial set of events is usually compiled by conducting a literature search and interviewing key experts in the fields being studied. This initial set is then refined by combining some closely related events, eliminating others, and refining the wording for others.

Once the event set is determined, the next step is to estimate the initial probability of each event. These probabilities indicate the likelihood that each event will occur by some future year. In the initial application of cross-impact and in some current applications, the probability of each event is specified assuming that the other events have not occurred. Thus, the probability of each event is judged in isolation, and the result of the cross-impact analysis is to adjust those initial probabilities for the influences of the other events.

The other approach to estimating initial probabilities assumes that the expert making the probability judgments has in his mind a view of the future that serves as a background for his judgments. Thus, in estimating the probability of each event, he takes into account the probabilities of the other events. In effect, he is cross-impacting the events in his mind, and to ask him to disregard the effects of other events would be to invalidate much of his expertise. In this approach, the initial probabilities and impact judgments reflect the expert's view of the expected future situation. The cross-impact runs are used to show how changes in that situation (the introduction of new policies or actions, the unexpected occurrence of an event, and the like) would affect the entire set of events.

These initial probabilities may be estimated by individual experts but more commonly are estimated by groups containing experts from the various disciplines covered by the events. Delphi questionnaires or interviews also can be used to collect these judgments.

The next step in the analysis is to estimate the conditional probability matrix. In the early cross-impact technique, an estimate of strength and direction of impact was made by specifying a number between $-1$ and $+1$. This impact number was then used in the quadratic equation presented earlier to calculate the impact. Current versions pose the impact question somewhat differently. Impacts are now estimated in response to the question "If event $m$ occurs, what is the new probability of event $n$?" Thus, if the probability of event $n$ was originally judged to be 0.50, it might be judged that the probability of event $n$ would be 0.75, if event $m$ occurred. The entire cross-impact matrix is completed by asking this question for each combination of occurring event and impact event.

When the initial probabilities have been estimated with reference to the other event probabilities (that is, not considering each event in isolation), there is some additional information that enters into the estimation of the impact matrix. For each event combination, there are bounds on the conditional probabilities that can exist. Selwyn Enzer, while with the Institute for the Future, first presented the case for these limits in the cross-impact literature (1972). These limits can be illustrated with a simple example. Suppose we considered two events, *n* and *m*, event *n* with a 50 percent chance of occurring in the next year and event *m* with a 60 percent chance of occurring. Thus, out of 100 hypothetical futures, event *n* would occur in 50 of them and event *m* in 60. Obviously, events *m* and *n* would occur together in at least 10 of the futures.

In this case, in answer to the question "If event *m* occurs, what is the new probability of event *n*?" We are limited in our responses. A conditional probability of 0 for event *n* is impossible, for example, since if event *n* never occurred when event *m* occurred, the "overlap" of 10 combined occurrences would not be possible. The initial probability estimates specified that event *n* occurs in 50 percent of our hypothetical futures. Since, in this approach, it was assumed that the estimate of 0.50 for the original probability of event *n* included a consideration of the 0.60 probability of event *m*, an inconsistency in judgment has occurred. Either the original probability estimate of event *n* does not actually take into account the 0.60 probability of event *m*, or the probability of event *n* given the occurrence of event *m* is not equal to 0. One of these judgments is incorrect because it leads to an inconsistency, but only the participants in the analysis can decide which judgment must be changed. They may decide that the initial probability estimate for event *n* did not fully account for the expected influence of event *m*, or they may decide that their original estimate of the probability of event *n* given the occurrence of *m* was too high. In either case, they have learned something about events *n* and *m* because of the cross-impact exercise. This learning process that occurs while the cross-impact matrix is being estimated is one of the major benefits of performing a cross-impact analysis.

The range of conditional probabilities that will satisfy this consistency requirement can be easily calculated. The initial probability of an event can be expressed as follows:

$$P(1) = P(2) \times P(1/2) + P(\bar{2}) \times P(1/\bar{2}) \qquad (1)$$

where: $P(1)$ = probability that event 1 will occur
$P(2)$ = probability that event 2 will occur
$P(1/2)$ = probability of event 1 given the occurrence of event 2
$P(\bar{2})$ = probability that event 2 will not occur
$P(1/\bar{2})$ = probability of event 1 given the nonoccurrence of event 2

This expression can be rearranged to solve for P(1/2):

$$P(1/2) = \frac{P(1) - P(\bar{2}) \times P(1/\bar{2})}{P(2)}$$

Since P(1) and P(2) are already known (the initial probability estimates) and P($\bar{2}$) is simply 1 − P(2), only P(1/2) and P(1/$\bar{2}$), the conditional probabilities, are unknown. By substituting zero for P(1/$\bar{2}$) (the
smallest value it could possibly have), the maximum value for P(1/2)
can be calculated. Thus

$$P(1/2) \leq \frac{P(1)}{P(2)} \tag{3}$$

Similarly, by substituting 1.0 for P(1/$\bar{2}$) (the largest possible value for
P(1/$\bar{2}$)), the minimum value for P(1/2) can be calculated:

$$P(1/2) \geq \frac{P(1) - 1 + P(2)}{P(2)} \tag{4}$$

Thus, the limits on the new probability of event 1 given the occurrence
of event 2 are:

$$\frac{P(1) - 1 + P(2)}{P(2)} \leq P(1/2) \leq \frac{P(1)}{P(2)} \tag{5}$$

Using equation (5), we can now calculate the limits for the example
used previously. If the initial probability of event *n* is 0.50 and for event
*m* is 0.60, the permissible values for the probability of event *n* given the
occurrence of event *m* are 0.17 and 0.83. Or, if the probability of event *n*
given the occurrence of event *m* is actually 1.0, then the initial probability of event *n* must be 0.60 or greater. Figure 2 presents the results of
these limits calculations for any combination of probabilities for occurring and impacted events.

Once the cross-impact matrix has been estimated, a computer program is used to perform a calibration run of the matrix. A run of the
matrix consists of randomly selecting an event for testing, comparing
its probability with a random number to decide occurrence or nonoccurrence, and calculating the impacts on all of the other events as a
result of the occurrence or nonoccurrence of the selected event. Impacts are normally calculated using odds ratios rather than the impact
formula used in the original technique. In order to apply the odds ratio
technique, the initial and conditional probabilities of the events are
converted to odds, using the following relationship

$$\text{Odds} = \frac{\text{Probability}}{\text{1-Probability}} \tag{6}$$

if each
of these
occurs

what is the probability of these events

| | E 1 .05 | E 2 .10 | E 3 .15 | E 4 .20 | E 5 .25 | E 6 .30 | E 7 .35 | E 8 .40 | E 9 .45 | E 10 .50 | E 11 .55 | E 12 .60 | E 13 .65 | E 14 .70 | E 15 .75 | E 16 .80 | E 17 .85 | E 18 .90 | E 19 .95 |
|---|---|---|---|---|---|---|---|---|---|---|---|---|---|---|---|---|---|---|---|
| **E 1 .05** (upper) | 1.00 | 1.00 | 1.00 | 1.00 | 1.00 | 1.00 | 1.00 | 1.00 | 1.00 | 1.00 | 1.00 | 1.00 | 1.00 | 1.00 | 1.00 | 1.00 | 1.00 | 1.00 | 1.00 |
| (lower) | .00 | .00 | .00 | .00 | .00 | .00 | .00 | .00 | .00 | .00 | .00 | .00 | .00 | .00 | .00 | .00 | .00 | .00 | .00 |
| **E 2 .10** (upper) | .50 | 1.00 | 1.00 | 1.00 | 1.00 | 1.00 | 1.00 | 1.00 | 1.00 | 1.00 | 1.00 | 1.00 | 1.00 | 1.00 | 1.00 | 1.00 | 1.00 | 1.00 | 1.00 |
| (lower) | .00 | .00 | .00 | .00 | .00 | .00 | .00 | .00 | .00 | .00 | .00 | .00 | .00 | .00 | .00 | .00 | .00 | .00 | .50 |
| **E 3 .15** (upper) | .33 | .67 | 1.00 | 1.00 | 1.00 | 1.00 | 1.00 | 1.00 | 1.00 | 1.00 | 1.00 | 1.00 | 1.00 | 1.00 | 1.00 | 1.00 | 1.00 | 1.00 | 1.00 |
| (lower) | .00 | .00 | .00 | .00 | .00 | .00 | .00 | .00 | .00 | .00 | .00 | .00 | .00 | .00 | .00 | .00 | .00 | .33 | .67 |
| **E 4 .20** (upper) | .25 | .50 | .75 | 1.00 | 1.00 | 1.00 | 1.00 | 1.00 | 1.00 | 1.00 | 1.00 | 1.00 | 1.00 | 1.00 | 1.00 | 1.00 | 1.00 | 1.00 | 1.00 |
| (lower) | .00 | .00 | .00 | .00 | .00 | .00 | .00 | .00 | .00 | .00 | .00 | .00 | .00 | .00 | .00 | .00 | .25 | .50 | .75 |
| **E 5 .25** (upper) | .20 | .40 | .60 | .80 | 1.00 | 1.00 | 1.00 | 1.00 | 1.00 | 1.00 | 1.00 | 1.00 | 1.00 | 1.00 | 1.00 | 1.00 | 1.00 | 1.00 | 1.00 |
| (lower) | .00 | .00 | .00 | .00 | .00 | .00 | .00 | .00 | .00 | .00 | .00 | .00 | .00 | .00 | .00 | .20 | .40 | .60 | .80 |
| **E 6 .30** (upper) | .17 | .33 | .50 | .67 | .83 | 1.00 | 1.00 | 1.00 | 1.00 | 1.00 | 1.00 | 1.00 | 1.00 | 1.00 | 1.00 | 1.00 | 1.00 | 1.00 | 1.00 |
| (lower) | .00 | .00 | .00 | .00 | .00 | .00 | .00 | .00 | .00 | .00 | .00 | .00 | .00 | .00 | .17 | .33 | .50 | .67 | .83 |
| **E 7 .35** (upper) | .14 | .29 | .43 | .57 | .71 | .85 | 1.00 | 1.00 | 1.00 | 1.00 | 1.00 | 1.00 | 1.00 | 1.00 | 1.00 | 1.00 | 1.00 | 1.00 | 1.00 |
| (lower) | .00 | .00 | .00 | .00 | .00 | .00 | .00 | .00 | .00 | .00 | .00 | .00 | .00 | .14 | .29 | .43 | .57 | .71 | .86 |
| **E 8 .40** (upper) | .13 | .25 | .38 | .50 | .62 | .75 | .87 | 1.00 | 1.00 | 1.00 | 1.00 | 1.00 | 1.00 | 1.00 | 1.00 | 1.00 | 1.00 | 1.00 | 1.00 |
| (lower) | .00 | .00 | .00 | .00 | .00 | .00 | .00 | .00 | .00 | .00 | .00 | .00 | .12 | .25 | .38 | .50 | .63 | .75 | .88 |
| **E 9 .45** (upper) | .11 | .22 | .33 | .44 | .56 | .67 | .78 | .89 | 1.00 | 1.00 | 1.00 | 1.00 | 1.00 | 1.00 | 1.00 | 1.00 | 1.00 | 1.00 | 1.00 |
| (lower) | .00 | .00 | .00 | .00 | .00 | .00 | .00 | .00 | .00 | .00 | .00 | .11 | .22 | .33 | .44 | .56 | .67 | .78 | .89 |
| **E 10 .50** (upper) | .10 | .20 | .30 | .40 | .50 | .60 | .70 | .80 | .90 | 1.00 | 1.00 | 1.00 | 1.00 | 1.00 | 1.00 | 1.00 | 1.00 | 1.00 | 1.00 |
| (lower) | .00 | .00 | .00 | .00 | .00 | .00 | .00 | .00 | .00 | .00 | .10 | .20 | .30 | .40 | .50 | .60 | .70 | .80 | .90 |
| **E 11 .55** (upper) | .09 | .18 | .27 | .36 | .45 | .55 | .64 | .73 | .82 | .91 | 1.00 | 1.00 | 1.00 | 1.00 | 1.00 | 1.00 | 1.00 | 1.00 | 1.00 |
| (lower) | .00 | .00 | .00 | .00 | .00 | .00 | .00 | .00 | .00 | .09 | .18 | .27 | .36 | .45 | .55 | .64 | .73 | .82 | .91 |
| **E 12 .60** (upper) | .08 | .17 | .25 | .33 | .42 | .50 | .58 | .67 | .75 | .83 | .92 | 1.00 | 1.00 | 1.00 | 1.00 | 1.00 | 1.00 | 1.00 | 1.00 |
| (lower) | .00 | .00 | .00 | .00 | .00 | .00 | .00 | .00 | .09 | .18 | .27 | .36 | .45 | .55 | .64 | .73 | .82 | .91 | .92 |
| **E 13 .65** (upper) | .08 | .15 | .23 | .31 | .38 | .46 | .54 | .62 | .69 | .77 | .85 | .92 | 1.00 | 1.00 | 1.00 | 1.00 | 1.00 | 1.00 | 1.00 |
| (lower) | .00 | .00 | .00 | .00 | .00 | .00 | .00 | .08 | .15 | .23 | .31 | .38 | .46 | .54 | .62 | .69 | .77 | .85 | .92 |
| **E 14 .70** (upper) | .07 | .14 | .21 | .29 | .36 | .43 | .50 | .57 | .64 | .71 | .79 | .86 | .93 | 1.00 | 1.00 | 1.00 | 1.00 | 1.00 | 1.00 |
| (lower) | .00 | .00 | .00 | .00 | .00 | .00 | .07 | .14 | .21 | .29 | .36 | .43 | .50 | .57 | .64 | .71 | .79 | .86 | .93 |
| **E 15 .75** (upper) | .07 | .13 | .20 | .27 | .33 | .40 | .47 | .53 | .60 | .67 | .73 | .80 | .87 | .93 | 1.00 | 1.00 | 1.00 | 1.00 | 1.00 |
| (lower) | .00 | .00 | .00 | .00 | .00 | .07 | .13 | .20 | .27 | .33 | .40 | .47 | .53 | .60 | .67 | .73 | .80 | .87 | .93 |
| **E 16 .80** (upper) | .06 | .13 | .19 | .25 | .31 | .38 | .44 | .50 | .56 | .62 | .69 | .75 | .81 | .87 | .94 | 1.00 | 1.00 | 1.00 | 1.00 |
| (lower) | .00 | .00 | .00 | .00 | .06 | .13 | .19 | .25 | .31 | .38 | .44 | .50 | .56 | .63 | .69 | .75 | .81 | .88 | .94 |
| **E 17 .85** (upper) | .06 | .12 | .18 | .24 | .29 | .35 | .41 | .47 | .53 | .59 | .65 | .71 | .78 | .82 | .88 | .94 | 1.00 | 1.00 | 1.00 |
| (lower) | .00 | .00 | .00 | .06 | .12 | .18 | .24 | .29 | .35 | .41 | .47 | .53 | .59 | .65 | .71 | .76 | .82 | .88 | .94 |
| **E 18 .90** (upper) | .06 | .11 | .17 | .22 | .28 | .33 | .39 | .44 | .50 | .56 | .61 | .67 | .72 | .78 | .83 | .89 | .94 | 1.00 | 1.00 |
| (lower) | .00 | .00 | .06 | .11 | .17 | .22 | .28 | .33 | .39 | .44 | .50 | .56 | .61 | .67 | .72 | .78 | .83 | .89 | .94 |
| **E 19 .95** (upper) | .05 | .11 | .16 | .21 | .26 | .32 | .37 | .42 | .47 | .53 | .58 | .63 | .68 | .74 | .79 | .84 | .89 | .95 | 1.00 |
| (lower) | .00 | .05 | .11 | .16 | .21 | .26 | .32 | .37 | .42 | .47 | .53 | .58 | .63 | .68 | .74 | .79 | .84 | .89 | .94 |

**Figure 2.** Limits for Conditional Probabilities

|                          |                        | The Probability of This Event Becomes: | | | |
| --- | --- | --- | --- | --- | --- |
| If This Event Occurs     | Initial Probability    | 1    | 2    | 3    | 4    |
| EVENT 1                  | 0.25                   | ///  | 0.50 | 0.85 | 0.40 |
| EVENT 2                  | 0.40                   | 0.60 | ///  | 0.60 | 0.55 |
| EVENT 3                  | 0.75                   | 0.15 | 0.50 | ///  | 0.60 |
| EVENT 4                  | 0.50                   | 0.25 | 0.70 | 0.55 | ///  |

**Figure 3.** Cross-Impact Probability Matrix

The impact of event $n$ on event $m$ is then calculated as the ratio of the odds of event $m$ given event $n$ to the initial odds of event $m$. Thus, the cross-impact matrix shown in Figure 3 would become the matrix shown in Figure 4 when odds are used in place of probabilities. The ratio of the new odds to the initial odds is used to define the event impacts. Thus, the occurrence of event 2 causes the likelihood of event 1 to go from odds of 0.33 to 1.50. The odds ratio expressing the occurrence impact of event 2 on event 1 is, therefore, 1.50/0.33 = 4.5. Figure 5 shows the entire odds ratio matrix corresponding to Figures 3 and 4.

A nonoccurrence odds ratio matrix can also be calculated from the information in the occurrence matrix in Figure 4. Again, using the

|                          |                        | The Odds of This Event Become: | | | |
| --- | --- | --- | --- | --- | --- |
| If This Event Occurs     | Initial Odds           | 1    | 2    | 3    | 4    |
| EVENT 1                  | 0.33                   | ///  | 1.00 | 5.67 | 0.67 |
| EVENT 2                  | 0.67                   | 1.50 | ///  | 1.50 | 1.22 |
| EVENT 3                  | 3.00                   | 0.18 | 1.00 | ///  | 1.50 |
| EVENT 4                  | 1.00                   | 0.33 | 2.33 | 1.22 | ///  |

**Figure 4.** Cross-Impact Odds Matrix

The Odds of This Event
Are Multiplied:

| If This Event Occurs | Initial Odds | 1 | 2 | 3 | 4 |
|---|---|---|---|---|---|
| EVENT 1 | 0.33 | //// | 1.5 | 1.9 | 0.67 |
| EVENT 2 | 0.67 | 4.5 | //// | 0.5 | 1.2 |
| EVENT 3 | 3.00 | .55 | 1.5 | //// | 1.5 |
| EVENT 4 | 1.00 | 1.0 | 3.5 | .41 | //// |

**Figure 5.** Occurrence Odds Ratios

equation

$$P(1) = P(2) \times P(1/2) + P(\bar{2}) \times P(1/\bar{2})$$

the probability of event 1 given the nonoccurrence of event 2, $P(1/\bar{2})$, can be determined. From these probabilities, the nonoccurrence odds ratios can be calculated just as the occurrence odds ratios are calculated.

Once the odds ratios have been determined, the calculations proceed as follows:

1. An event is selected at random from the event set.
2. A random number between 0.0 and 1.0 is selected. If the random number is less than the probability of the event being tested, the event is said to occur. If the random number is greater than the event probability, the event does not occur.
3. If the event (event j) occurs, the odds of the other events are adjusted as follows:

   New odds of event i = (Initial odds of event i) × (occurrence odds ratio of event j on event i)

   If the event does not occur, the same calculations are made but the nonoccurrence odds ratios are used.

4. Steps 1, 2, and 3 are repeated until all the events have been tested for occurrence.
5. Steps 1 through 4 (which represent one play of the matrix) are repeated a large number of times.
6. The frequency of occurrence of each event for all runs of the

cross-impact matrix determines the new or calibration probability of that event.

The calibration probabilities resulting from the program run will normally be within a few percentage points of the initial probabilities, since the cross-impact matrix was constructed to be consistent (to include the consideration of the influences of the events on each other). However, since consistency is insured only for event pairs, it is possible that inconsistencies in event triplets or quartets or higher orders may exist. The nonoccurrence impact matrix is calculated according to the assumption that the initial probabilities are consistent with each other. Thus, the nonoccurrence impacts should exactly balance the occurrence impacts. But these calculations are based on event pairs. The combined effects of two or more events on one event may cause some changes in the initial probabilities. If any of the calibration probabilities differ from the initial probabilities by more than a few percentage points, the matrix should be tested for these higher-order effects. This can be accomplished by rerunning the cross-impact program with a different string of random numbers. If the same probability shifts occur, they probably are the result of higher-order impacts; otherwise the shifts were simply the result of a particular random number sequence.

At this stage in the analysis, the cross-impact matrix is ready to be used for sensitivity testing or policy analysis. Sensitivity testing consists of selecting a particular judgment (an initial probability estimate or a conditional probability estimate) about which uncertainty exists. This judgment is changed and the matrix is run again. If significant differences occur between this run and the calibration run, it is apparent that the judgment that was changed is an important one. It may be worthwhile to spend more effort in making that particular judgment. If no significant differences appear, that particular judgment probably is a relatively unimportant part of the analysis.

Policy testing is accomplished by first defining an anticipated policy or action that would affect the events in the matrix. The matrix is then changed to reflect the immediate effects of the policy. This is usually accomplished either by changing the initial probabilities of one or more events or by adding a new event to the matrix. A new run of the matrix is then performed and compared with the calibration run. The differences are the effects of the policy. Often, unexpected changes will result. When this happens, these changes can be traced back through the matrix so that the chains of causality that led to the unexpected changes can be determined and the effects of the policy understood. Used in this way, the cross-impact matrix becomes a model of event interactions that is used to display the effects of complex chains of impacts caused by policy actions.

## A CROSS-IMPACT ANALYSIS EXAMPLE

The use of cross-impact analysis can be demonstrated by a simple example dealing with the electric utility industry. In such a study, events similar to those shown in Table 2 would be considered. While a larger number of events would normally be considered in a real study, these seven will serve to illustrate the technique. Table 2 also shows the initial probabilities for 1985 that might be estimated for these events. These probabilities are supposed to be a consistent set; thus, the estimate of 0.25 for event 1 includes the consideration that event 7 has a 0.50 likelihood, that event 4 has a 0.20 likelihood, and so on.

The next step is to estimate the event impacts. The first attempt at

## Table 2. Events Used in Cross-Impact Example

| Event | Probability of Occurring by 1985 |
|---|---|
| 1. The average real price of electricity for all users increases by 50 percent from the 1975 level. | 0.25 |
| 2. Nonuniform conservation efforts by electricity users result in a 4 percent reduction in average load and a 1 percent reduction in peak load. | 0.30 |
| 3. Strict new environmental standards are established on the strip-mining of western coal. | 0.50 |
| 4. The use of energy storage and load control systems by industry reduces industrial peak demand by 10 percent. | 0.20 |
| 5. A moratorium on new nuclear plants is passed by at least 10 states. | 0.10 |
| 6. Peak and seasonal pricing is adopted by the majority of U.S. utilities. | 0.75 |
| 7. The average yearly load factor increases by 15 percent. | 0.50 |

| If This Event Occurs: | Initial Probability by 1985 | The Probability of This Event Becomes: | | | | | | |
|---|---|---|---|---|---|---|---|---|
| | | 1 | 2 | 3 | 4 | 5 | 6 | 7 |
| 1. Electricity Price Increases by 50 percent | 0.25 | ▨ | 0.60 | 0.40 | 0.30 | 0.08 | 0.85 | 0.50 |
| 2. Conservation Reduces Average Load 4 percent and Peak Load 1 percent | 0.30 | 0.35 | ▨ | 0.50 | 0.20 | 0.10 | 0.90 | 0.25 |
| 3. Strict Environmental Standards Established for Western Coal | 0.50 | 0.40 | 0.30 | ▨ | 0.20 | 0.05 | 0.75 | 0.50 |
| 4. Energy Storage and Load Control Reduce Industrial Peak by 10 Percent | 0.20 | 0.15 | 0.15 | 0.50 | ▨ | 0.10 | 0.60 | 0.75 |
| 5. A Moratorium on New Nuclear Plants Is Passed by 10 States | 0.10 | 0.50 | 0.30 | 0.20 | 0.20 | ▨ | 0.75 | 0.50 |
| 6. Peak and Seasonal Pricing Is Adopted | 0.75 | 0.25 | 0.20 | 0.50 | 0.75 | 0.10 | ▨ | 0.65 |
| 7. Average Load Factor Increases by 15 Percent | 0.50 | 0.10 | 0.30 | 0.50 | 0.20 | 0.10 | 0.65 | ▨ |

**Figure 6.** Initial Estimates of Event Occurrence Impacts

these estimates is shown in Figure 6. Once these initial estimates have been made, it is necessary to check all of the estimates to make certain that they fall within the permissible limits (as shown in Figure 2). In this case, one of the estimates does not fit the limits for consistency. The probability of event 4 (energy storage and load control by industry) given the occurrence of event 6 (peak load pricing) was estimated to be 0.75. However, the limits on this probability are 0 and 0.27. The discrepancy is immediately obvious. The analyst is asserting that if peak load pricing occurs, industrial energy storage to cut peak load is very likely to happen (probability of 0.75). However, even though the initial probability of peak load pricing is high (0.75), the initial probability of industrial energy storage was estimated to be very low (only 0.20).

Obviously, if the occurrence of event 6 makes event 4 very likely, the fact that event 6 is very likely to occur means that the probability of event 4 cannot be low. Or conversely, it may be that the initial probabilities are, in fact, correct and the conditional probability is too high.

In this case, let us assume that the analyst decides that the occurrence of the event should indeed be more likely initially (0.40) because event 6 is very likely to happen and that the new probability of event 4 given the occurrence of event 6 is somewhat lower than before (0.50). This new matrix is shown in Figure 7.

Using the relationships discussed earlier, the nonoccurrence matrix can now be calculated, as can the occurrence odds ratios and the

| If This Event Occurs: | Initial Proba-bility by 1985 | The Probability of This Event Becomes: | | | | | | |
|---|---|---|---|---|---|---|---|---|
| | | 1 | 2 | 3 | 4 | 5 | 6 | 7 |
| 1. Electricity Price Increases by 50 Percent | 0.25 | | 0.60 | 0.40 | 0.45 | 0.08 | 0.85 | 0.50 |
| 2. Conservation Reduces Average Load 4 Percent and Peak Load 1 Percent | 0.30 | 0.35 | | 0.50 | 0.40 | 0.10 | 0.90 | 0.25 |
| 3. Strict Environmental Standards Established for Western Coal | 0.50 | 0.40 | 0.30 | | 0.40 | 0.05 | 0.75 | 0.50 |
| 4. Energy Storage and Load Control Reduce Industrial Peak by 10 Percent | 0.40 | 0.15 | 0.15 | 0.50 | | 0.10 | 0.60 | 0.75 |
| 5. A Moratorium on New Nuclear Plants Is Passed by 10 States | 0.10 | 0.50 | 0.30 | 0.20 | 0.40 | | 0.75 | 0.50 |
| 6. Peak and Seasonal Pricing Is Adopted | 0.75 | 0.25 | 0.20 | 0.50 | 0.50 | 0.10 | | 0.65 |
| 7. Average Load Factor Increases by 15 Percent | 0.50 | 0.10 | 0.30 | 0.50 | 0.40 | 0.10 | 0.65 | |

**Figure 7.** Final Estimates of Event Occurrence Impacts

nonoccurrence odds ratios. These matrices are shown in Figures 8, 9, and 10, respectively.

With this information in hand, the calibration run of the matrix can be made. The results of this run (shown in Table 3) show changes of no more than 0.02 for any event, indicating that the matrix is balanced.

The matrix now can be used for sensitivity and policy tests. The results of two such runs will be shown here. The first test assumes the passage of legislation setting strict standards for the mining of western coal (event 3). By setting the probability of this event to 1.0 and rerunn-

| If This Event Does Not Occur: | Initial Proba- bility by 1985 | The Probability of This Event Becomes: | | | | | | |
|---|---|---|---|---|---|---|---|---|
| | | 1 | 2 | 3 | 4 | 5 | 6 | 7 |
| 1. Electricity Price Increases by 50 Percent | 0.25 | | 0.20 | 0.53 | 0.38 | 0.11 | 0.72 | 0.50 |
| 2. Conservation Reduces Average Load 4 Percent and Peak Load 1 Percent | 0.30 | 0.21 | | 0.50 | 0.40 | 0.10 | 0.69 | 0.61 |
| 3. Strict Environmental Standards Established for Western Coal | 0.50 | 0.10 | 0.30 | | 0.40 | 0.15 | 0.75 | 0.50 |
| 4. Energy Storage and Load Control Reduce Industrial Peak by 10 Percent | 0.40 | 0.32 | 0.40 | 0.50 | | 0.10 | 0.85 | 0.33 |
| 5. A Moratorium on New Nuclear Plants Is Passed by 10 States | 0.10 | 0.22 | 0.30 | 0.53 | 0.40 | | 0.75 | 0.50 |
| 6. Peak and Seasonal Pricing Is Adopted | 0.75 | 0.25 | 0.60 | 0.50 | 0.10 | 0.10 | | 0.02 |
| 7. Average Load Factor Increases by 15 Percent | 0.50 | 0.40 | 0.30 | 0.50 | 0.40 | 0.10 | 0.85 | |

**Figure 8.** The Nonoccurrence Matrix

| If This Event Occurs: | Initial Odds by 1985 | The Odds Ratio Impacting This Event Is: | | | | | | |
|---|---|---|---|---|---|---|---|---|
| | | 1 | 2 | 3 | 4 | 5 | 6 | 7 |
| 1. Electricity Price Increases by 50 Percent | 0.33 | | 3.5 | 0.7 | 1.2 | 0.8 | 1.9 | 1.0 |
| 2. Conservation Reduces Average Load 4 Percent and Peak Load 1 Percent | 0.43 | 1.6 | | 1.0 | 1.0 | 1.0 | 3.0 | 0.3 |
| 3. Strict Environmental Standards Established for Western Coal | 1.0 | 2.0 | 1.0 | | 1.0 | 0.5 | 1.0 | 1.0 |
| 4. Energy Storage and Load Control Reduce Industrial Peak by 10 Percent | 0.67 | 0.5 | 0.4 | 1.0 | | 1.0 | 0.5 | 3.0 |
| 5. A Moratorium on New Nuclear Plants Is Passed by 10 States | 0.11 | 3.0 | 1.0 | 0.2 | 1.0 | | 1.0 | 1.0 |
| 6. Peak and Seasonal Pricing Is Adopted | 3.0 | 1.0 | 0.6 | 1.0 | 1.5 | 1.0 | | 1.9 |
| 7. Average Load Factor Increases by 15 Percent | 1.0 | 0.3 | 1.0 | 1.0 | 1.0 | 1.0 | 0.6 | |

**Figure 9.** The Occurrence Odds Ratios

ing the matrix, the effect of the occurrence of this event on all others can be displayed. In this case, the results (Table 4) are not surprising. The probability of a price increase (event 1) is increased as a direct result of the occurrence of event 3 and little else is changed. This is the expected result since event 4 has no impact on any of the other events except for a negative impact on event 5 (which does decrease in probability slightly).

The second run assumes that peak and seasonal pricing (event 6) is not implemented. The probability of this event is reduced to 0 and the

| If This Event Does Not Occur: | Initial Odds by 1985 | The Odds Ratio Impacting This Event Is: | | | | | | |
|---|---|---|---|---|---|---|---|---|
| | | 1 | 2 | 3 | 4 | 5 | 6 | 7 |
| 1. Electricity Price Increases by 50 Percent | 0.33 | | 0.6 | 1.1 | 0.9 | 1.1 | 0.8 | 1.0 |
| 2. Conservation Reduces Average Load 4 Percent and Peak Load 1 Percent | 0.43 | 0.8 | | 1.0 | 1.0 | 1.0 | 0.7 | 1.5 |
| 3. Strict Environmental Standards Established for Western Coal | 1.0 | 0.3 | 1.0 | | 1.0 | 1.6 | 1.0 | 1.0 |
| 4. Energy Storage and Load Control Reduce Industrial Peak by 10 Percent | 0.67 | 1.4 | 1.6 | 1.0 | | 1.0 | 1.9 | 0.5 |
| 5. A Moratorium on New Nuclear Plants Is Passed by 10 States | 0.11 | 0.9 | 1.0 | 1.1 | 1.0 | | 1.0 | 1.0 |
| 6. Peak and Seasonal Pricing Is Adopted | 3.0 | 1.0 | 3.5 | 1.0 | 0.2 | 1.0 | | 0.0 |
| 7. Average Load Factor Increases by 15 Percent | 1.0 | 2.0 | 1.0 | 1.0 | 1.0 | 1.0 | 1.9 | |

**Figure 10.** The Nonoccurrence Odds Ratios

matrix is rerun. The results are shown in Table 5. In this case, four events are affected by the change: 1, 2, 5, and 7. The causes of these changes can be traced from the impact matrices shown earlier. Event 4 (energy storage and load control by industry) is affected directly by the nonoccurrence of event 6. The probability of event 7 (load factor increases) is decreased by the direct influence of the nonoccurrence of event 6 but is also decreased by events 2 and 4. Event 4 has a positive impact on event 7, but since event 4 is less likely in this run, the net result is a negative impact on event 7. Event 2 has a negative impact on event 7, and its probability is increased in this run. Thus, the decrease in probability of event 7 results from the combined effects of events 2, 4, and 6.

**Table 3. Calibration Results**

| Event | Initial Probability | Calibration Probability | Change |
|---|---|---|---|
| 1. Electricity price increases | 0.25 | 0.23 | −0.02 |
| 2. Conservation reduces load by 4 percent and peak by 1 percent | 0.30 | 0.29 | −0.1 |
| 3. Strict environmental standards for coal | 0.50 | 0.50 | — |
| 4. Energy storage and load control by industry | 0.40 | 0.40 | — |
| 5. Moratorium on nuclear plants | 0.10 | 0.10 | — |
| 6. Peak and seasonal pricing | 0.75 | 0.75 | — |
| 7. Load factor increases by 15 percent | 0.50 | 0.50 | — |

The probability of event 2 is increased in this run partially as a result of the direct impact of event 6, but also as a result of the decreased probability of event 4 and the increased probability of event 1. Event 1 (price increases) is not directly affected by event 6, but it is affected by events 2, 4, and 7, each of which is directly affected by event 6.

Thus, several paths of impact appear in the run. Event 6 directly affects events 2, 4, and 7. Each of these events in turn impacts event 1.

**Table 4. Test of Occurrence of Event 3**

| Event | Initial Probability | Test Probability | Final Probability | Change |
|---|---|---|---|---|
| 1. Electricity price increases | 0.25 | 0.23 | 0.31 | 0.08 |
| 2. Conservation reduces load by 4 percent and peak by 1 percent | 0.30 | 0.29 | 0.32 | 0.03 |
| 3. Strict environmental standards for coal | 0.50 | 1.00 | 1.00 | — |
| 4. Energy storage and load control by industry | 0.40 | 0.40 | 0.39 | −0.1 |
| 5. Moratorium on nuclear plants | 0.10 | 0.10 | 0.07 | −0.03 |
| 6. Peak and seasonal pricing | 0.75 | 0.75 | 0.74 | −0.01 |
| 7. Load factor increases by 15 percent | 0.50 | 0.50 | 0.49 | −0.01 |

**Table 5. Test of Nonoccurrence of Event 6**

| Event | Initial Probability | Test Probability | Final Probability | Change |
|---|---|---|---|---|
| 1. Electricity price increases | 0.25 | 0.23 | 0.28 | 0.05 |
| 2. Conservation reduces load by 4 percent and peak by 1 percent | 0.30 | 0.29 | 0.43 | 0.14 |
| 3. Strict environmental standards for coal | 0.50 | 0.50 | 0.50 | — |
| 4. Energy storage and load control by industry | 0.40 | 0.40 | 0.27 | −0.13 |
| 5. Moratorium on nuclear plants | 0.10 | 0.10 | 0.10 | — |
| 6. Peak and seasonal pricing | 0.75 | 0.00 | 0.00 | — |
| 7. Load factor increases by 15 percent | 0.50 | 0.50 | 0.26 | −0.24 |

Event 1 and event 4 have further impact on event 2, and events 2 and 4 exert further impact on event 7.

It is exactly this kind of complicated impact pathways that cross impact is designed to evaluate. In a larger matrix, these pathways may become even more complex. The basic strengths of cross-impact analysis are that it is a way of evaluating the effects of these complex interactions and that the interactions can always be traced through the matrix by the analyst trying to discover the reasons for the results of interesting runs.

## ALTERNATIVE CROSS-IMPACT TECHNIQUES

The cross-impact approach described in the previous sections is the basic form of the most widely used approach to cross impact. Parts of this basic approach may be altered depending on the requirements of a particular analysis. For example, sequencing of events is often an important addition. Sequencing involves designating certain events as precursor events or action items that should always occur or be tested for occurrence before the other events, and designating certain other events as outcome or goal events that should always be tested for occurrence after all the other events. In this way, a rational order can be imposed on each of the Monte Carlo runs of the event matrix, so that the resulting causal pathways more readily reflect real world relationships.

A second modification that is sometimes employed is the creation of a figure-of-merit used to evaluate the results of several alternative outcomes. Each event is assigned a number corresponding to its importance to the interest groups affected by the outcomes, with the sign of the number indicating whether a positive or a negative change in probability is desirable. These importance weights are then multiplied by the change in probability for each event in a particular policy run. The sum of these products is the figure-of-merit for that policy. The policies with high figures-of-merit would be considered more effective than those with low or negative figures-of-merit.

As mentioned earlier, the basic approach might also be used with initial probability estimates that consider each event in isolation. In this approach, the analyst feels more comfortable in making initial probability estimates that assume the nonoccurrence of all other events than in making estimates that include the influences of those events. In this case, the first run of the matrix is not a calibration run but a run to produce probabilities adjusted for the likely impacts of other events in the base case. This, of course, was the original approach to cross impact as it was conceived by Gordon and Helmer.

A number of alternative approaches to cross-impact analysis also have been developed over the years. The literature is rich with alternative calculational methods and conceptual frameworks for the application of the cross-impact concept (Boucher and Stover, 1976).

For many applications, one of the major limitations of the basic cross-impact approach is that it deals with only "a slice in time." Revised probabliities are presented for some future year, but no information is generated about the transition from the current situation to the future state. Various alternative approaches deal with the development of a dynamic or continuous form of cross impact. The earliest work in this area was performed in 1970 at the Institute for the Future (Gordon, Rochberg, and Enzer, 1970). This approach (called the dynamic method of cross-impact analysis) added trends to the events in the cross-impact matrix. Each variable was identified as having dynamic behavior of one of three types: S-shaped growth (such as the probability of an event or the market penetration of a new product), exponential growth (such as GNP or population), and constant value (such as available land). Cross impacts were computed each year of the run for each variable and resulted in amended growth curves for each variable. The approach was tested with retrospective application to the increase in hybrid corn acreage and demographic transitions. Further research along similar lines has been continuing in other institutions.

Helmer has adopted a similar approach in his application of cross impact to gaming (Helmer, 1972). This approach also uses events and trends in the same cross-impact matrix but does not specify curve types for the trends. Any type of extrapolation for the trends is allowed, and impacts on the trends are calculated simply by adding or sub-tracting impact constants from the baseline trend values. As in other dynamic approaches, calculations are repeated for each time interval within the cross-impact run. Helmer uses the cross-impact approach as a major part of games designed to explore future conditions, the first application being to study variables and events important to the future states of the nation.

A third approach to dynamic cross-impact analysis was developed at the Monsanto Company (Craver, 1972, 1973; Kiefer, 1973). This ap-proach deals strctly with events and their probabilities of occurrence. A cumulative probability curve is developed for each event by specifying the probability of the event for two future years and then fitting an S-shaped curve to those points. Impacts are specified in terms of how the final probability of the event (the limit of the S-curve) would change and how the slope of the curve would change. A fairly complex computa-tional algorithm is used to calculate the final "cross-impacted" set of probability curves for each event. Monsanto has been using this tech-nique in its planning since the early 1970s with much success. The planning team at Monsanto contends that convening a meeting of people from different backgrounds to discuss the initial probabilities of the events and the event cross impacts has educational value that, in itself, justifies the use of cross impact, regardless of whether the impact calculations are subsequently performed.

Other approaches to the dynamic cross impact of events have been developed. Shozo Shimada (1971) and Keijiro Hagashi and Yoichi Kaya (1973) all have presented approaches that attempt analytic study of the joint probability density functions of event pairs to determine the cross-impact effects.

An approach to the dynamic cross impact that deals mainly with time variables rather than events has been developed by Julius Kane (1972). This approach, called KSIM, is similar to that developed at the Institute for the Future. Each variable is assigned a value between 0 and 1, where 0 and 1 represent the physical limits on the variable. Cross impacts are defined in terms of the strength of the effect of one variable on another. Impacts are calculated by weighting the strength of the effect of one variable on another by the distance from minimum value of the first variable. The output is in the form of values of each variable (with respect to the maximum and minimum values of that variable) versus time. The emphasis in this case is on developing an understand-ing of the qualitative behavior of the system as opposed to developing quantitative estimates of future values. The approach, which in fact develops a simple simulation model, focuses on facilitating communi-cation of information about system behavior.

Most of the approaches discussed so far develop revised probabilities for each of the events. These probabilities can then be used to construct scenarios by assigning occurrence or nonoccurrence to events on the basis of their revised probabilities. One approach that produces occurrence and nonoccurrence forecasts directly has been developed by Murray Turoff (1972). In this approach, the user specifies initial and conditional probabilities as in the basic approach. The method of using the conditional probabilities and calculating impacts is different, however. The final output is also different. A run of the matrix is performed by identifying which event has a probability closest to 0 or 1. This event is then assumed not to occur (if the probability is close to 0) or to occur (if the probability is close to 1). The impacts of the occurrence or nonoccurrence on all the other events are calculated, and the next event with probability closest to 0 or to 1 is identified. This procedure is repeated until all events have been exhausted. The result is a determination of which events will occur and which events will not occur. Thus, in effect, a scenario is defined that includes the occurrences of some events and the nonoccurrences of others. There is no reason to repeat this run a large number of times and to average the results, as in the basic Monte Carlo approach, because each run will be exactly the same since no random selections are involved. Occurrences and nonoccurrences are decided deterministically by perturbing the probability structure as little as possible at each step in the computations.

A use of the concept of cross-impact analysis that focuses on the impact pathways has been described by Geradin (1974). In this approach, a cross-impact matrix is constructed by specifying event impacts on a scale from $-10$ to $+10$. All those impacts below some arbitrary bounds ($1 - 7$ to $+7$, for example) are then set to 0, being considered too weak to influence the system greatly. With the remaining impacts in the cross-impact matrix (those impacts greater than $+7$ and less than $-7$, for example), the impact loops are traced. Second-degree loops will exist when event 1 affects event 2, and event 2 affects event 1. Third, fourth, and higher-order loops will also exist. An examination of these impact loops can then reveal the sensitive points of the system. If it is desirable that event 2 occur, for example, one would look for loops that contain positive impact on event 2 and see what other events in those loops might be sensitive to actions that could be taken by the interested groups.

## CURRENT RESEARCH ON CROSS-IMPACT ANALYSIS

Current work on cross-impact focuses mainly on two areas: investigation of the problems of consistency in cross-impact matrices and combinations of cross-impact with other forecasting techniques. Dalkey has done much of the work on consistency (1972). He has developed various rules and procedures for eliminating many of the inconsistencies that can arise in the estimates of initial and conditional probabilities. Jackson and Lawton also have studied the problem of inconsistency (1976). They have shown that inconsistencies can arise with respect to combinations of three or more events, even if the limits on conditional probabilities for event pairs are respected. They also have developed computational procedures for calculating the limits on combinations of event occurrences and nonoccurrences. They urge the use of these calculations with respect to the study of scenario probabilities.

Research at the Battelle-General Research Institute has considered the combination of cross-impact analysis with regression model forecasting (Duval, Fontela, and Gabus, 1974; Fontela and Gabus, 1974). In a forecasting study focusing on the Spanish economy, cross-impact analysis was used to develop plausible scenarios. A single run of the cross-impact model was used to define which events occurred and which did not. Next a scenario was described based on these event occurrences and nonoccurrences. Estimates were made as to what influence, if any, the scenario conditions would have on the exogenous parameters of a regression model of the Spanish economy. These estimates were then used to change the exogenous inputs to the regression model, and the model was used to forecast the major parameters of the Spanish economy.

Cross-impact analysis is also being used in conjunction with a trend forecasting procedure developed by The Futures Group called trend impact analysis (TIA) (Gordon and Stover, 1976). Most trend forecasts are based on the extrapolation of past data. TIA uses extrapolation to produce a baseline projection but then adjusts this projection to account for the impacts of future events. The baseline may be obtained in a variety of ways: it may be generated through the use of computerized curve-fitting techniques, as the output of simple regression equations or complex econometric or simulation models, as the result of physical or engineering calculations, and so on. In any case, this baseline is a projection of the parameter being studied that includes certain information about the past and certain assumptions about the future.

The second step in the TIA process is to identify future events, which, if they occurred, would alter the baseline projection. Once a set of potentially important events has been identified, the probability of occurrence of each event as a function of time is estimated. Cross-impact analysis is often used to develop consistent estimates of these probabilities. The next step is to estimate the impact of each event on the baseline projection, that is, to estimate the way in which the baseline would change if each event were to occur. These impacts are specified in terms of five parameters:

1. The time, in years, from the occurrence of the event until the trend begins to respond.
2. The time, in years, from the occurrence of the event until the impact on the trend is largest.
3. The magnitude, in percentage of the baseline curve, of that largest impact.
4. The time, in years, from the occurrence of the impacting event until the impact reaches a final or steady-state level.
5. The magnitude, in percentage of the baseline curve, of that final impact.

A computer program is then used to combine these probability and impact judgments to calculate the expected impact of the selected events on the baseline trend. The expected value of the combined impacts is computed by summing the products of the probabilities of the impacting events for each possible year and the magnitude of their impacts, taking into account their specified time lags. The program also calculates the uncertainty in the forecast resulting from the uncertainty in the baseline and the uncertainty about whether or not individual events will actually occur.

TIA is therefore a technique that produces a forecast of the future values of time-series variables and displays a measure of the uncertainty of those forecasts. These forecasts include the consideration of the effects of important future events on each other (through the cross-impact analysis) and on the projected variable (through the event to trend impact calculations).

Another promising line of current research involving cross-impact analysis is the combination of cross impact with computer modeling. At The Futures Group a new technique, probabilistic system dynamics (PSD), has been used since 1973 (Gordon and Stover, 1976; Stover, 1975). PSD combines system dynamics simulation modeling with a time-dependent version of cross-impact analysis. Figure 11 illustrates the combination of these two techniques. Events included in the cross-impact matrix, if they occur, may affect variables within the system dynamics model; relationships between two variables may change, new relationships may arise, or entirely new sectors may be added to the model. The model variables, in turn, may affect event probabilities. Thus, the sequence of calculations in a run of the entire model is as follows. Calculations are first performed in the system dynamics model for a particular time period. Some of these values are then transformed

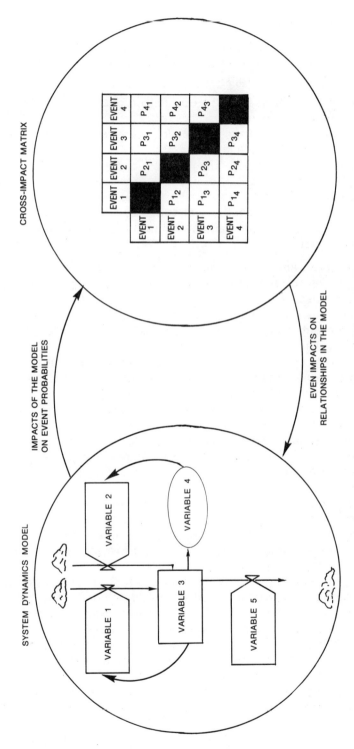

**Figure 11.** New Impact Loops in Probabilistic System Dynamics

to the cross-impact matrix, and the impacts of these variables on event probabilities are calculated. Next, the impacts of these new event probabilities on other event probabilities are calculated. These new probabilities are then transferred back to the model, where model changes in response to these probabilities are determined. Model calculations for the next solution interval are then performed. In this manner, the important influence of future discrete events is included in simulation models through the use of cross-impact analysis.

## CONCLUSION

Cross-impact analysis has been used in many studies since 1968. In many cases, its use has helped analysts improve their understanding of the complex interactions among the events being studied. Regardless of whether new information is gained from runs of the matrix, the heuristic nature of the cross-impact procedure itself, involving detailed consideration of the important events and their likely pair-wise interactions, often justifies the use of the technique.

In spite of these strengths, cross-impact analysis is limited in its application because it generally deals only with events. While the consideration of future events is crucial to the study of the future, most systems cannot be described fully with events only. For this reason, the major application of cross impact in the future will probably be in combination with other techniques. The basic cross impact and variations such as KSIM will probably continue to be used in special applications and for learning exercises, but cross impact will likely be used most often in combination techniques such as scenario construction, the Battelle regression equation approach, trend impact analysis, and probabilistic system dynamics.

## REFERENCES

Boucher, Wayne I., and John Stover. 1976. *An Annotated Bibliography of Cross-Impact Analysis*. Glastonbury, Conn.: The Futures Group.

Craver, J. Kenneth. 1972. "Technology Assessment by Cross-Impacts." Paper presented at the Engineering Foundation Conference on Technology Assessment held at Henniker, N.H. (July).

———. 1973. "A Practical Method for Technology Assessment." Paper presented at the First International Conference on Technology Assessment held in The Hague, The Netherlands (May).

Dalkey, Norman C. 1972. "An Elementary Cross-Impact Model." *Technological Forecasting and Social Change,* Volume 3, Number 3, 341–351.

Duval, A., E. Fontela, and A. Gabus. 1974. *Cross-Impact: A Handbook of Concepts and Applications.* Geneva: Battelle-Geneva (July).

Enzer, Selwyn. 1972. "Cross-Impact Techniques in Technology Assessment." *Futures,* Volume 4, Number 1, 30–51.

Fontela, Emilio, and Andre Gabus. 1974. "Events and Economic Forecasting Models." *Futures,* Volume 6, Number 4, 329–333.

Gerardin, Lucien A. 1974. *To Forecast Decisionmaking with System Analysis: Systematic Analysis to Foresee Alternative Futures.* Paris: Thompson-CSF-France (April).

Gordon, Theodore, J., and H. Hayward. 1968. "Initial Experiments with the Cross-Impact Matrix Method of Forecasting." *Futures,* Volume 1, Number 2, 100–116.

————, Richard Rochberg, and Selwyn Enzer. 1970. *Research on Cross-Impact Techniques with Selected Problems in Economics, Political Science and Technology Assessment.* Menlo Park, Calif.: Institute for the Future.

————, and John Stover. 1976. "Using Perceptions and Data About the Future to Improve the Simulation of Complex Systems." *Technological Forecasting and Social Change,* Volume 9, Numbers 1/2, 191–211.

Hayashi, Keijiro, and Yoichi Kaya. 1973. "Dynamic Cross-Impact Method." *Tokyo 12th Science Lecture Conference Abstracts* (August), 785–786. (In Japanese.)

Helmer, Olaf. 1972. "Cross-Impact Gaming." *Futures,* Volume 4, Number 2, 149–167.

Jackson, J. Edward, and William H. Lawton. 1976. "Some Probability Problems Associated with Cross-Impact Analysis." *Technological Forecasting and Social Change,* Volume 8, Number 3, 263–273.

Kane, Julius. 1972. "A Primer for a New Cross-Impact Language—KSIM." *Technological Forecasting and Social Change,* Volume 4, Number 2, 129–142.

Kiefer, David. 1973. "Cross-Impact Assesses Corporate Ventures." *Chemical and Engineering News* (April), 8–9.

Shimada, Shozo. 1971. *A Hybrid Cross-Impact Matrix Method.* Central Research Laboratory, Report HC–70–029. Tokyo: Hitochi, Ltd. (March).

Shimmen, Toru. 1973. "A Short Paper on Cross-Impact Analysis: A Basic Cross-Impact Model." Draft. Tokyo: Institute for Future Technology.

Stover, John. 1975. "The Use of Probabilistic System Dynamics in the Analysis of National Development Policies: A Study of Economic Growth and Income Distribution in Uruguay." *Proceedings of the 1975 Summer Computer Simulation Conference.* San Francisco, Calif. (July).

Turoff, Murray. 1972. "An Alternative Approach to Cross-Impact Analysis." *Technological Forecasting and Social Change,* Volume 3, Number 3, 309–339.

J. MICHAEL McLEAN[1]

# Simulation Modeling

In recent years, mathematical simulation modeling has become one of the most influential techniques used for thinking about the future. Furthermore, the methodological difficulties inherent in the modeling process represent to some extent a microcosm of those encountered in the more general domain of future research. The term *mathematical modeling* covers a wide and disparate range of activities, some of which are covered in other chapters in this Handbook.

This article is intended both as an introduction to simulation models for those completely unfamiliar with the subject, and as a survey and critical evaluation of the theoretical potential and practical utility of such models. As such, it represents an uneasy compromise between the demands of clarity and the need for a certain amount of quite esoteric technical discussion. We therefore begin with an extremely simplified discussion of the basic concepts involved in modeling and its underlying rationale. Later, many of the points made in the introduction are reviewed, thus raising the level of sophistication of the discussion as the article progresses.

## WHAT IS A SIMULATION MODEL?

Dictionary definitions of the word "model" incorporate three distinct commonplace usages. It is used as a noun implying representation, as an adjective implying a degree of perfection or idealization, and as a verb to show what something is like. All these ideas are, in fact, related to the usage adopted in the more specialized use of the word in such fields as cybernetics, systems theory, and forecasting. Fundamentally, a model represents a simplified version of reality; the construction and use of models involve a selective attitude toward information. Our mental processes use models all the time; whenever we think we manipulate concepts and these concepts are not in the real world, they are in fact models that represent the world around us. This kind of model is termed a *mental* model.

The kind of models we are discussing here are far removed from this basic notion of a mental model, yet the relationship can be easily traced. When we need to communicate with others, we must formulate our mental models into some symbolic form. We generally do this by the use of ordinary language. In using speech or writing, we make explicit our implicit mental models. Mathematical models are expressed not in everyday language but in the vocabulary of mathematics; variables and equations substitute for the nouns, verbs, and constructions of ordinary discourse. Simulation models are perhaps the most common variety of mathematical models; a simulation model attempts to reproduce the behavior of the system being modeled. Here we must make an important distinction between a *static* model and a *dynamic* model. A static model represents a system at a single point in time, whereas a dynamic model attempts to trace the behavior of a system at successive points in time. Thus, a simulation model is a mathematical representation of a system from which the behavior of the system over time can be inferred.

The final ingredient necessary for this rather brief definition of modeling is the role of the computer. Only the rare simulation model is not implemented on a computer; this is because it is a very complex and difficult task to work out the behavior of a model containing even a very small number of equations. Hence, simulation of real world systems has only become possible since the development of high-speed electronic computers that can manipulate data and perform calculations at a speed many million times faster than the most talented human calculator.

To summarize our definition, we can say that a simulation model imitates and represents the system under study in the form of a set of mathematical variables and a number of explicit relationships between them. These relationships are sufficient to determine the change in the model variables over time (the model behavior), this process usually being performed with the help of a computer. As we shall see, this definition is by no means complete. We shall return to many of the points raised here later in this chapter.

## WHY BUILD SIMULATION MODELS?

The basic motivation for building simulation models stems from the urgent need to understand how many complex social, economic, and technical systems work. Short-term forecasts may often be made on the assumption that certain social or economic trends will be maintained and that these trends can be estimated simply by looking at the past behavior of the key variables. For longer term forecasts, it may be all important to identify changes in such short-term trends. In order to do so, it is necessary to acquire a deeper understanding of the underlying mechanisms that generate the historical behavior of the system. Thus, while the purpose of a simulation model is to reproduce the historical behavior of a system and to project that behavior into the future for the purposes of forecasting, the focus of the modeling exercise should be the correct identification of the causal structure that produces that behavior. Knowledge of such an underlying causal structure is equivalent to the possession of a theory of the workings of a system. Now it must be accepted that for the wide range of socioeconomic phenomena in which the forecaster is interested there do not exist any completely adequate causal theories.

Given this situation, two courses of action are open to the modeler. He can either attempt to build a model solely on the basis of the available data relating to the behavior of the system, or he can attempt to construct a primitive theory based on plausible relationships between the model variables. Using the latter approach, the behavior of the system can be derived from the causal assumptions made and this model behavior checked against the available real world data. Examples of both approaches are prevalent in the forecasting literature, the first being epitomized by the large number of econometric forecasting models (Ball, 1967) and the second by the systems dynamics approach pioneered by J. W. Forrester (1968) and the multiplicity of models built using this approach. The differences between the various modeling approaches will be discussed in a later section; what we are trying to illustrate here are the different purposes for which each kind of model is constructed. In general, models constructed largely on the basis of the statistical analysis of time-series data are built to provide short- to medium-term prediction. For models based on an attempt to construct a theory, the resulting theory can be an end product in itself. The construction of such models is usually less concerned with prediction than with gaining knowledge—ideally, practical knowledge for understanding the present and choosing and realizing the future. This kind of modeling is thus much more concerned with "problem definition" (setting a framework within which potential future problems can be investigated) than with the solution of such problems.

In providing an explicit framework for thinking about the future of a particular aspect of the real world, models also possess great potential for facilitating communication between disparate individuals and research groups working on common problems. Ideally, computer simulation models can represent an improvement over "mental" models that may be fuzzy, incomplete, and imprecisely stated. Computer models can also help to bridge the gap between the several different perceptions of reality—models—adopted by the various academic disciplines.

In addition, simulation models can provide a much more accurate assessment of the dynamic behavior implied by a set of assumptions about the structure of a system. This is perhaps the most basic and least disputable advantage of computer modeling. The digital computer can certainly and precisely derive the solution to a large number of complex equations. Where those equations represent the causal structure of a system, the solution can be interpreted as an unambiguous projection of the future behavior of that system.

In summary then, we can say that there are three main factors underlying the motivation for building computer simulation models: a model can be a device for *prediction*, that is, as a method for deriving the future consequences of assumptions made about the present; a tool for *learning* about the way a system works; and a means of improving *communication* between different research groups and between researchers and the public.

In practice, these factors are rarely separable, and most modeling exercises will incorporate some combination of them in their stated objectives. The various possible combinations that can be obtained by placing greater or lesser emphasis on these elements can give rise to apparently disparate modeling approaches. These differences are further reflected in the wide range of modeling methodologies employed; a survey of these approaches forms the substance of the following section.

## A REVIEW OF MODELING APPROACHES

Models can be classified in many ways, and it is clear from the literature that, even within the limited category of computer simulation models, there is a wide range of available approaches. It is important to realize, however, that systems of classification—taxonomies—of models are inevitably limited by the fact that a large number of factors—dimensions of classification—need to be taken into account. In this section, we briefly discuss four of these dimensions, which we believe to be the most significant, but we emphasize that the full subtlety of different approaches to modeling can only be illustrated by detailed consideration of actual models. For this reason, we consider several detailed case studies in later sections; we do not attempt to draw any systematic conclusions concerning the relative merits and disadvantages of the various approaches at this early stage.

### SNAPSHOTS AND MOVIES

The first dimension along which computer simulation models can be placed is concerned with the way in which the model deals with time. At one extreme, time may not be included as an explicit variable; such models—*static* models—may seem particularly inappropriate for the purposes of forecasting. However, many forecasting projects using models have been based upon exercises in comparative statics. Examples of this approach are common in urban and geographic modeling in which the spatial dimension is of considerable importance. The gravity model of Lowry (1964) and its many derivatives that attempt to describe the pattern of industrial growth, best exemplify this approach. By calibrating such a model at, say, five-year intervals on the basis of extrapolated trends in population, industrial activity, and so forth, the changing patterns of urban structure can be deduced from a series of "snapshots" of the system. Another common example of a static model is the economic input-output matrix technique. This method, pioneered by Leontief some fifty years ago, is basically an economic accounting device in which direct material transfers between industrial sectors are arranged in the form of a matrix. The mathematical manipulation of this matrix can be used to highlight the ultimate effects of changes in supply and demand patterns when transmitted around the industrial system. The U.N. World Input-Output model (Leontief, 1974), which has only just been completed, extends the matrix to include natural resource inputs and outputs in the form of pollution and environmental damage. In this way, it is intended to examine the interrelationships between future economic growth and environmental issues. Progression over time is handled in the same way as with the Lowry models; levels of demand are estimated from projections of overall growth rates and the resulting patterns of global industrial activity, trade, natural resource usage, and environmental impact are compared at ten-year intervals.

In contrast to these static models, each of which can be likened to a series of still photographs, many other computer simulation models treat time as an explicit variable and thus resemble moving pictures. This analogy can be extended further inasmuch as such *dynamic* models usually develop in a series of short time steps, just as the appearance of movement is created in the cinema by the rapid display of a sequence of still pictures. Certain variables in the model are regarded as "level" or "state" variables; these level variables completely describe the state of the system at a particular time. A set of equations are then used to calculate the rates of change of the level variables, which are then updated to give the state of the system at the next time step. This process is repeated until the desired time span for the simulation has been covered. By making the time step sufficiently small, the desired degree of approximation to a completely continuous system can be obtained. This approach is the core of the systems dynamics technique of J. W. Forrester (1961, 1969), but the principles also apply to most other dynamic simulation models.

The main advantage claimed for dynamic rather than static models is their capability to include feedback effects. A feedback effect consists of a closed causal path that connects a level variable, via intermediate variables, to its own rate of change. The realization of the importance of feedback forms one of the underlying foundations of the field known as cybernetics or the systems approach. According to Forrester, "Feedback loops govern action and change in systems from the simplest to the most complex" (1971). The authors of *The Limits to Growth* model (Meadows, et al.. 1972, p. 121) assert,

even in the absence of improved data, information now available is sufficient to generate valid behavior modes for the whole system. This is true because the model's feedback loops structure is a much more important determinant of overall behaviour than the exact numbers used to quantify the feedback loops.

Despite the emphasis systems dynamicists place on feedback, it is not at all clear that either the methodological implications or the scientific basis of such an emphasis have been fully worked out. We shall return to this point frequently in this article.

## DESCRIPTIONS AND PRESCRIPTIONS

A useful and commonly used method of classifying models involves the extent to which they are intended to describe the way the system works and evolves, and to what extent they prescribe how a system could or should evolve. In fact, few models fall entirely into either category, and the distinction is not an easy one to make. Even a model intended purely as a descriptive model must, by the selective nature of all models, exclude some aspects of the real system being studied. The choice of factors to exclude often amounts to a prescriptive or normative view of the system. Consider, for example, a model concerned with future levels of economic activity; if the indicator chosen were to represent the overall level of activity, say GNP, then that model would almost certainly contain very different variables and relationships to a model which uses as an indicator the income of the poorest 10 percent of the population. Although the GNP-oriented model might be intended simply to describe the working of the economy, it would also contain the normative implication that income disparities were not an important factor for future consideration. Similarly, even an explicitly normative model, such as the Bariloche Foundation's World Model (Herrera et al., 1976) discussed later, will contain mechanisms that are regarded as descriptive and that are intended to set the bounds within which the normative assumptions of the model can be tested.

Despite the fuzziness of the distinction between descriptive and normative models, the terms are still meaningful when used in a relative sense. Certainly, we can say that some models are more normative than others, as the case studies given later will illustrate.

## BLACK BOXES AND STRUCTURES

We have already discussed the problems involved in the modeling of social systems for which we do not have an adequate theoretical framework. Modelers' responses to these problems have resulted in two contrasting approaches. The first is to build a model based as much as possible on available data, making the minimum number of theoretical assumptions. This approach leads to a model that tends to resemble the engineer's black box. Inputs to, and outputs from, the box can be measured but the contents and detailed inner workings of the box are not regarded as features that should be exposed to test or public scrutiny.

This concentration on empirical data implies that the adequacy of the model should be assessed with reference to the model's ability to produce the "correct" output from a given set of inputs. In contrast to this approach, many modelers have adopted the stance that the structure of the model is all important, that the adequacy of a model should be assessed by the plausibility of the detailed individual relationships built into the model.

Again, it is important to realize that "pure" examples of these opposite approaches cannot be found in practice. Indeed, many philosophers of the scientific method would assert that a model based only on empirical data could not be constructed. The very act of identifying data always involves the use of at least a primitive theory. Furthermore, no modeler would, or could, attempt to build a model in which only theoretical relationships could be found, in the sense that such theoretical relationships must be ultimately derived from experience, even if not justified explicitly in terms of empirical data.

Undoubtedly, the choice of one of these approaches is conditioned largely both by the relative extent and availability of theory and data concerning the particular system being modeled, and the ultimate purpose for which a particular model is intended. Beyond these considerations, however, it is possible to make some assessment of the limitations of the black box approach as a basis for assessing the effects of policy. In practice the input and output variables of the black box approach are often interpreted as policy and target variables, respectively. The simulation of policy-making thus reduces to the problem of selecting the right combination of input values in order to achieve the right values of the output variables. An acceptance of this model of policy-making relies on the assumption that the relationships between inputs and outputs are fixed for the time domain of the simulation.

Furthermore, the division of variables into those that can be affected directly by deliberate policy choices and those that reflect the effect of those choices is, of course, arbitrary. The history of many nations indicates that the range of variables that may be regarded by governments as policy variables can change drastically over time. Similarly, the nature of many historical, political, and economic changes can be identified with changes in the structural relationships between economic and social variables. Thus, we can say that, in general, black box models severely constrain the number of policy choices whose effects can be evaluated. This conclusion is especially relevant in the light of a recent article by Anthony Fedanzo, Jr., concerning the Strategy for Survival model (1974) built by Mesarovic and Pestel for the Club of Rome. This is perhaps the most sophisticated and complicated global forecasting model yet. The model embodies an approach described by its constructors as "multilevel, hierarchical modeling" and is directly oriented for the use of policy-makers. According to Fedanzo, the model is multilevel in that four of its sections (called strata) dealing with demography/economics, technology, ecology, and geophysics are treated in terms of relatively simple input/output submodels, i.e., black boxes. The policy decisions are simulated in other strata which control the four strata mentioned above. If this is, in fact, a true description of the model structure, it casts serious doubt on the ability of the model to simulate the effects of many kinds of policies.

This conclusion can only be advanced as tentative because of the extreme obscurity of the technical description of the model. As a prominent futures researcher has pointed out, "the reader who attempts to delve into the innards of the model in the back-up volumes will encounter monumental difficulties in deciphering the details" (Linstone, 197C, p. 331). This is a serious problem in itself, and we will return to the question of the relationship between the adequacy and clarity of models.

## DETERMINISM, OPTIMIZATION AND CHOICE

A deterministic model is one in which the numerical results produced are completely determined at the outset of the computer experiment. In contrast with this situation, it is possible to build models in which the modeler is allowed to monitor selected variables during the course of the calculations and to make adjustments to certain model parameters on the basis of a desired pattern of model behavior. As mentioned above, this latter approach is that adopted by the constructors of the Strategy for Survival model. A third alternative is that whereby the modeler chooses a desired outcome expressed in terms of a set of model variables in advance of the computer run, and the required variable monitoring and parameter adjustments are made automatically by a mathematical optimization routine incorporated within the model.

Models can thus be usefully classified by the extent to which they are goal-seeking and the methods by means of which goals, if any, are sought. This consideration is an especially important one in the context of socioeconomic forecasting models since, like the distinction between black-boxes and structures, it reflects the way in which the model deals with the effects of conscious policy-making. Thus, in general, descriptive models place less apparent emphasis on human policy intervention than does either the optimization or hierarchical decision stratum approach. We can also say that optimizing models are usually also normative models since the mathematical optimization routine usually is intended to represent the consistent implementation of a particular set of policies regarded as desirable by the model constructors. A significant group of exceptions to this generalization are to be found in models that claim to describe the real world on the basis of a theory which asserts that real world systems themselves operate so as to optimize the value of certain variables. For example, the body of economic theory known as neoclassical asserts, among other things, that a free market economy contains a sufficient wealth of feedback loops to enable it to retain a relatively stable equilibrium in the face of external perturbations, and to automatically anticipate and avert many potential crises without external policy intervention. This theory forms the basis of the Systems Analysis Research Unit's global model.

In fact, any system containing feedback processes can be regarded to some extent as goal-seeking. The great discovery of Adam Smith, that an economy which can be described by a completely determinist set of rules based on individual self-interest would appear to maximize the public good as if "led by an invisible hand," was an early example of a principle more recently rediscovered by systems researchers. That principle, stated by Norbert Wiener in 1948, asserts that there is nothing mysterious about purposive or goal-seeking behavior, that although in purposive behavior the future (in the form of some goal) seems to affect the present, such behavior can in fact be analyzed and generated entirely in cause-and-effect terms *providing* feedback processes are taken into account.

Mathematical optimization routines do, however, go one stage further along the goal-seeking dimension in the sense that they can alter the relative importance of the various feedback processes within the model. Human choice can go even further in choosing the objective function for the optimization process and by directly altering the structure of the model. Thus, the full scope of possible policy alternatives can ohly be simulated by allowing the full range of possible amendments to the model, from changes in input variables to changes in feedback processes and ultimately to radical alternatives in model structure.

## THE LIMITATIONS OF MODELING

So far, we have attempted to clarify the nature and purposes of computer simulation modeling, and we have briefly compared and contrasted various approaches to modeling that have been adopted. In this section, we assess the relative merits of the various approaches and attempt to draw some tentative conclusions about some of the limitations of modeling as a forecasting method.

Let us start with the assumption that the problems involved in thinking about the future of the real world are not organized in the same fashion as the problems of the academic disciplines. It follows that the full character of such problems can become evident only if a wide variety of causal relationships can be considered: economic, political, sociological, psychological, technical. It would seem likely that such an eclectic analysis can involve several different conceptualizations—informal models—of what it is that determines the nature and scale of the problems being studied. From our survey of modeling approaches we have seen that computer simulation modeling can, in theory, deal with this situation quite well.

The range and flexibility of modeling approaches outlined above would seem sufficient to transform a large number of disparate conceptualizations into a range of formal mathematical models. Some of these models might well be complementary, in which case a suitable array of them would provide a means for exploring determinants of the future from a number of contrasting viewpoints. Some would not be complementary, indicating both the inherent complexity of the problems and the existence of fundamental theoretical and ideological differences.

The question we must now address is whether conventional approaches to the construction of computer simulation models do in practice both incorporate a multiplicity of differing disciplinary viewpoints and highlight possible areas of consistency and contradiction between the different possible perceptions of a problem area. A superficial analysis of recent major forecasting models is sufficient to suggest that this is not the case. For example, it can be argued that each of the large-scale world models so far completed has been based upon a single conception of the nature of problems facing the world. Each modeling exercise chooses at the outset a particular approach, which then greatly determines the outcome of the exercise. Models are fundamentally statements of system structure, and in the case of many modeling approaches the model structure is greatly constrained by the choice of modeling techniques.

Even systems dynamics, which is perhaps the most flexible of modeling approaches, and which apparently does *not* constrain the choice of system structure at all, suffers from a closely related drawback. When a model is built to study a complex situation, two definite, if not distinct, research phases can be identified. First, there is the stage of problem-finding involving the formation of a conceptual structure that can then be translated into a set of mathematical equations for describing the system under study. In the second stage, this structure is used to derive the consequent behavior of the system, using complex mathematical techniques.

The concrete manifestation of the systems dynamics method consists of the range of computer programming languages, such as *DYNAMO* (Pugh, 1973), designed to cope with the second stage of the process. The apparent simplicity and appeal of these languages, known generically as Continuous System Simulation Languages (CSSL), has tended to shift attention from the vital task of producing an adequate model structure. Their ease of use enables the modeler to produce a working model with a minimum of time, effort, and thought, and encourages him to devote a disproportionate amount of time to the refinement and calibration of detailed numerical relationships. Once a dynamic model has been built using these techniques, its structure soon acquires an air of concrete permanence. Many man-years can then be happily employed in the evaluation of minor amendments, experimentation with varied parameter values, and general tinkering within a given model framework. The similarity of the structures of the agricultural subsystems of many varied world models, as noted by Clark and Cole (1976, p. 21), testifies to the hypnotic inertia of a certain choice of system representation.

One significant consequence of this pattern of model development is the tendency of models to become more and more complex as additional relationships and variables are added to the existing structure. Increasing complexity leads in turn to a reduced motivation to challenge the basic structural assumptions of the model. As the model grows larger and larger, the more important it becomes for the creators of the model to justify the time and effort expended in its construction. The very process of modeling thus comes to possess an inherent dynamic that discourages the modeler from ever questioning the extent to which the most appropriate structure has been selected.

In the context of models used for urban and regional planning, Sayer (1976) has remarked on the conceptual supremacy of a very limited range of established models, which despite their lack of confirmation tend to structure and constrain researchers' perceptions of urban systems. Furthermore, the dominance of particular model frameworks has been to some extent concealed by the variety of terms used to describe the models. The Lowry (1964) model, for example, has also reappeared in the recent literature under the guises of a gravity or entropy model. The tendency of urban systems dynamics' models to grow ever larger and more complex has also been documented (Lee, 1973). Perhaps the only modeling approach that has not encouraged this process is the econometric empirical method. Here instead we can detect a tendency toward the use of more and more sophisticated and time-consuming statistical methods for estimating model parameters (Fisher and Sheppard, 1972).

The central focus of this analysis of the limitations of simulation modeling is that any single forecasting technique is inherently inadequate (Encel et al., 1975, p. 91), that any idea of building a general model with which to examine all alternatives must be suspect. The positive prescription arising from this recognition is that a forecasting exercise will be more effective if it is based on the evaluation of many alternative models rather than a single model and a set of data. Insistence on a plurality of model structures should not be regarded as a demand for a preliminary phase in the modeling process, which would later be replaced by a "correct" model structure. We believe that structural pluralism should be an essential feature of any modeling exercise that claims to improve our ability to deal with real world problems. Nor should the modeler rest content with a specious plurality of model structure which is created by minor structural modification to a core model. Rather, the alternative structures should be developed in such detail that a problem already solved with the guidance of one model can be treated in a new and perhaps more detailed fashion with the aid of a fresh structure. The function of such concrete alternatives is to enable the assessment of the adequacy of forecasting models in a manner transcending mere comparison of the behavioral consequences of structural assumptions with available theory and data. However closely a forecasting model seems to reproduce a historical situation, however obvious the assumptions embodied within the model, and however necessary those assumptions seem to be to both the users and constructors of a model, its adequacy as a basis for forecasting can only be asserted after it has been confronted with alternative models. Therefore, the construction and detailed development of these alternative models should, if possible, precede any public pronouncement of the practical success or policy relevance of a forecasting model.[2]

## MUST MODELS BE COMPLEX?

There is an apparent serious drawback to the methodology outlined above: that is, it takes considerable time and effort to build alternative models. In order to deal with this problem, it is necessary to return to a number of basic questions concerning the relationship between the adequacy and complexity of models. It has already been pointed out by Clark and Cole (1976, pp. 110–112) that for a model to be of value it should be as simple as possible—the very purpose of modeling being the simplification and structuring of reality. Indeed, one of the most important theoretical advantages of model-building, the way in which underlying assumptions are made explicit, is often vitiated in practice by the extreme complexity of the representations chosen. The simpler a model is, the more easily it may be understood by the audience to whom it is addressed. This is especially important when policy recommendations based on a modeling exercise are presented to policymakers. If these recommendations are to carry any weight, their derivation must be clearly traceable from a comprehensible model.

There is also good reason to suppose that, in common with many other forms of intellectual and economic activity, model-building possesses a built-in tendency toward diminishing returns of scale. This feature is especially relevant when the model builder is concerned with a problem area categorized by a lack of a theoretical base, shortage of time-series data, and a high level of conflict between so-called experts. Given this all too common situation, the building of a range of explanatory models can be a most powerful heuristic device. In such circumstances, the production of a single elaborate, untestable, complex dynamic model can be regarded as an almost criminal waste of scarce research capacity.

An analogy between this kind of model-building and the seventeenth-century school of art and architecture known as baroque provides some interesting insights. The baroque school was characterized by its deliberate intention as propaganda through its dramatic intensity and emotional appeal, and its heavily and sometimes grotesquely ornate style, with unnecessary features added for ornament rather than for utility.

These features which in art or architecture might be merely ugly or overpowering can, in forecasting, become quite dangerous. Undoubtedly, computer simulation models do have an appeal that is derived solely from the use of a computer. Whatever the detailed content of the models, the combined use of high technology and an apparently rigorous mathematical treatment have considerable advantages as effective tools for propaganda. That the success of the "limits to growth" model as a propaganda exercise was in large measure attributable to the use of a computer has been acknowledged by the project's sponsors, the Club of Rome (Thiemann, 1973).

It is somewhat more difficult to justify the second baroque parallel: the assertion that much of the complexity of model structures is designed for ornament rather than for utility. It has certainly been demonstrated that many models can be greatly simplified while still retaining the same behavior patterns (Cuypers and Rademaker, 1973). Modelers often disaggregate their models (that is, add new relationships and variables) so as to anticipate the potential criticism that their models are too simple. This is, of course, a perfectly natural and practical step. On the other hand, it frequenly turns out that many additions and amendments to the model make no significant difference to model behavior. When this happens, it is again quite natural for the modelers to leave such changes in the model, even though they make no difference to the model results. In this way, the model acquires a great deal of redundant complexity. An alternative approach would be to restore the model to its previous state after each apparently unnecessary amendment has been made while retaining full details of any elaborations that were tried out.[3] Thus, the final model would be as simple as possible and potential changes of oversimplification could be defended on the basis of well-documented experiments performed during the process of model-building. Few model builders have, in fact, adopted this approach.

Having considered some of the potential advantages and practical drawbacks of computer simulation models as a basis for forecasting, we now examine the structure and results of some actual models.

## ALTERNATIVE MODELS COMPARED

It is impossible in this short chapter to examine more than a tiny fraction of the available range of published forecasting models. We limit ourselves here to a brief discussion of some features of perhaps the most ambitious of forecasting models which deal with selected aspects of the world systems—global models. Global models are probably the boldest attempts at multidisciplinary simulation modeling and, as such, are a natural subject for consideration here. It must be pointed out that there already exists a considerable body of analytic and critical literature on these models. The early MIT models of Meadows and Forrester have, in particular, attracted substantial attention (Cole, 1973a). Similarly, the later world models of Mesarovic-Pestel, the Japanese Club of Rome (Kaya and Suzuki, pp. 371–388), the Bariloche Foundation, and others have been discussed and analyzed in a recent publication that has already been referred to here many times (Clark and Cole, 1976). For deeper analysis and exhaustive bibliographies, the interested reader is directed to these reviews. Here we will consider just a few points arising from our previous discussion in connection with a comparison of two of these world models.

At the time *The Limits of Growth* was published, the world model, WORLD-3, which formed the basis for the book, represented the most ambitious attempt to apply computer simulation modeling to thinking about the future of the world. As such, it inevitably created a great deal of controversy on every level from the technical details of the modeling approach (Cole and Curnow, 1973b) to the motivation and ideology of the authors (Golub and Townsend, 1975). The general argument presented in *Limits*, which by now must be familiar to readers with even the briefest acquaintance with futures research, was that exponential increases in consumption and population would eventually exhaust the planet's natural resources, perhaps even in the near future. Even if this catastrophe were avoided, growing pollution levels would result in ecological collapse. One of the key assertions of the constructors of this model was that the "behavior mode" of the model was sufficiently robust to survive almost any conceivable structural modification; that the basic pattern of world economic development was that of "overshoot and collapse." As a result of the more detailed mathematical assessment of WORLD-3 which followed the publication of *The Limits to Growth*, at least three authors (Scolnik, 1973; Vermeulen and de Jongh, 1976, pp. 29–32; Cole and Curnow, 1973a, pp. 108–134) have been able to show that relatively minor changes of parameters and relationships in the model can lead to radically different outcomes for the future of the world system. For example, Scolnik (1973) shows that with less than 5 percent variation in a small number of key parameters (with an average variation of only 0.75 percent), the model shows a smooth trajectory of unlimited growth until the year 2300.

Here we see a dangerous pitfall in Gerhart Bruckmann's idea of a forecast which is "good enough" (1976). To many readers, the forecasts derived from WORLD-3 seemed to meet this criterion. Supporters of the *Limits* thesis argued that it made little difference whether the world economic system would collapse from a shortage of natural resources in twenty years or two hundred years, the important point being that without drastic modifications of the present world system such a disaster would be inevitable. Whether such a catastrophe is inevitable has not yet been determined with any certainty. What is now certain is that the Meadows model is not "good enough" to settle the question beyond any doubt. Even a comparison of WORLD-3 with alternatives consisting of minor structural variants of the original model is sufficient to provide an extremely powerful critical assessment of the model's adequacy and of the conclusions that were reached on the basis of it. It is possible to conjecture that an intellectual stimulus even greater than that of *The Limits to Growth* might have been provided if the talented team that produced WORLD-3 had themselves devoted some time to the production of a series of alternative models.

This task, as it turned out, was left to others. At an early presentation of the *Limits* model in Rio de Janeiro, a team of scientists from the Bariloche Foundation in Argentina decided that a response was necessary. The Bariloche team pointed out (Herrera, et al., 1976) that many development experts in the industrialized countries tend to view world problems as stemming from the massive growth of population in the developing world, with the consequent strain on the world's agricultural system and increased use of scarce resources of energy and minerals.

The reemergence of this view of world development as a race between population and scarce resources, first stated by Malthus early in the nineteenth century, has been greeted with concern by the Latin American scientists. They believe that, while control of population, measures to halt pollution, and the rational use of energy and minerals are essential, these efforts are only complementary to and dependent on more fundamental social, political, and economic changes required in the international system if the major problems of the world are to be challenged successfully. They identify the root causes of these problems in the uneven distribution of power, both between and within nations, resulting in oppression and exploitation. The deterioration of the physical environment is not an inevitable consequence of human progress but the result of a particular form of social organization.

The conceptual model of the Bariloche team thus involves a shift toward a society that is essentially socialist, based on equality and full participation of all its members in the decisions affecting them. In such a society, consumption and economic growth are regulated so as both to increase the welfare of all the population and to remain compatible with the natural environment. The team realized the necessity not only of describing their ideal society, but also of demonstrating that such a society could be viable in terms of the available economic and physical resources. The normative mathematical model was thus built to demonstrate the possibility that all countries and regions of the world could move from their present situations toward a world in which all its people could be provided with their basic needs—a world free from hunger and poverty.

This basic needs approach thus forms the central core of the mathematical model. The needs are defined in terms of nutrition, housing, education, and health. These needs are generously defined; for example, a nutrition target of 3,000 calories per person per day was set, a level regarded by most nutritionists as luxurious. The model is essentially an economic model in which the production system is the main driving force. Five production sectors are identified: agriculture, education, construction, capital goods, and consumption goods and services. The main function of the production system is to allocate capital investment and manpower between the sectors, not according to relative profitability but in such a way as to provide the best possible satisfaction of basic needs. This satisfaction is achieved by using an optimization routine that determines how resources are allocated between production sectors. Since the team observed a close relationship between life expectancy and the level of satisfaction of basic needs, it was decided that the optimization should seek to maximize life expectancy at birth.

The model also attempts to demonstrate the possibility of regional self-sufficiency; that most poor regions of the world can satisfy the basic needs of their people by relying on their own economic and natural resources. This applies not only to individual Third World countries but also to the pooling of resources by poor nations with similar problems. The model thus divides the developing countries into three continents—Latin America, Africa, and Asia—each bloc being treated as a separate entity. At this stage, three crucial differences between the Bariloche and *Limits* models should be evident. First, we can contrast the explicitly normative nature of the Bariloche work with that of the *Limits* model, which claimed to be a description of the way the world works. Second, we can compare the levels of aggregation of the two models: WORLD-3 treats the world as a single entity, whereas the Bariloche model deals with four separate geographical and economic regions, each with five production sectors. Third, Bariloche makes use of an optimization routine to simulate the effect of a set of consistently applied policy choices; where possible policy measures are dealt with in *Limits*, it is by means of ad hoc changes to initialization variables.

The results of the Bariloche model indicate that, with the exception of the Asian region, the basic needs targets can be met in the time span of a single generation—in Latin America by 1992 and in Africa by 2008. It can be argued that, as was the case with WORLD-3, these conclusions can be deduced directly from the major assumptions of the model. The Bariloche team assumes a completely equitable distribution of income within regions, the implementation of a radical and sophisticated planning mechanism for the allocation of investment, the total absence of resource shortages during the time span considered, and the continuation of technological progress at the rate experienced during the last few decades.

The assumption regarding technological progress is especially crucial. When the model is run assuming that technological progress gradually declines, reaching zero in the year 2000, the results show a different picture. In this case, only Latin America reaches the basic needs targets and then over a longer time period; in Africa and Asia, the economic system collapses. Debate concerning the future rate of technological progress was a key feature of many of the criticisms of the "limits to growth" thesis (Julien and Freeman, 1973, pp. 66–79), and it would seem that the Bariloche model has again emphasized the importance of this area of uncertainty.

A more fundamental criticism of the Bariloche model asserts that, by assuming away down-to-earth problems of actually bringing about change in the current world order, the Bariloche team manages to sidestep that area in which new thinking is most urgently required. In its present form, the model is clearly an inadequate guide to those policies which, in the real world, might encourage the satisfaction of basic needs. While it is easy to implement a device for the rational allocation of investment and labor where those variables are just electrons in a computer, it is a vast step to assume that such allocation can be made to work in the real world of factories, farms, men, and machines. Criticism along these lines can be elaborated indefinitely. To some extent, however, these criticisms are misplaced, for after all the model was only intended to provide a riposte to the newly emergent Malthusian position encouraged by the MIT world models. In this role, it certainly succeeds—at least to the extent of highlighting areas of critical uncertainty for the future of the world system.

It is interesting to speculate whether the Bariloche model is too baroque for its purpose. The inclusion of many sophisticated and detailed mechanisms in the model might seem difficult to justify in view of the uncertainty about the values of such key parameters as the rate of technological change. This point is especially crucial in the light of the three-year delay between the initial conception and the final completion of the model. In this period, the Malthusian ideas of *The Limits to Growth* have had a chance to settle firmly in the collected subconscious of many policy-makers the world over. In this sense, perhaps the Bariloche model arrived too late. Nevertheless, despite its late publication, the basic needs concept at the core of the model has at least penetrated the thinking of international organizations such as the ILO. Researchers at the ILO used the opportunity provided by a preview of the model to lay out the basic needs framework that dominated the 1976 ILO world conference (Jolly, 1976, pp. 363–365).

## NEW DIRECTIONS FOR MODELING

Three general conclusions can be drawn from the discussion so far: simple models are to be preferred to more complex, "baroque" models; the production of alternative models is a more constructive exercise than the building of a single structure; and modelers should be encouraged to take every opportunity to criticize and test their models as part of the model-building process. We have also noted earlier that most existing modeling technologies (in the form of programming languages, etc.) tend to detract modelers from the directions we regard as desirable. We would therefore like to round up this article with a brief and inevitably superficial survey of current research in the field of modeling methodology. A more adequate coverage of this topic can be found in a recent paper by the author (McLean and Shepard, 1976).

There is a considerable recent body of both theoretical and applied work on the use of directed graphs for simulation modeling. The practical application of this theory is epitomized by the work of Warfield (1974) and other members of the Battelle Memorial Institute (Baldwin, 1975); indeed, Battelle has been largely instrumental in disseminating the notion of interpretive structural modeling. This modeling approach concentrates on the use of unweighted and often unsigned binary graphs. This is equivalent to building the simplest possible models—those that study only the existence or nonexistence of interactions between the components of a system. This restriction has been encouraged by their use of either manual or relatively simple computational techniques for the analysis of such models. As a consequence, the dynamic evolution of the systems described has not been investigated.

Working along similar lines, Roberts (1971) has for some time now been developing structural models to analyze the future demand for energy. Roberts' analyses depend on a rather cumbersome use of mathematical theorems concerning various stability properties of models. We describe the techniques as cumbersome since, as does Battelle, little use is made of automatic analyses, and mathematical sophistication and extreme ingenuity substitute for computational power. Nevertheless, his work represents an extension of Battelle's since it is primarily concerned with forecasting the dynamic behavior of systems represented by simple structural models.

Since Roberts' analysis relies on rigorous mathematical theorems, in his early work he limited his model structures to signed digraphs, that is, models specified in terms of signed binary numbers only. The limitations of this kind of model for behavior mode analysis have been pointed out elsewhere (McLean, Shepherd, and Curnow, 1976b, pp. 18–19). The principal drawback is that using only binary numbers insures that all feedback processes in such a model are of equal importance, whereas in real world systems, some feedback loops can be described as dominant. The identification of such loops is an extremely powerful method of analysis (McLean and Shepherd, in press). Although F. S. Roberts (1975) has recently extended his methodology to include quantitative data, he still relies on manual (non-computerized) techniques of analysis (1975, pp. 703–724).

The work of Kane (1972, pp. 129–142) is very similar in both content and direction to that kind of modeling for which we have argued earlier in this article. Kane has produced a combined methodology/programming language to deal with cross-impact matrices that represent the structural dynamics of a system. His computer language, called KSIM, is designed as an alternative to existing dynamic simulation languages, with the emphasis placed on ease of use and the ability to quickly assess the implications of structural changes. Unfortunately, KSIM has a fundamental limitation built into the method by which system behavior is calculated. Kane makes the somewhat arbitrary assumption that all functional relationships expressed in the model take the form of a logistic curve; that is, that all state variables in a system described by a set of KSIM equations are only allowed to vary between an explicit upper and lower bound. While it is true, as Kane asserts, that "such growth and decay patterns are characteristic of many economic, technological, and biological processes" (1972, p. 133), it is also true that many of the variables commonly included in the methods of social and economic systems behave as if no such bounds existed.

The work of Moll and Woodside (n.d.) has corrected two of the limitations inherent in KSIM. They have implemented an interactive computer package, XIMP, in which either KSIM or Roberts' digraph models can be embedded. XIMP enables the modeler to modify and run simple models on-line, and in addition it contains capabilities for parameter identification, tracking optimization, sensitivity analysis, and stability analysis. While XIMP has not yet been tried out as a vehicle for model development, it would seem that it has great potential for such use.

A survey of progress in modeling methods would be incomplete without some mention of the work of the team at the Science Policy Research Unit (SPRU), of which the author is a member. A full description of this work is available (McLean, Shepherd, and Curnow, 1976b), together with an introductory article (McLean and Shepherd, 1976). The concrete manifestation of our research is a computer modeling package, SPIN, which has been tailored for the type of modeling for which we have outlined a case.

Four aspects of the package are especially relevant to our discussion. First, the package has been designed specifically for the rapid construction of alternative dynamic structural models. Second, we have concentrated on making the package easy to use in order to make the techniques available to the nonexpert modeler. Third, the package represents only a methodological framework; its only essential feature is the use of an interaction matrix representation of a linear model. Although it presently contains a number of what we term *techniques for the analysis of system structure*, which we have found to be of use for guiding model development, their use is optional and they can be replaced by other heuristics or ignored at the choice of the user. This flexibility reflects our greater commitment to an approach to modeling rather than to a particular set of methods. Finally, we would like to emphasize that our development of SPIN has been closely related to ongoing research at SPRU concerned with both the construction of new models and the analysis and evaluation of models already constructed by other researchers. This reflects our view that a sound methodological basis for systems research and modeling can best be established through confrontation with real world problems; that there is no question of a trade-off between theoretical research and practice, but rather a significant synergy to be obtained from their interaction.

Even this brief survey of modeling research tends to refute the recent assertion by Edward Roberts that "the key variants in model building approaches were available ten years ago or earlier" (1976, p. 231). What remains to be achieved, however, is the closer integration of these promising developments in methodological research with practical model-building exercises.

## CONCLUSIONS AND APOLOGIES

Readers familiar with the philosophy of science will perhaps recognize the ideas of Feyerabend (1963, pp. 3–39) in our plea for simplicity and pluralism in modeling. Perhaps a more significant inspiration can be found in the work of Popper (1959). Although we disagree with many details of Popper's epistemology, we would concur with his emphasis on the importance of a self-critical and skeptical attitude as a prerequisite for the growth of knowledge. In forecasting, as in other forms of human inquiry, no technique can do more than encourage the search for alternative conceptual structures. Firm motivation to exploit that technique is also required. We also feel that computer simulation modeling is only one of a wide range of possibilities for thinking about the future; no single method can offer a universal framework. We would hope that the critical attitude required for the most fruitful application of modeling would also motivate the futures researcher to seek out and explore alternative modes of inquiry as well as alternative models.

## NOTES

1. Science Policy Research Unit, University of Sussex. I would like to thank my friends at SPRU who have helped with general advice, especially John Clark, Ian Miles, and Paul Shepherd. The content of this article nevertheless remains my own responsibility.

2. Although it must be admitted that development may be impractical. In this case, we would require that any published model should not only make explicit the particular structural assumptions on which it is based, but also emphasize these assumptions and the possible alternatives.

3. Of course, the possibility of significant synergy between a number of "redundant" sections should also be investigated before such a course of action is taken.

## REFERENCES

Baldwin, M. M. (ed.). 1975. *Portraits of Complexity.* Battelle Monograph, Number 9 (June).

Ball, R. J. 1967. *Econometric Models. Mathematical Model Building in Economics and Industry.* London: Griffin.

Bruckmann, G. 1976. *Problems of Futures Research.* University of Sussex, England: Science Policy Research Unit. (Mimeo.)

Clark, J., and S. Cole, with R. C. Curnow and M. J. D. Hopkins. 1976. *Global Simulation Models.* London: John Wiley and Sons.

Cole, H. S. D., et al. 1973a. *Models of Doom: A Critique of "The Limits to Growth."* New York: Universe Books.

———, and R. C. Curnow. 1973b. "Backcasting with the World Models." *Nature,* Volume 245 (October 12).

———. 1973c. "An Evaluation of the World Models." H. S. D. Cole, et al., *Models of Doom: A Critique of "The Limits to Growth."* New York: Universe Books, 108-134.

Cuypers, J. G. M., and O. Rademaker. 1973. *An Analysis of Forrester's "World Dynamics" Model.* Eindhoven: Project Global Dynamica, Report U16 (1973-05-01).

Encel, S., et al. 1975. *The Art of Anticipation.* London: Martin Robertson.

Fedanzo, A. J., Jr. 1974. "Multilevel, Hierarchical World Modelling." *Technological Forecasting and Social Change,* Volume 9, Numbers 1/2, 35-49.

Feyerabend, P. K. 1963. "How to Be a Good Empiricist—A Plea for Tolerance in Matters Epistemological." In B. Baurin (ed.), *Philosophy of Science.* Volume 2. New York: Wiley Interscience, 3–39.

Fisher, G., and D. Sheppard. 1972. *Effects of Monetary Policy on the United States Economy.* Paris: Organisation for Economic Co-operation and Development.

Forrester, J. W. 1961. *Industrial Dynamics.* Cambridge, Mass.: MIT Press.

———. 1968. *Principles of Systems.* Cambridge, Mass.: Wright-Allen Press.

———. 1969. *Urban Dynamics.* Cambridge, Mass.: MIT Press.

———. 1971. *World Dynamics.* Cambridge, Mass.: MIT Press.

Golub, R., and J. Townsend. 1975. "Malthus, Multinationals and the Club of Rome." Unpublished paper, Sussex, England: Science Policy Research Unit, University of Sussex.

Herrera, A. O., et al. 1976. *Catastrophe or New Society.* Ottawa: International Development Research Center.

Jolly, R., 1976. "Conference Report." *Futures.* Volume 8, Number 4 (August), 363–365.

Julien, P. A., and C. Freeman. 1973. "The Capital and Industrial Output Subsystems." In H. S. D. Cole, et al., *Models of Doom: A Critique of "The Limits to Growth,"* New York: Universe Books, 66–79.

Kane, J. 1972. "A Primer for a New Cross-Impact Language—KSIM." *Technological Forecasting and Social Change*, Volume 4, 129–142.

Kaya, Y., and Y. Suzuki. 1974. "Global Constraints and a New Vision for Development—II." *Technological Forecasting and Social Change*, Volume 6, 371–388.

Lee, D. B. 1973. "Requiem for Large-scale Models." *Journal of the American Institute of Planners* (May), 163–178.

Leontief, W. 1974. "Structures of the World Economy." *American Economic Review.* Volume 64, Number 6 (December), 823–834.

Linstone, H. A. 1975. "Book Review: Mankind at the Turning Point." *Technological Forecasting and Social Change*, Volume 7, Number 3, 331.

Lowry, I. S. 1964. *A Model of Metropolis.* Santa Monica, Calif.: RAND Corporation.

McLean, M., and P. Shepherd. 1976. "The Importance of System Structure." *Futures*, Volume 8, Number 1 (February), 40–51.

———. In press. "Feedback Processes in Dynamic Models." *Applied Mathematical Modelling.*

———, with P. Shepherd and R. C. Curnow. 1976a. *Progress in Structural Modelling—A Biased Review."* Paper presented at the Third European Meeting on Cybernetics and Systems Research, Vienna (April).

———,P. Shepherd, and R. C. Curnow. 1976b. *Techniques for the Analysis of System Structure.* University of Sussex, England: Occasional Paper Series of the Science Policy Research Unit, Number 1 (February), 18–19.

Meadows, D., et al. 1972. *The Limits to Growth.* New York: Universe Books.

Mesarovic, M., and E. Pestel. 1974. *Mankind at the Turning Point.* New York: E. P. Dutton.

Moll, R. H. H., and C. M. Woodside. n.d. *Augmentation of Cross-Impact*

*Analysis by Interactive Systems Analysis Tools.* Carleton University, Canada: Technical Report Number S.E. 76–1, Department of System Engineering.

Popper, K. R. 1959. *The Logic of Scientific Discovery.* London: Hutchinson Educational.

Pugh, A. L., III. 1973. *DYNAMO II Users Manual.* Cambridge, Mass.: MIT Press.

Roberts, E. B. 1976. "On Modelling." *Technological Forecasting and Social Change,* Volume 9, 231.

Roberts, F. S. 1971. *Signed Digraphs and the Growing Demand for Energy.* Santa Monica, Calif.: RAND Corporation, R–756–NSF.

———. 1975. "Weighted Digraph Models for the Assessment of Energy Use and Air Pollution in Transportation Systems." *Environment and Planning,* Volume 6, 703–724.

Sayer, A. 1976. *A Critique of Urban Modelling.* London: Pergamon Press.

Scolnik, H. 1973. *On a Methodological Criticism of Meadows WORLD-3 Model.* Argentina: Fundacion Bariloche. (Mimeo.)

Thiemann, H. 1973. "Interview." *Europhysics News* (August).

Vermeulen, P. J., and D. C. J. de Jongh, 1976. "Parameter Sensitivity of the 'Limits to Growth' World Model." *Applied Mathematical Modelling,* Volume 1, Number 1 (June), 29–32.

Warfield, J. M. 1974. *Structuring Complex Systems.* Battelle Monograph, Number 4 (April).

Wiener, Norbert. 1948. *Cybernetics.* Cambridge, Mass.: MIT Press.

RICHARD  D.  DUKE

# Simulation Gaming

A decade ago, the term *simulation gaming* did not exist in the popular lexicon. The literature of the period referred instead to *operational-gaming*, a hyphenated adjunct to the newly developed field of operations research. Gradually, the term *gaming* began to appear in the academic press, most notably in papers relating to business, political science, and urban simulation. Today, references made to gaming are commonplace; the term is found in sources ranging from newspapers and national magazines to other public and semi-public documents.

Of course, the word "game," meaning a playful diversion or amusement, has been in common use for centuries. The evolution of games from a form of play to a serious undertaking can be traced back in time to war games—checkers and chess in their earliest forms. By the eighteenth century, military games were in use for the analysis of possible real-world battle situations. By the advent of World War II, military games were no longer "play," and "gaming" was used to describe an activity of serious purpose. Since World War II, military gaming has become increasingly sophisticated, and its importance as a policy-making tool is evidenced by the secrecy associated with military gaming activities.

World War II spawned at least five developments that have become important parts of gaming: computers, operations research, the mathematical theory of games, simulation, and the early business games. Gaming for social science purposes did not emerge in its own right until the early 1960s; the various gaming products of the ensuing decade reflect an initial confusion in its application. The dramatic increase in the use of gaming in the last decade has resulted both from the increased recognition of the technique's potential as well as from its diffusion through the social sciences for both academic and applied purposes.

Unfortunately, many interpretations of simulation gaming to date have been ill conceived. The technique has not been well understood, and enthusiastic proponents have used it beyond its capability. Gaming is not a predictive device, nor is it a panacea to be plugged into the problem of the moment. But it can be usefully employed for gaining perspective on complex systems, particularly for guiding speculation about future circumstances. Simulation gaming, properly employed, is a powerful tool both for conveying views and for explaining alternative situations.

These games serve four basic functions:

1. To transmit information (as is typical in a lecture format or through other conventional communication devices).
2. To extract information (as in a typical social science question-naire or other survey research instruments).
3. To establish multilogues between players (as, for example, a research team that is trying to articulate the problem under study).
4. To motivate players and to prepare them for some future experience.

Often, several of these purposes can be represented in a single game construct.

The following brief list of examples shows the range of content areas and types of users:

1. The Impassee Game used in Ghana by a group concerned with the development of a new market in Accra.
2. The At-Issue Game used in Monterey Bay, California, by the regional planning agency to examine the implications of a proposed new highway.
3. The Metro-Apex Game used by the federal government, in particular the Environmental Protection Agency, as an air pol-lution control training device.
4. The HEX Game developed for UNESCO as a human settlement planning game to be employed by Third World nations.
5. The Conceptual Mapping Game employed by a research and development firm in southern California to explore geothermal energy implications and alternatives as part of the national energy picture.
6. The SNUS (Simulated Nutrition System) Game developed for the United Nations Food and Agriculture Organization (FAO) in Rome and employed by them for nutrition planning in Third World nations (which will be discussed at the end of this chap-ter).

## THE PURPOSE OF SIMULATION GAMES

Man employs a variety of communication modes. These may be perceived as falling along a continuum and ranging from the simple to the complex. As they become more complex, their three basic components—language, communication technology, and pattern of interaction—become more sophisticated both individually and in their combined patterns. Simulation gaming is at the most sophisticated end of the continuum and typically employs multiple languages (including a game-specific language), a multilogue (as opposed to dialogue), and a sophisticated, interactive combination of communication technologies.

Simulation gaming is the one means conducive for presenting a dynamic model that is an abstraction of complex reality. Within the context of a game, we develop a highly organized jargon or special language that permits the various respondents to talk to each other with greater clarity than they would be able to through traditional communication modes. Games can be viewed as abstract symbolic maps of various multidimensional phenomena. As such, they serve as a basic reference or filing system for participants concerned with that phenomenon. If these constructs are properly elaborated, they can represent not only a present reality but also a future possibility or, more properly, alternative futures.

One caution is in order: simulation gaming is one of the most costly modes of communication for both construction and use. The potential user should therefore consider alternative modes carefully. Before proceeding with the gaming technique, every effort should be made to ascertain that the client's need cannot be met by some less cumbersome mode.

In approaching today's public policy problems, there is a crucial need for methods of communication and analysis that are future-oriented and that can convey the totality of an extremely complex and rapidly changing situation. Gaming fills this need.

Since World War II, a future-oriented perspective has become mandatory. There is an urgent need for information assimilated as heuristics, since the recurrent waves of new "facts" are too numerous and too fleeting in duration to be captured and assimilated by each new generation. Alternative futures must be advanced and selected, frequently where no useful precedent exists. Traditional modes of communication do not lend themselves to transmitting heuristics. We must devise new modes that are most effective in providing overview, holistic thought, or gestalt. As public policy issues increasingly reveal the interconnectivity among social, political, economic, and biological systems, the need for achieving systemic understanding is becoming more urgent. R. F. Rhyne has commented on this situation and its significance for policy-makers and citizens:

There is a macro-problem, an interweaving of adverse conditions that is more extensive, more richly structured by interior lines of interaction, and more threatening than any circumstance faced before all mankind.

The interweaving of problems in this era has forced attention to wider and more complex fields by each decision maker . . . The mode of understanding that is needed is one of gestalt appreciation rather than explicit knowledge of bits of data. This is true whether one views the current macroproblem as a citizen, a responsible executive agent in government or business, or a re-searcher. The extent of the field to be appreciated and the contraction of the time available for doing so interdicts the normal, experiential way of gaining deep appreciation, so vicarious routes are needed (1973).

Rhyne argues that decision-making is not a logically determinable process. He believes that the citizen, the policy researcher, or other decision-maker must first comprehend the whole—the entirety, the gestalt, the system—before the particulars can be dealt with.

Man thinks in images and transmits his images to others by means of language. This process requires that he translate his holistic image into a sequential string of component descriptions and that his listener attempt to reconstruct the image. Sequentiality is sufficient as long as the listener can hold initial components while he receives later ones; this requires that the pattern be simple. Because a mental holding process breaks down very quickly under the strain of today's com-plexities, another method of transmitting information must be devel-oped. We now need to find a vehicle of communication that will im-prove our ability to convey the patterns and comprehend the future, and that will permit larger segments of mankind to conduct more intelligent dialogues about these complexities. It is now apparent that man must deal not with a future but with *many* futures, and with the communications modes historically available to us, we are not very well equipped to think these through.

## TRADITIONAL EXPLORATORY MODES

What are the major stylistic differences in transmitting a comprehen-sion of a "complex reality" through traditional sequential communica-tion and through simulation gaming?

Figure 1 illustrates the communication process in a typical lecture or conference situation. There are several impediments to the discussion of a serious topic in this context, stemming from the problems of

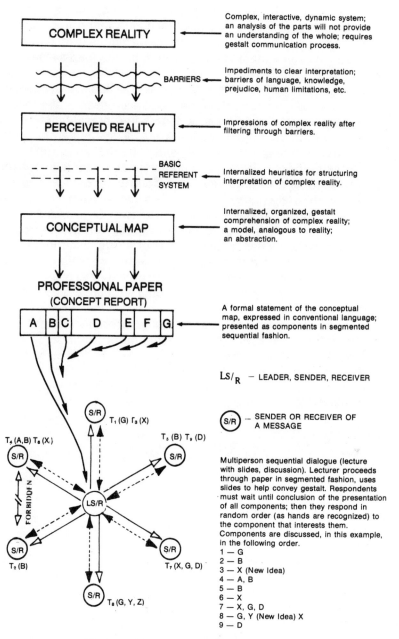

**Figure 1.** Multiperson Sequential Dialogue

perceiving and transmitting complexity, as well as from the mechanical aspects of engaging a group of people in dialogue. In the first instance, a complex topic must be abstracted to a manageable level and committed to some trial statement (usually written) that serves as a basis for discussion.

The figure starts with a complex reality that is all one fabric, although its pattern is partially obscure. Nonetheless, the process of abstracting and organizing inevitably results in a segmented presentation to the receivers. The choice of the term *complex reality* deliberately suggests a problem whose dimensions cannot readily be grasped in their entirety by human faculties. Barriers to complete and unambiguous understanding of reality include real limitations of understanding the subject in its particulars (lack of empirical or theoretical base), as well as human limitations in interpreting what is known (for example, it was obvious for a long time that the sun circled the earth every twenty-four hours—the empirical evidence clearly supported this fact; those who challenged this obviously perceived reality were in considerable jeopardy). Different humans will develop different perceptions of a problem, thereby prompting the need for sophisticated exchange of messages concerning the problem.

Humans organize their perceptions along different formats, even though they refer to the same reality. Each individual has some basic frame of reference that serves as an internalized heuristic for structuring personal interpretation of a complex reality. For example, if you were to request a statement from a sociologist, economist, geographer, political scientist, engineer, or urban planner concerning the problems of a major urban community, the structure of their responses would vary considerably, both in emphasis and organizational mode; there would be one reality, but many styles of perceiving and organizing abstractions of it.

The result of this personal process of winnowing an organized and manageable scheme from an impression of some complex idea is a conceptual map. This map is viewed as an internalized, organized, abstracted comprehension of complex reality that the holder chooses to transmit or discuss. In some sense it is a model, analogous to the reality. This conceptual map may or may not be committed to a formal written document. In simulation gaming, the conceptual map serves as a mental blueprint to aid in conveying complex systems. The conceptual map helps to classify, sort, and store information, and it provides a heuristic language to be used as a common symbol structure for discussing a given complex system. Data conveyed through a conceptual map cease to be mere bits of information; rather, they become heuristic wisdom. However, a conceptual map is not assimilated as a static structure or by static means; it is built iteratively over time.

Typically, this abstracted organized model of reality appears as a professional paper. (For gaming purposes, the term *concept report* is used.) Because of the limitations of written communication, the original reality appears in segmented form, and each chapter or section analyzes a logical component as though it truly existed in isolation. Normally, special devices are employed to emphasize the integrity of the reality; various graphics and statements indicating the linkage between components are used to suggest the actual dynamic. Consider the task of a research team that must present some radical new design for an internal combustion engine to the board of directors. The presentation is likely to be broken into presentations of the fuel system, the ignition system, the air intake and exhaust system, and so on. Contrast this approach to that of the team leader who presents a working model of the engine made of clear lucite (a simulation of the actual model) and responds to questions on its functional characteristics on demand from the board.

Having achieved an organized statement of complexity designed to serve as a starting point for discussion, we now encounter a mechanical problem. The report will be presented verbally to a group of potential respondents who may or may not have had prior access to the written statement. Upon completion of the presentation, discussion ensues. Respondents are selected in the order in which they seek recognition, or more commonly, in the case where multiple respondents wish to speak, in some random pattern. To avoid chaos, conventions governing these "discussions" are employed. Respondents are discouraged or prohibited from private exchanges, and all voices must be recognized by the chair and a response given. Courtesy demands that the chair recognize those wishing to comment according to temporal equity, rather than according to the logical content of the proposed comment. (The chair has no way to fathom who will address what aspect of the topic.) Time constraints force limits to a given exchange to allow time for other comments, but, unfortunately, the other comments may prove to be more or less relevant. Potentially interesting tangential ideas must be stifled to insure a fair airing of the author's views.

The result of this sequential dialogue format is a less than perfect airing of the differing perceptions of complex reality. Nonetheless, the technique does suffice in many instances and is widely used. A sequential presentation can be burdensome and exhausting, but, more importantly, complex reality is a system that can never be comprehended by the exclusive examination of the individual components. Communication in simulation gaming differs significantly from sequential communication in that it implies a less rigid transmission of ideas and emphasizes a heuristic understanding of some complex reality. Simulation gaming therefore permits the receiver a greater flexibility in addressing facets of complexity than is possible with a sequential presentation.

## EXPLORATION THROUGH SIMULATION GAMES

Figure 2 is concerned with establishing communication about the same kinds of complexity as in Figure 1, but in this instance the communication is through simulation gaming. The process of perceiving, abstracting, and organizing the problem is much the same as the process employed in preparing for a lecture, but the device used to facilitate communication about the topic is quite different.

In this instance, the basic abstraction (model) is stated in a concept report before being incorporated into the game itself. The game construct becomes a logical, even if highly abstracted, analogue to the complex topic. The game designer makes his presentation through the game rather than through a verbal presentation or organized text. Participants are asked to identify with certain perspectives and are required to conform to certain logical constraints within that setting. Discussion of the system is prompted by the deliberate introduction of circumstances that tend to sharpen perception of dynamic relationships. A variety of events, problems, or issues can be articulated, and their introduction into the gaming context (pulse) helps to focus the many discussions simultaneously underway. The discussions obtain their focus both from the basic model represented in the game and from a pulse. A pulse is a problem, issue, or new information presented to the players in the game. It is used to trigger an exchange of messages between the players and serves as a device for organizing the progress for the discussion. Because the pulse may be either prespecified or introduced as a result of participant need during play, there is considerable latitude in setting the agenda for discussion and in establishing the sequence of deliberation. This permits some escape from the rigid sequentiality of the formal lecture, which must go logically from beginning to end. The game construct is all of one piece and has no logical entry or exit point per se. It therefore allows the individual to enter into the multilogue from his own frame of reference or point of perspective. It also permits and encourages a vigorous ongoing discussion among changing and unstable coalitions of people who come together as their ideas coincide and who quickly break away to form new conversational units.

Because the respondent is roaming freely within a logical construct, he discerns its shape and characteristics by a series of vignettes of his own making. Instead of being constrained to an arbitrary and preordained path of inquiry, he is free to explore in a sequence that appears logical to him.

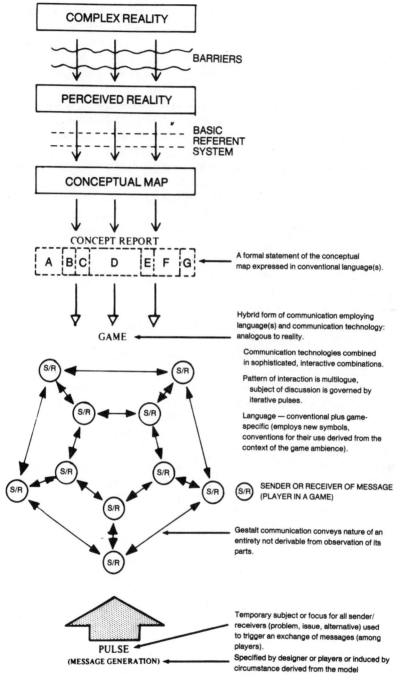

**Figure 2.** Communicating Through Simulation Gaming

In reviewing this method, it is important to differentiate between multilogue and many dialogues being conducted simultaneously. Multilogue is the organized simultaneous inquiry into some complex topic; contrast this format to that of a cocktail party, which is characterized by many simultaneous dialogues covering a broad array of disjointed subject matter.

Multilogue occurs quite naturally in some small group situations. It is frequently contrived deliberately as counterpoint to a lecture in a formal conference session. (Following a presentation, the attendees are broken up into small discussion groups, typically five to seven persons, and are subsequently returned to the original conference format.) Multilogue is the primary interaction pattern in simulation gaming.

Figure 3 explores in greater depth the dynamics of communication within a simulation gaming exercise. Complex reality is represented in the diagram as a hexagon, with the various modes representing decision points and all lines connecting these points representing potential information flows.

Several items of significance must be emphasized. First, the players are assumed to be engaged in different roles requiring varying perceptions of the reality modeled by the game. Because they are simultaneously engaged in the process, the message interchange pattern contains many concurrent dimensions and the term *dialogue* is insufficient to describe the process. Rather, it should be thought of as many parallel and simultaneous dialogues (multilogue), all pertaining to some aspect of a complex phenomenon. Serendipitous occurrence, both during the play of the game and in the organized critique that follows, will heighten the significance of these message exchanges in terms of what they convey to the player about the nature of the complex reality.

Whatever reality may be, there are always barriers to its perception, and the perceived reality that filters through those barriers becomes the basis for discussion. Because of the complexity involved, both abstraction and organization are required, and our internalized heuristics guide us in formulating a model of reality. This internalized model or conceptual map, whether or not independently committed to paper, becomes the basis for the construction of the game. If the process is successful, the game is in some sense analogous to reality.

This process of abstraction entails both the complex problem under consideration and the factors that are brought to bear on the system. These factors are independently analyzed, abstracted, and organized for later systemic introduction into the game. These are pulses, and their existence allows the participants to gain insight into the abstracted system. That is, the participants explore reality through the

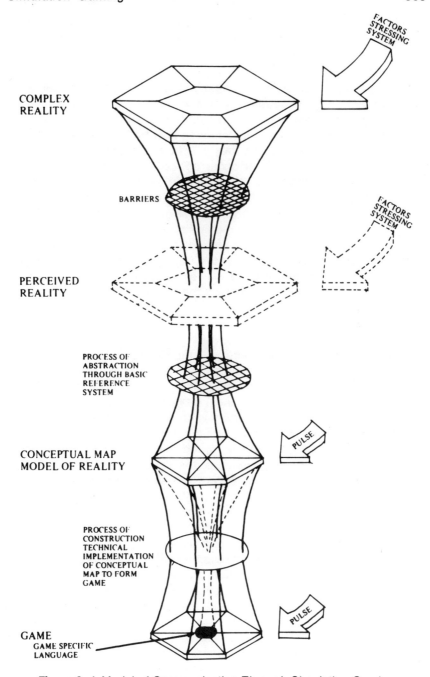

**Figure 3.** A Model of Communication Through Simulation Gaming

consideration of iterative pulses of information that focus them in their different perspectives on a common or shared problem, issue, or alternative. The pulse, then, becomes an organizational device, somewhat analogous to the organization of sentence structure, which encourages the multilogue to be focused on a shared phenomenon, even though many such dialogues may be simultaneously underway. It is this phenomenon that permits the serendipitous discovery of the nature of complexity. These pulses of information may be induced either by the designer or by the player, and they may be predetermined, random, or triggered by certain events or occurrences in the play of the game.

A game-specific language develops as the symbols used in the game acquire specific meanings for the participants through their experiences during the events of the game. This game-specific language may be deliberately designed into the game structure or acquired inadvertently by the players as jargon to assist multilogue. The game-specific language is a critical element in the gaming design. It must be sufficiently complex to improve discussion about a specific problem but simple enough to be learned during the normal course of play.

## SNUS—AN EXAMPLE

The Simulated Nutrition System Game (SNUS I) was developed for the Food Policy and Nutrition Division of the United Nations Food and Agriculture Organization as an aid in nutrition and planning education programs in Third World countries. The game was designed for play by a high-level ministerial staff, with the objective of increasing their understanding of the processes affecting nutrition, particularly in terms of national economic policy. It was hoped that through play they would become more conscious of many of the variables and the alternative futures with which they ought to deal in their real world roles.

The purpose of SNUS I is to initiate thoughtful discussion of issues, policies, and futures of national nutrition planning in developing countries. It provides an experience whereby fundamental linkages and problems of the nutrition system of a developing nation can be quickly understood and discussed via a common "language" created by SNUS I. The objectives of the discussion are an understanding both of the basic conceptual framework depicting the nutrition system and of the complex interaction of national level decisions on a nation's nutrition status.

The design of SNUS I anticipated its use as an introduction to nutrition planning seminars and short courses employed by the Food Policy and Nutrition Division's ongoing training programs. The game is currently being used in nutrition planning workshops, and kits have been distributed through the Food Policy and Nutrition Division of FAO, Rome, and the Office of Nutrition, U.S. Agency for International Development, Washington, D.C.

SNUS I represents a mythical developing nation (SNUSLAND), which manifests typical nutrition and economic development problems found in many developing nations. It can be recalibrated to approximate any nation, thus providing greater utility in differing training situations. SNUS I is a participant interaction simulation and does not require the use of a computer. Play takes approximately eight hours.

In each cycle of the game, some players take two different roles. During Phase I of each cycle, these players assume the roles of national ministers; in Phase II, they "change hats" and assume regional allegiances as members of either the urban, coastal, or farming regional teams. The nutrition planning team and the national planning team members continue to play the same role through Phase I and Phase II.

Phase I is primarily a budget arbitration and planning process in which the national ministers submit their budgets, propose policies, and evaluate national nutrition and development status. The arbitration process takes place in the national cabinet meeting where the budget proposals are weighed against one another within the constraints of the national budgetary funds available. After the policies and plans have been adopted in the cabinet meeting, the Minister of Finance allocates the budget to the ministries. The final step in Phase I is allocation of the ministerial funds to the regions.

Phase II begins with the players assuming their regional team roles. Production units begin to operate simultaneously in each region. After input requirements have been met for production, the commodity symbols are placed on the board. The commodities are transported to market, where they are sold to the middlemen by the "rich" and "poor" populations in each region. Food purchases are made according to effective diet demand as well as income and market price. Once food has been distributed, the nutrition planning team assesses the nutritional status of the nation, while the regional teams prepare their requests for aid from the national government.

Play is begun after the players have been briefed on the present status of SNUSLAND. The scenario of SNUSLAND can be modified by the operator when different problems or linkages are to be highlighted. The scenario provides a historic backdrop that helps bring the dynamics of the nutrition problems into focus. It also gives an overview of the political and economic structure, and of present constraints and bottlenecks to improving nutrition.

## SUMMARY

In simulation gaming, the conceptual map—an internalized, organized, overall comprehension of complex reality—serves as a mental blueprint to help convey complex systems. The conceptual map classifies, sorts, and stores information, and it provides a heuristic language to be used as a common symbol structure for discussing a given complex system. Data conveyed through a conceptual map cease to be mere bits of information and instead become heuristic wisdom. However, a conceptual map is not assimilated as a static structure or by static means; it is built up iteratively over time.

The basis for learning games derives from two basic characteristics of games: (1) the game is an environment for self-instruction, permitting multidimensional entry (and, therefore, simultaneous multiple sensing from different perspectives in a safe environment) and conveying heuristics (general and structural learning) in a responsive environment; and (2) the iterative character of games allows enlarged perception and logical mental closure with each iteration, thereby permitting an emphasis on gestalt or overview, the establishment of context as perceived to be relevant to the player, and reality testing through formal citiques.

In summary, learning occurs through simulation games because they represent abstract symbolic maps of multidimensional phenomena that serve as basic reference systems for tucking away bits and pieces of details that are transmitted. In particular, they assist in the formulation of inquiry from a variety of obtuse angles or perspectives. These perspectives are meaningful to the individual making the inquiry and can be transmitted only through a multidimensional, abstract, symbolic-mapping procedure.

The previous observations on the character of change in the world since World War II can be summarized as follows. Before World War II, the need for pragmatic information and fact, learned by rote, was imperative. In the new era, there is an urgent need for the acquisition of heuristics—a flexible set of highly abstract conceptual tools that will let the participant view new and emerging situations, having no precedent, in a way that permits comprehension. Simulation gaming holds strong promise for reestablishing the comprehension of totality, which is necessary for the intelligent management of any complex system.

Nearly everyone at some time or other has wanted a crystal ball to peer into the future. We now need a real world equivalent to the crystal ball. More than ever before, we need to be able to "reminisce" about the future, to explore "what if" questions in involved and highly speculative environments. These mythical constructs must be explicit, so that

those who have an interest in them can comprehend and, when necessary, challenge the relationship they represent. If these constructs were
built, we would have a model of a future reality that would be subject to
continuous modification and redefinition, dependent on the best judgment and information of those most likely to be affected.

Man has not one future but many futures to choose from, but this
choice is predicated on his ability to articulate the various possibilities
before they occur. It is beyond human comprehension to deal with the
present in a detailed and factual way, and it is equally impossible to do
so for alternative futures. Instead, we need heuristic, overview, or
gestalt perception from which we can derive an orientation toward the
future that will provide us with crude guidelines for action.

Simulation gaming is one prospect for assisting us with this task. A
game can provide an overview, a level of detail appropriate to the task
at hand, and mechanisms that illustrate the major dynamics of the
linkages among the system components. Gaming has particular potential because it enables the individual to approach complex problems,
from whatever perspective seems germane, in a coherent and logical
context, and to experiment in a basically safe environment. It allows the
individual to gain some sense of how the system responds to his
particular proposals.

## NOTE

1. This article and the accompanying graphics have been abstracted from
Duke (1974). *Gaming: The Future's Language.*

## REFERENCES

Duke, Richard D. 1974. *Gaming: The Future's Language.* New York: Halsted
Press.

Greenblat, Cathy S., and Richard D. Duke. 1975. *Gaming/Simulation: Rationale, Design and Applications.* New York: Halsted Press.

Rhyne, R. F. 1973. "Communicating Holistic Insights." *Fields Within Fields,*
Volume 5, Number 1, 93–104.

JOSEPH P. MARTINO

# Technological Forecasting

This chapter describes the field of technological forecasting, including its history and background, as well as the more common methods utilized. It also outlines the strengths and weaknesses of the methods discussed and indicates their most appropriate applications. Before discussing technological forecasting specifically, however, some general comments on forecasting are in order.

All forecasters utilize the same basic approach to forecasting. They attempt to identify patterns of behavior that are characteristic of their field of study, utilizing these patterns as a basis for projecting future outcomes. This approach is used by weather, economic, stock market, population, and social forecasters, as well as technological forecasters. The degree of success of forecasters in any field depends upon the extent to which (1) there are reliable patterns in past events, (2) these patterns are known to forecasters, and (3) forecasters can obtain the data needed to utilize these patterns in the generation of forecasts.

In some fields of knowledge, the patterns of behavior are clearcut and involve only a few variables, about which data can be readily obtained. In other fields, the patterns involve numerous variables, many of which may be only poorly known or for which the data may be sparse. For this second group of fields, forecasts will inevitably be less accurate or precise than in the first. This has nothing to do with the competence of the forecasters or with the methodology employed. It is a matter strictly of the state of knowledge of the field in which the forecast is to be made and of the amount of data available. Forecasters in various fields such as demography and meteorology approach their forecasting tasks differently, not because the different fields demand different methodologies, but because the problems they present to the forecaster are different in terms of the kind and extent of data available.

An important question for forecasting in any field is whether forecasting has any validity at all. Forecasting deals with events that are yet to take place. Since we can have no direct knowledge of the future, is it even possible to place forecasting of anything on a scientific basis? We can have direct knowledge only of the past, and even then, our direct knowledge is limited by the finite span of individual experience and by the partial availability of records (resulting from either the outright failure to keep records, or the accidental or deliberate destruction of records). Since science demands facts, data, and measurements, how can we place forecasting on a scientific basis when our subject matter is inherently unmeasurable?

The basic answer to this question involves the fact that science itself is an attempt to forecast. Every scientific law can be written in a form that is a statement of the future consequences of a given situation. That is, a scientific law is a statement that, given a specific set of circumstances, a specific outcome will occur. But how can this outcome be known? How can scientists be certain that a given constellation of circumstances must result in a specific outcome? Only because this specific pattern of circumstances and outcome has been observed repeatedly in the past, without fail. This observation may be in the form of a controlled experiment conducted in a laboratory, or it may be an elaborate observation based on careful measurement of a naturally occurring event. In either case, a scientific law is based on the repeated observation that a specific situation is followed by a particular outcome. However, scientists can never be absolutely certain that, at some time in the future, that same identical set of circumstances will not be followed by a totally different outcome. In other words, scientific laws are simply statements of patterns that have been observed in the past and that are expected to repeat themselves in the future. Scientists assume that these patterns they have observed are in fact valid and useful for prediction. This assumption has turned out to be a useful one, and scientific knowledge has undergrided the enormous changes that technology has made in our environment within the course of human history. Nevertheless, the scientists' only warrant for assuming the repeatability of patterns is that such an assumption has worked in the past. Since it has worked, the assumption can be utilized in the future as well.

The forecaster is in much the same situation as the experimental scientist. He derives patterns from past experience and assumes that these patterns will continue to be observed. His only justification for making this assumption is that it works. The activities of forecasting and of experimental science are thus closely related. The scientific basis of forecasting depends, then, not on any ability to obtain "facts" about the future, but on the utilization of the methods and logic of science, to identify patterns of behavior and to project these patterns. Since the forecaster must make do with fewer cases and less data than most scientists are able to acquire, his forecasts will have more uncertainty about them than will the statements of scientific law propounded by scientists. This uncertainty does not arise from any weakness in his methods relative to those of scientists, however. It arises solely from the practical difficulties of his chosen field of endeavor.

## HISTORY OF TECHNOLOGICAL FORECASTING

Techological forecasting, of one kind or another, is almost as old as the Industrial Revolution. Since excellent discussions of the "remote past" of the field are given elsewhere (Ayres, 1969; Bright, 1968), this topic will not be covered here. Suffice it to say that, while some of these early forecasts were good, many were far from the mark, and few, if any, utilized sound scientific principles in identifying the patterns that the forecasters projected.

Following the end of World War II, the U.S. government sponsored a number of sporadic attempts at technological forecasting. However, the "modern" development of the field can be dated to the 1960s. The first serious attempt to apply scientific methods to the forecasting of technological change was the work of Lenz, who coined the term *technological forecasting* for this activity. In his report, which was based on his 1958 Master's thesis, Lenz discussed most of the forecasting patterns available in all fields of endeavor and described applications of these patterns to the forecasting of technological change (1962). His discussion include growth curves, trend curves, precursorfollower relationships (akin to the leading indicators of the economist), and biological analogies. Very few methods have been added to the repertoire of the technological forecaster since Lenz's pioneering report. The most significant of these additions, the Delphi procedure (discussed later in this article), was actually invented prior to 1962 but was not published until 1964. In general, however, Lenz's report discussed essentially all the methods in current use for technological forecasting. The changes since 1962 have been in the direction of refining the methods rather than in developing a wide range of new methods.

During the 1960s, there was considerable activity within the U.S. government, particularly the Department of Defense, in the application of technological forecasting. In 1963, the Air Force prepared an elaborate forecast under the name Operation Forecast. The Army and Navy established technological forecasting as part of their formalized planning procedures. The Army, in particular, published an official technological forecast that was maintained by a permanent staff and updated periodically. While virtually all the forecasts prepared by the

Defense Department were classified, their existence and titles became generally known. A sampling of titles from this period can be found in Ayres (1969).

By the late 1960s, technological forecasting seemed to have come of age. One of the first conferences on technological forecasting was sponsored by the Industrial Management Center, organized by James Bright. While half of the papers presented were from military sources, the other half reflected purely civilian viewpoints. This fact indicated that technological forecasting was finding a home in industry as well as in government. At about this same time, two journals were founded: *Technological Forecasting and Social Change*, published in the United States, and *Futures*, published in England. While aimed at somewhat different audiences and having somewhat different editorial styles, both journals provided communications channels for the growing number of methodologists and practitioners who were attempting to improve technological forecasting methods. In 1968, the World Future Society also appointed a technological forecasting editor for its journal, *The Futurist*, and carried more or less regular columns and articles on the subject. Along with the journals and articles came a spate of books. Most of the early books represented the proceedings of conferences, or collections of published essays, but by the early 1970s, several books had appeared which had been written by a single author and which were intended for use as texts or introductions to the field of technological forecasting.

As with most new activities, there was a tendency to oversell technological forecasting. Some of its early practitioners promised much more than they could possibly deliver. Some organizations, to show they were "with it," established technological forecasting groups and activities. Reality quickly reasserted itself, however, and at the first economic downturn, many forecasting activities were dismembered as quickly as they had grown. Since some of these forecasting activities had been instituted mainly as window dressing, they never had any real impact on decisions and their demise was no great loss. Many of the overenthusiastic promoters of technological forecasting also quickly left the field, in search of greener pastures elsewhere. The period since 1972 has witnessed a slow but steady growth of the field, with wider acceptance of formal technological forecasting in industry and government. Academic acceptance is slowly but surely growing as well, with the establishment of futures research centers in many universities and courses in technological forecasting at still others. Thus, technological forecasting has reached a considerable degree of acceptance in industry, government, and the academic world, and may be looked upon as an activity similar to operations research or management science.

While presenting no panacea, it does have some useful contributions to make in a time of technological change. Its contributions must be integrated with those of other disciplines such as operations research, economics, and demographic forecasting.

## TECHNOLOGICAL FORECASTING METHODS

Technological forecasting methods are sometimes divided into exploratory and normative methods. Exploratory methods are utilized to project future developments on the basis of past history. Normative methods are used to determine what technology will be required to meet certain assumed problems or conditions of the future. Normative methods are highly akin to planning and are not actually justified on the basis of their similarity to the scientific method, given earlier in this article. Because of their difference in orientation and in basic justification, they will not be discussed further here. Instead, this article will concentrate on so-called exploratory methods. Those interested in normative methods and their relationship to planning are referred to sources such as Martino (1972).

All exploratory forecasting methods are really extrapolatory in nature. They start with a set of events that have taken place up to the time of the forecast, attempt to identify the patterns present in that history, and project these patterns into the future. It is not the case, of course, that extrapolative methods are limited to forecasting "more of the same." The use of extrapolative methods does not force the forecaster to project a "bigger and better" version of today's world. In fact, some extrapolation methods allow the forecaster to identify policy variables that can be manipulated and that can allow the decision-maker to alter the course of events and shape a future different from the past or present.

Exploratory methods, despite their common extrapolative nature, can be divided into purely extrapolative, explanatory, and auxiliary methods. Each of these types will be treated in turn.

### PURELY EXTRAPOLATIVE METHODS

Some forecasting methods do not require any knowledge of either the elements affecting change in the subject area or the interactions among those elements. They are thus purely extrapolative in nature. They assume that whatever has caused the patterns of the past will continue to operate to produce similar patterns in the future. When this assumption is valid, purely extrapolative methods can be highly useful, since they are simple to apply. The forecast is obtained simply by extrapolating the observed historical patterns. The two most commonly used methods of pure extrapolation are growth curves and trend curves.

### Growth Curves

Both the growth in size of individuals (i.e., height, weight, and so forth) and the growth in numbers of a population often exhibit a "lazy-S" shaped curve when plotted against time. The growth starts slowly, passes through a phase of rapid increase, and slows down again as some upper limit is reached. This curve has become known as a growth curve. It is found not only in its original field, biology, but also in technology. The growth in performance of some technical approach to solving a problem often exhibits the same lazy-S pattern. When a new device is first developed, it is often difficult to get it to work at all and improvement is slow. As the bugs are worked out of the new device, rapid improvement takes place and a plot of performance shows a steep rise. Finally, limits on improvement are set by the laws of chemistry and physics. As these limits are approached, additional improvement is harder and harder to squeeze out and the rate of improvement slows down. When plotted, the curve rises more slowly and almost flattens out. A typical growth curve is shown in Figure 1, which displays the history of improvements in the efficiency of steam engines. The points are the actual historical data, and the curve shown has been fitted to the data by mathematical means. (The curve is shown on a logarithmic scale. This permits the inclusion of a range of values covering several orders of magnitude but also has the unfortunate effect of straightening out the lower part of the lazy-S.) Once a growth curve has been fitted to the data and a mathematical equation has been obtained for the curve, the forecast is prepared simply by projecting the curve. If a forecast for some specific year is needed, it can be obtained by substituting the desired year into the mathematical formula. The resulting number is the forecast, and it is simply the projection of the historical pattern, under the assumption that the forces that formed the historical pattern will continue to act.

The particular application of growth curves is to those situations in which it is necessary to forecast the future behavior of some single technical approach to solving a problem. Such technical approaches are always bounded by some upper limit, and the forecaster is really interested in how performance will approach that upper limit. He thus fits an appropriate mathematical curve to the historical data and attempts to project the resulting curve toward the upper limit. In order to do so, he must calculate the fundamental upper limit, using knowledge

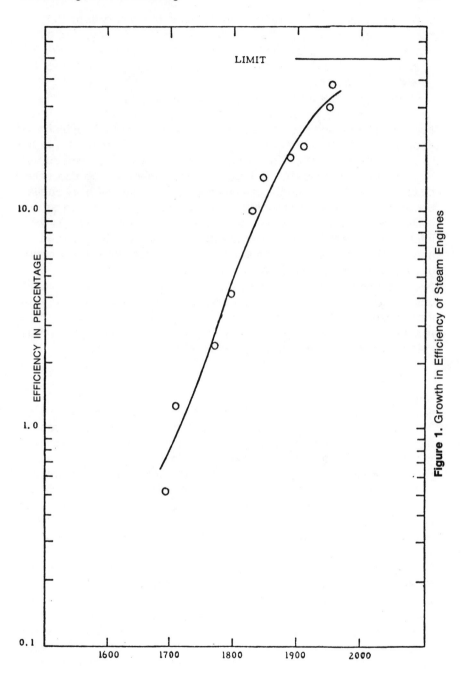

**Figure 1.** Growth in Efficiency of Steam Engines

of the physical, chemical, or other laws that establish the upper limit. In addition, he must choose the proper mathematical form for the curve. The Pearl Curve is probably the most widely used growth curve, but others such as the Gompertz, the von Bertalanffy, and the Fisher-Pry curves are also used.

In many cases, a technology has involved a succession of individual technical approaches during its total history. Each of these technical approaches has been subject to its own upper limit, but each technical approach in turn has a higher upper limit. A plot of the history of the overall technology then is a succession of intersecting growth curves. This situation is illustrated in Figure 2, which shows a portion of the history of the increase in the speed of aircraft. In the 1940s, propeller-driven aircraft were approaching their ultimate upper limit in speed, while the jet engine was coming on the scene. The first jets were inferior to contemporary propeller-driven aircraft, but the jets had the potential for much greater speed. The growth curves for the two technical approaches intersected as shown.

When a forecaster is faced with a technology whose history exhibits a succession of growth curves such as that shown in Figure 2, he is no longer concerned with the details of the individual growth curves. He is more concerned with the long-term trend of the technology. He must therefore utilize trend curves, which we will discuss next.

*Trend Curves*

Trend curves display the long-term behavior of some technology. The use of trend curves assumes that whatever factors produced the trend will continue to produce an extension of the trend. In particular, if the past has seen a succession of growth curves, with each curve reaching a higher limit, the trend forecast is based on the assumption that this behavior will continue. That is, new technical approaches will continue to be found to overcome the limits of their predecessor approaches. This pattern will continue until the overall technology itself approaches some fundamental upper limit that cannot be breached by any technical approach, such as the speed of light.

A typical long-term technological trend is shown in Figure 3. This figure shows the growth in productivity (passenger-miles per hour) of transport aircraft, from the mid-1920s until 1969. Although there is, of course, some scatter in the data, an overall trend is certainly present. The history of this technology includes many breakthroughs: pressurized cabins, swept wings, jet engines, and the like. Despite these many breakthroughs, involving a variety of individual technologies, the overall technology of passenger transport aircraft shows a steady, long-

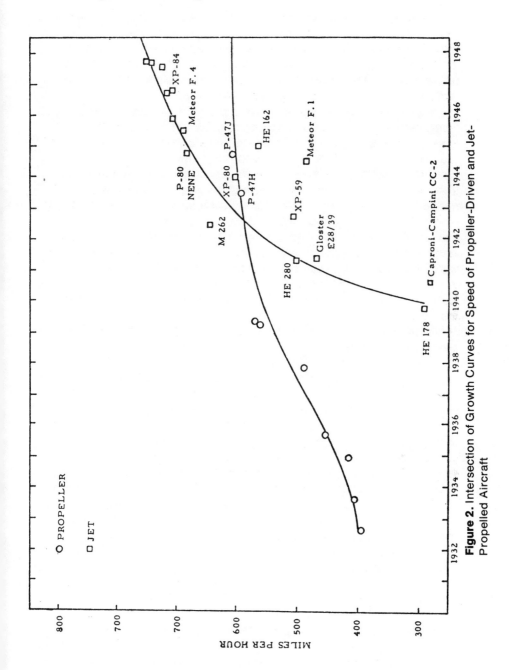

**Figure 2.** Intersection of Growth Curves for Speed of Propeller-Driven and Jet-Propelled Aircraft

term trend. In this particular case, the trend is one of exponential growth. There are no breaks or jumps in the curve as various breakthroughs are introduced into passenger transport. A particular set of factors, including economics and technology, governed the growth of passenger aircraft productivity for over forty years and produced a remarkably well-behaved long-term trend.

Exponential growth seems to characterize a great many technologies. Their performance seems to grow exponentially for periods of several decades. So long as the conditions that produced this trend are not expected to change, and so long as there are no unbreakable barriers set by fundamental physical laws, the forecaster may utilize trend extrapolation to obtain a projection of future performance. This method has an important advantage for the forecaster. It allows him to project beyond the upper limit of the technical approach currently in use, on the assumption that a new technical approach will be found when it is needed, just as new ones were found in the past when they were needed. The forecaster can make such a projection without having to identify the successor approach or to invent it if none can be identified. He need only assume that the future will be continuous with the past. This approach, however, requires the forecaster to identify some measure of performance that can be applied to several successive technical approaches (e.g., passenger aircraft can be compared on the basis of their productivity, without regard to method of propulsion, type of construction, and so forth). This approach also subjects the forecaster to the risk that the factors producing the trend in the past will not continue to operate unchanged and will instead act to produce some new pattern in the future. Since the forecaster has made no effort to identify those factors, he has no way of determining when some critical factor may change and invalidate his forecast.

The purely extrapolative methods of forecasting are usually simple to apply. Moreover, they are easy to present and understand. They are valid sufficiently often that their use is justified. However, they are vulnerable to unsuspected changes in critical conditions that may throw them off completely. Thus, the forecaster's projection may be invalidated by changes in background factors such as politics, economics, and technology.

### Explanatory Methods

In preparing his forecast, there are a number of techniques in which the forecaster is able to use knowledge of the factors that affect technological change and of the interactions that take place among those

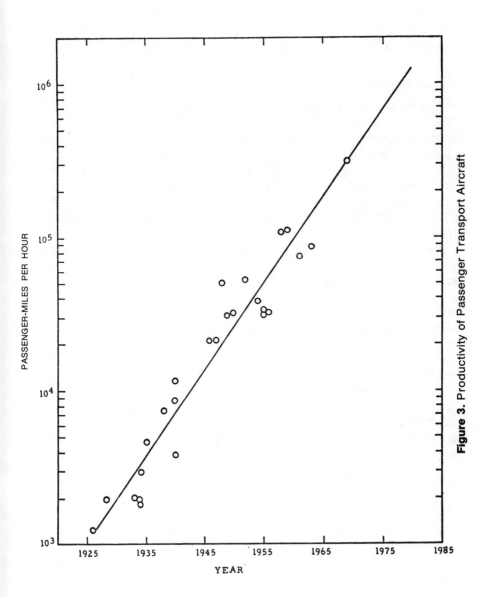

**Figure 3.** Productivity of Passenger Transport Aircraft

factors. These methods free him from the necessity of forecasting a continuation of historical trends. They permit him to take into account changes in background conditions and to allow for the effects these changes will have on the technology he is forecasting. Some of these methods are presented below.

### Correlation Methods

The forecaster can sometimes take advantage of correlations between the technology he is attempting to forecast and some other quantity that he can more readily measure or estimate. One of the most frequent correlations found between different technologies is a "leader-follower" relationship. Often, some technological advances are first demonstrated in a particular area and are then adopted in another area. If some pattern can be discovered that governs the rate of diffusion from the leader to the follower technology, this pattern can be used for forecasting purposes. Figure 4 shows one such correlation pattern. The upper line is the speed trend for combat aircraft. In the past, many advances in aeronautical technology were first incorporated in combat aircraft, and then, as their acceptability was demonstrated, they were subsequently adopted in commercial aircraft. The lower trend curve shows that there has been a leader-follower relationship between combat and commercial aircraft technology. However, the time lag for transfer of technology from combat to commercial aircraft seems to be growing in a consistent manner. The forecaster need not attempt to explain the reason for this growing lag. Once it is observed, however, he can utilize it to project future advances in speed of commercial aircraft on the basis of performance already attained in combat aircraft.

Other correlations besides leader-follower exist. One such correlation is shown in Figure 5. This plot shows both total installed hydroelectric capacity in the United States and the size of the largest single hydroelectric turbine, both as a function of time. The plot is on a logarithmic scale, which means that the virtually constant separation between the two sets of data corresponds to a virtually constant ratio between the total installed capacity and largest single unit. This type of correlation has been observed in many situations, especially in the chemical industry. Once such a correlation has been identified and validated in a sufficient number of cases, it can be used for forecasting purposes. This method allows the forecaster to take into account some of the background factors that may alter the rate of change in the performance of the technology hs is attempting to forecast.

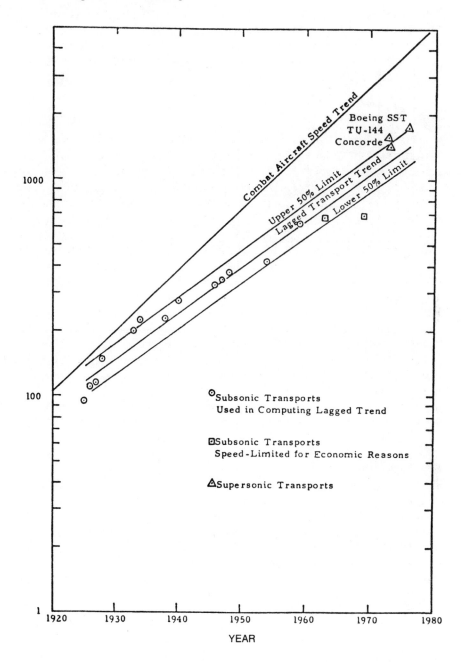

**Figure 4.** Correlation Between Speed of Combat Aircraft and Speed of Transport Aircraft

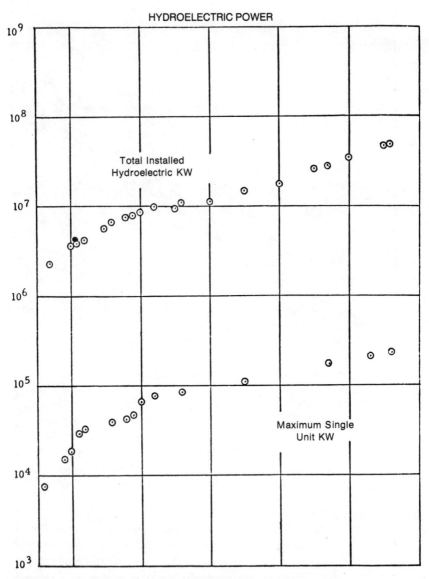

**Figure 5.** Parallel Growth in Total Hydroelectric Power and Maximum Hydroelectric Turbine Size

*Precursors*

Forecasters in many areas have learned to watch for precursors that have some established relationship with the topic they are interested in forecasting. Economists perhaps make the most extensive use of such leading indicators, but other types of forecasters also use them. The method of precursors is used by technological forecasters as well and can be a very powerful tool, especially for identifying potential break-throughs. Virtually every major technological advance of the past has been preceded by such precursors. These may include scientific advances that imply a potentially superior technology, or technological developments that are in themselves incomplete but that could give improved performance if combined with some other innovation that may not yet be available. The forecaster can make very effective use of these precursors to forecast technological change before it occurs. He must systematically gather information about precursors and interpret the information he has obtained. He must attempt to identify any patterns that may exist in the precursors. As he identifies more and more precursors, the patterns will become clearer, and he may be able to determine what pieces of the patterns are yet missing. He can then institute a deliberate search for those missing pieces. If a pattern he has been tracking is indeed a valid one, at some point he will have enough pieces that he can confidently state what other pieces are still missing and when they should be expected to appear. He can then forecast the technological change that will result from completing the pattern.

To illustrate this approach, consider the history of the jet engine. Table 1 lists a series of significant events in this history. Once the airplane was invented, there was interest in an improved engine for it. By 1921, three distinct proposals had been made for a jet engine, including not only a ram-jet but also piston-engine and turbine-driven compressors. In 1923, Buckingham of the National Advisory Committee for Aeronautics reported to the Army Air Service that jet engines were inferior to piston engines below speeds of 250 mph. Since the then-current aircraft speed was about 150 mph, it was clear that the jet was no immediate competitor for the piston-driven engine. As time passed, however, technological advance continued. In 1926, a theory was developed which permitted the design of more efficient compressors. In 1929, the turboprop engine was proposed, this being a combination of a propeller with a turbine engine that drove its own compressor. In 1929, the turbojet was again patented. At this point, Whittle determined that a jet engine would be practical if turbine-driven compressors could be obtained with a compression ratio of 4:1 and an

## Table 1. Major Events in the History of the Jet Engine

---

1910 Coanda proposes aircraft engine with piston-driven compressor
and jet exhaust
1913 Lorin proposes jet engine with compression by ram effect
(ram-jet)
1921 Guillaume patent on jet engine with turbine-driven compressor
1923 Buckingham reports to U. S. Army Air Service that jet engine fuel
efficiency inferior to piston engines below 250 mph
1926 Griffith develops theory for design of efficient compressors
1929 Griffith proposes aircraft engine with turbine-driven propeller
(turboprop)
1930 Whittle patent on jet engine with turbine-driven compressor
1931 Aircraft turbosuperchargers have compression ratio of 2:1,
efficiency of 62 percent
1935 von Ohain patent on jet engine with turbine-driven compressor
1939 He-178 jet flies with von Ohain engine in Germany
1940 Caproni-Campini CC-2 jet flies in Italy
1941 Gloster E28/39 jet flies with Whittle engine in England
1942 XP-59 jet flies with GE engine in United States

---

efficiency of 75 percent. These values were clearly within reach, and in 1935 another patent was granted on a turbojet engine. In 1939, 1940, 1941, and 1942, four different and independently invented jet aircraft were flown.

Each of the events in the table is a possible precursor for the ultimate breakthrough of the jet engine. Each one provided some additional warning of what was coming. After the work of Buckingham, the pattern of events started to become clear. One requirement for the jet engine was a sufficiently high aircraft speed; below that speed, there was no need for a jet engine. The improvements in turbine design theory and the determination of threshold values for turbine compression ratio and efficiency provided further warnings of what was coming. More-over, they identified additional pieces of the pattern to watch for. Thus, during the 1930s, a forecaster concerned with breakthroughs in aircraft propulsion should have been tracking progress in aircraft speed, com-pressor efficiency, and compression ratio. When these reached or crossed the thresholds he had set previously, he could forecast the advent of the jet engine.

The forecaster who wishes to exploit precursors must carry out a well-structured search for potential clues to what is coming. He must first observe the possibility of a developing pattern, which requires that he scan a wide range of sources that would be expected to carry clues to patterns of possible interest to him.

When the forecaster becomes aware of a potential pattern that might concern him, he next shifts from general scanning to a deliberate and purposeful search. He asks himself, if the first clues are in fact part of a pattern, what would the rest of the pattern look like. If the first clue is a scientific finding, he may then look for an application. Whatever the nature of the rest of the pattern, as he perceives it, he initiates a search for indicators of that pattern, in sources most likely to carry clues about the rest of the pattern. If he finds additional clues, this is evidence that the pattern he is tracking is a real one. When he obtains the clues, he elaborates the pattern. What is the meaning of the additional clues? What else do they point to? Has an application been attempted? If so, did it work? If it failed, why did it fail? What else might be needed to make it work? The answers to these questions indicate possible further clues to search for. As these additional clues are found, the pattern becomes more and more complete, until the forecaster is in a position to give a forecast with an acceptable degree of confidence.

Some of the clues the forecaster finds will be negative clues. That is, they will appear to be saying that the pattern he has been tracking is a false one and that the technology he is attempting to forecast will never be developed. It must be remembered that this answer may in fact be the correct one. Many promising technologies never do see application, for reasons that may have little to do with their technical performance. Others, after showing early promise of technical gain, do not pan out because of problems dealing with implementation of the technology. The forecaster may be tracking one of these technologies, and the negative answer will then be the correct one. However, only after the fact will it be known whether the important factors are external or exogenous variables. Such models can be utilized by decision-makers to guide their actions with regard to technological change. For instance, a decision-maker may be concerned about the level of R&D funding he should expend on the development of a particular technology. A forecaster might construct for him a model of the technology in which level of R&D funding is an exogenous variable. With such a model, the decision-maker can test the consequences of various levels of R&D funding and determine what is the best decision for him to make. This would be of far more use to him than would be a closed model, which would forecast the decision before he made it, as well as then forecasting the consequences for the technology.

Causal models are important because they allow the forecaster to take into account changes in the conditions that shape the future. These changes may be in the form of decisions that have already been made but whose impacts are yet to be felt (e.g., last year's enrollments in science courses will largely determine the number of science graduates three years hence), or they may be changes in the form of decisions that are currently under study and have not yet been made. Causal models may thus be used to examine the consequences of alternative policies under study, or to examine means for alleviating the consequences of changes that have already been made but whose impacts are yet to come.

Despite the emphasis on incorporating causes of change in the causal model, such models are still basically extrapolative in nature. They assume that the same factors that mattered in the past will matter in the future and that the relations between those factors will be the same in the future as they were in the past. Despite this inherently extrapolative nature, the causal model is a much more useful forecasting tool than any of the other extrapolative methods. Unfortunately, the state of the art of causal models for technological forecasting is still quite limited, although improvements are constantly being made.

Most of the models available are quite specialized. They are limited to such things as forecasting the cost of developing a new item of electronic equipment such as a radar, when the desired improvement in performance is specified, or forecasting the growth of productivity in a given industry when the level of R&D expenditure in that industry is known. The most successful instance of such causal models to date occurs in the area of predicting the rate of diffusion of an innovation through the adopting industry. Models are available that can predict the rate of diffusion (or adoption) when the relative profitability of the innovation, and its cost relative to other innovations adopted by the same industry, are known. Some of these models have been extended to include the impact of government regulations on the industry that is adopting the new technology. However, much work remains to be done on extending these models to all industries and on including other factors which are likely to be important but which have not yet been adequately studied. It can be expected, however, that the state of the art of causal models will improve and that the models available to the technological forecaster will increase in power and precision. Ultimately, such models may replace the other extrapolative methods described above, with the possible exception of the use of precursors.

### AUXILIARY METHODS

The exploratory methods discussed above are usually utilized for forecasting single areas of technology. If a broad area of technology is to be forecast, it is necessary to forecast different subareas separately. It may even be necessary to utilize different methods in each subarea. The problem arises when these individual forecasts are obtained. It then becomes necessary to combine them into an overall forecast. Two methods are in common use for this purpose: cross-impact matrices and scenarios. These methods are not in themselves forecasting techniques. Rather, they are means for combining forecasts, and in particular for determining whether the independently obtained forecasts are consistent with each other. A third auxiliary method sometimes utilized for combining independently generated forecasts is the surprise-free forecast. Each of these methods will be discussed below.

## Cross-Impact Matrices

The basis for a cross-impact matrix is a set of events that are forecast to occur within a specified period of time. Each event has associated with it a date when it is forecast to occur and a probability of occurrence. The date of occurrence may, of course, be a span of time rather than a single date. The events are listed in chronological order of occurrence and arrayed as the rows and columns of a matrix. Such a matrix is shown in Figure 6. The cells of the matrix represent the interactions among the events in the rows and columns. It should be noted that the matrix format is simply a bookkeeping scheme to assure that the forecaster considers all possible impacts; it does not have any of the formal properties of a mathematical matrix. From inspection of Figure 6, it can be seen that for any pair of events there are two interaction cells. Since it is assumed that interactions can occur only from the earlier event to the later event, one of these cells is redundant. It is customary to make use of this redundance by using one of the cells to record the impacts of occurrence of the earlier event, and the other to record the impacts of nonoccurrence of the earlier event. By custom, occurrence impacts are stored above the diagonal; nonoccurrence impacts are stored below the diagonal. For instance, if event $E_1$ takes place, the cell at Row $E_1$ and Column $E_3$ would record the impact on $E_3$ of the occurrence of $E_1$. If, conversely, $E_1$ fails to take place, the impact is recorded in the cell in Column $E_1$, Row $E_3$. In each case, the impacts are recorded in terms of the change in timing and change in probability of the impacted event. To use the matrix, the forecaster starts with the earliest event and uses some random device to determine whether or not the first event will take place. In either case, he then determines the impact of this outcome on all later events. These may be advanced or delayed, made more probable or less probable, and so forth. Once all impacts from the occurrence or nonoccurrence of the first event are accounted for, he then goes on to the second event. He continues in this manner until the list of events is exhausted and each has been tested to see whether or not it occurred. Complications in this operation arise when more than one event is forecast for the same time; when

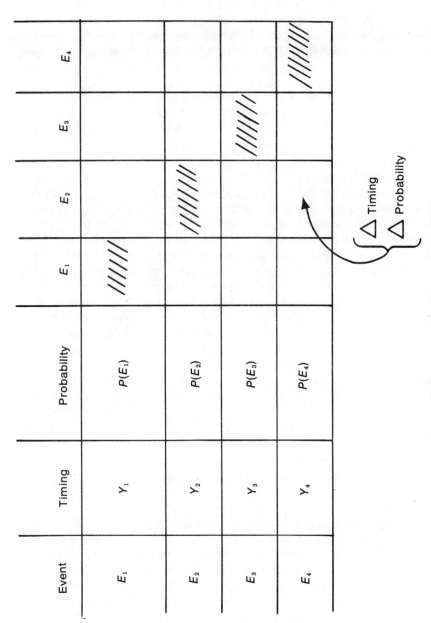

**Figure 6.** Example of a Cross-Impact Matrix

an event is forecast to occur within a time span rather than on a single date; when events interchange their chronological order as a result of impacts from earlier events; and when trends rather than discrete events are forecast. (All of these complications can be handled by methods given in References, especially Martino, 1972.)

Obviously, a single "play" of the matrix will not give the forecaster much information. The proper use of the cross-impact matrix involves a large number of such plays, followed by statistical analysis of the results. Each play generates one synthetic future history of the technology under examination, but because this synthetic future history contains many random events, it can in no sense be looked upon as a likely representation of the future. Only a statistical summary of a large number of such plays can be used as a forecast. Generally, the cross-impact matrix is computerized so that a large number of plays can be run through in a short time, with the statistical summary produced automatically.

The cross-impact matrix has two major applications. (1) It is used to check the consistency of the individual forecasts which go into it. If the forecasts are inconsistent, this fact will become apparent from anomalies that will appear in the results. (2) It is used to identify key events that have a great deal of leverage on the subsequent courses of events, through their occurrence or nonoccurrence. These key events represent "levers" by which the decision-maker can influence the future course of the technology being forecast.

The utility of the cross-impact matrix is completely dependent upon the correct specification of the cross impacts among the events in the matrix. If these statements of impacts are in error, the output of the matrix will likewise be in error. However, if the statements are correct or are based on the best information available, the cross-impact matrix can be used to make worthwhile policy recommendations. Thus, the cross-impact matrix is an important tool for the forecaster.

### Scenarios

The scenario differs from the cross-impact matrix in two ways. First, it is less rigorous, since it is primarily a verbal description of some future situation. Second, it is more detailed and provides a rich description rather than simply a list of events that are to take place. The scenario can be considered a written description of a single future history, which might have come from a single play of a cross-impact matrix.

An important use of the scenario is in identifying inconsistencies among individual forecasts. If there are such inconsistencies, they will show up as the forecaster attempts to place them within the same scenario. The inconsistent forecasts may require incompatible prior events or mutually exclusive sets of circumstances. Such things become more readily apparent when they are juxtaposed in a scenario. The scenario is less useful than the cross-impact matrix for identifying key events. The reason lies in the comparative lack of rigor of a scenario. Even though a scenario is written in which one event "causes" a succession of following events, this is not proof that the event will in fact cause such a change in circumstances. The cross-impact matrix, with much greater rigor, can be used for identifying key events.

The primary importance of the scenario lies in its ability to portray, in vivid and graphic language, the cumulative impact of an entire set of events. Thus, the scenario often makes a much greater impact on the reader than would the simple barebones listing of a set of events. The forecaster often takes advantage of this capability of the scenario by generating a family of scenarios covering a given set of events. One might be a "best case" scenario, in which everything favorable occurs; another might be a "worst case" scenario, in which everything goes wrong; and there may be one or more intermediate scenarios depicting less extreme situations. Each scenario attempts to depict what life would be like under the particular course of events portrayed as taking place. When used in this way, scenarios can be very helpful in leading nonspecialists to understand the consequences of various possible combinations of events.

### Surprise-Free Projections

The surprise-free projection is essentially a special class of scenario. Kahn and Wiener originated the term in their book (1967). They took a set of thirteen long-term trends, including population, literacy, and GNP, and projected these into the future along the same trends they had been following in the past. The projection is called surprise free because each of the major elements is assumed to follow its historical trend. As Kahn and Wiener showed, however, the "surprise-free" projection can still contain some surprises, as the trends interact with one another to produce a situation different from today's world (even though it is implicit in the interactions among trends). They then used this surprise-free world as the "standard" world which they could compare with alternative worlds resulting from a major change in one or more of the basic trends. The surprise-free projection, along with the variants produced by altering one or more of the basic trends, can be used to give some indication of which variables may be important to the decision-maker who wants to reshape the future.

## RELATED TECHNIQUES

This section discusses two techniques that are not strictly fore-casting methods but that have been quite useful to technological fore-casters. They are really tools with many uses, including the preparation of forecasts. These techniques are Delphi and computer simulation.

### Delphi

In some cases, the forecaster finds that the best way to prepare a forecast is to utilize the judgment of experts in the field. He may require their judgment of the rate of progress, the impact of some external event on rate of progress, and the like. One obvious way to utilize expert judgment is to ask a single expert. However, as it is commonly believed that "two heads are better than one," the use of several experts is preferable to the use of a single expert. Groups of experts have at least as much information available to them as does any single expert in the group. Also, they can consider at least as many factors that may be relevant to the issue as can any member of the group. In fact, it is generally assumed that groups possess more total information and can consider more factors than can any single member. Thus, a group should be able to provide better expert judgment than can any single member. The only question is how to extract this judgment from the group in an efficient manner, which avoids the problems of conventional committee action. As is well known, committees often tend to take on a life of their own and pursue courses of action that have little or nothing to do with the purpose for which they were organized.

Delphi was developed to overcome the disadvantages of conventional committee action. Delphi is characterized by anonymity, controlled feedback, and statistical response. The group interaction in Delphi is anonymous, in the sense that comments, forecasts, and the like are not identified as to their originator but are presented to the group in such a way as to suppress any identification. The other panel members can thus respond to them without regard to their personal feelings about the originator. In addition, since the interaction is anonymous, the members of the panel feel fewer inhibitions about changing their minds, since they do not thereby suffer any "loss of face." The interactions among panel members are controlled by a panel director or monitor, who filters out material not related to the purpose of the group. The usual problems of group dynamics are thus completely bypassed. Finally, the panel viewpoint is summarized statistically rather than in terms of a majority vote. Thus, the degree of agreement among panel members is displayed explicitly, with every panel member's position included in the final statement. The procedure for conducting a Delphi sequence is outlined in Table 2, which describes its use for preparing a forecast.

In the first round, the panelists are informed of the general area in which they are to forecast, what time frame they should consider, and any constraints they should take into account (such as actions by specific groups or individuals and expected levels of funding). The panelists then respond individually to the director with lists of events they expect to occur during the time period considered, under the constraints stated at the outset. Thus, at the end of the first round, the director receives a set of events. No single panelist has seen the entire set, however.

In Round 2, the director provides each panelist with a complete set of events returned from Round 1. In preparing this list, he may consolidate like events, delete uninteresting or unimportant events, and the like. For each event, the panelists estimate the date of occurrence. However, in some cases, they may be asked for several dates, each associated with a specific probability of occurrence. For instance, they may be asked to estimate dates by which the event is 10, 50, and 90 percent likely to have occurred. If the event is a trend rather than a single event, the panel members may be asked to estimate dates by

**Table 2. Steps in a Delphi Sequence**

---

*Round 1*

Panelists receive general instructions
Panelists respond with items (events, trends, etc.)

*Round 2*

Panelists receive list of items
Panelists respond with estimates (dates, etc.) for each item

*Round 3*

Panelists receive list of items, medians, and quartiles of estimates
Panelists respond with revised estimates, statements supporting "outlying" estimates

*Round 4*

Panelists receive list of items, revised medians and quartiles, and summaries of statements
Panelists respond with revised estimates, additional supporting statements, comments on statements of other panelists

---

which it will have reached certain levels (e.g., "have captured 50 percent of the market for devices of that type"). Thus, for each item, the director receives a distribution of dates representing the initial opinions of the panel members. For each event, he determines a median date (i.e., the date such that 50 percent of the estimates are earlier and 50 percent later), and the two quartile dates (i.e., dates such that 25 percent of the estimates are later and 75 percent earlier).

In Round 3, the director provides each panelist with the list of events and the median and quartile dates for each event. The panelists reconsider their earlier estimates, in the light of the statistical summary of the estimates from the other panelists, and provide new estimates of dates for each event (which may include sticking with their earlier estimates). Those panel members whose revised estimates are "outliers", i.e., before the first quartile or later than the third quartile from the second round, are also expected to provide justification for their "extreme" positions. This justification may include logical arguments or supporting facts that demonstrate why, in their opinion, the majority of the panel members made estimates that were "too late" (or conversely, "too early"). The director receives, for each item, a new distribution of dates for each event and a set of arguments for advancing or delaying the date for each event.

In Round 4, the director provides each panel member with the set of events, revised medians and quartiles for each event (based on the responses to Round 3), and a summary of the arguments for advancing or delaying the estimate for each event. The panelists respond with new estimates, with justification if their new estimates fall outside the revised quartiles, and with any comments they wish to make on any of the arguments made during the previous round.

At the conclusion of the four rounds, the panel director has a set of events forecast to occur, a forecast date for each event (the median date from the last round), some information on the degree of uncertainty in the forecast (derived from the difference between upper and lower quartile dates), and a summary of the arguments for advancing or delaying the forecast date. Thus, he not only has a forecast but also some measure of its uncertainty and an understanding of what factors are important in influencing the date of occurrence of each of the events.

Several modifications of this sequence are possible. The panel may in effect skip the first round by receiving at the outset a list of events of interest to the panel director. Also, if the panel reaches complete agreement or displays hopeless polarization, the final round may be deleted as unnecessary. In such cases, the entire sequence may be collapsed to two rounds.

The outcome of a Delphi sequence is, of course, nothing but opinion. The results of the sequence are only as valid as the opinions of the experts who made up the panel. Therefore, Delphi should be utilized when expert opinion is needed. Moreover, if the questionnaire is poorly constructed, the panel output is degraded. Thus, the Delphi panel must consist of experts in the area to be forecast, and the questions must be constructed carefully. When these conditions are met, Delphi represents an efficient way of extracting opinion from a panel without the distortions that often accompany conventional committee activity. (For more information on Delphi, see Martino, 1972, Linstone and Turoff, 1975, as well as the Delphi chapter in this Handbook.)

### Computer Simulation

All the forecasting methods described above can be carried out manually. However, in many cases these manual methods can be tedious and subject to human errors of data manipulation. This is true even of extrapolating a trend and even more so of something as complex as utilizing a cross-impact matrix. Using a causal model is often impossible without the aid of a computer to trace out the interactions of all the variables.

These problems of time and precision frequently lead forecasters to the use of computer simulation. Computer simulation provides a means by which the computer can be utilized to carry out large numbers of calculations in a short time. A computer simulation may extrapolate a wide variety of trends quickly and accurately; play out a cross-impact matrix many times within a few seconds; and make several runs of a causal model, each with different values for one or more variables.

Computer simulation is important because it enables the consequences of a model, forecast, or set of forecasts to be explored in detail, even though the forecasts themselves may be too complex for the forecaster to understand them readily by direct examination. Changes in the values of individual variables, changes in policy, and the like can be examined rapidly, and the effects of alterations in input can be determined readily through changes in output.

As with any other use of the computer, the results are no better than the data that go in. The computer programmer's slogan, "garbage in, garbage out," is as valid for forecasting by computer simulation as it is for any other computer application. The function of the computer is to perform, rapidly and precisely, the same operations a human being could perform less rapidly and less precisely. If the computer does the wrong thing, however, the result is just as wrong as if the mistake had been made by a human being. The computer simply makes the mistake more rapidly than does the human. In short, the results of a forecast are in no way improved by computerizing them. The computer is a useful tool, but it does not replace the forecaster.

## CONCLUSION

This article has discussed many forecasting techniques. Some involve rigorous analysis of purely quantitative data, and others are completely subjective. In between are methods that utilize a mixture of judgmental data and quantitative data. Each of these methods has its own strengths and weaknesses. Each should be used in those applications where its strengths are important and its weaknesses of lesser importance. The art of the forecaster lies, in no small measure, in being able to select for each application the precise technique that has the strengths needed and whose weaknesses are not significant.

Many other forecasting methods are available besides those described above. Most of these, however, tend to be more restricted in application. They are appropriate only for much more limited circumstances. Those given above are the most widely used and are suitable for the vast majority of cases with which the technological forecaster is confronted. Likewise, the user of forecasts will find that most of the forecasts he receives will have been prepared using one or another of the methods described above.

Since we can never have any facts about the future, a factual "science" of the future is clearly impossible. However, it can never be proven with certainty that continued repetitions of a controlled experiment will give identical results. Hence, science itself is based on the assumption that the future will be like the past, in certain very specific ways. Science has succeeded because it has sought an understanding of reality, which can be expressed in terms of simple "laws" of great generality. Science continues to accept these laws only because they continue to provide adequate predictions of the outcome of specific situations. When a deviation between law and experiment is found, it is ultimately resolved by stating a more correct version of the law (e.g., replacement of Newton's laws of motion with Einstein's more precise laws). Forecasters can validate their forecasting methods in the same way. They can seek explanations of the course of past history and test these explanations against a variety of circumstances. As long as these explanations continue to provide adequate predictions, they can continue to be used for forecasting purposes. This means that forecasters have just as much justification for believing in the adequacy of the laws of nature they have discovered. In both cases, this belief is founded on exactly the same process of test and validation. Thus, forecasting is a "scientific" process in exactly the same way that science itself is. Just as scientists do, forecasters connect historical facts with future outcomes through theories and laws that have been tested and validated in a variety of circumstances.

The forecasting methods described here should not be considered as final or ultimate. They are continually being refined and improved, as can be seen readily through reference to any of the journals mentioned earlier. It must be expected, then, that with the passage of time, better methods will be available. However, it is not necessary to wait for these improved methods. The methods currently available are adequate for the solution of many problems confronting our society. While improvement in these methods is needed, the methods are already good enough that they should be employed much more widely than they are at present.

## REFERENCES

Ayres, Robert U. 1969. *Technological Forecasting and Long-Range Planning.* New York: McGraw-Hill.

Bright, James R. (ed.). 1968. *Technological Forecasting for Industry and Government.* Englewood Cliffs, N.J.: Prentice-Hall.

Kahn, Herman, and Anthony Wiener. 1967. *The Year 2000: A Framework for Speculation on the Next Thirty-three Years.* New York: Macmillan Co.

Lenz, Ralph C., Jr. 1962. "Technological Forecasting." Report ASD-TDR-62-414. Wright-Patterson Air Force Base: U.S. Air Force.

Linstone, Harold A., and Murray Turoff, 1975. *The Delphi Method: Techniques and Applications.* Reading, Mass.: Addison-Wesley Publishing Co.

Martino, Joseph P. 1972. *Technological Forecasting for Decision-Making.* New York: American Elsevier.

JOSEPH F. COATES

# Technology Assessment

This chapter reviews methods and techniques applicable to technology assessment. Technology assessment is a class of policy studies which systematically examine the effects on society that may occur when a technology is introduced, extended, or modified. It emphasizes those consequences that are unintended, indirect, or delayed. It contains several basic assumptions:

- New technological knowledge creates new ignorance.
- More information and analysis, rather than less, promotes better decisions.
- Technology assessment is a policy tool useful in business as well as government.
- Organization of certainty and uncertainty in order to define strategies and tactics for managing any particular technology is a major policy need.
- In the long range, indirect and unanticipated effects of a technology are often more significant than the immediate or planned consequences.
- Technology assessment is likely to be iterative and part of an interlocking set of studies.
- Decisions will be made.

These basic points if kept in mind resolve many otherwise conflicting strategies.

Because policy studies are intended to influence decision-making and policy formulation, one must shape and define what their contents should be. Not everything relevant to the subject enters into a policy study; it should include only those things that will lead to influencing the decision process. In my experience, good studies are almost always iterated. You do it once to understand the problem; you do it a second time to get it right; you do it a third time to burnish the results. The

SOURCE: *Chemtech* (June 1976), 372–383. Reprinted with permission of *Chemtech*, the polydisciplinary magazine of the American Chemical Society © 1976.

second round is the longest, the third the briefest. It may turn out that with experience we can collapse this process into fewer stages, but it is well to plan on at least three stages.

These comprehensive (holistic) new policy studies are unlike most planning that attempts to build on certainty—on what we know. Since we are exploring the implication of *new* technology, the newer the technology, the more intrinsic irreducible uncertainties there will be. Technology assessments and EISs build on both certainty and uncertainty. Useful actions that flow out of such study must be based on organization and identification of the implications of these uncertainties and certainties. That is a new and exciting premise for analysts, planners, and decision-makers.

Technology assessment has been widely practiced in the Executive Branch in the last half dozen years, and there are at least a dozen major studies and numerous minor ones that have successfully explored the widest range of impacts implied by one or another technology or project (V. Coates, 1972; Jones, 1973). The National Environmental Policy Act of 1969 (P.L. 91–190) and the Environmental Impact Statements it requires further stimulated interest in assessing long-range consequences of technology.

## RESULTS OF A TECHNOLOGY ASSESSMENT

The action consequences of a technology assessment must be acknowledged early since they should influence the study's structure. It is also important to recognize them explicitly since two widely held beliefs demean the value of assessments. On the one hand, some label technology assessment as a means of stifling needed advancement. On the other hand, others view technology assessment as a new whitewash to assuage the public about the preordained.

Against this background it is useful to identify some of the rich consequences that may follow from a soundly structured technology assessment (Figure 1).

What might happen as a result of a good impact study goes well beyond "good and bad," "do or don't" advice. For one thing, it should be grist for the mill of all parties of interest, to everybody who is concerned, whether he is an advocate, a concerned lay citizen, a possible adversary, or the decision-maker. Whether or not one is influenced by the technology, one needs intellectual input for one's thought process and attitude formation. One should be able to think better about an issue having been exposed to a reasoned impact statement.

It is extremely important to look at the output side of the impact study

Modify project to reduce disbenefits and/or to increase benefits
Identify regulatory or other control needs
Define a surveillance program for technology as it becomes operational
Stimulate R&D to:
    Define risks more reliably
    Forestall anticipated negative effects
    Identify alternative methods for achieving goals of technology
    Identify corrective measures for negative effects
Identify control needs
Encourage development of a technology into new areas
Identify needed institutional changes
Provide sound inputs to all interested parties
Identify new benefits
Identify intervention experiments
Identify possible impacts
Identify partial or incremental implementation
Prevent technology from developing (an unusual but not impossible outcome)

**Figure 1.** Possible Consequences of a Successful Technology Assessment

process because what people are going to do with the impact statements should strongly influence the inputs into the study. If you do not consider the possibility of formal surveillance and monitoring as an output, then you will never organize the study to focus on what sort of things should be subjects for surveillance and monitoring. If you never consider whether regulation is adequate, you will never put the pieces into the study that will allow you to identify the regulatory gaps. If you never entertain the possibility of stepwise implementation, then you will never shape the impact study with the considerations that will allow you to find an incremental approach.

## WHAT TO INCLUDE

Several things need to be said about how technology assessment relates to established disciplines. Put in the negative, technology assessment is not a branch of engineering or of economics or of political science. It is neither a branch of law nor a new thrust in operations research. While any particular study may draw upon one or more of these disciplines, technology assessment is different and distinct from each.

The second point to be made is that there is a general desire to identify methodology associated with any problem, since there is the hope that once a fixed methodology is recognized people will learn to use it in the way they learn multiplication tables, input/output analysis, and the like. Technology assessment does not work quite that way. The techniques and methods brought to bear in an assessment are a function of the problem, the group for whom the assessment is being made and its authority, and the budget available for the study. While technology assessment is more an art form that must be actively created and framed to fit the individual problem, there is a relatively definable set of categories, components, or modules, what one might call a metamethodology, that must be satisfied in a comprehensive assessment (Figure 2).

Early, one learns that the client is likely to be unclear as to what the problem is. Thus, the initial framing of the problem may require frequent reworking during the study in order to put in a form to permit decision-related output.

Rarely is a project confined to a single option; usually a variety of alternatives must be considered. For analytical purposes, one may want to select a subset of alternatives because it may be necessary to examine only them to determine impacts and consequences.

Identification of impacts requires a combination of broad experience, skills, imagination, and creativity. There are no fixed procedures by which one can anticipate consequences of a given technology. In some cases, the technology itself may suggest where to look for impacts. For example, with a weather modification technology, the physical system suggests to a first approximation where one would look for effects. In some cases, the technology may be so diffuse, as with a picture telephone or a medical innovation, that one must go to one or another method of exhaustion to identify impacts.

Many qualitative and quantitative tools may be brought to bear to evaluate the significance of impacts one has identified. Tools of economic analysis, social surveys, scaling techniques, and others are included here, but one can expect that the evaluation is likely to be a

Examine problem statements
Specify systems alternatives
Delay project
Evaluate impacts
Identify the decision apparatus
Identify action options for decision apparatus
Identify parties at interest
Identify macrosystem alternatives (other routes to goal)
Identify exogenous variables or events possibly having an effect on 1-8
Draw conclusions and recommendations

**Figure 2.** Components of Technology Assessment

mixed bag of relatively hard and soft outputs. Economic analysis is likely to be a crucial first analytic tool. By no means is it close to the limits of issues and consequences associated with any rich technology, such as geothermal energy development, kidney transplants, or tax reform. Consequently, the economic analytical techniques, however important and powerful they may be, are only an opening stage in a full analysis. Morgenstern (1972) has reviewed the critical issues that contemporary economists cannot handle well or at all. Most are germane to technology assessment.

The decision apparatus relevant to the problem should be identified explicitly and the range of responsibilities of individual components defined as far as is feasible. With many complex problems, there are overlapping and partial responsibilities in government and in the private sector. Frequently, multinational or international organizations have some responsibility for a technology.

Defining decision options and alternatives open to the decision apparatus is something of a creative enterprise. It is relatively unusual for much imagination to be brought to the management of technology. One must attempt to innovate with regard to action options and alternatives. The failure to do this often leads to vague, uncertain, or sterile options and conclusions, or to wishbook recommendations while overlooking important opportunities for social invention and innovation.

One must examine all the above to come to a set of wise conclusions and recommendations. In general, it is best not to come to a precise and definitive single set of exclusive recommendations. A menu of alternatives and an analysis of their consequences are better fare for the decision-maker.

It is important to identify who, in fact or in principle, has a stake in the technology and in its possible impacts and consequences. This is important not only from an analytical viewpoint in helping identify impacts and consequences. It is also important from a decision point of view in indicating who may influence the range and kind of action options which the decision-maker has before him. The parties at interest, after all, are those who will, or should have, the strongest influence on the decision apparatus. It is by no means simple and straightforward to identify such parties since many will emerge only after the project has been implemented or is about to be.

Exogenous factors should have a prominent place in any technology assessment. By exogenous factors, I mean those changes in society, its goals, its orientation, or its technology which could have an influence on the primary technology or factors interacting with it. These exogenous factors may vary anywhere from another new technology to an economic upturn or downturn, change in the international situation, or modification of legislation. Again, as with impacts, the identification of exogenous variables is a partially analytical and partially creative exercise. It is in this element of an assessment that one moves into the tricky and elusive areas of social, institutional, technical, economic forecasting and state-of-society assumptions.

As part of a technology assessment, it is important to recognize and analyze the impacts of variations on the technology under consideration. However, there is another set of technological alternatives to be considered, and these are what one might call macro-alternatives. For example, the various ways of removing oil from the north slope of Alaska would not comprise macro-alternatives but, rather, systems alternatives. Macro-alternatives might be the development of geothermal resources, the cutting down on the demand for energy, or building superports to increase oil imports. Similarly, if one were examining alternatives to the picture telephone, the macro-alternatives might involve cheaper air transportation or cable television.

## TECHNIQUES

Several studies have treated the methods and techniques applicable to technology assessments. In the review of some twelve comprehensive technology assessments, Jones briefly noted some of the methods and techniques used and provided selective illustrations (1973). In an earlier study, V. T. Coates (1972) reviewed eighty-nine studies indicating the techniques and methods used. Perhaps the most comprehensive, up-to-date treatment is the monograph by Hetman of the Organization for Economic Co-operation and Development (OECD) (1973).

These studies report the use of many generic techniques, such as systems analysis, systems engineering, simulation, modeling, trend projection, and some specific techniques such as cost/benefit, input/output, and Baysian analysis. In addition, these studies found technology assessment projects that utilized:

| | |
|---|---|
| Content analysis | Expert panels, conferences, workshops, briefings, |
| Historical surveys | |
| Historical analogy | Questionnaires, surveys, hearings |
| Delphi | Rule-making procedures, including hearings |
| Compilation and analysis of all available information | |
| Artistic judgment | On-site or field investigation |

Since any discipline or profession may be germane to a particular assessment, it would be inappropriate to imply that the foregoing is comprehensive. Consequently, an indeterminate number of methods and techniques may find a place in any specific study. I would thus like to concentrate on methods thought to be less familiar to the average reader, and attempt to relate them to the elements outlined above.

## DELPHI

Many techniques applicable to impact assessments result from futures research, particularly from developments of World War II (Ayers, 1969; Martino, 1972; Jantsch, 1966). One of the most versatile and generally applicable of these techniques is consensus forecasting or the Delphi technique (Figure 3) as developed by Helmer, Dalkey, and associates at RAND Corporation.

Before discussing Delphi, it is appropriate to mention that most systematic attempts to examine the future afford additional benefits distinct from the precision and reliability of the forecast. These heuristic and didactic benefits include the demand for making assumptions explicit; sharing these explicit assumptions and identifying divergent assumptions; and the effective, conscious, systematic definition of consequences of that divergency. An additional benefit from systematic attempts to examine the future is almost always a broadening of the range of alternatives being considered. Complementing that is a general sensitization of the complexities and interactions that influence alternative futures. Finally, a more diffuse benefit is the general discipline in thinking demanded by a comprehensive, exhaustive, and systematic analysis and synthesis.

The Delphi technique is an attempt to improve the utilization of experts in analysis, evaluation, and forecasting. It uses informed intuitive judgments in a format other than the committee meeting.

The committee approach to problem analysis has a number of drawbacks. A major one is that most committees do not make either their reasoning or their assumptions explicit. Committees also tend to operate by seeking a consensus; thus, minority views and alternatives tend to get buried before a final report is written. Often a "bandwagon" syndrome takes hold, putting pressure on committee members to "go along." In many instances, an authoritative (or vocal) panel member can drive the panel onto a bandwagon. Finally, in a committee meeting, it is often difficult for the individual to change his mind once he has taken a position.

Most of the drawbacks of committee operation result from the interaction of the personalities of the committee members. This implies that a better situation for using experts would be some kind of "meeting"

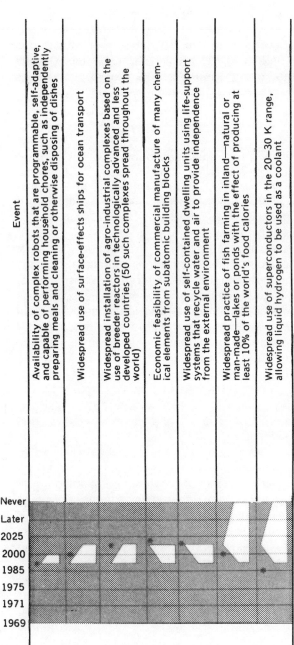

**Figure 3.** Displaying Delphi Results

Forecasts of the time of occurrence of events discussed are presented. The polygons depict the final range or opinions generated by the group. The high point on the bar indicates the median date at which the panelists judged there was a 50% chance the event would occur. The shorter legs of the polygon define the limits of the upper and lower quartiles, and the bar itself the interquartile range. The asterisk denotes the median date of occurrence forecast by the subset of respondents who rated themselves "expert" or "generally familiar" with the event in question. The respondents also developed an extensive list of prospective consequences they felt might be expected as a result of the forecast technological and scientific developments. Each of these consequences was judged as to its likelihood of being a result of the event, and assuming it should occur, whether it was favorable or unfavorable

SOURCE: Theodore J. Gordon and Robert H. Ament, "Forecasts of Some Technological and Scientific Developments and Their Societal Consequences," September 1969, Institute for the Future Report No. R-6.

without face-to-face confrontations, but with adequate communication, interaction, and feedback among individuals. Note that the mere elimination of face-to-face contact alone is not sufficient. The Delphi technique has been suggested as a means to overcome these difficulties.

In its simplest form, the Delphi technique is a carefully designed series of individual interrogations (usually conducted by written questionnaires) interspersed with information and opinion feedback. Here is a simple illustration.

Suppose a panel of experts is convened to estimate the year by which the employment rate among the black population will be the same as that for the white population. Each panel member responds individually in writing with an initial estimate. The person running the panel arranges the results of this first round from highest to lowest and determines the median and the interquartile range. The interquartile range is the interval containing the middle 50 percent of responses.

The second round begins with the results of the first round being sent to each panelist. The respondents are then asked to make a new estimate. *If their estimates are outside the interquartile range, the respondents are asked to indicate why their judgments were so different from the majority judgment.* This step forces those with extreme views to either stand behind them—with explicit reasoning—or to move into the majority's range if no strong convictions are held by the respondents.

In the next round, responses (now spread over a smaller interval) are summarized again, and all the respondents are given a summary of reasons offered by those who have taken extreme positions. Another revision is requested based on the reasoning presented. A respondent whose response is still outside of the interquartile range is required to indicate why he remains unconvinced by opposing numbers. In a fourth round, these criticisms are resubmitted to the entire panel and a final revision of estimates is requested. The median of these responses could then be taken as approximating the group judgment or, more significantly, the range of responses may be presented, representing an ordered, weighted series of judgments, so that one now does not come up with a single answer, but a set of answers with associated priorities.

In the majority of cases where the technique has been applied, there seems to be a convergence of opinion. In some instances, polarization around more than a single "answer" has been observed. In other cases, two or even three modes or peaks may result.

The working of this Delphi technique depends on a number of factors. In the first instance, there is always the question of who is an expert when a panel of experts is convened. Little advice can be proffered here on that. The only useful hint in the direction of distinguishing "good" experts from "bad" is to ask for self-evaluation within the context of the Delphi game. If the responses to a particular question are weighted to attach more significance to those answers coming from people who indicated (in the private context of the Delphi technique) that they were more expert in some areas than others, it might be possible to converge to a more accurate response.

Of major importance in the operation of the panel is that interaction and feedback be kept as free as possible. Since experts in different disciplines use different languages, the group running the Delphi must phrase its questionnaires and models so that all respondents understand them.

In conclusion, it might be said that Delphi is a rational way of obtaining a collective judgment uninfluenced by the psychological obstacles that influence conventional panel meetings.

A panel of ten or so people can be run by one person. As a rule of thumb, figure 2 hours work per panelist per complete Delphi. Expired time for Delphi depends on speed of processing answers and delays in sending them to the panel.

The Delphi technique has evolved extensively in the last few years and in general is applicable to any situation to which quantitative values may be assigned, whether these are dates, weightings, or scalings. Consequently, it is applicable to almost any area of inquiry. Among the recent developments associated with the technique is the computer-assisted Delphi in which one is able to participate over an undetermined, lengthy period (Turoff, 1972).

Reflecting some of the difficulties associated with the Delphi technique, Gordon and associates (1974) have been moving back to a structured interview format. In some cases, the Delphi interviews are not conducted anonymously or by mail, but in face-to-face interviews. In some sense, this comprises a sophisticated variation on conversation. The literature of the Delphi is extensively reviewed in a collection of readings by Linstone and Turoff (1975).

The technique has been severely criticized by Sackman (1974). As with any generally applicable technique, Delphi is subject to abuse, notably poor construction, inadequate testing, hasty and inadequate analysis, and failure to analyze the basis for divergent opinions. It is also worth noting that the technique has been applied in a few instances to resource allocation, where again the critical feature is that the quantitative element is the resource to be allocated.

## CROSS-IMPACT ANALYSIS

One disadvantage of the Delphi technique is that it tends to treat each component of the analysis as an independent variable. A more sophisticated, complex technique, called cross-impact analysis, has been developed in which individual components of the forecast are not only independently evaluated, but evaluated in relation to each other. For example, factor A may have a relatively low probability of occurrence. Similarly, factor B may have a relatively low probability of occurrence. But the probability of factor A's occurring may be increased if factor B is realized.

Note that the Delphi and the cross-impact techniques are in no way limited to the analysis of experts, but can also be turned to exploring different outlooks of experts and nonexperts, or groups with various professional backgrounds.

## TREND EXTRAPOLATION

Trend extrapolation as well as other futures-related techniques are widely used in forecasts of all sorts. They have their legitimate place in technology assessment when used as a guide to the analysis of present trends as well as a clue to what kinds of normative judgments should be made.

Normative forecasting is a term used to describe goal-related predictions in which the forecast is premised on the identification of activities required to achieve a particular goal (Ayers, 1969; Martino, 1972; Jantsch, 1966).

## STRUCTURING THE PROBLEM

It frequently is the case that in attempting to unfold the impacts of a given technology, the technology itself provides a logical backbone for at least identifying first-order consequences and for suggesting second- and third-order consequences. For example, in one study of means to increase snowfall in Colorado, the movement of the air mass which releases the snow and then continues to move downwind provided one physical system for searching out impacts. The snowfall, its evaporation, its melting, its consequent runoff into the river provided another conceptual backbone against which to search out impacts. Unfortunately, in many cases the problem does not so readily lend itself to this kind of structuring, as for example, with the consequences of alternative work schedules or video-telephone or birth control technology.

In these cases, one may move to what would be called methods of exhaustion, which are basically techniques based on experience that provides checklists against which one can systematically search out impacts of a technology. For environmental impact statements, the U.S. Geological Survey put forward Circular 645 which provides a 100

$\times$ 88 matrix or some 8,800 cells relating classes of effects of a technology to places in the ecosphere that may be affected (Leopold, et al., 1971). The checklist does not define what is important; it merely provides a structured list of suggested impacts to look for. It has the additional advantage of facilitating presentation of results by allowing one to systematically display conslusions from a study as to where major and minor impacts may occur.

## MORPHOLOGICAL ANALYSIS

Morphological analysis is another technique for the exhaustive search for effects. It has been extensively discussed in the literature but relatively little used except by its inventor, Fritz Zwicky, the aeronautical engineer who has used it in searching systematically for aircraft propulsion systems. The method basically depends upon asking a series of questions about a technological development, the set of questions being exhaustive of all possible questions one could ask about the technology. One then provides a full range of all potential answers to each question. For example, with regard to planning a community health clinic, one might ask such questions as: Where could it be located? What kinds of people would it serve? What medical services would it perform—and so on. Against each of these questions, one would then attempt to provide all conceivable answers. One then proceeds by systematically selecting all permuted combinations of the answers to each question. Obviously, the possibility becomes extremely large, but one quickly realizes that many combinations are incompatible or unrealizable. Consequently, the total number of alternative systems to be explored in depth rapidly diminishes but nevertheless remains large (Zwicky, 1957).

## DECISION AND RELEVANCE TREES

Related methods of exhaustion are the decision tree and the relevance tree which attempt to develop all possible options and alternatives with regard to technology. The branches are critical decisions that exclude other major options.

The practical use of the relevance tree in technology assessment is beautifully illustrated in a recent study of geothermal energy resource development by Gordon and associates (1974). The tree covers some seventy pages of their report. The tree is useful not only for organizing factors but also for stimulating imagination and insight into crucial elements of the technology and possible points of impact or consequence. It is also valuable as a check or a challenge and as a means of codifying impacts suggested by other independent means.

Other methods of exhaustion particularly focused on technology assessment have been developed by Louis Mayo of George Washington University and by Philip Bereano of Cornell University. Bereano's work particularly relates the attempt to introduce human values as a centerpiece in the conceptualization and conduct of the analysis. He has carried forth one brief unpublished analysis using this approach with regard to the Alaska pipeline.

## ECONOMIC TECHNIQUES

Virtually any technique of economics has its place in a technology assessment. Among the techniques receiving substantial use input/output analysis, which is a tool for tallying and organizing the interrelationships of economic activities and productivities of one sector of the economy to all other sectors including itself. So, for example, if one sets up an input/output analysis table involving 188 sectors of the economy, and one of those sectors is the concrete and cement industry, the table would present the contributions the concrete industry makes to each of the 188 sectors of the economy, including itself. The development of this technique in the last twenty years has become a major factor in economic analysis. It is now a standard tool in government (Leontief, 1966) and is rapidly proliferating in new uses such as the striking of energy balances and the application to national and international pollution issues.

The centerpiece of the application of economic techniques is cost-benefit analysis, which has been widely described. For example, cost-benefit techniques applicable to control of automobile emissions have been extensively applied and reviewed (U.S. Senate, 1974a). This report illustrates the strengths, as well as the practical policy limits, of cost-benefit techniques. A recent review of cost-benefit studies in auto safety highlighted the role of assumptions about the scope of factors entering into an analysis. This report also highlights the difficulty of "costing out" injuries and deaths, as well as a problem common to most comprehensive impact studies, that of data quality (U.S. Senate, 1974).

*Benefit-Cost and Policy Analysis 1973* (Haveman, 1974) is a new annual replete with detailed papers on cost benefits on such things as the automobile, the Alaska pipeline, flood alleviation, environmental control, income maintenance, health insurance, and many other subjects. It should be valuable both to novice and experienced analysts.

## RISK ANALYSIS

A variant on cost-benefit has been called risk-benefit analysis. A National Academy of Engineering Symposium put together an interesting, instructive set of readings on this methodology (1971). The particular issue of the value of a life is a central source of vexation in many analyses and is exemplary of a larger class of consequences that are either difficult to cost out because of lack of data or present conceptual, intellectual, and emotional obstacles to cost analysis. With regard to the practical attempts to do this, the experience of the legal community in dealing with suits for compensation for loss of life has been pulled together in an interesting, brief monograph (Zeitlin, 1962).

An excellent brief book by Reutlinger reviews techniques for project appraisal under conditions of uncertainty (1970).

With regard to the more general area of effects, such as aesthetic ones which present difficulties in directly costing, Sprague of the U.S. Geological Survey developed an interesting technique which I call the "At Least" method. Conceptually, this technique involves costing out the price of a remedy to a disutility and then putting before the decision-maker the question of whether he is willing to pay that much. If the answer is yes, the decision system is prepared to pay so much to eliminate a disutility, then the disutility must be worth "at least" that much. If the system is reluctant to pay that much, then the disutility is probably not worth that much.


SYSTEMS ANALYSIS

Systems analysis is a powerful tool applicable to technology assessment. As Blumstein points out:

A systems analysis focuses successively on

A particular system—a collection of people, devices, and procedures intended to perform some function

The function of the system—the job it is supposed to perform

Measures of effectiveness by which one can measure or calculate how well alternative system designs perform the function

Alternative system designs to be compared

A mathematical model with which one can calculate the measures of effectiveness associated with each alternative system design (1967).


It is clear that this broadsweeping conceptual approach can be a unifying principle in any analysis. However, the emphasis on mathematical modeling, on quantitative measuring, and so forth, precludes the adequate treatment of many factors central to technology assessment, such as the means by which one identifies an impact, the identification of decision apparatus, the generation of possible options and alternatives.

## SIMULATION

Closely related to systems analysis is the application of mathematical techniques to the simulation of a physical system. This can have broad application in the analysis of many problems. For example, where water, meteorology, networks, traffic flows, or other readily modeled systems are a critical part of the technology, these tools can play a major part in a technology assessment.

## MODELING

A more general category than simulation is modeling, which can include simulation. Specific mathematical modeling techniques of general interest are systems dynamic modeling, which enjoyed a recent wave of public awareness, particularly through the book *The Limits To Growth* (Meadows, et al. 1972), and the numerous systematic criticisms of that approach to the study of major policy issues. The more recent work by Mesarovic and Pestel carries the concept of global modeling a step further. They have taken a regional and more subtle approach than did Meadows and their associates (Mesarovic and Pestel, 1974).

Dynamic modeling, of course, is not limited to a macro-world problem, but can be applied to any system in which a relatively small number of variables can be identified and mathematical relationships among components defined in order to form the basis of the computer-assisted analysis. A particular variant on dynamic modeling, KSIM, developed by Kane, is applicable to simulation as a didactic and heuristic tool for understanding the implications for policy of variables interacting over time.

The particular value of the KSIM approach is that it permits a small group to work out its basic assumptions, however divergent, about the fundamental factors influencing and influenced by a major development, such as a supertanker port site off a specific city, a new energy conservation regulation, or an agricultural development. It then permits the group to go forward from that point in terms of their own assumptions to trace the implications over time (say thirty years). Since this is done with the aid of a computer, in real time a group may "play" the variables and begin to develop a feel for the sensitivity of the system to their assumptions. While the heuristic and didactic values of this interactive approach should not be underestimated, one must guard against the enthusiasm which it engenders in misconstruing it to be a true analytical technique. In my view, it is only a valuable antecedent to an in-depth analysis.

A process for structuring complex systems, developed by Warfield at

Battelle, known as Interpretive Structural Modeling, is a group activity in applying logical reasoning to complex issues. One might, for example, with such a technique, working with a group from diverse, conflicting backgrounds, take as a model problem identification of the factors that influence the structure, organization, and operation of a municipal welfare system. Having identified those factors, the structural modeling system permits the group to determine the interrelationships and networkings among the elements in the system. The factors that are fundamental can be related to those that are derivative in the system. Again, the technique is one for dealing with complexity in a preliminary way, to codify and to organize what would normally remain uncertain and subjective (Warfield, 1974).

The Signed Digraph is also valuable for preliminary organization of interactions among critical variables. Figure 4 shows the relationship among the set of variables dealing with a particular system. The system of signs not only points out the interrelationships, but also gives further logical information about transitivity of the effects and likely points of successful intervention. The Signed Digraph may be regarded as the early state of a system dynamic modeling, or it may be handled solely as a qualitative tool (Roberts, 1971).

Other examples of mathematical modeling are found in the major study on climatic implications of atmospheric pollution, which is looking at the effects of fleets of supersonic aircraft on the atmosphere and Earth. The mathematical modeling of the physical systems is a principal tool in understanding the chemical and physical interactions of that total system.

## PHYSICAL MODELING

Physical modeling can also play a part in technology assessment. For example, in a study of the proposed extension of New York City's Kennedy Jetport (Gates, 1971), the study team took advantage of the existence of a large-scale physical model of New York waterways installed at the Waterway Experiment Station in Vicksburg, Mississippi. It played a substantial part in developing an understanding of the implications of extending the jetport.

## SCENARIOS AND GAMES

Scenarios are mainly attempts to systematically develop complex statements of future world states. It is a major technique for exploring future implications. Scenarios can vary all the way from statements of a few hundred words to elaborate, complex descriptions of situations

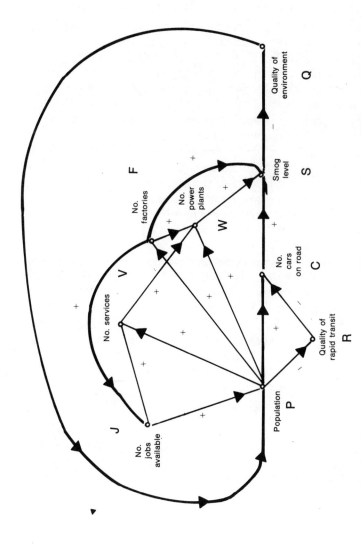

**Figure 4.** Simplified Signed Digraph for Air Pollution in a Given Region (Roberts, 1971). A useful interpretation is to assume that a + sign on the directed edge x to y means that, all other things being equal, variable x "augments" variable y. Put otherwise, an increase (decrease) in variable x leads to an increase (decrease) in variable y. A − sign then means that, all other things being equal, variable x "inhibits" variable y, or an increase (decrease) in x leads to a decrease (increase) in variable y. (In this sense, the sign might be conveniently thought of as a sort of first derivative of a function relating y to x.)

that specify initial positions, attitudes, data, and orientations for parties to the scenario. In the latter case, the situation is often referred to as a game. These particular kinds of "serious games" have been described in useful detail by Abt (1970). Scenarios and game-playing have also been done with the assistance of computers and are particularly applicable to the evaluation of military hardware in simulated combat situations. Scenarios, however, may also be played out in a playacting mode in which each of the participants in the game comes forward with a position in terms of his present state-of-knowledge. These positions, actions, and so forth are all collected, and the new state-of-the-game is put forward in the next round.

Some have even gone so far as to suggest that psychodrama may be a useful tool for some assessment purposes. While serious games of the strategic sort are generally of limited value as research tools, they do have substantial value as educational devices and in sensitizing players to some of the complexities of the situation.

I have had some interesting experiences in sensitizing groups to the complexities and conceptual approaches to technology assessment by game-playing with groups of 20 to 100 people. We play out the first day at a "think-tank" planning a year-long project on a technology assessment of a specific subject. The first day at work comprises a good two-hour game, playing out defining the issues to be investigated, methods, techniques, approaches, and so forth (Figure 5).

Even such sophisticated subjects as cost-benefit analyses lend themselves to group game-playing. For example, I conducted a workshop in which the group, working entirely with its own resources, calculated the costs and benefits of automobile pollution by going through a series of exercises to first map the scope and range of effects to be included. It then defined a group of costing variables, worked out on a consensus basis the rough ranges of values to be assigned to death, injuries, etc., and then proceeded with the calculations. While again one must not take the outcome of such efforts too seriously, it does become clear that when these efforts are compared with full-fledged cost-benefit studies, a great deal of credibility is lent to the value of the technique (Coates, 1972).

## MOOT COURTS

Moot courts have been applied to several technologies as a way of understanding and anticipating the kinds of issues and perspectives that would be developed in a real court situation. This comprises, of course, a variation on the serious game.

| Study techniques | Structuring the problem | The systems alternatives | Possible impacts | Evaluating impacts | Identifying decision makers | Identifying possible action options for decision makers | Parties at interest | Macro systems alternatives | Exogenous variables stage of society | Conclusions and recommendations | Participation of parties at interest | Presentation of results |
|---|---|---|---|---|---|---|---|---|---|---|---|---|
| Historical surveys | • | • | • |  | • | • | • | • | • | • |  |  |
| Input/output | • |  |  | • |  |  | • |  |  |  |  | • |
| Compilation of prior work | • | • | • | • | • | • | • | • | • | • |  |  |
| Cost-benefit | • |  |  | • |  |  | • |  |  |  |  | • |
| Systems analysis | • | • | • | • |  | • |  | • |  |  |  |  |
| Risk-benefit | • |  |  | • |  |  | • |  |  |  |  | • |
| Systems engineering | • | • | • | • |  |  |  | • |  |  |  |  |
| Simulation | • | • | • | • |  |  | • |  | • |  | • | • |
| Expert panels, workshops | • | • | • | • | • | • | • | • | • |  | • | • |
| Modeling | • | • | • | • |  |  | • |  | • |  | • | • |
| Hearings | • | • | • |  | • | • | • | • | • | • | • | • |
| Interpretive structural modeling | • |  |  |  | • |  | • |  |  |  | • | • |
| Field or on-site investigation | • |  | • | • | • |  | • |  |  |  | • |  |
| Signed digraph | • |  | • | • | • | • |  |  |  |  |  | • |
| Trend extrapolation and analysis |  |  | • | • |  |  |  |  | • |  |  | • |
| Physical models |  |  | • | • |  |  |  |  |  |  |  | • |
| Delphi | • | • | • | • | • | • | • | • | • |  | • |  |
| Scenarios/games | • | • | • | • | • | • | • | • | • | • | • | • |
| Cross impact | • | • | • | • |  | • |  |  | • |  | • |  |
| Moot courts |  |  | • | • | • | • | • |  |  | • | • | • |
| Check lists | • | • | • |  | • | • | • |  |  |  |  | • |
| Telecommunication participation |  |  | • | • | • | • | • |  | • | • | • | • |
| Morphological analysis | • | • |  |  |  |  |  | • |  |  |  |  |
| Syncons |  |  | • | • | • | • | • | • | • | • | • | • |
| Historical analogy | • |  | • | • | • | • | • |  | • | • | • |  |
| Survey techniques |  |  |  | • |  |  | • |  | • | • | • | • |
| Decision/relevance tree | • | • | • | • | • | • |  |  |  |  |  | • |
| Ballots |  |  |  | • |  |  | • |  | • | • | • | • |
| Fault tree | • |  | • | • |  |  |  |  |  |  |  | • |
| Decision theory |  |  |  | • |  | • |  |  |  | • |  | • |
| Scaling |  |  |  | • |  |  |  |  | • | • |  | • |
| Brainstorming | • | • | • |  | • | • | • | • | • | • | • |  |
| Graphics |  |  |  | • |  |  |  |  |  |  | • | • |
| Judgment theory |  |  |  | • |  | • |  |  | • |  |  |  |
| Dynamic modeling | • | • | • | • |  |  |  |  | • | • |  | • |
| KSIM | • | • | • | • |  |  |  |  | • | • | • | • |

**Figure 5.** Elements in a Comprehensive Technology Assessment

## PARTICIPATION TECHNIQUES AND TECHNOLOGIES

The need to bring in parties of interest, stakeholders, diverse points of view, as well as to effectively involve decision-makers and those directly influencing them in understanding the complexities and subtleties of a technology is central to the development of an effective public policy. A variety of techniques, particularly exploiting growing communications capability in cable TV, computers, and various telecommunications hookups have been described in substantial detail by Carroll (1971), Pool (1973), and Etzioni (1971).

Related to these participation techniques is what one might call a variety of sensitization techniques in which the principal value is to bring about mind changing in order to broaden the participants' outlook on the complexity of the problem and the need to bring in new issues.

Coming out of the work in the futures area, such techniques as Syncon would fall in the category of sensitization. Syncon is a technique using the physical arrangements of people coupled with roving experts and closed circuit television to bring large numbers of people actively into discussion on a complex issue and gradually build a larger and larger body of understanding, and even a consensus on points of agreement and disagreement. The participants are assembled in a pie-shaped arrangement, separated into wedges by curtains or draperies. Each wedge may contain one or a few dozen people. As the discussion of the issues proceeds in each of the wedges and a consensus is built, a curtain is drawn apart and wedges are combined, thereby raising the discussion to a new level of sophistication. Within the wedges, closed circuit television is available so one may examine what is going on in the other wedges, or even interrogate and draw from them. The technique has been used several times, and the practitioners are becoming more skilled with it. In at least one situation, it has been broadcast over local public television to educate a wider community.

"Telecommunications and Democracy" was the subject of a one-day symposium at the 141st Annual Meeting of the American Association for the Advancement of Science in New York, January 30, 1975.

## SURVEY TECHNIQUES

Obviously, survey techniques are a central tool in understanding public views. Technology for surveys is continually evolving. An example is the project Minerva of Etzioni and his associates, involving citizen interaction and feedback on telecommunications systems (1971).

## DECISION THEORY

Decision theory is a growing social technology that has a major role in technology assessment, particularly with regard to quantifying alternatives for the decision-maker (Tribus, 1969). One specific example, the decision to seed hurricanes, is conveniently available as worked out by Howard and associates (1972).

## SCALING

Scaling techniques should be a major input to any assessment. In general, one should assume, until proved otherwise, that virtually any set of related considerations can be usefully scaled one way or another (Stevens, 1951).

## BRAINSTORMING

Brainstorming as both a structured and unstructured exercise for the free-flowing generation of ideas is central to any team activity working with a complex problem. One can brainstorm in any of its variants with any degree of sophistication.

## GRAPHICS

The concept of the crisis room developed by the military, or the situation room used by both the military and NASA involving elaborate, complex, sophisticated information and display techniques, has been applied to a limited extent to civil sector problems.

The application of these and other graphics techniques in public policy decision-making has been reviewed by Ewald (1973). That paper reviews twenty-five projects and activities in which graphics are a central part of the policy-related technology. Feinberg has made a specific study on kinostatistics, that is, the attempt to use graphic and cinematographic techniques for presenting social data with or without the assistance of computers (1972).

## JUDGMENT THEORY

Hammond of the University of Colorado has done basic work on the characteristics of human judgment. Why do people judge a matter the way they do? What policies do they really follow in complex situations? What policies do they really follow in complex situations? Let me illustrate with one of his classic cases, a labor-management dispute.

Consider the issues in the annual negotiation. Let us say we identify the issues as A, B, C, D, . . . and so on. What you find experimentally is that labor may be emphasizing A, B, C, D, while management may find issues C, D, E, and F important to them. The conflict has to do with resolving their views and hence their actions on those issues. What Hammond's studies show is first that people are unable, unless helped, to identify the true weight they assign to these various components. We seem to be unable to think through that C is really very important to us and we really don't give a hoot about D or E. That's hard for people to come to. Even harder is to realize what is important to the opposition. By a system of interrogation and regression analysis, Hammond is able to assign for each side the relative weight they, in fact, give to each element. Having assigned those relative weights, he then finds he can do a number of interesting things. First of all, he can define a set of optimal solutions to the conflict. He can define a set of solutions faster and probably better than will come out of the dispute because he can optimize across all the weighted variables. The second thing he finds is that if he tells one side what its weighting or what both sides' weightings are, he can enormously accelerate the resolution of the conflict by the participants. Hammond finds that he can train people to make better judgments faster. For example, he has a neat little game which in about thirty tries "teaches" you to be a credit manager at a bank; you learn by assigning weightings as a bank credit manager does. He calculates your correlation and you have a unique measure of your learning, and so of your ability to mimic or duplicate the credit manager.

In general, in utilizing judgment theory, Hammond asks people a set of questions, and the questions involve different choices. By an analysis of the responses to those questions, he is able to determine the weighting you assign to each of the underlying components. For example, in the bank manager case, you're given five bits of data: the sex of the applicant, his credit rating, his monthly income, and what he wants use the money for, etc. You just go through a case and you make a judgment: give the loan, not give the loan. When you've gone through a set of these, Hammond quickly analyzes (with an automated system) weights you really gave to each factor. Then you get the feedback from the expert's judgment so you can rather quickly make the same kind of judgments.

Hammond has computer-assisted display techniques to facilitate all this. This has a lot of promise to it and is scientifically very sound. This is an interesting bit of social technology applicable to many aspects of assessment, choice, and value-judgment (Hammond and Summers, 1972; Hammond and Brehmer, 1973).

CONCLUSION

The relative applicability of the above techniques to the ten modules or elements of a technology assessment are displayed in Figure 5. As one can see, it ain't easy. But it is necessary . . . decisions will be made.

REFERENCES

Abt, Clark C. 1970. *Serious Games*. New York: Viking Press.

Ayers, Robert U. 1969. *Technological Forecasting and Long-Range Planning*. New York: McGraw-Hill.

Blumstein, Alfred. 1967. "Systems Analysis and the Criminal Justice System." *The Annals*, Volume 374 (November), 92–122.

Carroll, James D. 1971. "Participatory Technology." *Science* (February), 647–653.

Coates, Joseph F. 1972. "Calculating the Social Costs of Automobile Pollution." *Science and Public Policy Study Group Newsletter* (June/July).

Coates, Vary Taylor. 1972. *Technology and Public Policy: The Process of Technology Assessment in the Federal Government*. Washington, D.C.: George Washington University, Program of Policy Studies in Science and Technology.

Etzioni, Amitai, Eugene Leonard, Harvey A. Hornstein, Peter Abrams, Thomas Stephens, and Noel Tichy. 1971. *"Minerva*: A Participatory Technology System." *Bulletin of Atomic Scientists* (November), 4–12.

Ewald, William R., Jr. 1973. *Graphics for Regional Policy Making, a Preliminary Study*. National Science Foundation, Office of Exploratory Research and Problem Assessment.

Feinberg, Barry M. 1972. *Kinostatistics: Communicating a Social Report to the Nation*. Washington, D.C.: National Science Foundation, Bureau of Social Science Research, Inc. BSSR: 532.

Gates, David M., et al. 1971. *Jamaica Bay and Kennedy Airport*. Washington, D.C.: National Academy of Sciences-National Academy of Engineering, No. 1871.

Gordon, T., et al. 1974. *A Technology Assessment of Geothermal Energy*. Glastonbury, Conn.: The Futures Group (R164–46–11).

Hammond, K. R., and B. Brehmer. 1973. "Distrust Among Nations: A Challenge to Scientific Inquiry," in L. Rappoport and D. Summers (eds.). *Human Judgment and Social Interaction*. New York: Holt Rinehart.

_____, and D. A. Summers. 1972. "Cognitive Control." *Psychological Review*, Volume 79, 58–67.

Haveman, R. H., et al. 1974. *Benefit-Cost and Policy Analysis 1973*. Chicago: Aldine Publishing.

Hetman, Francois. 1973. *Society and the Assessment of Technology*. Paris: Organisation for Economic Co-operation and Development.

Howard, R. A., J. E. Matheson, and D. W. North. 1972. "Decision to Seed Hurricanes." *Science*, Volume 196, 1191–1201.

Jantsch, Erich. 1967. *Technological Forecasting in Perspective*. Paris: Organisation for Economic Co-operation and Development.

Jones, Martin V. 1973. *A Comparative State-of-the-Art-Review of Selected U.S. Technology Assessment Studies*. Washington, D.C.: National Science Foundation.

Kane, Julius. 1972. "A Primer for a New Cross-Impact Language—KISM." *Technological Forecasting and Social Change*, Volume 4, 129–142.

Kloman, H. (ed.). 1975. "A Mini Symposium: Public Participation in Technology Assessment." *Public Administration Review*, Volume 35, Number 1 (January/February), 67–80.

Leontief, Wassily. 1966. *Input-Output Economics*. New York: Oxford University Press.

Leopold, Luna B., Frank E. Clarke, Bruce B. Hanshaw, and James R. Balsley. 1971. *A Procedure for Evaluating Environmental Impact*. Washington, D.C.: U.S. Geological Survey, Circular 645.

Linstone, H., and M. Turoff (eds.). 1975. *The Delphi Method: Techniques and Applications*. Reading, Mass.: Addison-Wesley Publishing Co.

Martino, Joseph P. 1972. *Technological Forecasting for Decision-making*. New York: American Elsevier.

Meadows, Donella H., Dennis L. Meadows, et al. 1972. *The Limits to Growth*. New York: Universe Books.

Mesarovic, M., and E. Pestel. 1974. *Mankind at the Turning Point*. New York: E. P. Dutton.

Morgenstern, O. 1972. "Thirteen Critical Points in Contemporary Economic Theory: An Interpretation." *Journal of Economic Literature*, Volume 10 (December), 1163–1189.

National Academy of Engineering, Committee of Public Engineering Policy. 1971. *Perspectives on Benefit-Risk Decision-Making*. Washington, D.C.

Pool, Ithiel de Sola (ed.). 1973. *Talking Back: Citizen Feedback and Cable Technology*. Cambridge, Mass.: MIT Press.

Price, Charlton R. 1974. *Conferencing Via Computer: Cost/Effective Communications for the Era of Forced Choice*. Washington, D.C.: George Washington University, Program of Policy Studies in Science and Technology, Innovation Information and Analysis Project.

Reutlinger, Shlomo. 1970. *Techniques for Project Appraisal Under Uncertainty*. Baltimore, Md.: Johns Hopkins Press. Occasional Paper No. 10.

Roberts, Fred S. 1971. *Signed Digraphs and the Growing Demand for Energy*. Santa Monica, Calif.: RAND Corporation. R–756–NSF.

Sackman, H. 1974. *Delphi Assessment: Expert Opinion, Forecasting and Group Processes*. Santa Monica, Calif.: RAND Corporation. R–1283–PR.

Stevens, S. S. 1951. "Mathematics, Measurement, and Psychophysics," in S. S. Stevens (ed.). *Handbook of Experimental Psychology*. New York: John Wiley and Sons, 1–49.

Tribus, Myron. 1969. *Rational Descriptions, Decisions, and Designs*. Elmsford, N.Y.: Pergamon Press.

Turoff, Murray. 1972. *"Delphi Conferencing: Computer Based Conferencing* with Anonymity." *Technological Forecasting and Social Change*, Volume 3, 159–204.

U.S. Senate, Committee on Commerce. 1974. *Need to Improve Benefit-Cost Analyses in Setting Motor Vehicle Safety Standards*. Comptroller General of the United States, Washington, D.C.: U.S. Government Printing Office. Report No. 3–164497(3).

———, Committee on Public Works. 1974a. "The Costs and Benefits of Automotive Emissions Control." Volume IV of *Air Quality and Automobile Emissions Control*. National Academy of Sciences-National Academy of Engineering. Washington, D.C.: U.S. Government Printing Office. Serial No. 93–24.

Warfield, J. N. 1974. *Structuring Complex Systems*. Columbus, Ohio: Batelle Memorial Institute. Battelle Monograph No. 4.

Zeitlin, Leon, 1962. *Life's Value in Cash*. London: Oswald Wolff.

Zwicky, Fritz. 1957. *Morphological Astronomy*. New York: Springer-Verlag.

DENIS F. JOHNSTON

# Social Indicators and
# Social Forecasting

## THE CONCEPT OF SOCIAL INDICATORS

Attempts to define social indicators (SIs) and to differentiate them from social statistics or other forms of social information reflect both the evolution of the social indicators movement and the plurality of objectives envisioned for this nascent activity. The first influential contemporary work on this subject opened with the following definition:

This volume as a whole is devoted to the topic of social indicators—statistics, statistical series, and all other forms of evidence—that enable us to assess where we stand and are going with respect to our values and goals, and to evaluate specific programs and determine their impact (Bauer, 1966).

This timely publication was accompanied by an upsurge of research activity and related developmental efforts, both within government and among private research groups, aimed at improving our capacity to evaluate social programs, monitor social changes, and provide comprehensive assessments of the condition or "well-being" of the society as a whole (Sheldon and Moore, 1968). One important outcome of this activity was a governmental report that introduced the idea of social reporting. In this report, Mancur Olson provided the following modification of Bauer's definition:

A social indicator, as the term is used here, may be defined to be a statistic of direct normative interest which facilitates concise, comprehensive and balanced judgments about the condition of major aspects of a society. It is in all cases a direct measure of welfare and is subject to the interpretation that, if it changes in the "right" direction, while other things remain equal, things have gotten better, or people are "better off." Thus statistics on the number of doctors or policemen could not be social indicators, whereas figures on health or crime rates could be (U.S. Department of Health, Education and Welfare, 1969).

Meanwhile, a number of academic researchers were veering toward a more "value neutral" and analytically powerful conception of social indicators. This conception is exemplified by the following definition, which stresses the function of social indicators as structural components of a social system model:

The term *social indicators* comprises those social statistics which possess the following attributes: (1) they are components in a sociological (including socio-psychological, demographic and ecological) model of a social system or some particular segment or process thereof; (2) they can be collected at a sequence of points in time and accumulated into a time-series; and (3) they can be aggregated or disaggregated to levels appropriate to the specifications of the model (Land, 1970, 1975).

Finally, Richard Stone offered a looser and less formal conceptualization, which allows for a broad range of social indicators designed to serve different purposes:

Social indicators relate to some area of social concern and they may serve the purposes of curiosity, understanding or action. They may take the form of simple data series or they may be synthetic series obtained by applying a greater or lesser amount of processing to data series. . . . Social indicators form a subset of the data series and constructs actually or potentially available and are thus distinguished from other statistics only by their suitability and relevance for one of the purposes mentioned (United Nations Statistical Office, 1975).

These alternative definitions demonstrate that no single line of development can hope to encompass the diversity of needs and perceptions that underlie the widespread interest in social indicators. Bauer's concept and that of Olson share a direct concern for normative evaluation and a strong pragmatic orientation toward the assessment of social programs, but Olson's definition excludes nonstatistical forms of evidence. Of greater significance is the difference between Olson's view of the normative significance of SIs and Land's view that SIs are functionally integrated in "systems" models. Stone's concept recognizes that different kinds of SIs may serve different but equally useful purposes. These purposes have been summarized in a report of the President's Commission on Federal Statistics:

Quantitative social information (indicators) is required for: (1) the establishment of social goals and priorities; (2) the evaluation of public programs; (3) the development of a system of social accounts that could provide guidance among alternative interventions; and (4) increasing our knowledge of the functioning of society and enhancing our capability in social prediction. (Sheldon, 1971).

Sheldon's article goes on to describe the three types of social indicators needed to satisfy these requirements. First, problem-oriented or direct policy-relevant indicators are needed for the purpose of informing policy decisions and evaluating ongoing programs. Second, descriptive indicators are needed in order to permit the assessment of both the current status of society and trends occurring through time. Third, analytic indicators are called for—i.e., measures that reflect functional interrelations among major components of models of some specified system or subsystem of the society. In summary, when a particular measure or data set is selected as a social indicator, the underlying rationale may be that the data are thought to reflect the effectiveness of a particular program, or that they depict a significant trend or characteristic related to some aspect of "well-being," or that they provide some explanatory insight with respect to a development or condition of interest.

A fuller appreciation of the potential usefulness of social indicators can be gained by considering them as interrelated sets of information or as "social accounting" schemes. Both Springer (1970) and later Zapf (1975) have identified five major functions to be performed by a system of social indicators or social accounts. First, there is the basic measurement function whereby the current status of the society and emerging trends in major social processes may be described. Second is an evaluative function, requiring measures in the form of benefit-cost ratios to be utilized in assessing the performance of specified programs or social functions. Third is what Springer terms "the specification of control mechanisms." This function requires both an analysis of the interaction between social structures and social performance in specified areas of concern (Zapf's accounting function) and the marshaling of explanatory information relating to "experientially tested knowledge of causal connections" (Zapf's explanatory function). Fourth, a system of social indicators would serve to identify gaps (and redundancies?) in our knowledge of the status and performance of the major segments of society. Springer terms this the "feedback" function, since it would permit a better determination of data needs and priorities. Finally, there is the function which Springer calls "anticipating the future." In Zapf's terms, this function is expressed in direct relation to policy-making—i.e., "harnessing the above functions in systematic institutionalized action in support of an active social policy."

A fundamental issue in regard to the development of such a system of social indicators is the nature of the paradigm that might guide that development. Springer outlines two alternatives here: a descriptive paradigm and a normative paradigm. The descriptive paradigm can be viewed as a system of descriptive categories, incorporating a time dimension and arranged according to the main structural-functional sectors of the society. Such a model enjoys two advantages: it is conceptually familiar, and it can utilize data from major data collection agencies that tend to be organized in a similar manner—for example, health data from the National Center for Health Statistics, education data from the National Center for Education Statistics, or employment data from the Bureau of Labor Statistics. The descriptive paradigm suffers certain disadvantages as well. It would provide the same kinds of information that are presently available, albeit within a more comprehensive frame of reference. It would not offer either the analyst or the decision-maker anything really new; their highly selective perceptions of social reality, filtered through a screen of conventional disciplinary and subject-matter boundaries, would remain unaffected. A further disadvantage stems from the ease with which existing bodies of data can be fitted to such a paradigm. The danger here is twofold: first, the data selection process is likely to be heavily biased in favor of statistical series of well-established reliability and familiarity. This implies a preponderance of descriptive statistics relating to the conventional demographic, social, and economic characteristics of the population and a paucity of attitudinal data reflecting public perceptions, feelings of satisfaction, and the like. Second, and more importantly, a descriptive format cannot adequately fulfill the function of "anticipating the future," beyond providing a data base for trend extrapolation. Nor does it offer much guidance in specifying control mechanisms; the recognition of structural regularities, as reflected in a particular time series, does not imply the identification of their underlying causes (Spilerman, 1975).

Descriptive statistics, particularly in time-series form, are of course essential in developing forecasts. They also serve as indicators of significant improvements or retrogression in certain areas of life—e.g., unemployment, mortality, and crime rates. Further insights may be gained when trends in such rates are analyzed by means of multivariate techniques, such as the unsurprising discovery that crime rates in the United States are positively associated with the rate of unemployment and the more interesting discovery that the rate of morbidity also bears such a relation with unemployment (Brenner, 1971). However, neither descriptive indicators nor the associations observed among them offer much by way of explanatory insight for the policy-maker; at best, they reveal what is going on and where we stand, not why things happened as they did. A further objection to the descriptive paradigm is that it is designed to focus attention on what we think we know rather than on what we need to learn. It does not lend itself to the elaboration of alternative possibilities for the development of society, nor does it facilitate the exploration of the network of positive and negative consequences (benefits, costs, and associated trade-offs) that may follow the pursuit of any given set of social goals (Olson, 1970).

The normative paradigm calls for the construction of a system of social indicators organized with reference to their significance for a specified set of social goals and priorities. The intuitive appeal of such a model is obvious, since it accords with the view that social indicators can only be distinguished from other social statistics on the basis of their normative significance. In principle, this paradigm would also liberate the selection of social indicators from excessive concentration on available statistics and conventional measurements. It would give greater emphasis to the need for new indicators in those areas or aspects of social life that are inadequately reflected by our existing social statistics and measurements. With such a paradigm, finally, social indicators work would tend to concentrate more on research and development efforts and less on the marshaling and publication of selected data from existing sources.

The main disadvantage of a normative paradigm is that it requires the specification of goals and priorities around which the social indicators would be developed. Recent experience in the United States and elsewhere is instructive in this regard. The fifteen "national goals" announced by the President's Commission on National Goals (1960) illustrate the kind of difficulties encountered in such undertakings. The goals are either too sweeping and abstract to permit meaningful evaluation of progress toward their attainment, or they reflect unobjectionable human aspirations (e.g., "justice" or "equity") that defy expression in tangible terms. For example, such goals as "the preservation and perfection of the democratic process," or "the advancement of knowledge and innovation on every front" can scarcely be objected to as expressions of desirable social goals, but they are seriously deficient as statements of objectives toward which progress may be measured. Equally unassailable and empirically useless are such typical goal statements as "the optimal use of available resources" (with reference to the objective of community development) or "maximizing the individual's creative potential" (with respect to educational goals).

A fundamental requirement for any expression of a goal which is to be used in normative assessment is an estimate, however crude and tentative, of the social investment called for in its pursuit. A further requirement is that the postulated goals be viewed as a set, in order to recognize their mutual interactions. In brief, what is needed is a matrix of goals and requisite inputs, supplemented by a cross-impact analysis of the interactions and consequences of the different programs or policies required for the pursuit of these goals. Even a crude judgment that the attainment of Goal A (or, more precisely, the attainment of a specified level with respect to an agreed-upon indicator of Goal A) would facilitate, impede, or have no effect upon the attainment of Goal B would greatly enhance the process of setting priorities by identifying those critical "intervention points" where appropriate policies would have desirable multiplier effects (Gordon, 1968).

In view of the experience of the Commission on National Goals, it is understandable that the later efforts of the National Goals Research Staff did not extend to specifying a set of national goals (despite its name), but were directed instead toward initiating public discussion of emerging national trends and options. The announced theme of the staff report makes this objective clear:

This report is designed not as a listing of specific goals to be sought, but as a springboard for discussion and an aid to decision. It does not presume to say *what* our choices should be. Rather, it defines the questions, analyzes the debates and examines the alternative sets of consequences (National Goals Research Staff, 1970).

Two points can be made with respect to this approach. First, if normative analysis of emerging social trends and developments is to be attempted, some set of goals must be specified. If such specification is not regarded as the proper function of a National Goals Research Staff, the task must be carried out in some other manner—perhaps by a private commission. Second, it is important to distinguish between national goals as prescriptions for government action and social goals as postulates for analysis. National goals can only be established through popular consensus, as expressed through the legislative enactments of representative government. But social goals can serve to inform the legislative process and the public it serves by exploring alternative sets of social goals and the consequences of their pursuit (Terleckyj, 1975).

## TYPES AND USES OF OUTLOOK STATEMENTS

In order to review some of the methods employed in developing social forecasts (or outlook statements), it is helpful to distinguish among the different types of outlook statements that can be prepared. In particular, the terms *prediction*, *projection*, and *forecast*, which are often used interchangeably, may be defined as having different characteristic properties and uses. These three types by no means exhaust the subject. For example, the preparation of scenarios or the issuance of authoritative prophecies, particularly those intended to be self-fulfilling, represent additional modes whereby the future may be explored. However, these additional procedures, together with the broad spectrum of multivariate analytic methods and computerized simulations, may be viewed as means for generating outlook statements of the above types.

1. *Predictions*—To many social scientists, the ability to predict systematically is the ultimate test that scientific understanding has been achieved. Since this type of outlook statement, unlike the guess, hunch, or inspired intuition, involves the application of a known "covering law" to the phenomenon in question, it is often regarded as essentially similar to explanation. This similarity is well described as follows:

.... explanation in terms of laws argues that prediction and explanation are simply different uses of the same schema. In prediction we are said to be in possession both of the hypothesis and the statement of initial conditions from which the prediction-claim is derivable. In explanation, on the contrary, the explicandum (that which is being explained) is assumed to hold and we attempt to find the statements of initial conditions and the hypothesis which jointly entail it. ... According to this view, if we can justifiably predict that an event will occur, then we can also give an explanation of why the event occurred. The explanation and prediction are supported by exactly the same information, i.e., the relevant generalization and the statement of initial conditions (Brown, 1963).

This "symmetry" thesis has been extended to cover functional analysis as well as nomological explanation (Hempel and Oppenheim, 1948; Hempel, 1959). By this extension, the explanations of the functionalists may be used in prediction in precisely the same sense as the conventional explanations in terms of governing laws. In either case, by this view, explanations and predictions are essentially deductive arguments, differing only in their temporal direction with respect to the "explicandum."

From this line of reasoning it follows that the search for "covering laws" must be given first priority in pursuing both explanatory power and predictive ability, and that these goals are inseparable. Unfortunately, the innumerable generalizations that abound in the social science literature offer little basis for formulating the kinds of "covering laws" that have proved useful in the physical sciences. The complex interactions that characterize all but the most trivial instances of social behavior—the interplay of biological, psychological, and cultural factors; our inability to identify, isolate, and measure the effects of these factors; and the imprecision of even the most straightforward measurements of social phenomena—effectively guarantee that any generalizations arrived at are either so abstract as to have little applicable significance or so qualified as to apply only to highly restricted domains (Goodman, 1965).

In practice, if not in theory, it is also true that the ability to explain or understand some phenomenon does not necessarily imply ability to predict it, whereas effective "predictions" can sometimes be made without understanding the determinants of the phenomenon predicted. Most analyses of social behavior rely upon cross-sectional information, where some of the critical factors affecting temporal variations in the phenomenon under study are likely to be constant (Spilerman, 1975). Under these circumstances, satisfactory explanations do not yield reliable predictions. Conversely, many forms of human behavior demonstrate fairly steady directions of change over time, or, more rarely, reliable cyclical patterns of change, so that extrapolations of observed trends, devoid of any "understanding" of underlying determinants, may yield quite reliable predictions. These considerations suggest that the task of developing useful outlook statements should not be too closely identified with the more conventional aims of scientific research (Massenet, 1963).

2. *Projections*—At first glance, projections may simply be described as conditional predictions. They typically display the same format: an assumed system whose governing principles (or covering law), combined with a specified set of initial conditions, provide a basis for deducing future states of the phenomenon in question. The crucial difference between predictions and projections, however, consists in the factual status of their underlying conditions. The typical "If . . . , then . . ." form in which projections are properly expressed offers a clue to this difference. The assumed determinants in a projection need not reflect known causal relationships. In fact, some of the most useful kinds of projections either require no understanding of underlying determinants, or else they reflect assumptions that are deliberate simplifications of the actual situation that is perceived. The first and most familiar instance is the extrapolation of observed trends in some periodic measure of interest. Of course, such extrapolations fail whenever the assumed trend is disturbed. Furthermore, neither their "success" nor their "failure" can be explained without appealing to factors that were not systematically taken into account in their preparation. Nevertheless, continued use of much "naive" extrapolations in the development of projections suggests, at least, that they work reasonably well most of the time. With many social phenomena, turning points are far less frequent than continuations of trend, at least in the short run.

A less familiar example of projections that do not reflect known conditions are those involving assumptions that are deliberately contrary to current reality, or for which no real world instance is known. For example, the future population of an area may usefully be projected on the assumption of zero in- or outmigration, where only the cumulative effects of mortality and fertility can have an effect. Similarly, the future age distribution of a population can be projected on the assumption of zero mortality from certain specified causes of death. Both can be most useful for analytic purposes, although neither is likely to correspond with actual events.

Given the present state of our understanding of social behavior, efforts to anticipate the future must find expression in the form of projections rather than predictions. Given the more debatable argument that social behavior is uniquely characterized by voluntaristic and purposive elements, projections are the only procedure at our disposal, since any set of determinants, however well grounded on empirical evidence, must be viewed as conditional rather than absolute.

3. *Forecasts*—According to the terminology we propose, a forecast may be regarded as a projection that has been selected as representing the "most likely outcome" from among a set of alternative projections. Forecasts in the social sciences therefore serve as substitutes for the outright predictions of the more exact sciences and must accordingly reflect realistic or at least plausible combinations of assumed conditions. Forecasts differ from projections with respect to their purpose rather than the methodology of their preparation. Whereas projections, at least in principle, are designed to delineate a range of possible alternative outcomes, forecasts represent reasoned judgments that some particular outcome is deemed suitable to serve as a basis for a program of action. Ideally, projections provide a range of alternatives for consideration; forecasts provide a basis for action.

Two broad subgroups of projections may be distinguished: exploratory and normative (Jantsch, 1967; Ayers, 1969). Exploratory (or heuristic) projections are designed to reveal the possible consequences of assumed sets of determinants and initial conditions. These may correspond to known or realistic conditions, or they may be counterfactual. In contrast, normative projections are designed to delineate alternative paths toward the attainment of a specified goal or target. Unlike exploratory projections, they are constrained by the need to reflect, at their starting point, actual conditions and determinant factors insofar as these can be known or estimated. They are similarly constrained at their point of termination, which is the specified goal.

The above distinction corresponds to that between a descriptive and a normative paradigm for developing systems of social indicators, as described in the preceding section. With the descriptive paradigm, time series of descriptive indicators could be utilized in developing alternative projections, reflecting different assumptions as to their mu-

tual effects or interactions. With the normative paradigm, social indicators would be devised to reflect the attainment of specified goals
and to monitor progress toward their attainment.

If past history offers scant comfort to those who seek to predict
future events or to anticipate future trends and developments, it also
provides ample evidence that the attempt to do so is inescapable.
Projections, and the forecasts which may be selected from a set of
projections, constitute essential ingredients in a wide variety of activities. First and foremost, they serve an anticipatory function by providing some assessment of a probable future condition or situation,
which can then be accommodated or modified by appropriate action.
Our frequent and glaring failures to anticipate actual future conditions
overshadow the fact that innumerable day-to-day actions are successfully predicated on just such prior anticipations. Only the failures are
noted because only the failures are disturbing.

Second, projections—or the forecast selected from among them—
are an essential input in program development. All planning and the
development of programs for their implementation is inherently future-
oriented. If such plans are to be developed rationally, they must therefore incorporate some systematic assessment of the future environment in which they are expected to take effect. If we plan anything, we
must forecast something (Cazes, 1972; de Neufville, 1975; Little, 1975).

Third, projections are an essential, though sometimes implicit, ingredient in program evaluation. Attempts at program evaluation, particularly in areas involving social behavior, commonly encounter the
problem that program benefits or effects cannot be estimated with
nearly the confidence or precision that surrounds estimates of program
costs. This is especially the case when costs are viewed in the narrow-
est sense of administrative allowances for resource inputs. The researcher recognizes in this difficulty the truism that the impact of any
social program is entangled in a web of cross impacts reflecting the
totality of factors and interactions operating in the given situation. This
problem can sometimes be overcome by conducting social experiments, where matched control groups may be compared with experimental groups before and after the stimulus (program) has taken
effect. But such a solution is as rare as it is expensive. More commonly,
it is necessary to resort to the preparation of exploratory projections of
the course of development that might be anticipated in the absence of
the program in question, so that a comparison of that projection with
actual program-related outcomes may yield an estimate, however,
crude, of program impacts or benefits. Such projections are also required in estimating the relative benefits from equivalent expenditures
in alternative programs.

Fourth, projections may be required to provide essential links in a chain of conjecture where the final projection builds upon those that logically precede it. Projections of GNP require, among other things, a projection of labor supply, which, in turn, requires a projection of the size and age distribution of the population of working age, which itself entails some projection of future mortality, net migration and, possibly, fertility. . . . etc.

Fifth, projections serve a critical function in public information. Our justifiable concern with the manipulative or propagandistic elements that may be found in projections or other outlook statements prepared solely for public effect should not obscure the fact that projections, if freed of such influences, have a unique educational value. Another truism is apposite here: the effectiveness of many social programs or policies depends upon public perceptions of the need for that program or policy. More generally, public consideration of issues confronting the society and the proposals for dealing with these issues is seriously handicapped by the absence of outlook statements that set forth the possible consequences of alternative courses of action.

Finally, projections serve an informational function for policy planners at a stage prior to decision-making. In performing this function, alternative projections can expand awareness of the "degrees of freedom" that may exist in a given situation and that may thus prompt consideration of alternative courses of action which might not otherwise be recognized.

The above overview prompts a few general remarks concerning the challenging but hazardous enterprise of anticipating the future. One of the most frequently quoted remarks (Gabor, 1964) aptly expresses the limits of the possible in this area: "The future cannot be predicted, but futures can be invented." This notion clearly differentiates efforts to design alternative futures from efforts to predict what will, in fact, happen (Boguslaw, 1971). But if these designs are intended to serve as possible guidelines for policy rather than as mere intellectual stimulants, they must incorporate a realistic assessment of our actual conditions and the forces that have created these conditions. The challenge is to achieve a sense of our becoming which recognizes the reality of our being. When we allow that reality to dictate our future, we commit the historicist fallacy (Bell, 1964; Miles, 1975). When we allow our hopes and aspirations to dominate our thinking, we commit the idealistic fallacy. The caustic remarks of one prominent critic of futurology are a useful reminder that the future is not likely to correspond to either our predictions or our dreams:

What the future-predictors, the change-analysts, and trend-tenders say in effect is that with the aid of institute resources, computers, linear programming, etc. they will deal with the kinds of change that are *not* the consequences of the

Random Event, the Genius, the Maniac, and the Prophet. To which I can only say: there really aren't any; not any worth looking at anyhow (Nisbet, 1968).

## THE ROLE OF SOCIAL INDICATORS IN SOCIAL FORE-CASTING

Strictly speaking, any outlook statement, whether it merits designation as a prediction or as a projection, forecast, prophecy, or outright guess, is an extrapolation from our perception of the present. Here again, Nisbet (1968) makes the trenchant observation that our projections, Delphi exercises, scenarios, and the like tell us very little about the future, but are quite revealing about the present as perceived by social analysts and technicians through the filter of their adopted methodologies and values. This profound truth is based on the sound epistemological principle that all knowledge, whether pertaining to the past, present, or "future," must take the form of ideal constructs whose components can only reflect current notions of relevance and scientific acceptability and current perceptions of reality (Frank, 1954; Kuhn, 1962).

The above observation, despite its skepticism with regard to our capacity to foretell the future, provides a sound pragmatic foundation for the employment of social indicators in the development of projections. The most obvious example of such use is the trend extrapolation of selected indicators (when available in time-series form) by means of some curve-fitting technique, plotted against time. Such exercises, despite their transparent simplicity, are often useful in relation to phenomena that are not ordinarily subject to sudden changes of major magnitude. An example that comes to mind is the extrapolation of observed trends in age-sex specific rates of mortality, or in such rates classified by cause of death.

The most serious limitations of such exercises stem from their arbitrariness and their weak explanatory power. They are arbitrary in the sense that no series of observations arranged chronologically, however smooth or linear they may be, can offer a valid "prediction" of the locus of the future points or values. Temporal sequences carry no implications of causal determination. The employment of conventional criteria, such as "least squares lines," is equally arbitrary. Furthermore, except for the adjustments that may be carried out judgmentally to correct for perceived changes in definitions, remove or adjust "aberrant" observations, and the like, the observed trend is taken as is, and its extrapolation neither requires nor supplies any understanding of the influences that may have shaped it. The accuracy of the resultant projection ultimately depends on the extent to which the net effect of unknown determinants, influences, and disturbances in the future remains similar to their net effect in the past. Thanks to the principle that *natura non facit saltum*, there exists a considerable variety of measurable social phenomena for which such trend extrapolations may yield usefully reliable information. In general, however, the degree of confidence that may be associated with such projections is in inverse proportion to the length of the projection period.

Such projections, as long as they are not confused with predictions, can be of great value by depicting where we are likely to be at some specified future date in the absence of major changes in underlying conditions and influences. Unlike the more sophisticated forecasting models, trend extrapolations need not assume a surprise-free future. What they assume, more precisely, is that the net effect of future surprises, interacting with other influences, will be about the same as it has been over the period of observation. What these extrapolations cannot tell us, of course, is how an observed trend might be modified in a desired direction, or why it has developed as it has. Above all, they can never provide forewarning of major turning points in the trend they reflect; they invariably fail at just the time when questions of how and why are most pressing.

A more challenging and potentially rewarding use of social indicators in social forecasting is that of "unrestricted reduced form equations" (Spilerman, 1975). Here, the indicator of interest (the dependent variable) is associated with a number of independent and exogenous variables whose influence upon the dependent variable is determined by ordinary least squares analysis. On the assumption that these influences shall remain invariant over the projection period, future values of the dependent variable can be "predicted" from known or assigned future values of the independent variables. For example, an indicator of health status may be observed (either cross sectionally or over time) to bear some relation to indicators of nutrition, available preventive health services, housing conditions, and the like. Expressed quantitatively, these relations, together with assumed future values of the independent variables, can be used to project future health status.

There are three sets of conditions under which such relationships might yield projections of acceptable reliability. First, though rarely, measurable variables may be found whose values "lead" those of the variable of interest in a consistent manner. In such cases, observed values in the leading indicator can be used to "predict" future values of the lagging indicator, up to the duration of the lead or lag period. Given the usual delays in recording current observations, such periods are usually too short to permit more than very short-range projections.

Exceptions to this limitation can be found, however, particularly in demographic analysis, where successive birth cohorts of a population can be used to forecast, with some reliability, the volume of movement into a number of socially significant categories. Examples are initial entry into elementary school five or six years ahead, graduation from secondary school and initial entry into college or into the labor force seventeen or eighteen years ahead, and, albeit with rapidly diminishing precision, initial family formation twenty to twenty-five years ahead.

Second, but even more rarely, some or all of the independent variables may be subject to control or manipulation, so that their future values can be assigned in relation to specified policy objectives. In developing sets of normative projections, such a procedure is often adopted in order to reveal the implications of the values that are assigned. A familiar example is the projection of future employment by occupation or by major sectors of the economy on the assumption that future labor demand will have a specified relation to future labor supply.

Third, and far more common, is the circumstance in which each of the associated variables must be projected independently—an unfortunate circumstance that implies an endless regression of regressions. A further limitation, particularly in the case of long-range projections, is the need to assume stability (or, given a behavioral model, a predictable trend) in the structure of the relationships expressed in the initial equation. From an analytic viewpoint, these requirements are salutary inasmuch as they impose stringent demands to clarify assumptions and specify relationships in full detail. From a practical viewpoint, however, these requirements require data of high quality and imposing quantity. No matter how far the subdivision of a given phenomenon and its determinants may be carried, it is ultimately necessary to assume, assign, or extrapolate future values for the components one ends up with. At that point, the exercise of considerable judgment becomes inescapable.

Social indicators, even when they are not available in time-series form, can function usefully both as warning indicators, signaling a need for remedial action, or as baseline estimates, from which normative projections toward specified goals may be developed. In the health area, for example, single-time measurements of the incidence of physical defects (hearing and vision impairments, tooth decay, and the like) offer advance warning of potential future demand for health care services. Similar single-time observations of educational performance offer similar warnings of potential demand for remedial education or training. This usage of social indicators is implicitly prognostic, even though it does not necessitate their introduction in formal projective models. In fact, the most important purpose underlying the presentation of a wide variety of descriptive indicators before both policymakers and the interested public is to prompt consideration of these indicators in terms of possible future conditions they portend. In this sense, social indicators are valuable for the questions they provoke rather than the answers they contain. (Johnston, 1970, 1971).

When single-time measures are selected as social indicators, the presumption is, of course, that the replication of these measures at stated intervals would, in time, greatly enhance their informational value. Thus, such measures, if selected wisely, may be viewed as candidates for priority consideration in future data collection efforts. But such selection implies a need for a research capability to search the existing body of data for measures that merit replication (Duncan, 1969). In addition, there is a need to consider the necessity and possibilities for developing measures or indicators in those areas of social life that are inadequately covered by existing data collection activities. For example, the development of indicators reflecting changes in such areas as levels of aspiration, levels of group attachment and intergroup hostility or tolerance, and levels of alienation or anomie have been recommended (Campbell, 1971; Campbell, Converse, and Rodgers, 1976). Indicators of this type would provide a basis for assessing the status of the society independently of its evaluation in terms of its level of material affluence, general prosperity, productivity, and similar conventional criteria. Here also, when such indicators are collected at periodic intervals, they can provide a basis for illustrative projections of possible future states, though the interpretation of such trends is even more contentious than that of the more familiar and "objective" descriptive indicators (National Opinion Research Center, 1972).

Two broad research and development efforts now underway offer some promise in identifying appropriate social indicators among existing social statistics, and, more importantly, in specifying indicators for those aspects of life that are not adequately represented. The first of these efforts is under the guidance of the Organization for Economic Co-operation and Development (OECD) in Paris, and the second is under the direction of the United Nations Statistical Office (UNSO) in New York. The OECD effort has begun by establishing a number of goal areas or areas of concern for each of which several more specific subareas are identified. These, in turn, are being examined by expert groups and consultants with the aim of specifying agreed-upon measures or indicators relating to each area (OECD, 1973, 1976). The United Nations effort has adopted a different approach, but with a similar objective. Based on the initial work of Richard Stone, it has developed a comprehensive System of Social and Demographic Statistics (SSDS) which, if implemented, would provide periodic information on human "stocks" and "flows" with respect to the several subsystems in the society. Such estimates could then be linked to the corresponding economic stock and flow data stemming from the system of national accounts, so as to yield estimates of costs and benefits associated with these movements (United Nations Statistical Office, 1975).

The following table outlines both the OECD and the UNSO goal areas and subsystems, respectively:

| OECD List of Major Goal Areas | UNSO List of SSDS Subsystems |
|---|---|
| 1. Healthfulness of life | 1. Health |
| 2. Individual development through learning | 2. Learning activities. |
| 3. Employment and the quality of working life | 3. Earning activities and the inactive |
| 4. Time and leisure | 4. Leisure and time accounts (separate subsystems) |
| 5. Personal economic situation | 5. Social Security and welfare distribution accounts (also earning activities) |
| 6. The physical environment | 6. Housing conditions |
| 7. The social environment | 7. Population size and composition and families and households (separate subsystems) |
| 8. Personal safety and the administration of justice | 8. Delinquency |
| 9. Social opportunity and participation | 9. Social class, stratification, and mobility. |

As seen in this aggregated form, the OECD and UNSO efforts clearly encompass the major structural-functional components of society with similar broad categories. These two efforts are quite different, however, with respect to their potential for both social indicator development and social forecasting. The OECD effort offers a more immediate payoff, since it focuses on descriptive indicators which can, in many cases, be obtained from available data. The UNSO effort, on the other hand, calls for the establishment of a comprehensive data base employing a unified system of concepts, definitions, and classifications so as to permit estimation of stocks and gross flows into and out of each of the subsystems over time. The OECD efort can be expected to generate significant improvements in the data collection activities of member countries and in the establishment of internationally comparable concepts and measurements in the intermediate term—five to ten years. The UNSO effort promises to yield indicators of far greater explanatory power, but only if and when the proposed data system can be put into operation—and that is a long-term prospect. However, both efforts, of necessity, can only proceed incrementally. In some countries, including the United States, selected areas of social behavior, such as the transitions through the school system and into the labor force, may be represented with sufficient reliability for some purposes from data now available. Within the labor force itself, movements of employees among occupations and sectors of the economy may also be estimated with acceptable accuracy. These transitions (or transition probabilities) can, in turn, provide a basis for projecting prospective future movements, linked, of course, to projections of population and labor force. These transition probabilities, particularly when they become available in time-series form, would themselves constitute useful derivative indicators.

It is evident that social indicator development along the lines suggested above does not offer a panacea for the difficultues that beset social forecasting efforts. Social indicators cannot provide new or improved forecasting techniques; they can only offer an enriched data base to which these techniques may be applied and more systematic criteria to determine where such forecasting efforts might bear fruit. These are, to be sure, important benefits. They suggest some convergence of interest between social indicator development efforts and the efforts of those concerned with long-term futures analysis (Henderson, 1974; Henshel, 1976; Harrison, 1976).

Social indicators, even if restricted to exclusively statistical measures, offer considerable potential for employment in the more qualitative forecasting techniques—particularly in connection with Delphi exercises and the construction of future scenarios. Their use in Delphi exercises could take the form of a matrix of current status indicators supported by available time series in these indicators, which a panel of respondents would be expected to consider in suggesting possible future values of these measures. Presented in matrix form, such indicators could also be used to elicit views as to their possible cross impacts (Helmer and Rescher, 1960). Equally promising is their potential role in supplementing the range of conventional socioeconomic data employed in the construction of scenarios of the future. Such scenarios, which have been strongly criticized for their almost exclusive reliance upon economic and technological factors, could usefully incorporate the kind of corrective insights that social indicators, particularly subjective or perceptual indicators, could provide (Encel et al., 1975; Miles, 1975).

If the future cannot be predicted, the ultimate value of social forecasts must rest upon criteria other than their accuracy. The history of errant social forecasts is, of course, notorious. Less familiar, but equally deserving of notoriety, are the forecasts whose fortunate authors achieve high repute because of the purely accidental circumstance that their forecast turned out to be accurate. Even a clock that has stopped is accurate twice each day! More appropriate criteria include timeliness, relevance, and plausibility of underlying assumptions. Most importantly, social forecasts should possess heuristic value—that is, they should offer explorations of the possible. This requirement applies to normative projections as well as to purely exploratory ones, since alternative paths toward the achievement of a specified goal suggest, at least, that no single path is mandatory.

Short of accurate prediction, social forecasts can serve two general functions: advance warnings and explorations of the possible. In providing advance warnings, the role of appropriate social indicators is self-evident. Such measures can point to impending needs or imbalances and thereby prompt consideration of remedial actions. Of course, when such advance warnings are viewed as predictions or prophecies, they can rebound upon their developers in interesting ways. Since they are obviously intended to be self-denying, their "failure" to predict accurately is their success, and vice versa.

The role of social indicators in the development of exploratory projections is equally central, inasmuch as they can provide additional dimensions to the areas under consideration and a fuller awareness of the alternatives that are potentially available. In fulfilling these two functions, social forecasts help us to escape both the determinism resulting from problems left too long untended and that resulting from a failure to recognize the freedom of action we may in fact possess (Bell and Mau, 1971).

The directions to be taken in improving our capabilities with respect to these general functions can only be set forth with some temerity. To begin with, quantitative forecasting procedures alone cannot be relied upon to yield an adequate awareness of alternative goals that might be pursued or the priorities that might be called for. But qualitative procedures that commonly incorporate a distinct value orientation cannot possibly reflect the range and interactions of the many relevant factors in any systematic fashion. These different forecasting methods must be fused. That such a convergence may be in prospect is suggested by three current lines of development. First, there is the growing sophistication of the practitioners of the arts of model-building, systems analysis, computer simulation, and the like, as regards the inescapable— and pervasive—elements of judgment that infuse their efforts (Morgenstern, 1963; Stekler, 1970; Streissler, 1970). Second, there is the rediscovery, shared with equal dismay by numbers of pure and applied scientists alike, that typical social problems are somehow qualitatively different from primarily technical problems that have proven so amenable to applied engineering solutions (Hardin, 1968; Crowe, 1969). Finally, there is a growing perception, shared by such scholars as Emery and Klages and most elegantly expressed by Bertrand de Jouvenel, that if the social sciences are to serve human aspirations, they must combine the search for causal understanding with an exploration of human values and the creative possibilities they express (Emery, 1968, 1975; Klages, 1968; de Jouvenel, 1967).

It is evident that improved social indicators can play a key role in bringing about some convergence between the value-neutral efforts of conventional social scientists and the value-oriented concerns with social assessment and normative forecasting. Much less evident is the direction to pursue in achieving such improvement. The limitations of available social indicators have been summarized by Sheldon and Freeman (1970). These scholars have pointed out, first, that social indicators cannot be relied upon to increase the objectivity of sociopolitical policy development, for the fundamental reason that the social goals and values that determine these policies cannot be validated by an appeal to statistical descriptions of past or current conditions. What we are and have been may tell us what we are in process of becoming, but not what we should aspire to being. Second, they stress the limited potential of social indicators for purposes of program evaluation, since program impacts can seldom be isolated from a host of uncontrolled influences by statistical manipulation alone. Third, they argue, as does Bertram Gross, that social indicators cannot be neatly arranged in a social accounting scheme so as to yield either an aggregate index of social welfare or direct comparisons of the well-being associated with different aspects or components of that abstract quality (Sheldon and Freeman, 1970; Gross, 19766).

In view of these limitations, Sheldon and Freeman propose that social indicators should be developed with the more modest but attainable objective of providing a more adequate monitoring of the changing status and characteristics of society. Such an objective greatly weakens the distinction between social indicators and social statistics in general. If societal monitoring is and should remain a fundamental objective of social indicators development, a more challenging aim can be added: the construction of indicators designed to provide new perspectives both on our accepted institutions and practices and on the alternative modes of action and organization that challenge these traditions (Chenriot, 1972; Gross and Straussman, 1974; Miles, 1975).

If the normative significance of social indicators, as contained in the definitions we began with, is to be retained, valuational considerations must play an integral role in their development. To many practitioners in the field, particularly those who regard social indicator development as an integral part of normal social science research, the above argument appears to suffer from a basic confusion. Indicators, they point out, are value-neutral; the normative significance of any datum lies, as does beauty, in the eyes of the beholder. In other words, the determination that a particular indicator reflects an improvement or a deterioration is entirely a function of the valuational perspective of the observer. Of course, that is true, and it serves as a reminder, if any is needed, that the technical job of devising and testing valid and reliable social measurements can only proceed according to the conventional scientific standards of objectivity, verifiability, and so on. But the significance of social indicators lies in their use; to be meaningful in that sense is to be relevant to some set of values or goals (Young, 1968; Sheldon and Parke, 1975).

The arguments concerning the role of values in social science are both classic and interminable. One source of the difficulties is readily apparent: the scientist cannot legitimately adopt, qua scientist, the role of advocate. Less apparent may be the excessive reliance upon the models and metaphors of physical science. Peter Winch, among others, argues for the need to recognize a crucial distinction between understanding social and natural phenomena. In the case of social phenomena, understanding requires the preservation of the internal relation between the concept and its social setting, including its valuational or normative significance. Winch expresses this distinction by contrasting the historical and mechanical explanation: "Historical explanation is not the application of generalizations and theories to particular instances; it is like applying one's knowledge of a language in order to understand a conversation rather than like applying one's knowledge of the laws of mechanics to understand the workings of a watch" (1958).

The classic position of those who espouse a value-free social science is deceptively simple. Social scientists, like their counterparts in the physical sciences, can inform us as to the most effective means of attaining our (given) objectives. In addition, they can inform us as to the possible or probable consequences of pursuing given objectives. They cannot, as scientists, prescribe these ends. But the actual roles played by many social and physical scientists do not conform to this neat division between analyzable means and given ends. In the first place, our means become our ends, at least over the short run, and must therefore be evaluated in their own right; the ends do not justify any means. Second, scientists are increasingly confronted by the need to cope with complex problems involving both technical and moral issues. As Paul Diesing has noted (1950, 1955, 1962), modern societies are pluralistic with respect to both their means and their ends. They encompass, albeit with shifting emphasis, different types of rationality that govern the performance of the major sectors of the society. These types include legal and moral rationality, related to the discovery and application of rules and generalizations; technical and economic rationality, related to the calculation of efficient means in cost-benefit terms; and social and political rationality, related to human creativity. Diesing warns of the dangers resulting from applying the technical and economic norms of rationality outside the sphere of strictly technical and economic functions. This argument suggests the need for indicators that reflect the multiplicity of systems of rationality which share legitimacy in any society. At present, only the economic sector, with its norm of efficiency in the application of scarce means to alternative ends, offers the possibility of realistic evaluation of system performance in monetary, cost-benefit terms, although even here, difficulties abound (Lowe, 1965, 1969). As for the other sectors of society, governed by the norms appropriate to noneconomic systems of rationality, appropriate criteria for such evaluation remain to be established (Cole, 1976).

If social indicators and the social forecasts derived therefrom are to be relevant to the needs of decision-makers, they must be both normatively significant and descriptively adequate. The art of decision-making, whether public or private, macro or micro, involves granting some recognition to each of the different systems of rationality without according ultimate legitimacy to any one of them. Societies cannot successfully pursue purely economic goals, or purely technical goals, or purely political goals, without experiencing the collapse of one or another of their subsystems. Thus, social indicators must be developed independently of, and as supplements to, the indicators appropriate to the technical and economic spheres of activity. And, too, they must ultimately reflect the nontechnical and noneconomic norms appropriate to these other spheres (Toulmin, 1961; Taviss, 1969; Sawhill, 1974).

Social values are themselves important objects of scientific study, and a monitoring of changes in values by means of appropriate indicators is itself a major objective of social indicator development (Iklé, 1967; Taviss, 1969; Baier and Rescher, 1969). But the fact that values may and do change over time does not alter the fact that both the assessment of the current state of a society and the formulation of policies designed to guide its future development imply a normative standpoint. Decision-making is inherently meaningless except insofar as it expresses some value or derived goal. The purpose of any decision is to bridge the gap between one's current situation and some preferred state; such a gap cannot be perceived, nor a preferred state identified, except in terms of one's values. Thus, social indicators must not only serve as benchmarks in our efforts to ascertain our current status and direction of change; they must also illuminate the values that are implicit in these trends and conditions, and, in the form of exploratory and normative projections, they must also illustrate our potential for further development. Insofar as social indicators are able to fulfill these requirements, they can eventually provide the kind of informational and evaluational foundation for rational and democratic decision-making which Shackle has described so eloquently: "In a predestinate world, decision would be illusory; in a world of perfect knowledge, empty; in a world without natural order, powerless. Our intuitive attitude to life implies non-illusory, non-empty, non-powerless decision" (1961).

It may be appropriate to close with de Jouvenel's reminder to those decision-makers and informed publics who are expected to utilize the ultimate results of the efforts at social indicator development and social forecasting: "Designers of statistics are indeed philosophers, however unwilling to claim the name, and are fully aware that different aspects of reality can be lit up if alternative sets of concepts are used" (1967). *Caveat emptor.*

The views and interpretations expressed in this article are solely the author's and do not necessarily reflect those of the Office of Management and Budget.

## REFERENCES

Ayers, Robert U. 1969. *Technological Forecasting and Long-Range Planning.* New York: McGraw-Hill.

Baier, Kurt, and Nicholas Rescher (eds.). 1969. *Values and the Future.* New York: Free Press.

Bauer, Raymond A. (ed.). 1966. *Social Indicators.* Cambridge, Mass.: MIT Press.

Bell, Daniel. 1964. "Twelve Modes of Prediction—A Preliminary Sorting of Approaches in the Social Sciences." *Daedalus* (Summer), 845–880.

Bell, Wendell, and James A. Mau. 1971. "Images of the Future: Theory and Research Strategies." In Wendell Bell and James A. Mau (eds.), *The Sociology of the Future.* New York: Russell Sage Foundation, 6–44.

Boguslaw, Robert. 1971. "The Design Perspective in Sociology." In Wendell Bell and James A. Mau (eds.), *The Sociology of the Future.* New York: Russell Sage Foundation, 240–258.

Brenner, M. Harvey. 1971. *Time Series Analysis of Relationships Between*

*Selected Economic and Social Indicators.* Washington, D.C.: U.S. Department of Labor. Manpower Administration Report Number 81-07-69-22.

Brown, Robert. 1963. *Explanation in Social Science.* Chicago: Aldine Publishing.

Campbell, Angus. 1971. "Social Accounting in the 1970's." *Michigan Law Review,* Volume 23, Number 1 (January), 2-7.

———, Philip E. Converse, and Willard L. Rodgers. 1976. *The Quality of American Life.* New York: Russell Sage Foundation.

Cazes, Bernard. 1972. "The Development of Social Indicators: A Survey." In Andrew Shonfield and Stella Shaw (eds.), *Social Indicators and Social Policy.* London: Heinemann Education Books, 9-22.

Cole, Sam. 1976. "Long-term Forecasting Methods." *Futures,* Volume 8, Number 4 (August), 305-319.

Crow, Beryl L. 1969. "The Tragedy of the Commons Revisited." *Science,* Volume 166 (November 28), 1103-1107.

de Jouvenel, Bertrand. 1967. *The Art of Conjecture.* (Translated from the French by Nikita Lary.) New York: Basic Books.

de Neufville, Judith Innes. 1975. *Social Indicators and Public Policy.* Amsterdam, Oxford, New York: Elsevier Scientific Publishing Co.

Diesing, Paul. 1950. "The Nature and Limitations of Economic Rationality." *Ethics,* Volume 61, Number 1 (October), 12-26.

———. 1955. "Non-economic Decision-Making." *Ethics,* Volume 66, Number 1 (October), 18-35.

———. 1962. *Reason in Society.* Urbana, Ill.: University of Illinois Press.

Duncan, Otis Dudley. 1969. *Toward Social Reporting: Next Steps.* New York: Russell Sage Foundation.

Emergy, Fred E. 1968. "Concepts, Methods, and Anticipations." In Michael Young (ed.), *Forecasting and the Social Sciences.* London: Heinemann Educational Books, 41-70.

———, and E. L. Trist. 1975. *Towards a Social Ecology: Contextual Appreciations of the Future in the Present.* London: Plenum.

Encel, Solomon, Pauline K. Marstrand, and William Page (eds.). 1976. *The Art of Anticipation—Values and Methods in Forecasting.* New York: Pica Press.

Frank, Phillip G. 1954. *The Validation of Scientific Theories.* Boston: Beacon Press.

Gabor, Dennis. 1964. *Inventing the Future.* Harmondsworth, Middlesex: Penguin-Pelican Books.

Goodman, Nelson. 1965. *Fact, Fiction, and Forecasts.* 2d ed. Indianapolis: Bobbs-Merrill.

Gordon, T. J. 1968. "New Approaches to Delphi." In James R. Bright (ed.), *Technological Forecasting for Industry and Government.* Englewood Cliffs, N.J.: Prentice-Hall, 134-143.

Gross, Bertram M. 1966. "The State of the Nation: Social Systems Accounting." In Raymond A. Bauer (ed.), *Social Indicators.* Cambridge, Mass.: MIT Press, 154-271.

———, and Jeffrey D. Straussman. 1974. "The Social Indicators Movement." *Social Policy,* Volume 5, Number 3 (September/October), 43-54.

Hardin, Garrett. 1968. "The Tragedy of the Commons." *Science,* Volume 162 (December 13), 1243–1248.

Harrison, Daniel P. 1976. *Social Forecasting Methodology: Suggestions for Research.* New York: Russell Sage Foundation.

Helmer, Olaf, and Nicholas Rescher. 1960. *On the Epistemology of the Inexact Sciences.* Santa Monica, Calif.: RAND Corporation.

Hempel, Carl G. 1959. "The Logic of Functional Analysis." In Llewellyn Gross (ed.), *Symposium on Sociological Theory.* New York: Row, Peterson, 271–307.

———, and Paul Oppenheim. 1948. "Studies in the Logic of Explanation." *Philosophy of Science,* Volume 18, 135–175. Reprinted in Herbert Feigl and May Brodbeck (eds.). 1953. *Readings in the Philosophy of Science.* New York: Appleton-Century-Crofts, 319–352.

Henderson, D. W. 1974. *Social Indicators: A Rationale and Research Framework.* Ottawa: Economic Council of Canada.

Henriot, Peter J. 1972. *Political Aspects of Social Indicators: Implications for Research.* New York: Russell Sage Foundation.

Henshel, Richard L. 1976. *On the Future of Social Prediction.* Indianapolis: Bobbs-Merrill.

Iklé, Fred Charles. 1967. "Can Social Predictions Be Evaluated?" *Daedalus* (Summer), 733–758.

Jantsch, Erich. 1967. *Technological Forecasting in Perspective.* Paris: Organisation for Economic Co-operation and Development.

Johnston, Denis F. 1970. "Forecasting Methods in the Social Sciences." *Technological Forecasting and Social Change,* Volume 2, 173–187. Reprinted in Albert Somit (ed.). 1974. *Political Science and the Study of the Future.* Hinsdale, Ill.: Dryden Press, 68–88.

———. 1971. "Social Indicators and Social Forecasting." *Cahiers du Centre de Recherches Science et Vie,* Volume 2 (September), 41–83.

Klages, Helmut. 1968. *Soziologie zwischen Wirklichkeit und Möglichkeit— Plädoyer für eine Projektive Soziologie.* Köln und Opladen: Westdeutscher Verlag.

Kuhn, Thomas S. 1962. *The Structure of Scientific Revolutions.* Chicago: University of Chicago Press.

Land, Kenneth C. 1970. "On the Definition of Social Indicators." Paper presented at the annual meeting of the Population Association of America (April).

———. 1975. "Social Indicator Models: An Overview." In Kenneth C. Land and Seymour Spilerman (eds.), *Social Indicator Models.* New York: Russell Sage Foundation, 5–36.

Little, Dennis L. 1975. "Social Indicators and Public Policy." *Futures,* Volume 7, Number 1 (February), 41–51.

Lowe, Adolph. 1965. *On Economic Knowledge, Toward a Science of Political Economics.* New York: Harper and Row.

———. 1969. "Toward a Science of Political Economics," and "Economic Means and Social Ends—A Rejoinder." In Robert L. Heilbroner (ed.), *Economic Means and Social Ends.* Engelwood Cliffs, N.J.: Prentice-Hall, 1–36, 167–199, respectively.

Massenet, Michel. 1963. "Les méthodes de prévision en sciences sociales." *Futuribles,* Number 66.

Miles, Ian. 1975. *The Poverty of Prediction.* Lexington, Mass.: Lexington Books.

Morgenstern, Oskar. 1963. *On the Accuracy of Economic Observations.* 2d ed. Princeton, N.J.: Princeton University Press.

National Goals Research Staff. 1970. *Toward Balanced Growth: Quantity with Quality.* Washington, D.C.: U.S. Government Printing Office.

National Opinion Research Center, University of Chicago. 1972–    . *General Social Surveys.* Chicago: University of Chicago, and Williamstown, Mass.: Roper Public Opinion Research Center.

Nisbet, Robert A. 1968. "The Year 2000 and All That." *Commentary,* Volume 45 (June), 60–66. Reprinted with a postscript in Albert Somit (ed.). 1974. *Political Science and the Study of the Future.* Hinsdale, Ill.: Dryden Press, 257–278.

Olson, Mancur. 1970. "An Analytic Framework for Social Reporting and Policy Analysis." *Annals of the American Academy of Political and Social Science,* Volume 388 (March), 112–126.

Organisation for Economic Co-operation and Development (OECD). 1973. *List of Social Concerns Common to Most OECD Countries.* Paris.

–––––. 1976. *Measuring Social Well-Being: A Progress Report on the Development of Social Indicators.* Paris.

President's Commission on National Goals. 1960. *Goals for Americans.* New York: American Assembly.

Sawhill, Isabel V. 1974. "Social Indicators, Social Accounting and the Future of Society." In Albert Somit (ed.), *Political Science and the Study of the Future.* Hinsdale, Ill.: Dryden Press, 114–127.

Shackle, George L. S. 1961. *Decision, Order and Time in Human Affairs.* Cambrdige: Cambridge University Press.

Sheldon, Eleanor Bernert. 1971. "Social Reporting for the 1970's." In the President's Commission on Federal Statistics, *Federal Statistics,* Volume II, Chapter 7. Washington, D.C.: U.S. Government Printing Office, 403–435.

–––––, and Howard E. Freeman. 1970. "Notes on Social Indicators: Promise and Potential." *Policy Sciences,* Volume 1 (Spring), 97–111.

–––––, and Wilbert E. Moore (eds.). 1968. *Indicators of Social Change.* New York: Russell Sage Foundation.

–––––, and Robert Parke. 1975. "Social Indicators." *Science,* Volume 188 (May 16), 693–699.

Spilerman, Seymour. 1975. "Forecasting Social Events." In Kenneth C. Land and Seymour Spilerman (Eds.), *Social Indicator Models.* New York: Russell Sage Foundation, 381–403.

Springer, Michael. 1970. "Social Indicators, Reports, and Accounts: Toward the Management of Society." *Annals of the American Academy of Political and Social Science,* Volume 388 (March), 1–13.

Stekler, Herman O. 1970. *Economic Forecasting.* New York: Praeger Publishers.

Streissler, Erich W. 1970. *Pitfalls in Econometric Forecasting.* Westminster: Institute of Economic Affairs.

Taviss, Irene. 1969. "Futurology and the Problem of Values." *International Social Science Journal,* Volume 21, Number 4, 574–584.

Terleckyj, Nestor E. 1975. *Improvements in the Quality of Life—Estimates of Possibilities in the United States, 1974–1983.* Washington, D.C.: National Planning Association.

Toulmin, Stephen. 1961. *Foresight and Understanding.* New York: Harper and Row.

United Nations Statistical Office. 1975. *Towards a System of Social and Demographic Statistics* (ST/ESA/STAT/SER.F/18). New York: United Nations.

U. S. Department of Health, Education and Welfare. 1969. *Toward a Social Report.* Washington, D.C.: U. S. Government Printing Office.

Winch, Peter. 1958. *The Idea of a Social Science and Its Relation to Philosophy.* London: Routledge and Kegan Paul.

Young, Michael. 1968. "Forecasting and the Social Sciences." In Michael Young (ed.), *Forecasting and the Social Sciences.* London: Heinemann Educational Books, 1–36.

Zapf, Wolfgang. 1975. "Systems of Social Indicators: Current Approaches and Problems." *International Social Science Journal,* Volume 27, Number 3, 479–497.

# Part IV

# Substantive Areas for Futures Research

While the previous section of the Handbook raised the question of "How?" this one speaks to "What?" What are the content areas of futures research? What are the substantive disagreements among futurists?

The opening chapters introduce the two principal, competing perspectives on the future: one proclaims that everything is going very well, and the other warns that things are not going very well at all. Optimism and pessimism are as old as *Homo sapiens,* but when they occur in a technologized civilization, they take on an enormous significance. Inappropriate beliefs can be an invitation to catastrophe.

Herman Kahn may be the best known futurist because of his ability to provoke and, at times, to persuade. Although his interest in modern warfare might seem to indicate an affinity for the darker side of things, Kahn is convinced of the strength and benefit of industrial advance, and thus finds himself at the head of the school of optimists. If people heed the doomsayers, he argues, then their decisions are likely to be mistaken ones and will have tragic consequences.

In "The Optimistic Outlook," Kahn and his colleague William Brown explain why the prospects for the future are sanguine and why the problems others foresee are not really so ominous. Among the issues aired in this chapter are the toll industrial culture is taking on the environment and the upcoming supply of food, energy, and raw materials. The ensuing chapters explore these subjects in greater depth.

Writing in opposition to Kahn and Brown, Victor Ferkiss contributes "The Pessimistic Outlook." A scholar of the history of ideas, Ferkiss establishes a historical and contemporary context for the exercise of pessimism. He shows that the traditional worry of humanity exchanging its soul for material prosperity remains at the core of pessimistic thought, but has recently been supplemented by less philosophic predicaments regarding population and the environment. At the close of his chapter, he chastizes Kahn for portraying the pessimists as dangerous: "It is those who argue that everything will be all right if we continue our present course and choose to ignore warnings of possible catastrophe who menace the future."

In his chapter, Ferkiss recalls that the publication of the *Limits to Growth* in 1972 rekindled the debate between optimists and pessimists. This book, a product of Jay Forrester's global simulation efforts at the Massachusetts Institute of Technology, was assembled by several of Forrester's colleagues and students. The advances Forrester has made possible in the computerized simulation of large systems has assured him a place in history. Forrester has played an important role in the newly reopened debate between scholars like Kahn who see no need for imposing limits on industrial growth and those like Ferkiss who see great need. As Forrester maintains in his chapter, the debate has progressed to the point where it can now be more finely focused.

These two contrasting outlooks for the future reappear in a different guise in the following two chapters. Daniel Bell, most well known for his projections of postindustrial society, sketches the features of this upcoming economy. Premised on the continued upthrust of science and technology, the economy as he sees it will become ever more devoted to the production of services rather than goods, and the labor force will become increasingly dominated by white-collar and professional workers. Postindustrial economy will not displace the industrial economy, but will build on it, much as the industrial built on the preindustrial. Since Bell's view of the future entails the evolution of industrial society along optimistic lines, it is no wonder that Herman Kahn frequently cites Bell in his articles and speeches.

Hazel Henderson has a different perspective. The industrial economy, she states, is not in the process of purifying itself, but rather in the throes of dying, having exhausted its potential. "Will we continue moving toward producer-oriented, capital-intensive, centralizing, and hazardous technologies (and accept the burgeoning risks and the price of government regulation and necessary control)," she asks, "or will we opt for simpler, cheaper, less violent, decentralized technologies, which conserve capital, energy, and resources, and therefore require more people to own and operate them and which, since they are benign, require less regulation?" Identifying herself with *The Limits to Growth* camp, she finds the first path untenable. The second is not only possible, but there are signs that this counter-economy, as she calls it, is already beginning to appear.

The next five chapters deal with more specific aspects of the debate between optimists and pessimists: population, food, raw materials, energy, and the environment. Will overpopulation become so pervasive that hordes of humans will threaten the survival of the planet? An unlikely prospect, according to Tomas Frejka's projections. Following an explanation of basic demographic concepts, Frejka indicates why population experts can say with reasonable confidence that the world population growth rate is beginning to slacken and that a plateau at approximately double the present number of human beings is likely for the twenty-first century.

Will food supplies hold up? In Lester Brown's view, the problems ahead are considerable, although not insuperable. The global food economy is threatened by several factors, including a precipitous decline in reserves and a rapid increase in the dependence of all nations upon one food-producing region. "A world of cheap abundant food with surplus stocks and a large reserve of idled cropland may now be history," he states.

While Brown is not very optimistic about the upcoming supply of food, Indira Rajaraman is more hopeful about the future availability of the mineral resources required by industrialized life. In her chapter, she reviews forecasts that have been made for the global availability of non-renewable resources. The studies are short of the ideal, she says, but the results are good enough to permit solid conclusions: an ample supply through the year 2000, with chances for shortages increasing thereafter. Most imperiled is the supply of fossil fuels.

It is on this shortage that James O'Toole focuses in "Energy for the Future." O'Toole's analysis is based in part on a Delphi study conducted by the Center for Futures Research at the University of Southern California, which polled people knowledgeable in energy matters. Although he projects that we will run out of petroleum, certain short-term adjustments and long-term innovations can combine to improve our energy projects.

In his sobering chapter, Barry Commoner warns that if we continue to handle the resources of industrialization as carelessly as in the past, the environment will no longer be able to sustain human life. Commoner describes why disregard for essential ecological systems can only end in catastrophe. Such seemingly innocuous developments as the depletion of water-borne oxygen or the introduction of polyvinal plastics herald the beginning of the end. How much time do we have? "One can try to guess at the point of no return—the time at which major ecological degradation might become irreparable. In my own judgment, a reasonable estimate for industrialized areas of the world might be from twenty to fifty years, but it is only a guess."

The next four chapters examine various aspects of life in the future as it may be influenced by technological choices. H. Wentworth Eldredge sketches fifteen futures for urban life; the actual future will depend on which technologies are adopted and to what extent. He believes that the least attractive options are the most likely to occur, although some of the more exciting possibilities (such as floating cities) may prove to be irresistible.

Arthur C. Clarke's faith in technology is naturally reflected in his chapter. "The purpose of human life," he states boldly, "is information processing"—and machines will advance this purpose. The communications technology which he forsees for the near future will lead to the "United States of Earth." What is more, the next stage will be communication beyond Earth.

Thomas McFaul, who explores a more problematic area of technological progress, reaches a more cautious conclusion than Clarke. The technology associated with biomedicine is developing so swiftly, and is colliding with ethical and legal standards so forcefully, that it demands constant vigilance. McFaul provides an overview of the questions that will have to be resolved as this technology advances.

The last of these four chapters, Christopher Dede's "Technology and the Future," reviews much that has been discussed throughout this section of the Handbook. He summarizes the several schools of thought on technology, which has become a primary object of concern for futures researchers. Dede restates the ongoing debate between optimists and pessimists on technological growth and identifies which thinkers he feels will eventually produce the resolution.

The next two chapters document the growing importance of futures activity to the two American sectors that are most concerned with shaping the future— the polity and education. In "Futures in the Political Process," William Renfro and Marvin Kornbluh summarize the new congressional foresight provisions, efforts to establish political goals through citizen participation, and the contributions of federal agencies to forecasting and goal-setting.

In "Futures in Education," Harold Shane and Roy Weaver explain how futures research has taken hold in the educational sphere. Not only have educational planning and curriculum development been important areas for futures research, but so have all the efforts to create a better future through improvements in schooling.

The last two chapters of Part IV extend the scope of futures research even further. In the context of increasing global tensions between the haves and the have-nots, Ervin Laszlo examines the pessimistic position (which has evolved from "doom" to "gloom") and the optimistic (which is stuck at "bloom"). According to Laszlo, the inadequacies of the present world system are becoming more conspicuous, especially to those nations trying to cope with swelling populations and soaring expectations. As a consequence, Laszlo foresees the arrival of new modes of international order based on collective self-reliance.

If Earth-bound ways of life are to play themselves out, then perhaps the answer will be extraterrestrial colonies. In "Settlements in Space," Magorah Maruyama discusses the range of cultural patterns that may be invented for these colonies, once Earth-derived psychological and social difficulties are overcome. This topic provides Maruyama with an opportunity for productive speculation.

HERMAN KAHN
and WILLIAM M. BROWN

# The Optimistic Outlook

It now appears that the 1975–1985 decade is destined in certain ways to mark one of the most important turning points in world history. The world's population is estimated to be growing about 2 percent a year. The Gross World Product (GWP), which is more difficult to assess, seems to have increased on the average about 5 percent a year since 1950, or at a per capita rate of about 3 percent a year. If these rates were to continue, world population would double every thirty-five years, GWP in fourteen years, and GWP/capita in twenty-three. But all three growth rates, on the average, already have started (or will soon do so) a more or less slow but long-term decline. They may have already reached their peak and almost certainly will before 1990.

If this decline actually occurs, then scholars and publicists who have extrapolated trends on the basis of recent all-time high rates (see, for example, Figures 1–5) will have suggested incorrect expectations about the world's future and the underlying mechanisms at work. The longer the range of the projection is extended, the more misleading the popular metaphor of explosive or exponential growth will become.

Undoubtedly, many readers have been won over to the many current arguments that the world could not sustain recent growth rates be-cause many mineral resources would rapidly approach exhaustion, while pollutants would increase to levels that would deteriorate our lungs, dim our vision, poison our water, and cause irreparable struc-tural or climate damage. Even if the above tragedies were not likely to occur, would not the very complexity and rapidity of this unrelenting exponential growth overwhelm our capacity for adjustment (e.g., create impossible requirements for fast, complex decision-making, or, simply through the effects of "future shock," create devastating problems)? Would not the implied international dependence increasingly demand a world government, a development that seems clearly unlikely in the absence of war or major calamity and that may not even be desirable? What about problems associated with the increasing income gaps both within and between countries which so many believe will soon lead to high levels of violence?

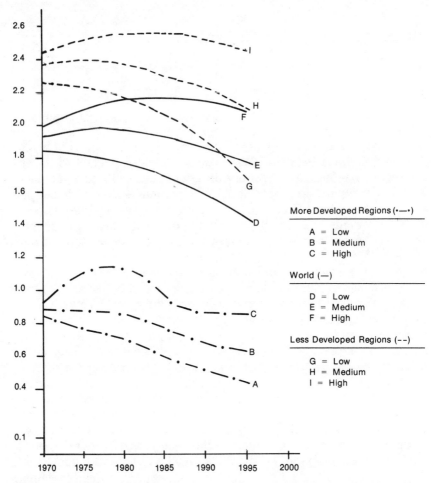

**Figure 1.** Percent Annual Rate of Growth as Assessed in 1973 (based on pre-1970 data)

SOURCE: U.N. World Population Projections, 1973

| REGION | POPULATION IN MILLIONS | | | | | ANNUAL RATE OF GROWTH (PERCENT) | | | | |
|---|---|---|---|---|---|---|---|---|---|---|
| | MEDIUM | HIGH | LOW | ** CONSTANT | OLD* MEDIUM | MEDIUM | HIGH | LOW | ** CONSTANT | OLD* MEDIUM |
| WORLD TOTAL | | | | | | | | | | |
| 1970 | 3,621.0 | 3,621.0 | 3,621.0 | 3,621.0 | 3,631.8 | 1.93 | 1.99 | 1.85 | 1.98 | 2.0 |
| 1975 | 3,987.7 | 3,999.9 | 3.971.5 | 3,998.3 | 4,021.8 | 1.97 | 2.09 | 1.82 | 2.14 | 2.1 |
| 1980 | 4,401.0 | 4,441.4 | 4.350.6 | 4,449.6 | 4,456.7 | 1.98 | 2.15 | 1.77 | 2.27 | 2.0 |
| 1985 | 4,858.1 | 4,946.2 | 4,753.9 | 4,983.7 | 4,933.5 | 1.91 | 2.15 | 1.69 | 2.36 | 1.9 |
| 1990 | 5,345.9 | 5,508.3 | 5,173.7 | 5,607.2 | 5,438.2 | 1.86 | 2.13 | 1.57 | 2.45 | 1.8 |
| 1995 | 5,866.1 | 6,126.5 | 5,596.7 | 6,337.5 | 5,961.4 | 1.76 | 2.09 | 1.39 | 2.55 | 1.7 |
| 2000 | 6,406.6 | 6,803.0 | 5,998.8 | 7,200.1 | 6,493.6 | | | | | |
| MORE DEVELOPED REGIONS | | | | | | | | | | |
| 1970 | 1,084.2 | 1,084.2 | 1,084.2 | 1,084.2 | 1,090.3 | 0.88 | 0.93 | 0.84 | 0.93 | 1.0 |
| 1975 | 1,132.8 | 1,135.9 | 1,13.0 | 1,136.0 | 1,147.4 | 0.87 | 1.01 | 0.76 | 0.95 | 1.1 |
| 1980 | 1,183.0 | 1,194.6 | 1,174.9 | 1,191.0 | 1,210.1 | 0.85 | 1.03 | 0.70 | 0.92 | 1.0 |
| 1985 | 1,234.3 | 1,257.6 | 1,213.6 | 1,246.8 | 1,275.0 | 0.76 | 0.95 | 0.59 | 0.83 | 0.9 |
| 1990 | 1,282.3 | 1,318.5 | 1,253.3 | 1,399.6 | 1,336.5 | 0.67 | 0.86 | 0.50 | 0.77 | 0.9 |
| 1995 | 1,326.0 | 1,376.5 | 1,285.2 | 1,350.6 | 1,396.1 | 0.62 | 0.85 | 0.44 | 0.75 | 0.8 |
| 2000 | 1,367.7 | 1,436.0 | 1,313.7 | 1,402.3 | 1,453.5 | | | | | |
| LESS DEVELOPED REGIONS | | | | | | | | | | |
| 1970 | 2,536.8 | 2,536.8 | 2,536.8 | 2,536.8 | 2,541.5 | 2.36 | 2.43 | 2.26 | 2.41 | 2.5 |
| 1975 | 2,854.9 | 2,863.9 | 2,840.5 | 2,862.3 | 2,874.4 | 2.39 | 2.51 | 2.23 | 2.59 | 2.4 |
| 1980 | 3,218.0 | 3,246.8 | 3,175.8 | 3,258.6 | 3,246.6 | 2.37 | 2.55 | 2.16 | 2.74 | 2.4 |
| 1985 | 3,623.7 | 3,688.6 | 3,537.3 | 3,736.9 | 3,658.5 | 2.29 | 2.55 | 2.06 | 2.84 | 2.3 |
| 1990 | 4,063.6 | 4,189.8 | 3,920.4 | 4,307.6 | 4,101.7 | 2.22 | 2.51 | 1.90 | 2.93 | 2.1 |
| 1995 | 4,540.1 | 4,750.0 | 4,311.5 | 4,986.9 | 4,565.3 | 2.08 | 2.44 | 1.66 | 3.01 | 2.0 |
| 2000 | 5,038.9 | 5,367.1 | 4,685.1 | 5,797.9 | 5,040.1 | | | | | |

* As assessed in 1968.
** No change in age-specific fertility rates.

**Figure 2.** Data for U.N. World Population Projections

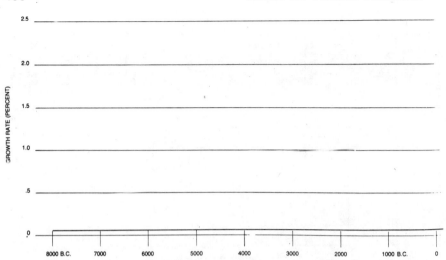

SOURCE: Ronald Freeman and Bernard Berelson, "The Human Population," *Scientific American* (September 1974), pp. 36–37.

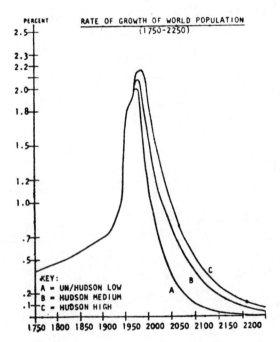

**Figure 3.** World Population Growth in Historical Perspective (8000 B.C. to 8000 A.D.)

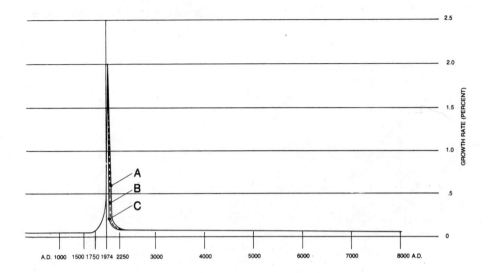

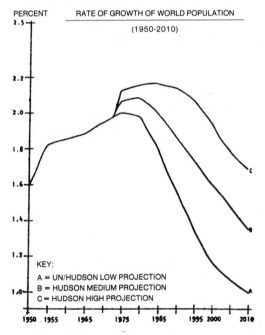

NOTE: All the above curves share the same assumption; they simply put the data into an increasingly broader time perspective.

NO. OF CHILDREN
PER WOMAN

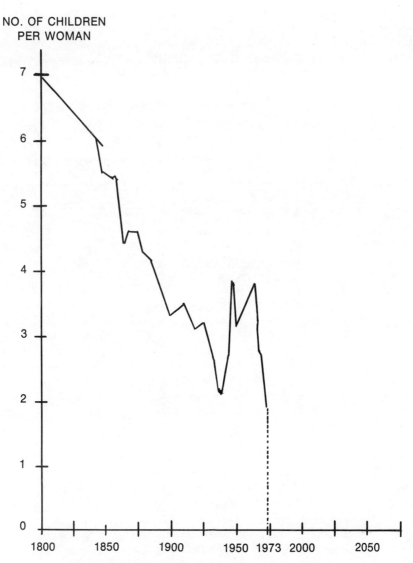

**Figure 4.** Total Fertility Rate in the United States

SOURCE: Based on data in *TIME,* September 16, 1974, 56.

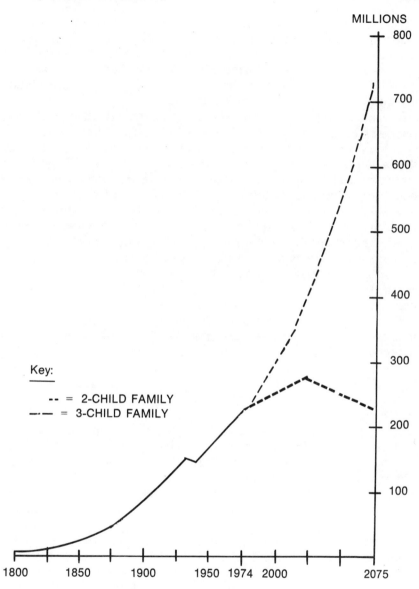

**Figure 5.** U. S. Population Projections

SOURCE: Based on data in *TIME,* September 16, 1974, 56.

What about changing priorities among our values and even changes in the values themselves? Of all the ways to express these fashionable problems, changing priorities and values appear to be the most relevant, in a causal sense, to the more or less gradual decrease in average growth rates that we should expect. And, initially, changing priorities probably will be more important than changing values.

This kind of preference is manifested, for example, when death rates decrease but retirement benefits increase in affluent societies. Thus, children are less needed to provide security for old age. Furthermore, the expense and difficulty of raising children are usually greater with increased urbanization or as domestic help grows scarcer in developed countries. All of these factors tend to make large numbers of children a less welcome choice, even if the basic values have not changed—and these tend to change also, if a bit later. It should be pointed out that in most circumstances direct government programs intended to reduce population growth rates are remarkably ineffective, in the short and medium run, at least as compared to "spontaneous" corrective measures that arise out of the basic trends, and in turn affect first the changing priorities and then the changing values. Practically the only exceptions are government programs that disseminate family planning information. These programs are very likely to be more important than exhortations for public cooperation or other official policies that try to restrain population growth rates. We believe that the restraint of population growth is very likely to occur, but mostly for a variety of personal reasons, not because of lurid, imaginative descriptions of future starvation, resource limitation, and pollution, or the actual occurrence of these events. Moreover, the pace of change will be determined by these individual decisions and on the whole will not be hurried, unless the basic trends are hurried. (See, for example, the remarkable changes in the fertility rate of U.S. females from 1800 to 1974, shown in Figure 4. Almost all of these changes occurred before the recent changes in birth control technology and without government exhortation.)

Recently, we have heard a lot about exponential growth, especially from those who contend that such growth, or perhaps any growth, cannot be tolerated much longer. Yet, it is little more than a commonplace observation that few growth curves in nature can be exponential or "geometric" for very long. Rather, they tend to follow the so-called logistic or (slightly mislabeled) S shape, roughly represented by the two solid lines in Figure 6.

It is at the unique inflection point of any such S curve that a continuously increasing rate of growth changes to a continuously decreasing rate of growth. Such curves have been forecast by the United Nations

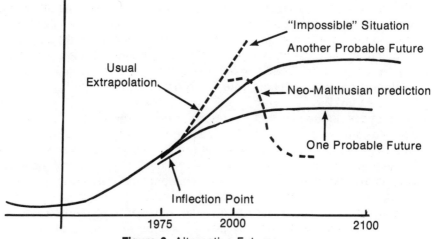

**Figure 6.** Alternative Futures

(see Figures 1-3), the Hudson Institute (see Figure 3), and others. We believe they forecast a reasonable representation of future trends in world population. These curves are more or less summarized in Figure 7.

The change in population growth rates indicated implicitly above and shown explicitly and in more detail on the following pages is self-evident. If correct, it illustrates the special character of today's issues and the dramatic change likely to occur in the very near future. Note

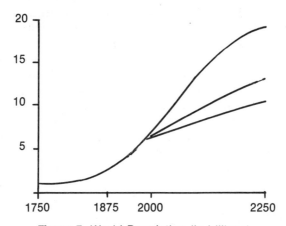

**Figure 7.** World Population (in billions)

that the curves show both the U.N. and Hudson projections of the low, medium, and high outcomes. The Hudson Institute's analysis concludes that world population growth is more uncertain than the U.N. projections would indicate. In either case, however, the point is the same: within this decade or so, we expect to enter a new phase of history, one with declining rates of growth, first for world population and then GWP.

We have suggested that the future dramatic reduction of population growth rates indicated in the figures will result not from the limitation of physical resources but from social forces that will gradually produce changing priorities, followed by new values. The following developments are expected to occur as a consequence of evolving long-term trends that are visible in nearly every developing culture: (1) increasing urbanization and then suburbanization, perhaps evolving into megalopolies; (2) increasing literacy and education leading to the growing relative importance of the "knowledge industries"; (3) increasing affluence through economic growth, accompanied by more leisure-time activities; (4) increasing concern with personal and national safety, environmental purity, and other quality of life issues; and (5) the individual's desire to restrict family size to an optimum (generally smaller) size with the assistance of improving birth control technology, and the promotion of similar trends elsewhere through suitable family planning programs. Under current conditions in most countries, growing worldwide affluence and *embourgeoisement* tend to encourage smaller families. Although these trends are strongest in affluent societies, they are evident to some extent almost everywhere. In each of the advanced societies—Western and Eastern Europe, the Soviet Union, Japan, North America, Australia, and New Zealand—as the population has become healthier, more industrialized, and wealthier, the birthrate has dropped substantially (see Figure 5). All of these countries seem to be rapidly approaching population equilibrium. That is, if the trends in the age-specific birthrates of various age cohorts continue they will gradually lead to zero or negative population growth in the next fifty years.

Many upper-middle-class people in these countries are beginning to lose their taste for economic growth. This group led the movement toward fewer children, and it is not unlikely that their values will be adopted by the rest of the population when they reach similar levels of affluence, or at least not long after. In general, as affluence becomes more widespread, an increase in it often seems less desirable at least if it requires sacrificing other desires. (E.g., the children of affluent people today tend to prefer more leisure and travel to greater savings and increased effort at work.)

To put this matter into yet another perspective, we believe that mankind is now moving into an historic period with unusual economic prospects. For the past 10,000 years, most people have lived or subsisted at very low material standards—roughly between $50 and $300 per capita, approximately equivalent to those of Indonesia or China today. In this dawning new era, a new plateau of relative material abundance can be predicted as the common lot of mankind: within the next century current U.S. and European standards could become almost a world norm in underdeveloped countries, give or take a factor of 2.

We are well aware that such a prospect for mankind directly contradicts most current projections of severe resource shortages and growing environmental horrors. Serious though some of these concerns are, the plausible and, we believe, realistic scenarios that have been studied at the Hudson Institute suggest overall optimism about the world's chances for a better material future. Our analysis leads to projections showing that the world population will level out near the end of the twenty-first century between 10 to 28 billion people, with an average per capita income of from $10,000 to $20,000 derived from a GWP of $100 to $300 trillion. Such figures are, of course, rough estimates and do not consider enormous calamities (such as large-scale nuclear warfare). The reasonably possible are distinguished from the possible but relatively unlikely, which would perhaps increase the uncertainty in the range of expected results two to ten times.

Of course, no iron law of history ordains that growth rates must start to decline before we reach 1980 or 1990, or that we will be able to deal competently with some of the very real problems of growth that remain when the rates are declining. Any reading of the future must be based on the evidence of the past and present and on as careful an analysis of likely future problems and issues as can be made. Based on such studies, we have concluded that, beyond this decade, the world will rarely, if ever, witness economic growth rates as high as those experienced during the first seventy-five years of this century, except as small or sporadic deviations from a gradual trend toward increased comfort and abundance. The rates will not increase unless some key basic changes in current trends are made. Many tragedies of supply and adjustment and other problems will probably occur, but all of them will seem resolvable eventually or tolerable from an historic perspective at least as judged by likely middle-class criteria or as proven by the actual course of events. Indeed, it seems likely that historians of the twenty-first century will find that our generation became most concerned about exponential growth just when this growth began losing its explosive character through natural processes and just as the gradual adjustment to a new, unprecedented abundance had begun.

Specifically, what are some of the principal points of contention that are of such concern that many citizens now choose or claim to cast their choice for zero or much reduced growth? The list would certainly include the physical problems related to environmental pollution, food, energy, and nonrenewable metal resources. Let us consider each in turn.

## ENVIRONMENTAL DISTURBANCES

As few may realize, the worldwide environmental movement of the 1960s produced much more than a new national conscience about environmental quality. It has led to a *major victory* in Japan, North America, and northwest Europe, and, to a lesser but quite significant degree, in most of the other affluent nations of the world, and even in some of the less affluent ones. The victory may not yet be completely apparent because it is still in process. In some of the less affluent nations, it may quite properly be delayed somewhat or even partially reversed, at least until the costs in slower economic development become acceptable. Even in the three most dedicated areas—Japan, North America, and northwest Europe—it may take observers five to ten years to see the full impact of recent trends on environmental cleanliness.

Despite this victory, this period will not be one of repose. There will be a constant battle between the more militant environmentalists and those who feel the financial "oppression" of the clamor for rapid solutions—especially those expenses for retrofitting existing installations to rectify past "carelessness" or for "too early" adoption of costly and unreliable interim environmental technologies. Generally, however, the majority will opt for compromise—protection of the environment where it is practical and useful, and encouragement of economic growth when it is most productive and the environment is believed less important (e.g., oil from Alaska). The battles will be fought continually and openly with many setbacks. There will be thousands of specific skirmishes; progress in the Trans-Alaska Pipeline, continental offshore oil drilling, and perhaps some strip mining of coal will be called setbacks by some, victories or reasonable compromises by others. The victories will be won by the moderate majority who are willing to pay reasonable costs, both directly and indirectly, to achieve clean air and clean water, without carrying a policy to an extreme. In particular, they will tolerate a small amount of aesthetic and environmental damage in some areas where such damage is justified for economic stability or further growth, as long as most populated or recreational areas are steadily improved and enlarged. Their environmental objective is not *zero* damage or no pollutants but steady improvement in the overall quality of life by reasonable standards, including economic stability and economic growth, where feasible.

Most of the conflict will not be over life and death issues, but over aesthetic and quality-of-life issues—and often about relatively marginal matters. All will agree that the environment cannot everywhere be left completely in its original pristine purity if the nation is to operate normally. A house, a motor, a factory, a port, or an oil well—all disturb the environment and create some pollution. The problem we will always face is one of where and how much? How much environmental disturbance shall we allow in the future and for how long? How much shall we correct the abuses of the past and how soon? In determining and later redetermining these compromises (probably over and over again), we can expect a continuing struggle between the opposing forces. Only the fanatics will feel a personal defeat (or a defeat for mankind) each time a power plant is built, an oil tract leased, or a pipeline built. The majority will gradually learn that new power plants are cleaner and safer than ever before, that oil can be found with new protection against danger of spillage, and that pipelines can be built with only temporary scarring over small areas. This is indeed progress, progress for which the environmentalists who fought the early battles deserve much credit. But a full victory will require a decade or more—an interval that will seem an eternity to the fanatic—until it is completed.

Let us remember the major gains already achieved in Pittsburgh and London where choking emanations no longer offend the senses. Or the cleanup of the Willamette River and the improvement of aquatic life in Lake Erie, which many wrote off in the last decade. Both the Hudson River and the Thames River now have many species of fish in them that have not been seen for decades. (Some of the more extreme environmentalists commented, "They must be mutations which like garbage.") Who but fanatics would question the profound impact which the expenditure of $200 to $300 billion during the next decade in the United States will have on pollutants from motor vehicles, industries, urban waste, and farms? Many mistakes and setbacks will certainly occur, but ten or fifteen years from now, and almost certainly by the year 2000, it is very likely that we will look back with great pride on our accomplishments. We will breathe the clean air, drink directly from the rivers, and smile with pleasure at the aesthetic landscape—undoubtedly while we haggle over whether or when some of the restrictions should be changed by another 5 percent. In any reasonable historical perspective, that outcome will be termed a clear victory for environmental protection and a great improvement that will be obvious to all except the extremists.

At the moment, the more extreme environmentalists seem to have unusually great influence, which probably has diminished recently. For example, during a recent (November 1974) election, voters defeated two California referendums, one for a mass transit system and one to prevent dams on wild and scenic rivers. A reasonable guess, barring unexpected environmental or economic surprises, is that during the next several years the political balance will move toward decisions that give greater weight to the economic impact of environmental protection. Part of the motivation would arise from the strains of the current stagflation and energy issues, and part from the growing realization that the costs for immediate and total implementation appear to be much larger than those previously estimated and publicized. Consequently, over the next few years, we expect to see greater leniency toward requests for stretching out compliance with some of the more difficult or costly changes (e.g., auto exhausts, $SO_2$ removal, thermal effluents). Such a stretching out, however, would not change our conclusion that within a decade the quality of the overall environment will improve profoundly.

Such congressional actions as forcing some relatively arbitrary deadlines and decisions on the automobile industry were not a bad strategy to get action started. If the legislators had tried to be more reasonable from the very beginning, the resulting compromises almost unquestionably would have been excessive. It was only by creating arbitrary and artificial deadlines and changes in the rules (that may result in inflicting more or less unjust punishment on various industries and groups) that it became possible to get the programs moving so rapidly. At this point, however, we should remember that these deadlines and changes in the rules *were* arbitrary and artificial. At present, minor compromises may often have large beneficial economic effects and yet slow down the total environmental program relatively little.

With respect to political decisions, it might be reasonable for policymakers to envisage three major categories in the relationship between environmental control and land use. One category would include the most protected regions such as special wilderness areas (e.g., mountains, national parks, lakes, and some deserts) which, by common consent, would be kept in a state of nearly pristine purity and in which any noticeable polluting activity would be strictly forbidden or severely controlled. The second category would involve the areas in which people spend most of their time—the residential, industrial, commercial, and farming districts. This category is the one in which the major struggles to define an optimum environment would, and we believe properly should, be waged for at least the next decade. The third category would be defined as one in which "junkpiles" of one kind or another, for economic or technological reasons, would be tolerated for greater or lesser periods of time. For example, strip-mining operations until the land is restored; oil fields until they are depleted; pipelines or transmission lines until they are obsolete.

Indeed, by choice there might not be complete or satisfactory restoration in some cases. With respect to this third category, we would encourage the current trend: to set legal standards to assure that any major disturbances which are not self-healing would be restored, *if practical*, but more or less gradually and in reasonable consonance with the economics of the local situation. The time periods involved could vary from months to decades, but rarely centuries. It may be particularly galling for a neo-Malthusian or an environmental extremist to accept this third category as necessary, yet we would assert that it is a normal and necessary consequence of any industrial society, past, present and future, and will remain so. The time requirements for restoration, however, or the degree thereof, may be appropriate subjects for continuing debates, but not the principle that this is a big country where certain limited areas are more or less expendable.

In retrospect, it seems strange that the environmental movement fought the Trans-Alaska Pipeline (TAP) with such vehemence. How could they have failed to realize that this great economic venture required the use of only about 15 square miles of very remote land (out of a total of more than 600,000 square miles, or much less than 0.01 percent of the Alaskan area), located in regions so remote that, except for the workers, it could be seen only by a few of the most adventurous tourists? Moreover, for most tourists it would constitute an impressive and even desirable sight. Once the pipeline was properly designed, its impact on wildlife would be negligible, or possibly even of some small benefit (for example, as an occasional refuge from the arctic wind). But the main point here is how easily the opposition avoided noticing that, during the pipeline's brief existence of perhaps a few decades, there would still be the remaining 599,985 square miles, or more of Alaskan wilderness to be admired in its undisturbed state! Why did they concentrate upon the mere 15 square miles and, in advance, find the image so distasteful? Even today, they ignore the fact that the unfortunate delay in starting the TAP not only added billions to its original cost, but for about four years (1973–1977) also required us to pay about $5 billion annually to foreign producers for our fuel requirements. The total bill in extra costs and foreign exchange is in excess of $25 billion. The delay may even necessitate some very unfortunate foreign policy compromises. Historically, the 15 square miles may yet become one of the most costly bits of real estate in the world—$2 million per acre. Some of the environmentalists pressed as hard as they did in the TAP case for an ulterior ideological motive—that of blocking industrial growth with little attention given to the economic impact.

There may be some lessons in this example that can set the stage for more reasonable decisions in the future. Consider the strip mining of coal which now seems to be urgently needed to achieve our goal of energy independence. Where the land and the environment can readily be stored to approximately their original condition, we would contend that there should be little argument about whether the strip mining should be approved. Where the restoration to the original condition is not feasible but a reasonably aesthetic substitution can be designed, then, again, it should not create much of a decision problem—perhaps a debate to choose which form of restoration would be most desirable. A more difficult case would be one, for example, in which a particularly arid climate prevents either a restoration to nearly original conditions or a pleasing alternative. When desirable re-landscaping appears impossible or uneconomic, under what circumstances might either a partial restoration or a less than desirable aesthetic substitute be acceptable? Such instances, if in fact they occur at all, would seem to be the ones over which any major environmental struggles should be fought. The eventual decisions would presumably result from a combination of (1) the effective arguments about the environmental consequences, (2) the importance of the project to the country, (3) the cost to the country of "expending" the area (i.e., we would like again to emphasize that not all areas may be worth "saving"), and (4) (as always) the most political clout.

We are not asserting here that no subtle, long-term, complex, and difficult environmental issues will arise. We doubt very seriously that any will appear which cannot be solved through international cooperation. Here we are thinking of such issues as reduction of the ozone layer, heating or cooling of the earth, and contamination of the seas. Most of the environmental issues that are taken seriously can be handled by purely national programs. A few need regional programs, but none really needs a world government, although a few may require worldwide programs. One of the reasons we need affluence, industrial growth, and advanced technology is that, without them, it may be impossible to deal with many of these esoteric issues. For example, a poor country may feel it is absolutely necessary to use DDT; a richer country can use more expensive insecticides. Indeed, in the long run, we will have to use various kinds of low-pollution agriculture to produce food. Whether this will be possible will depend very much on the standard of living of the countries concerned. While the developed world would not be very much affected if the controlled environment or other low-pollution agriculture resulted in grain prices of $300 to $400 per ton, such a change would be disastrous for the poor countries.

## FOOD PROBLEMS AND GROWTH

The problem of food is basically economic: Who pays for it and with what predictability and reliability? Solutions to the problems of an adequate food supply for every country of the growing world will not be easily found or, if found, may take longer and be less reliable than those for the "principal" pollution problems. This conclusion is not based on the lack of land, resources, technology, or capital but mainly on government policies, poor management, and, on occasion, just plain bad luck.

The trouble seems to arise—especially among the less developed countries (LDCs)—from a combination of (1) cultures that have traditionally lived on the brink of starvation and have tolerated some malnutrition; (2) the sporadic and haphazard nature of such natural calamities as drought, plant disease, insect plagues, frost, and excessive untimely rains; (3) the unfortunate rapid growth of population in some LDCs which have benefited from high leverage health care easily transmitted in the form of cheap medicines and vaccines; and (4) the great political (as well as technical) difficulties in transferring modern agricultural technologies to some of the LDCs with large populations. These countries need assistance the most and have resisted or have only very slowly been receptive to even obvious agricultural needs, such as increases in irrigation and fertilizer use.

Yet, many LDCs (Mexico, the Philippines, Brazil, Taiwan, Korea) have made astonishing progress. Also, there are increasing efforts to assist those who still need help by furnishing aid through technology, supplies, and equipment, as well as by direct shipments of grain after natural calamities. For the least advantaged countries, we must hope that a slowing of population growth, coupled with the gradual infusion of improved agriculture, will eventually result in abundance. Hopefully, the combined efforts of all countries will produce a sufficient supply to circumvent malnutrition or starvation threats within the next few years and, by the end of the century, improved nutrition for all.

Almost nowhere on the Asian subcontinent, where the great threats of inadequate food supplies now exist, is there such a shortage of land or water that food production could not be *more than doubled* with modern techniques. India, the classic example, has as much arable land as the United States, much greater ability for multiple cropping, and a potentially bountiful supply of water from Himalayan rivers, aquifers, and monsoon rains. It is not beyond reason to expect that, with an effective approach to self-help, India could become a food *exporting* country. But the effort has to be made in India by Indians; the United States can help, but not as much as is generally believed. (India *did* become self-sufficient in agriculture for a few years in the late

1960s. During this time, the Indian government, perhaps because of unusually good weather and a premature optimism about the expected harvests from the "Green Revolution," regrettably changed its policy emphasis from agriculture to industry.)

Although it is popular to speak of the *world* food problem, a severe problem exists only in certain countries, where shortages have occurred sporadically if not chronically, for centuries. Nevertheless, it has become politically acceptable (or even laudatory) to claim that the developed countries, especially the United States, are the cause of these problems, and even to accuse them of having robbed the LDCs of their wealth over the years. Yet, the very countries in which the bulk of the severe food shortages chronically exist (the nations of South Asia) are those which have consistently received aid for decades, often in the form of massive food shipments, for which they have seldom paid (nor are they likely to). A more valid charge that the South Asians could reasonably level at the United States and other developed countries is that some of our aid has been too effective. That is, it has removed formerly fatal diseases to such an extent that the population growth rate has doubled in recent years, in turn causing a rapid increase in the demand for food. Of course, no one would now recommend a return to poor health and premature death as the remedy to the burgeoning demand for food.

It should be emphasized that most LDCs, including the Asian communist countries, have no particular food problem, barring an occasional temporary problem, such as a severe drought. Indeed, within the last few decades, the list of LDCs which regularly cope reasonably well with their food needs has grown far larger than the list of those which do not. The group of countries that are still unable to supply their own nutritional needs is composed of the poorest third of the LDCs (by population). Perhaps 85 percent of the 900 million people involved are the South Asians of India, Bangladesh, Pakistan, and neighboring small countries. Most of the others are in sub-Saharan Africa and in scattered regions of South and Central America. Clearly, the major problem to be solved is that of helping the peoples of South Asia to become as self-sufficient in food production as most other developing nations. Unfortunately, this is not too hopeful a conclusion because the desired results seem to depend upon appropriate and timely changes in policy occurring within these countries. Yet, the attempts to find an appropriate solution through national and international action, as well as through private efforts, are generally increasing.

For the balance of this century, the prognosis is quite favorable for two-thirds of humanity (the richest, the more dynamic, the "coping" LDCs, and communist Asia), but quite ambiguous for the poorest third of the world. We cannot be confident that hunger and malnutrition will disappear. On the contrary, unhappily, much suffering and great problems are likely to be witnessed. These problems can be greatly mitigated, however, and possibly solved by creating sensible programs within and outside the troubled areas. On the other hand, the suffering might be further aggravated through unwarranted beliefs that solutions through economics and technology are impossible, or by wide acceptance of the currently popular poetic image that Malthus is being resurrected and is coming to claim the long-awaited vindication of his prophecy.

None of the above discussion about food production has considered the more novel technical approaches to the future production of calories and proteins by means of food factories. Some of the techniques now under development that could produce almost limitless amounts of edible, perhaps very palatable, foods include the conversion of cellulose by enzymes, of petroleum or petroleum waste by the growth of single-cell high-protein organisms, and the intensive growth of plants in scientifically controlled, pollution-free environments. The last-named technique could give annual yields from 10 to 100 times that available through conventional modern farming, using fewer inputs of water and fertilizer than currently. This technique is unusually suitable for arid climates and has been commercially developed in several countries. Each new scientific advance in food production can be expected to be phased in more or less rapidly, in accordance with its competitiveness and the growing demand, and to contribute its share to human abundance and eventually to general affluence. At a minimum, various food factories can soon be expected to be of great value in preventing future malnutrition.

During the 1974 World Food Conference in Rome, the discussion of the potential for hunger and malnutrition in the world reached new heights. The conference left a widespread impression that such problems could be with us "eternally." Perhaps they will. If so, this outcome seems more likely to occur if the no-growth segment of public opinion wins out over that of continued economic growth. Only the latter segment can substantially increase the world's wealth and technology, which are the major tangible assets for overcoming the threat of hunger. To develop this theme further, let us consider, for example, a particular hypothetical world 200 years from now. Such a world has, on average, increased its GNP/capita (at least for the less developed countries) at a modest rate of 2.3 percent annually; this rate is quite small compared to many recent examples. The arithmetic is simple but compelling. On the average, each person in the LDCs would have an annual income 100 times greater than that of today. Even the poor would have become rich by today's standards. The "untouchable" Indian could have an income equivalent to that of a middle-class American today.

But, we may ask, would there be enough food if, after that 200 years, the world population reached 20 billion, about five times the current population? The answer to that question is a simple, yes!—if we are referring to what is economically and technically feasible. For example, as we mentioned above, it has been shown in present commercial practice that, by use of plastic greenhouses or other types of controlled-growth chambers, the annual production per acre of many edible plants could be increased from ten to more than a hundredfold, while requiring only minimum amounts of water and nutrients, since very little is wasted. High yields occur because *several* crops annually may be scientifically grown in an *optimum* environment free of disease and pests. This approach is capital intensive. Even if it resulted in relatively high production costs, as much as $500 per ton of grain or its equivalent (an almost impossibly high figure), it would still be feasible for the wealthy world we have visualized. About 15 to 20 percent of the average income would be spent for food at these high prices and at current American standards of consumption. This form of agriculture could reduce the required farm acreage to *less* than that in cultivation today, freeing land for other useful purposes. This argument does not imply that this agricultural practice would be widely used in that rich hypothetical world of the future. But it does imply that if such a solution does *not* evolve, it is only because superior alternatives are adopted, resulting in better or cheaper nutrition, or both. In 200 years, we could certainly expect to find solutions much better than those that can be adapted from today's technology.

## ENERGY PROSPECTS

The problem of energy sufficiency in the world, which today may be characterized as a transient socioeconomic problem rather than one of technology or resources, is in process of solution. Few senior analysts doubt that the resolution will require more than one or two decades at most, and, with luck, possibly less than a few years. Undoubtedly, the near-term solution will combine (1) the conservation of energy to alleviate the present economic strains through the many ways already made popular (better insulation, smaller vehicles, mass transit, and the like); (2) some changes induced by higher energy costs, expressed in new energy-efficient designs for homes, industries, transport, and commerce; and (3) the vigorous development of new sources of energy both through increased exploration for conventional fuels, with the application of advanced technology for improving efficiency, and the harnessing of new energy sources.

All of these measures are familiar except perhaps for new sources of energy from advanced technology. This approach is now being pursued through research, some of which may be commercially feasible before the end of this century. So many promising techniques exist that are independent of fossil fuels that it is now almost inconceivable that an abundance of new energy from these sources will not be phased into extensive commercial exploitation early during the twenty-first century, and perhaps sooner. Some of the possibilities are as follows:

*Solar electrical power:* Two sources are through the use of relatively inexpensive arrays of solar cells and through large-area radiant reflectors. The supply is "unlimited" in abundance, clean, and may eventually be furnished cheaply.

*Nuclear power:* Although uranium reactors may always involve a residual worry about leaks, disasters, or effective waste control, the technology is here and, undoubtedly, the safety can be improved steadily over time. If necessary, we could live with current problems and uncertainties. Moreover, nuclear energy without such safety problems, through *fusion*, has never appeared more promising, and we might well witness the first commercial installation in this century. The fusion reactor is nearly free of serious radioactive threats in any of its present designs and, if successful, offers hope for almost complete safety through more advanced designs now being studied. In the advanced concepts, the reactions would not leave any radioactive waste to be disposed of directly or indirectly. In addition, the power potential is unlimited.

*Ocean gradient power:* Theoretical designs and current pilot plant operations are underway. If and when they are successful, a clean renewable source, effectively unlimited in its potential, will become available. Additional side-benefits would be pure water and nutrients for aquaculture.

*Cellulose conversion:* A pilot plant is now being designed to convert cellulose into glucose from which alcohol can be readily synthesized. The process offers good hope for annually converting billions of tons of a renewable resource, cellulose, into a clean fuel, alcohol, with a potential energy yield several times that obtained currently from all the world's fossil fuel sources. This is only one example (and not the most advanced or promising) of many approaches to the conversion of biological materials to fuels.

*Geothermal energy:* The interior of the earth contains enough energy to supply the needs of a profligate world for billions of years. The problem is to develop this source economically in many places. Technical solutions are being sought to overcome the problems of reaching, tapping, and conveying this energy rapidly to the earth's surface at a cost competitive with other techniques. Nature has demonstrated one approach by showing that water properly delivered into deep crustal fractures will return as great geysers of steam. If we can economically create by engineering what nature has done by chance, then clean, unlimited power from the earth's interior is in mankind's grasp. The prospects appear good in many areas of the world.

Clearly, although we may feel the pinch of high-priced energy today, the long-run prospects offered by a few of the more promising possibilities offer potentially inexpensive and enormous, perhaps inexhaustible, supplies of nonpolluting energy. This is a sound basis for developing worldwide affluence during the next century.

## METAL RESOURCES

The nonrenewable resources most often discussed, namely, the industrial metals, are more easily examined by grouping the metals into three appropriate categories.

The first group comprises five important metals that are in such abundant supply that they are essentially inexhaustible. These are iron, aluminum, magnesium, titanium, and silicon. A second category includes four metals, copper, cobalt, manganese, and nickel, which are found accreting in nodules located on the ocean floor. About twenty large industries or consortiums are currently developing new ocean mininng techniques for these metals. The nodules have been found to exist in such huge quantities and in so many areas that they are believed to be forming faster than they can be mined and processed for human use. Most experts believe that one or more of the many possible mining techniques will soon (within ten to twenty years) be commercially successful—certainly well before any exhaustion of standard mine sources can occur.

What of the other principal industrial metals? These are mainly chromium, zinc, lead, tin, gold, silver, and mercury. Although none is on the verge of exhaustion, if the demand for any of these metals increases, then we can expect the price to rise to the point where it is in reasonable balance with supply. The price would affect and be affected by (1) successful exploration for new sources; (2) improved technology for mining residual ores of lower concentration; (3) improved recycling; (4) substitution of the other minerals in adequate supply or plastics (which are becoming increasingly effective each year as metal substitutes); and (5) new engineering designs which can circumvent or reduce the need for high-priced metals. In addition, the ocean contains every industrial metal in dissolved or suspended particles, in quantities that are enormous compared to any foreseeable demand. Even at present, there are certain indications of new approaches that might soon lead to commercial mining of the ocean water for the desirable mineral content. However, even if the ocean continues to resist such commercial extraction, there seems to be little reason for any major concern about appropriate metals for the world's economy. None of the metals in this last group is indispensable; they are only convenient to man's current needs and styles of living.

## CONCLUSION

Rather than present a technical essay, we have chosen to illustrate how some of the more difficult international problems can be understood and approached in order to find satisfactory solutions. During the next few years, increasing worldwide time and attention will be given to these problems. As a result, there should be a greater likelihood that they will be successfully resolved. All in all, we remain optimistic about the potential of man's future. We can only hope that man does not throw away his potential through foolish political behavior or misplaced concern about nonexistent or badly formulated growth issues.

VICTOR FERKISS

# The Pessimistic Outlook

Modern civilization is coming to an end. The signs of this demise are to be found not only in objective political and economic factors but above all in the psychological realm. For the first time since the beginning of modern, secular, industrial civilization, the optimism which characterized and energized that civilization at its height is being replaced among most intellectuals and political activists of the West by concern, fear, and, in some quarters, despair. Even if many of these fears turn out to be unfounded or exaggerated, the fact remains that a sea-change in the collective consciousness has taken place: what was once taken for granted has now become problematic.

The generally held optimism of the past had several components. First, it was believed that humanity was gaining increasing control over the forces of nature through science and technology and that ultimately this control would become absolute. A corollary of this concept was the belief that the triumph of technology would eventually result in an era of material abundance for all human beings, satisfying not only basic human needs but providing the basis for a universally affluent society. It was further assumed that this technologically conditioned universal abundance could mean the realization of mankind's age-old dreams of utopia, that it would make possible the creation of a society in which abundance would ensure the elimination of conflict, oppression, exploitation, and unhappiness. Through control over nature and material growth the millennium would be brought to pass. Some still cling to these once unquestioned beliefs, but more and more their faith is being challenged by logic and events—as well they might, for these beliefs are almost certainly false.

Pessimism about the future is nothing new. Classical civilization was dominated by cyclical theories of history in which societies rose, flourished, and fell in a manner analogous to the passage of the seasons in the natural order (Eliade, 1954). During the decline of the Roman Empire, commentators bemoaned the end of the world as they knew it; even in the Christian Middle Ages, men clung to the classical concept that the golden age was in the past. But it was Christianity that laid the basis for the idea of progress as the eschatalogical concepts of Parousia and the millennium became secularized. Men began to see in science and technology the instruments for redemption not in a supernatural order but on earth (Polak, 1973). The ancient scourges of hunger, disease, and even war would in time be exorcised as mankind conquered nature through science and did away with the scarcities that bred misery and conflict. Utopian speculation was the inevitable extrapolation of the belief in science and technology as earthly saviors, and by the time of the American and French revolutions men confidently looked forward to a new era of peace and plenty. At first, the Industrial Revolution was regarded as the instrument for transforming these dreams of the past into reality as expanding multitudes were housed and fed, and time, distance, ignorance, and disease were increasingly overcome by human artifice.

Even at the apogee of nineteenth-century optimism, however, pessimism remained alive, if only as the creed of a crotchety minority. The Industrial Revolution and mass democracy, regarded as its foreordained offspring, had their critics among a minority of intellectuals and supporters of the old order. The romantic movement deplored the "single vision" of the moderns, as Blake put it (Roszak, 1972). Conservative sociologists criticized the loss of community and its replacement by impersonal contractual relationships (Bramson, 1961), and critics such as Samuel Butler cried havoc at the rise of the machine (Butler, 1872). In the beginning, this strand of pessimism could be construed as simply the disappointed reaction of a conservative class and their intellectual epigoni to the rise of democracy and the cultural triumph of the common man. Their strictures against the Industrial Revolution, "materialism," and the rise of the masses as a requiem for privileges lost and/or a shield for privileges they sought to retain, represented the narrow complaint of those who in Tom Paine's words pitied the plumage while ignoring the dying bird.

The fear of what kind of future mass industrial society was creating continued to spread, even to those who did not consider themselves conservatives and partisans of the old order. A powerful dystopian tradition arose in fiction to counter the earlier utopianism. Books such as Zamiatin's *We* (1924), Capek's *R.U.R.* (1921) (which gave us the term *robot*), and above all, Huxley's *Brave New World* (1932) became popular. A critique of the "machine age" was apparent in movies such as Chaplin's *Modern Times.* This tradition reached its zenith in Jacques Ellul's influential nonfiction work, *The Technological Society* (1964). European-oriented sociologists, alarmed at the seemingly unaccountable rise of Hitlerism in one of the world's most advanced industrial societies, created the concept of mass society, the conformist consequence of the industrial age (Ferkiss, 1969, pp. 69–76). From a slightly different perspective, the left-wing writer George Orwell created a classic political satire in *1984* (1949), a date which has become a popular symbol of a dreaded possible future. Increasingly, the intellectuals (of the developed Western world, at least) began to look askance at mass industrial society and its results, so much so that C. P. Snow in *The Two Cultures and the Scientific Revolution* (1959) could accuse them of forgetting the vast benefits science and industrialism had conferred upon the ordinary run of humanity.

Yet, one thing must be kept in mind about this first wave of pessimism about the future which science and technology were creating for mankind. The basic thesis of those who held this pessimistic view was that rational, secular, scientific, technologically based industrial civilization and its attendant affluence were having undesirable, even frightening, second-order effects. Mechanization was destroying traditional culture, impoverishing humanity spiritually, replacing excellence with mediocrity, threatening freedom, replacing variety with uniformity and individuality with conformity, substituting ugliness for beauty, destroying nature, turning man into a machine, and, in general, making possible, indeed inevitable, the spectacle of mankind exchanging its soul for material prosperity. Almost without exception, the critics of the industrial age (a notable early exception is Friedrich George Juenger [1956]) assumed that, however high and undesirable the price, the Faustian bargain was being kept. Science and technology, they maintained, could deliver unbounded power and prosperity in return for whatever losses of freedom and integrity humanity had to suffer. The problem of the present age, the Russian Orthodox philosopher Berdyaev wrote in an aphorism popularized by Aldous Huxley (1932, epigraph), is not the disappointment that utopia is impossible but the fear that it is possible.

The pessimism common among the contemporary cultural elite introduces a new element. In addition to agreeing with the pessimists of the past about the desirability of the Faustian bargain, thoughtful and informed men and women are increasingly coming to believe that this bargain will not and cannot be kept, and that the treasures for which humanity has been selling its soul are fools' gold. This new element changes the nature of the debate fundamentally. The past criticisms of technological messianism were primarily arguments over values, over whether the price paid for affluence and growth were too high. The present criticism hinges on questions of fact, whether there will be enough food for future generations to eat, enough water to drink, enough air to breathe, enough capacity to deal with the pollutant byproducts of growth. The issue is no longer simply one of whether we

face a future of mediocrity or tyranny, but whether mankind can physically survive.

This new pessimism did not spring full blown from the computers of
the Club of Rome or from the eloquence of the orators of Earth Day,
although they dramatized it for the Western, especially American, world
(Meadows et al., 1972; Environmental Action, 1970). It has earlier roots,
in movements of thought once obscure but now increasingly prominent, once separate but now increasingly convergent. The two most
important precursors of the contemporary pessimistic outlook were the
population and conservation movements. Serious concern over the
total size of population was largely the product of the mid-twentieth
century. Prior to this time, those concerned with population, population
growth, and birth control were primarily interested in the immediate
side-effects of large families from a humanitarian standpoint as, for
instance, Margaret Sanger or, like many elitist or racially oriented
geneticists, in the perceived possibility that the "wrong kind" of people
were breeding faster than the better. (These origins of the population
movement have done much to cloud the issues involved in overpopulation and make it difficult culturally and politically to deal with the
problems of overall population size on its merits.) Only in recent decades has the advancing science of demography—and the threatening
advance of world population—begun to impress on public opinion the
most salient fact about world population, that Malthus (given the qualifications expressed even in his original theory) was essentially correct
and that population tends to increase geometrically while means of
subsistence lag behind. Beginning with works that appeared in the
1950s such as Fairfield Osborn's *Our Plundered Planet* (1948) and
William Vogt's *The Road to Survival* (1948) and culminating in the
phenomenal popular success of Paul Ehrlich's *The Population Bomb*
(1968), both leaders and the general public in most of the world have
come to realize that, whatever their precise nature, there are upper
limits on the number of people the planet can support at even minimal
levels of physical subsistence.

Population is, of course, only one term in the population-resources
equation upon which human prosperity and survival rest. In a seculari-
zation of the Christian assumption that God would provide for all of his
future creatures, those who projected unlimited growth long assumed
the unlimited availability of resources. As the idea of progress became
secularized, man became the active agent in the processes of Providence. It was increasingly assumed that science and technology could
not only unlock treasures destined for man's use, though hidden in
prior ages, but also that through a kind of universal alchemy they could
transform man's physical planetary heritage in such a way that it could

provide subsistence for uncountable millions. It must be noted that the availability of unlimited usable resources is not a datum but an assumption. No religious thinker would have expected Providence to somehow repeal the laws of nature and preserve the feckless from disaster; yet, secular thinkers assumed that science could enable mankind heedlessly to ignore possible future shortages. What is significant about neo-pessimism is not that the falsity of the assumption of unlimited abundance has been proved but that a gratuitous assumption is now being questioned.

By the mid-nineteenth century many voices throughout the Western world argued that certain resources were being used up at such a rate that they were rapidly being exhausted. So it was that the conservation movement was born. From the outset (most notably in the United States), a conflict arose between those who favored conservation for the purpose of avoiding waste, and thus maximizing the use of resources, and those who wanted to preserve stocks of resources in their natural state for aesthetic or spiritual purposes. This conflict was embodied in the divergence of the ideas of such pioneer American conservationists as Gifford Pinchot and John Muir at the beginning of the present century. Finally, as early as the middle of the nineteenth century, the interrelationships among population, resources, and other elements in the environment were beginning to be grasped. In the work of such men as George Perkins Marsh (1864), the foundations of the modern concept of ecology—as distinguished from the more narrowly oriented but underlying biological sub-specialty of the same name— were being laid. Now it was necessary to combine these various insights into a common perspective on the world, to give a sense of urgency to what heretofore had been long-range predictions of eventual disaster, and to popularize what had been the knowledge or belief of a relatively small minority.

To specify the precise historical origins of contemporary neo- pessimism is difficult and leads necessarily to somewhat arbitrary generalizations. The explosion of conscious fear for the future of the planet dramatized by Earth Day in 1970 was preceded by several important precursor events. One, the significance of which is often lost upon commentators, was World War II. World War I was perhaps more horrifying than World War II in terms of the sufferings of actual combatants, and many regarded it not only as the termination of La Belle Époque but also as the end of civilization itself. "The lights are going out all over Europe," Sir Edward Grey said; "We shall not see them lit again in our lifetime" (Tuchman, 1963, p. 146). But, for Americans especially, World War I could be regarded as only a temporary aberration, the "war to end wars," which was to herald the coming of the good society. World War II ended that illusion. The horrors of the Hitler regime in industrial and "civilized" Germany—above all the Holocaust—made many feel, however subconsciously, that the world they thought they knew was not as stable as they had once believed, that the earth could open under the feet of men and women at any time. The atomic bomb added dramatically to that impression, particularly after its "secret" became the possession of a totalitarian enemy. The widespread belief of human beings that, despite the "Strangelovian" reasonings of the prophets of limited nuclear warfare, it was now possible for a third world war to literally wipe out human civilization reintroduced into popular and intellectual consciousness the ancient assumption that the mighty works of men were really as dust and that the day of judgment might well be at hand. No matter what the position of the hands of the clock on the *Bulletin of Atomic Scientists,* all sensitive men and women knew that the clock was running, and, save for absolute universal nuclear disarmament, it could never be stopped, only clumsily and precariously reset from time to time. At least one of the scientific organizations devoted to the present world crisis, the former Scientific Committee for Public Information, had its origins in the efforts of Barry Commoner and his associates to monitor the hazards of nuclear fallout prior to the Test Ban Treaty.

From the beginnings of the Industrial Revolution, men and women had deplored the impact on nature of the industrial processes upon which the new prosperity was based; the "dark Satanic mills" had long been with us. The worst effects of industrialism, however, impinged primarily on the exploited working classes. The more affluent could escape them, and even if they deplored them, their cries of anguish could be regarded as reactionary aestheticism. By the mid-twentieth century, a paradox developed in which larger and larger numbers of people became affluent—in part as a result of mass industrial society—and began to deplore the adverse side-effects of industrial society, especially in the United States. Americans had always resolved many of their problems by picking up and moving westward, and California became the epitome of the American dream. Once the Pacific was reached, however, there was no place left to flee. The publicity given the horrendous smog that began to be a regular feature of life in Los Angeles in the 1950s symbolized for yearning Americans a new sense of closure and entrapment. The dramatic oil spills at Santa Barbara in the early 1960s only highlighted the fact that American life was not necessarily getting better, that in the process of becoming rich we were destroying many of the amenities we had sought.

Two events in the 1960s dramatized the fact that unless mankind took better care of its common Mother Earth, global political disaster was possible. One event was technological, the other political. In the late 1960s, for the first time human beings were able to leave the confines of Earth's surface and venture out into space. Yet, oddly enough, this triumph of technology over nature instilled in many a new sense of human limitations. Pictures taken from the Apollo spacecraft gave man his first opportunity to see the planet whole and to grasp its finiteness and its identity as an isolated system. The bleakness of the moon and the testimony of the astronauts demonstrated that this green and blue speck in our solar system was not only our ancestral home but also the sole body hospitable to human habitation. This new consciousness was one of the factors leading to Earth Day in April 1970. Inspired by leading environmentalists, notably Senator Gaylord Nelson of Wisconsin, meetings were held in cities throughout the United States calling attention to the fragility of Earth's ecosystem. These meetings warned that headlong pursuit of economic growth and technological power could destroy the planet's viability, and would inevitably impoverish and threaten human life throughout the globe (Environmental Action, 1970).

Overnight, the environment became a national issue. A movement arose with its own organizations, ranging from quiet pressure groups to semi-violent activists, and even with its own flag and colors (Environmental Action, 1971). Nowhere was the movement stronger than on college campuses, where it became a new cause that often absorbed or superseded previous concerns about peace, poverty, and civil rights, often to the chagrin of promoters of these causes (Neuhaus, 1971). These promoters failed to realize what many of the young did— that if the earth became uninhabitable for mankind, none of these other problems would have meaning. Concern over population growth, resource conservation, pollution, and environmental degradation coalesced into a new movement which regarded them as parts of an overall world crisis. For the first time in history, informed people throughout the world were confronted with the possibility that industrial civilization was not only threatening the good things of life but also life itself.

The pessimistic view of the future involves a number of propositions about the nature of the world and the human condition, all of which have complex ramifications. But it rests on two basic propositions which its exponents have sought to implant into the general consciousness. The first is that the earth is a single system (in some respects an ecosystem) in which everything that takes place potentially affects everything else to a greater or lesser degree. Explosion of an atomic bomb in Nevada or China poisons a mother's milk in Turkey or Tibet. DDT used on farms in Argentina or Africa can destroy the marine life in distant seas. Changes in air temperature caused by industrial activity can affect the polar ice caps, and cutting down trees in the Amazon can deplete the oxygen supply of the entire world. The nature and incidence of the effects of particular actions may be debatable, but that they have secondary effects across continents and into the future can no longer be argued. Just as problems in one area or one realm of life affect others—climactic changes influencing economics, economics affecting politics, politics in turn involving decisions that have an impact on climate, e.g., the Soviet plans for turning major rivers southward for irrigation purposes—so also solutions are as interrelated as problems. In a sense there is only one total global problem, however complex its ramifications—what one of the founders of the Club of Rome, the Italian industrialist Aurelio Peccei, called the "world problematique" (Peccei, 1969). In itself, this proposition of the interrelatedness of the globe is neither pessimistic nor optimistic in its implications, although it does suggest the difficulty of discovering and implementing solutions. To this proposition pessimists add the further caveat that various elements of the world problem, especially its negative elements, have been increasing exponentially. This is not simply a modification of the basic Malthusian proposition; it is also an empirical generalization that can be made from observable data. Population has been growing exponentially over the last 100 years at least. Consumption of various minerals and even of water has been growing exponentially. So have various indices of pollution. It is a simple mathematical exercise to extrapolate these growth curves to the point where population becomes enormous, resources nonexistent, and pollution unbearable (Ehrlich and Ehrlich, 1970). Analogues with natural, especially biological, processes suggest that all curves are S-curves and reach asymptotes after which they turn downward and backward. Such growth will ultimately stop. But if growth is not consciously halted by a human agency it will be by such scourges as famine, disease, and natural disasters.

By combining the propositions that the world's problems are all interrelated and that certain exponential rates of growth are inherently disastrous, one can only conclude that the world as a whole is headed for disaster unless somehow the world's course can be changed. The question becomes, in the words of the title of a broadcast series produced by CBS TV in the early 1970s, "Can the World Be Saved?"

Is such concatenated disaster likely or inevitable? Many of the particular propositions leading to and creating these general propositions were combined in a computer-generated scenario using the model of systems dynamics developed by Professor Jay Forrester of the Massachusetts Institute of Technology (Forrester, 1971). In 1972, the Club of

Rome published a little book called *The Limits to Growth* (Meadows, et al., 1972), with great attendant publicity. The book argued that, unless certain trends were checked, the interactions of population growth, resource use, industrial productivity, and pollution generation would lead to the global collapse of industrial civilization by the first decades of the twenty-first century. This model of doom was widely accepted in many influential academic and political quarters. Ironically, it was accepted in large measure because, unlike earlier broadside attacks on contemporary industrial civilization, it was itself the product of advanced technology, its methodology being rationalistic and quantitative rather than romantic and impressionistic. Science, which once seemed to promise that utopia was at hand, now appeared to be telling us that, as a result of the unlimited expansion of a science-based socioeconomic system, disaster was imminent. Since its publication, *The Limits to Growth* and its central theses have been widely criticized in terms of both data and methodology (Cole, et al., 1973). Moreoever, subsequent reports of the Club of Rome have disaggregated, if not substantially modified, its conclusions (Mesarovic and Pestel, 1974). But despite the creation of facile scenarios for continued progress by various individuals and groups such as the Hudson Institute, no one has yet produced an overall model of the future comparable to *The Limits of Growth* in empirical complexity and theoretical rigor and leading to substantially less pessimistic conclusions. The existence of this model has put the possibility of doom on the intellectual agenda of every thinking human being. More than that, it has provided a backdrop for different and more particular pessimistic forecasts, in much the same way as in earlier centuries the quasi-knowledge of particular triumphs of science led most human beings to believe in the inevitability of progress.

In recent years, a large literature pessimistic of the human future has arisen. Many of the scenarios suggested or propositions advanced are mutually exclusive in the long run but not necessarily so in the shorter term. That is, nuclear war can destroy civilization before famine undermines it, but this does not mean, as some authors may suggest, that we are not now moving in the direction of both disasters. Just as particular exponents of pessimistic viewpoints claiming scientific legitimation differ, so the pessimistic dystopian literature of contemporary science fiction, which has helped popularize a mood of pessimism, also differs. The same author sometimes suggests alternative futures for mankind which are almost equally bleak (Brunner, 1969, 1973). Nonetheless, it is possible to extract and comment upon certain prevalent themes in the literature of pessimism.

Perhaps the most widely accepted single factor leading to a pessimistic view of the future is population growth. Even if the growth of world population should stop at under 7 million, as the most optimistic demographers believe possible, this would be an enormous increase over the present population level. This vast increase leads those who decry it to anticipate certain dire consequences: shortages of food reaching famine proportions, which will in turn lead to misery and to internal and external wars; greatly increasing pollution; and scarcity of a variety of finite resources, not the least of which is space (Ehrlich, 1968, 1974). Fear of these consequences of population increase is widespread among the educated of the world, especially in the West. It has already been a factor in lowering birthrates among some groups and has figured in government policy. Those who argue that the world population is more likely to level off at 15 billion people or so (Kahn, 1976, p. 7), but that this will be all right since technology will unlock new resources to take care of them, do little to assuage this fear since the evidence is far stronger for the first element in this proposition than for the second.

Fear of increasing pollution and its effects is also widespread, particularly among the more educated and affluent of the Western world. It is a common observation that pollution stems largely from economic growth, and it is feared that the increase in economic growth will inevitably mean an increase in pollution. Pollution is condemned for its effects on the amenities of life and on human health—however difficult it is to measure these health effects because they are cumulative and negatively synergistic (Schwartz, 1971). Although pollution is often the effect of economic growth, it can also retard it. For example, water polluted by industrial use is often useless for irrigation, and various forms of chemical and atmospheric pollutants can negatively affect the productivity of agriculture and fisheries. Just as the population pessimists fear a "standing room only" world populated by starving billions, so those who are the most pessimistic about pollution foresee a world of unbreathable air, undrinkable water, and widespread danger and ugliness. Unchecked pollution can mean slow disaster as well as spectacular catastrophes such as localized killer smogs. Perhaps the most extreme case of disaster through pollution would be nuclear mishaps in a society based on nuclear energy. Nuclear accidents could kill millions and seriously harm countless others (Ruedisli and Firebaugh, 1975, pp. 262–272).

The scarcity of resources is increasingly being perceived as a national and international problem. The shock of the first Arab oil embargo, however shortlived its immediate effects, was an obvious turning point. Insofar as modern industrial societies are dependent upon exponentially increasing use of materials, most of which are in finite even if not in short supply, these societies are increasingly threatened with economic dislocation or even collapse and the attendant social conflicts and breakdowns; international wars over dwindling, scarce resources; and, at the very least, a change in the economic balance of power in the world from the dominance of raw material consumers to that of raw material producers. This change in the balance of power would reverse a trend as old as the expansion of Western civilization and would entail unmeasurable economic, political, social, and cultural consequences (Ashby, 1976).

All of the above disasters can be thought of first in physical and then in political and cultural terms. Some futurists are pessimistic because they believe that, even if mankind could continue to support a growing population through technology, in the process technology and science would, to a greater or lesser degree, threaten the very humanity of the race. Fear is still widely expressed that computers may lead to regimentation and the destruction of privacy; that automation may create regimentation and/or meaningless anomic leisure; and that genetic discoveries will ultimately destroy traditional family and sex roles, deprive man of his biological identity, or as a result of science's creation of new and uncontrollable life forms, lead to catastrophes (Taylor, 1969). The old fears about science and the machine as enemies of human freedom and identity have been supplemented by fears that science cannot deliver the goods in terms of material sustenance. The present fear is that the world of the future may be *both* mechanized and impoverished.

Some pessimists see total disaster as the outcome if mankind continues on its present course. According to various doomsday scenarios all the forces of destruction, acting in a cumulative and mutually reinforcing manner, will lead to an "ecocatastrophe." For example, the pressures of population on scarce resources will lead to minor wars which will wreak havoc on the ecosystem, causing crop failures, famine, disease, and eventually all-out nuclear war (Ehrlich, 1969; Watt, 1974). For such extreme pessimists, man's very ability to survive as a biological species is increasingly in jeopardy. Ironically, these prophets of doom have been joined and reinforced psychologically, if not logically, by a growing number of thinkers who argue that nature itself is increasingly restive and is preparing to assault the proud towers of technological civilization with catastrophes of its own making—a new ice age, a resumption of massive volcanic activity, or some other abrupt change in the balance of nature which would reinforce the effects of human heedlessness (Webre and Liss, 1975).

Not all pessimists carry their pessimism to such extremes. Many argue that even if the human race and/or human civilization as we know it is not imminently threatened by global catastrophe, the pressures of shortages and pollution and the dangers of our technology, especially nuclear technology, can or will lead to famine, pestilence, and war. Some believe the very complexity of modern technological civilization will lead to inevitable organizational breakdown (Vacca, 1973). For this school of pessimists, the human race will avert physical catastrophe, but only at the cost of what some might regard as social catastrophe.

This point of view is somewhat similar to the argument that it may be physically possible to avert the ecological doomsday toward which we are heading, but it may not be politically and socially possible to take the necessary measures in time.

Even many who hold that we can avert disaster through social invention and social discipline could be classified as pessimistic inasmuch as most contemporary thinkers would consider the means they describe as necessary to be culturally repressive. An example is the argument of the noted economist Robert Heilbroner, that an authoritarian society operating under some system of military or monastic socialism can deal with shortages, pollution, and nuclear proliferation (1974, 1975). Such seers argue in effect that we can avoid physical doomsday or major catastrophe only at the cost of cultural regression, which many regard as doom itself.

To what extent is the pessimistic view justified? The prophets of doom are under attack from the optimists from two different angles, on the basis of arguments that are logically independent of one another. The first line of argument amounts to "blaming the messenger," a kind of massive *argumentum ad hominum.* The optimists claim that some foresee disaster for humanity because they mistakenly identify humanity with their own class, race, or nation. The current attack on the cultural fruits of technology and its ability to support an ever-increasing population, it is alleged or implied, is akin to the attacks that entrenched reactionaries made on the democratizing the liberating effects of the Industrial Revolution. It is the white, upper and upper-middle classes who are concerned about environment, ecology, population, and mechanization because they see their special privileges or life-styles threatened (Neuhaus, 1971). The doomsayers are indeed all basically birdwatchers, uninterested in the real concerns of the majority of the nation's, or the world's, inhabitants who are poor and want and need economic growth, even at the cost of the mass production that replaces handicrafts or the oil refineries that replace bird sanctuaries (Johnson, 1973). Pessimism is racist and classist, the jeremiad of a declining and selfish upper class. What is true within the advanced industrial nations is even more true on a world scale. Pessimism about what the future will be like if present trends continue is the attempt of an international elite of groups and nations to prevent the growth of others to equal status. Pessimism is rampant in countries such as the United States and among some in Western Europe because they see their role in the world declining. On the other hand, optimism is the normal pose for those in the rapidly developing nations and the socialist camp who are now at last coming into their own.

Undoubtedly, this line of argument has some plausibility. It is in fact the more educated and affluent in the world who are most pessimistic and fearful of actual or imminent loss. Even if this is true, it may only prove that they are the most clearsighted about the dangers that threaten the world as a whole; every movement of thought and action in history has been the creation of minorities. Even if the reasons can be found to account for the reception of certain ideas by certain audiences, this does not say anything about the objective truth of propositions about the future.

The question of the validity of the pessimist position about the future, then, must turn on questions of fact and data and their interpretation. Insofar as the pessimists' critics seriously address the substance of the pessimistic argument rather than resort to personal denunciations of pessimists as elitists, leftists, romantics, and the like, or to such simple, quasi-religious affirmations as "any problem created by technology can be solved by more technology" or "mankind has always survived in the past and always will in the future," the criticism of pessimism takes two basic forms. One is the argument that pessimists overaggregate the data with which they deal and oversimplify the issues involved. It is illegitimate, it is claimed, to talk of the world as a whole going to pieces on the basis of averages or the combination of various converging factors since in the real world every part of the globe is in a different state. Some may starve while others may prosper; even with shifting wind currents, not all parts of the earth will be equally polluted. Therefore, projections of overall trends tell us little. Certainly, they do not tell us that at some hypothetical future date the world will go over some brink as a total unit. By the same token, the concept of technology is an oversimplification. Some technologies pollute or devour resources, while others help to alleviate pollution or to stretch out resources. Some technologies menace human freedom or identity, and other technologies contribute to human freedom and integrity. Statements about the future based on averages or grandiose statements about the "dangers posed by technology" are inherently and necessarily false.

The second line of attack is that in any event pessimists are overly deterministic in their view of the future. Sometimes this argument descends to the facile assertion that things may look bad but "something will turn up." However, it often results from a sober and sophisticated view of history and social dynamics. Such a view notes that predictions often prove false because the behavior of individual and combined factors cannot be accurately predicted in advance, and that statements based on such prediction must always be regarded as likely to be false, at least in the form in which they are set forth (Nisbet, 1974). At any rate, it is alleged, human beings can do something about the future. We do not live in a deterministic universe.

How justifiable are such criticisms of the pessimistic view? First, it should be emphasized that, despite the claims of computer programmers on both sides, the arguments between the optimists and pessimists are subject to the same kind of scientific proof as that involved in laboratory experiments, or even in arguments about the role of antislavery sentiment in causing the American Civil War. Human beings observe phenomena in the world about them and construct schemes for regularizing their observations and making them intelligible. Various observations and data can be fitted into varying schemes, and we choose these schemes (called paradigms by some historians of science [Kuhn, 1970]) on the basis of their simplicity, relevance to significant questions, and demonstrated (after-the-fact) ability to help us predict and manipulate the world about us. At present, optimism and pessimism are conflicting paradigms about the human future into either of which virtually all agreed-upon or asserted data can somehow fit. Therefore, while controversy about particular facts (such as the world's "estimated" oil reserves about which the basic data are dreadful), can sharpen the argument and strengthen the logical structure of the conflicting paradigms, it is of little use in proving either true or false. Judgments about which is more valid and useful will have to be made on the basis of canons of credibility that are difficult, if not impossible, to verify in the strict scientific sense.

In this writer's opinion, however, the pessimistic view of the future is nearer to the truth than the optimistic and, on the whole, more functionally useful for creating a humane future. It is highly unlikely that doomsday is imminent, if by this is meant some kind of global catastrophe that will render the world unfit for human habitation. But population continues to increase at rates greater than the ability of the earth to sustain it, and the maldistribution of wealth between areas of different population levels persists. Economic development is not taking place on an adequate scale in the Third World and cannot do so through the use of large-scale technology within the economic framework of capitalism. The population of much of the globe will never achieve the living standards of the currently most fortunate, if by this is meant living in the same manner through the use of the same technological means. Resources are being depleted faster than substitutes can be found, and nuclear energy provides no panacea. Pollution is on the increase and threatens not only health and amenities, but also the stability of local and global ecosystems. Despite rising interest in liberatory technology, powerful economic and political forces and sheer cultural inertia continue to push mankind toward a mechanized society. The issue is not whether it is theoretically possible that by the year 2000 technology will solve these problems and provide a higher real standard of living in conditions of freedom. Rather, the issue is whether such a solution can be developed given the economic stresses existing within the relevant time framework. Tomorrow's problems cannot be solved by the day after tomorrow's technology, financed by the economies of the day after that. Even if presently available and economically feasible technologies could solve our global problems, there is little evidence that the social and political forces necessary to put them to work exist or will emerge. If catastrophe is required to convince human beings of the necessity of taking action, the technical feasibility of such action to prevent catastrophe is irrelevant.

There will therefore be a gradual diminution of living standards in most parts of the world, even as other areas may prosper. Accordingly there will be accelerated conflicts, increased social and political breakdown, and gradual loss of amenities and freedom. These events will occur if the present belief systems and modes of life of modern industrial society persist. This prediction, however pessimistic, is obviously provisional. It assumes that change in belief systems will not take place. Changes are in fact possible in our perceptions of the world, and in our social and political institutions (Ferkiss, 1974; Stavrianos, 1976). Hence, pessimism about the future can only be justified if it is assumed that we live in a deterministic universe and that, foreseeing catastrophe, we cannot take the measures necessary to avert it.

The question then becomes that of which paradigm, the optimistic or the pessimistic, is more functional, not simply in describing the future but in creating it in accordance with our desires to avoid doomsday or any of its less horrendous variations. Optimists argue that if we keep on going as we are everything will work out. The greatest menace to the future, they contend, is pessimism which, by causing us to doubt our ability to succeed in the future, becomes a self-fulfilling prophecy (Kahn, et al., 1976, p. 25). Such an approach is logical only if one assumes an analogy with a runner who is approaching his goal along the correct track and may fail to reach it if he becomes discouraged and slows down or quits in despair. This approach is entirely false, however, if in fact the runner has become confused and is running in the wrong direction, away from his goal.

If the goal of mankind is a sustainable society for the human race in which subsistence, justice, and freedom are available to all, then to ignore the misdirectedness of present lines of development is to betray the future and to make some version of doomsday inevitable. It is those who argue that everything will be all right if we continue our present course and choose to ignore warnings of possible catastrophe who menace the future. It is the pessimists who have for the most part grasped that it is not the human species or civilization itself that is necessarily doomed but the present order of things and the world view that underlies it. Willingness to perceive danger is the first step toward averting it. The case for pessimism rests not only on the greater preponderance of data in its favor but its usefulness, even necessity, as a prelude for building the future.

## REFERENCES

Ashby, Sir Eric. 1976. "A Second Look at Doom." *Encounter*, Volume 46 (March), 16–24.

Bramson, Leon. 1961. *The Political Context of Sociology.* Princeton, N.J.: Princeton University Press.

Brunner, John, 1969. *Stand on Zanzibar.* New York: Ballantine Books.

———. 1973. *The Sheep Look Up.* New York: Ballantine Books.

Butler, Samuel, 1872. *Erewhon.* London: Trubner.

Capek, Karel. 1961. *R.U.R.* London: Oxford University Press. (Originally published in 1921.)

Cole, H. S. D., Christopher Freeman, Marie Jahoda, and K. L. R. Pavitt (eds.). 1973. *Models of Doom: A Critique of the Limits to Growth.* New York: Universe Books.

Editors of *The Ecologist.* 1972. *Blueprint for Survival.* New York: New American Library.

Ehrlich, Paul R. 1968. *The Population Bomb.* New York: Ballantine Books.

———. 1969. "Eco-catastrophe". *Ramparts*, Volume 8, (September) 24–28.

———, and Anne Ehrlich. 1970. *Population, Resources, Environment.* San Francisco: W. H. Freeman.

———. 1974. *The End of Affluence.* New York: Ballantine Books.

Eliade, Mercea. 1954. *The Myth of the Eternal Return.* Princeton, N.J.: Princeton University Press.

Ellul, Jacques. 1964. *The Technological Society.* New York: Alfred A. Knopf. (First published in 1954.)

Environmental Action National Staff. 1970. *Earth Day—The Beginning.* New York: Bantam Books.

———. 1971. *Earth Tool Kit.* New York: Pocket Books.

Ferkiss, Victor. 1969. *Technological Man.* New York: George Braziller.

———. 1974. *The Future of Technological Civilization.* New York: George Braziller.

Forrester, Jay. 1971. *World Dynamics.* Cambridge, Mass.: Wright-Allen Press.

Heilbroner, Robert F. 1974. *An Inquiry into the Human Prospect.* New York: W. W. Norton.

———. 1975. "The Human Prospect—Second Thoughts." *Futures*, Volume 7, 31–40.

Huxley, Aldous. 1932. *Brave New World.* New York: Doubleday-Doran.

Johnson, Willard R. 1973. "Should the Poor Buy No Growth?" *Daedalus*, Volume 102 (Fall), 165–189.

Juenger, Friedrich George. 1956. *The Failure of Technology.* Chicago: Henry Regnery.

Kahn, Herman, with William Brown, and Leon Martel. 1976. *The Next Two Hundred Years.* New York: William Morrow.

Kuhn, Thomas. 1970. *The Structure of Scientific Revolutions.* Chicago: University of Chicago Press.

Marsh, George Perkins. 1864. *Man and Nature.* New York: Scribners.

Meadows, Donella H., Dennis Meadows, et al. 1972. *The Limits to Growth.* New York: Universe Books.

Mesarovic, Mihajlo, and Eduard Pestel. 1974. *Mankind at the Turning Point.* New York: E. P. Dutton.

Neuhaus, Richard J. 1971. *In Defense of People.* New York: Macmillan Co.

Nisbet, Robert A. 1974. "The Year 2000 and All That." In Albert Somit (ed.), *Political Science and the Study of the Future.* New York: Dryden Press, 257–267.

Orwell, George. 1949. *1984.* New York: Harcourt Brace.

Osborn, Fairfield, 1948. *Our Plundered Planet.* Boston: Little, Brown and Co.

Peccei, Aurelio. 1969. *The Chasm Ahead.* New York: Macmillan Co.

Pirages, Dennis, and Paul R. Ehrlich. 1974. *Ark II.* New York: Viking Press.

Polak, Fred L. 1973. *The Image of the Future.* New York: Elsevier.

Roszak, Theodore. 1972. *Where the Wasteland Ends.* New York: Doubleday.

Ruedisli, Lon C., and Morris W. Firebaugh (eds.). 1975. *Perspectives on Energy.* New York: Oxford University Press.

Schwartz, Eugene S. 1971. *Overskill.* Chicago: Quadrangle Books.

Snow, C. P. 1959. *The Two Cultures and the Scientific Revolution.* Cambridge, England: Cambridge University Press.

Stavrianos, L. S. 1976. *The Promise of the Coming Dark Age.* San Francisco: W. H. Freeman.

Taylor, Gordon Rattrey. 1969. *The Biological Time Bomb.* New York: Signet Books.

Tuchman, Barbara, 1963. *The Guns of August.* New York: Dell Books.

Vacca, Roberto. 1973. *The Coming Dark Age.* New York: Anchor Books.

Vogt, William. 1948. *The Road to Survival.* New York: William Sloane Associates.

Watt, Kenneth E. F. 1974. *The Titanic Effect.* New York: E. P. Dutton.

Webre, Alfred L., and Philip H. Liss. 1975. *The Age of Cataclysm.* New York: G. P. Putnam's Sons.

Zamiatin, Eugene. 1924. *We.* New York: E. P. Dutton.

JAY W. FORRESTER

# Sharpening the Debate Over the Future

The debate on growth needs a sharpened focus. Much of the past discussion has been too general to couple with practical issues. A more effective resolution of growth questions might follow from three changes in perspective: (1) More emphasis on social limits and on the trade-off between physical limits and social limits; (2) more attention to solutions at the national level where effective institutions exist, rather than at the world or regional levels where institutions are weak compared to the forces created by growth and by limits; and (3) more awareness of intermediate modes of dynamic behavior that lie between the short-term business cycle and the long-term life cycle of growth.

## SOCIAL LIMITS

The first change of perspective should be from physical to social limits. Much of the limits to growth debate has focused too narrowly on physical constraints. Restricting debate to physical limits invites hope that technology can circumvent such limits. Indeed, technology might do so for quite some time. But any expectation that shortages of energy and food can be overcome will be used by people and governments as an excuse to avoid facing the issues posed by growth of population and social stress.

Through growth in population, a reduction of physical pressures can be transformed into an increase in social pressures. If physical limits seem less threatening, then concern about population growth will be temporarily relaxed. If physical support appears possible, the easy course is to ignore population growth. But rising population density is surely at the root of many social stresses. Crowding, psychological pressures, and lack of individual purpose, arising from increased population and a more complex technological society, accentuate frustration and antisocial behavior. Pushing back physical limits has encouraged population growth, but, as a consequence, rising population density will shift pressures to social limits.

Social limits already exert growing pressure in the form of drug addiction, kidnappings, aircraft hijackings, sabotage, revolution, and a returning threat of atomic war. Technological complexity also produces more subtle pressures in the form of questioning the legitimacy of institutions. Social limits are not relieved by more emphasis on technology. Quite the contrary, increased technology has increased per capita income while creating a more complex and vulnerable society. A complex technological society is at the same time harder to understand, more difficult to accept, and easier to disrupt. Complexity increases frustration and disenchantment, while also increasing vulnerability to either individual or organized interference.

In public debate over physical limits, the desirability of technological success is seldom questioned. For example, in the present energy shortage, the first question should not be, "Can technology provide unlimited energy?" Instead, we should ask, "If unlimited energy were available, should we want it?" To ask for unlimited energy is to favor shifting the restraint on growth from physical limits to social limits. Energy can be converted to food for support of population that will then be more apt to grow until social breakdown occurs. Society should want to choose the least traumatic mix of growth-limiting pressures. We will most likely do better with distributed than with concentrated pressures. Rather than limit growth by social stresses alone, a combination of social and physical pressures probably will generate a smoother transition from growth to equilibrium. Some social threats, some energy and materials shortages, some inadequacy of food, and some pollution would exert a balanced set of restraints until people began to accept the inherent trade-off between the rising population and falling quality of life.

Therefore, the debate over physical limits seems unbalanced. It can divert governments and the public from the ultimate necessity of striking a compromise between population, standard of living, and quality of the natural environment. The issue of physical limits obscures a rising threat from social limits. As population growth continues, aided and abetted by intensifying technology, complexity increases. With greater complexity comes stronger tendencies for social breakdown and at the same time more vulnerability to disruption. The debate on growth has so far been largely between environmentalists on one side and economists and technologists on the other. The issues should be broadened to include more input from sociologists, political scientists, and theologians. The nonphysical side of man needs stronger representation.

## NATIONAL FOCUS FOR ACTION

The second change in perspective should be from world limits to national limits. Although the problem of growth in a finite world can be stated on a one-world basis, solutions seem likely to come only from the national level because only national institutions have the power to act.

The limits to growth debate has concentrated on the entire world or on major regions. *The Limits to Growth* coalesced the world into one system (Meadows et al., 1972). Such a single aggregate is useful for stating the problem. The book, *Mankind at the Turning Point*, divided the world into several regions (Mesarovic and Pestel, 1974). Subdivision into major areas is useful for looking at differences between dissimilar regions. The United Nations debates food shortages and economic development as world problems; such broad and general treatment is useful for alerting member nations to the issues. However, implementation of effective policies for restraining growth and achieving a desirable equilibrium cannot be expected on a uniform world or regional scale.

For areas larger than countries, no authority capable of dealing with growth exists. Neither the United Nations nor the regional confederations have power to strike a balance in the trade-off between population and standard of living. Nor is it clear that the trade-off should even be desired at the world level.

A wide range of compromise is possible between size of population and conditions for living. Different cultures might choose different compromises. Some countries would allow a higher population and accept a lower standard of living, and others would take steps to stabilize population before the capacity of its geography had become so fully committed.

If countries retain the freedom to choose the trade-off between population and standard of living, then physical equality between countries is not possible. Different countries will arrive at different balances. Freedom of choice and worldwide equality are incompatible. If there were to be physical equality on a global scale, some authority would be required to impose uniform standards for the balance between population density and geographical capacity. While such external imposition of population standards is most unlikely to be accepted, without such standards, material equality will be impossible.

Most countries are now acting as if their shortages could forever be met from the outside, but as worldwide limits to growth are ever more closely approached, there is less slack in the world system. International trade has depended on such slack. Although many countries have supported their population growth with imports, as every area becomes more heavily loaded, less is available for others. The time is approaching when each country must more and more meet its growth-induced needs from within its own borders.

If a country believes that solutions for its stresses can be found outside, then failure to achieve solutions would naturally be attributed to others. When both the source of the problem and the potential solution are believed to lie across the border, such is the basis for war. Unless population is to be restrained by war and genocide, nations must look inward. If each nation comes to terms with its own geographical capacity, international tension can be reduced.

Suggesting that nations think in terms of self-suffiency is not a favorable proposal to the developed countries. Most industrial countries have been living beyond their geographical means. They have imported energy and resources at low prices, depressed by excess world supply. They have exported manufactured goods at high prices, sustained by a world shortage of industrial capacity. The imbalance is reversing, however. Energy and resources are becoming scarce, and prices will rise. Manufacturing capacity and technical skills are becoming widespread, and relative prices will fall. To live within their own capabilities, most industrial countries face a more traumatic transition than many developing countries. Of all the developed countries, Japan is probably the most vulnerable. Without foreign energy, foreign resources, and foreign markets, in the not to distant future life in Japan will be far different. Close behind Japan in vulnerability are Western Europe and then the United States. Countries with sufficient energy and resources are rapidly acquiring industrial knowledge and plant capacity to manufacture with their own labor for their own markets.

If industrial countries see their plight as having been caused by countries that withdraw supplies and markets, then war is apt to be chosen as the obvious solution. If, however, industrial countries recognize their own growth as having been the cause of social and economic pressure, then internal adaptation, with any necessary reduction in standard of living, becomes an appropriate solution. Through a general recognition that growth pressures come from national, not international, actions, we may avoid atomic war as the ultimate limit to growth.

This proposal to put limits to growth in the national context is quite the reverse of most present discussions for sharing and for human equality that imply that others have created the problems and must be responsible for solutions. Such is the basis for distrust and conflict.

Any course of action has weaknesses and disadvantages. Three are of particular concern in choosing the national route for dealing with growth. First, countries that limit population and thereby sustain attractive living conditions must be able to police their borders and prevent inundation by people from countries where population has grown beyond the national capacity. Some countries may be so small or have such unfavorable border conditions that they cannot adopt policies of self-sufficiency. Such countries will probably be absorbed into larger political units. Second, individual freedom to migrate across national borders will be severely restricted when overpopulation is recognized as the critical limit in every country. Third, some international discipline will still be needed to prevent any one country from serving itself at the expense of other countries. For example, a country must not be allowed to discharge pollutants that threaten other countries or the rights of others in the oceans and atmosphere. These issues are more limited and manageable than trying to cope on a uniform worldwide basis with population control, equality, common standards for quality of life, and yielding of national sovereignty to a powerful central authority.

Thus, this second change of perspective from limits to growth as a single world issue would lead to decentralization of limits for separate handling by individual nations. Each nation could then address the questions of how much population it could support at a desired standard of living; how it could develop its future without taking environmental capacity from others; and how it could discourage population from rising above the target level. No country, rich or poor, seems to have accepted such internal questions as its top priority. Instead, most countries are using external issues of world energy, distribution of food, and international investment as ways to divert their citizens from the difficult task of shaping their own future. I see no promising avenue but to reverse foreign adventurism, turn inward, establish national self-sufficiency in each country, and solve global problems by taking appropriate action separately in each part of the world. This position should enhance national and global stability in a world of geographic and cultural diversity.

## INTERMEDIATE DYNAMICS

The third change in perspective should be from exclusive concern with the life cycle of growth to the multiplicity of dynamic modes inherent in a national economy.

Different groups tend to be concerned with different time behaviors in our social system. In the time dimension, a growing minority is presently concerned with the very long run, while most people in commerce and government do not look beyond the short-term business cycle. For those who are interested in stresses arising from growth and who are seeking a viable long-run equilibrium, the life cycle of growth extends several hundred years backward and at least a hundred years forward, and encompasses the period of exponential growth, the transition period of growth being suppressed by environmental forces, and a future equilibrium. In contrast, the business-cycle perspective is only some five years wide. With such different time horizons, lack of serious communication between the two groups is almost inevitable. Failure to see things the same way is unavoidable because, in the time dimension, the two groups have little in common.

The economic system contains intermediate modes of behavior that may serve to bridge the gap in viewpoints. The literature of politics, public attitudes, and economics is rich in discussion of important changes occurring over several decades. Our social systems contain the diversities of structure necessary to create many simultaneous modes of behavior spread throughout the time range from a few months to a few centuries.

The intermediate dynamic modes in society are important. Not only do they fill the behavior spectrum between the extremes, but, more importantly, they generate symptoms that confuse and mislead those who focus on either extreme. Changes whose characteristic time intervals are in the fifteen- to sixty-year range can easily be misinterpreted as belonging to either the business cycle or to the life cycle of growth. When intermediate modes are attributed to one extreme or the other, the extremes are incorrectly perceived and the middle ground of dynamic behavior is lost as a common basis for communication.

After the work on *World Dynamics* (Forrester, 1971) and *The Limits to Growth* (Meadows et al., 1972), the MIT System Dynamics Group has been looking at the full range of time spans of behavior in social and economic change at the national level. We belive that social and economic change must be linked together and that the design of improved national policies will be of the greatest practical effectiveness.

MIT has been developing a system dynamics model (J. Forrester, 1961, 1968, 1971, 1975; Meadows, 1973, 1974; N. Forrester, 1972; Mass, 1975) of the national economy. The model contains some fifteen industrial sectors, worker mobility networks between sectors for both labor and professionals, and household, demographic, financial, and government sectors. When fully assembled, the model will have nearly a hundred times as much detail as *The Limits to Growth* model.

Simulation studies have thus far been conducted with one and two industrial sectors of the National Model (of some fifteen ultimate sectors). Even this limited part of the whole economy generates simultaneously a wide range of periodic fluctuations. Several different modes of cyclic behavior originate from the interactions of inventories, production rate, acquisition of labor and capital, and supply interconnections between different sectors.

In a complex economic structure, many different dynamic modes of fluctuating activity can exist simultaneously. Much puzzling economic behavior probably arises from multiple modes superimposing their patterns of interaction. If identities of the separate modes are not recognized, symptoms arising from one part of the system may be misinterpreted and applied to policy control points in some entirely different part of the system. Policy is then ineffective because it only remotely relates to the symptoms that inspired the policy.

An extensive literature deals with each of three different modes of periodic fluctuation in the economy—the business cycle, the Kuznets cycle, and the Kondratieff cycle.

The business cycle, the well-known short-term fluctuation of business activity, appears as varying production rates and employment, with peaks of activity separated by some three to seven years. Business cycles lie within the experience of most persons and are the focus of attention in the press and in governmental policy debates.

The much less generally recognized Kuznets cycle (Abramovitz, 1961; Gordon, 1951) exists as a statistical observation that many time series in the economy seem to exhibit a periodicity of fifteen to twenty-five years. The source of the Kuznets cycle has been a subject of debate. It has received little public attention because other cyclic modes in the economy are of sufficient magnitude to mask the Kuznets cycle from popular awareness.

Finally, the Kondratieff cycle (Kondratieff, 1935; Garvy, 1943) is a fluctuation in the economy characterized by intervals of about fifty years between peaks, which are separated by long valleys of stagnation.

Simulation studies with the new MIT System Dynamics National Model of the economy have shown that physical relationships and decision-making policies in the production of consumer durables and capital equipment can generate simultaneously all three major periodicities—the business, Kuznets, and Kondratieff cycles (Forrester, 1975). The short-term business cycle can be generated by interactions among backlogs, inventories, production, and employment without requiring involvement of capital investment or changes in consumer income. The Kuznets cycle is consistent with policies governing production and the acquisition of capital equipment. The fifty-year Kondratieff cycle can arise from the structural setting of the capital-equipment sector, which supplies capital to the consumer-goods sector but also at the same time must procure its own input capital equipment from its own output.

Those concerned about the hazards of growth may be misled by the Kondratieff cycle. Much of the upward thrust of economic activity in the last three decades may be a consequence of expansion in the capital sectors that seems to go with the rising phase of the long wave. If so, the economic processes will not sustain themselves forever. When capital expansion has run its course, accompanied by heavy debts and nonsustainable rates of public and private borrowing, an internal readjustment must begin. In such a readjustment, capital sectors decline, unemployment increases, people move back toward food and consumer-products sectors, and growth is suspended or reversed. Such conditions may confuse the limits to growth debate. Those attempting to reduce unemployment and increase short-term economic growth may blame the downturn on environmentalists and adherents of an equilibrium society. On the other hand, proponents of equilibrium may misinterpret a downturn in the long wave as arrival of a nongrowth future. Instead, the downturn, like the upward phase, may be only a consequence of imbalance. If so, the end of growth would not represent a sustainable equilibrium.

A period of slackening growth, arising as a consequence of internal dynamics of the Western economies, should be taken as an interlude in which to accelerate discussion of future alternatives.

## SUMMARY

The limits to growth debate deals with the most important issue of our times, but the particular form of the debate often fails to produce effective action. Discussion could be led into more practical channels by three changes in perspective.

First, emphasis should shift from concentration on physical limits to a greater concern for social limits. The controversy over physical limits creates a public impression that growth is desirable if physical limits can be overcome. However, to the extent that physical limits are pushed back, or are merely expected to be pushed back, emphasis on stabilizing population will be reduced. But rising population density almost certainly leads to increased social stress. Social stress appears as mistrust between groups, personal alienation from society, disrespect for government, civil strife, and international conflict. Social breakdown looms as the ultimate limit to growth. So far, limits to growth has been a subject for environmentalists, economists, and technologists. As the trade-off between social and physical limits becomes more apparent, discussion should be broadened to include social, religious, and political viewpoints.

Second, emphasis should shift from world limits and world solutions to national limits and a national balance between population and environmental capacity of a particular country. The debate on limits to growth has tended to focus on the world as a whole, major regions, and on issues outside any particular country. Such an external perspective implies that any problem belongs to or is caused by someone else. No country, however, can evade the social and physical limits to growth. Furthermore, only nations have effective political processes. Using the external perspective, people see difficulties as being imposed from the outside and war against others as the solution. By contrast, from the internal perspective, a country would perceive world pressures as the consequence of local pressures and striking an internal balance as the solution. Until the inner perspective becomes widely established, major war is increasingly likely as the limit to growth.

Third, emphasis should converge from extremes represented by the short-term business cycle and the broad sweep of the life cycle of growth to include fluctuations of intermediate duration in economic affairs. Different groups tend to concentrate on different behavior modes in society. The public, business, and government are enmeshed in short-term business cycles. At the other end of the time spectrum, proponents of an equilibrium society deal almost exclusively with the life cycle of growth. Over the life cycle of growth, growth gives way to a transition region of conflicting pressures that eventually lead to some future form of equilibrium. However, between the business cycle and the life cycle of growth are dynamic changes running for several decades. Such intermediate modes are usually ignored or misinterpreted by those interested in either extreme of time span. Of particular importance is the possibility of a fluctuation in the economy of some fifty years duration known as the Kondratieff cycle.

If a Kondratieff cycle exists, it should significantly affect thinking about both the business cycle and the life cycle of growth. The business cycle has usually been interpreted without regard for the possibility of its being superimposed on an intermediate fluctuation such as the Kondratieff cycle. Interaction between the Kondratieff cycle and the business cycle may have led to erroneous explanations of recessions and depressions, and to inappropriate policies for economic stabilization. At the same time, the rising phase of a Kondratieff cycle may have been confused with long-term growth. A fifty-year intermediate fluctuation that influences symptoms of both business cycles and the life cycle of growth could serve as a bridge for closing the communication gap between short-term and long-term interests.

Those who would be leaders toward a sustainable future must thread their way through the multiple cross-currents in social and economic change. Effective leadership must be built on sensitivity to important trade-offs, awareness of institutional influence, and knowledge of the social processes shaping the future. Toward these ends, the most important trade-off lies between social and physical limits; the institutional choice should favor the nation over multinational organizations; and the analysis of social processes should emphasize the intermediate changes occurring over several decades that create expectations, cause population movement, and restrict economies.

## REFERENCES

Abramovitz, Moses. 1961. "The Nature and Significance of Kuznets Cycles." *Economic Development and Cultural Change,* Volume 9, (April), 225–248.

Daly, Herman E. 1973. *Toward a Steady-State Economy.* San Francisco: W. H. Freeman.

Forrester, Jay W. 1961. *Industrial Dynamics.* Cambridge, Mass.: MIT Press.

———. 1968. *Principles of Systems.* Cambridge, Mass.: Wright-Allen Press.

———. 1971. *World Dynamics.* Cambridge, Mass.: Wright-Allen Press.

——. 1975. *Collected Papers of Jay W. Forrester.* Cambridge, Mass.: Wright-Allen Press.

———. 1976. "Business Structure, Economic Cycles, and National Policy." *Business Economics,* Volume 11, Number 1 (January), 13–24.

Forrester, Nathan B. 1972. *The Life Cycle of Economic Development.* Cambridge, Mass.: Wright-Allen Press.

Garvy, George. 1943. "Kondratieff's Theory of Long Cycles." *Review of Economic Statistics,* Volume 25, Number 4 (November), 203–220.

Gordon, Robert A. 1951. *Business Fluctuations.* New York: Harper and Row.

Kondratieff, N. D. 1935. "The Long Waves in Economic Life." *Review of Economic Statistics,* Volume 17, Number 6 (November), 105–115.

Mass, Nathaniel J. 1975. *Economic Cycles: An Analysis of Underlying Causes.* Cambridge, Mass.: Wright-Allen Press.

Meadows, Dennis L., and Donella H. Meadows (eds.). 1973. *Toward Global Equilibrium: Collected Papers.* Cambridge, Mass.: Wright-Allen Press.

———, et al. 1974. *Dynamics of Growth in a Finite World.* Cambridge, Mass.: Wright-Allen Press.

Meadows, Donella H., Dennis Meadows, et al. 1972. *The Limits to Growth.* New York: Universe Books.

Mesarovic, Mihajlo, and Eduard Pestel. 1974. *Mankind at the Turning Point.* New York: E. P. Dutton.

# The Postindustrial Economy

The concept "postindustrial" is counterposed to that of "pre-industrial" and "industrial." A preindustrial sector is primarily *extractive,* its economy based on agriculture, mining, fishing, timber, and other resources such as natural gas or oil. An industrial sector is primarily *fabricating,* using energy and machine technology, for the manufacture of goods. A postindustrial sector is one of *processing* in which telecommunications and computers are strategic for the exchange of information and knowledge.

In recent years, the world has become dramatically aware of the strategic role of energy and natural resources as limiting factors of industrial growth, and the question is raised whether these limitations do not modify the onset of a postindustrial sector.

To this, there is an empirical and a theoretical answer. As a practical fact, the introduction of postindustrial elements, which are capital-intensive, does depend—in the timing, rate of diffusion, and extensivity of use—on the productivity of the other sectors. The development of an industrial sector depends in considerable measure on the economic surplus of an agrarian sector; yet, once industrialization is under way, the productivity of the agrarian sector itself is increased through the use of fertilizer and other petrochemical products. Similarly, the introduction of new information and processing devices may be delayed by rising costs in the industrial sector or lagging productivity, but once introduced they may be the very means of raising that productivity.

Theoretically, one can say that postindustrial society is, *in principle,* different from the other two. As a theoretical principle, the idea of industrialism did not derive from an agrarian mode. And similarly, the strategic role of theoretical knowledge as the new basis of technological innovation, or the role of information in recreating social

SOURCE: Excerpted from the Foreword: 1976 from *The Coming of Post-Industrial Society: A Venture in Social Forecasting* by Daniel Bell. © 1973 by Daniel Bell, © 1976 by Daniel Bell. Basic Books, Inc., Publishers, New York. Reprinted by permission of Basic Books, Inc.

processes, does not derive from the role of energy in creating a manufacturing or fabricating society. In short, these are, *analytically,* independent principles.

Broadly speaking, if industrial society is based on machine technology, postindustrial society is shaped by an intellectual technology.
And if capital and labor are the major structural features of industrial
society, information and knowledge are those of the postindustrial
society.[1] For this reason, the social organization of a postindustrial
sector is vastly different from an industrial sector, and one can see this
by contrasting the economic features of the two.

Industrial commodities are produced in discrete, identifiable units,
exchanged and sold, consumed and used up, as are a loaf of bread or
an automobile. One buys the products from a seller and takes physical
possession of it. The exchange is governed by specific legal rules of
contract. But information and knowledge are not consumed or "used
up." Knowledge is a *social* product and the question of its costs, price,
or value is vastly different from that of industrial items.

In the manufacture of industrial goods, one can set up a "production
function" (i.e., the relative proportions of capital and labor to be employed) and determine the appropriate mix, at the relative costs, of
each factor. If capital is embodied labor, one can talk of a labor theory
of value.

But a postindustrial society is characterized not by a labor theory but
by a knowledge theory of value.[2] It is the codification of knowledge that
becomes directive of innovation. Yet knowledge, even when it is sold,
remains also with the producer. It is a "collective good" in that, once it
has been created, it is by its character available to all. Thus, there is
little incentive for any single person or enterprise to pay for the production of such knowledge unless they can obtain a proprietary advantage,
such as a patent or a copyright. But, increasingly, patents no longer
guarantee exclusiveness, and many firms lose out by spending money
on research only to find that a competitor can quickly modify the
product and circumvent the patent; similarly, the question of copyright
becomes increasingly difficult to police when individuals or libraries
can Xerox whatever pages they need from technical journals or books,
or individuals and schools can tape music off the air or record a
television performance on video disks.

If there is less and less incentive for individual persons or private
enterprises to produce knowledge without particular gain, then the
need and effort fall increasingly on some social unit, be it university or
government, to underwrite the costs. And since there is no ready
market test (how does one estimate the value of "basic research?"),
there is a challenge to economic theory to design a socially optimal

policy of investment in knowledge (e.g., how much money should be spent for basic research; what allocations should be made for education, and for what fields; in what areas do we obtain the "better returns" in health; and so on), and how to "price" information and knowledge to users.[3]

In a narrower, technical sense, the major problem for the postindustrial society will be the development of an appropriate "infrastructure" for the developing *communications* networks (the phrase is Anthony Oettinger's) of digital information technologies that will tie the postindustrial society together. The first infrastructure in society is transportation—roads, canals, rail, air—for the movement of people and goods. The second infrastructure has been the energy utilities—oil pipeline, gas, electricity—for the transmission of power. The third infrastructure has been telecommunications, principally the voice telephone, radio, and television. But now with the explosive growth of computers and terminals for data (the number of data terminals in use in the United States went from 185,000 in 1970 to 800,000 in 1976) and the rapid decrease in the costs of computation and information storage, the question of hitching together the varied ways information is transmitted in the country becomes a major issue of economic and social policy.

The "economics of information" is not the same character as the "economics of goods," and the social relations created by the new networks of information (from an interactive research group communicating through computer terminals to the large cultural homogenization created by national television) are not the older social patterns—or work relations—of industrial society.[4] We have here—if this kind of society develops—the foundations of a vastly different kind of social structure than we have previously known.

The postindustrial society, as I have implied, does not *displace* the industrial society, just as an industrial society has not done away with the agrarian sectors of the economy. Like palimpsests, the new developments overlie the previous layers, erasing some features and thickening the texture of society as a whole. It might be useful to highlight some of the new dimensions of postindustrial society.

1. *The centrality of theoretical knowledge.* Every society has always existed on the basis of knowledge, but only now has there been a change whereby the codification of theoretical knowledge and materials science becomes the basis of innovations in technology. One sees this primarily in the new science-based industries—computers, electronics, optics, polymers—that mark the last third of the century.

2. *The creation of a new intellectual technology.* Through new mathematical and economic techniques—based on the computer linear

programming, Markov chains, stochastic processes, and the like—we can utilize modeling, simulation, and other tools of system analysis and decision theory in order to chart more efficient, "rational" solutions to economic and engineering, if not social, problems.

3. *The spread of a knowledge class.* The fastest growing group in society is the technical and professional class. In the United States this group, together with managers, made up 25 percent of a labor force of eight million persons in 1975. By the year 2000, the technical and professional class will be the largest single group in the society.

4. *The change from goods to services.* In the United States today, more than 65 out of every 100 persons are engaged in services. By 1980, the figure will be about 70 in every 100. A large service sector exists in every society. In a preindustrial society, this is mainly a household and domestic class. (In England, it was the single largest class in the society until about 1870.) In an industrial society, the services are transportation utilities, and finance, which are auxiliary to the production of goods, and personal service (beauticians, restaurant employees, and so forth). But in a postindustrial society, the new services are primarily human services (principally in health, education and social services) and professional and technical services (e.g., research, evaluation, computers, and systems analysis). The expansion of these services becomes a constraint on economic growth and a source of persistent inflation.

5. *A change in the character of work.* In a preindustrial world, life is a game against nature in which men wrest their living from the soil, the waters, or the forests, working usually in small groups, subject to the vicissitudes of nature. In an industrial society, work is a game against fabricated nature, in which men become dwarfed by machines as they turn out goods and things. But in a postindustrial world, work is primarily a "game between persons" (between bureaucrat and client, doctor and patient, teacher and student, or within research groups, office groups, service groups). Thus, in the experience of work and the daily routine, nature is excluded, artifacts are excluded, and persons have to learn how to live with one another. In the history of human society, this is a completely new and unparalleled state of affairs.

6. *The role of women.* Work in the industrial sector (e.g., the factory) has largely been men's work, from which women have been usually excluded. Work in the postindustrial sector (e.g., human services) provides expanded employment opportunities for women. For the first time, one can say that women have a secure base for economic independence. One sees this in the steadily rising curve of women's participation in the labor force, in the number of families (now 60 percent of the total) that have more than one regular wage earner, and in the rising

incidence of divorce as women increasingly feel less dependent, economically, on men.

7. *Science as the imago.* The scientific community, going back to the seventeenth century, has been a unique institution in human society. It has been charismatic, in that it has been revolutionary in its quest for truth and open in its methods and procedures. It derives its legitimacy from the credo that knowledge itself, not any specific instrumental ends, is the goal of science. Unlike other charismatic communities (principally religious groups and messianic political movements), it has not "routinized" its creeds and enforced official dogmas. Yet, until recently, science did not have to deal with the bureaucratization of research, the subordination of its inquiries to state-directed goals, and the "test" of its results on the basis of some instrumental payoff. Now science has become inextricably intertwined not only with technology but with the military and with social technologies and societal needs. In all this, a central feature of the postindustrial society—the character of the new scientific institutions—will be crucial for the future of free inquiry and knowledge.

8. *Situses as political units.* Most of sociological analysis has focused its attention on classes or strata, horizontal units of society that exist in superior-subordinate relation to each other. Yet, for the post-industrial sectors, it may well be that situses (from the Latin *situ,* location), a set of vertical orders, will be the more important loci of political attachment. There are four *functional* situses—scientific, technological (i.e., applied skills: engineering, economics, medicine), administrative, and cultural; and five *institutional* situses—economic enterprises, government bureaus, universities and research complexes, social complexes (e.g., hospitals, social service centers), and the military. My argument is that the major interest conflicts will be between the situs groups, and that the attachments to these situses might be sufficiently strong to prevent the organization of the new professional groups into a coherent class in society.[5]

9. *Meritocracy.* A postindustrial society, being primarily a technical society, awards place less on the basis of inheritance or property (though these can command wealth or cultural advantage) than on education and skill. Inevitably, the question of a meritocracy becomes a crucial normative question.

10. *The end of scarcity?* Most socialist and utopian theories of the nineteenth century ascribed almost all the ills of society to the scarcity of goods and the competition of men for these scarce goods. In fact, one of the most common definitions of economics characterized it as the art of efficient allocation of scarce goods among competing ends. Marx and other socialists argued that abundance was the precondition

for socialism and claimed, in fact, that under socialism there would be no need to adopt normative rules of just distribution, since there would be enough for everyone's needs. In that sense, the definition of communism was the abolition of economics, or the "material embodiment" of philosophy. Yet, it is quite clear that scarcity will always be with us. I mean not just the question of scarce resources (for this is still a moot point) but that a postindustrial society, by its nature, brings new scarcities which nineteenth- and early twentieth-century writers had never thought of. The socialists and liberals had talked of the scarcities of goods; but in the postindustrial society there will be scarcities of information and of time. The problems of allocation inevitably remain, in the crueler form, even, of man becoming *homo economicus* in the disposition of his leisure time.

11. *The economics of information.* Information is by its nature a collective, not a private, good (i.e., a property). In the marketing of individual goods, it is clear that a "competitive" strategy between producers is to be preferred lest enterprise become slothful or monopolistic. Yet, for the optimal social investment in knowledge, we have to follow a "cooperative" strategy in order to increase the spread and use of knowledge in society. This new problem regarding information poses the most fascinating challenges to economists and decision makers in respect to both theory and policy in the postindustrial society.

## NOTES

1. By information I mean, broadly, the storing, retrieval, and processing of data, as the basis of all economic and social exchanges. This would include: (1) Records: payrolls, government benefits (e.g., Social Security), bank clearances, credit clearances, and the like; (2) Scheduling: airline reservations, production scheduling, inventory analysis, product-mix information, and so forth; and (3) Demographic and library: census data, opinion surveys, market research, knowledge storage, election data, and so forth.

By knowledge, I mean an organized set of statements, of facts or ideas, presenting a reasoned judgment or an experimental result that is transmitted to others through communication media in some systematic form.

2. A parallel argument has been made by the German Marxist scholar Jurgen Habermas, who has written:

... technology and science (have) become a leading productive force, rendering inoperative the conditions for Marx's labor theory of value. It is no longer meaningful to calculate the amount of capital investment in research and development on the basis of the value of unskilled (simple) labor power, when scientific-technical progress has become an independent source of surplus value, in relation to which the only source of surplus value considered by Marx, namely the labor power of the immediate producers, plays an ever smaller role.

Jurgen Habermas, *Toward a Rational Society* (Boston: Beacon Press, 1970), 104.

To that extent, too, one can say that knowledge, not labor, is a social product and that Marx's analysis of the social character of production applies more fully to knowledge than to the production of goods.

3. The seminal work on this question of collective goods is Mancur Olson's *The Logic of Collective Action* (Cambridge: Harvard University Press, 1965). The question of the "economics of information" has come to absorb the attention of the Harvard economists Kenneth Arrow and Michael Spence. For some initial reflections, see Kenneth Arrow, "Limited Knowledge and Economic Analysis," *American Economic Review,* March 1974, and Michael A. Spence, "An Economist's View of Information," in Carlos A. Cuadra and Ann W. Luke (eds.), *Annual Review of Information Science and Technology,* Volume 9 (Washington, D.C., 1974).

4. One intriguing way in which cheap communications technology creates new social patterns is the use of the citizens' band radio as a form of coordinated action. In 1974, independent truckers could create vast slowdowns on a thousand-mile chain of roads in the Midwest by radio communication for selected blockade points. In one sense, this is little different from the pattern of riverboat pilots exchanging information which Mark Twain described so hilariously in *Life on the Mississippi,* but in this, as in so many instances, the characteristic of modernity is not the nature of the action but its scale, rapidity, and coordination.

For an authoritative elaboration of these technical questions, see the monograph *The Medium and the Telephone: The Politics of Information Resources,* by Paul J. Berman and Anthony Oettinger, Working Paper 75-8, Harvard Program on Information Technology and Public Policy. For this and other materials on information technology, I am indebted to my colleague Professor Oettinger.

5. What is striking is that in the communist world, it is quite clear that situses play the major role in politics. One analyzes the play of power, not in class terms, but on the basis of the rivalries among the party, the military, the planning ministries, the industrial enterprises, the collective farms, the cultural institutions—all of which are situses.

HAZEL HENDERSON

# The Emerging Countereconomy

The Dark Age following the collapse of Rome was anything but dark. Rather, it was an age of epochal creativity, when values and institutions were evolved that constituted the bedrock foundation of modern civilization. It is true that this creativity was preceded by imperial disintegration—by the shrinkage of commerce and cities, the disappearance of bureaucracies and standing armies, and the crumbling of roads and aqueducts and palaces. This imperial wreckage explains, but scarcely justifies, the traditional characterization of the early medieval period as "dark." It was an age of birth, as well as death, and to concentrate on the latter is to miss the dynamism and significance of a seminal phase of human history.

L. S. Stavrianos, *The Promise of the Coming Dark Age*

The system which we call "an economy" is continually changing and evolving, with new enterprises growing at its advancing edge while older corporations and institutions die and dissolve (Henderson, 1976). In this process of decay, they release their components of capital, land, human skills, and talents to be reabsorbed into the fledgling companies and new enterprises in the leading sector for their further development. Since an economy is also a living system, composed of live biological units, i.e., humans in dynamic interaction with the energy and resources around them, it conforms to the basic laws of physics (as we know them) and the same entropy-syntropy cycles of decay and regeneration as do all biological systems. The First Law of Thermodynamics proposes that matter-energy can be neither created nor destroyed, from which we can infer that for some systems or components of systems to grow, others must die and decay so that their elements can be reutilized. The Second Law of Thermodynamics, the Entropy Law, states that all these cycles of building up and breaking down involve the use of energy, some of which is lost as waste heat. Since this degraded energy cannot be reconstituted, the system is said to be very slowly evolving, qualitatively and irreversibly toward greater disorder and entropy. This trend is locally countered by living organisms in their evolutionary drive toward higher complexity and order via structure, knowledge, information, and the like, i.e., negentropy. Two economists, employing vastly expanded time/space horizons, Kenneth Boulding (1968) and Nicholas Georgescu-Roegen (1971), have stressed the importance of this general perspective as a context for economic analysis. A new hybrid school of thermodynamic-economic analysis has emerged from their insights (Odum, Hannon, Berry, Long, Slessor, Lovins, Daly et al.) and has been developing its methodology under the auspices of the International Federation of Institutes for Advanced Study in Stockholm.[1]

This basic model of the entropy-syntropy cycle and the irreversible evolution of all natural and biological systems is crucial to our understanding of the particular subsystem we call our economy, as well as in helping us see current economic difficulties in longer time perspectives, as the onset of the decline of industrialism. This decline, although it will undoubtedly prove uncomfortable, will likely only affect the unsustainable modes of production and consumption it has fostered. With leadership and foresight, it may release nutrients to spur the development of the already visible "counter-economy" now beginning to flourish in the interstices of the industrial system. In this chapter, without benefit of official government statistics (few agencies even conceive of the counter-economy), I shall attempt to sketch its contours and some of its features.

First, it is necessary to state my underlying assumptions, shared by many others (Forrester, Meadows, Heilbroner, Georgescu-Roegen, Tinbergen, Daly, Schumacher, Mesarovic et al.),[2] that currently defined, real growth of GNP in mature, industrial countries—the United States, Japan, and those of Western Europe—is exhausting its potential. Economic growth is now constrained both by the internal structure and dynamics of these societies and by external factors. Examples of these factors are the worsening planetary population-resource ratio, climatic uncertainties, the new and legitimate militancy of the countries of the Southern Hemisphere, and the increasingly visible social costs of world trade (including destabilizing interdependencies imposed by so-called free markets: synchronously oscillating economies; chronic unemployment and disruption of labor patterns; culturally inappropriate technology transfer, and so forth (Henderson, 1974 c).

I also assume, therefore, that these mature industrial societies are already experiencing a fundamental transition from economies that maximize production, consumption, and resource-throughput, based on nonrenewable resources (fossil fuels and uranium), to economies minimizing resource-throughput and material consumption and shifting to conservation, recycling and a basic of renewable resources, and managed in the interest of sustained-yield productivity (Henderson, 1976a). While economists struggle to address these new conditions and unfamiliar variables, those whose vision has remained unclouded can see that this transition is obvious and that it can be inferred from extremely simple metaphors, e.g., "There is no such thing as a free lunch," "Nothing fails like success," the aspect of "growth as cancer." They also see that, indeed, average citizens in these societies have learned to tune out their leaders and mass media, and are well on their way to understanding the true situation, in spite of the obfuscations of intellectual "day-laborers" and the divinations of "experts." As I have noted elsewhere (Henderson, 1974a), signs of the death of the industrial order can no longer be explained away. They have reached above the threshold of sensory awareness in many of these countries, where citizens can smell the foul air and water, are losing hearing from rising noise levels, and can sense the rising urban disorder in slums, unsafe streets and curtailed services, and near brushes with insolvency.

It is fairly self-evident that these mature industrial societies could not continue expanding at past rates, simply because such rates are always in relation to the size of a base. Any citizen knows that as a base grows, the rate of its expansion must sooner or later decline, whether one is looking at the rate of increase of today's shares in IBM or Xerox, compared with their past spectacular performance, or the rate of growth in the size of oil tankers, airplane, or human settlements. (The only current exception to this rule appears to be bureaucracies, but they too may be reaching an apogee—a subject on which I will expand later.) And yet, there is still a great deal of handwringing in Washington today about falling rates of economic growth (GNP-defined) and falling rates of technological innovation and "productivity" (inadequately defined), when the base for calculating such rates—the giant U.S. sociotechnical system—is the largest on the planet. Surely we know by now that human cultures have a habit of rising and then declining as they exceed some resource limit, run out of technological adaptability, or simply lose creative cultural steam. Karl Polanyi may well have been correct when he said that industrialism and the package of social legislation which installed the free market system in England and gave rise to the Industrial Revolution was a rare aberration in human history. Until that period, humans had normally employed two other major production and resource-allocation systems, based on reciprocity and redistribution (Polanyi, 1944). Therefore, we may now have to countenance the proposition that industrial culture and our own petroleum age may be a somewhat brief episode in human history, but that this may not be an unmitigated disaster, or even a disaster at all. So I am not impressed when U.S. rates of technological innovation and productivity are compared, with official horror, to the higher rates of Japan (with a base approximately an order of magnitude smaller than our own). I am not upset when warned that new "science and technology gaps" are widening and Congress is urged by science and high-technology promoting groups to appropriate ever more tax dollars to save us from this fate. Their underlying assumption in all these exhortations is that the health of the scientific and technological enterprise, as currently defined and constituted, is coterminous with the health of the country as a whole. Many now reject this proposition, including myself—but that is another story.

It is therefore my contention that, since such a vast sea-change in the structure of mature, industrial countries is now underway, much of their intellectual paraphernalia has also now been rendered obsolete (Henderson, 1976d). Apparent paradoxes abound, which are usually signals that paradigmatic shifts are required. The continuing crisis in economics, particularly the denouement of macro-economic management, is accompanied by crises in sociology, psychology, and even physics. Two insistent dilemmas are now almost unavoidable in any industrial society: (1) Advancing technological complexity systematically destroys free market conditions, making laissez-faire policies ever less workable, while at the same time we humans have not yet learned how to plan such societies. (2) Advancing technological complexity also destroys the necessary conditions for democratic political governments to function, since legislators and even heads of state, let alone the average voter, cannot master sufficient information to exert popular control of technological innovation. At the same time, the hazardous nature of new technologies often requires societal regulation and policing that erode or abrogate civil liberties, i.e., some complex technologies (for example, nuclear power) are *inherently* totalitarian (Henderson, 1976c).

Human societies are only now beginning to systematically review strategies (some long forgotten or in the cultural traditions of so-called primitive societies) to deal with the destabilizing social effects of technological changes and innovations. Clearly, the free market model of consumer-driven innovation is unworkable, for all the reasons argued by Francois Hetman in *Society and the Assessment of Technology* (1973). More obviously, if the market model were operating, there would not exist in most industrial countries the growing mass movements and protests demanding political control of technology, technology assessment, "appropriate technology," "liberatory technology," "demo- (rather than aristo-) technology," "alternative technology," and all the other slogans and rallying cries used by these movements in the United States, Canada, the United Kingdom, France, Norway, Sweden,

Denmark, The Netherlands, Australia, New Zealand, and Japan. The death-prattles of traditional, market-oriented economists about "deregulation," "getting the government off the backs of business" (their latest sophistries being the justification of almost any public or private project, however exorbitant, dangerous, or mismatched with human needs, on the grounds of "creating jobs"), and returning to the mythical state of grace of "the free market" are today greeted with ever greater public incredulity. Neither business nor government leaders seem willing to face an axiom of our complex, interdependent, unmodelable, unmanageable socio-technical societies. Each order of magnitude of technological mastery and managerial scale *inevitably* calls forth an equivalent order of magnitude of necessary government effort to coordinate and control and maintain an uneasy "social homeostasis." Any honest debate about deregulation must address this metalevel issue concerning the entire direction of our technological societies. I.e., will we continue moving toward producer-oriented, capital-intensive, centralizing, and hazardous technologies (and accept the burgeoning risks and the price of government regulation and necessary control), or will we opt for simpler, cheaper, less violent, decentralized technologies, which conserve capital, energy, and resources, and therefore require more people to own and operate them and which, since they are benign, require less regulation (Henderson, 1975)?

The metalevel trade-off facing all mature industrial societies is essentially between complexity, division of labor, and specialization on the one hand, and the levels of communication, coordination, and general transaction costs incurred on the other (Henderson, 1977). Today's economic policy and investment decisions are no longer simply choices between more roads, schools, and chemical factories, or between nuclear or solar energy. They involve this societal, metalevel trade-off, as well as others, including those between centralization and decentralization, capital- versus labor-intensive production patterns, and the even more crucial choice concerning the society's flexibility.

Such meta-choices are beyond human capabilities and even our most advanced modeling methodologies at present, for indeed these choices are involved with the evolution of our species. Most species make such choices over eons and, unconsciously, through their genes and the processes of natural selection and ecological succession. These evolutionary choices in the development path of species also involve these meta-trade-offs and the "economics of flexibility," i.e. "spending" flexibility now versus "storing" future flexibility. The mode nature chooses involves profligate sacrifice of individual members of a species, before a set of adaptations is selected for genetic "hard-programming" of the genotype itself. These concepts are discussed at greater length by Gregory Bateson in *Steps to an Ecology of Mind* (1975), in which he brilliantly generalizes from such evolutionary genetic concepts to human and social systems. He notes, "In all homeostatic systems, higher systems of control must lag behind event sequences in the peripheral circuits . . . so as to permit stochastic processes of trial and error to experiment with adaptations." Timing is all. A too-rapid genetic adaptation to change may only maladapt the species for the next set of environmental perturbations. The paradox is exquisite: "Nothing fails like success." That humans are now at the point in their own evolution where these formerly genetic, evolutionary choices are emerging as conscious, cultural decisions is evident in the nature of these metalevel policy choices which industrial societies face today (Henderson, 1977). The counterculture and citizen protest movements of the 1960s, which are forming the nucleus of the emerging counter-economies based on self-reliant, decentralized, ecologically harmonious life-styles, are far from faddish. They are deadly serious and must be explicitly documented and reinforced, since they represent the best repositories of social and cultural flexibility during the decline now underway in many mature industrial countries.

The evolutionary dilemma summarized by the aphorism "Nothing Fails Like Success" can be restated in the terms of anthropology as the Law of the Retarding Lead. This law holds that the best adapted and most successful countries have the greatest difficulty in adapting and retaining their lead in world affairs and, conversely, that the backward and less successful societies are more likely to be able to adapt and forge ahead under changing conditions. In his new book, *The Promise of the Coming Dark Age,* L. S. Stavrianos uses these principles to argue that for the crowded, ecologically depleted planet of today, Western societies must now flounder. In contrast, societies adapting from the Chinese, communal model of self-reliant development and mass-participation; from the Yugoslavian model of worker self-managment; and from the counterculture, citizen action, community-control models now being developed in the counter-economies in the Western industrial countries may be able to synthesize unique development strategies of their own (Stavrianos, 1976). Stavrianos, Forrester, Goldsmith, Illich,[3] I, and others have argued that if Western societies are to become regenerative and sustainable societies, they may indeed have to learn from the so-called less developed countries, as well as relearn much traditional wisdom and skill from their own pasts in order to reinforce, augment, and culturally reward the emerging counter-economies in their midst.

In the face of the current transition of industrial societies and the efforts at reconceptualizing the new situation, it is not surprising that levels of cognitive dissonance are increasing. In the United States, in spite of a decade of predictions of their transience, we see the durability of the counterculture, the environmental movement (which, according to Harris and Opinion Research, is stronger than ever),[4] the consumer and public interest advocacy, the women's liberation and minority rights movement, as well as the diffusion of their new values and life-style options. In addition, statistics now document the new reverse migration from cities to rural areas, and the dropouts now include the middle class and middle-aged seeking relief from the rat race in simpler, more dependable life-styles. Even the election of President Jimmy Carter in 1976 was an indication of the general disaffection with the "business as usual" approach to government. For he won through a coalition of those groups for whom the U.S. economy was not working—labor, the less affluent, small business, small farmers, environmentalists, blacks, women, and other minorities—and without massive corporate and special interest campaign funds.

In any period of cultural transition, the dominant organs of a society often increase the efforts to reassure the public, while their leaders privately express doubt and fear. This is not surprising, since it is precisely these institutions of government, business, academia, labor, and religion, as well as their leaders, which are in decline and whose power is threatened and eroding. The information-gathering and disseminating media, the statistics and the indicators are all geared to measure the society's well-being in terms of the well-being of these existing institutions. Therefore, the growing shoots of the society are unmeasured and overlooked, and will remain insufficiently monitored and studied as possible new social models. Industrialized societies face a similar situation today, but we cannot afford to wait until the conceptual wreckage of industrialism is sifted and composted. We need to study the counter-economy at the same time that we are examining our now inappropriate statistics (e.g., GNP, unemployment statistics, and measures of productivity and efficiency) which are now generating dangerous illusions.[5] New perceptions, concepts, values, and paradigms can gradually generate more realistic models and provide more appropriate statistics; the ferment of new efforts in this area is some cause for encouragement.

To aid in this reconceptualization process, I will review the various features of the growing edges of industrial societies as I have observed them over the past ten years: what is being born quietly amid the decay and the inevitable contraction of intermediation and world trade, based on obsolescent doctrines of comparative advantage; the development of new models of social, rather than GNP-defined, per capita averaged economic growth; and the resurgence of pride and vigor among many of the world's ethnic and indigenous peoples as the old power centers lose their nerve.

It is premature to envision a planetary counter-economy, since much pragmatic experimentation will be needed before the ancient and now irrelevant dogmas and conflicts over capitalism versus communism can be transcended. Both systems are based on technological determinism and inadequate notions of industrial efficiency and progress, and both display an anthropocentric blindness to ecological dimensions and human potential. Economics itself has become an inoperative category, an academic relic useful for accounting in microtransactions. Its terminology is necessary only in order to communicate with those socialized into its conceptual habits, who, unfortunately, still exert an enormously dangerous measure of influence in our resource-allocation systems (Henderson, 1976f). Some of the most interesting and significant manifestations of the counter-economies in the United States, Canada, the United Kingdom, the Scandinavian countries, The Netherlands, Japan, Australia and New Zealand, include:

1. The growth of counter-media and alternative publishing (a measuring rod of the counter-economy). For example, in the United States, *Prevention* (nearly 2 million circulation), *Organic Gardening* (1 million), *Rolling Stone* (approximately 1.5 million), *Mother Earth News* (300,000), and *The Whole Earth Catalog* and *Epilog;* the proliferation of regional magazines dealing with ecological life-styles and appropriate technology; some eighty publishing ventures operated by feminists; the rise of the black press; and the hundreds of small, often cooperatively owned book publishers and distributors.

2. The alternative marketing enterprises. For example, the *Alternative Christmas Catalog,* which, instead of materialistic goods and junk gifts, offers a vast selection of "psychic gifts" such as subscriptions to counter-culture magazines and newsletters and memberships in various counter-culture, public interest and citizen organizations; the growth of organizations marketing rural crafts, such as quilts, embroidery, clothes, and toys to urban department stores, often on a nonprofit basis; the alternative merchandising media now offered to small rural business and crafts by the burgeoning counterculture media and their inexpensive advertising rates and well-defined audiences; highly professional public interest advertising agencies, the best known of which in the United States is the Public Media Center of San Francisco, which does not take ordinary commercial clients, but rather citizen organizations and their social causes.[6] Another new mode is the development of alternative marketing groups such as Oxfam's "Bridge" in Britain, which catalogs and links small, rural producers of hand-crafted goods and art in the Third World with affluent, concerned

consumers in Britain. These new trading links operate in a nonprofit, people-to-people fashion, thereby avoiding profit-motivated trading channels and multinational enterprises.[7] Another mode is that of staging both rural and urban "fairs," where various sectors of the countereconomy can nucleate and cross-fertilize. These fairs feature new lifestyle speakers, book stalls, booths for local citizen organizations, and commune-made arts and crafts. The Toward Tomorrow Fair in Amherst, Massachusetts, recently featured five acres of alternative technology exhibits by small businesses in solar energy, wind power, bioconversion, flushless toilets, do-it-yourself housing, and home and garden tools. It attracted 7,000 people and has now become an institution. Similar fairs and festivals, such as the Cousteau Society's Involvement Days and those concerned with improving nutrition and holistic health, draw similar crowds. They augur new lateral linkages and networks that are insulated from traditional industrial merchandising and are based on emerging value systems impervious to the materialistic Madison Avenue "hard sell."

3. The growing interest in household economics, i.e., the economics of use-value rather than market-value. In *The Center* magazine (1976), Professor Sol Tax has proposed that we begin looking at the possibilities of the family rather than large corporations as the corporate unit and that we alter our tax structure and laws, where necessary, to favor this smallest unit of economic and social organization.

In 1780, over 80 percent of all Americans were self-employed in household economies or small businesses (People's Bicentennial Commission, 1975). Today hundreds of thousands of small entrepreneurs and family farms and enterprises have been driven out of business by so-called economies of scale based largely on unrealistically low energy prices and cheap, subsidized capital investment (Henderson, 1976b). Most of our citizens have become industrial peasants, dependent on jobs with corporations or government, while only 10 percent remain their own bosses. In *Home, Inc.,* Scott Burns estimates that if our national statistics were to include the value of households and the work performed by men and women in them, the total would be equal to the entire amount paid out in wages and salaries by every corporation in the United States (1975). Burns notes that government statisticians only value the household when it breaks down, i.e., they know the cost of welfare, aid to dependent children, and social services and thus could impute negatively the value of viable households. In addition, he observes that while income tax laws allow corporations to deduct and depreciate items of capital equipment, householders are forced to treat their own productive assets, e.g., sewing machines, ovens, freezers, yogurt makers, and home tools as if they were consumer goods (Burns, 1975). A survey in 1969 by Ismail Sirageldin, *Non Market Components of National Income,* measured the total value of all goods and services produced by the household sector in 1965 as about $300 billion (Burns, 1975). The increasing protest at the statistical blackout perpetrated for so long on the household economy, is, of course, being spearheaded by women, who have been consistently ignored by economists' definitions of productivity and value as well as excluded from the GNP and their rightful access to retirement security. Many women fight these gross injustices by going outside the home and competing successfully in the market economy, while many others, together with concerned men, fight to restore the proper place of the family in our economic life and to strengthen its role in the vital nurturing and socializing of the young and in maintaining intergeneration cohesion. Many others in the counter-culture work to enlarge the definition of the family to include communes and intentional families of all kinds, based not only on sex roles, but also on work and companionship. Most of our economic statistics are devised to plot the market system rather than to trace the full and real dimensions of our total economic system. So far, the sparse academic efforts to overhaul the GNP to include the value of the household economy and subtract the soaring social costs of market activities, such as Tobin and Nordhaus's Measure of Economic Welfare (MEW) and, more recently, Samuelson's Net Economic Welfare (NEW), have been minor adjustments. Such efforts have never been promoted by the economics profession, in spite of general acknowledgment of the glaring errors in GNP-measurements of economic growth (Henderson, 1973a).

4. The growth of the various movements for alternative technology. These movements are flourishing in all mature industrial societies, particularly Britain, the Scandinavian countries, the United States, and Canada. There is almost a surfeit of studies and statistics related to the characteristics of dominant modes of industrial scientific and technological development, since technological productivity and technology transfer are issues of keen interest in national and international trade. However, the emerging economies based on more culturally and ecologically appropriate technology have been totally ignored by most agencies of government in the countries where these movements exist. One can only infer the size of this sector from advertising lineage in alternative media and by the best-seller status of its proponents, such as E. F. Schumacher's *Small Is Beautiful,* Robert Pirsig's *Zen and the Art of Motorcycle Maintenance,* and Ivan Illich's *Tools for Conviviality* and *Energy and Equality,* and the flowering of special magazines in this field, such as Canada's *Alternatives;* Britain's *The Ecologist, Undercurrents, Resurgence,* and *Appropriate Technology;* Australia's *Earth*

*Garden, Grass Roots,* and *The Powder Magazine;* and the United States' *Journal of the New Alchemists, Co-Evolution Quarterly, Rain, Science for the People, Workforce, Shelter, Self-Reliance,* and scores of others (Rivers, 1975).

5. The rebirth of populism and the co-operative movement, neighborhood and block development, "sweat equity" urban renewal, land trusts, and the increased bartering of skills and home-produced goods and services. The Co-operative League of the U.S.A., in its 1975 review, states that more than 50 million Americans now belong to co-operatives. These include co-op banks to provide credit that commercial banks deny; 22,879 credit unions; 2,034 insurance plans with over 7 million members; 1,700 nursery schools; 8,000 farmers' marketing co-ops; 999 electric co-ops in rural areas serving 6.5 million customers; 258 student housing co-ops; 241 rural telephone co-ops serving 750,000 subscribers; 102 fishing co-ops with 7,098 members; 125 memorial societies to provide dignified burial rites serving 500,000 people; and, most recently, food co-ops, now numbering 223 and serving 577,000 consumers.[8] A bill to establish a national co-operative bank came close to passage in the 1976 Congress and will, no doubt, be passed during the Carter Administration. This bill will help counteract the discrimination co-ops have suffered at the hands of commercial, multinational banks. Many local organizations are campaigning to set up state-owned development banks modeled after the successful state Bank of South Dakota, in order to make credit available to small-scale farmers (which the U.S. Department of Agriculture now proposes to consign to oblivion by dropping them from its statistics) and local community development corporations and co-ops. The Massachusetts Community Development Finance Corporation may be one of the first in the field. It is already authorized, has an initial appropriation of $10 million, and will buy stock in enterprises owned in common by the residents of any geographical area in Massachusetts.[9] Meanwhile, grassroots community organizations are springing up, based on the spectacularly successful model of ACORN in Arkansas, a coalition of poor homeowners, farmers, sharecroppers, workers, and urban residents of all races. The solidarity of this group has shown how local satrapies controlling millions of dollars of tax money can be captured by determined voters who study their own local political systems carefully; and how utility rate increases can be fought, as they have also been reduced in California and other states by the Lifeline coalitions. Horrified at the success of these grassroots efforts, utilities have launched emergency counterattacks in the form of stepped-up lobbying and advertising (charged to their customers' bills), while deposed political hacks in Arkansas and editorials in Little Rock newspapers

talked of "the Lilliputians who banded together and tied down Gulliver."[10] All of these new co-operative, neighborhood-based, political and economic activities are costly. Moreover, designing new statistics for them demands intellectual creativity since few official measures are available and since status quo institutions and media often are successful in playing down such activities or blacking out reporting of them in commercially controlled media.

6. The rising worker-participation and self-management movements. These movements are more active in Western Europe and Canada than in the United States or Japan. Western Europe's political traditions facilitate the dissemination and cohesion of efforts to gain more influence over the quality of working life. In the United States, the labor movement has thus far reaped more material rewards through traditional bargaining strategies for higher wages. This situation is now changing because recently, real incomes have remained unchanged for protracted periods and because faltering U.S. growth can no longer assure workers of steady employment, let alone a large share of a growing pie. In Japan, worker demands for self-management have been headed off by the commitment of Japanese management to lifelong employment and all-embracing welfare benefits. As the Japanese economy is being further weakened by its raw material and energy dependence and reliance on unrealistic levels of exports, corporate executives are adopting Western-style mass layoffs. This tactic will result in the radicalization of the Japanese labor force, with uncertain outcomes. Western European countries such as Sweden, Norway, Germany, France, and Britain are making almost daily accommodations to the pressure from unions—from Sweden's Meidner Plan to shift substantially the ownership of Swedish industries to their workers, to Germany's worker-management parity on boards of steel companies, to the milder forms of job-enrichment that are becoming commonplace in Western Europe and the United States and Canada (Henderson, 1976e).

U.S. management is well aware of the radical implications of these experiments. In some cases, as workers have successfully organized production, achieved productivity gains, and worked out salary differentials in their own committees, they have gained the confidence to ask the taboo question, "What are all these managers doing, and aren't they just featherbedders?" At this point, many of the experiments are quietly discontinued, since the workers are challenging "the divine right of capital" (Henderson, 1976e). In Britain, this issue, which underlies the ancient war between labor and capital, has erupted into class warfare. As one worker put it, "There isn't going to *be* any production until it's fair. We know we are a poor country, and it's a luxury, but let's get on with the class war and settle it" (Henderson, 1976e). The model for much worker self-management experimentation is Yugoslavia, where the concept of private property is similar to that of our own Founding Fathers. For example, Ben Franklin clearly distinguished between legitimate ownership of property for the purpose of individual autonomy and self-reliance, and property endlessly accumulated when it could "commence a tyranny" on others (People's Bicentennial Commission, 1976b).

7. The resurgence of ethnic and indigenous peoples all over the planet. For example, the extraordinary secret summit meeting held in Trieste in 1975 by the oppressed ethnic minorities of Europe—the Basques, Catalans, Galicians, Croats, Occitanians, Bretons, Irish, Scots, Welsh, Corsicans, Sardinians, Flemings, Frisians, and Piedmontese—where they shared their vision of "a Europe of Peoples,"[11] "the American Indian Movement in the United States, and the demands of Canada's native residents of the Yukon and Northwest Territories for the return of their lands.[12] These populations now recognize that metropolitan power centers are unable to meet their needs, and, indeed, that these exploitative relationships must now be resisted openly and severed. Pioneer research in this field is being conducted by Elise Boulding, whose study, *The Underside of History,* will appear shortly. *The New Internationalist* reviewed these global struggles in its December 1976 issue. If these ethnic peoples are able, as seems likely, to forge stronger links with the growing world feminist movement and with citizen action movements in the industrialized countries, the prospects for their contribution to a saner, more just world system are exciting (Henderson, 1976g). Many of the goals of these ethnic peoples are similar to those of the counterculture and citizen action movements: curbing the excesses of the profit system, creating new principles of accountability of both corporate and bureaucratic power and wealth, making science and technology serve democratically determined social and human goals, decentralizing decision-making and public access to information and government, ending discrimination based on race and sex, and drawing on the wisdom of traditional cultures to redesign life-styles harmonious with each other and the natural environment.

8. The global ecology movement and feminist movement. Both are providing unique roles in social transformation since they operate within the industrial elite. The male-dominated industrial societies find it impossible not to deal with the wives of corporate and government bureaucrats who have become their uncomfortable social consciences. In addition, many executives must defend the daily decisions of their institutions to their ecologically minded sons and daughters.

9. The building of new coalitions in industrial countries between formerly fragmented citizens groups, which is continuing. In the United States in the 1960s, many formerly disparate local groups fought air pollution in New York and California, and some tried to clean up local rivers or stop roads or airports, but with little knowledge of each other's activities. After Earth Day in 1970, people realized more than before the necessity for united efforts to protect the environment and the planetary biosphere (Henderson, 1968, 1971). Similar convergences occurred around the concept of corporate accountability, when consumer and environmental advocates and civil rights, women, and student movements joined with antiwar groups and counterculture forces.[13] Today, new and older elements of the labor movement, rural voters, small business people and farmers, grassroots and neighborhood groups, and appropriate technology advocates are coalescing and are forming a new holistic conceptualization of the decline of the industrial system itself. An example of the workings of such new coalitions was a conference on Working for Environmental and Economic Justice and Jobs in May 1975, attended by 300 leaders from labor, environmental, and social justice organizations. They met to push for labor-intensive public projects and private investments, and to support the goals of a full-employment economy and reordered corporate and government priorities.[14] Similar conferences are scheduled in Ohio, California, New York, and other states. A new coalition, which I helped found in 1974, Environmentalists for Full Employment, assists in uniting local environmentalist, labor, and minority and social welfare forces to focus on the many more jobs available in less capital-intensive, resource- and energy-conserving technological options. These coalitions are expressing a group consumer demand for mass transit, solar and wind energy, and recycling and bioconversion industries—demands that cannot be voiced in the marketplace. Their political efforts will soon create new sectors of the economy, just as they created the pollution control industries (Henderson, 1971) and the $50 million solar industry in the United States.

One of the most interesting aspects of the counter-economy and one of its greatest services is its creation of new images of the future, new alternatives in technology, work, life-styles, family arrangements, and societal roles. As Elise Boulding has noted, a nation that loses its power to imagine its future must become directionless and falter. The misty outlines of viable alternative futures can now be recognized in many industrial countries. Those for whom the status quo is still providing comfortable livings and meaningful lives are naturally impatient at the efforts of citizen movements and public interest advocates. They also scoff at the futurists for their scenario-building, hypothesizing, and explorations of values. And yet, the process of reconceptualization is a vital activity.

## NOTES

1. See, for example, Energy Analysis, Report Number 6, International Federation of Institutes for Advanced Study, Sturegaten 14, Stockholm, 1974.

2. See, for example, Forrester (1974), Heilbroner (1975), Georgescu-Roegen (1971), Tinbergen (1976), Daly (1973), Schumacher (1973), and Mesarovic and Pestel (1975).

3. See, for example, Forrester (1974), Goldsmith (1972), and Illich (1973).

4. Harris Survey, December 1975, *Chicago Tribune,* and Opinion Research Survey, December 1976, Princeton, N.J.

5. See, for example, Henderson (1973a, 1973b, 1974b, 1976b).

6. Public Media Center, because of its low overhead and salaries, offers campaigns at approximately one-tenth the cost of conventional advertising agencies. Some of its clients include Ralph Nader's Critical Mass and Americans for a Working Economy, a predominantly neo-classical view of the workings of the U.S. economy.

7. Bridge Alternative Marketing, OXFAM, 274 Banbury Road, England.

8. *Co-op Facts and Figures,* The Co-operative League of the U.S.A., Washington, D.C., 1975.

9. *Self-Reliance,* June 1976, Washington, D.C., p. 8.

10. *Acorn News,* November 1976, Little Rock, Ark., Volume 6, Number 8.

11. *The New York Times,* July 8, 1975.

12. *The New Internationalist,* December 1976, 22–23.

13. See White House Conference, 1972.

14. See *Environmentalists for Full Employment Newsletter,* Number 3, Fall 1976, p. 1, 1985 Massachusetts Avenue N.W., Washington, D.C. 20036.

## REFERENCES

Bateson, Gregory. 1975. *Steps to an Ecology of Mind.* New York: Ballantine Books.

Boulding, Elise. 1977. *The Underside of History: A View of Women Through Time.* Boulder, Colo.: Westview Press.

Boulding, Kenneth. 1968. *Beyond Economics.* Ann Arbor: University of Michigan Press.

Burns, Scott. 1975. *Home, Inc.* New York: Doubleday.

Daly, Herman E. 1973. *Toward a Steady-State Economy.* San Francisco: W. H. Freeman.

Forrester, J. 1974. *World Dynamics.* Cambridge, Mass.: MIT Press.

Georgescu-Roegen, Nicholas. 1971. *The Entropy Law and the Economic Process.* Cambridge, Mass.: Harvard University Press.

Goldsmith, Edward. 1972. "The Blueprint for Survival." *The Ecologist* (January), 14.

Heilbroner, Robert. 1976. *An Inquiry into the Human Prospect.* New York: W. W. Norton.

Henderson, Hazel. 1968. "Should Business Tackle Society's Problems?" *Harvard Business Review* (July/August), 77–85.

———. 1971. "Toward Managing Social Conflict." *Harvard Business Review* (May/June), 82–90.

———. 1973a. "Limits of Traditional Economics: New Models for Managing a Steady-State Economy." *Financial Analysts Journal* (May), 28–30, 32, 79–80, 83–84, 86–87.

———. 1973b. "Ecologists Versus Economists." *Harvard Business Review* (July) 28–30, 32, 34, 36, 152–157.

———. 1974a. "Citizen Movements." *Annals of the American Academy of Political and Social Science* (March), 34.

———. 1974b. "The Entropy State." *Planning Review,* Volume 2, Number 3 (May), 1, 3, 4.

———. 1974c. "Resources and the Future of Wealth and Scarcity" (Unpublished paper). Lake Itasca, Minn.: Lake Itasca Seminar on the Future of Business.

———. 1975. "Forcing the Hand of the De-Regulators." *Just Economics* (October), 10–13.

———. 1976a. "The Coming Economic Transition." *Technological Forecasting and Social Change,* Volume 8, Number 4, 337–352.

———. 1976b. "Farewell to the Corporate State." *Business and Society Review* (Spring), 49–56.

———. 1976c. *Technology at a Crossroads.* Des Moines, Iowa: The Damon Lecture, American Association of Industrial Arts Convention (April).

———. 1976d. "Ideologies, Myths and Paradigms: Changes in Operative Social Values." *Liberal Education* (May), 143–157.

———. 1976e. "Redefining the Rights and Responsibilities of Capital." Paper presented at the Minneapolis Foundation Conference on the Future of the Free Enterprise System, Brainerd, Minn.

———. 1976f. *On Productivity and Technological change.* Hearings on the Future of Economic Growth, Joint Economic Committee, 94th Congress (November).

———. 1976g. "Citizen Movement for Greater Global Equity." *International Social Science Journal,* Volume 28, Number 4 (December), 773–788.

———. 1977. "Inflation: A View from Beyond Economics." *Planning Review,* Volume 5, Number 2 (March), 3–7, 12, 28.

Hetman, Francois. 1973. *Society and the Assessment of Technology.* Paris: Organization for Economic Co-operation and Development.

Illich, Ivan. 1973. *Tools for Conviviality.* New York: Harper and Row.

Mesarovic, M., and E. Pestel. 1974. *Mankind at the Turning Point.* New York: E. P. Dutton.

People's Bicentennial Commission, 1975a. *Common Sense Two.* New York: Bantam Books.

———. 1975b. *Voices of the American Revolution.* New York: Bantam Books.

Polanyi, Karl. 1944, *The Great Transformation.* New York: Beacon Press.

Rivers, Patrick. 1975. *The Survivalists.* London: Methuen.

Schumacher, E. F. 1973. *Small Is Beautiful: Economics As If People Mattered.* New York: Harper and Row.

Stavrianos, L. S. 1976. *The Promise of the Coming Dark Age.* San Francisco: W. H. Freeman.

Tax, Sol. 1976. "Proposal for a New Institution: The Family as a Corporate Entity." *The Center Report,* Volume 9, Number 1 (February), 6–7.

Tinbergen, Jan. 1976. *Reshaping the International Order.* New York: E. P. Dutton.

White House Conference on the Industrial World Ahead. 1977. *Business in 1990.* Washington, D.C.: U.S. Government Printing Office.

TOMAS FREJKA

# Future Population Growth

In 1696, Gregory King projected the population of the United Kingdom for 600 years—up to 2300 A.D. (King, 1696). If his projection had proved accurate, the British population would have numbered about 8 million in 1975 and not its actual 56 million inhabitants. Given the state of the art in his time, King was no doubt at a comparative disadvantage; yet, even today, it would be difficult to find a scholar willing to make a serious population forecast for such an extensive time period. This does not imply that demographers have nothing to say about future population trends. To the contrary, we are reasonably certain about a number of features of future population growth, and in many ways population projections are more reliable than numerous other types of reflections about the future.

Even though King's projection was far from accurate, he cannot be faulted for his approach to the problem:

1. He assembled the best available data on the United Kingdom population, but unfortunately all that he had was an estimate of the total population.

2. He studied and evaluated past growth trends and wound up with a remarkably good estimate: it took the United Kingdom 435 years to double its 1696 size.

3. On the basis of this estimate, King made a guess that the next population doubling would take 600 years.

The same approach is used today for preparing and computing population projections; the major difference is that more information and experience and advanced methods are available.

1. In most cases, we know more about the population in question than its total size. We usually have information about such characteristics as age and sex composition, health and mortality, fertility behavior, marital patterns, geographical distribution and mobility, occupation, income and wealth distribution, and educational levels. Of course, the available data differ in quality from one country to another; for example, the data for Sweden are better than those for Sri Lanka, which in turn has better data than Senegal.

2. Nowadays, not only do we have knowledge about past trends of

total population size of a country, but we can also make comparisons between countries. Furthermore, there are usually data on the historical changes of various population characteristics. As the science of demography develops, it provides us with a continuously improving understanding of the systems that underlie the surface of population change.

3. The ability to formulate assumptions about future trends depends to some extent on the quality of data and knowledge described above. However, there is hardly a guarantee that a projection, especially into a similarly distant future, will not be off the mark as much as King's was in the seventeenth century. The point is that prediction is not the only function of population projections. Another function of constructing population projections is to illustrate the growth consequences of differing assumptions. Thus, for instance, a major part of the analysis in the 1972 Report of the Commission on Population Growth and the American Future is based on projections assuming Americans—numbering 209 million in 1972—would continue to have either three-child or two-child families: "One hundred years from now, the 2-child family would result in a population of about 350 million persons, whereas the 3-child family would produce a total of nearly a billion" (Commission on Population Growth and the American Future, 1972, p. 22).

The Commission on Population Growth and the American Future, even with all its detailed information (seven huge volumes of papers) about many structural and qualitative features of the population and with good knowledge of past trends, decided to work with alternative projections rather than only with one predictive projection as King did in his time. Furthermore, projecting a mere 100 years into the future, the range between the alternatives in 2070—650 million—was three times larger than the initial 1970 U.S. population. The calculations showed that if the two-child family pattern persisted, the population would be 70 percent larger in 100 years; a three-child family pattern would result in a five-fold increase in population size. Since we know what basic assumptions were used in computing these projections, we can evaluate and discuss them, especially because some (although very little) time has passed since the projections were made.

U.S. fertility after the Depression, particularly in the post-World War II period, deviated from its long-term decline and produced the baby boom of the 1950s, in which three- to four-child families were commonplace. By the time the projections quoted above were computed in 1972, average fertility of the U.S. population had declined abruptly. In 1957, the *total fertility rate**—a rather vivid, albeit imperfect, measure of

---

* All demographic concepts that are italicized the first time they appear in the text are defined and discussed in the Appendix.

the total number of children born per woman—had been 3.8, but by 1972 it had fallen to 2.0. That is, an imaginary woman passing through her childbearing years would have borne almost four children had she conformed to 1957 fertility patterns, but only two children had she followed 1972 fertility patterns. Between 1972 and 1976, fertility continued to decline and reached an all-time low in 1976; in that year, the total fertility rate was slightly less than 1.8.

This cursory look at U.S. fetility trends, as well as the fact that we do have some understanding of what caused these trends and similar trends in other countries, enables us to make certain judgments about the above projections:

1. In view of the childbearing behavior of the recent past, future population growth trends are more likely to approximate the numbers associated with the two-child family assumption, i.e., a U.S. population of about 350 million in the 2070s rather than the growth trends associated with the three-child family assumption.

2. If the 1972–1976 fertility levels were to persist over time, the United States would have a population smaller than 350 million in the 2070s.

3. Based mainly on analogy rather than on a profound sociological, psychological, and economic analysis, one should not rule out a reversal of fertility trends, namely, a new baby boom, in which case one would have to modify judgments listed under points 1 and 2 above. If such a fertility increase were to occur soon and if it would last for as long as the previous baby boom, the U.S. population in 2070 would be larger than the 350 million.

4. As the relatively large generation born in the 1950s passes through the prime childbearing years, if it were to have children at present rates, i.e., 10 to 20 percent below the two-children average, the U.S. population would still be growing at a rate of about 0.5 percent per year for at least twenty years. Given the growth momentum caused by the post-World War II baby boom, it is unlikely that the American population will stop increasing for some years to come. The total fertility rate would have to decline to a 1.2 level and remain there throughout the 1970s and 1980s in order to bring about immediate zero population growth (Frejka, 1968).

Thus far, we have discussed some ways in which fertility trends could shape the size of the U.S. populaton over the next 100 years. We have not discussed how mortality and migration trends might enter the picture; we have hardly discussed population growth trends of the near future; we have not even mentioned the desires and attempts of nations to modify population growth trends, and how and why these views and actions developed and were implemented—and how effective they appear to be.

Mortality trends and migratory movements shape population growth trends in interaction with fertility behavior. Modern population projections are carried out using the so-called component method: one takes the base population divided into age and sex groups and then projects each group by applying assumed mortality, migration, and fertility patterns.

For countries, such as the United States, that have achieved low mortality and where almost all children survive into adulthood, it is relatively simple to establish assumptions about future mortality trends. U.S. mortality, for instance, declined significantly in the late nineteenth century and throughout the first half of the twentieth century. Since the late 1950s, further decline has been limited. Average *life expectancy* at birth for white males increased from about forty-eight years at the beginning of the century to almost sixty-eight years by 1960 (Taeuber, 1972, p. 29) and has remained at that level since then; for white females, the increase in life expectancy was even larger, from fifty-one years in 1900 to seventy-four years by 1960 and to seventy-six years in 1972. Not surprisingly, the U.S. Bureau of the Census in its most recent population projections assumes only minor mortality declines in the future (U.S. Bureau of the Census, 1975).

Immigration and emigration are subject to many economic and social factors, but because U.S. legislation contains specific stipulations, the Census Bureau assumes 400,000 annual legal immigrants with a reasonable degree of confidence. The actual annual number of immigrants is higher as a result of illegal immigration, but it is not known by how much. Estimates of the total number of illegal immigrants in the United States in the mid-1970s go as high as 12 million persons (Keeley and Tomasi, 1976). Although the actual figure is probably lower, there is undoubtedly substantial illegal immigration which, if continued, will considerably influence future U.S. population growth. Also, the annual number of permanent emigrants from the United States is unknown, but in the mid-1970s it was still considerably smaller than the number of immigrants.

Having assembled basic demographic knowledge on the current state and past trends of the U.S. population, one can maintain that the population in 2070 is likely to be around 350 million inhabitants. At the same time, however, it should be noted that this projection is based on the following assumptions: average fertility behavior oscillating around the two-child family, a slight improvement in health and thus mortality conditions, and an average flow of 400,000 immigrants per year. How close to this projection the actual U.S. population in 2070 will be will depend on the extent to which these assumptions prove true.

It has become a standard procedure to periodically review population projections. Between 1947 and 1975, the United States published twelve sets of projections, usually with three or four different combinations of assumptions to accommodate ranges of future possibilities (U.S. Bureau of the Census, 1975). Nevertheless, the demographic situation was changing so rapidly that occasionally a few years after the projections had been computed the actual population was no longer within the projected range. According to the 1947 projections, the 1950 U.S. population was projected to be between 145 and 148 million, but in reality it was 152 million; and according to the 1971 projections, the 1975 population was projected to be between 216 and 218 million but it was actually 213 million.

These population projections rapidly rendered themselves obsolete as a result of unexpected fertility trends. In the late 1940s, fertility increased more than anybody had assumed it would, and in the early 1970s, fertility continued to decline instead of leveling off as was assumed.

Population projections *not* involving fertility assumptions, i.e., projections concerned only with specific population segments that are already born when being projected, can be relatively more reliable than "complete" population projections. It is, for example, a relatively simple task for the Census Bureau to project the population of voting age over the next fifteen years or so because the persons subject to the projection are alive at the time of computation (U.S. Bureau of the Census, 1976). Thus, it was determined that by November 1976 there would be 150 million U.S. inhabitants of voting age. This number had to be adjusted because it included people who were not eligible to vote, such as aliens and inmates of prisons, mental hospitals, and other institutions. In a similar way, a rather high degree of accuracy can be achieved in projecting the school-age population at different levels of schooling, entrants to the labor force, the population of retirement age, and any other specific age-sex group of population, provided the base population of the projection has already been born at the time of computation. Thus, at least for the low mortality nations, one can say that short-term projections of population segments alive at the time of computation should be quite accurate. However, even short-term projections of total populations—especially of the segments that are yet to be born—are much less reliable, particularly as base data for social and economic planning purposes.

Much of what has been said about the U.S. population applies to other low mortality-low fertility countries. Since there exists a rather loose, albeit distinct, relationship between socioeconomic conditions, life-styles, and demographic patterns, these are the countries of the world that have been comprehensively modernizing for at least a number of decades, if not centuries, and are commonly known as the developed countries. Close scrutiny will reveal significant variations also in their demographic features: in 1974, the German Democratic Republic, for instance, had a total fertility rate of less than 1.6, with a *crude birthrate* equal to 10 births per 1,000 inhabitants per year, whereas Czechoslovakia had a total fertility rate of 2.5 and a crude birthrate of 20 per 1,000 (Mauldin, 1976). Nevertheless, in their basic attitudes and background, populations of the developed countries are relatively homogeneous. They have had a long history of improving public health and effective preventive medicine resulting in high life expectancies; they have had a long history of economic and social change, increasing literacy and levels of education, and profoundly transformed life-styles—all of which are consistent with relatively low fertility. With only a few exceptions, in the mid-1970s the developed countries have adopted fertility behavior corresponding roughly to the two-child family pattern, and in about half of these countries fertility is below *the replacement level.* Yet, very few of the populations in the developed countries have ceased to grow because the current generations of parents are still relatively large and thus, even with low fertility, enough babies are being born to more than offset the number of people dying.

The demographic situation of the so-called developing countries is different. In the not too distant past, practically all the developing countries had low rates of population growth because high fertility was counterbalanced by high mortality. During the first half of the twentieth century, and particularly after World War II, various modernizing elements spread to or were gradually adopted by many developing countries. These developments resulted in a decline in mortality, at first in Latin America, then in Asia, and more recently in Africa. However, current mortality differentials among the developing countries are vast. Some countries, such as Costa Rica, Cuba, Venezuela, Mauritius, and Sri Lanka, have life expectancies almost equal to those of the developed countries—certainly over sixty years, possibly close to seventy years. Other countries, such as Egypt, Iran, Peru, Brazil, India, and Thailand, have experienced rapid mortality declines, but there is room for considerable decline; their life expectancies range between fifty and sixty years. Several countries, especially the African, have high mortality; their life expectancies are below fifty years, often by a substantial margin.

On the whole, even with the recent precipitous mortality decline, average life expectancy is still about twenty years shorter in the developing world than in the developed countries. The huge mortality differentials among developing countries and the fact that most of them do have higher mortality than the developed ones is expressed also in the range of *crude death rates*—from below 10 per 1,000 inhabitants per year in many Latin American and several Asian countries to above twenty, occasionally even close to thirty in countries of sub-Saharan Africa.

By comparison, fertility declines are not nearly as widespread nor have they, in most countries, been as large as mortality declines. Mauldin (1976) estimates that the average crude birthrate for the developing countries declined by almost 15 percent over the twenty-five-year period 1950–1975, from an initial crude birthrate of 42 per 1,000 to 36 per 1,000 in 1975. Apparently, there are still many countries in Asia and especially in Africa, where fertility behavior has changed only very little, if at all, and where women on the average are bearing around six children and often more. Among the larger countries in this group are Nigeria, Ethiopia, Zaire, Morocco, Bangladesh, Pakistan, Iran, Burma, and Mexico. There are also many countries, most notably in East and Southeast Asia but also in Central and South America, where fertility decline is spreading, although with widely varying intensity. In these countries, the number of children born per woman is between four and six. Larger countries in this category include Egypt, Indonesia, India, Thailand, the Philippines, Brazil, and Colombia. There are also a few developing countries, most of them with small populations, that have experienced a pronounced fertility decline; their total fertility rate was below four in the mid-1970s. A single African country is in this group—Mauritius. This category also includes some Asian countries—Hong Kong, Singapore, South Korea, Sri Lanka, Taiwan, and Fiji (actually Oceania); and some Central and South American countries—Barbados, Chile, and Trinidad and Tobago.

On the whole, fertility in the developing countries was still rather high over the past twenty-five years. As a result, these countries have a large proportion of young people: around 40 percent of the population are below age fifteen, about 25 percent are in the prime childbearing ages of fifteen to twenty-nine, and only about 5 percent are over age sixty.

The recent combination of rapidly declining mortality and relatively high fertility has brought about rates of population growth of unprecedented levels. In practically all developing countries in the early 1970s, *the rate of natural increase* (the crude birth rate minus the crude death rate) was above 2 percent per year, often around 3 percent or even higher. The doubling time for a population growing around 3 percent per year is twenty-three years, at 2 percent per year thirty-five year and, for comparison, at 0.5 percent per year 140 years.

The significance of a young age structure becomes even more evident when it is realized that as a consequence of declining mortality, an increasing number of children will survive to adulthood and presumably form families, i.e., marry and have children of their own. In this way, a young age structure alone provides a significant reservoir of future population growth.

The People's Republic of China is not only the largest of the developing countries, but it is also a country for which we have almost no precise quantitative, demographic data. Experts differ in their opinion as to what extent the Chinese central government itself knows these facts, but whatever the case may be, national population data are not published. Consequently, foreign experts have tried to estimate the current demographic properties of China's population, if for no other reason than that it constitutes approximately one-fifth of the world's population. Unfortunately, these estimates vary considerably. Estimates of China's 1975 population range from 800 to 978 million inhabitants; estimates of her crude birthrate range between 14 and 37 per 1,000 inhabitants, her crude death rate between 6 and 15 per 1,000, and the rate of natural increase between 0.8 and 2.4 percent per year (Brackett, Ravenholt, and Goldman, 1976). Regardless of the wide range in numerical estimates, a reasonable consensus exists among almost all those who are knowledgeable about China's population policies and the direction of basic demographic trends. As a result of a comprehensive concern and integrated actions, health conditions are good, mortality has declined to relatively low levels, and fertility has declined and is certainly lower than in many other developing countries; hence, the rate of natural increase also could be relatively small.[1]

The enormous diversity among countries in fertility and mortality trends and levels adds up to the global demographic picture shown in Figure 1. The picture is a simplified one: in addition to concealing the heterogeneity, it also hides the probability that—as many believe and have attempted to document—the rate of natural increase of the developing countries has during very recent years reached a turning point and has started to decline. Since this probable, incipient descrescendo of the population growth rate of the developing countries is clearly reinforced by the currently diminishing rate of natural increase in the developed countries, it seems beyond doubt that the world population growth rate in the mid-1970s is falling.

Will the current decline in the world's population growth rate continue or even accelerate? Or will it be reversed? How long might it take for the population in the developing countries to reach a rate of growth similar to the one in the developed countries in the 1970s? What seem to be the population growth prospects for the near and more remote future? Of the world? Of the developed countries? Of the developing countries?

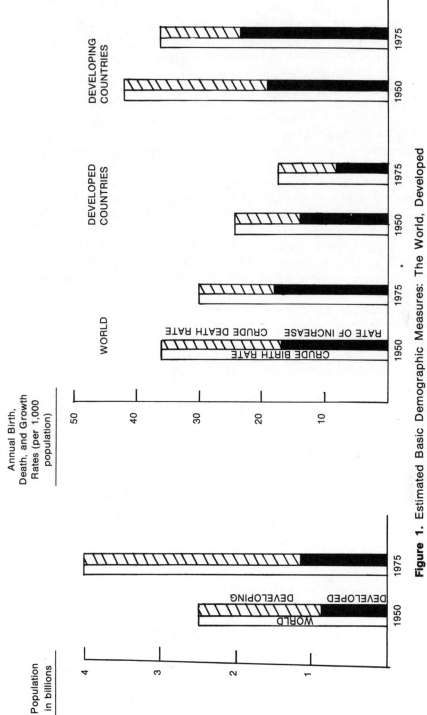

**Figure 1.** Estimated Basic Demographic Measures: The World, Developed Countries, and Developing Countries, 1950–1975

SOURCES: Population Division (1975); Mauldin (1976).

Experience has taught us that attempts to extrapolate from past trends and to regard the results as reliable predictions are seldom useful. A more meaningful understanding of possible future population growth can be gained by outlining various hypothetical developments and discussing the chances each has to materialize.

As a starting point, let us assume that fertility behavior at the replacement level is adopted on a worldwide basis, namely, that the average couple bears as many children as are needed to guarantee the survival of two of them to adulthood (each adult is "replaced" by one child). If such fertility patterns were adopted in the mid-1970s and maintained thereafter, the total population of the developed countries would grow from its 1975 size of 1.1 billion to 1.3 billion in the year 2000 and 1.4 billion in 2050—a growth of 25 percent between 1975 and 2050. In the developing countries, the 1975 population of about 2.9 billion would increase to 3.6 billion in the year 2000 and 4.4 billion in the year 2050—a growth of over 50 percent between 1975 and 2050. Even if this assumption were at all possible, the world would have almost 6 billion inhabitants by the year 2050.

Barring man-induced or natural catastrophes of major proportions, these calculations appear to be unrealistically low for the developing countries and consequently for the whole world. In the developing countries, average fertility is about twice as high as that assumed above: in the mid-1970s, fertility and mortality patterns imply four children surviving to adulthood for every two adults of child-bearing age. Only about one-third of the population in the developing countries may be experiencing unusually steep fertility declines at present, whereas changes in the fertility behavior of the other two-thirds are moderate and gradual, and for some of them of no significant consequence at all.

Evidently, one has to make some less radical assumptions about fertility decline in the developing countries as a whole in order to illustrate more feasible alternatives. One possibility is to assume that current levels of fertility would be transformed to the two-child family pattern by the turn of the century. Compared with the historical experience of the developed countries in the late nineteenth and early twentieth centuries, this would still be a startlingly rapid change, and thus we label this illustration the "rapid demographic transition." If, however, the fertility decline in the developing countries were to require an amount of time comparable to that experienced by the developed countries, one could assume that fertility behavior in the developing countries would be transformed to the two-child family level by the middle of the twenty-first century. This time frame is referred to as "the traditional demographic transition." To many, this assumption may seem rather conservative, which provides some justification for considering the calculations that result from this assumption as an illustration of growth patterns on the high side.

To return to the developed countries, the projection assuming a continuing two-child family pattern in the developed countries is a reasonable but not necessarily correct assumption. There is no guarantee that a prolonged deviation from such a trend in either direction could not occur. In Eastern Europe and the Soviet Union, fertility oscillated around this level during the early and mid-1970s; in the remainder of Europe and in North America, however, fertility has continued to decline below the replacement level and, as of late 1976, is not showing signs of a trend reversal. Nevertheless, even if we were to assume continued fertility below replacement (say 10 percent) for the developed countries, it would not make a significant difference in terms of future growth of the world population in the coming 50 to 100 years. With a fertility level 10 percent below replacement, the population of the developed countries would number 1.3 billion in the year 2000 and 1.2 billion in the years 2050, instead of 1.3 and 1.4 billion, respectively, with a continuous two-child family fertility pattern. Furthermore, the nature of world population growth is going to be determined increasingly by population growth trends in the developing countries because the population of these countries in 1975 was almost 75 percent of the world's population. As a result of anticipated low growth rates in the developed countries, its proportion in the world population is bound to increase, possibly to as much as 90 percent by the second half of the twenty-first century. Thus, for the following calculations, a long-term two-child family fertility pattern in the developed countries is applicable.

It remains to be mentioned that mortality throughout the world is assumed to continue to decline and eventually (during the first half of the twenty-first century) to reach the low levels currently prevailing in Scandinavia. Such an assumption presumes limited further mortality decline in most of the developed countries and more or less significant but gradual further mortality decline in the developing countries. Should major epidemics, wars, famines, or environmental deterioration occur in the future, of course, mortality would not continue to decline at the rates assumed.

The data assembled in Table 1 illustrate the parameters of hypothetical future world population growth:

1. The first projection is labeled the "illusory demographic transition" for a good reason. It assumes worldwide fertility at the replacement level commencing in the mid-1970s and remaining at that level thereafter. It might be reasonable to assume this for the developed

**Table 1. Hypothetical Trends of World Population Growth, 1975–2100**

| Type of Projection | Region | Population in Billions | | | | |
|---|---|---|---|---|---|---|
| | | 1975 | 2000 | 2050 | 2100 | |
| The Illusory Demographic Transition | | | | | | |
| Two-child family fertility pattern adopted universally in mid-1970s in both developed and developing countries | Developed Countries | 1.1 | 1.3 | 1.4 | 1.4 | |
| | Developing Countries | 2.9 | 3.7 | 4.4 | 4.6 | |
| | WORLD TOTAL | 4.0 | 5.0 | 5.8 | 6.0 | |
| The Rapid Demographic Transition | | | | | | |
| Two-child family fertility pattern adopted in developed countries in mid-1970s and in developing countries by the year 2000 | Developed Countries | 1.1 | 1.3 | 1.4 | 1.4 | |
| | Developing Countries | 2.9 | 4.5 | 6.5 | 6.8 | |
| | WORLD TOTAL | 4.0 | 5.8 | 7.9 | 8.2 | |
| The Traditional Demographic Transition | | | | | | |
| Two-child family fertility pattern adopted in developed countries in mid-1970s and in developing countries by the year 2040 | Developed Countries | 1.1 | 1.3 | 1.4 | 1.4 | |
| | Developing Countries | 2.9 | 5.3 | 11.6 | 13.9 | |
| | WORLD TOTAL | 4.0 | 6.6 | 13.0 | 15.3 | |

SOURCE: Frejka (1973).

countries, but in practically all the developing countries, such a radical reduction of fertility simply could not occur. Available evidence, knowledge, and experience indicate that average fertility levels in the developing countries are going to be significantly higher than is assumed in this projection for at least a decade or two. Consequently, the computed world population growth trends are understated. One can state with a considerable degree of confidence that the world population is going to number more than 5 billion inhabitants in the year 2000 unless an unexpected major reversal of mortality trends takes place. With a lesser degree of confidence but not without justification, one can assert that the world population is likely to reach a number higher than 6 billion inhabitants during the twenty-first century.

2. Evidence seems to be accumulating (Kirk, 1971, 1976) to support the notion that the "traditional demographic transition" projection can be considered an illustration of the upper limits of future world population growth. In a number of developing countries—with varying social, economic, climatic, historical, and religious conditions—for which reasonably good documentation of recent fertility trends exists, a distinctly more rapid decline of fertility has occurred than was the case in the demographic transition of many of the now developed countries. Keeping in mind the qualifications and assumptions, one can state that world population is not likely to be larger than 6.5 billion in the year 2000 and that it is not likely to reach 13 billion by the middle of the twenty-first century. On demographic grounds, however, one cannot categorically rule out the traditional transition projection because it is conceivable that the demographic transition in the developing countries, as it seems to be underway in the mid-1970s, might decelerate considerably, i.e., the fertility decline might slow down and/or the mortality decline could accelerate.

3. By this process of elimination, one arrives at the rather broad conclusion that future world population growth is likely to take place between the two extremes illustrated by the illusory and the traditional demographic transitions. One might even go one step further in order to provide a more concrete picture and say that—viewed with a 1976 perspective—it seems plausible to assume that world population in the year 2000 will number about 6 billion inhabitants and could be almost stabilized at approximately 8 billion by the middle of the twenty-first century (see Figure 2).

At present, i.e., in the mid-1970s, probably more than ever before in human history, many national (and local) governments and international organizations are not merely passive observers of demographic trends but are actively involved in influencing the directions of population change. World, national, and subnational demographic

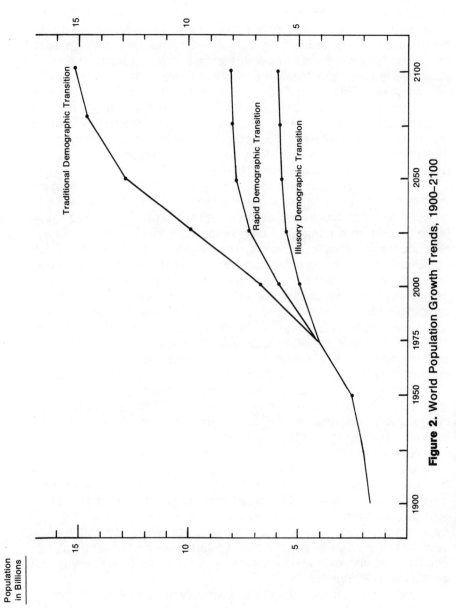

**Figure 2.** World Population Growth Trends, 1900–2100

SOURCE: Frejka (1973).

trends—growth of populations, trends of mortality, migration, fertility—are an expression of myriad conscious and subconscious decisions, which are in turn shaped by the economic and psychic welfare-maximizing activities of the families concerned and by the social environment, including governmental policies. Policies that have an impact on demographic trends include both those that are designed to do so and many others for which such impact is a secondary consideration or an unforeseen side-effect. With regard to national welfare, the governments of nation-states are the centers where the current demographic properties and trends of the population are evaluated and decisions are made as to whether these trends should be modified (Demeny, 1975).

According to a 1974 study by the United Nations, out of 148 governments, 85 considered their national population growth rates acceptable, 42 considered them excessive, and 21 considered their growth rates deficient (U.N. Secretariat, 1975). The perception of deficient population growth rates has resulted in serious population policy measures mainly in developed countries. It "appears that nations in particularly sensitive positions, as perceived locally (for example, Argentina, France, Israel), and nations with birth rates near or below replacement (for example, Bulgaria, Greece, Hungary, Japan, Poland, Rumania) are not comfortable in those situations and seek remedies against 'demographic decline' " (Berelson, 1974, p. 773). In the developing countries, population policies designed to curb growth rates prevail. Thirty-three governments with 76 percent of the population of the developing countries have policies to reduce the population growth rate, and another thirty-one governments with an additional 16 percent of the population in the developing countries support family planning activities for other than demographic reasons (Nortman and Hofstatter, 1976).

The extent of the effect of population policies on demographic trends is difficult to assess because numerous other components of the changing social environment influence demographic behavior simultaneously. Yet, the experience of many countries has demonstrated that demographic trends are not only the result of the "normal" flow of events but are also modified by population policies. Policies regulating international migration, especially in tightly administered areas, tend to be the most effective policy measures (Davis, 1974); policies improving public and personal health conditions and thus lowering mortality tend to have a similar record (Stolnitz, 1975); and policies attempting to modify fertility behavior vary considerably in their effectiveness. According to Berelson (1974, p. 788), ". . . across the world it may be fair to say that developing countries have done better in lowering birth rates than the developed countries have done in increasing them; or, perhaps alternatively, that it is easier to lower birth rates by policy measures than to raise them." However difficult it might be to assess the extent of impact, for instance of the antinatalist policies in the developing countries (Freedman and Berelson, 1976), nobody will dispute the proposition that fertility in almost all the countries with such policies would currently be higher than it is had there not been such policies.

Future growth trends of any national population will reflect a complex interaction of numerous factors that in sum amount to the interaction between a nation's population growth momentum—positive, stable, or negative—and its determination to modify this momentum. Consequently, since a large and increasing proportion of the world's population resides in the developing countries, the future size of the world population depends to a large degree on the extent to which fertility trends in the developing countries are modified.

## APPENDIX
## SELECTED DEMOGRAPHIC CONCEPTS

The population size of an area is rarely constant; it grows because of births (and immigration) and diminishes because of deaths (and emigration). Two ways of measuring fertility are represented by the concepts of crude birthrate and total fertility rate. The *crude birthrate* is a measure that provides information on the relative frequency of births: the annual number of births of the area per 1,000 inhabitants. A more refined measure, *the total fertility rate,* provides some insight on the average childbearing behavior of individual women. The logic for this construct is to show the total number of children an imaginary woman would bear in her lifetime if she lived through her childbearing years and bore children in accordance with the current age patterns of fertility, that is, the frequency of births to women at different ages within their reproductive years fifteen to forty-nine. Fertility at the *replacement level* is the specific level of fertility that provides for a number of children to be born, such that each member of the parent generation is replaced by one child surviving to adulthood. Replacement level fertility is customarily expressed in terms of a specific total fertility rate. In countries with low mortality, a total fertility rate slightly over 2.0 will have a sufficient margin (allowing for mortality) to provide for replacement, whereas total fertility rates of 4.0 and over may correspond to fertility at the replacement level in high mortality situations. Replacement level fertility does not necessarily imply a zero population growth rate. If a relatively large proportion of the population is in the prime childbearing ages and fertility is at the replacement level, the combination will result in a positive rate of natural increase. The *rate of natural increase* can be calculated as the difference between the crude birthrate and the crude death rate. The *crude death rate* is analogous to the crude birthrate: the total number of deaths in a year per 1,000 inhabitants. Another measure indicating mortality levels is the *expectation of life at birth* (*life expectancy*). This measure corresponds to the number of years the imaginary average person can expect to live if he/she were to go through life and be subject to the risks of death prevailing for each age at a particular time and place.

## NOTE

1. Most recently, Banister (1977) has attempted to prove that the government of the People's Republic of China does possess reasonably reliable information about the demographic properties of its population. The evidence she has accumulated would indicate that in 1973 the population of China numbered 890 million and that in 1972 the crude death rate was between 7 and 8 per 1,000, the crude birthrate 25 to 27 per 1,000, and the rate of natural increase approximately 1.9 percent per year. Banister also discusses 1975 demographic measures—a crude death rate of 6 to 7, a crude birthrate of 21 to 22, and a rate of natural increase of about 1.5 percent—but these data are considerably less reliable than those for 1972.

## REFERENCES

Banister, Judith. 1977. "The Current Vital Rates and Population Size of the People's Republic of China and Its Provinces." Ph.D. dissertation, Food Research Institute, Stanford University.

Berelson, Bernard (ed.). 1974. *Population Policy in Developed Countries.* New York: McGraw-Hill.

Brackett, James W., R. T. Ravenholt, and William Goldman. 1976. "World Fertility, 1976: An Analysis of Data Sources and Trends." *Population Reports: Family Planning Programs,* Series J, Number 12 (November), J-205-J-206.

Commission on Population Growth and the American Future. 1972. *Population and the American Future.* Washington, D.C.: U.S. Government Printing Office.

Davis, Kingsley. 1974. "The Migrations of Human Populations." In *The Human Population,* a Scientific American book. San Francisco: W. H. Freeman, 53-68. [Originally *Scientific American,* Volume 231, Number 3 (September), 92-105.]

Demeny, Paul. 1975. "Population Policy: The Role of National Governments." *Population and Development Review,* Volume 1, Number 1 (September), 147-161.

Freedman, Ronald, and Bernard Berelson. 1976. "The Record of Family Planning Programs." *Studies in Family Planning,* Volume 7, Number 1 (January), 1-40.

Frejka, Tomas. 1968. "Reflections on the Demographic Conditions Needed to Establish a U.S. Stationary Population Growth." *Population Studies,* Volume 22, Number 3 (November), 379-397.

———. 1973. *The Future of Population Growth: Alternative Paths to Equilibrium.* New York: John Wiley and Sons.

Keely, Charles B., and S. M. Tomasi. 1976. "The Disposable Worker: Historical and Comparative Perspectives on Clandestine Migration." Paper presented at the annual meeting of the Population Association of America, Session on Clandestine Migration, Montreal (April 30).

King, Gregory. 1696. *Natural and Political Observations and Conclusions upon the State and Condition of England, 1696.* Reprinted in *The Earliest Classics: John Graunt and Gregory King.* Germany: Gregg International Publishers Limited, 1973.

Kirk, Dudley. 1971. "A New Demographic Transition?" In *Rapid Population Growth: Consequences and Policy Implications.* Baltimore, Md.: Johns Hopkins Press, 123–147.

———. 1976. "The Accelerating Decline of Fertility in the Demographic Transition." (Manuscript.)

Mauldin, W. Parker. 1976. "Fertility Trends: 1950–75." *Studies in Family Planning,* Volume 7, Number 9 (September), 242–248.

Nortman, Dorothy, and Ellen Hofstatter. 1976. "Population and Family Planning Programs: A Factbook." *Reports on Population and Family Planning,* Number 2, 1–102. 8th ed.

Population Division, Department of Economic and Social Affairs of the United Nations Secretariat. 1975. *Selected World Demographic Indicators by Countries, 1950–2000.* ESA/P/WP.55, May 28. (Mimeo.)

Stolnitz, George J. 1975. "International Mortality Trends: Some Main Facts and Implications." In *The Population Debate: Dimensions and Perspectives, Papers of the World Population Conference, Bucharest, 1974,* Volume I, 220–236.

Taeuber, Irene B. 1972. "Growth of the Population of the United States in the Twentieth Century." In *Demographic and Social Aspects of Population Growth,* Charles F. Westoff and Robert Parke, Jr. (eds.), Volume 1, 17–84. Washington, D.C.: U.S. Government Printing Office.

U.N. Secretariat. 1975. "Population Policies and Programmes." In *The Population Debate: Dimensions and Perspectives, Papers of the World Population Conference, Bucharest, 1974,* Volume II, 583–605.

U.S. Bureau of the Census. 1975. *Projections of the Population of the United States: 1975 to 2050.* Population Estimates and Projections, Series P–25, Number 601 (October).

———. 1976. *Projections of the Population of Voting Age for States: November 1976.* Population Estimates and Projections, Series P–25, Number 626 (May).

LESTER R. BROWN

# The Prospects for Food

As we move into the final quarter of this century, the world food economy appears to be undergoing a fundamental transformation. Two developments stand out. One, the comfortable reserve of surplus stocks and excess production capacity that the world has enjoyed over the past generation may now be history. Two, the world is becoming overwhelmingly dependent on North America for its food supplies. Together these two developments add up to a new role and responsibility for North America.

Only a few years ago the world had not only surplus stocks and excess production capacity, but it appeared that both would be around for a long time to come. Suddenly, within a span of a few years, they have largely disappeared. Today the entire world is living hand to mouth, trying to make it from one harvest to the next. Global food insecurity is greater now than at any time since the years immediately following World War II, making weather in the principal food-producing countries a major global economic and political concern.

A measure of growing worldwide food deficits, grain exports from North America have doubled during the 1970s, expanding from 56 million tons in 1970 to nearly 100 million tons during fiscal year 1976. Of the 115 countries for which data are readily available, all but a few now import grains. Those countries which remain as significant exporters at the global level can be numbered on the fingers of one hand. Two of these, the United States and Canada, dwarf the others. The two together export enough grain to feed the 600 million people of India.

The reasons for growing dependence on North American food supplies are manifold. Growing population pressure triggers new food demands as it simultaneously speeds up the deterioration of food systems; agriculture is widely mismanaged; and new affluence whets appetites in the OPEC countries and elsewhere. The causes of the growing deficits vary, and often a combination of factors is responsible, but the effects are the same: ever greater pressure on North American food supplies.

As a result of these trends, North America today finds itself with an almost monopolistic control of the world's exportable grain supplies, a situation for which there is no historical precedent. In a world of food scarcity, where there may not be enough food to go around, North America must decide who gets how much food and on what terms. The governments of the United States and Canada have not consciously sought this responsibility, any more than the countries of the Middle East have planned their geographical location astride the world's richest oil fields; but they must reckon with it nevertheless.

In recent years, shortages of food have contributed to global double-digit inflation and to severe nutritional stress among low-income people everywhere. In some of the poorer countries, shortages have boosted death rates, reversing postwar trends. National political leaders in the food-deficit countries, rich and poor alike, are growing uneasy over future access to food supplies. Profound changes in the world food economy have brought into question the basic assumptions underlying our food policies, forcing us to rethink how we relate our food resources to the rest of the world.

## NEW SOURCES OF GLOBAL FOOD INSECURITY

Throughout much of the period since World War II, the world has had two major food reserves: stocks of grain held by the principal exporting countries and cropland idled under farm programs in the United States. During the 1960s and early 1970s some 50 million acres out of a total U.S. cropland base of 350 million acres were held out of production to support prices. Stocks of grain held by the exporting countries were readily available for use when needed. Cropland idled under farm programs in the United States could be brought back into production within a year. Together grain stockpiles and cropland reserves provided security for all mankind, a cushion against any imaginable food disasters.

As recently as early 1972, it seemed likely that surplus stocks and cropland idled under farm programs would be part of the landscape for the foreseeable future. Then, suddenly, things began to change. The global demand for food, fueled by the relentless growth of population and by rising affluence, began to outstrip the productive capacity of the world's farmers and fishermen. The world fish catch, which had tripled between 1950 and 1970 and moved to a new high each year, turned downward for three consecutive years. Most of the idled U.S. cropland was returned to use beginning in 1973 and all of it thereafter, but still food reserves were not rebuilt.

In 1961, the combination of reserve stocks of grain in exporting countries and idle cropland in the United States amounted to the equivalent of 105 days of world grain consumption. By 1972, stocks still equalled 69 days of world consumption. Then reserves began to drop rather abruptly—to 55 days in 1973 and still further to 33 days in 1974. The 1975 carryover stocks remain precariously low, and all hopes for rebuilding them to safe levels vanished with the poor 1975 Soviet harvest. U.S. Department of Agriculture (USDA) estimates of carry-over stocks in 1976, largely determined by the 1975 harvest, indicated an even lower level than in 1975 (See Table 1.)

The third source of global food insecurity and instability in the mid-1970s is the near total dependence of the entire world on one region—North America—for its exportable food supplies. Considering that both countries within the region are affected by the same climatic cycles,

## Table 1. Index of World Food Security, 1961–1976

| Year | Reserve Stocks of Grain[1] | Grain Equivalent of Idled U.S. Cropland | Total Reserves | Reserves as Days of Annual Grain Consumption |
|---|---|---|---|---|
| | | (Million Metric Tons) | | |
| 1961 | 163 | 68 | 231 | 105 |
| 1962 | 176 | 81 | 257 | 105 |
| 1963 | 149 | 70 | 219 | 95 |
| 1964 | 153 | 70 | 223 | 87 |
| 1965 | 147 | 71 | 218 | 91 |
| 1966 | 151 | 78 | 229 | 84 |
| 1967 | 115 | 51 | 166 | 59 |
| 1968 | 144 | 61 | 205 | 71 |
| 1969 | 159 | 73 | 232 | 85 |
| 1970 | 188 | 71 | 259 | 89 |
| 1971 | 168 | 41 | 209 | 71 |
| 1972 | 130 | 78 | 208 | 69 |
| 1973 | 148 | 24 | 172 | 55 |
| 1974 | 108 | 0 | 108 | 33 |
| 1975 | 111 | 0 | 111 | 35 |
| 1976[2] | 100 | 0 | 100 | 31 |

1. Based on carryover stocks of grain at beginning of crop year in individual countries for year shown. the USDA has recently expanded the coverage of reserve stocks to include importing as well as exporting countries; thus the reserve levels are slightly higher than those heretofore published.

2. Estimates by USDA.

SOURCE: Based on USDA data and author's estimates.

with a poor crop in one all too often associated with a poor crop in the other, complete reliance on the United States and Canada is even riskier than it first seems.

The fourth disruptive factor was a decision made by Soviet political leaders to offset crop shortfalls with imports. Since recent year-to-year fluctuations in the Soviet grain harvest have exceeded the normal annual gains in the world grain crop, this decision further destabilizes the world food economy. This policy, apparently made in early 1972, may not be an irreversible one, but neither will it be easily abandoned. Soviet herds and flocks have been building steadily throughout the 1970s as a result of this policy. So too have the expectations and appetites of Soviet consumers.

Thus, four major factors contribute to instability in the world food economy today: the decline of grain reserves; the disappearance of idled cropland in the United States; the dangerous dependence of the entire world on the food surplus of one geographic-climatic region; and the decision by the Soviet government to offset shortfalls through imports rather than through belt-tightening. All but one, the heavy dependence on North America, have emerged quite recently.

The high costs of food price instability take many forms—economic, political, and social. Consumers, particularly the poor, obviously suffer. Most families do not find it easy to adjust to wide fluctuations in food prices. These same fluctuations in turn make it more difficult for producers to decide how much to plant and how much to invest in inputs. Dairymen and cattlemen everywhere have been caught in an impossible bind between the price of milk or beef and the cost of grain. The result is predictable. Thousands have been driven out of business, leading to erratic flows of milk and meat to market and to discontent among consumers.

Governments are beleaguered by violent fluctuations in food prices too. Unstable markets wreak havoc with foreign exchange budgets, particularly those of developing countries heavily dependent on food imports, and undermine government efforts to combat inflation. Indeed, soaring food prices have contributed directly to the unprecedented global inflation of the mid-1970s.

## NORTH AMERICAN BREADBASKET

North America has emerged as the world's breadbasket only since World War II. Its rise is best measured by looking at the net grain-trade flows among various geographic regions. An aggregate of all grains is a useful indicator of food trends, since grains supply more than half of man's food energy supply when consumed directly and a sizable segment of the remainder when consumed indirectly. From the production side, grains occupy more than 70 percent of the world's cropland area. Net regional data, which exclude trade among countries within a region, help isolate more clearly the basic trends in the world food economy.

Prior to World War II, all geographic regions, except Western Europe, were net exporters. North America was not the only exporter nor even the leading one. During the 1934-1938 period, Latin America was exporting an average of 9 million tons per year, while North America exported only 5 million tons. Eastern Europe, including the Soviet Union, was exporting 5 million tons annually, exactly the same as North America.

All this has now changed beyond recognition. Asia has developed a massive deficit. It is now importing some 50 million tons of grain per year, most of it taken by three countries—Japan, China, and India. Africa, Latin America, and Eastern Europe (including the U.S.S.R.) have all become food-deficit regions too. Western Europe, continually a major importer, has been the only stable element through the period; its imports rarely moved outside the 20 to 30 million ton range.

North America's unchallenged dominance as a global food supplier began in the 1940s. The scale of exports expanded gradually during the 1950s and 1960s. During the 1970s, North America grain exports have nearly doubled in response to the explosive growth in import demand from around the world. (See Table 2.)

Why has one region emerged as a supplier of food to the rest of the world? If one were to select the single dominant factor transforming

### Table 2. The Changing Pattern of World Grain Trade[1]

| Region | 1934–1938 | 1948–1952 | 1960 | 1970 | 1976[2] |
|---|---|---|---|---|---|
| | (Million Metric Tons) | | | | |
| North America | + 5 | +23 | +39 | +56 | +94 |
| Latin America | + 9 | + 1 | 0 | + 4 | − 3 |
| Western Europe | −24 | −22 | −25 | −30 | −17 |
| E. Europe & U.S.S.R. | + 5 | — | 0 | 0 | −27 |
| Africa | + 1 | 0 | − 2 | − 5 | −10 |
| Asia | + 2 | − 6 | −17 | −37 | l47 |
| Australia & N.Z. | + 3 | + 3 | + 6 | +12 | + 8 |

1. Plus sign indicates net exports; minus sign, net imports.
2. Preliminary estimates of fiscal year data.
SOURCE: Derived from FAO and USDA data and author's estimates.

world trade patterns in recent decades, it would be varying rates of population growth. Certainly the conversion of Asia, Africa, and Latin America to deficit status was population related. Population growth has been less influential in Eastern Europe, while one of the keys to Western Europe's stability as a food importer has been its modest population growth.

A comparison of North America and Latin America illustrates the devastating effects of rapid population growth. As recently as 1950, North America and Latin America had roughly equal populations, 163 and 168 million, respectively. The difference since then explains much of the changing trade pattern. While North America's population growth has tapered off substantially since the late 1950s, Latin America's has escalated at an explosive rate. Several Latin American countries, such as Mexico, Venezuela, Peru, and Brazil, have population growth rates of 3 percent or more per year, a rate which, if it continues, will lead to a *nineteenfold population increase within a century.* If North America's 1950 population had expanded at 3 percent per year, it would now be 341 million rather than the actual 236 million. At current per capita consumption levels, those additional 105 million people would absorb virtually all exportable supplies and North America would be struggling to maintain self-sufficiency.

## KEY ACTORS ON THE GLOBAL SCENE

The preceding section discussed the changing pattern of world food trade in terms of geographic regions, sketching out a panoramic view of historical change. This section focuses on several key countries or groups of countries that are contributing to changing trade patterns and are destined to influence future food-trade trends.

### JAPAN

Japan is far and away the world's largest grain importer, importing more than any other two countries combined. The reasons are obvious. The government is upgrading diets for a population equal to nearly half that of North America and squeezed into an area smaller than California. In 1975 Japan imported nearly 20 million tons of grain, making it more dependent on imports than on its own production. (See Figure 1.)

Through centuries of change, Japan kept its cereal imports at a fairly low level. But as population pressure began to mount several decades ago, the Japanese turned to the oceans for their animal protein and began to reserve their limited land resources for the intensive production of rice. As a result, they now grow the rice they need but make inordinate claims on the world's fisheries.

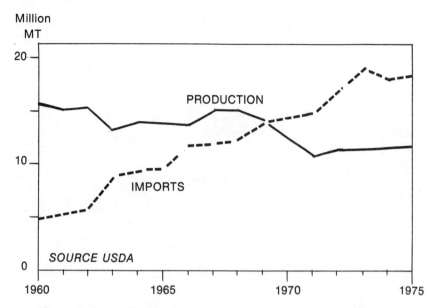

**Figure 1.** Japan: Production and Imports of All Grains, 1960–1975

As incomes and purchasing power have risen, many Japanese consumers have begun to prefer livestock products to fish. Consumption of pork and poultry products is now on a par with that of other industrial countries, but per capita annual beef intake is still only nine pounds, a small fraction of the hundred pounds or more consumed in the United States and Canada.

Postwar prosperity has enabled Japanese consumers to enrich their diets, but imports of grain have subsequently shot up to 20 million tons per year. Since 1970, grain imports, consisting largely of feedgrains but also including sizable quantities of wheat, have exceeded domestic grain production. One might say that Japan today relies on imports to feed 62 percent of its 110 million people.

Japanese economic projections for the next decade show food imports continuing to rise as a result of further moderate population growth and rising incomes. Japanese consumers now vie for more livestock products; with reasonable prices, consumption will continue to climb. We can only speculate as to when Japan's imports of cereals will level off, but it is not likely to be soon.

Japan received a great deal of credit for the sharp reduction in its birthrate during the years immediately following World War II. Since then, however, its population has continued to grow at 1 percent or more per year, and now grows at a rate nearly double the North American rate of natural increase. Recent signs suggest that the Japanese are again preparing to discourage population growth actively, and they could quite reasonably move toward population stability over the next decade if they decide to do so.

### CHINA

Visitors to China in recent years almost always comment on the seemingly excellent nutritional condition of the population. Journalists, econonists, scientists, and doctors all come away with the same impression. The obvious clinical signs of malnutrition, present in almost every other low-income country, appear to be almost wholly absent in China.

The success of Chinese efforts in nutrition can probably be attributed more to improvements in distribution than to production gains. The latter have been creditable but not spectacular. China has imported several million tons of grain per year since 1960, a total of 78 million tons from 1960 to 1975. These heavy imports of grain, largely wheat, were financed at least in part by modest exports of higher value rice. From 1970 to 1975, China apparently imported more grain than India but, having done so, China has seemingly achieved adequate nutrition for its population while India is far from it. (See Table 3.)

Chinese success in agriculture cannot be viewed apart from the social reforms and regimentation that have resulted in a rare degree of social equity not only within the rural sector but between the rural and urban sectors as well. Another strength of the Chinese system is the organization of consumer and production teams to permit the mobilization of excess or seasonally idle labor for rural road construction, reforestation, and the construction of terraces and irrigation reservoirs and canals. Enormous earth-filled irrigation dams have been built almost entirely by human muscle power.

Its achievements granted, Chinese agriculture is not without prob-

### Table 3. China: Imports of Grain, 1961–1975

(Million Metric Tons)

| | | | | | |
|---|---|---|---|---|---|
| 1961 | 5.6 | 1966 | 5.6 | 1971 | 3.0 |
| 1962 | 4.6 | 1967 | 4.9 | 1972 | 4.8 |
| 1963 | 5.4 | 1968 | 4.4 | 1973 | 7.7 |
| 1964 | 6.3 | 1969 | 3.9 | 1974 | 7.0 |
| 1965 | 5.9 | 1970 | 4.6 | 1975 | 4.4 |

SOURCE: China: A Reassessment of the Economy. A compendium of papers submitted by the Joint Economic Committee, U.S. Congress.

lems. It has many. Pressures on agricultural resources are evident in the shift of land from soybeans to cereals. As recently as the 1930s, China supplied 90 percent of the soybeans entering the world market. Within the last few years, it has not only lost this exportable surplus but has even begun to import soybeans, almost exclusively from the United States.

An indication of the seriousness with which the Chinese leadership views the agricultural problem is its willingness to compromise ideologically and to turn to foreign engineering firms, primarily American, to build fertilizer plants. No less than thirteen massive new nitrogen fertilizer complexes are under construction. Upon completion, these plants should virtually eliminate China's heavy dependence on imported fertilizer. Nonetheless, returns on additional fertilizer use in China are dependent on comparable increases in other inputs and upon further progress in basic agronomic research. Without them, yield gains from additional massive quantities of fertilizer will diminish rapidly.

China may ultimately solve its food problem, but probably as much by its aggressive action on the population front as on the food front. Estimates of current population growth (and one must underline "estimate" because not even the Chinese seem to have precise data) hover around 1.6 percent per year, a rate comparable to that of the United States in the late 1950s.

Despite the downplaying of the issue in official pronouncements in international forums, the Chinese leaders have been among the first to perceive the need to sharply curtail population growth. With the possible exception of Singapore, no government has confronted the population threat so directly as China. The leadership has not only provided family planning services and created the social conditions conducive to lowering fertility rates, but it has also reshaped important economic and social policies so as to discourage large families. The birthrate appears to be dropping precipitously. If it continues to decline, China's population growth rate could dip to 1 percent by the end of this decade or shortly thereafter. If it can continue to move toward the clearly defined goal of population stability, then China could finally solve its food problem and, by eliminating its need for imports, could help solve the world's food problem.

## INDIA

India's future food situation is surrounded by large question marks. The outlook appeared quite bleak in the mid-1960s until the government redesigned its food policies and priorities, giving agriculture the support it deserved. This reshaping of economic policies, combined with the advent of the high-yielding strains of wheat and rice, gave Indian agriculture a dramatic boost. During the six-year span between 1965 and 1971, India succeeded in doubling its wheat crop, a performance unmatched by any other major country. By 1972, India was teetering on the brink of self-sufficiency in cereals. Malnutrition was still rampant among the poor but, in economic terms, India's farmers were producing about all that the market would absorb. India actually provided massive food aid to refugees from Bangladesh and to the newly independent nation itself. For a brief period, it ranked second after the United States as a food-aid donor. (See Figure 2.)

Since the high watermark of Indian agriculture in the early 1970s, there have been numerous setbacks, some external to the Indian economy. In the spring of 1975, the USDA estimated that the Indian wheat crop was reduced by a million tons simply because of a shortage of fuel to operate irrigation pumps. Then too, India, more than most other countries, has been adversely affected by the short supply and high price of fertilizer. Heavy dependence on fertilizer imports reflects in part the inefficiency of India's domestic fertilizer plants. The problem is not a lack of agricultural potential; India is capable of producing far more food than is now produced. But India has not been able to put together the resources, the priorities and the policies essential to continued rapid development of its agriculture.

The hydra-headed economic problems of the 1970s are exacerbated by ecological abuse. Deforestation, overgrazing, desert en-

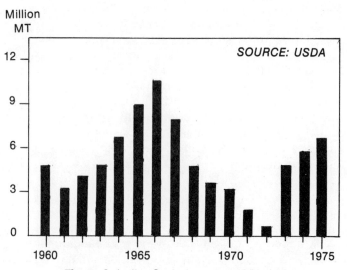

**Figure 2.** India: Grain Imports, 1960–1975

croachment, and increased flooding resulting from the destruction of natural vegetation are all beginning to take their toll of India's food production. The productivity of a vast semiarid area, covering a fifth of the country, is threatened by these forces. Soil erosion and the silting of irrigation reservoirs also have a measurable negative effect on food output.

On the population front, India has succeeded in modestly reducing its birthrate, but it still has a long way to go. It remains to be seen whether India can reduce its dependence on imported foodstuffs, or whether this dependence will become absolute and crippling in the years ahead as a result of continuing high birth rates, unfavorable economic forces, and negative ecological trends.

### U.S.S.R.

The agricultural production potential of the Soviet Union is severely constrained both by its natural environment and by the organization of its agriculture. Soviet agriculture is, by and large, low rainfall agriculture comparable to that of the Great Plains of Canada and the United States. The U.S.S.R. has severe winters and a short growing and grazing season. It has no choice region like the U.S. corn belt that combines rich soils and high, dependable rainfall.

In addition to these natural constraints, Soviet agriculture must contend with some basic institutional inefficiencies. Collectivization has dampened individual incentive. Almost universal reliance on dual purpose breeds of livestock for milk and meat has resulted in production inefficiencies: the Soviet Union is using more grain per capita than the United States to provide fewer (per capita) pounds of meat for its consumers. Despite great organizational efforts, and the allocation of tremendous amounts of grain to the meat-producing sector, the Soviet system cannot provide comparable quantities of meat for its consumers, who now consume scarcely half the meat consumed by Americans and Canadians. This is where political expediency joins hands with agricultural inefficiency. (See Figure 3.)

The Soviet decision to offset crop shortfalls with massive imports rather than via the more traditional method of belt-tightening by consumers is the most destabilizing single factor in the world food economy today, one that is enormously costly to consumers everywhere. The instability derives not so much from the scale of Soviet grain imports as from their unpredictable and secretive nature. The question now before the international community is how to reconcile the erratic need for imports with the urgent need to maintain some semblance of stability in the world grain market.

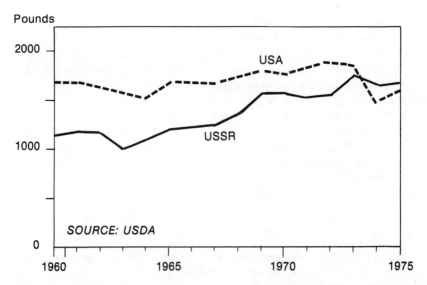

**Figure 3.** United States and Soviet Union: Per Capita Annual Grain Use, 1960–1975

The Soviet Union will probably be importing grain for the forseeable future. A recent speech by Soviet agricultural leader and Communist party spokesman, Fedor Kulakov, which was published in full in both *Pravda* and *Izvestia,* suggests that the return on recent investment in Soviet agriculture has disappointed the leadership. Indeed, the Soviets may be contemplating a shift in investment emphasis toward the exploitation of minerals and other raw materials for export. Even after a decade of heavy investment in agriculture, they still find that satisfying consumer needs requires large grain imports. Since there is little evidence to suggest any reduction in Soviet dependence on food imports in the years ahead, North America should gear both its production and export policies to the new reality of heavy Soviet dependence on imported grain.

### BRAZIL

For at least a generation, writings on world food prospects have alluded to the potential of Brazil, and particularly of the Amazon Basin, as a source of food for the world. Unfortunately, as we face global food shortages and are forced to reassess reality, it is becoming clear that Brazil is by no means a cornucopia. Although it has recently emerged as a soybean exporter, it is far from fulfilling its mythical legacy as a major supplier of food for the world. Indeed, in 1973, Brazil imported more grain than any country in the Western Hemisphere. Even with food from abroad, Brazil's Northeast still contains one of the largest areas of abject poverty and malnutrition found anywhere in the world.

What has happened to the notion that Brazil could someday feed the world? First, only a minute percentage of the area of the vast Amazon Basin is potentially cultivable with present food prices and prospective farming technologies. Even development of the pockets of agriculturally promising land will require extensive investment in transportation, drainage, research, credit, and marketing facilities. The problem is not so much that Brazil has not been able to expand its food production; it has, and at a fairly impressive rate. But Brazil is faced with a prodigious growth in the demand for food, as a result of a rapid rate of both population and economic growth. The population of Brazil grows at nearly 3 percent per year. In addition, its economy has been growing by an impressive 8 to 10 percent yearly over the past decade. Together, these two sources of growth in demand are raising food needs by some 4 percent per year, good weather or bad.

To meet new demands Brazil needs to increase agricultural output over an extended period of time far more rapidly than any major country has yet succeeded in doing. A sustained 4 percent annual growth in food production makes essential a heavy continuing investment in agriculture. In addition, it requires rapid innovation in agriculture that in turn requires the development of a wide range of new technologies and their immediate dissemination and acceptance by farmers. With an agricultural research system that is underdeveloped and poorly financed and a rural population that is still partly illiterate, the problems involved here are glaringly evident. Finally, with landholdings highly concentrated among a small percentage of the population, a redistribution of land is urgently needed to give those who work it a stronger incentive to raise its productivity.

But even all this is not enough. Brazil's current population growth rate of nearly 3 percent will, if it continues, result in the present population of 108 million multiplying to over 2 billion in a century, just four generations hence. Brazil would have to contend with a population larger than that of China and India combined well before this time in the next century. Without a strong commitment to family planning, the prospect of Brazil becoming a major supplier of grain to the world is a myth and not a harmless one.

## OPEC

The unprecedented accretion of wealth and purchasing power in oil-exporting countries over the past few years is now being reflected in their expanding food imports. Not only is the increase in purchasing power a very sharp one, but the number of people involved also represents a substantial portion of the world's population. The thirteen OPEC countries have a combined population of 268 million, nearly half of which is in Indonesia. Market size aside, the level of food consumption, especially of high protein foods, in OPEC countries is modest. Given the relatively low food consumption base, many new petrodollars will become food dollars.

In countries where oil exports are large and populations relatively small, as in Iraq, Iran, or Venezuela, food consumption per person is likely to rise in a meteoric fashion. Overall, the scale of food imports to OPEC countries seems certain to increase dramatically in the years ahead. If oil prosperity begins to spread beyond the urban elite, diets will be rapidly upgraded. Considering the historical neglect of agriculture in most of these countries, any sharp increase in demand will have to be satisfied initially by imports.

Most OPEC nations are semi-arid, and many are faced with severe ecological stresses in agriculture. Both Algeria and Nigeria suffer from overgrazing, deforestation, and the spread of the Sahara Desert. Nigeria, with a population variously estimated at from 60 to 80 million people, must deal with intense population pressures at a time when the system of traditional slash and burn cultivation is being undermined in some areas. As recovery periods between plantings are shortened to keep pace with the demand for food, soils are no longer able to regenerate their fertility.

A primary use of the new oil wealth is investment in agriculture. Ecuador, Nigeria, Iran, and Iraq are multiplying their financial commitment to agriculture. But continuing rapid growth in food output requires more than capital. The support system for agriculture includes an indigenous research capacity, technical advisory services, farm credit services, roads and market and, in many instances, reforms in land tenure. Viable agriculture also assumes the availability of tillable land and water.

The rate of expansion in the agricultural output of these countries will accelerate, but the decisive question is how fast the acceleration will be relative to that of the demand for food. Nearly all OPEC countries have food deficits, and in some they are substantial. Algeria, for example, relies heavily on imported wheat to sustain its population. The poor 1975 wheat harvest may result in an import need of close to 2 million tons, more than double the average of the past ten years. (See Figure 4.)

As increased purchasing power in OPEC countries converts into greater demand for livestock products, including poultry, many countries are implementing programs to rapidly expand food production.

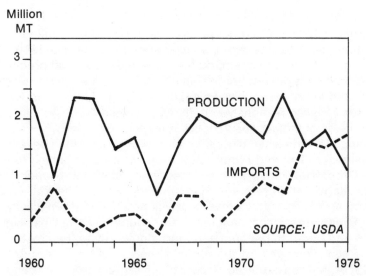

**Figure 4.** Algeria: Production and Imports of All Grains, 1960–1975

Some expect to double poultry and egg output within a period of two or three years: Iraq, for example, which has not traditionally imported feedgrains, is projected to import nearly a million tons annually by the end of the current decade in order to support its burgeoning poultry and livestock industry.

Ecuador has expanded its food output only 5 percent over the past three years. Yet, while production limps along, the demand for food is soaring, because of both population growth and the infusion of oil money into the economy. The result, as of mid-1975, is an acute domestic shortage of food and a need for a sharp increase in imports.

OPEC's food picture is clouded by Indonesia. If the oil dollars begin to filter down to the lower income groups, they will convert almost immediately into a demand for additional food. Can the Indonesian agricultural economy respond to this growth in demand? In the short run at least, it is doubtful. Because Indonesia supports a large population, even modest increases in per capita food import requirements would result in a large market demand for food imports.

From a social point of view, increasing the purchasing power of more than a quarter of a billion of the world's lower income people is unquestionably desirable. New buying power would mean more and better food and would greatly reduce malnutrition. But from an analytical point of view, the claims on the world's exportable food supplies are very steep and abrupt. In addition, they come at a time when there is little slack in the world farm economy.

### THE GREEN REVOLUTION COUNTRIES

In addition to OPEC, another group of countries, the so-called Green Revolution countries, deserves special attention. The mid-1960s witnessed the launching of a remarkable effort to expand food production in the food-deficit poor countries, an effort centered around the development and international dissemination of high-yielding dwarf wheats and rices. Highly responsive to fertilizer, these new strains could double yields of indigenous varieties if managed properly.

Coming at a time when per capita food production in the developing world was declining and requests for food aid were beginning to pour in, the Green Revolution was heralded as an exciting advance. India doubled its wheat crop in a six-year period; Mexico, the Philippines, Pakistan, and Turkey all increased cereal production dramatically.

The Green Revolution enabled many countries to cut back grain imports and some to become exporters. India, riding the crest of the Green Revolution, was on the verge of cereal self-sufficiency in the early 1970s. Mexico exported 10 percent of its grain crop between 1965 and 1969, though the production gains were eventually overwhelmed by one of the world's fastest population growth rates. (See Figure 5.)

By the mid-1970s, Mexico was importing one-fifth of its grain needs.

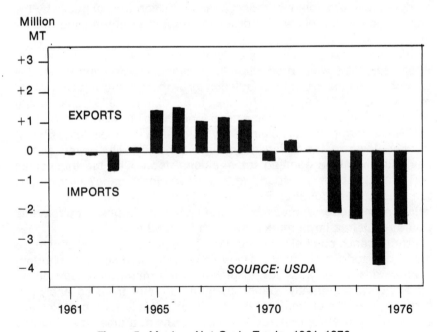

**Figure 5.** Mexico: Net Grain Trade, 1961–1976

The Green Revolution enabled the Philippines to end a half century of dependence on imported rice and to become a net exporter of rice during the late 1960s; today it is again importing rice on a large scale. Agriculture made measurable gains in these countries, but the advances were simply eaten up by the relentless growth in population.

During the early years of the Green Revolution, many of those involved in launching it, including Norman Borlaug, the originator of the miracle seeds, and myself, cautioned that the new seeds should not be viewed as a solution to the food problem. The only ultimate solution to the food problem in these countries was and is to put the brakes on population growth. The new seeds were simply buying time, perhaps another fifteen to twenty years, to get population growth under control. Half of that time has now passed. Though there has been some progress on the family planning front, it is clear from the data cited above that it is not nearly enough, and that time will not be bought so cheaply again.

## A DISTURBING REVERSAL

One of the most disturbing trends in the world food economy during the 1970s has been the downturn in grain yield per hectare. (See Figure 6.) This new trend shows up in recently published USDA data that cover all grains except rice (for which reliable worldwide yield data are not

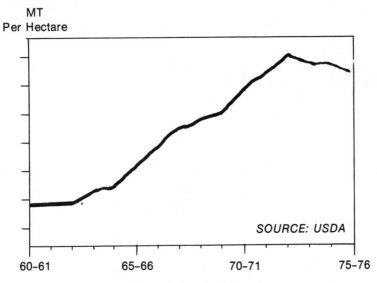

**Figure 6.** World Grain Yield per Hectare

readily available). If the average world grain yield during the period from 1960 to 1975 is plotted as a three-year sliding average in order to smooth out the fluctuations associated with weather, a disturbing trend emerges. From 1960 until 1972 this three-year average increased each year, but then in 1973 it turned downward, dropping further in 1974 and still further in 1975. At its peak in 1972, the average grain yield per hectare was 1.91 metric tons, but over the next three years it dropped to 1.84 metric tons, a decline of 4 percent. The crucial question is: why did this occur?

Aside from weather, which may or may not have been a major determinant, there are at least five factors that contributed to this downturn in world grain yields per acre: (1) the release for production of the 50 million acres of idled, below-average fertility cropland in the United States that, added to the global cropland base, almost certainly reduced the average crop yield; (2) the high cost and tight supply of energy; (3) the high cost and tight supply of fertilizer; (4) the buildup of population pressures that reduce the fallow cycles of shifting cultivators in large areas of West and East Africa, Central America, the Andean countries, and Southeast Asia to the point where fallow periods are now too short to allow soil fertility to regenerate; and (5) the growth of the demand for firewood in developing countries to such an extent that local forests could not keep pace and that more and more animal dung was used as fuel and less and less as an essential source of soil nutrients.

Together, these five factors apparently led to the downturn in world grain yields during the 1970s. There may well be others. Among these five it is impossible to measure individual contributions or indeed even to rank them in order of importance. Since many of these conditions still obtain, the critical question now is: when will the upward trend resume and how vigorous will it be?

## FUTURE FOOD PROSPECTS

Outlining a global food strategy requires at least some notion as to what the future food situation will be, as to whether food is more likely to be abundant and cheap or scarce and dear. The conditions under which the world's farmers and fishermen will attempt to expand food output during the final quarter of this century are quite different from those prevailing during most of the quarter century just ending. In most respects, it will be more difficult to increase food production than it was in the past.

None of the basic resources required to expand food output—land, water, energy, fertilizer—can be considered abundant today. The enormous growth of both economic and agricultural output during the second quarter of this century depended largely on a seemingly boundless supply of cheap energy. There is no prospect of a return to cheap energy in the foreseeable future.

Expanding the cultivated land area is also becoming more difficult and costly. Indeed, in some countries, the area under cultivation is actually declining as a result of desert encroachment, soil erosion, or urban sprawl. There are only a few places in the world where fertile new land awaits the plow: the Republic of Sudan, the tsetse fly belt in sub-Saharan Africa (assuming the tsetse fly can be eradicated), and parts of the interior of Latin America.

Scarce though new land is, the lack of water may be the principal constraint on future efforts to expand world food output. From 1950 to 1970, there was a virtual explosion in irrigated areas as large new irrigation projects were undertaken in China, India, and numerous other developing countries. Irrigated area was expanding by nearly 3 percent per year, but the annual increase from now until the end of the century will be scarcely 1 percent, since most of the choice dam sites have already been exploited.

The real cost of fertilizer, particularly widely used nitrogen fertilizer, declined substantially throughout most of the period since World War II. Cheap fertilizer played a major role in the impressive expansion of food production in the industrial countries of North America, Europe, and Japan, but, because the cost of fertilizer is closely tied to the cost of energy, we cannot expect a return to cheap fertilizer either.

At midcentury, the world fishing industry was brimming with optimism. Seemingly inexhaustible supplies of fish could be netted as fast as fishing technologies improved and capital investment expanded. This optimism was well founded. The world fish catch expanded from 22 million tons in 1950 to 70 million in 1970. Then suddenly, with little warning, it declined for two consecutive years, at least partly as a result of overfishing. An increasingly common phenomenon, overfishing now affects oceanic fisheries as widely separated as the haddock fishery in the North Atlantic and the anchovy fishery in the South Pacific. Some marine biologists think the world catch of table grade fish may be approaching its maximum sustainable limit. Others envision brighter prospects, but not even the most hopeful foresee future gains even remotely approaching those of the past twenty-five years.

In a number of oceanic fisheries, efforts to expand the catch further have led to overfishing, depletion of stocks, and an actual decline in catch. Additional investment in fishing capacity brings not only a diminishing return per unit of investment, but in many fisheries an actual negative return. What is not yet widely realized is that a similar predicament may engulf agriculture in parts of the world where population pressure is mounting. Extending food production onto marginal land is already leading to overgrazing, deforestation, desert expansion, soil erosion, silting of irrigation reservoirs, and increased flooding.

In some developing countries, these negative forces may soon override the drive to step up food output through additional capital investment and technological innovation. We may witness in the not too distant future sustained absolute declines in national food production in some developing countries, namely those with the most rapid population growth, because of these ecological stresses. This backsliding will be without precedent in the modern world and, I dare say, our success in anticipating such a reversal may not be any greater than our success in predicting the declining catch in oceanic fisheries.

In the industrial countries, diminishing returns on key agricultural inputs such as fertilizer and energy may severely constrain efforts to expand food output rapidly. In the early 1950s, each additional pound of fertilizer in the American corn belt raised corn yields by some 15 to 20 pounds. Today, an additional pound of fertilizer applied in the same corn field may yield an additional 5 pounds. The use of chemical fertilizer has not yet reached the saturation point in any of the industrial countries, but for some the point may not be far off. By contrast, the production response to fertilizer in the developing countries, where usage rates are low, is still quite high.

Hindsight now enables us to identify specific technological advances or factors that have led to quantum jumps in world food output. Among these were the hybridization of corn, the rapid spread in the use of chemical fertilizer in industrial countries following World War II, and, more recently, the rapid spread of the high-yielding dwarf wheats and rices in the Green Revolution countries. As we look over the shoulders of agricultural researchers today, it is difficult to see any technological advances on the drawing board which will lead to comparable quantum leaps in world food output.

In summary, the scarcity of basic resources required to expand food output, the negative ecological trends which are gaining momentum year by year in the poor countries, and the diminishing returns on the use of energy and fertilizer in agriculture in the industrial countries lead me to conclude that a world of cheap abundant food with surplus stocks and a large reserve of idled cropland may now be history. The present augurs a somewhat grimmer future, one of more or less chronic scarcity enlivened only by sporadic surpluses of a local and shortlived nature. Current dependence on North America will likely continue to increase, probably being limited only by the region's export capacity.

INDIRA  RAJARAMAN

# Forecasts for Nonrenewable Resources

Every periodic recurrence of concern over the adequacy for future economic expansion of the world's endowment of mineral resources seems to set in its wake a recurrence of the counter view, that it is pointless to try to quantify long-term demand and supply in any way. So many imponderables, chiefly technological, are thought to influence the future course of events—enough to render any exercise in long-term projection devoid of meaning or consequence. The latest resurgence of concern over the long-term outlook was sparked dramatically by the first Club of Rome study (Meadows et al., 1972), with its forecast of total depletion within the next century. This provoked a good deal of criticism in response, based essentially on the expectation of technological solutions to shortages as and when they arise and on a belief in the potential abundance of the earth, an abundance needing only human ingenuity to be released and become available.[1]

It is certainly true that there are at any time continuing developments in the technology of exploration and recovery, so that ore bodies of lesser accessibility and lower quality become economic to mine. Even conventional techniques of exploration have not been exhaustively applied to all parts of the world. Recycling is a further possibility that can extend the supply. Finally, on the demand side, technological improvements in the efficiency of materials use are expected to continue as will the substitutions of materials that are relatively more abundant for materials relatively less so.

All these factors notwithstanding, there does not seem to be a case for leaving the materials availability problem to the market, unless it is believed that solutions will be found swiftly and flexibly to shortages as and when they are reflected in market prices. A more reasonable assumption is that there will be short-run inelasticities and inflexibilities within the system, so that periodic shortages could cause severe dis-

SOURCE: From "Non-renewable resources. A review of long-term projections" by Indira Rajaraman, which was published in *Futures*, Volume 8, Number 3, June 1976 (Copyright of IPC Science & Technology Press Limited, Guildford, England). Reprinted with permission of IPC Science & Technology Press Limited.

locations. No better example can be found than the recent oil crisis, although the shortage was precipitated for reasons other than physical scarcity. There is a great need, therefore, for a careful continuing evaluation of the total endowment of each mineral resource and of its "life" at foreseeable rates of consumption, so that areas of impending shortage can be identified well in advance.

This chapter is a review of studies that have made a contribution in this direction by projecting future demand, or by estimating the total stocks of nonrenewable resources that are known to exist or are likely to be discovered with further exploration or with foreseeable improvements in exploration technology. It must be emphasized that the computations made here of the "life" of these stocks at projected rates of demand are not to be interpreted as estimates of the number of years before total depletion or doomsday. Rather, they must be regarded as estimates of the lead time available for the exploration of solutions at both the demand and supply ends of the materials availability problem (short of the ultimate and least attractive solution of slowing growth rates). In any comprehensive monitoring of the implications of continued economic growth, there are, of course, further dimensions that need to be considered such as environmental pollution and damage. These, however, fall outside the scope of this chapter.

Demand projections are reviewed in the section that follows, and estimates of mineral endowment in the section after that. Ideally, long-term demand and supply are best determined simultaneously within the framework of a dynamic model with a range of solutions for alternative contingencies. There are many interdependencies that need to be taken into account. Different materials can often satisfy the same need, and the extent to which they are substituted for one another is a function (among other factors) of the relative supply outlook. Each material is needed as an input for the production of other materials and is used complementarily with others, so that the demand for each is a function of the total materials mix. Finally, all of these relationships are a function in turn of the choice of technology, which itself changes over time.

The studies reviewed below do not take into account all of these relationships. Nevertheless, they do provide an adequate basis for an initial look into the crucial question of the resource base for future world economic growth.

## DEMAND PROJECTIONS

In projecting future demand for raw materials, there is no implication that these in any way represent projections of need. Demand at all times is an important policy variable for dealing with potential shortages; possible instruments range from the technological to the institu tional or sociopolitical, such as greater energy conservation or improved recycling of nonenergy materials. The projections covered here are to be viewed, rather, as first approximations to what is likely to prevail, given the assumptions each makes on technological change, recycling, and conservation.

The rate of growth of future demand for a raw material is a function both of future growth in Gross Domestic Product (GDP) and of future changes, if any, in the intensity of use of the material per unit of final output. Since both components are likely to vary according to country or region, materials demand is best projected on a disaggregated region or country level, and then aggregated to obtain the global forecast.

The intensity of use of any material per unit of total output is a function of two variables. The first is the composition of total output. Broad trends in the composition of output in industrialized nations— toward service—indicate that the use-intensity for materials will decline on the whole in these countries, and that it will rise on the whole in countries trying to industrialize. Within the broad trend, however, individual materials will be affected differently according to the rates of growth of the particular activities in which each is used.

The second variable is the use-coefficient of a material in its various uses, which can change through intermaterial substitution or the technological improvements that have historically lowered use-coefficients over time, such as more efficient fuel use and stronger and lighter alloys. (Technological change is frequently the cause of many changes in output composition as well—new products, new means to satisfy old wants.) Intermaterial substitution in its turn is influenced by relative prices, which in turn reflect relative global availability. Thus, the future demand for a raw material is a function, among other factors, of its estimated future supply. This is an important interdependence.

Ideally, as mentioned earlier, global demand projections should be made within the framework of a dynamic model with several regional subsystems. None of the three studies reviewed below adopted such an approach, which would have involved a mammoth undertaking.[2] The first study, and the one that covers the largest number of minerals, is the 1970 edition of *Mineral Facts and Problems,* a publication of the U.S. Bureau of Mines (U.S. Department of Interior, 1970). The second is a 1971 study done by Resources for the Future as part of a larger study carried out for the United States Commission on Population Growth and the American Future (Ridker, 1972). Finally, there is the 1972 study made for a few selected materials by a research team headed by Wilfred Malenbaum for the National Commission on Materials Policy (1972). All three studies project demand up to the year 2000.

The projections in *Mineral Facts* are done separately for two sectors, the United States and the rest of the world; not surprisingly, the U.S. projections are the more carefully constructed. These are based on the assumption of a 4 percent rate of growth of Gross National Product (GNP) in constant prices. A range is estimated for the year 2000 of total output of each of the major products or activities in which each mineral is used, based on the projected growth in GNP, along with its estimated composition in the terminal forecast year. "High" and "low" values are then established for the mineral input required for these outputs, taking into account possible changes in use-coefficients. For the rest of the world, no explicit assumptions are made as to future rates of growth of GNP or its composition. Projected rates of demand for the rest of the industrialized world are assumed to be roughly equivalent to those for the United States. For developing countries, these rates are adjusted according to a rough judgment as to whether these countries would require a more, or less, rapid rate of increase in the use of the material.

For nonenergy resources, the Resources for the Future study uses the projections in *Mineral Facts* for demand outside the United States, and makes independent projections *only* for the United States. These are arrived at through a dynamic input-output model, although the possibilities the model offers for varying use-coefficients are not exploited. The use of fixed technical coefficients in long-term projections is always a serious shortcoming, but the other shortcomings—the use of the casual *Mineral Facts* projections for the rest of the world—are even more serious. (For energy materials, the study uses a different procedure altogether; this will be examined later in the section.)

The Malenbaum study is the only one that arrives at global projections on the basis of a more than twofold division of the world, and the only one in which future demand is estimated equally carefully for each regional subdivision. There are ten of these. A global rate of growth of GDP of 3.8 percent is assumed; rates for individual regions fall between 3.4 percent and 4.2 percent except for Japan (5 percent). The U.S. growth is projected at 3.75 percent, slightly under the global average. Intensity of use per unit of total output is then projected separately for each of these regions, and materials demand in the terminal forecast year obtained as a product of projected GDP and intensity of use. Projections of intensity of use are done graphically as a function of per capita income, with reference to the historical trend in both the region in question and, except for the United States, in regions at similar levels of per capita income. There is a large element of judgment in these trend extrapolations, not always carefully justified. Nevertheless, their general direction and magnitude are generally plausible; with a few exceptions (noted below), the Malenbaum estimates are the most accurate of the three.

The Malenbaum study does not, unfortunately, cover many minerals (Table 1). The list covered here has therefore been limited accordingly and has been expanded only to include some major materials not covered in the Malenbaum study. A comprehensive set of projections must, of course, include mercury and silver, among other materials; such a study would be most useful and is anxiously awaited.

*Mineral Facts* was very comprehensive in terms of number of minerals included, but, as has just been seen, it has severe methodological limitations. These were the projections used in *The Limits to Growth*. In this connection, a curious if minor error was noticed here with respect to the use in this study of the figures from *Mineral Facts.* Percentage growth rates are supplied in *Mineral Facts* separately for the United States and the rest of the world; overall growth rates must be obtained from the sum of U.S. and non-U.S. consumption in the terminal years. The authors of *The Limits to Growth,* however, use the rest-of-the-world growth rates and term them global rates, which they are not. Since the global rates in general are lower than the rest-of-the-world

**Table 1. Projected Rates of Annual Increase in Demand up to the Year 2000**

| | | USBM[1] (%) | | RFF[2] (%) | | | | Malenbaum[3] |
|---|---|---|---|---|---|---|---|---|
| | | High | Low | High | Low | High[4] | Low[4] | (%) |
| *Nonferrous* | | | | | | | | |
| Aluminum | World | 7.52 | 5.06 | 6.89 | 4.75 | 6.68 | 4.44 | 5.86 |
| | USA | 7.27 | 4.99 | 4.89 | 3.94 | 3.71 | 2.77 | 5.20 |
| | R of W[5] | 7.66 | 5.11 | | | | | 6.25 |
| Copper | World | 5.68 | 3.46 | 5.32 | 3.11 | 5.25 | 3.02 | 3.76 |
| | USA | 5.23 | 3.68 | 3.03 | 2.00 | 2.31 | 1.40 | 2.85 |
| | R of W | 5.80 | 3.41 | | | | | 4.07 |
| Lead | World | 2.75 | 1.55 | 2.59 | 1.79 | 2.50 | 1.74 | |
| | USA | 3.62 | 1.16 | 3.49 | 2.38 | 3.21 | 2.19 | |
| | R of W | 2.32 | 1.62 | | | | | |
| Tin | World | 1.79 | 0.20 | 2.07 | 0.14 | | | |
| | USA | 1.60 | 0.59 | 1.21 | 0.56 | | | |
| | R of W | 2.31 | 0.00 | | | | | |
| Zinc | World | 3.29 | 2.22 | 3.37 | 2.50 | 3.12 | 2.25 | 3.69 |
| | USA | 3.32 | 1.25 | 3.64 | 2.52 | 2.90 | 1.70 | 2.87 |
| | R of W | 3.27 | 2.49 | | | | | 3.95 |

**Table 1 (Continued)**

| | | USBM[1] (%) | | RFF[2] (%) | | | | Malenbaum[3] |
|---|---|---|---|---|---|---|---|---|
| | | High | Low | High | Low | High[4] | Low[4] | (%) |
| *Ferrous and ferroalloys* | | | | | | | | |
| Iron | World | 2.47 | 1.40 | 2.52 | 1.45 | 2.50 | 1.43 | 3.82 |
| | USA | 2.32 | 1.37 | 2.90 | 1.80 | 2.51 | 1.53 | 2.14 |
| | R of W | 2.50 | 1.40 | | | | | 4.16 |
| Chromium | World | 3.34 | 1.98 | 3.32 | 2.02 | | | |
| | USA | 3.30 | 2.02 | 3.21 | 2.19 | | | |
| | R of W | 3.35 | 1.97 | | | | | |
| Cobalt | World | 2.13 | 0.94 | 2.41 | 1.10 | | | |
| | USA | 2.43 | 0.86 | 3.25 | 1.37 | | | |
| | R of W | 1.97 | 0.98 | | | | | |
| Manganese | World | 3.34 | 2.29 | 3.41 | 2.32 | | | |
| | USA | 2.23 | 1.47 | 2.80 | 1.76 | | | |
| | R of W | 3.49 | 2.41 | | | | | |
| Molybdenum | World | 4.69 | 3.68 | 5.07 | 4.06 | | | |
| | USA | 4.18 | 3.16 | 5.16 | 4.11 | | | |
| | R of W | 5.00 | 4.00 | | | | | |
| Nickel | World | 4.01 | 2.80 | 3.49 | 2.49 | | | |
| | USA | 3.96 | 2.76 | 3.21 | 2.19 | | | |
| | R of W | 4.04 | 2.83 | | | | | |
| *Nonmetallic minerals* | | | | | | | | |
| Phosphorus | World | 6.15 | 4.04 | 6.12 | 4.20 | | | |
| | USA | 4.78 | 2.95 | 4.57 | 3.59 | | | |
| | R of W | 6.61 | 4.43 | | | | | |
| Potassium | World | 5.35 | 3.90 | 5.45 | 4.20 | | | |
| | USA | 4.71 | 2.77 | 5.19 | 4.19 | | | |
| | R of W | 5.54 | 4.21 | | | | | |
| Fluorine | World | 5.28 | 4.37 | | | | | 5.26 |
| | USA | 4.61 | 3.70 | | | | | 4.40 |
| | R of W | 5.60 | 4.69 | | | | | 5.62 |
| *Fossil fuels* | | | | | | | | |
| Solid | World | 2.98 | 1.35 | 1.39[6] | | | | 3.57 |
| | USA | 5.28 | 2.91 | 2.13 | | | | 2.87 |
| | R of W | 1.96 | 0.76 | 1.16 | | | | 3.72 |

## Table 1 (continued)

| | | USBM[1] (%) | | RFF[2] (%) | | | | Malenbaum[3] |
|---|---|---|---|---|---|---|---|---|
| | | High | Low | High | Low | High[4] | Low[4] | (%) |
| Fluid | World | 5.17 | 2.93 | 4.81 | | | | 4.41 |
| | USA | 4.22 | 1.25 | 2.50 | | | | 3.20 |
| | R of W | 5.55 | 3.53 | 5.55 | | | | 4.93 |
| Natural gas | World | 5.62 | 4.03 | 4.96 | | | | 3.37 |
| | USA | 3.43 | 1.92 | 2.78 | | | | 2.24 |
| | R of W | 7.71 | 6.05 | 6.87 | | | | 4.74 |
| *Nuclear fisson fuels* | World | 10.87[7] | 10.30 | 19.99 | | | | 10.69[9] |
| | USA | 10.60 | 10.11 | 19.77 | | | | 13.43 |
| | R of W | 11.10 | 10.51 | 20.56 | | | | 9.40 |
| *All fuels*[8] | World | | | 4.72 | | | | 4.33[10] |
| | USA | | | 3.54 | | | | 3.60[10] |
| | R of W | | | 5.18 | | | | 4.67[10] |

1. From U.S. Bureau of Mines, *Mineral Facts and Problems.*

2. The Resources for the Future study did not make independent estimates for the rest of the world, using instead the rates projected by the U.S. Bureau of Mines, *except* in the case of fuel consumption.

3. Projections from paper prepared by W. Malenbaum.

4. These estimates assume that an active attempt will be made to improve the percentage contribution of recycled materials to total consumption. All the other rates in the table are based on the assumption that the percentage contribution from recycling will be no greater than in the base year.

5. Rest of world.

6. Only a single set of projections were made by the Resources for the Future study for fuel consumption, with no high or low variants.

7. Rates are provided separately for uranium and thorium in the study by the U.S. Bureau of Mines. These data have been aggregated in terms of quantities to obtain the growth rates presented here.

8. The U.S. Bureau of Mines study did not project demand for overall fuel consumption.

9. The Malenbaum study does not make a separate estimate for nuclear fuels; estimates are made only for fossil fuels and for a residual "other" category that includes hydraulic and other minor sources of energy in addition to nuclear energy.

10. Aggregate demand here is projected in terms of metric tons rather than, as in the Resources for the Future study, in units of heat equivalent; the latter would have been the more correct because of the wide variation in energy potential per unit weight.

component, the use of the latter contributed toward making doomsday somewhat more imminent than it would otherwise have been.

In all three studies, recycling is assumed to make no greater proportional contribution to the consumption of nonenergy materials than in the base year, with the exception of a few alternative projections for the United States in the study by Resources for the Future.

Of all the metals in Table 1, the highest rates are projected for aluminium on the assumption of a continuing substitution for copper and other metals, especially in structural and electrical applications, because of both its special properties and its present and potential abundance. (As will be seen in the next section, however, these potential sources have not yet been quantified.) Data on historical trends in the Malenbaum study reveal that the intensity of use for the metal rises as per capita income increases, at a diminishing rate for industrialized countries, but at particularly dramatic rates at the early stages of industrialization. The study, however, projects future intensity increases much too conservatively in the light of past trends. For this metal, then, the range specified by the U.S. Bureau of Mines study is probably the most reasonable (U.S. Department of Interior, 1970). For the remainder of the metals, the Malenbaum estimates where available are the most plausible (1972). Copper is projected to decline in developed countries because of substitution by aluminium and plastics and to rise in developing countries despite such substitution, primarily because of changes in output composition. Intensity increases are foreseen also for iron and zinc in newly industrializing nations. Future requirements for iron in particular, for infrastructure and agricultural and industrial equipment in these countries, will be enormous and cannot possibly be compatible with the forecast range in *Mineral Facts* of 1.4 to 2.5 percent (U.S. Department of Interior, 1970). Correspondingly, the use-intensity of zinc, which is used to protect iron and steel against corrosion, and of ferro-alloys whose use is linked closely to that of iron, must be expected to increase. There is a problem here, however. No estimates were made in the Malenbaum study for any of these metals other than zinc (1972). Since future ferrous demand in developing countries is grossly underestimated in *Mineral Facts,* the estimates made for ferroalloys for these countries in the same study must clearly also be subject to the same underestimation factor. The forecast ranges in the U.S. Bureau of Mines study for lead and tin, on the other hand, are quite reasonable; both metals are highly substitutable, with nickel, zinc, and plastics the chief substitutes for lead, and aluminium and plastics for tin (U.S. Department of Interior, 1970).

Of the nonmetallic minerals, all three materials, phosphorus, potassium, and fluorine, can be seen to have very high projected growth rates indeed, especially in developing countries. The first two are indispensable plant nutrients and are demanded chiefly as inputs for the manufacture of fertilizer. Even at the high rates projected, per capita use of phosphate and potash fertilizer in the year 2000 in the rest of the world will be far below present levels of per capita use in the United States. Thus, these rates of increase in future demand essentially represent lower bounds on what will be needed if world agricultural lands are to be cultivated to their maximum capacity. For fluorine, the third material in the category, an estimate is made in the Malenbaum study (1972). The estimate is close to the high of the forecast range in *Mineral Facts* (U.S. Department of Interior, 1970). A sharp rise in intensity of use is projected for newly industrializing countries in the Malenbaum study. Fluorine was used in the past principally as a flux additive in the steel industry, but now it is increasingly being used as a chemical additive to certain plastics, and in the production of synthetic cryolite for aluminium refining—both fast growing industries. Very little fluorine is recovered, or recoverable, for reuse.

In the projection of demand for fuels, it is much preferable to work from projections for energy in the aggregate toward projections for materials that can satisfy that demand. The substitutability between these materials, actual and potential, is quite high, and the demand for each could deviate quite substantially from projected rates if assumed patterns of fuel use do not hold. Projections for individual component materials must, therefore, be treated with some latitude. It is only the overall rate that can be determined with some accuracy.

The *Mineral Facts* estimates were not made in the aggregate; a forecast range was provided only for each fuel taken individually (U.S. Department of Interior, 1970). Further, an estimate of the overall forecast range from energy taken as a whole cannot be obtained by aggregating the individual highs and lows because the assumptions with respect to intermaterial substitution would not be consistent.

The projections in the other two studies, however, were done initially in the aggregate. In the Resources for the Future study (Ridker, 1972), the procedure used for energy forecasting was different from that used for the other minerals. For both the United States and rest-of-the-world demand, an intensity-of-use analysis was done along the lines of the Malenbaum study. A median global growth rate of GNP of 3.5 percent was assumed. Both studies predicted rising intensities of energy use in developing countries. On the whole, the slightly higher rates predicted by the Resources for the Future study may well prove to be the more correct. Even these rates might turn out to be underestimates if the mining of other minerals should be done in increasingly energy-intensive ways. The demand for energy is especially closely interlinked with the demand for other minerals and with the techniques used for their exploration and recovery. If, as is eventually probable, the world's raw materials should be recovered from increasingly inaccessible and low-grade deposits, energy intensities could rise very steeply even in industrialized countries like the United States.

In terms of component materials, the most dramatic rise in the Resources for the Future study is for nuclear fuels (Ridker, 1972), which are forecast to replace coal in electricity generation to a very large extent. The extent of this substitution seems somewhat exaggerated; the Malenbaum estimates for coal and nuclear fission fuels are probably more realistic (1972). For the rest, the slightly higher projections of Resources for the Future are preferable.

Fossil fuels are used primarily to generate energy but not exclusively. They have important nonenergy uses as metallurgical reductants and as chemical raw materials in petrochemical and fertilizer manufacturing. It is implicitly assumed in the studies covered here that nonenergy demand for these materials will rise at the same rate as projected energy demand.

## ESTIMATES OF MINERAL ENDOWMENT

There are two dimensions to the estimation of total mineral endowment: geological certainty and cost of recovery. Until recently, there was no standard terminology or categorization that could automatically convey the coverage of the estimate. A scheme recently suggested by V. E. McKelvey of the U.S. Geological Survey is described briefly below. It is used in estimates put forward by the U.S. Bureau of Mines and by the Geological Survey.

Identified resources are those that are known to exist. Unidentified resources are those that have not yet been discovered, and are subdivided into the categories of *hypothetical* and *speculative* resources. Identified resources are then broken down by feasibility of recovery—basically into two groups: those resources termed *reserves* that are exploitable at today's prices and technologies, and those termed *subeconomic resources* that are not presently exploitable. It is possible to further subdivide the latter according to the price at which each subeconomic deposit will become economic to mine, but since these prices are so much a function of other prices (such as those of energy), it is not very useful to do so. Total reserves are sometimes further classified by level of certainty—from measured or proved reserves through indicated to inferred reserves. All of these categories are essentially finer subdivisions of what is basically known to exist.

The relevant figure for today is the total stock of reserves. This total provides the lead time for the further expansion of reserves, either with the "discovery" of resources that were formerly only hypothesized to exist, or with the development of technologically more efficient means of recovery. The most optimistic estimate of this lead time is obtained by dividing reserves by current annual consumption, the "static index." More realistic estimates are obtained by providing for the projected increases in demand.

If reserves are not added to within this period, rising prices will give rise to a secondary expansion of reserves as formerly sub-economic resources become economically recoverable. The lead time provided by total identified resources, then, is the maximum time period available within which further discoveries must be made that will transfer resources into the identified category. In the absence of technological improvements, however, it would take enormous price increases before all sub-economic resources could become economically recoverable—price increases that could choke off demand entirely. The actual lead time available for further exploration and discovery will, therefore, be much smaller than that provided by total identified resources.

The hypothetical and speculative categories are meant to cover total undiscovered world resources, but they should not be interpreted as covering the total ultimately available. Techniques for the estimation of undiscovered resources at any time are a function of the state of geological knowledge and foreseen technological possibilities (in terms of mineable depths, etc.). By summing the resource estimates across all levels of geological certainty and feasibility of recovery, estimates can be obtained of the lead times for the development of these as yet unforeseen possibilities.

An estimate of ultimate resources is sometimes made by looking at the metal composition of common rock and estimating the total amount thus available in, say, the upper mile of the earth's crust. These estimates of the "crustal abundance" of each mineral are not presented here because energy requirements would be so enormous for the mining of such a low-grade resource, and environmental obstacles so formidable, that the possibility lies beyond what can even be speculated upon today.

Estimates for the various categories of resources are presented in Table 2 for each mineral. The figures are obtained for the most part from publications of the U.S. Geological Survey and pertain to the year 1973 (U.S. Department of Interior, 1974a), or in some cases, 1972 (U.S. Department of Interior, 1974b). Except in the case of energy materials, systematic estimates of world resources are available only from this agency. The publications in question are very comprehensive; estimates for each mineral are pieced together from a careful survey of all the relevant literature.

Estimates of aluminium resources are provided in terms of esti-

## Table 2. Estimates of World Endowment[1]

| | Unit | Reserves[2] | Identified[3] | Unidentified[4] | Total |
|---|---|---|---|---|---|
| | | | Resources | | |
| **Nonferrous[5]** | | | | | |
| Aluminium | | | | | |
| (bauxite) | $10^6$ ton | 3 600 | | | abundant |
| Copper | $10^6$ ton | 370 | 750 | 720 | 1 470 |
| Lead | $10^6$ ton | 144 | 1 644 | 210 | 1 854 |
| Tin | $10^6$ ton | 4.7 | 22.4 | 18.8 | 41.2 |
| Zinc | $10^6$ ton | 131 | 1 665 | 3 941 | 5 606 |
| | | | | | |
| *Ferrous and ferroalloys[5]* | | | | | |
| Iron | $10^6$ ton | 97 | 253 | | |
| Chromium[6] | $10^6$ ton | 466 | 1 215 | 1 008 | 2 223 |
| Cobalt | $10^6$ ton | 2.7 | 4.5 | | |
| Manganese[7] | $10^6$ ton | 1 625–3 250 | 3 550–7 100 | 2 500–5000[8] | |
| Molybdenum | $10^6$ ton | 4.7 | 31.5 | 1 100[8] | |
| Nickel | $10^6$ ton | 46 | 70 | | |
| | | | | | |
| *Nonmetallic minerals[5]* | | | | | |
| Phosphorus | $10^6$ ton | 6 614 | 6 614 | 9 920[8] | |
| Potassium | $10^6$ ton | 109 280[9] | | | |
| Fluorine | $10^6$ ton | 132 | | | 409[10] |
| | | | | | 1 650[11] |
| | | | | | |
| *Fossil fuels* | | | | | |
| Coal, all | | | | | |
| ranks[12] | $10^6$ ton | 1 400 000[15] | 9 500 000 | 7 300 000[8] | [16] |
| Petroleum[13] | $10^9$ bbl | 625[16] | | | 7 700[17] |
| Tarsands[13] | $10^9$ bbl | | | | 915 |
| Oilshale[13] | $10^9$ bbl | | 3 098 | 9 250 | 333 200 |
| Natural gas[14] | $10^{12}$ ft$^3$ | 1 897[16] | | | 24 275[17] |
| | | | | | |
| *Nuclear fission fuels[5]* | | | | | |
| Uranium | $10^6$ ton | | 1.1[15] | 3.3[15] | 4.4[15] |
| Thorium | $10^6$ ton | | 0.4[15] | 2.3[15] | 2.7[15] |

1. For the most part the data pertain to the year 1973 and are taken from *Commodity Data Summaries 1974.* If the figures were not available from the above, they were obtained from *U.S. Mineral Resources.* These data pertain to the year 1972.

2. The rate or range used for each mineral is that selected previously in prices.

## Table 2. (continued)

3. Those resources known to exist, includes reserves and subeconomic reserves—those not exploitable at current prices.

4. These have not yet been discovered but are hypothetical or speculative resources.

5. Million short tons (of metal content where applicable).

6. Derived on the basis of 0.28 short tons of chromium from one long ton of chromium ore.

7. Based on 0.25–0.50 short tons of manganese from one long ton of ore.

8. These estimates do not include speculative resources.

9. This estimate is for 1968 and is taken from *Mineral Facts.*

10. The total is for fluorspar alone.

11. Total estimated fluorine content of phosphate rock.

12. The estimates for coal are for reserves or resources in the ground. The present recoverability factor is about 50%.

13. Barrels (42 gallons) of recoverable oil. For petroleum an average recoverability factor of 30% is used.

14. Cubic feet of recoverable gas. The present recoverability factor is about 80%.

15. These figures pertain to the year 1974. "Reasonably assured resources" are shown here under "identified" for the nuclear fission fuels.

16. Alternative estimates are available from the World Energy Conference; see text.

17. The World Energy Conference report tried to quantify the results of a U.S. Geological Survey report that placed every country with on- or offshore oil possibilities in one of several broad ranges of recoverable potential (this is in addition to what is already recorded for the country as reserves). Summing the upper and lower bounds of these ranges, the World Energy Conference obtained a world range; the midpoint of this range was summed here with the estimate of reserves to obtain the total estimate. These data pertain to the year 1972.

mated bauxite resources alone. Although other aluminous materials exist and are thought to be abundant, no quantitative estimates were available of their extent. For the remaining materials, the table is self-explanatory. Estimates of unidentified resources were not available in all cases, and where only partial estimates were provided (for the hypothetical but not the speculative category), a total estimate is not given in the table. No figures are presented in the table for potassium. Estimates for potassium resources are not given in the latest publications of the U.S. Geological Survey, possibly because sea water is expected to be an ultimate unlimited source of the material. A necessary condition for the economical recovery of potassium from sea water, however, will be an abundant supply of energy.

For energy resources, an additional source was available in the 1974 report of the World Energy Conference (World Energy Conference, 1974). These estimates were obtained from official responses to questionnaires sent out to every country. The report, however, does not provide independent estimates for all the resource categories or for all the fuels, and fills in the gaps with figures from U.S. Geological Survey publications. The procedure followed in Table 2 has been to give the World Energy Conference estimate only where none is available from the Geological Survey, and to mark those categories for which alternative estimates are available from the World Energy Conference. Total coal resources are estimated by the World Energy Conference at 11.85 trillion ($10^{12}$) short tons, considerably below the estimate provided by the U.S. Geological Survey of 16.8 trillion ($10^{12}$) short tons for the identified and hypothetical categories alone. Recoverable oil reserves, on the other hand, are given a higher estimate of 640 billion barrels, but recoverable gas reserves are estimated at 1855 trillion cubic feet, slightly under the U.S. Geological Survey estimate.[3] The World Energy Conference is the only source of estimates for the nuclear fission fuels, although no breakdowns were available of identified resources into reserves and sub-economic resources.

Absolute figures of mineral endowment, however, do not convey very much in and of themselves. They have to be related to figures of present consumption, and this is done in Table 3. The static index can

**Table 3. Life Span of World Mineral Endowment[1] at Projected Rates of Demand**

|  | Static Reserve Index (years) | | Resources at Projected Demand[2] (years) | | |
|---|---|---|---|---|---|
|  | 1968[3] | 1972[4] | Reserves | Identified Resources | Total Resources |
| *Nonferrous* | | | | | |
| Aluminium | 115 | 317 | 43–56 | | |
| Copper | 42 | 54 | 29 | 43 | 59 |
| Lead | 27 | 38 | 26–29 | 93–132 | 97–139 |
| Tin | 17 | 18 | 14–18 | 49–80 | 70–141 |
| Zinc | 22 | 21 | 15 | 65 | 97 |
| *Ferrous and ferroalloys* | | | | | |
| Iron | 220 | 200 | 57 | 80 | |
| Chromium[5] | 397 | 274 | 70–94 | 97–138 | 115–167 |
| Cobalt[5] | 109 | 108 | 56–74 | 69–104 | |
| Manganese[5] | 97 | 295 | 17–90 | 93–121 | |

**Table 3. (continued)**

| | Static reserve Index (years) | | Resources at Projected Demand[2] (years) | | |
| --- | --- | --- | --- | --- | --- |
| | 1968[3] | 1972[4] | Reserves | Identified Resources | Total Resources |
| Molybdenum[5] | 78 | 53 | 26–29 | 59– 72 | |
| Nickel[5] | 157 | 66 | 32–39 | 40– 50 | |
| *Nonmetallic minerals* | | | | | |
| Phosphorus | | 520 | 58–77 | 58– 77 | |
| Potassium | 7668 | | | | |
| Fluorine | 22 | 54 | 25 | | 44 |
| | | | | | 73[6] |
| *Fossil fuels* | | | | | |
| Coal | | 419 | 73 | 131 | |
| Petroleum | 31 | 35 | 20 | | 63 |
| | | | | | 145[7] |
| Natural gas | 39 | 47 | 24 | | 68 |
| *Nuclear fission fuels* | | | | | |
| Uranium | | | | 17 | 29 |
| Thorium[8] | | | | | |

1. See Table 2 for sources.

2. The rate or range used for each mineral is that selected previously in this article as the most reasonable.

3. Using reserve estimates for 1968, at primary consumption in 1968. Figures from *Mineral Facts and Problems*.

4. Annual figures of primary consumption are published with very much more of a time lag than annual production figures. For this index, therefore, annual production figures had to be used, obtained from *Minerals Yearbook 1972*. An average was taken of production in the years 1970–1972 so as to even out stock changes.

5. The range of rates used for these ferroalloys is subject to an underestimation factor. See text for explanation.

6. For total fluorine endowment, includes that obtainable from phosphate rock.

7. This is for the total endowment of petroleum, including that obtainable from tarsands and oilshale.

8. Demand for thorium is not very large at present. It is actually lower than the 1.1 thousand short tons produced annually as a byproduct of monazites mined for their rare-earth content. Demand for thorium is not expected to increase substantially until well into the breeder-reactor era.

be seen to have gone up since 1968 in many cases, indicating that new discoveries, improving technology, rising prices, or all three have caused the reserve total to increase by more than annual consumption over the period.

Starting from annual average levels of primary production during the period 1970–1972, the table presents figures for the number of years' lead time at the rates of projected demand increase selected in the previous section as the most reasonable. The number of years provided by a certain stock of a mineral starts with the year 1972. If reserves or resources of any mineral are to last until the end of the century, their life span at projected rates of consumption increase must equal or exceed twenty-nine years.

Those minerals with a reserve life span of twenty-nine years or a little under are copper, lead, and molybdenum. All three, however, are estimated to have large sub-economic or undiscovered deposits, in the form of deep sea nodules and elsewhere. Those minerals whose reserve life span falls well short of the end of the century are tin, zinc, fluorine, petroleum, and natural gas. The case of uranium has to be disregarded because the development of nuclear fission as a source of energy is very recent, and exploratory activity to date has not as a result been exhaustive; present estimates of total endowment will surely be revised substantially. Further, the introduction of the breeder reactor is likely to cause a sharp reduction in the demand for newly mined uranium because stockpiles of residual uranium isotopes from present reactors could fuel the breeder which is less selective in terms of isotopes needed. The breeder reactor is expected to utilize about 60 percent of the potential energy in natural uranium as compared to 1 percent in nonbreeder reactors. Eventual rates of increase in the demand for uranium should, therefore, be much lower than the rates projected in Table 1. No estimates are given in Table 3 of the life span of thorium resources, since demand for the material is not expected to amount to much until late in the breeder-reactor era.

Of the five materials mentioned above with insufficient reserves, zinc probably presents the least problems. Large sub-economic and unidentified resources of zinc are estimated to exist. The remaining four could be problem areas. In the case of tin, unidentified resources are not very large because it is an old metal with well-known geological associations. The life span of these resources is large only because it is estimated that demand will not grow at very high rates; aluminium and plastics are expected to substitute for tin in many of its uses. Even so, there will be some uses for which substitutes will be difficult to find, and tin may well be in very short supply until suitable alternatives are found.

Fluorine is estimated to exist in large quantities in fluorspar and phosphate rock, but the life span of these is not very large at projected rates of consumption increase. Further, there is no possibility of a decline in these rates of increase in the foreseeable future because fluorine is needed for the very materials—aluminium and plastics—which are expected to substitute for other, less abundant, materials. This is but one example of the complex interconnections between resources, and of the many obstacles that stand in the way of solving a shortage in any one area of materials use.

In the case of petroleum and natural gas, large resources are estimated to exist, particularly if the tarsand and oilshale deposits become widely exploitable. However, at projected rates of demand increase, these deposits will not last many years. There are many uses of oil and gas for which no immediate substitute is in sight, except perhaps for liquid or gaseous fuels produced from coal. But coal resources themselves are not that large relative to consumption. It must also be remembered that the endowment and life span estimates for coal are for reserves or resources in the ground; the present recoverability fraction is only about 50 percent.

## CONCLUSIONS

The studies reviewed here leave considerable scope for improvement; this has been emphasized throughout. Materials projections must be done on a collective rather than an individual basis, taking into account all production interrelationships, and all substitutabilities and complementarities in use. The difficult problem of technological forecasting must be quantitatively faced, and ranges of coefficients specified; most of all global projections must be aggregated from country or regional estimates, and secondary forecasts made after working into the model the likely policy action toward recycling or conservation. Within the limitations of the studies covered here, however, and keeping in mind the corresponding limitations on the number of minerals covered, it does seem possible to arrive at the following tentative conclusions.

For the remainder of this century, the time span for which the demand projections reviewed here were made, the global outlook is reasonably optimistic. Of the major minerals covered, all those with reserves falling short of the year 2000 are estimated to have large resources that should extend their availability, certainly up to the end of the century.

As to the longer run, the outlook does not appear quite as promising. Total mineral resources as presently estimated are large but will not last very long if consumption continues to grow at the rates projected for the remainder of this century. While it is certainly possible that in the longer run the demand for nonenergy materials may rise at lower rates than these, the demand for energy-producing materials may, by the same token, rise at much higher rates. Technologically induced reductions in the use-coefficients for nonenergy materials are frequently obtained only at the expense of higher use-coefficients for energy; substitution-induced reductions are frequently obtained at the expense of the accelerated use of petroleum-based plastics. In industralized countries, changes in the composition of output toward services will mean lower rates of use for nonenergy materials that at the same time it could mean higher rates of use for energy in transport and in other leisure-time activities.

On the supply side, nonenergy minerals might become available in the future only at levels of energy-use much greater than those prevailing today. This will be true even where secondary recovery is feasible because recycling is energy-intensive. In the case of those minerals like potassium, needed for fertilizer for which no reduction in demand growth is possible and where recycling is not feasible, primary recovery in the longer run from sea water and other such sources will involve very energy-intensive operations indeed.

Thus, energy use is likely to grow in the long run at rates even higher than those projected for the remainder of this century. Resource lead times for energy-producing materials are therefore likely to be lower than those computed—although, of course, there is considerable scope for improvement in the efficiency of both use and recovery of conventional fuels. The focus here on nonrenewable resources excludes from consideration hydraulic geothermal, solar, and other possible energy sources, of a nondepletable nature. Such sources, however, do not provide a *substantive* alternative today because of the special geophysical and climatic conditions necessary for their exploitation. (In particular local settings where these conditions do exist, of course, these forms of energy will be all important.) In the very long run, nuclear fusion offers the possibility of a widely available, abundant source of energy, but the lead time for the development of this possibility is essentially provided by the global stock of nonrenewable resources alone.

As mentioned at the outset of this chapter, no consideration was given to the environmental costs of future minerals recovery. There is a trade-off, once again, between energy use and environmental damage, though not all such damage can be countered through energy-intensive corrective operations. Indeed, energy recovery itself will in the future be done in environmentally hazardous ways (offshore petroleum breeder reactors) . Thus, the future availability of materials, both energy and nonenergy, will be constrained by political, social, and biological limits to the tolerance of environmental damage. There may be further political and institutional constraints to the recovery of minerals from the sea and other areas where thorny issues of territorial rights arise. Much will depend on the success of international regulation and cooperation.

The global focus of the paper necessarily obscures the outlook at the national level. Nations are not equally endowed with raw materials. Nowhere is the geographical bunching of deposits more extreme than in the case of the fuels. Thus, while limits to growth may never be reached in a global sense, they may well be reached in countries insufficently endowed with either mineral resources or the means to acquire them. Depletion in such areas of the world could well occur much before the end of the century despite the optimistic outlook for this period at the global level. Once again, international cooperation will be a necessity for staving off localized doomsdays.

## NOTES

1. A bibliography of much of this literature is available in World Bank Special Task Force, 1972, *Report on the Limits to Growth,* Washington, D.C., mimeographed. Other relevant publications are Beckerman (1974) and Cole et al. (1973).

2. One study that has been done along these lines, but is not available for review, is a United Nations Technical Study headed by Wassily Leontief on the impact of prospective environmental issues and policies on the International Development Strategy of the Second United Nations Development Decade.

3. Estimates for petroleum and natural gas are also made by the *Oil and Gas Journal.*

## REFERENCES

Albers, J. P., et al. *Summary Petroleum and Selected Mineral Statistics from 120 Countries, Including Offshore Areas.* Washington, D.C.: U.S. Department of Interior, Geological Survey Professional Paper, Number 817.

Beckerman, Wilfred. 1974. *In Defence of Economic Growth.* London: Jonathan Cape.

Cole, H. S. D., et al. 1973. *Thinking About the Future.* London: Sussex University Press.

Malenbaum, Wilfred. 1972. "Materials Requirements in the U.S. and Abroad in the Year 2000." Philadelphia, Pa.: National Commission on Materials Policy. (Mimeo.)

Meadows, Donnella, A., Dennis Meadows, et al. 1972. *The Limits to Growth.* New York: Universe Books.

Ridker, Ronalf G. (ed.). 1972. *Population, Resources and the Environment.* Volume 3 of Research Reports for the U.S. Commission on Population, Growth and the American Future, Washington, D.C.: U.S. Government Printing Office.

U.S. Department of Interior, Bureau of Mines. 1970. *Mineral Facts and Problems.* Washington, D.C.: USBM Bulletin, Number 650.

———. 1972. *Minerals Yearbook 1972,* Volume 1. Washington, D.C.

———, Bureau of Mines and Geological Survey. 1974a. *Commodity Data Summaries 1974.* Appendix I to *Mining and Minerals Policy,* Washington, D.C.

———, Geological Survey. 1974b. *U.S. Mineral Resources.* Washington, D.C.: Geological Survey Professional Paper, Number 820.

World Energy Conference. 1974. *World Energy Conference Survey of Energy Resources.* New York.

JAMES O'TOOLE

# Energy for the Future

During the 1970s, the nation became obsessed with a vision of an oil barrel being inexorably drained, eventually leaving us bereft of the energy that drives our civilization. The initial source of this nightmare—the Arab Oil embargo—left America with a crisis mentality. The world, or so it seemed, was going to hell in a barrel of oil. But as queues of autos at gas stations have disappeared and oil has once again begun flowing, cooler heads have prevailed. It is now commonly accepted that there is enough oil to last the world for at least another twenty years. This fact is little reason for complacency. The oil will clearly run out one day, and, long before then it will become much too expensive to waste as our civilization has become accustomed to doing. Thus, to avoid a real energy crisis in the 1990s—one that might well destroy industrial civilization—it is necessary to start conserving energy now and to find alternatives to fossil fuels.

Since energy is seldom used directly (we need technology to harness energy for productive purposes), it is incumbent upon society to develop new technologies so that they will be in place when the oil runs out. Unfortunately, we are not likely to find the new technologies needed for the future because we continue to evaluate and assess technologies by standards developed during the early Industrial Revolution. Such standards are inappropriate for postindustrial societies concerned with pollution, diminishing resources, overpopulation, the quality of goods, and the quantity and quality of jobs.

Although the environment has changed, the way society thinks about technology remains stagnant. For example, in the energy area, there is almost complete faith bordering on fanaticism in the inevitability of "the grand technological solution." The orthodox vision is of a dramatic technological solution, like some *deus ex machina* descending and saving the day for modern man. Nuclear fusion, in-situ coal liquefaction, hydrogen fuel from electrolysis, ocean thermal gradients, and

SOURCE: James O'Toole, *Energy and Social Change* (Cambridge, Mass.: MIT Press, 1977). Reprinted by permission of MIT Press © 1977.

solar power (either from collectors in orbit or from collectors paving the desert) are often advanced as attractive long-range solutions to the world's energy problems. The grander the technology, in fact, the more attractive it seems. After all, the bigger it is and the further off its development, the more it will cost—which means a bigger share of a bigger pie for everybody involved. Indeed, fusion should keep thousands of physicists and engineers occupied for at least another half century—solving the problem, at least, of unemployment among the highly skilled.

But there are several problems inherent in the big technology solution to energy problems:

1. It is extremely costly and thus requires government financing and consequent bureaucratic controls.
2. It is difficult to estimate the effects on the environment, climate, or atmosphere, but by definition these are likely to be greater than with smaller technologies.
3. Its development cannot be guaranteed—some technological breakthroughs (such as antigravity) are always "just ten years away."
4. Its time lag between laboratory demonstration and wide-scale commercial implementation is lengthy. For example, fission was demonstrated in 1942, but the first commercial reactor was not working until 1967. Even now, only 5 percent of U.S. electrical needs are met by fission. Indeed, because of environmental issues these time lags appear to be growing.
5. Development of grand options dries up intellectual and financial capital that could be better applied to dozens of more promising, less-expensive options.

There is no reason to be sanguine about grand solutions to America's energy problems. Hydrogen auto fuels and nuclear fusion will not be available for at least fifty years. Nor are we soon to see large amounts of electricity generated by centralized solar power plants; only 1 percent of U.S. electricity is forecasted to be produced in this fashion by 1995 (O'Toole, 1976).

Nevertheless, mankind must clearly evolve from primitive energy hunters and gatherers to sophisticated energy farmers. This transformation will entail moving beyond reliance on the relatively haphazard process of discovering fossil fuels, to the scientific processes of cultivating and harvesting renewable energy derived from tides, wind, hydro, solar, chemical, and mechanical sources. This change might well include nuclear fusion someday, but possibly not soon enough to meet the inevitable running down of petroleum and natural gas resources.

One thing the change implies is a long-term trend away from the centralization of energy supplies toward many decentralized, independent, alternative sources. This promises not only a more broadly based energy system (hence one less vulnerable to the vicissitudes of resource availability), but also a less bureaucratically controlled system.

The probable energy future is one in which oil, gas, coal, nuclear, and geothermal sources will all have a place for many generations, and these sources will be gradually augmented by solar and other currently uneconomical technologies. To insure that these long-term changes will not lead to sudden dislocations will require the immediate intitiation of some rather mundane steps: (1) conversion to a more electric economy; (2) the development of superbatteries (portable, high-energy-density, high-power-density storage devices), and (3) the gradual phasing-in of methanol as an auxiliary auto fuel.

## THE ADVANTAGES OF ELECTRICITY

The most pressing energy problem is to reduce the consumption of petroleum and gas without creating severe economic hardships (Enzer, 1975). Of the many alternatives that have been discussed for achieving this reduction, one has received too little attention in light of its many merits. This option is to increase the use of more plentiful fuels by converting them to electricity. Several major difficulties would have to be overcome to make this approach effective, including the expensive changeover to technologies that can utilize electricity. Still, a gradual shift to an electric economy has many distinct advantages.

First, electricity is a suitable form of energy for use with today's plentiful coal and nuclear fuels and with most of tomorrow's prospective energy sources (such as advanced nuclear, geothermal, and solar forms). It is also a good form for converting solid waste to useful energy. Hence, it is not a dead-ended medium, but one with a flexible future. Moreover, electricity is highly versatile; it can be used for almost every application currently satisfied by petroleum and gas, except when these materials are used in lubrication and as feedstock in the petrochemical industry. Finally, it is pollution-free at the use end. This attribute, which concentrates the pollution at the generators, permits antipollution efforts to be more focused and hence probably more effective.

Increased use of electricity poses some major associated problems: (1) it is highly capital-intensive; (2) its use is cyclic and thus requires a capacity that is more than double average consumption; (3) a long time is needed to bring additional capacity into service; (4) although it concentrates its pollution at generating stations, these stations are major polluters (and when they are nuclear-fueled, they present safety hazards as well as the major issue of how to dispose of radioactive wastes); and (5) the use of electricity for personal transportation appears unattractive relative to petroleum in the short run.

On the other hand, with sufficient time and capital, electricity can easily be substituted for most industrial uses and for mass transportation. Although it is presently limited in personal transportation vehicles by the relatively poor performance of current batteries, an improved battery would make electric automobiles ideal replacements for cars powered by internal combustion engines.

Widespread use of electric automobiles would mitigate the capital problem associated with electric power stations by reducing the cyclic use pattern of electricity; it would raise the load factor considerably. This increase would occur because electric vehicles would typically be used in the daytime and be recharged (and hence consume electricity) at night. An increased load factor would mean that less capacity would satisfy more demand; hence, there would be less capital cost per unit consumed. From this perspective, increased efforts to replace petroleum- and gas-consuming devices by electrical devices is an attractive option in both the near and the longer terms.

What must still be resolved is the near-term effect that a massive switch to electricity would have on our petroleum consumption. Studies of electric automobiles have been underway for many years. These studies have failed to identify an attractive vehicle. However, they have used as their standard the performance of the internal combustion engine. If the design criteria were to develop the best transportation vehicle for use as the second (or third) car in the typical U.S. family (in an environment where petroleum is simply not available), the results might be vastly different. For example, using the present electric car, it has been shown that a 20 mph vehicle with a 50+ mile range can be developed.

Major advances have been made in electric vehicle technology in the past several years, and many light trucks and vans for urban and local delivery service may be electric-powered within the next decade. Other transportation areas that offer opportunities for electric substitution include freight and passenger trains. Similarly, it has been decades since an electrically powered trolley-bus was designed for use in American cities. Such cars, buses, trucks, and trains would offer many advantages if petroleum prices continue to rise as we envisage.

Turning to the residential sector, a comparison of gas space heating and electric heat pump environmental conditioning reveals other potential advantages of innovative uses of electricity. At present, a great fraction of residential gas and oil consumption is used in space heating, while the rest is used in water heating, cooking, air conditioning, clothes drying, and other minor uses. With the application of the heat pump, space heating by electricity would offer a major savings in primary fuel use. The heat pump puts out more usable heat than it takes in as input energy. The heat energy source is the outside environment rather than fuel combustion. It is simply an air conditioning system operating in reverse. The heat pump is actually less costly than a gas furnace with air conditioning today, and will soon be less costly than a gas furnace alone as fuel prices rise in the next year or two. The commercial sector closely parallels the energy use patterns of the residential sector and therefore provides similar opportunities for electric substitution. (The heat pump is a good idea even when not generated electrically. The pump, of course, can be powered by any energy source.)

In the industrial sector, process steam is the largest end use of energy. In this case, the most difficult problem is the logistics of getting steam to the user. In the future, large industrial complexes could be built in clusters around steam-generating facilities. In this configuration, requirements for process steam can be met by electric boilers or by waste heat from other energy conversion processes.

In summary, we are facing a period in which reducing consumption of imported petroleum and natural gas will receive the highest national priority. Domestic supplies of these fuels are declining, and new reserves have been slow in coming into the inventory. If we were to reduce consumption by fiat by rationing gasoline, we would face major economic dislocations. Hence, we must gradually convert our home, industrial, and transportation energy systems to the use of more plentiful fuels. The most flexible and least disruptive way of achieving this is a gradual transition to an electric economy.

The electrical use patterns thus created would ease the capital burden on the electric utilities and would probably decrease the cost of electrical energy. Pollution and radioactive waste disposal would still be problems. But on balance, pollution would be reduced and concentrated at the generating stations. The remaining problems of waste disposal, safety, and improved batteries require further research.

## THE EFFECTS OF SUPERBATTERIES

A 50 percent probability of development of superbatteries in the next fifteen years, and 90 percent probability within twenty years, has been forecasted.[1]

The battery may well be to the postindustrial era what the stirrup was to feudalism. Should a breakthrough in portable electrical energy storage devices occur, it would revolutionize the energy and transportation situation in America. Such a development would initially be used in electrically propelled cars, buses, and trucks. This would permit a greater shift in basic fuels from petroleum and gas to coal and nuclear power. It would also change the cost trade-off associated with solar energy systems because the batteries would permit decentralized solar energy to be used and stored so that they provided not only light and heat during the night hours, but also energy for personal transportation vehicles.

Roof space for solar collectors would become a valuable commodity as energy provision decentralized and became an individually collected commodity. Windmills, currently inefficient largely because of a problem of storing the energy they generate, would also become a more attractive energy source. Electric utilities would become more efficient because they would be able to run their plants at maximum capacity, storing energy for use during peak periods. Inefficient electrical generation plants would be quickly phased out because the nation would have more capacity than needed.

The area of greatest growth in energy capacity would be in individual homes and commercial and industrial buildings. Utility-produced electricity would be used only to supplement energy needs that could not be met by individual systems.

This technology would also find immediate application in underdeveloped countries because it would free them from the continuous need to import petroleum. The price of petroleum would drop on the world market, and the concern over its depletion would dwindle considerably. Petroleum would be used in very few applications, primarily in the petrochemical areas and for such specialized purposes as aircraft fuel.

The environmental impact of such a breakthrough would be immense. Most air pollution problems would disappear. However, the problems of transportation and traffic congestion would remain. Without the need to conserve energy, mass transportation systems may be even more difficult to implement.

The industrial activity that would be promoted by the demand for energy storage devices, solar collectors, and new vehicles would be extremely large. Many industries would also be phased out of production, leading to a major period of industrial transition.

The battery seems like such an obvious response to the problems of energy availability—then why has it received so little attention relative to other potential energy sources? Obviously, the superbattery is not, in itself, a full solution to the problems outlined above. To fully realize the potential of the battery, an efficient transducer is needed to convert sunlight into electricity. This breakthrough may be as difficult to achieve as the battery itself. Moreover, the battery is quite threatening to many large industries in the United States, most notably coal, petroleum, and autos. Still, some automakers have apparently spent research money to develop a better battery and battery-operated cars. However, because they use the performance criteria of the internal combustion engine car (speed and acceleration) in their battery vehicle designs, they find that electric cars using current lead acid batteries have a limited range (48 to 58 miles) (Compton, 1974).

Probably more of a constraint is that there is no battery lobby in the scientific establishment. At the National Science Foundation and the Energy Research and Development Administration, big science is represented by nuclear interest groups, coal interest groups, and solar interest groups, but there just does not appear to be enough potential for big money to attract universities and private laboratories to the relatively mundane task of developing a better battery. "Leave it to the Japanese. There is no Nobel prize to be won in batteries," the scientific community seems to be saying. (Indeed it appears that Toyota has recently produced a prototype electric car with a driving range of from 112 to 125 miles [U.N. Institute for Training and Reseach, 1975]. Sadly, in the short run at least the scientific incentive in America seems to be working against the development of the battery: No big research money + no moon-shot-scale publicity + no glamor = no battery.

## THE GRADUAL SUBSTITUTION OF METHANOL

Even without a superbattery, some things can be done to reduce reliance on petroleum. In 1975, consumers in industrialized nations started paying a price for gasoline at service station pumps that exceeds the costs of an equivalent amount of energy from a nuclear reactor (Hoffman, 1974). This little-noticed milestone presages that date within the next three decades when synthetic nonfossil fuels become cheaper than gasoline. George Hoffman has shown how synthetic fuels will gradually come to be economical vis-à-vis fossil fuels (1974). His econometric model shows that there will be no major dislocations as one form of automotive fuel gradually becomes more economical than its predecessor. (The progression in his model is from petroleum, to shale oil, to kerogen, to coal liquefaction, and ultimately to hydrogen.) The price of synthetic fuel will not reach parity with fossil fuels until the year 2025, however. Hoffman's study indicates that it is not too early to start conceiving, planning, and designing the nonfossil fuel industry of the next century because it will soon become economical to start using methanol as an additive in gasoline. Hoffman has also undertaken a cost-benefit analysis of the relative merits of methanol, cryomethane, methane, and hydrogen; he has concluded that either methanol or cryomethane are the auto fuels of the future.

What is significant about Hoffman's findings is that methanol, like the superbattery, is receiving relatively little attention from industry and government. Moreover, increased methanol production—when made from animal waste and garbage—like the battery, can be achieved in relatively less capital-intensive modes, in more decentralized plants, and would help to break the world's reliance on petroleum. Methanol is not as economically or socially promising as the battery, but it is ironic that the U.S. oil industry is making heavy investments in coal and shale while ignoring a potentially more acceptable source of fuel. Moreover, one lesson is clear from a review of energy technologies: it is unwise to place all of one's future hopes on just one or two alternatives.

## CHOOSING THE RIGHT TECHNOLOGIES OR NO TECHNOLOGY AT ALL

The rising price of energy by itself will force substitution and change in the American economy. Still, choices will have to be made. Higher prices do not eliminate the need to plan; rather, they heighten the requirement to understand the long-term consequences of the options open to decision-makers. For example higher energy prices open up five aggregate alternatives:

1. Substituting energy for energy—an abundant resource like coal for a scarce one like natural gas.
2. Substituting capital for energy—adopting a new, more energy-efficient technology.
3. Substituting a product for energy—making a dress out of cotton rather than nylon, or making liquid detergents rather than powdered detergents.
4. Substituting processes for energy—installing windows that open in office buildings.
5. Substituting labor for energy—assembling a radio by hand instead of mechanically.

Which of these substitutions to make will depend on the industry in question and on the analysis of the second- and third-order consequences of the alternatives. Businessmen, economists, and engineers tend to favor the first two options because these are consistent with the traditional concepts of economic efficiency. However, changes in values, new environmental concerns, and notions of corporate social responsibility will force future-oriented executives to weigh also the costs and benefits of the latter three forms of substitutions.

Especially important in such deliberations will be choosing technologies appropriate to the future. In the past, the appropriate type and scale of technology could be determined through the optimization of what economists call "production functions," which are basically equations used to find the best mix of labor, capital, and natural resources to produce a good. It is unlikely that industrialists will be able to rely only on this quantitative method of achieving profit maximization in the future. "The one best way," "optimization," "maximization," and "industrial efficiency" are, as Daniel Bell reminds us, not the only concepts that will impinge themselves on the decision-making process in industry in the late twentieth century. Already, industrial organizations are finding that society will not permit them to pursue a single goal (profit maximization). Indeed, as executives of most of the leading firms in America are beginning to recognize, businesses are becoming social institutions with many constituencies and many goals. As we see today, businesses are not only under pressure from stockholders to use capital efficiently to increase productivity and profits, but there are new pressures, too: from conservationists to use processes that are environmentally sound, from the government to use energy efficiently, from consumers to produce safe and durable goods, from unions and society to create jobs, and from workers to provide satisfying jobs.

The managers' traditional task of choosing the right technologies and the right production mix is therefore more important than ever, but the factors influencing their decisions are concomitantly more complex and the consequences of their options less clear. A new calculus will be needed for effectively choosing technologies in the future. This calculus—if it can be called that—must incorporate the new qualitative concerns of the society along with the traditional quantitative concerns of management for industrial efficiency.

How would this calculus be applied? There is no reason to believe that there will be any magic formula; technologies and processes will differ from industry to industry and from plant to plant. Nor is there any reason to predict a sudden and massive abandoning of current plants and machines. More likely, the shift will be gradual as new plants and equipment are introduced to replace obsolete capital goods. Within these broad parameters, it will probably be necessary for future executives to choose processes that move toward the ends of the technological continuum illustrated in Figure 1 and away from the middle-range technologies that were developed in the latter part of the industrial era.[2]

It is clear that middle-level technologies are suited for industrial eras

**Figure 1.** The Technological Continuum

|                               | Low Technology | Middle Technology | High Technology |
| ----------------------------- | -------------- | ----------------- | --------------- |
|                               | ◄───────────── Trend ──────────────► |        |                 |
| 1. Energy efficiency          | Very high      | Low               | Medium          |
| 2. Capital use efficiency     | High           | Medium            | Very high       |
| 3. Productivity               | Medium/Low     | Medium            | Very high       |
| 4. Quality of goods           | High           | Low               | High            |
| 5. Environmental soundness    | High           | Low               | Medium          |
| 6. Worker satisfaction        | Very high      | Low               | High            |
| 7. Labor intensity            | Very high      | Medium/Low        | Medium/High     |

characterized by cheap energy, surplus capital, high consumer demand for mass-produced goods, little environmental concern, and a poorly educated work force. Because the future appears antithetical to all these characteristics, it seems likely that industry will move either to the high productivity of high technology or to the high quality of low technology.

In the auto industry, for example, growing pressures for energy and capital efficiency, productivity, and worker satisfaction would probably lead managers over the next twenty years to produce cars either through fully automated processes (an assembly line without semi-skilled production workers) or by teams of highly skilled manual workers. Which way the industry or company will go will depend on the price of its product, union pressures, and dozens of other factors too numerous to list here. What is important is that it is improbable that the industry will be able to stay in the middle of the continuum. Moreover, moving either way from the center will require the invention of new technologies.

Low-technology solutions need not entail a return to backbreaking labor. For example, Volvo has shown that new low technologies can be highly productive and labor-saving, and require as much engineering genius as high technologies. In its plant at Kalmar, Sweden, Volvo has replaced the assembly line with 250 individual car carriers—18-foot long platforms that deliver cars to twenty-five different assembly teams. Not only is the monotony of the assembly line avoided, but also the painful necessity of working in the uncomfortable overhead position typical of assembly lines has been replaced by the ability of the car carriers to be tipped on their side, thus allowing the worker to perform his tasks at a normal eye-level position. What is being discovered around the world is that there is *choice* where technology is concerned.

A Mead Company paper mill in the South has recently designed its technology to meet human needs instead of arranging human organization to meet the needs of technology. The entrepreneurial challenge is to find technologies that are environmentally sound, energy-efficient, and satisfying for workers.

What would happen to productivity if substitutes were made to the low rather than the high end of the continuum? E. F. Schumacher argues that the gross productivity of society can actually be increased by applying the appropriate technologies:

As I have shown, directly productive time in our society has already been reduced to about 3½ percent of "total social time" [all the collective time of adults, including sleeping, eating, watching television, and doing jobs that are not directly productive], and the whole drift of modern technological development is to reduce it further, asymptotically, to zero. Imagine we set ourselves a goal in the opposite direction—to increase it sixfold, to about twenty percent, so that twenty percent of the total social time would be used for actually producing things, employing hands and brains and, naturally, excellent tools. . . . At one-sixth of present-day productivity, we should be producing as much as at present. There would be six times as much time for any piece of work we choose to undertake—enough to make a really good job of it, to enjoy oneself, to produce real quality, even to make things beautiful. (Schumacher, 1975).

The technological continuum illustrates not only the alternatives for a given industry but also the probable general drift of the American economy as a whole. What is important to understand about the aggregate effects of a shift from middle technologies is

1. The shifts will be gradual.
2. The shifts will go both ways—not just to the high or just to the low end. The Schumacher view that only small is beautiful is inappropriate in our advanced economy. The high productivity of high technology actually helps to support more workers in services and low-technology jobs.
3. We do not know which industries will go which way at this time.
4. The shifts will be voluntary responses to market and social pressures.
5. Shifts to low technology do not necessarily entail abandoning modern technology or high productivity.

Basically, the shifts forecasted have four antecedents in the contemporary economy. First, the United States is already moving toward a services economy and is beginning to rely on foreign nations to provide many mass-produced and some energy-intensive goods. These shifts are likely to continue for as long as there is a less-developed world and for as long as some underdeveloped countries have ready access to cheap natural gas and oil. Second, American industries are beginning to adopt the so-called sociotechnical philosophy that technologies can be designed to meet social needs. Third, there is some rekindled interest in the production of goods by craftsmen. Fourth, some mass-produced goods that contribute only to waste or planned obsolescence are being abandoned (beverage cans). None of these incipient trends constitutes a revolution, but it is not a revolution that is being forecast. Rather, it would seem that higher energy costs, when combined with the larger package of new social and economic demands, will encourage substitutions of products or processes or labor for energy.

## ULTIMATE ABUNDANCE?

In the very long run, there is good reason for optimism about the supply of energy. In the midst of the energy crisis of 1973 and 1974, it was easy to slip into pessimism by forgetting that the world economy ultimately operates on the laws of supply and demand. Eventually, increases in the price of a commodity bring a host of restoring forces into play. The recent increase in the price of crude oil was so dramatic that the restoring forces generated may not be felt for a decade—but they will be felt.

To be more specific, the price increase will eventually trigger unprecedented activity in the exploration for new fossil fuel deposits, unearthing enough to meet man's needs for another two decades. The higher price will significantly alter the curve of rapidly increasing consumption and will put a variety of other long-term forces into play: national energy policies aimed at greater fuel economy, reduced consumption, or national self-sufficiency. Even if the energy research and development programs do not result in immediate stores of new energy, every step along the road toward practical solar energy conversion, controlled nuclear fusion, and similar innovations will increase the nervousness of those who sit atop the large, known reserves of petroleum. Eventually, these countries will be tempted to unload large amounts at bargain prices while there is still some demand in the marketplace.

It may take several years for a country like the United States to make the transition from passenger automobiles that average 10 miles per gallon to those averaging 35 miles per gallon, but such a transition is clearly under way. As more and more countries (England, Norway, Mexico, China) become major petroleum producers, any thought of an international cartel to maintain an artificially high petroleum price will vanish. Increased mining and use of coal along with a proliferation of nuclear reactors will further increase the availability of energy, even in the short term. It is with good reason that more and more economists are writing of the coming energy glut.

In any one of at least a dozen technological areas, a breakthrough could occur at almost any time that would have the effect of significantly increasing the quantity of energy available relative to human needs. Controlled fusion is one of the more highly publicized examples of this sort, but there are numerous more probable candidates. For example, solar energy would begin to play a major role if any one of several developments occurred: (1) a more efficient solar collector at a moderate price; (2) an inefficient but very cheap solar collector; (3) an inexpensive transducer for the direct conversion of sunlight into electricity; or (4) the development of a portable high-capacity energy storage device that could effect a very profound change for the better in the efficiency with which energy is consumed.

No doubt, ultimate abundance is still an iffy proposition. But the factors most likely to turn *if* into *when* are high energy prices brought about by market pressures and the unconstrained imagination of American entrepreneurs.

The short-run future forecast here is basically optimistic, and the normative long-run future described is equally sanguine. Nevertheless, I feel compelled to conclude with a caveat. Because there will be no short-term crisis, we fear that complacency may obviate the steps necessary to achieve the long-term abundance we forecast. Although energy will be readily available for the next decade, in the short run it is necessary to begin to change energy practices. Energy prices need to be greatly increased *now* if a long-term crisis is to be avoided. Unfortunately, by mid-1976, American consumers were being lulled into complacency by the relaxation of the OPEC cartel on oil prices and were again wasting electricity in their homes, buying big cars, and joy-riding. Many industries were becoming sloppy again in their conservation policies. Most distressing, the administration had backed off from its former proposals to deregulate and raise energy prices.

Although an economy of abundance is an "iffy" proposition, complacency is the factor most likely to lead to an economy of scarcity in the long run.

## NOTES

1. This section is based on Enzer, (1975a). By battery, I mean any high-density, high-powered energy storage device—including flywheels. Some efficient heat storage devices are already available. In Britain, many homes have storage heaters that are cheaply warmed using off-peak electrical capacity.

These storage devices are simple, brick-like substitutes that remain warm for as long as twenty-four hours.

2. The technological continuum is an enlargement of the automation continuum discussed briefly in Lawler and Hackman (1971). In some ways, this formulation may appear inconsistent with the concept recently revealed in Schumacher (1975). Most of the differences center on these points: Schumacher's constructs are designed for developing countries, whereas mine are suggested only for the United States; and Schumacher's "intermediate technologies" are, in the main, low technology on my continuum.

## REFERENCES

Compton, W. Dale. 1974. "Energy Conversion and Storage Technology—The Sodium-Sulfur Battery." In Jay Holmes (ed.), *Energy, Environment, Productivity,* Washington, D.C.: National Science Foundation, 25–30.

Enzer, Selwyn. 1975a. *Some Societal Impacts of Alternative Energy Policies.* Menlo Park, Calif. Institute for the Future, Special Report WP–21.

———. 1975b. *Alternative Futures for California.* Los Angeles: University of Southern California, Center for Futures Research.

Hoffman, George. 1974. *"The U.S. Fuel Industry in the 21st Century."* Paper commissioned by the University of Southern California Center for Futures Research, Los Angeles.

Lawler, Edward E., and J. Richard Hackman. 1971. "Corporate Profits and Employee Satisfaction: Must They Be in Conflict?" *California Management Review,* Volume 14, Number 1, 46–55.

O'Toole, James. 1976. *Energy and Social Change.* Cambridge, Mass.: MIT Press.

Schumacher, E. F. 1975. *Small Is Beautiful: Economics As If People Mattered.* New York: Harper & Row.

U.N. Institute for Training and Research. 1975. *Important for the Future,* Volume 1, Number 1 (September).

BARRY COMMONER

# The Impending Environmental Catastrophe

In the last few years, the environmental crisis has entered forcefully into the political arena, not only in the United States, but also in Sweden, England, Germany, Japan, Italy, and the Soviet Union. During the preparations for the 1972 United Nations Conference on the Human Environment, it became a subject of international debate.

In the United States, the political impact of environmental issues is so strong as to generate, in some quarters, the suspicion that many of them are really politics dressed up as ecology. As a result, ecology suffers somewhat from the kind of "credibility gap" that has been observed in the neighborhood of the White House in recent years. And like some recent U.S. presidents, ecologists are sometimes suspected of escalating an admittedly bad situation into a catastrophic one—by claiming that environmental deterioration is not merely a threat to the quality of life, but to life itself, that the very survival of human beings on the earth is at stake. Even a "numbers game" has evolved: "How long," people want to know, "do we have to live?" Environmentalists' answers range from about 100 to rather few years. One has even asserted that if the crisis is not on its way to solution by 1972, he will give up the campaign, for it will then be too late (Ehrlich, 1970).

How real is the environmental threat to human survival? How much time *do* we have? Or is the issue of survival only scare tactics, an exaggeration made in the presumably good cause of forcing public action on the declining quality of life?

The issue of survival can be put into the form of a fairly rigorous question: are present ecological stresses so strong that—if not relieved—they will sufficiently degrade the ecosystem to make the earth uninhabitable by man? If the answer is yes, then human survival is indeed at stake in the environmental crisis. Obviously, no serious discussion of the environmental crisis can get very far without confronting this question.

It should be said at the outset that while this question is a fairly

SOURCE: *The Closing Circle.* Reprinted by permission of Barry Commoner © 1972.

rigorous one, any answer is a matter of judgment, not of fact. Nevertheless, it is a judgment that can, and should, be related to actual data and scientific principles.

My own judgment, based on the evidence now at hand, is that the present course of environmental degradation, at least in industrialized countries, represents a challenge to essential ecological systems that is so serious that, if continued, it will destroy the capability of the environment to support a reasonably civilized human society. Some number of human beings might well survive such a catastrophe, for the collapse of civilization would reduce the pace of environmental degradation. What would then remain would be a kind of neobarbarism with a highly uncertain future. The reasoning behind this judgment is described in what follows.

To begin with, it is prudent to take note of the inherent limitations of any discussion that hopes to comment on the future course of ecological change. Extension from past data to future trends—the process of extrapolation—has many pitfalls. The most serious difficulty is that any such numerical extension necessarily assumes that the future process will be governed by the same mechanisms that have controlled past events. Mark Twain's (1917) observation on the Mississippi River is pertinent here:

> In the space of one hundred and seventy-six years the Lower Mississippi has shortened itself two hundred and forty-two miles. That is an average of a trifle over one mile and a third per year. Therefore, any calm person, who is not blind or idiotic, can see that in the Old Ooelitic Silurian Period, just a million years ago next November, the Lower Mississippi River was upward of one million three hundred miles long, and stuck out over the Gulf of Mexico like a fishing-rod. And by the same token any person can see that seven hundred and forty-two years from now the Lower Mississippi will be only a mile and three-quarters long, and Cairo and New Orleans will have joined their streets together, and be plodding comfortably along under a single mayor and a mutual board of aldermen. There is something fascinating about science. One gets such wholesale returns of conjecture out of such a trifling investment of fact.

This is a useful warning. It is particularly relevant to ecological events, for as shown earlier, their inherent complexity often leads to sudden, qualitative changes in response to gradual, quantitative ones. For this reason, estimates of the future condition of an ecosystem can easily be confounded by the emergence of such qualitative changes as the predicted quantitative effects intensify.

Only few quantitative extrapolations of the changing state of the environment can be made with reasonable accuracy. Probably the firmest estimate is that regarding the depletion of oxygen in U.S.

surface waters. From the yearly rate of increase in the amount of organic wastes intruded into surface waters, the total amount of oxygen required to degrade them can be estimated for future years. Then, this quantity can be compared to the total oxygen content of U.S. surface waters. The time at which the two values become equal signals a statistical crisis: that the total oxygen content of surface waters is then insufficient to support the ecological purification of the total influx of organic waste. According to a 1966 report of the U.S. National Academy of Sciences, on the basis of present trends this will occur at about the year 2000. Of course, this does not mean that the oxygen content of every U.S. river and lake will then go to zero. If the present trend is maintained, some bodies of water would reach that point much sooner. Others, perhaps a stream in the distant reaches of the Rockies, might not change in oxygen content at all. However, although it is rather crude and purely statistical, this computation is a useful—and ominous—prediction. It tells us that within the next thirty years we can expect many of our rivers and lakes to meet the fate of Lake Erie and to become incapable of supporting the ecological cycle that accomplishes the self-purification of surface waters.

One possible response to this prediction is "So what?" If most of our rivers and lakes become foul with decaying organic matter, could we not get used to the odor, purify the water needed for domestic and industrial use by technological means (for example, by using the inexhaustible supply of power that the AEC promises in order to distill pure water from foul), and go about our business? The answer is that the predicted quantitative change in surface waters will probably generate qualitative changes in the ecosystem, which could gravely threaten human survival.

In natural aquatic systems, the organic matter content is rather low. In turn, this severely limits the number and variety of microorganisms (bacteria and molds), most of which require organic matter, that can live in these systems. In the soil ecosystem, matters are very different. Here high levels of organic matter are common and a great variety of bacteria and molds that live on it inhabit the soil. Now, it is commonly found that among these numerous soil microorganisms are many that cause disease in animals and man. This can be demonstrated by a simple laboratory experiment. A pinch of soil is added to a flask of sterile organic nutrient medium, and the microorganisms are allowed to grow for a time. Then the resulting microbial culture is injected into a mouse; the animal is almost certain to die of an infection. When such soil cultures are studied in detail, numerous species of bacteria and molds that are known to cause a variety of animal and human diseases, some of them fatal, can be identified.

Although the soil harbors this reservoir of pathogenic micro-organisms, they actually cause disease only rarely. Typically, this oc-curs when soil happens to penetrate an unprotected part of the body. For example, heavy inhalation of dusty soil can lead to lung disease. Ordinarily, such contact is limited because the soil is held in place by the roots of plants. If, as a result of ecological degradation, dust-bowl conditions develop, such lung diseases may occur more frequently. So long as the natural integrity of the ecosystem is maintained, animals and man are to a large degree isolated from soil-borne infections.

Now let us return to surface waters. These are, of course, in intimate contact with the soil and its burden of pathogenic microorganisms. Moreover, people come into equally intimate contact with water—by swimming in it, drinking it, or inhaling spray. There is, therefore, a ready physical path leading from the soil and its pathogens, through the water, to man. Nevertheless, soil-borne disease ordinarily remains rare in man. The reason is clear: in natural conditions, surface waters are a very effective *biological* barrier to the movement of pathogenic microorganisms from the soil to man because the water ordinarily contains insufficient organic matter to support the growth of the patho-gens. Since the organisms do not reproduce in the nutrient-poor water, the few that may enter it from the soil become highly dilute and even-tually die off; the statistical probability that they will invade the body of, let us say, a swimmer is negligible.

However, in the next thirty years or so, as many rivers and lakes become unnaturally burdened with organic matter, the natural biologi-cal barrier between soil and man will break down. Some of the patho-gens might grow and reproduce in the water, reaching concentrations that make a human infection far more likely than before. For this reason, the projected ecological change in surface waters is much more serious than a smelly nuisance. It may expose human beings to a host of new and unaccustomed diseases for which immunity may be lacking. This is the real danger in the extensive pollution of surface waters with organic matter.

Unhappily, there is at least one hint that this process may have already begun. In 1965, a new disease, now known as men-ingioencephalitis, was reported from Florida. It occurred typically in teen-age children several days after prolonged swimming during warm summer months in a pond or river. A severe headache develops, leading to coma, and, with a high frequency, to death. The cause of this disease has now been established—it is an amoeba, a microscopic protozoan, that is very commonly found in soil. Apparently, the amoeba enters the body from infected water through the nose and massively invades the victim's brain membranes. The ecological basis of the disease now seems clear. In the soil, this amoeba is usually found in an inactive form, a cyst. When a high concentration of bacteria develops in the neighborhood of the cyst, their secretions stimulate it and an active amoeba emerges which then lives on the bacteria. It seems likely, then, that in organically polluted streams and ponds there may be enough bacteria to activate the amoebic cysts as they enter the water from the soil, where they are plentiful. Feeding on the bacteria, the amoebae then reproduce in the water, becoming sufficiently concentrated to invade successfully the brain of the unlucky swimmer (Callicott, 1968).

A hint that other soil organisms may be growing in polluted water comes from New York harbor. There it has been observed that despite a considerable improvement in the numbers of bacteria released into the harbor from sewage outlets, the bacterial count has increased by several hundred percent in recent years. It is possible that this change is a result of the growth of soil bacteria in the polluted waters around New York.

Breakdown of the water barrier between man and the soil has other, equally serious implications. Among the common molds found in soil are certain species that are known to produce a very active carcinogen, aflotoxin. These, too, grow on organic matter. Recent studies by an associate of the Center for the Biology of Natural Systems at Washington University show that many soil molds—including those that produce aflotoxin—can be isolated from streams heavily polluted with organic matter.[1] Should these organisms become common, we will be faced with another serious hazard to health. Some of the molds normally found in soil, but which have now been detected in polluted water, can cause serious infections if they become established in the body (for example, in a wound). Unfortunately, some current medical practices increase the likelihood of such infections. For example, changes in body levels of steroid hormones, such as result from the use of cortisone or of contraceptive pills, may increase susceptibility to such mold infections.

The rapid spread of water pollution is exemplified by the results of a recent survey of European beaches (Novick, 1971). The survey showed that visitors to most of the beaches of France, Spain, Belgium, and Italy are twice as likely to acquire an infection if they go swimming than they are if they stay out of the water. From the Italian Riviera to the beaches of the Dutch coast, heavy organic pollution from sewage and industrial wastes and the accompanying high bacterial count has become prevalent. The rate of deterioration appears to be accelerating in recent years; this should be regarded, I believe, as a warning of possible catastrophic health problems in the coming years.

It is this kind of warning of things to come that leads me to conclude that *if* we permit most of our surface waters to become heavily polluted with organic matter, we may be faced with outbreaks of new, serious diseases that could go a long way toward rendering major parts of the land uninhabitable. The increasing pollution of surface waters with organic matter breaks down the natural ecological separation of man and animals from soil pathogens and may open up a veritable Pandora's box of disease and toxic hazards. If we do not check the present course of water pollution, I believe that the multiple effects of these hazards may in the future become an intolerable threat to human health. And in this case, the future is something like the next thirty years.

One important reason why new ecological dangers often arise in the course of gradual, quantitative changes is the phenomenon of synergism. A common example of this effect was mentioned earlier: if the levels of sulfur dioxide and a carcinogen in polluted air are both doubled, the resultant hazard is much more than doubled, because sulfur dioxide inhibits the lung's self-protective mechanism and makes it more susceptible to the carcinogen. In synergism, the overall effect of a complex biological insult is always greater than the sum of the effects of its separate parts.

Such synergistic interactions can occur within the body and thereby intensify the effects of environmental hazards. An example is the interaction between NTA and metals such as mercury and cadmium.[2] When laboratory animals are exposed to NTA in the presence of mercury and cadmium levels, a tenfold increase in fetal abnormalities occurs. This is the observation that has barred the use of NTA in detergents. The NTA/mercury-cadmium synergism is typical of the tendency of metals to form complexes with certain types of organic compounds that may sharply differ, in their chemical and biological properties, from either of the separate constituents.

Synergistic interactions can also occur within the ecosystem. An example is the impact of organic water pollutants on the hazard from mercury pollution. Very considerable amounts of metallic mercury have been dumped into rivers and lakes in the United States, Canada, and elsewhere by chloralkali plants. As it lies on the bottom of a lake or river, metallic mercury is relatively innocuous. But if the bottom mud is rich in bacteria and especially if the oxygen content is low, bacterial action converts the metal to an organic form, methyl mercury. This is very soluble in water, enters the bodies of fish, where it causes the widespread occurrence of unacceptable levels of mercury. This means that pollution of surface waters by organic matter seriously intensifies the hazard of mercury pollution. Recent studies also suggest that another element, arsenic—which has entered surface waters as a contaminant of phosphate (from detergents and other sources)—may follow a similar course.[3] Bacteria seem to be able to methylate arsenic and convert it to a highly toxic organic form. As a result of such interactions, we must anticipate that new *kinds* of environmental hazards may suddenly emerge as the levels of organic matter in surface waters gradually increase. Mercury deposited on river and lake bottoms many years ago can remain there, harmlessly, for many years, then, quite suddenly, as organic pollution intensifies, the ecological status of the bottom mud is changed and mercury emerges as a serious environmental hazard.

Heavy industrialization pours increasing amounts of toxic metals into the air: mercury, lead, nickel, and cadmium, for example. From the air, these metals are carried down to the soil by rain and snow where they accumulate. The ecology of the soil is very vulnerable to the toxic effects of these metals, for they may inhibit the growth of necessary soil bacteria and of plants. In addition, new unnatural complexes of these metals with organic compounds in the soil may be formed. The NTA experience warns that some of these may become new environmental dangers. It is well within the bounds of reasonable extrapolation, I believe, that if we continue to accumulate such metals in the soil, its ability to support plant life—to produce food crops and timber—might eventually be reduced catastrophically. It is also possible that new metal-organic complexes that are harmless to crops will pass through them to man, in food, where they may not be so harmless.

Pollution of air with the oxides of sulfur is a similar hazard. The situation is best known in Northern Europe, where Swedish data, for example, show a progressive increase in the acidity of rain and snow over recent years (Albone, 1970). This unnatural influx of acid into the soil is bound to have serious effects on plant growth and may already be reducing the rate of timber production. But again, the greater danger may be from qualitative changes in the growth of soil microorganisms and in the chemical interactions among soil constituents in these new, unnatural conditions. Pollutants which accumulate in the soil may drastically upset its vital ecological balance.

Those pollutants that do not end up in the soil are eventually deposited in the oceans, which have begun to accumulate persistent pesticides (it has recently been computed that about 25 percent of all the DDT produced is now in the ocean) and other synthetic organic pollutants. Relatively little is known, as yet, about the impact of these pollutants on the vital ecological systems in the ocean. These systems produce most of the oxygen in the atmosphere through photosynthesis. Although there is no evidence of changes of the oxygen content of the air, there are some indications that photosynthetic activity of marine organisms may be inhibited by DDT and other pollutants.

Another reason why we must expect the unexpected in environmental pollution is that new effects are so often set in motion long before we are aware that the problem exists. Consider the following sequence of events.

In the 1950s, the plastic industry developed new types of flexible, synthetic materials—polyvinyl plastics—with good wearing properties. They found a ready market in automobile upholstery, so that within a decade the interiors of nearly every American car contained yards of the new plastic. Since then nearly everyone has been in contact with the material. Many people have noticed on entering a plastic-upholstered car, which has had its windows closed for a day or so—especially in the summer heat—that the steering wheel is slippery and that the inner window surfaces are coated with a slippery, transparent film. Car drivers—myself included—have tolerated this effect for a number of years without complaint (which, for myself, I now painfully regret). But in a space capsule, matters are not so relaxed. Here NASA technicians noticed the same effects, but took them seriously because the film spoiled the efficiency of optical equipment. For this reason, NASA barred the use of polyvinyl plastics in space equipment about five years ago.

Now the scene shifts to hospital blood banks. There important glass equipment used to store and transfuse blood and other fluids was replaced by polyvinyl equipment about ten years ago. This was an apparently advantageous step, for the new equipment, unlike the old, was unbreakable.

The scene shifts again, this time to military hospitals in Vietnam, where the new plastic transfusion equipment is in extensive use. Here in the last few years a new medical phenomenon "shock lung," a sometimes fatal disorder, is noticed in the wounded after transfusions, especially of long-stored blood. The effect was reported in medical journals in 1959, but not related to the transfusion process.

Now it is 1970. At the Carnegie Institution's embryology laboratory in Baltimore, Dr. Robert De Haan is having a problem with an experiment. He finds that cultures of embryonic chick heart cells, which he has studied successfully for some time, are mysteriously dying. After some effort he discovers the cause: some toxic material is leaching out of polyvinyl containers into his culture medium, killing the cells. He soon informs a colleague, Dr. Robert J. Rubin of the Johns Hopkins Hospital, of this finding. Dr. Rubin is concerned, because this same material may be leaching from polyvinyl blood transfusion equipment. His studies confirm this expectation. Material incorporated into the polyvinyl plastic in the manufacturing process, which is designed to make it flexible, readily enters the stored blood. He finds the plasticizer and its metabolic breakdown products in the blood, urine, and tissues of patients receiving blood that has been stored in polyvinyl bags. He finds, too, that the plasticizer causes blood platelets to become sticky and clot—a condition that probably explains "shock lung."

All this is reported in a scientific journal in October 1970. In this paper, the authors point out that their results may account for the earlier observation of plasticizers in some foods, which are often packaged in polyvinyl-coated containers. One of these reports attracts the attention of Mr. F. C. Gross, now at NASA, but formerly a chemist with the United States Food and Drug Administration. He had been working on the spaceship plasticizer problem. He telephones Dr. Rubin and points out that human exposure to plasticizers is not limited to blood transfusions or to plastic-packaged foods, but includes as well the air that many car passengers breathe.[4]

Meanwhile, back in the scientific journals, now that the issue has been raised, one can find earlier studies which show that plastics contain not only plasticizers having toxic effects, but also other additives, known as "stabilizers," that are usually even more hazardous. In one 1968 scientific report, we read:

One of the most successful stabilizers in the plastics industry for PVC (polyvinyl chloride) formulations are the organotin compounds [i.e., tin-containing organic compounds]. Unfortunately they are also among the most toxic. Even though this toxicity is widely known, organotin stabilizers are still used in certain plastics for medical use (Guess and Haberman, 1968, p. 313).

Now that the alarm has been sounded, researchers are busy studying the toxic effects of the numerous varieties of stabilizers and plasticizers used in modern plastics. Eventually their results will show, it is to be hoped, what dangers we have endured in the last decade from automobile upholstery, food packages, medical and dental equipment, plastic toys and water hoses, and the new "wet-look" plastic garments. The present scientific results already show that the effects may be subtle and slow to appear. For example, some of the materials have significant effects on cell growth. And lurking in the background is the potentially ominous fact that the basic material used in many of these plastic additives—phthalic anhydride—is also a constituent part of the molecule of a now notorious substance—thalidomide.

Concerned with the chemical link between a substance known to cause serious fetal deformities and the phthalic acid derivatives used as plasticizers, several researchers at Baylor University in Texas have studied the effects of the latter on developing chick embryos. In their words, "The purpose of this work was to determine whether certain esters of phthalic acid which are used in the formulation of polyvinyl chloride plastics, were capable of producing adverse effects in the developing chick embryo" (Bower et al., p. 314).

Here is their summary of the results:

Dibutoxyethyl phthalate was capable of causing teratogenesis [embryonic defects- in these embryos. Congenital malformations such as crania bifida [cleft skull] and anophthalmia [malformed eye] were observed in newly hatched chicks receiving this phthalate ester into the yolk sac before the third day of embryonic life. Also marked exophthalmia, resulting from the absence of bone tissue forming the orbit of the eye, and blindness due to failure of the cornea to develop were other malformations observable in chicks treated with the phthalate ester. The data suggested that dibutoxyethyl phthalate, di-2-methoxyethyl phthalate and octyl isodecyl phthalate are capable of causing damage to the central nervous system of the developing chick embryo. This was manifested after hatching by grossly abnormal behavior of chicks such as tremor, non-purposeful bodily movement, and a total incapability of either standing or walking normally (Bower et al., p. 314).

What is the point of this story? It is *not* reported here in order to suggest that we are all about to perish from exposure to plastic automobile upholstery. All that can be said at this time about the hazard to health is that there may be one. What our experience with the plasticizer problem reveals is something much more serious than the harm that it might engender. It reminds us of our ignorance—that we are hardly aware of the potential hazards from hundreds of similar substances that have so quickly become ubiquitous in our environment. It warns us that the blind, ecologically mindless progress of technology has massively altered our daily environment in ways that may, much later, emerge as a threat to health. Unwittingly, we have created for ourselves a new and dangerous world. We would be wise to move through it as though our lives were at stake.

There is a final threat to ecological survival that hardly needs to be documented here—nuclear war. A decade ago, the military and their supporters could still pretend that victory was possible in a nuclear war. In the face of repeated evidence by the independent scientific community, led by Linus Pauling and others, the pretense was maintained for a while. Now, although the nuclear threat to survival is acknowledged, the United States and presumably other nuclear powers are in a constant state of readiness to launch a suicidal war. However, no political leader appears to be willing any longer openly to claim that civilization could survive a nuclear war.

These are the kinds of considerations that lead to my judgment that the present course of environmental degradation, if unchecked, threatens the survival of civilized man. Although it might be convenient if the environmentalist, like some occult seer predicting the end of the world, could set a date for this catastrophe, the exercise would be futile and in any case unnecessary. It would be futile because the uncertainties are far too great to support anything more than guesses. One can try to guess at the point of no return—the time at which major ecological degradation might become irreparable. In my own judgment, a reasonable estimate for industrialized areas of the world might be from twenty to fifty years, but it is only a guess.

In any case, this guesswork is unnecessary. For it seems to me that the world is now no longer willing to tolerate even the present level of environmental degradation, much less its intensification. It is now widely recognized, I believe, that we are already suffering too much from the effects of the environmental crisis, that with each passing year it becomes more difficult to reverse, and that the issue is not how far we can go to the brink of catastrophe, but how to act—now.

## NOTES

1. The study referred to here is being carried out by John Noell, Junior Fellow of the Center for the Biology of Natural Systems.

2. For a summary of this problem, see *Medical World News,* January 22, 1971, pp. 47–57. It is important to note that the scientific basis of the present views of the NTA hazard is still rather weak. Only one, as yet inadequately reported study, has been completed thus far, although more are in progress. Much more information is needed before the hazard can be evaluated.

3. For a review of this problem, see *Chemical and Engineering News,* July 5, 1971, pp. 22–34.

4. For a general account of the development of the medical problems associated with the plasticizers used in these plastics, see the articles by Robert De Haan, *Nature,* Volume 231 (1970), p. 85; and by R. J. Jaeger and R. J. Rubin in *Lancet,* 1970-II (1970), p 151. See also *Chemical and Engineering News,* April 26, 1971, p. 3 (letter from Frederick C. Gross regarding NASA's experience with volatile plasticizers in plastics).

## REFERENCES

Albone, Eric. 1970. "The Ailing Air." *Ecologist,* Volume 1, Number 3 (September), 97–107.

Bower, R. K., et al. 1970. "Teratogenic Effects in the Chick Embryo Caused by Esters of Phthalic Acid." *Journal of Pharmacology and Experimental Therapeutics,* Volume 171, Number 2, 314–324.

Callicott, J. H. 1968. "Amebic Meningioencephalitis Due to Free-Living Amebas of the Hartmanella (acanthamoeba)-Naegleria Group." *American Journal of Clinical Pathology,* Volume 49 (January), 84–91.

Ehrlich, Paul R. 1970. "An Interview with Paul Ehrlich." *Look* (April 21).

————. 1968. *The Population Bomb.* New York: Ballantine Books.

Guess, W. C., and S. Haberman. 1968. "Toxicity Profiles of Vinyl and Polyolefinic Plastics and Their Additives." *Journal of Biomedical Materials Research,* Volume 2 (September), 313–335.

National Academy of Sciences-National Research Council. 1966. *Waste Management and Control.* Washington, D.C., Publication 1400.

National Academy of Sciences. 1971. "Chlorinated Hydrocarbons in the Ocean Environment." Washington, D.C.

Novick, Sheldon. 1971. "Last Year at Deauville." *Environment,* Volume 13, Number 6 (July/August), 36–37.

Singh, A., et al. 1971. "Teratogenicity of a Group of Phthalate Esters in Rats." Abstracts, Tenth Annual Meeting, Society of Toxicology.

Twain, Mark. 1917. *Life on the Mississippi.* New York: Harper and Brothers.

H. WENTWORTH ELDREDGE

# Urban Futures

Today there is much talk of visionary urban futures. For example, Justus Dahinden's *Urban Structure for the Future* is a collection of futuristic city scapes (1972); whether we shall see them is another story. The investment in steel and concrete, not to mention emotional attachment and habit patterns, will make it impossible to change rapidly. As an example of this slowness, one has only to ponder the grandiose City of Tomorrow, General Motors' dream world of the New York's World Fair of 1939 which was supposed to arrive in about twenty-five years with its fancy aerial roadways and even fancier quasi-helicopters. But something new is coming and signs of it are abroad.

Given the multigroup society of the present United States with widely divergent value systems, overriding democratic values with heavy egalitarian overtones preclude any reductionism to *one national pattern* for societal-physical urbanism. A naive, simplistic perception of "human nature" is not remotely feasible in modern Western nations, even though there is a tendency to approach it in totalitarian nations. The enormous powers of the intellectual, technical, and even behavioral and organizational technologies make it possible both to have diversity and to meet human needs for the first time in history. We do have some options for our urban futures, despite the energy crunch. In post-industrial society with its heavy emphasis on the knowledge industry, there is bound to be a multiplicity of variants on patterns already visible in the 1970s.

To select a few searches for options: *Futures Conditional,* guided by that lively socioeconomist Robert Theobald, is an attempt to imagine various future scenarios for the next thirty years (1972). Paul Goodman early saw *Seeds of Liberation* in new thought patterns that would free humanity for building, first better societal futures and later physical structures (1964). In 1966, the American Institute of Planners launched a massive inquiry directed by William R. Ewald, Jr., into the next fifty years. This was an attempt to inform American (and the world's) professional city planners as to the rich variety of the feasible roads ahead.[1]

An amazing variety of authors—many of them exceptionally perceptive—from a wide spectrum of doers and thinkers at least concur to form the clear message that bumbling along with "more of the same" would be hopelessly inadequate. In "The Possible City," urban design student Kevin Lynch stresses that "mobility, access and communication are indeed the essential qualities of an urbanised region—its reason for being (1968, p. 145). This thought has been echoed by transportation specialist Wilfred Owen who emphasizes that access to activity nodes—jobs, dwellings, and recreation—is the key to civilized community development (Owen, 1972, pp 132–133). Even a hard-headed urban administrator, Roger Starr, executive director of New York's Citizen's Housing and Planning Council, bewailing the incessant critical attacks on "the city" by utopian types such as Lewis Mumford, Jane Jacobs, Herbert Gans, Victor Gruen, et al., knows that the balancing of the multiplicity of values (held by divergent groups *now*) is already an almost impossible task (Starr, 1967). It is bound to be worse in the future as groups multiply and pathways further divide.

If market choices are to be largely replaced by designed options under a National Urban Policy (NUP), then widespread societal-physical alternative possibilities must be built for multiple present and future life-styles. Minimum standards can probably be set; egalitarianism, heavily reinforced—and resisted—by increasingly scarce resources, will be quite likely to create iron maxima. But within these very wide parameters a NUP can offer the citizenry several attractive modes of life. Undoubtedly, both monetary and societal costs will be involved in making large numbers of available options, but the stunting of society by uniformity suggests immediate high societal costs and potential high monetary costs for the failure to provide options. Thus, it would appear that one of the most overwhelming tasks of NUP planners is to make readily available rewarding, feasible options in diverse physical and societal forms.

Traditionally, planners have tended to think in terms of multipurpose or multifunctional cities; this seems a rather narrow conclusion to reach after a long human experience drawn from governmental, religious, recreational, learning, trading, and industrial types of cities. The future could see specialized cities with clues elaborated from the above list of existent forms with such revised types as: (1) the ceremonial city (Washington), (2) the university city (Oxford as it was), (3) the research city (Novosibirsk), (4) the artistic city (Aspen), (5) the fun city or Hedonopolis (Cannes), (6) the communications or media city (see Option 14 below), (7) the museum city (Nara), including Museums of the Future (Mesa City of Soleri), (8) experimental cities of varied types (health, new social relations, communal economic developments), or (9) any combination of the above. In fact, each venture could be considered as an experiment (McHale, unpublished) and so treated. Actually, sharply differentiated satellite cities in a metropolitan area within a core city could offer rewarding variations.

In the following pages, I offer a realistic catalogue of feasible, relatively "surprise-free" urban options ahead. It assumes that no major economic, military, or ecological catastrophe will befall the world in the next three decades. Given multigroup society with divergent life-styles and values, holistic planners must offer a wide spectrum of choice. Despite both physical and societal utopianists, it is more than likely that in the year 2000 A.D., postindustrial society will be surprisingly like the present, only—hopefully—"better." These fifteen options are not mutually exclusive, and much overlapping is evident[2]; within options, there are clearly various sub-options that are not pursued here. Further, the emphasis tends to be on the physical-spatial framework and on location, which together do not determine societal structuring. Much social diversity is possible within similar man-made physical environments as within similar natural physical environments; the relationship between design and behavior is not one-to-one. These options are grouped under two categories: Type A—almost certain to continue; and Type B—generally visionary environments. No attempt is made to weigh formally the importance of the various options. Certain options clearly occur within the territory of larger urban forms, and others are relatively free-standing entities or activity centers. What effects a widespread appreciation of the energy crisis will have on all this is not yet clear.

## TYPE A: ALMOST CERTAIN TO CONTINUE

*Option 1. Megalopolis or urban region.* This is modern society's fate. THE PACIFIC BELT (Japan), BOSWASH (Boston to Washington), and RANDSTAD (Holland) are already here. Can such sprawling territorial giantism be redeveloped by opening up "density breaks" (similar to "fire breaks" in a forest) and by creating varied activity nodes to restructure interaction and upgrade the quality of life in such vast agglomerations? These have been defined as "man heaps" by Lewis Mumford, and "conurbations" by the English. Obviously, a multitude of life-styles are possible and existent in megalopolis.

*Option 2. Metropolitan central city* (500,000 and up), as a high-activity area with "cosmopolitan," sophisticated recreation, jobs, and living. The French regional *metropoles d'equilibre* fit this pattern; high-rise, vertically zoned buildings could serve as an experiment. Both "straight" and "counter" cultures can find room here. This is the locus of high-pressure private and public development in the United States as "the city fights back" to lure the middle-class into returning from the suburbs to live and to interact. It means modern office buildings, pedestrian malls, and walkways with interesting and diverse shops, recreational and cultural facilities—in short, the lure of the bazaar which has given variety to urban life. "New Towns" in this category, as they most certainly belong, attempt to divide the city into some semblance of meaningful communities (at least at the level of simple services).

*Option 3. Smaller central city* (50,000 to 500,000), with similar qualities but on a less national and more regional scale. The possibility exists of creating an *entire* community spirit. Town housing would exist, along with vertically zoned buildings with possible class and ethnic mixtures. Somewhere between a 250,000 and 500,000 population seems to be presently the critical mass for the full spectrum of city functions. Quality of life efforts would pay off richly here. The 1970 U.S. census indicates that cities in this group have continued to grow where metropolitan central cities (Option 2) are leveling off.

*Option 4. Small central city or town* (up to 50,000), still less national-regional interaction and more on a localized scale. Here local realities would be adjusted more clearly to varied natural environments and with specific functions, such as the research city, shore city, recreation city, university/learning/information city, and mountain city.

*Option 5. Satellite cities* for Options 2 and 3 to gain the putative benefits of Option 4. These are closely linked to new communities, but they could be upgraded existent towns or cities.

*Option 6. Inner suburbs,* a subset for all three major city types (2, 3, 4), which must be divided into "communities" serving various life-styles according to economic class, vocational and/or leisure interests, religion, ethnicity, race—high-rise and low-rise (townhouses/cluster housing). There should be a great variety of suburban types to suit various life-styles. The United States has its special problem in white-black antagonisms, and unless adequate optional suburban space (both integrated and nonintegrated) is made available for blacks to leave the central city, the ghetto problem will continue. Undoubtedly, suboptions regarding whether to integrate must be made available to face the hard reality of continuing prejudice. Patently, this applies also to outer suburbs and to new towns; here derelict land can be used as new green space for recreation and relief.

*Option 7. Outer suburbs,* similar but of a less "urban" character. Varied life-styles are stressed by design both physical and societal; a greater attempt is made through cluster housing to create "community." Some high-rise buildings in open settings are inevitable.

*Option 8. Exurbia.* Quasi-rural existence because of advanced transportation, "urbanistic" in quality; not unrelated to "the wired city" and the four-day work week. This option is made possible by the electric pump, septic tank, and four-wheeled drive vehicle; it is the haunt of "hillbilly" types and seclusive "intellectuals." This option is high-cost scatteration, but is immensely rewarding for certain personality types, who may be either incompetent, truly creative, or merely hiding from the horrid urban world (Spectorsky, 1955). It is increasingly the haunt of the counterculture and very suitable for new experimental family/community variants. Alpine recreational resorts possibly fit this category; the seashore has been pretty generally usurped by sprawl.

*Option 9. New towns* (or lately *New Communities*). Building new cities has held a great attraction for mankind; the sentiment "leave the messy clutter behind and start afresh" might even be traced back to mobile hunters striking the befouled encampment to move on to virgin areas. New towns are simply dwellings, jobs, recreation—a wide spectrum of services and controlled size. Most certainly, the current furor about new cities/towns/communities indicates a deep-seated dissatisfaction with existent urban forms. This is unquestionably the area for widespread experimentation both with physical forms and with societal structure, although they are presently somewhat oversold as a universal panacea. The enormous costs for the needed infrastructure of a massive new cities program to cope with a significant percentage of the expected 80 to 100 million new Americans (35 million new households $\pm$) by the twenty-first century boggles the imagination. To build for only 25 percent (20 to 25 million persons) would require 200 towns of 100,000 inhabitants, each costing between \$2-5 million in public and private investment, leading to an overall cost of \$1 billion at least.[3] While much will have to be spent to house, amuse, and provide jobs for the expected hordes, it is most unlikely that tapping the vast existing urban infrastructure would even approach such projected expenses, although the possible benefits of thousands of new towns might be extraordinarily great.[4]

New towns can consist of free-standing independent communities (Brasilia and Novosibirsk Academic City); groups of related free-standing, functionally divergent communities (Lewis Mumford's ideal); satellite communities with high self-employment (London ring new towns); extensions of cities—really glorified, quasi-independent suburbs (Long Island Levittowns and Stockholm's semi-satellite cities); and "New Towns in Town" (NTIT), lively tissue grafts to existing internal city structures (Fort Lincoln, Washington, D.C.) (Perloff 1966).

The ill-fated Minnesota Experimental City (MSC)—the brainchild of oceanographer, physicist, and meteorologist Athelstan Spilhaus and

aided by among others, Buckminster Fuller, urbanologist Harvey Perloff, and economist Walter Heller—was to be built by private financing
on 50,000 acres, 120 miles north of Minneapolis with a maximum
population of 250,000.[5] To date, this is perhaps the most obviously
experimental physical and societal effort. The plans were to roof over
the downtown area; partially fuel the municipal power plant by garbage;
install cable TV to approximate "the wired city" (Option 15); mix farms
and factories; and house people in megastructures complete with wa-
terless toilets, people-movers, and universal computer-managed
charge accounts. This project was shelved when the necessary cash
could not be raised.

New City Vaudreuil, which will house and provide jobs for 150,000
residents, is to be built by the French government in the Basse-Seine
region outside Paris. It will be the world's first urban center without
noise or pollution, and all green zones in the general area are to be
preserved, as was announced by President Pompidou. The city's traffic
will flow underground; factory smoke is to be carried off by underground conduits, the gasses being burned at the source; apartments
and business buildings are to be soundproofed; and all refuse moved
through underground conduits is to be used in adding to the city's
requirements for central heating.

These are merely some of the most "advanced" examples of new
community thinking. Others include the architecturally striking Brasilia
and Chandigarh, and the older Washington, Canberra, and New Delhi
(the British imperial city stage). The thirty-odd British new towns are
globally renowned; by 1963, probably well over 1,000 new towns of
various shapes and sizes had been identified (Osborn and Whittick,
1963, pp. 141–148). According to a 1973 report of the Department of
Housing and Urban Development, there are already 1,000 new towns
in the U.S.S.R. alone. The best known U.S. examples are Columbia
(Maryland), Reston (Virginia), Flower Mound (Texas), Jonathan (Minnesota), and Irvine (California). All are privately financed and all are in
varying degrees socially and physically innovative primarily in amenities.
The semi-satellite cities coupled to the public urban transit system of
Stockholm (they do not provide jobs for more than half the resident
population) have also attracted worldwide attention. Stockholm's town
centers are very reminiscent of American shopping centers but without
that ugly, naked parking necklace of automobiles. The Dutch have
done a splendid job in reclaiming the Zuider Zee for new town development. Tapiola, a tiny gem for only 17,000 persons, by adroit use of both
green and blue (water) space, has cheered the world with the realization that pleasant urban living is possible. Japan with characteristic zeal
dotted the hinterland of Tokyo with quasi-new towns composed of

rather barren, high-density dwellings. The prime example is Tama New Town which will house 410,000 people on 7,500 acres (the same acreage, incidentally, as Reston, which is designed to house 75,000 with high recreational amenities). At Tama, tenants, generally middle income, are to be selected by lot and divided into "neighborhoods" of 15,000 people. Most dwellers are expected to commute to Shinjuku (New Town in Town) or through it to central Tokyo for work (Hud, 1973). India is planning a "New Bombay" for a potential population of 2 million (Kaye, 1973).

As is well known, Israel has constructed a variety of new towns/new communities. The larger ones are for port or industrial purposes, and the smaller for agricultural development, and often for defense, under an urban settlement hierarchy system based on Christaller (Strong, 1971, pp. 170–173). Connected with the physical siting of population are the renowned versions of communal settlements: the *kibbutz* and *moshav*. Thus, the twin experimental functions of new communities are exhibited in Israel: technological virtuosity and fresh social patterning.

Noteworthy in new community development worldwide is the great variety of new governmental authorities or public corporations created to get on with the job. Traditional government has obviously been too wooden to do so. For example, the original or Mark I postwar new towns in Britain were designed to draw off the central city population in the London region. However, such new towns or massively developed old towns are now perceived as potentially powerful development nodes for furthering national urbanization policy with high technology, industry, higher education, and population distribution.[6] Even Herbert Gans, the egalitarian sociologist, believes that, treated delicately, new communities could make positive contributions to the nasty desegregation muddle there[7]. And so perhaps will "Soul City," the black New Town in North Carolina near Raleigh-Durham under the leadership of Floyd B. McKissick with a planned population of 50,000.[8] While the U.S. government is officially dedicated to sponsoring new communities in the Housing Acts of 1970 and 1972, thus far, its action has hardly been impressive. Unfortunately, no overall plans have been formulated.

*Option 10. A rural/agricultural setting.* This option could now be brought more easily into "urbanistic" living patterns by transportation and telecommunications. Unlike the U.S. mode of isolated homesteads, European agricultural life has long been town/village centered. Clearly, the increasing world population will need more and more food, while a declining proportion of the population will continue to opt for an agricultural life-style. Of course, for a considerable period of time, islands of "backward" rural culture will be preserved in Asia, Africa, Latin America, and possibly portions of North America. Such areas could offer a rewarding life-style for the actual inhabitants and "museums for living" (small residual forms throughout the world) for the denizens of more urbanized habitats.

## TYPE B. VISIONARY ENVIRONMENTS

These environments could be either physical or societal, or, more likely, some combination of both. They might serve as the temporary experiences of many or as the permanent life-style of a few.

*Option 11. Megastructures or "mini-cities."* These have fascinated mankind at least since the Tower of Babel (Dahinden, 1972). A Disneyland project, "The Community of Tomorrow," which has been proposed as a whole *enclosed* model town for 20,000 persons on fifty acres *only,* is to be part of the Florida Disney World. In addition, Paolo Soleri has recently visibly revealed his concept of giant supraterrestrial human hives housing up to hundreds of thousands of persons (Soleri, 1969). Soleri's rather fuzzy, complicated, intuitive, and communalistic notions about group life have influenced his often cantilevered bridgelike structures. Thus, his work naturally fits in with far-out commune options as well.[9] It will be interesting to see what kind of clients his constructions attract.

Apparently, the term *megastructure* (mega meaning giant) was the invention of Fumihiko Maki of the Japanese Metabolist Group in 1964. Habitat, designed by the Israeli architect Moshe Safdie and prepared for Expo 1967 in Montreal, was at first a near-financial disaster. It has now become a much publicized example of the "plug-in," "clip-on" structure;[10] it is turning out to be both a financial and a societal success. Taby, a satellite community outside Stockholm, houses 5,000 people in one group of vast, curved structures, flanked by eight tower blocks containing another 3,000 people. Meanwhile, in Denmark at Gladsaxe about 15 miles from Copenhagen, five 16-storey slabs, each 300 feet long, extend in tandem. According to a *New York Times* article in the mid-1960s, this construct seems to negate the warm humanism of Danish planning. As the *Times* reports, the buildings are factory-made prefabs and are assembled on site: "These slabs are aligned with formal, rigid, relentless horizontality."

Responsible officials have even flirted with the idea of building megastructures (human hives) directly in town. In 1966, New York Governor Nelson Rockefeller proposed a futuristic design for Battery Park City. It consisted of massive towers for the lower tip of Manhattan, high connective bridges, and dozens of apartments with a high pedestrian mall surrounded by other rabbit-warren dwellings on a large land fill totaling more than 90 acres. After lengthy interchanges with the New

York City fathers, *The New York Times* reported in 1970 that the plan toned down into a less grandiose format and was being re-thought.

In effect, vertically zoned buildings with garages and services below ground; and retail trade at ground level rising to business offices, schools, and finally to varied dwellings topped by the inevitable penthouse give promise of things to come. Theoretically, many of these megastructures are capable of infinite expansion or contraction that might be one partial answer to an increasingly mobile society.

*Option 12. The water city.* Scarcity of usable shoreland and possibly usable shallow water have led recently to large-scale "futuristic" designs for enormous activity nodes on reclaimed land or on stilts in shallow water. In the December 1967 issue of *Playboy,* Buckminster Fuller advocated a design for Japan in Tokyo Bay which would make use of his newly beloved tetrahedron shapes as piles. Given the population densities and typical minimal family space of the Orient, the water city-megastructure idea does not seem out of place now and may be a necessity in the future. Fuller carried his ideas further in a late 1968 article in *The New York Times.* He proposed the Triton Floating Community of 30,000 persons with structures up to twenty storeys; these fero-concrete platforms could be built in shipyards and towed to usable places just offshore existing coastal cities to be anchored in water up to 20 or 30 feet in depth. This proposal was financed by the U.S. Department of Housing and Urban Development; a trial construction nearly came to fruition in Baltimore harbor. At present there is a scheme to develop an artificial island off Tokyo. Earlier in his *Tokyo 1960* plan, Kenzo Tange had brilliantly explored the Tokyo Bay project.[11] Of course, there have been precursor water cities: Swiss Neolithic Lake Dwellings; Bangkok's *klongs* (canal life); Hong Kong's sampan colony at Victoria; Borneo's and New Guinea's stilt villages; and even Fort Lauderdale. And after all, most of the southern tip of Manahattan Island was once under water. Tange's plan called for a reconstruction of the central city and for a huge expansion, in megastructure form, into Tokyo Bay—both linear and in form—to take care of a 1980 estimated population of 20 million for the metropolitan area of the Japanese capital.

Based on research conducted at the Athens Center of Ekistics on the City of the Future Project, John G. Papaioannou concluded "that floating settlements on the oceans are expected to be considerably less costly than settlements on different land (mountains, swamps, deserts, frozen soil, etc.)"[12] some 70 to 100 years hence when the earth is trending toward one world city, Doxiadis' Ecumenopolis.

*Option 13. Underwater, underground and space habitations,* on a scale large enough to be significant. Jacques Cousteau collaborated in the design of a floating island to be built off the coast of Monaco which would have undersea features: ". . . more comfortable dwelling quarters may be floating stably a hundred feet or so below the surface where any wave motion is so damped out as to be unnoticeable" (*Congressional Record,* November 15, 1965).

The habitation-cum-fortress underground house is something new, although underground factories were well known in Nazi Germany and the United Kingdom during World War II. In addition, there was France's ill-fated Maginot Line. The salubrious atmosphere of huge salt mine caverns could conceivably serve for community experimentation. *Sousterrain* dwellings, which could have temperature control and immediate construction savings, could be built, especially in hot desert areas and quite possibly in sub-Arctic regions. Certainly burying certain structures and services below ground is already in progress in the central city. There are innumerable multi-storey underground parking garages in many cities (Paris, for example), and increasingly, sub-surface delivery roadways and shopping areas are being utilized.

The avowed (and partially endowed) purpose of the Committee for the Future is to develop extraterrestrial space to ease the environmental burden and to open "the solar system for humanity beginning with the establishment of a lunar community available to people of all nations." Unlikely as some of these science fiction solutions may appear today, they may in time at least offer recreational locations for people seeking new experiences.[13]

*Option 14. Communes and other societal innovations.* Recent new societies in the United States with presumed behavioral innovations are generally the efflorescence of the counterculture. They are largely and consciously simplistic in technology and in societal structuring. Even elementary contact with anthropology and history would suggest that middle-class, capitalist, and nationalist habitations/life-styles with certain economic, political, religious, familial, and recreational institutions hardly exhaust the possibilities for human arrangements. Nor does a minimal connection with the long story of utopian schemes and real utopian communities lead one to assume that it all began with "Walden Two" (Skinner, 1948).[14]

Despite the often jejune aspects of such experimental communal utopias and the relatively few persons involved in them, the present impact is being felt, no matter how faintly, by a whole generation of American youth and their foreign imitators. In these communes they see an appealing alternative to modern traditional Western civilization. In short, a counterpoint theme, no matter how unsubstantial, has been established.

Physical communes are in a sense concrete expressions of utopia, the no-place ideal world, to which the forefathers of most Americans emigrated from their assorted homelands. They and their descendants continued to pursue the dream across the wide and once beauteous continent until everything stopped in 1893 (the end of the frontier) on the shores of the Pacific. The more extreme seekers of the perfect/ ideal life probably founded more utopian colonies in the New World than elsewhere (although Robert Owen was English and Charles Fourier French). A catalogue of the better known nineteenth-century ventures in America would include the celibate New England Shakers (so-called because of their curious dancing-shuffling worship) who early preached "the careful craftsmen"; the Owenites at New Harmony in Indiana, a socialist-communist community; and Brook Farm, a poetic Phalanx with high-minded pretensions in almost anarchist interaction dedicated to "the honesty of a life of labor and the beauty of a life of humanity" (Richter, 1971, p. 129). The Oneida community, believing in "Free Love and Bible Communism," was started in 1847 and continued in altered form as Oneida Ltd.—a successful silver firm.

In their search for "freedom" and "love" and in their escape from crude materialism to production "for use rather than profit," these nineteenth-century experiments sound very familiar to us today. America's penchant for revivalist religious movements such as the Seventh Day Adventists and the Mormons has produced somewhat similar far-out societal designs. The extended adolescence imposed by the American educational system, because of the economic necessity of keeping the young out of the job market for as long as possible, is clearly in evidence in the romantic reaction to industrialism found in the encyclopedic *The Last Whole Earth Catalogue* (1971). The Hippie communes, both urban and rural, number about 3,000 in the United States. If each group consisted of ten people (in the Minneapolis area, twelve communes investigated there had a total of *116* members)[15] the total population of American communes would thus be only 30,000 in a nation of 210 million. Such a small number hardly heralds the Revolution.

Hippie core-values, the extreme example of these minimum-physical-planning/maximum-societal-planning variants, are an interesting summary of the counterculture: free, sensually expressive (anti-intellectual), immediate, natural, colorful/baroque, spontaneous, primitive, mystical, egalitarian, communal (Davis, 1971).

This largely societal option has been included here because it is clearly "innovative" and "revolutionary" (often in puerile ways) in its implications for standard society and in its message about the "failures" of industrial society. It could be just the tip of the iceberg of dissatisfaction with the industrial culture of Western society. Minimal space seems to be the *only* physical planning expense involved; the commune people make their own societal plans. Such exotics must not be crushed, even if someone else has "to tend store." Apparently, the affluent West can afford masses of the idle rich, nonproducing young-sters, idling oldsters, and the unemployed; surely then it can afford a few tens of thousands of experimenters seeking a better life on earth.[16]

Communes, as defined here, obviously do not exhaust the possi-bilities for societal innovation in urban areas. In 1971, Julius Stulman developed a creative systems approach to housing, which was largely economic. It included (1) an executive, professional, intellectual hous-ing center, (2) new, noncompetitive shared-value orientation, (3) "hous-ing as a self-renewing function which adjusts and develops as individ-uals, opportunities and communities evolve" (no on-site maintenance), (4) multiple consumer choices, (5) creation of new credit sources due to housing as a "containerised unit—with registered, computerised, bonded and insured controlled units," (6) "Mutual Insurance Fund" to include youth participation and leisure-time homebuilding as inputs with, finally (7) "registered bankable certificates of the units for a house complex" easily exchangeable as a restless population moves above (Stulman, 1971).

*Option 15. "The wired city."* As a result of the phenomenal growth of cable TV (potentially capable of two-way transmission), as well as the almost infinite potential of multichannel electronic interaction through "people's satellites,"[17] a nonterritorial, high-intensity participatory com-munity fitted to the "post-civilized" or information society, could await us.[18] Despite piecemeal research, very considerable argumentation, a few limited experiments,[19] and a galloping electronic technology, it seems unlikely that the multiplicity of ordinary and new functions will be much in operation in even the most sophisticated nations before the twenty-first century. The bits of the picture puzzle are slowly being fitted together but they still do not form a whole. It appears that the basic scenario will be a national cable/microwave grid of metropolitan networks reinforced or supplanted with satellite connections and even-tually lasers.[20] Computers serving both as storage facilities and as analysts with display capabilities will be at the center of this intellectual technology (Martin and Norman, 1970, p. 66). In the United Kingdom, consideration is already being given to setting up a national computer grid. In "the wired city," every dwelling will have its typewriter-like keyboard with printout capabilities and display screen in the home information/recreation/business center. (Additional home terminals are naturally possible.) This equipment will not be cheap, and trained intelligence will be needed to operate it. This brings up future questions of equity, egalitarianism, and the massive financing and maintenance of such "public services."

Here are some of the bits yet to be assembled in a potential non-territorial, electronic society, partially substituting the transmission of ideas for the transportation of people and goods, and freed to a certain extent from spatial considerations.[21] As transportation expert Wilfred Owen has pointed out:

The significance of communications as a substitute for transport derives from the fact that while the unit costs of transportation continue to rise as quality declines, telecommunications tends to increase in quality and decline in cost. Distance is important in transportation, but with communication satellites distance is almost irrelevant (1972, p. 132).[22]

Here is a portion of what "the wired city" might provide:

- *Information storage available by computer/TV*
  National data bank on the total society (with all the safeguards of privacy)
  National library
  National music library
  National theater/cinema library
  National health records and diagnostic information
  Scientific information service
  Crime information
  Credit information
- *Home service facilities*
  All banking and transactions ("the end of money")
  Shopping (plus delivery)
  Recreation (passive and active)
  Crime prevention
  Education in the home for children *and* adults
  Automatized cooking
  Visiting via videophone
  Printout news (*The New York Times* nationwide)
  "Mail" delivery electronically (on time)
- *Advanced societal innovations*
  Public opinion surveys
  Sampling to replace voting
  "Participatory democracy"[23]
  TV surveillance of public (and private) places
  New industrial/business locations
  New employment patterns (4-day, 3-day, even 2-day work week in a *work place* away from the dwelling)
  New population distribution
  "Home visits" by the doctor and specialist

Increased physical and societal design capabilities
New and powerful techniques for mass behavior, control, and
   surveillance
Systems design and guided social change (Boguslaw, 1965)[24]

All is clearly not sweetness and light in this future city. What if evil "philosopher kings" should occupy central positions in the national-international network? If "euphoria" characterized the initial reaction to the two-way TV, coaxial cable, computer, people's satellite syndrome, one already sees signs of alarm prior, hopefully, to advanced *protective action* (including active ombudsman functions) before the need arises.[25] Finally, for the loyal fans of the central city, "the wired city" is already posing quite a problem as people stay away from downtown, especially for evening recreation, with simple-minded, existent TV as one reason.

   The U.S. Department of Housing and Urban Development has commissioned a study on the impact of advanced telecommunications technology on American cities during the next twelve years (Cetron, 1973, pp. iv–v). The study concludes that:

- The advent of telecommunications technology (TCT), while highly beneficial to some segments of society, will prove detrimental to others.
- The positive impact of TCT will be felt primarily in the middle-class suburbs, while the negative impact will be concentrated in the central cities.
- TCT will not play a highly visible role in the major urban development of the next twelve years. Unless specifically anticipated by federal and local planning, any impact will not be properly understood and regulated until considerable damage has been done.
- The primary urban impact of TCT will be to reduce the economic viability of the central city by accelerating (though not directly causing) the delocalization of business and commerce.
- The social impact of TCT will be found at least as much in the indirect effects of TCT on the fiscal strength of cities as in the direct effects of new gadgets on the life-styles of individuals.
- The sector most affected by TCT will be the service sector, in which processes involving paper transactions will be particularly sensitive to technological substitution.
- It is unlikely that the central city population will derive much benefit in the next decade from such "luxury" applications of TCT as shopping or working at home.

- The most important *positive* impact of TCT in central cities will be in the areas of technical education (especially in programs designed to develop job skills among inner-city residents), routine city services (especially in transit systems, policy and fire protection), and remote medical or diagnostic services.

## CONCLUSION

Having explored at some length goals for a good society and alternative urban futures, it is apparent that more of the same will likely be the lot of Western urbanism for the rest of this century and probably well into the next. "Peripheral sprawl will undoubtedly be the dominant form of future urban growth throughout the US" (Downs, 1970) and the Western world. This will probably be true for the socialist nations as well; a degree of urban chaos is predictable for the developing countries. It is most likely that there will be no urban systems-break; visionary options will occur only here and there. The standard world projection of *one spread city* (Regional Plan Association, 1962), slopping untidily into the next is all too likely for those nations that are unwilling or unable to direct their growth and that do not have sufficient consensus and capital resources. Superior intentional societies and ordered environments still seem to be beyond our grasp (Reed, 1972).

## NOTES

1. *The Next Fifty Years* commemorated the fiftieth anniversary of the founding of the American Institute of Planners. Published by the University of Indiana Press (Bloomington, Ill.), it consists of three volumes: *Environment and Man* (1967), *Environment and Change* (1968), and *Environment and Policy* (1968).

2. The urban future could be sliced differently. Compare Anthony Downs, "Alternate Forms of Future Urban Growth in the United States," *Journal of the American Institute of Planners*, January 1970, 4. Incidentally, using ten key variables involved in urban development (with several arbitrarily chosen values for each), Downs indicates the logical possibility of 93,312 potential forms of future urban growth (p. 3).

3. Extrapolated loosely from Walter K. Vinette, *Paper Number Three, The Scenario for Minnesota's Experimental City.*

4. Downs further says in "Alternate Forms of Future Urban Growth in the United States" that "non-metropolitan new cities or expanded communities are not likely to capture any significant fraction of the nation's future urban growth in spite of their current vogue in planning literature" (p. 11).

5. From *Time* magazine, February 26, 1973. Sadly, the project was abandoned in April 1973; funds ran out.

6. Compare Lawrence Susskind and Gary Hack, "New Communities in a National Urban Growth Strategy," *Technology Review*, February 1972, 30–42;

also "New Communities," an American Institute of Planners Background Paper, Number 2, 1968.

7. Revised version of a paper presented for the Symposium on "The Human Dimensions of Planning," UCLA, June 1972.

8. "The Planning Process for New Town Development: Soul City," a Planning Studio Course, Fall 1969, Department of City and Regional Planning, University of North Carolina, Chapel Hill, under David Godschalk.

9. See Ralph Wilcoxen, *Paolo Soleri: A Bibliography.* According to *The New York Times* (November 4, 1973), Soleri stated, "The only way to keep autos out of the city is to build a city without streets."

10. Compare William Zuk and Roger H. Clark, *Kinetic Architecture.* To quote the book's jacket cover: "Exciting open-ended planning: proposed and actual structures that are *replaceable, deformable, incremental, expandable, reversible—even disposable.*" [Editor's italics.] Compare also Peter Cook (ed.), *Archigram.*

11. The team of architects led by Kenzo Tange designed a *Plan for Tokyo* in the April 1961 English issue of the *Japanese Architect.*

12. "Future Organization Patterns: A Long-Range World Wide View," a paper prepared for presentation at the Second International Future Research Conference, Kyoto, Japan, in 1970.

13. SYNCON (130 Spruce Street, Philadelphia, Pa. 19106) is their elaborate physical and intellectual system to relate varied disciplines in a holistic effort to solve primarily urban problems, including an interplanetary, international kibbutz or "Unibutz."

14. Compare W. H. G. Armytage, *Yesterday's Tomorrows: A Historical Survey of Future Societies.*

15. Michael Carr and Dan MacLeon, "Getting it Together," *Environment,* (November 1972). The study was conducted under the auspices of the American Association for the Advancement of Science.

16. This most certainly is not to encourage elaborate planning provisions for odd groups searching for instant Nirvana through drug utopias—a not inconsiderable subset or variant of existent communal experimentation. Compare Richard Blum, *Utopiates: The Use and Users of LSD-25.*

17. For example, ANIK, the Canadian internal satellite.

18. Sloan Commission on Cable Television, *On the Cable: The Television of Abundance,* is a fairly straight-line projection of more-of-the-same TV pattern, only with more choice up to the turn of the century. More imaginative alternative potentials could have been rewardingly explored; the societal planning lead time to cope with "the wired city" is shorter than one thinks.

19. Jonathan New Town, Minneapolis, Minnesota; Tama New Town, Japan; and Washington New Town, County Durham, England.

20. This, of course, could be international, as Euro-vision has already accomplished for one-way television.

21. Compare Melvin M. and Carolyn C. Webber, "Culture, Territoriality and the Elastic Mile," 1967, in *Taming Megalopolis,* Volume 1, 35–54, which considers the existent professional nonterritorial community.

22. Compare the hyperoptimistic "30 Services That the Two-Way Television Can Provide" by Paul Baran in *The Futurist*, October 1973.

23. Project Minerva (Electronic Town Hall Project) has already carried out preliminary exercises in 803 households of a middle-class high-rise housing complex in one of the nation's largest cities where residents aired their views about security problems from the comfort of their own homes. Amitai Etzioni, who is conducting the experiment, believes he could carry this out with 40,000 persons according to studies from the Center for Policy Research, Inc., 475 Riverside Drive, New York City.

24. As well as explaining latent capabilities for powerful symbiotic man-machine interaction, Robert Boguslaw, in *The New Utopians: A Study of System Designs and Social Change* (Englewood Cliffs, N.J.: Prentice-Hall, 1965), wisely explored paranoid possibilities in Chapter 8, "The Power of Systems and the Systems of Power."

25. These terms are the main headings for portions of the James Martin and Adrian R. D. Norman book, *The Computerized Society.*

## REFERENCES

Armytage, W. H. G. 1968. *Yesterday's Tomorrows: A Historical Survey of Future Societies.* Toronto: University of Toronto Press.

Baran, Paul. 1973. "30 Services That the Two-Way Television Can Provide." *The Futurist,* Volume 3, Number 5 (October), 202–210.

Blum, Richard. 1963. *Utopiates: The Use and Users of LSD-25.* New York: Dodd, Mead and Co.

Boguslaw, Robert. 1965. *The New Utopians: A Study of System Designs and Social Change.* Englewood Cliffs, N.J.: Prentice-Hall.

Carr, Michael, and Dan MacLeon. 1972. "Getting It Together." *Environment,* Volume 14, Number 5 (November), 2–9.

Cetron, Marvin. 1973. *An Analysis of the Impact of Advanced Telecommunications Technology on the American City.* Washington, D.C.: Forecasting International Ltd.

*Congressional Record.* November 15, 1965. "Extension of Remarks of the Honorable Claiborne Pell, October 22, 1965."

Cook, Peter (ed.). 1973. *Archigram.* New York: Praeger Publishers.

Dahinden, Justus. 1972. *Urban Structures for the Future.* New York: Praeger Publishers.

Davis, Fred. 1971. *On Youth Sub-Cultures: The Hippie Variant.* New York: General Learning Press.

Downs, Anthony. 1970. "Alternate Forms of Future Urban Growth in the United States." *Journal of the American Institute of Planners,* Volume 36, Number 1 (January), 3–11.

Etzioni, Amitai. 1973. "Project Minerva." *Center for Policy Research Newsletter,* Number 8 (January), 1–3.

Ewald, William R., Jr. (ed.). 1967–1968. *The Next Fifty Years.* Bloomington, Ill.: University of Indiana Press.

Goodman, Paul (ed.). 1964. *Seeds of Liberation.* New York: George Braziller.

Kaye, Dena. 1973. "Across the Gateway and into the Curry." *Saturday Review/World,* Volume 1, Number 1 (September 11), 70–76.

*The Last Whole Earth Catalog.* 1971. New York: Random House.

Lynch, Kevin. 1968. "The Possible City." *The Next Fifty Years,* Volume 3, *Environment and Policy.* Bloomington, Ill.: University of Indiana Press.

McHale, John. "Future Cities: Notes on Typology." (Unpublished draft.)

Martin, James, and Adrian R. D. Norman. 1970. *The Computerized Society.* Englewood Cliffs, N.J.: Prentice-Hall.

Osborn, F. J., and Arnold Whittick. 1963. *The New Towns: The Answer to Megalopolis.* New York: McGraw-Hill.

Owen, Wilfred. 1972. "Telecommunications and Life Styles." *The Accessible City.* Washington, D.C.: Brookings Institution.

Perloff, Harvey S. 1966. New Towns in Town. Washington, D.C.: Resources for the Future.

Reed, Paul. 1972. *Intentional Societies and Ordered Environments.* Monticello, Ill.: Council of Planning Librarians.

Regional Plan Association. 1962. "Spread City: Projection of Development Trends and the Issues They Pose: The Tri-State New York Metropolitan Region 1960–1985." *RPA Bulletin,* Number 100 (September).

Richter, Peyton E. (ed.). 1971. *Utopias: Social Ideals and Communal Experiments.* Boston: Holbrook Press.

Skinner, B. F. 1948. *Walden Two.* New York: Macmillan Co.

Sloan Commission on Cable Television. 1971. *On the Cable: The Television of Abundance.* New York: McGraw-Hill.

Soleri, Paolo, 1969. *Archology—The City in the Image of Man.* Cambridge, Mass.: MIT Press.

Spectrosky, A. C. 1955. *The Exurbanites.* New York: Berkeley Publishing Co.

Starr, Roger. 1967. *Urban Choices: The City and Its Critics.* Baltimore, Md.: Penguin Books.

Strong, Ann Louis. 1971. *Planned Urban Environments.* Baltimore, Md.: Johns Hopkins University Press.

Stulman, Julius. 1971. "Creative Systems in Housing." *Fields Within Fields,* Volume 4, Number 2, 112–132.

Susskind, Lawrence, and Gary Hack. 1972. "New Communities in a National Urban Growth Strategy." *Technology Review,* Volume 74, Number 4 (February), 30–42.

Theobald, Robert (ed.). 1972. *Futures Conditional.* Indianapolis: Bobbs-Merill.

U.S. Department of Housing and Urban Development. 1973. *Information Series 20, HUD International* (January 15).

Vinett, Walter K. 1972. *Paper Number Three, The Scenario for Minnesota's Experimental City.* Minneapolis, Minn.: University of Minnesota.

Webber, Melvin M., and Carolyn C. 1967. "Culture, Territorality and the

Elastic Mile." In H. Wentworth Eldredge (ed.), *Taming Megalopolis,* Volume 1. Garden City, N.Y.: Doubleday Anchor, 35–53.

Wilcoxen, Ralph. 1969. *Paolo Soleri: A Bibliography.* Monticello, Ill.: Council of Planning Librarians.

Zuk, William, and Roger H. Clark. 1970. *Kinetic Architecture.* New York: Van Nostrand Reinhold.

ARTHUR C. CLARKE

# Communications in the Future

It is probably true that in communications technology anything that can be conceived, and which does not violate natural laws, can be realized in practice. We may not be able to do it right now, owing to ignorance or economics, but those barriers are liable to be breached with remarkable speed.

For man is the communicating animal; he demands news, information, and entertainment almost as much as food. In fact, as a functioning human being, he can survive much longer without food—even without water—than without information, as experiments in sensory deprivation have shown. This is a truly astonishing fact; one could construct a whole philosophy around it.

So any major advance in communications capability comes into widespread use just as soon as it is practicable—and often sooner; the public can't wait for the "state of the art" to settle down. Remember the first clumsy phonographs, radios, and tape recorders? And would you believe the date of the first music broadcast? It was barely a year after the invention of the telephone. On April 2, 1877, a "telegraphic harmony" apparatus in Philadelphia sent "Yankee Doddle" to sixteen loudspeakers—well, soft-speakers—in New York's Steinway Hall. Alexander Graham Bell was in the audience, and one would like to know if he complimented the promoter—his now forgotten rival, Elisha Gray, who got to the Patent Office just those fatal few hours too late.

Gray was not the only one to be caught by the momentum of events. When news of the telephone reached England 100 years ago through Cyrus Field's cable, the chief engineer of the Post Office was asked whether this new Yankee invention would be of any practical value. He gave the forthright reply: "No, sir. The Americans have need of the telephone—but we do not. We have plenty of messenger boys."

Before you laugh at this myopic Victorian, please ask yourself this question: would you, exactly 100 years ago, ever have dreamed that the

---

Reprinted by permission of the Massachusetts Institute of Technology and the editors of *Technology Review*.

time would come when this primitive toy would not only be in every home and every office, but would also be the essential basis of all social, administrative, and business life in the civilized world? Or that one day there would be approximately one instrument for every ten human beings on the planet?

Now, the telephone is a very simple device, which even the nineteenth century could readily mass produce. In fact, one derivative of the carbon microphone must be near the absolute zero of technological complexity. You can make a working—though hardly hi-fi—microphone out of three carpenter's nails, one laid across the other two to form a letter H.

The extraordinary—nay, magical—simplicity of the telephone allowed it to spread over the world with astonishing speed. When we consider the much more complex devices of the future, is it reasonable to suppose that they too will eventually become features of every home, every office? Well, let me give you another cautionary tale.

In the early-1940s, the late John W. Campbell, editor of *Astounding Stories* and undoubtedly the most formidable imagination ever to be flunked at MIT, pooh-poohed the idea of home television. He refused to believe that anything as complex as a TV receiver could ever be made cheap and reliable enough for domestic use. Public demand certainly disposed of that prophecy. Home TV became available in the early neo-electronic age—that is, even *before* the solid-state revolution. So let us take it as axiomatic that complexity is no bar to universality. Think of your pocket computers again and march fearlessly into the future, trying to imagine the ideal, ultimate communications system, the one that would fulfill all possible fantasies.

Since no holds are barred, what about telepathy? Well, I don't believe in telepathy, but I don't *dis*believe in it either. Certainly some form of electronically assisted mental linkage seems plausible; in fact, this has already been achieved in a very crude form, between men and computers, through monitoring of brainwaves. However, I find that *my* mental processes are so incoherent, even when I try to focus and organize them, that I should be very sorry for anyone at the receiving end. Our superhuman successors, if any, may be able to cope; indeed, the development of the right technology might force such an evolutionary advance. Perhaps the best that *we* could manage would be the sharing of emotional states, not the higher intellectual processes. So radio-assisted telepathy might merely lead to some interesting new vices—admittedly, a long-felt want.

Therefore, let's stick to the recognized sense channels, of which sound and sight are by far the most important. Although one day we will presumably develop transducers for all the senses, just because they are there, I suspect that the law of diminishing returns will set in rather rapidly after the "feelies" and "smellies." These may have some limited applications for entertainment purposes, as anyone who was pulverized by the movie *Earthquake* may agree.

The basic ingredients of the ideal communications device are, therefore, already in common use even today. The standard computer console, with keyboard and visual display, plus hi-fi sound and TV camera, will do very nicely. Through such an instrument (for which I've coined the ugly but perhaps unavoidable name "comsole"—communications console) (Clarke, 1975), one could have face-to-face interaction with anyone, anywhere on earth, and send or receive any type of information. I think most of us would settle for this, but there are some other possibilities to consider.

For example: what about verbal inputs? Do we really need a keyboard? I'm sure the answer is "Yes." We want to be able to type out messages, look at them, and edit them before transmission. We need keyboard inputs for privacy and quietness. A reliable voice recognition system, capable of coping with accents, hangovers, ill-fitting dentures, and the "human error" that my late friend Hal complained about, represents something many orders of magnitude more complex than a simple alphanumeric keyboard. It would be a device with capabilities, in a limited area, at least as good as those of a human brain.

Yet, assuming that the curves of the last few decades can be extrapolated, this will certainly be available sometime in the next century. Though most of us will still be tapping out numbers in 2001, I've little real doubt that well before 2076 you will simply say to your comsole: "Get me Bill Smith": Or if you *do* say: "Get me 212–345–5512," it will answer, "Surely you mean 212–345–5521." And it will be quite right.

Now a machine with this sort of capability—a robot secretary, in effect—could be quite expensive. *It doesn't matter.* We who are living in an economic singularity, if not a fiscal black hole, have forgotten what most of history must be like.

Contrary to the edicts of Madison Avenue, the time will come when it won't be necessary to trade in last year's model. Eventually, everything reaches its technological plateau, and thereafter the only changes are in matters of style. This is obvious when you look at such familiar domestic objects as chairs, beds, tables, knives, forks. You can make them of plastic or fiberglass or whatever, but the basic design rarely alters.

It took a few thousand years to reach these particular plateaus; things happen more quickly nowadays even for much more complex devices. The bicycle took about a century; radio receivers half that time. This is not to deny that marginal improvements will go on indefinitely, but after a while all further changes are icing on a perfectly palatable cake. You may be surprised to learn that there are electrical devices that have been giving satisfactory service for half a century or more. The other day someone found an Edison carbon filament lamp that has apparently never been switched off since it was installed. And until recently, there were sections of Atlantic cable that had been in service for a full century!

Now, it's hard to see how a properly designed and constructed solid-state device can ever wear out. It should have something like the working life of a diamond, which is adequate for most practical purposes. So when we reach this state of affairs, it would be worth investing more in a multipurpose home communications device than an automobile. It could be handed on from one generation to the next, as was once the case with a good watch.

It has been obvious for a very long time that such audiovisual devices could complete the revolution started by the telephone. We are already approaching the point when it will be feasible—not necessarily desirable—for those engaged in what is quaintly called "white-collar" jobs to do perhaps 95 percent of their work without leaving home. Of course, few of today's families could survive this, but for the moment let's confine ourselves to electronic, not social, technology.

Many years ago I coined the slogan: "Don't commute—communicate!" Apart from the savings in travel time (the *real* reason I became a writer is that I refuse to spend more than thirty seconds moving from home to office), there would be astronomical economies in power and raw materials. Compare the amount of hardware in communications systems, as opposed to railroads, highways, and airlines. The number of kilowatt hours you expend on the shortest journey would power several lifetimes of chatter, between the remotest ends of the earth.

Obviously, the home comsole would handle most of today's first-class mail; messages would be stored in its memory waiting for you to press the playback key whenever you felt like it. Then you would type out the answer—or alternatively call up the other party for a face-to-face chat.

Fine, but at once we have a serious problem: the already annoying matter of time zones. They are going to become quite intolerable in the electronic global village where we are all neighbors, but a third of us are asleep at any given moment. The other day I was awakened at 4:00 A.M. by the *London Daily Express*, which had subtracted 5½ hours instead of adding them. I don't know what I said, but I doubt if my views on the Loch Ness Monster were printable.

The railroads and the telegraph made time zones inevitable in the nineteenth century; the global telecommunications network of the twenty-first may abolish them. It has been suggested, at least half seriously, that we will have to establish a common time over the whole planet—whatever inconvenience this may cause to those old-fashioned enough to gear themselves to the day-night cycle.

During the course of the day—whatever *that* may be—you will use the home comsole to call your friends and deal with business, exactly as you use the telephone now—with this difference. You'll be able to exchange any amount of tabular, visual, or graphical information. Thus, if you're an author, you'll be able to wave that horrid page one type in front of your delinquent editor on Easter Island, or wherever he lives. Instead of spending hours hunting for nonexistent parts numbers, engineers will be able to *show* their supplier the broken dohickey from the rotary discombobulator. And we'll be able to see those old friends of a lifetime, whom we'll never again meet in the flesh.

Which raises an interesting problem. One of the great advantages of Mr. Bell's invention is that you can converse with people *without* their seeing you, or knowing where you are, or who is with you. A great many business deals would never be consummated, or even attempted, over a video circuit; but perhaps they are deals that shouldn't be, anyway.

I am aware that previous attempts to supply vision—such as the Bell Picturephone—have hardly been a roaring success. But I feel sure that this is because of cost, the small size of the picture, and the limited service available. No one would have predicted much of a future for the very first "Televisors," with their flickering, postage-stamp-sized images. Such technical limitations have a habit of being rather rapidly overcome, and the *large screen, high definition* Picturephone-Plus is inevitable.

The possibilities of the comsole as an entertainment and informaton device are virtually unlimited; some of them, of course, are just becoming available, as an adjunct to the various TV subscription services. At any moment, one should be able to call up all the news headlines on the screen and expand any of particular interest into a complete story at several levels of thoroughness—all the way, let us say, from the *Daily News* to *The New York Times*. For the first time, it will be possible to have a news service with immediacy, selectivity, *and* thoroughness.

The electronic newspaper, apart from all its other merits, will also have two gigantic ecological plusses. It will save whole forests for posterity, and it will halve the cost of garbage collection. This alone might be enough to justify it and to pay for it.

Like many of my generation, I became a news addict during World War II. Even now, it takes a definite effort of will for me not to switch on the hourly news summaries, and with a truly global service one could spend every waking minute monitoring the amusing, crazy, interesting, and tragic things that go on around this planet. I can foresee the rise of even more virulent forms of news addiction, resulting in the evolution of a class of people who can't bear to miss anything that's happening, anywhere, and spend their waking hours glued to the comsole. I've even coined a name for them—Infomaniacs.

I used to think how nice it would be to have access, in one's own home, to all the books and printed matter, all the recordings and movies, all the visual arts of mankind. But would not many of us be completely overwhelmed by such an embarrassment of riches and solve the impossible problem of selection by selecting nothing? Every day I sneak guiltily past my set of the Great Books of the Western World, most of which I've never even opened. What would it *really* be like to have the Library of Congress—*all* the world's great libraries—at your fingertips? Assuming, of course, that your fingertips were sufficiently educated to handle the problem of indexing and retrieval. I speak with some feeling on this subject because for a couple of years I had the job of classifying and indexing everything published in the physical sciences, in all languages.

With the latest techniques, it would be possible to put the whole of human knowledge into a shoe box. The problem, of course, is to get it out again; anything misfiled would be irretrievably lost. Another problem is to decide whether we mass produce the shoe boxes, so that every family has one, or whether we have a central shoe box linked to the home with wide-band communications.

Probably we'll have both, and there are also some interesting compromises. Years ago I invented something that I christened, believe it or not, the *Micropaedia Brittannica.* But my *Micropaedia* would be a box about the size of an ordinary hardcover book, with a display screen and alphanumeric keyboard. It would contain, in text and pictures, *at least* as much material as a large encyclopaedia plus dictionary.

However, the main point of the electronic *Brittannica* would not be its compactness but the fact that, every few months, you could plug it in, dial a number, and have it updated overnight. Think of the savings in wood pulp and transportation!

It is usually assumed that the comsole would have a flat TV-type screen, which would appear to be all that is necessary for most communications purposes. But the ultimate in face-to-face electronic confrontation would be when you could not tell, without touching, whether the other person was physically present; he or she would appear as a perfect 3D projection. This no longer appears fantastic, now that we have seen holographic displays that are quite indistinguishable from reality. So I am sure that this will be achieved some day; I am not sure how badly we need it.

What could be done, even with current techniques, is to provide 3D, or at least widescreen Cinerama-type pictures for a single person at a time. This would need merely a small viewing booth and some clever optics, and it could provide the basis for a valuable educational-entertainment tool, as Dennis Gabor has suggested (1972). It could also give rise to a new industry—personalized television safaris. When you can have a high-quality cinema display in your own home, there will certainly be global audiences for specialized programs with instant feedback from viewer to cameraman. How nice to be able to make a trip up the Amazon, with a few dozen unknown friends scattered over the world, with perfect sound and vision, being able to ask your guide questions, suggest detours, request closeups of interesting plants or animals—in fact, sharing everything except the mosquitoes and the heat!

It has been suggested that this sort of technology might ultimately lead to a world in which no one ever bothered to leave home. The classic treatment of this theme is, of course, E. M. Forster's *The Machine Stops,* written more than seventy years ago as a counterblast to H. G. Wells. Yet, I don't regard this sort of pathological sedentary society as very likely. "Telesafaris" might have just the opposite effect. The customers would, sooner or later, be inspired to visit the places that really appealed to them, mosquitoes notwithstanding. Improved communications will promote travel for *pleasure*; and the sooner we get rid of the other kind, the better.

So far, I have been talking about the communications devices in the home and the office. But in the last few decades we have seen the telephone begin to lose its metal umbilical cord, and this process will accelerate. The rise of walkie-talkies and citizen's band radio is a portent of the future.

The individual, wristwatch telephone through which you can contact anyone, anywhere, will be a mixed blessing which, nevertheless, very few will be able to reject. In fact, we may not have a choice; it is all too easy to imagine a society in which it is illegal to switch off your receiver, in case the chairman of the People's Cooperative wants to summon you in a hurry. But let's not ally ourselves with those reactionaries who look only on the bad side of every new development. Alexander Graham Bell cannot be blamed for Stalin, who was once aptly described as "Genghis Khan with a telephone."

It would be an underestimate to say that the wristwatch telephone would save tens of thousands of lives a year. Everyone of us knows of tragedies—car accidents on lonely highways, lost campers, overturned boats, even old people at home—where some means of communication would have made all the difference between life and death. Even a simple emergency SOS system, whereby one pressed a button and sent out a HELP! signal, would be enough. This is a possibility of the immediate future; the only real problem—and, alas, a serious one—is that of false alarms.

At this point, before I lose all credibility with the engineers who have to produce the hardware, I'd better do a once-over-lightly of the electromagnetic spectrum. This is, I think, unique among our natural resources. We've been exploiting it for less than one lifetime and are now polluting much of it to the very maximum of our ability. If we stopped using it tomorrow, it would be just as good as new, because the garbage is heading outwards at the speed of light. Too bad this isn't true of the rest of the environment.

Do we have enough available bandwidth for a billion personal transceivers, even assuming that they aren't all working at once? As far as the home equipment is concerned, there is no problem, at least in communities of any size. The only uncertainty, and a pretty harrowing one to the people who have to make the decisions, is how quickly coaxial cables are going to be replaced by glass fibers, with their millionfold greater communications capability. Incidentally, one of the less glamorous occupations of the future will be mining houses for the rare metal, copper, buried inside them by our rich ancestors. Fortunately, there is no danger that we shall ever run out of silica.

I would also suggest that optical systems, in the infrared and ultraviolet, have a great future not only for fixed, but even for mobile, personal communications. They may take over some of the functions of present-day transistor radios and walkie-talkies, leaving the radio bands free for services that can be provided in no other way. The fact that opticals have only very limited range, owing to atmospheric absorption, can be turned to major advantage. You can use the same frequencies millions of times over as long as you keep your service areas 10 or 20 kilometers apart.

It may be objected that light waves won't go round corners or through walls. Elementary, my dear Watson. We simply have lots of dirt-cheap—because they are made from dirt!—optical wave guides and light pipes deliberately leaking radiation all over the place. Some would be passive, some active. Some would have very low-powered optical-to-radio transducers in both directions, to save knocking holes in walls and to get to awkward places. In densely populated communities, one would always be in direct or reflected sight of some optical transmitter of repeater. But we must be careful how we use the ultraviolet. People who talked too much might get sunburned.

When you are cycling across Africa, or drifting on a balsawood raft across the Pacific, you will, of course, still have to use the radio frequencies—say the 1,000 to 10,000 megahertz bands, which can accommodate at least the million voice circuits. This number can be multiplied many times by skillful use of satellite technology. I can envisage an earth-embracing halo of low-altitude, low-powered radio satellites, switching frequencies continually so that they provide the desired coverage in given geographical regions. NASA has recently published a most exciting report on the use of the very large (kilometer-square!) antennas we will soon be able to construct in space.[1] These would permit the simultaneous use of myriads of very narrow beams which could be focused on individual subscribers, carrying receivers that could be mass produced for about ten dollars. I rather suspect that our long-awaited personal transceiver will be an adaptive, radio-optical hybrid, actively hunting the electromagnetic spectrum in search of incoming signals addressed to it.

The invariably forgotten accessory of the wristwatch telephone is the wristwatch telephone *directory*. Considering the bulk of that volume for even a modest-sized city, this means that our personal transceivers will require some sophisticated information-retrieval circuits and a memory to hold the few hundred most used numbers. So we may be forced, rather quickly, to go the whole way and to combine in a single, highly portable unit not only communications equipment, plus something like today's pocket-calculators, plus data banks, plus information processing circuits. It would be a constant companion, serving much the same purpose as a human secretary. In a recent novel I called it a "Minisec" (Clarke, 1975). In fact, as electronic intelligence develops, it would provide more and more services, finally developing a personality of its own, to a degree that may be unimaginable today. Except, of course, by science fiction writers. In his brilliant novel, *The Futurological Congress*, Stanislaw Lem gives a nightmare cameo which I can't get out of my mind. He describes a group of women sitting in complete silence while their handbag computers gossip happily to one another.

One of the functions of science fiction is to serve as an early warning system. In fact, the very act of description may prevent some futures, by a kind of exclusion principle. Far from predicting the future, science fiction often exorcises it. At the very least, it makes us ask ourselves: "What kind of future do we really want?" No other type of literature poses such fundamental questions, at any rate explicitly.

The marvelous toys that we have been discussing will simply remain toys, unless we use them constructively and creatively. Now, toys are all right in the proper place; in, fact they are an essential part of any childhood. But they should not become mere distractions or ways of drugging the mind to avoid reality. We have all seen unbuttoned beer-bellies slumped in front of the TV set, and transistorized morons twitching down the street, puppets controlled by invisible disk jockeys. These are not the highest representatives of our culture, but, tragically, they may be typical of the near future. As we evolve a society oriented toward information, and as we move away from one based primarily on manufacture and transportation, there will be millions who cannot adapt to the change. We may have no alternative but to use the lower electronic arts to keep them in a state of drugged placidity.

In the world of the future, the sort of mindless labor that has occupied 99 percent of mankind, for much more than 99 percent of its existence, will, of course, be largely taken over by machines. Yet, most people are bored to death without work—even work that they don't like. In a workless world, therefore, only the highly educated will be able to flourish, or perhaps even to survive. The rest are likely to destroy themselves and their environment out of sheer frustration. This is no vision of the distant future; it is already happening, most of all in the decaying cities. So perhaps we should not despise TV soap operas if, during the turbulent transition period between our culture and real civilization, they serve as yet another opium for the masses. This drug, at any rate, is cheap and harmless, serving to kill Time for those many people who like it better dead.

When we look at the manifold problems of our age, it is clear that the most fundamental one—from which almost all others stem—is that of ignorance. And ignorance can be banished only by communication, in the widest meaning of the word. The best educational arrangement, someone once remarked, consists of a log with a teacher at one end and a pupil at the other. Unfortunately, there are no longer enough teachers, and probably not enough logs, to go around. One thing electronics can do rather well is to multiply teachers. As you doubtless know, at this very moment a most ambitious and exciting social experiment is taking place in India, where NASA's ATS-6 satellite is broadcasting educational programs to several thousand villages. ATS-6 is the only communications satellite in existence powerful enough to transmit signals that can be picked up on an ordinary TV set, augmented by a simple parabolic dish, like a large umbrella made of wire mesh. Although it is impossible to put a value on such things, I believe that the cost of this experiment will be trivial compared with the benefits. And the ground segment is remarkably cheap, in terms of its coverage. Would you believe 4,000 people round one TV set? Or a 3-meter diameter village antenna made of *dried mud*?

Of course, there are some critics, as reported recently by Dr. Yash Pal, the able and energetic director of the Indian Space Applicaton Centre.[2]

In the drawing rooms of large cities you meet many people who are concerned about the damage one is going to cause to the integrity of rural India by exposing her to the world outside. After they have lectured you about the dangers of corrupting this innocent, beautiful mass of humanity, they usually turn round and ask: "Well, now that we have a satellite, when are we going to see some American programmes?" Of course, they themselves are immune to cultural domination or foreign influence.

I'm afraid that cocktail party intellectuals are the same everywhere. Because *we* frequently suffer from the modern scourge of information pollution, we find it hard to imagine its even deadlier opposite—information starvation. For any outsider, however well meaning, to tell an Indian villager that he would be better off without access to the world's news, entertainment, *and knowledge* is an obscene impertinence, like the spectacle of a fat man preaching the virtues of fasting to the hungry.

I don't wish to get too much involved in the potential—still less the politics—of communications satellites, because they can take care of themselves and are now multiplying rapidly. The world investment in satellites and ground stations now exceeds a billion dollars and is increasing almost explosively. After years of delay and dithering, the United States is at last establishing domestic satellite systems; the U.S.S.R. has had one for almost a decade. At first, the Soviet network employed *non*synchronous satellites, moving in an elongated orbit that took them high over Russia for a few hours every day. However, they have now seen the overwhelming advantages of stationary orbits, and several of their comsats are currently fixed above the Indian Ocean.

We are now in the early stages of a battle for the mind—or at least the eyes and ears—of the human race, a battle that will be fought 36,000 kilometers above the equator. The preliminary skirmishes have already taken place at the United Nations, where there have been determined attempts by some countries to limit the use of satellites which can beam programs from space directly into the home, thus bypassing the national networks. Guess who is scared.

As a matter of fact, I tried to frighten the United States with satellites myself, back in 1960, when I published a story in *Playboy* (Clarke, 1960) about a Chinese plot to brainwash innocent Americans with pornographic TV programs. Perhaps "frighten" is not the correct verb, and in these permissive days such an idea sounds positively old-fashioned. But in 1960 the first regular comsat service was still five years in the future, and this seemed a good gambit for attracting attention to its possibilities.

Fortunately, in this area there is an excellent record of international cooperation. Even countries that hate each other work together through the International Telecommunications Union, which sets limits to powers and assigns frequencies. Eventually, some kind of consensus will emerge, which will avoid the worst abuses.

A major step toward this consensus was taken on August 20, 1971, when the agreement setting up INTELSAT (the International Telecommunications Satellite Organization) was signed at the State Department. I would like to quote from the address I gave on that occasion:

I submit that the eventual impact of the communications satellite upon the whole human race will be at least as great as that of the telephone upon the so-called developed societies.

In fact, as far as real communications are concerned, there are as yet no developed societies; we are all still in the semaphore and smoke-signal stage. And we are now about to witness an interesting situation in which many countries, particularly in Asia and Africa, are going to leapfrog a whole era of communications technology and go straight into the space age. They will never know the vast networks of cables and microwave links that this country has built at such enormous cost both in money and in natural resources. The satellites can do far more and at far less expense to the environment. . .

. . . I belive that the communications satellites can unite mankind. Let me remind you, that, whatever the history books say, this great country was created a little more than a hundred years ago by two inventions. Without them, the United States was impossible; with them, it was inevitable. Those inventions were, of course, the railroad and the electric telegraph.

Today we are seeing on a global scale an almost exact parallel to that situation. What the railroads and the telegraph did here a century ago, the jets and the communications satellites are doing now to all the world.

And the final result—whatever name we actually give to it—will be the United States of Earth.

I would like to end with some thoughts on the wider future of communications—communications beyond the earth. And here we face an extraordinary paradox, which in the centuries to come may have profound political and cultural implications.

For the whole of human history, up to that moment 100 years ago it was impossible for two persons more than a few meters apart to interact in real time. The abolition of that apparently fundamental barrier was one of technology's supreme triumphs; today we take it for granted that men can converse with each other, and even see each other, wherever they may be. Generations will live and die, always with this godlike power at their fingertips. Yet, this superb achievement will be ephemeral; before the next 100 years have passed, our hard-won victory over space will have been lost, never to be regained.

On the Apollo voyages, for the first time, men traveled more than a light-second away from Earth. The resulting 2½-second round-trip delay was surprisingly unobtrusive, but only because of the dramatic nature of the messages—and the discipline of the speakers. I doubt if the average person will have the self-control to talk comfortably with anyone on the Moon.

And beyond the Moon, of course, it will be impossible. We will never be able to converse with friends on Mars, even though we can easily exchange any amount of information with them. It will take at least three minutes to get there, and another three minutes to receive a reply (Coupling, 1952).

Anyone who considers that this is never likely to be of much practical importance is taking a very shortsighted view. It has now been demonstrated, beyond reasonable doubt, that in the course of the next century, we could occupy the entire solar system. The resources in energy and material are there; the unknowns are the motivation—and our probability of survival, which may indeed depend upon the rate with which we get our eggs out of this one fragile planetary basket.

We must *assume* that eventually very large populations will be living far from Earth—light-minutes and light-hours away, even if we only colonize the inner solar system. However, Freeman Dyson has argued with great eloquence (1973) that planets aren't important, and the real action will be in the cloud of comets out beyond Pluto, a light-day or more from earth.

Looking further afield, it is now widely realized that there are no fundamental scientific obstacles even to interstellar travel.[3] Although Dr. Purcell once rashly remarked that starships should stay on the cereal boxes, where they belonged, that's exactly where moonships were, only thirty years ago.

So the finite velocity of light will, inevitably, divide the human race once more into scattered communities, sundered by barriers of space and time. We will be as one with our remote ancestors, who lived in a world of immense and often insuperable distances, for we are moving out into a universe vaster than all their dreams.

But surely, it is not an empty universe. No discussion of communications and the future would be complete without reference to the most exciting possibility of all—communications with extraterrestrial intelligence. The Galaxy must be an absolute Babel of conversation, and it is only a matter of time before we can hear the neighbors. They already know about us, for our sphere of detectable radio signals is now scores of light-years across. Perhaps even more to the point is the fact that several microsecond-thick shells of X-ray pulses are already more than ten light-years out from earth, announcing to the universe that, somewhere, juvenile delinquents are detonating atom bombs.

Plausible arguments suggest that our best bet for interstellar eaves-dropping would be in the 1,000 megahertz, or 30 centimeter, region. The NASA/Stanford/Ames Project Cyclops report, which proposed an array of several hundred large radio telescopes for such a search, recommended a specific band about 200 megahertz wide—that lying between the hydrogen line (1420 MHz) and the lowest OH line (1662 MHz). Dr. Bernard Oliver, who directed the Cyclops study, has waxed poetic about the appropriateness of *our* type of life seeking its kind in the band lying between the disassociation products of water—the "water-hole."[4]

Unfortunately, we may be about to pollute the water-hole so badly that it will be useless to radio astronomers. The proposed MARESAT and NAVSTAR satellites will be dunked right in the middle of it, radiating so powerfully that they would completely saturate any Cyclops-type array. Barney Oliver tells me: "Since the Cyclops study, additional reasons have become apparent for expecting the water-hole to be our contact with the mainstream of life in the Galaxy. The thought that we, through our ignorance, may blind ourselves to such contact and condemn the human race to isolation appalls us."

The conflict of interest between the radio astronomers and the communications engineers will get more and more insoluble, until, as I suggested many years ago (Clarke, 1965), we move the astronomers to the quietest place in the solar system—the center of the lunar Farside, where they will be shielded from the radio racket of Earth by 3,500 kilometers of solid rock. But *that* answer will hardly be available before the next century.

Whatever the difficulties and problems, the search for extra-terrestrial signals will continue. Some scientists fear that it will not succeed; others fear that it will. It may already have succeeded, but we don't yet know it. Even if the pulsars *are* neutron stars, so what? They may still be artificial beacons, all broadcasting essentially the same message: "Last stop for gas this side of Andromeda."

More seriously, if the decades and the centuries pass with no indication that there is intelligent life elsewhere in the universe, the long-term effects on human philosophy will be profound—and may be disastrous. Better to have neighbors we don't like than to be utterly alone. For that cosmic loneliness could point to a very depressing conclusion—that intelligence marks an evolutionary dead-end. When we consider how well, and how long, the sharks and the cockroaches have managed without it, and how badly we are managing *with* it, one cannot help wondering if intelligence is an aberration like the armor of the dinosaurs, dooming its possessors to extinction.

No, I don't *really* believe this. Even if the computers we carry on our shoulders are evolutionary accidents, they can now generate their own programs—and set their own goals.

For we can now say, in the widest possible meaning of the phrase, that the purpose of human life is information processing. I have already mentioned the strange fact that men can survive longer without water than without information. Therefore, the real value of all the devices we have been discussing is that they have the potential for immensely enriching and enlarging life, by giving us more information to process—up to the maximum number of bits per second that the human brain can absorb.

I am happy, therefore, to have solved one of the great problems the philosophers and theologians have been haggling over for several thousand years. You may, perhaps, feel that this is rather a dusty answer, and that not even the most inspired preacher could ever found a religion upon the slogan "The purpose of life is information processing." Indeed, you may even retort: "Well, what is the purpose of information processing?"

I'm glad you asked me that . . .

## NOTES

1. Aerospace Corporation Report, *Potential Space System Contributions in the Next Twenty-Five Years,* 1975. For the Summary, see Volume 2 of the House of Representatives Subcommittee of Space Science and Applications, *Future Space Programs, 1975.*

2. "Some lessons during the setting up of SITE," a talk at UN/UNESCO Regional Seminar on Satellite Broadcasting Systems for Education and Development, Mexico City, September 2-11 1975.

3. See, for example, the "Interstellar Studies" issues of the *Journal of the British Interplanetary Society.* Just forty years ago, amid general incredulity, the journal started to publish studies of vehicles that could carry men to the Moon.

4. "Project Cyclops: A Design Study of a System for Detecting Extra-terrestrial Intelligent Life" (NASA/Ames CR 114445).

## REFERENCES

Clarke, Arthur C. 1960. "I Remember Babylon." *Playboy* (May).

———. 1963a. *Glide Path.* New York: Harcourt Brace Jovanovich.

———. 1963b. "You're on the Glide Path—I Think." *IEEE Transactions on Aerospace and Navigational Electronics,* Volume ANE-10, Number 2 (June).

———. 1965. *Voices from the Sky.* New York: Harper and Row.

———. 1975. *Imperial Earth.* New York: Harcourt Brace Jovanovich.

Coupling, J. J. 1952. "Don't Write; Telegraph." *Astounding Science Fiction* (March).

Dyson, Freeman. 1973. "The World, the Flesh and the Devil." In Carl Sagan (ed.), *Communications with Extraterrestrial Intelligence,* Appendix D. Cambridge, Mass.: MIT Press.

Gabor, Dennis. 1972. *The Mature Society.* New York: Praeger Publishers.

THOMAS R. McFAUL

# Biomedical Issues for the Future

Within the past two decades, changes in biomedical technology have come with great rapidity and have raised an array of profound questions about the future. Underlying all these questions is the realization that a biomedical revolution is altering our traditional understanding of human life. The implications of this revolution are staggering and ominous.

At the same time, the conduct of biology and medicine, like science in general, occurs within a socially acceptable moral and legal framework. Values and legal procedures shape biomedical practice in particular and science in general. The relationship of biomedicine to the future is a microcosm of the complex macrocosmic relationship of science to society. It involves not only changes in biomedical technology, but also how these changes affect and are affected by other social forces such as religion, philosophy, morality, and the legal process. In this chapter we shall focus on the interaction between changing biomedical technology, values, and the law, because it is chiefly out of this nexus of converging forces that the biomedical future will take shape.

We will begin by discussing some of the major normative concerns that are shaping legal policy and defining acceptable biomedical practice. We start with the normative concerns because, as we will see, these will reappear as we proceed through specific biomedical issues. Then we will examine specific issues as they relate to three stages in the life cycle: beginning-of-life, during-life, and end-of-life. Frequently, these issues are presented in an unsystematic fashion. By using these three stages of the life cycle, our discussion of specific issues will proceed in a coherent manner. We will conclude with future projections.

## NORMATIVE AND POLICY DILEMMAS

Four major issues surround changing biomedical practices. These are sanctity versus quality of life, informed consent, determination of participation in biomedical decisions, and formulation of a comprehensive biomedical social policy.

## SANCTITY VERSUS QUALITY OF LIFE

The sanctity versus quality of life issue is at its core a debate about "humanness." It centers on the temporal points at which biological life becomes or ceases to be viewed as human life. Sanctity of life proponents hold that from the moment of conception biological life is synonymous with human life. The sanctity of life position in its conservative form leads to the insistence that every effort be made to maintain biological human life until it is no longer possible to do so. Sanctity of life proponents usually oppose abortion and all forms of euthanasia or mercy killing, and ground their sanctity of life principles in traditional religious or philosophical beliefs.

The quality of life position is of more recent origin and is more likely to define human life in terms of psychological, cultural, intellectual, moral, and relational indicators of "personhood." It can be theologically or philosophically based. Recent innovations in medical maintenance technology have made it possible to sustain biological life long after the cessation of these "personhood" indicators. Some of the most confounding biomedical futures questions emerge precisely at this point. How is society going to treat biological life when personhood as measured by these indicators is either not a human possibility (beginning-of-life) or no longer a human possibility (during-life and end-of-life)? The sanctity versus quality of life debate embraces such issues as abortion, genetic manipulation, refusal of treatment, and euthanasia, among others. Together they span the three stages of the life cycle.

## INFORMED CONSENT

Informed consent means that participation by patients in a treatment program or by human subjects in an experiment must be based on (1) adequate knowledge about the nature and possible consequences of the program or experiments and (2) voluntary agreement to participate. Informed consent is designed to protect patients and human subjects from coercive treatment or experimental exploitation and experimenters from lawsuits. The principle of informed consent recognizes that the decision to be practiced or experimented "on" rests ultimately with the patient or human subject and that it is the responsibility of the medical professional to supply the experimenter with adequate information so that the patient or human subject can decide whether the benefits of volunteering for treatment or experimentation out-weigh the risks. The principles of confidentiality and truth-telling are closely related to informed consent and frequently appear in discussions about informed consent. The question of informed consent cuts across all three stages of the life cycle in such issues as artificial insemination; organ transplants; behavior control; and experimentation on children, prisoners, and the aged.

## DETERMINATION OF PARTICIPATION

Determination of participation differs from informed consent in three main respects. Informed consent refers to the rights of patients and human subjects. Determination of participation refers to the questions of (1) who can legitimately participate in biomedical decisions, (2) who decides when the patient or human subject is too incompetent to decide, and (3) who decides when the decisions of the patient or human subject affect the lives of others related in one way or another to the patient or human subject.

Some of the most compelling biomedical dilemmas bear on these three questions which span all three stages of the life cycle. Fetal and *in vitro* experiments are now technologically possible. Should they be encouraged? Who decides? The recent New Jersey Supreme Court decision in the case of Karen Ann Quinlan has taken a major step forward in determining who decides when a patient has suffered irreversible brain death. Can children, the mentally incompetent, or the acutely senile aged be used as experimental subjects? Under what conditions and who decides?

## BIOMEDICAL SOCIAL POLICY

The issue that brings together all biomedical dilemmas is the need for society to articulate a comprehensive biomedical social policy. The biomedical revolution has given rise to novel ethical and legal problems in a variety of areas such as abortion, *in vitro* research, genetic screening and manipulation, human subjects research, behavior control, transplants, scarce resources, and euthanasia. In the absence of policies that regulate activities in all these areas, society is left without the guidelines by which to monitor potential abuses by those who control the application of these new and powerful technological forces.

Is such a comprehensive policy likely to emerge in the future? If so, what kinds of provisions will it contain? If not, what is likely to emerge as an alternative? We shall address these questions in the final section of this chapter.

We will now turn to the three stages of the life cycle and discuss the biomedical dilemmas that are most likely to occupy the forefront of concern for the foreseeable future. All of these dilemmas are in various stages of resolution. In some cases, social consensus on how to deal with the social change implications of some biomedical practices has begun to emerge. Other cases are too recent in origin for widespread public agreement; resolution lies in the distant future. Still others are situated somewhere in between these two points.

## BEGINNING-OF-LIFE ISSUES

"Beginning-of-life issues" refer to those biomedical practices and dilemmas that apply to the pregnancy cycle.

### ABORTION

We begin with abortion, one of the oldest biomedical issues. The practice of abortion dates back as far as 4,600 years in ancient China. Proscriptive legislation against abortion existed in the Sumerian Code of 2000 B.C. Over the centuries, the abortion debate has flamed passions on both sides of the issue.

The abortion issue is in may ways exemplary of several of the new dilemmas of biomedical futures. The technology of abortion is now highly advanced. However, as in the past, no worldwide consensus yet exists over the rightful application of this technology. Although societies everywhere are still divided over the issue of abortion, a recent study suggests that the world is moving in a liberalizing direction. Since 1966 several countries have taken steps to liberalize abortion practices. Tietze and Lewit (1977) suggest that this liberalizing trend has led to new studies of abortion practices, more open release of data (estimates of the annual number of induced abortions range from 30 to 55 million), better medical procedures, and lower mortality rates. Changes in U.S. laws over the past ten years have paralleled the world trend (also see Callahan, 1970).

In the past, the United States traditionally found itself on the conservative end of the abortion issue. On January 22, 1973, the U.S. Supreme Court rendered a decision in *Roe vs. Wade* and *Doe vs. Bolton* that moved America suddenly to the permissive end of the abortion continuum without denying the legal rights of those on the conservative end. Historically, legal statutes and their sanctity of life justifications favored the fetus.

Increasingly, the courts have favored the rights of the pregnant woman and the quality of life arguments on her behalf. Proponents of liberalization held that rights of self-determination in matters of reproduction were being denied women. Sanctity of life principles were themselves being undermined with the compulsory birth of unwanted children. Restrictive laws do not prevent abortions; they only drive them underground where women become prey to potentially lethal abortion practices. Overpopulation threatens the quality of human life and augments already apparent ecological problems.

Thus on this crucial beginning-of-life issue the Court has opened quality of life options without prohibiting sanctity of life ones. It has extended to the pregnant woman and her consulting physician the right of participation in the decision to abort.

The right of participation, however, is bracketed by specific time periods during pregnancy. During the first trimester, the woman's right to decide whether to abort is primary. The state has no right to intervene. During the final two trimesters, the rights of participation are less specifically defined. The state may intervene on behalf of the woman in cases where the fetus threatens her life, whatever the circumstances. During the final trimester, the state may intervene on behalf of the fetus if it is viable (which is presumed to occur around twenty-eight weeks) and does not threaten the life of the woman. Other issues, such as the role of the father or parents in the case of teenagers in the decision to abort, were not resolved in the Court's decision (Annas, 1976). Sooner or later, the Court will also address these questions. In the absence of a comprehensive social policy, the Court has no alternative but to proceed in piecemeal fashion.

The liberalizing of biomedical practices, such as abortion, invariably generates conservative counter-responses. While the responses vary from issue to issue, they can be characterized as a call against the possibility of dehumanization. This ever-present danger within current and future biomedical practice should not be dismissed flippantly. Anyone who thinks that biomedical or any other technological innovations are value-neutral, inherently good, or free of moral ambiguities should read about the practice of biomedicine under Nazism and the verbatim transcripts of the Nuremberg trials (Alexander, 1949; "Biomedical Ethics and the Shadow of Nazism," 1976). We will say more about this matter later.

The concerns of conservatives over dehumanization in the abortion issue focuses chiefly on the attitudes of the living toward fetal life, which is wholly incapable of self-protection. At what point do permissive abortion practices lead to the insidious transformation of care of fetal life into the view of fetal life as "cheap life" to be destroyed by anyone, anywhere? Will the forces of dehumanization unleashed by liberalizing the abortion laws, ask sanctity of life proponents, create a domino effect that will lead to infanticide or the elimination of "defective" persons such as the mentally retarded, physically handicapped, senile, or others?

Advocates of liberalizing biomedical practices in the future accuse conservatives of fear-mongering with speculations about falling dominoes. But conservatives point out the historical episode of Nazism as an ever-present possibility. So great is this possibility and so heinous the outcome, they say, that society ought not even to open this Pandora's box. Liberals, on the other hand, hold that society can and must proceed cautiously and that liberalizing attitudes and legislation in one area does not ineluctably lead to dehumanization in any other area. The alternative to sancity of life is not denigration of life but quality of life, which by definition seeks to enhance personhood rather than destroy it.

### FETUS/ABORTUS RESEARCH

The legalization of abortion and advances made in abortion technology have brought other biomedical dilemmas into high relief. How should society treat (1) fetuses about to be aborted or (2) live abortuses? Are they fit subjects for experimental research? The question of the propriety of research on live abortuses applies equally to spontaneous abortions and induced ones. The Court's abortion decision confronts us with the issue of fetus/abortus experimentation because of the now potential availability of live abortuses, or as Paul Ramsey calls them "a new sort of human research subject that is live enough not to be dead, not yet mature enough to be an infant, yet a human being enough to deserve protections" (Ramsey, 1975, p. 59).

What right should society extend to fetuses and abortuses? Who may consent on behalf of the fetus/abortus? Is it appropriate to run experiments on condemned fetuses? If so, can experiments be conducted only during the time of abortion? Or in advance? And how far in advance of the actual moment of abortion? Should research on the fetus be therapeutic only, that is, to increase its life possibilities? Or should it be done for nontherapeutic purposes, simply to increase scientific biomedical knowledge so that other fetuses will benefit in the future, even though the research fetus will not have life? Should the fetus be killed or allowed to die in the process of abortion? Should aborted fetuses, whether spontaneous or induced, be kept alive *artificially* for either therapeutic or research purposes? What role should informed consent play? And who should decide?

To date, the Supreme Court has not heard a case on these crucial questions. At the same time, heated debate over the status of the fetus/ abortus as a fit subject for research has entered the public forum.

California has enacted the most conservative legislation to date. California law makes it unlawful for physicians to do scientific research on a live abortus except to save its life. Such legislation could become a model for other states.

The 1975 Report of the National Commission on the Protection of Human Subjects endeavors to balance therapeutic and nontherapeutic purposes in fetal research. The commission permits nontherapeutic fetus *in utero* research where information cannot be obtained by alternative means. It also requires that research impose minimal or no risk to the well-being of the fetus. The commission also requires the informed consent of the mother and specifies that the father must not object to the research. Under no conditions should inducements, monetary or otherwise, be offered to procure an abortion for research purposes.

On the crucial issue of fetus *ex utero* research, the report states that nontherapeutic research may be conducted if the fetus is less than twenty weeks gestational age, if no significant procedural changes are introduced into the abortion procedure in the interest of research alone, and if no intrusion into the fetus is made which alters the duration of life. Out of the debate and turmoil that surround fetus/abortus research a social policy is beginning to take shape. This policy reflects a fundamental moral concern with the therapeutic needs of the fetus/abortus, but it also attempts to accommodate the need to discover scientific information that might one day enhance the life possibilities of future fetuses ("Research on the Fetus," 1975, p. 74).

### IN VITRO RESEARCH

The dilemmas inherent in the question of fetus/abortus research are carried one step further in another beginning-of-life issue: *in vitro* experimentation. *In vitro* means literally "in the glass" and refers to any fertilization of the human ova which occurs outside the body of a female, either through a mixture of donor sperm and ova or by any other means. In other words, to use the popular idiom, we are talking about "test tube" pregnancy.

With *in vitro* research, the pregnancy process is altered dramatically. Life is no longer reproduced in the female body; rather, it is reproduced in a laboratory setting. The technology of *in vitro* experimentation has existed since the 1940s. The Italian biologist Daniele Petrucci fertilized a human egg in his laboratory in 1961, and he kept it alive for twenty-nine days. When the fetus became seriously deformed, Petrucci let it die but not before it developed a noticeable heartbeat. Later, he sustained the life of an *in vitro* fetus for fifty-nine days before a laboratory error caused its death. Petrucci discontinued his research after the Vatican condemned him for the experiments.

While laboratory reproduction technology exists, it is far from perfected. The inevitable questions arise. Should such experimentation continue? What are its implications? What are its potential uses? What are its potential abuses?

The implications of *in vitro* research are vast. *In vitro* pregnancy opens the door to potential unrestricted fetus/abortus research. Every detail of the pregnancy cycle can be studied microscopically. Every form of manipulation is possible, including genetic manipulation, which we will discuss in the next section. The ultimate implication, of course, is total control of the biological life process itself from the moment of conception.

Needless to say, here is one issue that engenders widespread debate. Conservatives dread the thought of it. Radical biomedical researchers cannot wait and wonder why all the fuss. Sanctity of life proponents scream against potential abuses to innocent human life. They point to the grotesque fetuses that were reproduced in experiments like those of Petrucci's. They invoke images of Huxley's *Brave New World*. Quality of life advocates, on the other hand, try to remain cognizant of the moral dangers inherent in such a technology but are likely to support cautious momentum in the direction of *in vitro* experimentation. They argue that the potential advantages of such research include the elimination of defective genes, better knowledge to insure safer "natural" pregnancies, nonnatural pregnancy options for couples who want them, embryo transplants for childless couples who want them, and so on.

As in the case of fetus/abortus research, public policy is also beginning to form around *in vitro* experimentation. Government policy on human subjects calls for the creation of an advisory board to determine the moral appropriateness of research done on human subjects as a means of safeguarding against potential abuses. The board must take into account community standards, legal issues, technological feasibility, and available guidelines governing each research situation before *in vitro* experimentation is permitted.

### GENETIC MANIPULATION

*In vitro* research and genetic manipulation are closely coupled as beginning-of-life issues. Genetic manipulation means the conscious attempt to modify in some way the genetic foundations of human life. Beginning-of-life genetic issues can be subsumed under two broad headings—negative and positive eugenics. According to James B. Nelson,

Negative eugenics is the attempt to eliminate hereditary defects that have already occurred in individuals or to prevent those who carry defective genes from passing them on to their offspring. Genetic counseling, genetic screening programs, and genetic therapy are its major forms . . . positive eugenics is concerned about improving the race through various forms of controlled reproduction (Nelson, 1973, pp. 99–100).

The idea behind negative eugenics is to curtail the introduction of defective genes into the gene pool by encouraging people who carry them not to reproduce. About 1,000 possible genetic defects are known to exist. The practice of withdrawing amniotic fluid is not new; starting in the mid-1950s scientists developed the technology for photographing and cataloguing the sex chromosomes of the fetal cells found in the fluid. Through the technique of amniocentesis administered between the thirteenth and eighteenth weeks of pregnancy, about 100 serious genetic disorders can now be detected.

These technological innovations force the issue of informed voluntary consent versus coercion. How far should the state go in making genetic screening mandatory? Under what conditions, if any, can the state contravene the right of couples to reproduce where the act of procreation results in children with genetic defects? Should mentally retarded people below a specific IQ level be sterilized to insure that the quality of life of future generations not be impaired? Or does the sanctity of life principle guarantee every individual the right to reproduce? With the increasing practice of amniocentesis and the legalization of abortion, should society adopt a policy of therapeutic abortion to prevent the birth of genetically defective fetuses?

Many of these controversial human rights questions are still unresolved at both the moral and legal-legislative levels. At the same time, some policies are emerging. Several states have begun to pass laws making genetic screening mandatory for such genetic diseases as sickle cell anemia, phenylketonuria (PKU), Tay-Sachs disease, and others. Recently, Maryland passed the first comprehensive mandatory screening law, one which might serve as a model for other states (Powledge, 1973, pp. 6–7).

Genetic counseling centers have also begun to appear throughout the United States and around the world. In the late 1940s, Dr. Sheldon Reed initiated a program of negative eugenics that has to date mushroomed into the establishment of several hundred counseling centers around the world. The area of genetic counseling, screening, and therapy is one that promises a bright future in a society becoming more conscious of its genetic foundations.

The development of negative eugenics techniques is not nearly as threatening to the current social order as is positive eugenics. In negative eugenics, counseling and therapy help eliminate potential negative personal and social consequences, and occur within the context of normatively acceptable methods of reproduction. Positive eugenics, on the other hand, is more ethically and politically explosive because it involves the aggressive application of new reproduction technologies that compete with traditional mores.

These new technologies include artificial insemination by husband or donor (AIH or AID), *in vitro* fertilization and embryo transplants, and the two most radical of all, cloning and manipulation of the DNA (deoxyribose nucleic acid) structure. DNA is the body's genetic code carrier, the fundament of human and all other forms of biological life. To manipulate DNA is to modify the very structure of life. Cloning refers to the replication of identical individuals through cell separation and manipulation during the early stage of embryonic growth. Body organs might also be cloned.

In the past few years, cloning and DNA technologies have advanced dramatically. These advances have predictably generated widespread disagreement over potential uses and abuses. After lengthy study and under carefully monitored conditions, the University of Michigan and other research centers have begun research in the controversial area of recombinant DNA (Committee B, 1976). Until now, most of the legislative and policy responses to issues of genetic manipulation have been in the area of negative eugenics. Advances in cloning and recombinant DNA technologies promise that more attention will be given to the social change problems raised by positive eugenics. How far society ultimately will be willing to go in manipulating the human genetic structure through positive eugenics and what forms of protection from abuse will develop are open questions.

An examination of abortion, fetus/abortus research, *in vitro* experimentation, and genetic manipulation suggests that we are a society in search of effective regulatory policies. Rather than the development of a comprehensive set of guidelines on these crucial beginning-of-life issues, we are witnessing the accumulation of laws and regulations that emerge out of case-by-case exigencies. Does this same pattern repeat itself on the critical during-life issues?

## DURING-LIFE ISSUES

"During-life issues" refer to those biomedical practices and dilemmas that apply to the time of life between birth and the end-of-life.

As we will see in the next section, advances in biomedical technology have muddled the question of death. Thus, when we refer to during-life issues, we mean those that emerge after pregnancy terminates in live birth but do not apply directly to the dilemmas surrounding human death. In real life, such distinctions are often artificial, but for purposes of analysis, they are useful.

### HUMAN SUBJECTS

We have already discussed some of the moral and policy problems related to the use of fetuses or abortuses as experimental subjects. We now want to enter more deeply into a discussion of the use of experimental subjects in general. Over the past thirty years, several ethical and legal codes that define the appropriate uses of human subjects for biomedical experimentation have been formulated.

When the horrors of Nazi biomedical practice were revealed for the first time after World War II, the world was stunned by the abuses of such practices. This gave rise to the Nuremberg Code of 1949 which was the first major effort in modern times to develop a code of conduct for research on humans. Since then, numerous other codes have been developed. They include the International Code of Medical Ethics of the World Medical Association (WMA), 1949; the WMA's 1954 Principles for Those in Research and Experimentation; the Declaration of Helsinki, 1964 (Beecher, 1970); and, most recently, the National Commission on the Protection of Human Subjects.

Human subject abuses are not restricted to this pathological case. Nazism represents the extreme but not the exclusive example of research conducted with a willful disregard of the rights of patients. In his now classic 1966 article, Henry Beecher gave case after case examples of unethical research in standard, socially accepted American biomedical practice. These and other revelations of continuing human subject abuses have driven deeply into our current social consciousness the following realization: future vigilance against the violation of the rights of human subjects must be constant.

To combat potential abuses, virtually every legal or ethical code of research insists that informed consent of the human subject is absolutely essential. In addition, two other factors are crucial in biomedical experimentation. One is the ever-present distinction between therapeutic and nontherapeutic research. We have already alluded to this distinction in our discussion of fetus/abortus research. Therapeutic research is intended to benefit directly the immediate patient and may or may not benefit future patients. Nontherapeutic research is designed to benefit future patients with little chance of benefiting the immediate patient.

The second is the risk-benefit factor. In cases where novel therapeutic experiments are conducted as a last hope possibility for a patient, risks may vastly outweigh benefits. This is legitimate. In nontherapeutic research, however, all relevant research codes insist that animal experiments be conducted prior to human experiments. Until research is done on animals to determine risks versus benefits, research on human subjects is disallowed.

In effect, we have witnessed in the past three decades the establishment of a set of procedures that carry both moral and legal force. These procedures are the social parameters that bracket the development and application of biomedical technology. They are designed to protect against the dehumanizing use of these new technologies. Human subject research that is based on informed consent; is therapeutic; and is of high benefit and low risk is both moral and legal. Research that is not based on informed consent; is nontherapeutic; and is of high risk-low (possibly no) benefit is immoral and illegal.

While human subject research on legally competent adults is not entirely free of moral or legal ambiguities, the most difficult cases involve experiments on children, prisoners, the mentally incompetent, and, as we have seen, fetuses and abortuses. In these cases, concepts such as proxy consent, protection committees, supplementary judgments, and so on have all been proposed as ways of handling situations in which voluntary informed consent cannot be given.

The National Commission on the Protection of Human Subjects along with other federal guidelines address these issues. In the case of prisoner subjects, a prison must be accredited before research can be done there; accreditation requires adequate food and shelter, the presence of adequate daily activity to eliminate unusual boredom, and the opportunity to earn money in other ways besides research. Thus, efforts are made to minimize impediments to voluntary consent (Brody, 1976, p. 165).

In the case of children, the courts allow the parents proxy consent where therapeutic low-risk research is involved, or even high-risk research in life and death situations. In nontherapeutic research, the courts support the rights of children not to be used by their parents as experimental subjects. According to Howard Brody (1976, p. 167), national guidelines state that

if the experiment can be done on animals or on adults, and all the necessary information obtained in that way, it ought not be done on children. If the experiment cannot be done on adults or animals in order to determine the estimated level of risk, then it cannot be determined whether a favorable ratio exists, and the experiment ought not be done on children. If the risks can be estimated from animal or adult experiments, but additional information is still needed before therapeutic application can be made, the experimentation on children may be considered.

The most problematic moral and legal issues surrounding the use of children as experimental subjects involve nontherapeutic research. The debate on this issue continues (McCormick, 1976; Bartholome, 1976), although a strong moral and legal consensus generally prohibits it.

### BEHAVIOR CONTROL

The technologies of behavior control are expanding very rapidly. These technologies can be grouped roughly into three categories: psychoactive drugs, behavior modification techniques, and psychosurgery. Psychosurgery involves operating on the brain but is distinct from neurosurgery in that it applies to cases evidently not related to some form of organic pathology.

While psychosurgery represents the extreme case, the technologies of behavior control as a group raise some enormous dilemmas for the future. According to Willard M. Gaylin, these include the problems of consent, the distinction between experimental (nontherapeutic) and therapeutic control, the organic versus inorganic relationships of brain functions, therapy versus social control or engineering, and the problems of human autonomy (Gaylin, no date). The growing technologies of behavior change present new opportunities for enhancing the quality of life. They may be used for easing human suffering and for eliminating incurable diseases. On the other side, their potential for abuse is vast.

The issue of psychosurgery has surfaced forcefully in the past few years with all its attendant uses and especially abuses given widespread exposure. Psychiatrist Peter R. Breggin is the main *agent provocateur*. In 1971, Representative Cornelius Gallagher inserted into the *Congressional Record* Breggin's 25,000-word diatribe against psychosurgery (Breggin, 1972). Shortly after Representative Gallagher's action, two bills calling for a moratorium on psychosurgery and further investigations were introduced into the House and Senate. California also became enmeshed in the controversy. On July 21, 1973, the governor of Oregon signed into law a bill that regulates the practice of psychosurgery. The law calls for the creation of a review board, insists on voluntary and informed consent, and calls for proxy consent in the case of guardians (Oregon laws, 1973). The National Commission also permits the practice of psychosurgery under carefully regulated conditions.

The one area of biomedical practice that reflects more than any other the careful enunciation of comprehensive guidelines is human subject experimentation. The National Commission Reports are now the starting point for all such discussions. Commission guidelines specify the procedures and articulate the ethical and legal principles that direct research activities on human subjects.

## END-OF-LIFE ISSUES

"End-of-life issues" refer to those biomedical practices and dilemmas that apply to problems of human dying. End-of-life is not being applied in an age-specific sense; rather, it refers to death at whatever age after birth and in any variety of circumstances.

### TRANSPLANTS AND SCARCE RESOURCES

Organ malfunctioning is one of the major causes of human death. Not all organs, of course, are indispensable to the maintenance of life. Others are. Much of the recent dramatic and popular coverage of biomedical practice has focused on the replacement of these indispensable organs, such as the kidney and heart, with either donor or artificial ones. Transplant technology has made major advances in the past three decades. Kidney transplants began in 1951. In 1961, the first immunosuppressive drug, asathioprine, was developed. Immunosuppressives help overcome the problem of rejection of a foreign organ by the recipient's body. They paved the way for Dr. Christian Barnard's December 3, 1967, cardiac transplant in Louis Washkansky.

Unlike the case of *in vitro* fertilization, in which sanctity of life and quality of life advocates strongly differ, on the transplant issue they are frequent allies. Widespread moral and legal consensus exists over the transplant issue. The Uniform Anatomical Gift Act (UAGA) defines the moral and legal conditions of transplant procedures. It is valid in all fifty states (Sadler et al., 1968). The provisions of the UAGA stipulate that any mentally competent person at least eighteen years of age can will *as a gift* his/her body or any of his/her parts upon death for transplantation or research. Organs may neither be bought nor sold. The decision to donate rests solely with the donor. Neither the state nor the medical profession has rights in the decision. The moral principle of the patient's consent finds legal expression and helps curtail potential abuses of the transplant technologies.

Many of the criticisms of the UAGA emerge at this point. The supply of available organs is perpetually less than the demand for them. Many proposals advocate the development of more efficient ways to meet transplant needs. One such proposal advocates that organs be removed routinely from the dead and preserved for later use unless forbidden by the patient or family. Some nations, such as Israel and Sweden, have enacted such legislation, as has the state of Virginia on a limited basis. Whether the UAGA will eventually be modified to include such an option remains to be seen. In the meantime, in order to meet transplant needs for kidneys, corneas, hearts, pituitary glands, and a host of others, thirty-five states have adopted the technique of using the driver's license to identify volunteer organ donors. This allows for the opportunity of rapid removal of organs in the event of accidental death before loss of oxygen renders them useless.

The scarce resources problem raises another important transplant issue: Who shall live when not all can live? James Childress (1970) addresses this question in an article of the same title. He raises the question of random selection versus selection on the basis of some criteria of social usefulness. He opts for the former because every potential patient has an equal chance of selection. No one is unjustly excluded by social usefulness criteria that could not possibly have universal support or that bias selection in favor of some and not others. Kidney patients now secure dialysis treatment through federal funding, but the scarcity problem still persists in other areas.

With advances in cloning technology and the creation of artificial organs, the problem of scarcity could disappear. Some advocate the routine "harvesting" and "banking" of organs (Gaylin, 1974) to alleviate organ scarcity. Until such changes come to pass, if they do at all, society is left with an admixture of selection practices and a biomedical problem in the process of resolution.

The UAGA recognizes the importance of donor organs but also protects patients' rights by requiring strict safeguards verifying the death of the donor. The American Medical Association guidelines specifically insist that donor death must be determined by physicians other than those performing the transplant. Thus, we are brought to the final cycle-of-life issue: death itself.

### DEFINING DEATH AND EUTHANASIA

Recent advances in cardiorespiratory technology have dramatically altered the dying process. Quite simply, the machinery now exists to sustain heart and lung functions long after the brain has become irreversibly inoperative. The brain is the physiological basis of personality and sociality. Through artificial means, the body can be maintained in a vegetative state long after brain death has resulted in the cessation of these human capacities.

These technological advances have raised three interrelated questions. (1) When does death occur? (2) What are the moral responsibilities and legal rights of the dying person? (3) What are the moral responsibilities and legal rights of those, other than the dying person, involved in the dying process, i.e., the physician, family, and others?

Recent legislative and court actions have begun to resolve some of these pressing issues, and we now have a glimpse of what future biomedical practice might look like in these areas. In 1970, the state of Kansas took the first step to enact into law a definition of death. The Kansas law makes either the "absence of spontaneous respiratory or cardiac function" or the "absence of spontaneous brain function" the medical-legal definition of death. While such definitions are designed in part to facilitate organ transplants, they have been criticized, chiefly for two reasons. First, technology changes so quickly that precise and permanent definitions are ill advised. Second, since the rate of deterioration and final cessation of body parts varies so widely, unanimity of opinion over the definition of death and the precise point in time when the *event* of death occurs in the *process* of dying is impossible to establish. Opinions vary widely (Harvard Medical School, 1968; Veatch, 1972; Morrison, Kass, 1971).

More recently, the New Jersey Supreme Court and the California legislature have taken a different tack. Rather than define death per se, they have begun to define the legal rights of dying persons and others relative to certain stages or events in the dying process. In effect, these decisions are beginning to reflect the moral and legal consensus now building around the quality of life conception of human life.

Traditionally, American law has been complicated and confused on the legal and policy questions surrounding death. The only issue on which unquestioned clarity has existed is direct euthanasia or mercy killing. It is first degree murder for a physician to directly bring about the death of a patient, even though the motive is mercy. In actual fact, no physician ever tried for direct euthanasia in the United States has ever been found guilty. Euthanasia, however, can be passive as well as active or direct. Passive euthanasia involves *withholding* or *ceasing* life-prolonging procedures once they have been started. Prior to the Quinlan case, the law showed considerable confusion over passive euthanasia. Out of this confusion, according to James B. Nelson (1973, p. 141), practical procedures nonetheless emerged.

Doctors were in a position to shape their own law in dealing with these situations. As yet there have been no convictions in American law for a physician's failure to provide treatment which might have prolonged life. Legally it is clear that there is always potential liability here, but the law thus far has always been interpreted so that everything hinges upon the special relationship existing between a particular doctor and a particular patient.

The Karen Quinlan case has brought some clarity to this confusion. On March 31, 1976, the New Jersey Supreme Court defined the conditions under which the practice of passive euthanasia is legal. If life-prolonging treatment has begun and a patient is declared permanently comatose, the parents or guardian of the patient may request withdrawal of treatment after consultation with attending physicians and the "Ethics Committee" or similar body of the institution in which the patient is hospitalized. The court decision also frees parents, guardians, physicians, hospital, or others from any civil or criminal liability. In effect, the court has declared that when the capacities of personality and sociality have irretrievably ceased, the requirement to prolong physical life is no longer unconditional.

Although precedent-setting, the Quinlan case addresses only those circumstances in which treatment has been initiated. Many issues are left unresolved. Two of the most important are (1) the issue of the right to *withhold* treatment on a brain death patient, and (2) whether brain death patients should be maintained mechanically while their organs are harvested.

On August 30, 1976, the California legislature passed the Natural Death Act which allows a legally competent adult to sign a "directive to physicians" instructing them to withdraw *or* withhold artificial life-prolonging treatment when a patient is declared "terminal" and death is imminent. This is the first so-called death-with-dignity legislation to be passed, even though bills have been introduced in several states such as West Virginia, Florida, and Idaho. The California law is highly restrictive and does not cover those who have *not* signed such a directive, whose treatment involves natural means, and whose death would be imminent only if lifesaving procedures were not used. Thus, on the crucial issue of withholding treatment on a brain-dead patient the act is silent. Because of these restrictions, the Natural Death Act has come under heavy criticism (Garland, 1976, pp. 5-6; Labacqz, 1976). At the same time, some important steps have been taken in the direction of resolving the dilemmas raised by recent changes in biomedical technology. Moral and legal momentum is shifting in the direction of support for some forms of passive euthanasia. Whether it will continue in the direction of active euthanasia only the future will tell.

On the important end-of-life issues, the Uniform Anatomical Gift Act has begun to provide guidelines for all important organ transplant procedures. In the area of euthanasia, we have yet to see the emergence of a moral consensus or the systematic development of a comprehensive policy that will define human rights and responsibilities in those areas in which the process of dying is complicated by powerful technologies that maintain body functions beyond the death of the brain.

## FUTURE PROJECTIONS

We have focused on the relationship between the technological, moral, and legal dimensions of the ever-changing field of biomedicine. What projections can we make about biomedical issues for the future?

We can anticipate that the pace of technological innovation will quicken, and most likely we will be dazzled by what biomedical technology will bring in the future. The new technologies, however, will not emerge in a moral and legal vacuum. Historically, scientific medical practice has never been "on its own." Rather, from the time of the Hippocratic Oath, society has sought the assurance that the practice of medicine would be nurtured by a humane vision of life. It has not always succeeded, and the horrors of Nazism reflect the decadent depths to which humanity can plunge. In the last thirty years, since the articulation of the Nuremberg Code, international efforts to elaborate new guidelines suggest that we are at least "on the way" toward developing a new Hippocratic Oath equal to the ethical and legal problems of current and future medical research and practice.

A number of ethical principles are beginning to emerge as near absolutes. At the head of the list stands the principle of voluntary informed consent. Closely behind are values such as maximum benefit-minimum risk, preference for therapeutic versus nontherapeutic applications, and recognition and preservation of the rights of patients and human subjects.

Legislative and court actions and emerging social policies that surround biomedical practices, limited though they are, embody these principles. Laws and policies in the areas of abortion; human experimentation, whether on competent adults, children, prisoners, the mentally incompetent, the aged, or fetuses/abortuses; *in vitro* research; psychosurgery and other behavior-control technologies; DNA experiments; organ transplants; or euthanasia and the rights of the dying reflect an underlying concern over these ethical principles.

As we have seen, the ethical, legal, and social policy resolutions affecting biomedical practice vary from issue to issue throughout the life cycle. Despite this unevenness, the cumulative impact over the past few decades of individual efforts by courts, legislatures, international organizations, health and medical associations, physicians, scientists, ethicists, theologians, philosophers, and others suggests the possibility, if not the probability, of developing in the future comprehensive and international guidelines that will regulate biomedical practice and carry both legal and moral force.

The emergence of such a policy, however, is contingent upon the ethical and political context of changing biomedical practices. Government agencies largely control research funding and thereby influence where the next research advance is likely to occur. With technological advance, new ethical and legal problems are created, and each in turn must be addressed. Thus, while biomedical research will proceed at varying rates of speed from issue to issue, the long-range cumulative impact will most likely be in the direction of developing comprehensive guidelines for assessing and shaping technological innovations in the biomedical field. As biomedical technologies advance and unravel the secrets of biological and human life, we can expect that the post-World War II emphasis on the humane application of these technologies will continue.

Such a projection should not be construed as a prediction. The humane application of biomedical technologies rests on continuities in the present ethical and political structures of societies around the planet and on maintaining the human rights momentum generated after 1945. The humane unfolding of the future is *not* inevitable, and the call for complacency is ill advised. Recent Watergate revelations testify to the fact that we are always in danger of drifting in the direction of erosion of human rights.

A humane vision of life lies at the basis of a humane biomedical future, and the preservation of democratic procedures will help insure that such a vision will be nurtured and made manifest. Legislative regulation opens policy to public scrutiny and implies that the wishes of the public are being enforced through appropriate guidelines. To the extent that this vision and these procedures are eclipsed by contravening future events, the planet runs the risks of returning to horrors already visited on millions, and indeed, exposure to worse horrors the mind has not yet imagined. The biomedical revolution carries the seeds of curse as well as blessing.

## REFERENCES

Alexander, Leo. 1949. "Medical Science Under Dictatorship." *New England Journal of Medicine,* Volume 241 (July 14), 39–47.

Annas, George J. 1976. "Law and the Life Sciences: Abortion and the Supreme Court: Round Two." *The Hastings Center Report,* Volume 6 (October), 15–17.

Augenstein, Leroy. 1869. *Come, Let Us Play God.* New York: Harper and Row.

Bartholome, William G. 1976. "Parents, Children and the Moral Benefits of Research." *The Hastings Center Report,* 6 (December), 44–45.

Beecher, Henry K. 1966. "Ethics and Clinical Research." *New England Journal of Medicine,* Volume 274 (June 16), 1354–1360.

―――. 1970. *Research and the Individual: Human Studies.* Boston: Little, Brown and Co.

"Biomedical Ethics and the Shadow of Nazism." 1976. *The Hastings Center Report.* Special Supplement (August).

Breggin, Peter R. 1972. "The Return of Lobotomy and Psychosurgery." *Congressional Record,* Volume 118 (February 24).

Brody, Howard. 1976. *Ethical Decisions in Medicine.* Boston: Little, Brown and Co.

Callahan, Daniel. 1970. *Abortion: Law, Choice & Morality.* New York: Macmillan Co.

Childress, James F. 1970. "Who Shall Live When Not All Can Live?" *Soundings,* Volume 53 (Winter), 339–362.

Committee B. 1976. "Report Committee to Recommend Policy for the Molecular Genetic and Oncology Program." University of Michigan (March).

Cutler, Donald R. (ed.). 1969. *Updating Life and Death: Essays in Ethics and Medicine.* Boston: Beacon Press.

Etzioni, Amitai. 1973. *Genetic Fix.* New York: Macmillan Co.

Fletcher, Joseph. 1954. *Morals and Medicine.* Boston: Beacon Press.

Frankena, William K. 1973. *Ethics.* 2d ed. Englewood Cliffs, N.J.: Prentice-Hall.

Garland, Michael. 1976. "Politics, Legislation, and Natural Death—The Right to Die in California." *the Hastings Center Report,* 6 (October), 5–6.

Gaylin, Willard. 1974. "Harvesting the Dead," *Harper's Magazine* (September), 23–30.

―――. No date. "The Problem of Psychosurgery." Hastings-on-Hudson, N.Y.: Institute of Society, Ethics, and the Life Sciences.

Gustafson, James. 1970. "Basic Ethical Issues in the Bio-Medical Fields." *Soundings,* Volume 53 (Summer), 151–180.

―――. 1975. *The Contribution of Theology to Medical Ethics.* Milwaukee: Marquette University Theology Department.

Harvard Medical School, Ad Hoc Committee of the Harvard Medical School to Examine the Definition of Brain Death. 1968. "A Definition of Irreversible Coma." *Journal of the American Medical Association,* Volume 205 (August 5), 337–340.

Hastings Center. 1976–1977. *Bibliography.* Hastings-on-Hudson, N.Y.: Institute of Society, Ethics, and the Life Sciences.

Labacqz, Karen. 1976. "AB 3060: Boon or Boondoggle?" *Ethics & Policy: Notes, Ideas, & Review Quotations from the Center for Ethics and Social Policy* Berkeley, Calif.: Graduate Theological Union.

McCormick, Richard A. 1976. "Experimentation in Children: Sharing in Sociality—A Reply to Paul Ramsey." *The Hastings Center Report,* Volume 6 (December), 41–46.

Mendelsohn, Everett, et al. (eds.). 1971. *Human Aspects of Biomedical Innovation.* Harvard Studies in Technology and Society. Cambridge, Mass.: Harvard University Press.

Morison, Robert. 1971. "Death: Process or Event?"; Kass, Leon R. "Death As an Event: A Commentary on Robert Morison," *Science* Volume 173 (August 20), 694–702.

Nelson, James B. 1973. *Human Medicine*. Minneapolis, Minn.: Augsburg Publishing House.

Oregon Laws. 1973. Chapter 616, 1361–1368.

Powledge, Tabitha. 1973. "New Trends in Genetic Legislation." *The Hastings Center Report,* Volume 3 (December), 6–7.

Public Law 93-348. 1974. "Title II. Protection of Human Subjects of Biomedical and Behavioral Research" (July 12).

Ramsey, Paul. 1970. *The Patient as Person*. New Haven, Conn.: Yale University Press.

———. 1975. *The Ethics of Fetal Research*. New Haven, Conn.: Yale University Press.

"Research on the Fetus." 1975. National Commission on the Protection of Human Subjects of Biomedical and Behavioral Research, Bethesda, Md.

"Research Involving Prisoners." 1977. National Commission for the Protection of Human Subjects of Biomedical and Behavioral Research, (January 14).

Sadler, Alfred M., Jr., et al. 1968. "The Uniform Anatomical Gift Act: A Model for Reform." *Journal of the American Medical Association,* Volume 206 (December), 2501–2506.

Shannon, Thomas, (ed.). 1976. *Bioethics*. New York: Paulist Press.

Sigerist, Henry E. 1951 and 1961. *A History of Medicine*. 2 vols. New York: Oxford University Press.

Thomas, Lewis. 1974. "Commentary: The Future Impact of Science and Technology on Medicine." *BioScience,* Volume 24 (February), 99–105.

Tietze, Christopher, and Sarah Lewit. 1977. "Legal Abortion." *Scientific American,* Volume 236 (January), 21–27.

Vaux, Kenneth. 1974. *Biomedical Ethics*. New York: Harper and Row.

Veatch, Robert M. 1972. "Brain Death: Welcome Definition or Dangerous Judgement?" *The Hastings Center Report,* Volume 2 (November), 10–12.

Walters, LeRoy (ed.). 1975. *Bibliography of Bioethics*. Volume 1. Detroit: Gale Research Co.

Wertz, Richard W. (ed.). 1973. *Readings on Ethical and Social Issues in Biomedicine*. Englewood Cliffs, N.J.: Prentice-Hall.

CHRISTOPHER DEDE

# Technology and the Future

Technological capability may be the most important force in shaping the present from a myriad of alternative futures. Political choices and economic trends and discontinuities play a major role in determining which alternative futures will become most probable. Nonetheless, the advent of a single new technology—or the emergence of unforeseen secondary or tertiary effects in an existing technology—can completely redefine the possible futures open to our society. Furthermore, the "technological style" of a culture tends to influence the values and types of thought accepted by its members. Thus, the fact that cultures are often characterized first by their level of technological development (hunting, agricultural, industrial, or postindustrial) may reflect a differential denominator more fundamental than economic system, ideology, or mores.

One way of visualizing technology's power to reshape the futures we can attain is to conceptualize a "tree" of alternatives. We stand on the trunk of the tree (the present) looking upward toward the branches (the major alternative futures). Each step we take up the trunk toward the branches (each decision we make in the present) chops off a branch (greatly reduces the probability of a cluster of possible futures). By the time we reach the branches—when the future becomes the present— all the branches are gone but one (the trunk), and a new set of alternative futures stretches upward.

Political choices and economic decisions usually remove branches (foreclose options). Technological breakthroughs, however, create branches and expand alternatives. For example, the development of a low-cost, low-weight, high-capacity electric storage device would radically reshape the futures open to us, as electric motors would become preferable to internal combustion engines in all applications. In contrast, a political or economic decision to utilize the catalytic converter or to reduce the speed limit, or even to fund mass transit, has less impact. Technology often defines the realm of the possible within which political and economic forces interact, and reshapes the value systems that direct political and economic choices.

One social force that rivals technology in its power to redefine our futures is social invention: the creation of new symbolic models for organized human activity. The institution of marriage, for example, is a social invention; the emergence of "wife" and "husband" roles, fidelity, and nuclear child-raising has fundamentally altered the nature of our society. Some social inventions under development today (sophisticated behavior modfication, an economic system combining the best aspects of capitalism and socialism) could open a host of new future branches.

Unlike prehistoric cultures, however, our society so heavily emphasizes technological "fixes" that social inventions account for little of the rapid expansion of future options we now see taking place. Prior to the development of writing and agriculture, all cultures utilized social inventions as their major approach to problem-solving (Mumford, 1967). For example, kinship networks and taboos against incest together minimized organized aggression; elaborate incest proscriptions insured marriage outside of one's own tribe, and the kinship relationships thereby engendered reduced the chances of intertribal warfare and enhanced communication. Now, our approach to the same problem is technological: a mutual balance of terror promoted by nuclear overkill capability. Our heavy reliance upon a research and development approach often results in predominantly technological, rather than social, redefinition of possible futures.

Given the scope of technology's influence on our future options, one current dispute among major futures researchers must be seen as *the* crucial issue in the field: is a continuation of our present policy toward technological development essential to attaining a desirable future, or a sure way of guaranteeing an undesirable future? One school of thought (including Herman Kahn, Daniel Bell, Arthur C. Clarke, and Buckminister Fuller) holds that only a continuation and intensification of our present approach toward technology can save us from economic stagnation, deteriorating political relationships with have-not countries, and eventual devastating shortages of food, energy, and resources. An opposing school (including the limits to growth group, Willis Harman, Robert Theobald, and Jim Bowman) forecasts that only a drastic change in our present policies toward technological development can save us from economic collapse, military confrontation with have-not countries, and eventual deterioration via resource shortages, pollution, social unrest, and the emergence of fascism. Which of these viewpoints should present-day decision-makers believe—or is neither fundamentally correct? The *quantitative* effect of our technological prowess on the shape of things to come is agreed to be very large, but what is the overall *qualitative* impact?

This debate in futures research is similar in some aspects to the periods of paradigm change Kuhn describes in *The Structure of Scientific Revolutions.* An established method for shaping reality (our present approach to technological development) is challenged by those who see a new class of problems this method will be unable to solve. Meadows, Roszak, and Harman depict contemporary problems such as pollution and the arms race as intrinsic flaws within our technological policy—anomalies that will worsen so long as we pursue solutions through present methods.

Proponents of the established method, however, see these same problems as temporary side-effects that will yield when adequate resources are devoted to their solution. Futurists such as Fowles point to the past and present successes of our current technological approach as reasons why we should not precipitously leap to some untested alternative (1976).

As in the scientific revolutions depicted by Kuhn, neither side can prove the other is wrong. Each school of thought selects historical incidents and present trends thought to be representative, and from these constructs a case that the majority of possible futures supports its point of view. Kahn's multifold trend (1972, p. 8) is an accumulation of the successes of our technological approach, extrapolated on the assumption that present problems will yield as easily to technology as did historic challenges. Harman's list of obsolete assumptions made by technocrats (1974, p. 64) is, like Luther's ninety-five theses tacked to the church door, a compilation of fallacies within the present policy which vitiate its chances of solving the crises now faced, successful as the past record has been. Thus, the dispute centers on whether our contemporary problems of pollution, arms race, resource limitations, overpopulation, and terrorism are somehow so fundamentally different from the past challenges which technological development has mastered that a new method of problem-solving is required.

Like the scientists in the middle of a Kuhnian debate, we cannot arrive at a choice between these two schools of thought—or choose some other, as yet unarticulated alternative—solely by rational means. The inexact epistemology of futures research prohibits a "proof" of the correctness of either position (Dede, 1973), nor does either viewpoint accept the methods of analysis and forms of evidence accumulated by the other. However, in making our leap of faith guided by educated intuition (as scientists ultimately must), we can look for perspectives that clarify the issues involved by contrasting the assumptions made by each side. This article, then, will attempt to illuminate the future of technology—the most crucial question in futures research—by examining some "cleavage terms" that separate the two viewpoints about technology into opposing premises.

One important cleavage concept in understanding the future of technology is the issue of the uniqueness of the crises we now face. John Platt has compiled the following list of trends during the last 100 years (1969, p. 1117):

increase in speed of travel by a factor of 100
increase in control over infectious disease by a factor of 100
increase in energy resources by a factor of 1,000
increase in data handling speed by a factor of 10,000
increase in power of weaponry by a factor of 1 million
increase in speed of communications by a factor of 10 million

This 100 year period contrasts with approximately 8,000 years since the development of agriculture (the beginning of historic societies) and 500,000 to 2 million years since the first hunting tribes (the beginning of the human race).

The relative amounts of time involved can be envisioned by imagining that the human race has been on earth for only 1 hour. Fifty-nine minutes and 40 seconds into that hour, agriculture was developed. One quarter of 1 second ago, the Industrial Revolution began in England. During the last one-tenth of 1 second, the trends listed above occurred.

Using this metaphor, the uniqueness of the present can clearly be seen. Most of human history has encompassed a very gradual accumulation of power to affect the physical and social environment. During some short periods, such as in the early irrigation cultures, this power accreted at a more rapid rate (Mumford, 1967). However, no period in the development of the species comes close to matching the last century in magnitude of power rapidly acquired—and focused in crucial, civilization-shaping areas such as energy resources, weaponry, communications, and travel.

Those who favor a continuation of our present technological thrust tend to interpret this concept of the uniqueness of the present as supporting their viewpoint. Technology, Bell argues, has succeeded in creating a powerful and benign industrial base, which now can be used as the foundation for postindustrial society. Arthur C. Clarke sees these accomplishments as a fulcrum by which power can be accumulated for another century, if we have the courage to continue our support of technological expansion.

Even those technocrats who do not see the immediate past as unmitigated progress and who have some doubts about the desirability of being guided by a technological "invisible hand" still see the sorcerer of science as the only hope of controlling the sorcerer's apprentice of technology. Platt (1969, p. 1120) himself urges that we forestall the dangers and side-effects of the powers gained from these trends by scientific task forces (similar to the Manhattan Project) devoted to technologically based solutions. Kahn (1972, pp. 205–219) foresees his "1985 Technological Crisis" as surmounted only by new technologies.

In contrast to these supporters of our present technological approach, those who advocate radical change see the uniqueness of the present as favoring their position. The very successes of the past are seen as having bred a host of dangerous and unprecedented problems. Harman (1974, p. 7) lists accomplishments such as control over disease, automation, and material affluence as engendering the corresponding crises of overpopulation and problems of the aged; unemployment, underemployment, and inflation; and pollution, resource depletion, and anomie. Rather than a secure and benign base on which to build, Mesarovic and Pestel (1974) envision industrialization as a dangerously unstable house of cards, urgently needing to be shored up by changes in political, economic, and cultural mores.

Because the present is unique, the novel dangers associated with our technological prowess are seen as irreducible through conventional wisdom—in fact, perhaps worsened by present policies. Theobald sees technology as a tool so thoroughly utilized that the problems now remaining are those immune to technological solution. Roszak and Harman both depict the crises we face as intrinsic products—not side-effects—of industrial development, amenable to solution only from a new perspective outside of the "technological imperative." Given the absence of consensus on the existence of a positive correlation between affluence and happiness (beyond a threshold level of prosperity), these critics argue that the conservative approach is to restrain technological advance until the intensity of the problems it has created is greatly reduced.

The discrepancy between technological and social invention that the past century has fostered is also cited as part of the uniqueness of the present. Social inventions tend to increase our ability to control our technological power to affect the physical and social environment. For example, the God/King, the organized priesthood, and the city were all social inventions that aided in harnessing the powers gained from the discovery of agriculture (Mumford, 1967). Many of the crises today are not unsolvable in theory but seem uncontrollable in practice because we cannot apply our technological skills delicately, swiftly, and in a localized manner. The rate of social invention in the past century has been quite low; our schools, political institutions, and economic system have experienced no comparable improvement in this period. A pause in technological development might allow these areas of social invention to advance to a corresponding sophistication, thereby restoring some degree of balance between the two areas.

On balance, careful examination of the concept of the uniqueness of the present has favored those who advocate a change in our present attitudes toward technology. The blessings associated with recent trends do seem inextricably mixed with fairly intractable problems, and each technological solution to a technological problem seems to beget secondary and tertiary effects which in turn generate a multitude of new problems. (The atomic bomb as a means of limiting war and the phosphate detergents as a solution to the biodegradability problem of soaps are two classic examples of this phenomenon.) Furthermore, the novelty of our present situation vitiates the arguments that technology's past successes auger well for the future. Historical study by and large seems to advocate social inventions as the best means to control a rapid technological expansion.

To counter these attacks, the proponents of present technological policy have advanced a set of arguments that can best be understood via a second cleavage concept, the "tiger-by-the-tail" idea. Technology is seen as having reached a level from which we must continue to advance because of the danger of remaining in our present stage, a danger caused both by resource limitations and by the gap between the have and have-not countries. Our present technological prowess seems able to provide affluence for some but not for all, and may be just inefficient enough in its use of resources to sustain short-term growth while causing eventual collapse through long-term resource depletion.

Arthur C. Clarke dramatizes this argument with his metaphor of "the cliff." He sees industrial civilization as having reached the base of a steep and lofty cliff, which must be climbed if the race is to survive. The resources at the base of the cliff are rapidly being depleted, and the population dependent on these resources continues to grow as the Third World countries move into the industrial stage of development. If America seizes the initiative and climbs the cliff (reaches the next stage of technological advance) before the resources at the base are too exhausted to make the assault feasible, then with our newly acquired "high" technologies we can pull the rest of the world up the cliff, to enjoy a modern-day Garden of Eden. If America hesitates, however (whether from caution or from waiting for the less developed countries to attain parity), the resources at the base of the cliff will be too depleted for a successful assault, and we will all perish miserably through fighting over an ever-diminishing supply of necessities.

The image these proponents of technology conjure up is analogous to that of Neanderthal man freezing to death a few scant feet above a huge vein of coal. With fusion or solar power linked to technologies highly efficient in terms of resource utilization (i.e., Fuller's example of a communications satellite using one ten-millionth the copper of a nationwide network of telephone wire), a "high" technology can be envisioned which might allow a very large population to live in prosperity. Now that technology has advanced to its present stage, Clarke argues, we must continue or be doomed; the industrialization begun two centuries ago is now irreversible.

This "tiger-by-the-tail" concept of technology is less flattering than proponents of our present policy would like, but it does provide a powerful answer to the "uniqueness of the present" arguments. Few advocates of a change in our attitude toward technology would maintain that we could reverse technological development without the collapse of civilization as we know it, and to freeze technology at its present level without simultaneously making other changes (such as massive redistribution) would not relieve any of the crises we now face. The evidence is quite convincing that the next stage of advance in technology (to fusion or solar power, communications by satellite, sophisticated resource utilization devices, and low-pollution electric engines) will require a "quantum leap" in resources committed to research and development and will necessitate a coordinated, deliberate effort. Thus, those who would refute the "tiger-by-the-tail" argument advanced by proponents of technology must show that a technological approach to our current crises has less chance of succeeding and higher risks than some other, concretely specified alternative.

One such counterargument used to illustrate the risks of a purely technological effort to scale "the cliff" is the theory that the higher the level of technology utilized by a civilization, the greater the amount of social conformity required within that civilization. In other words, an inverse relationship seems to exist between technological sophistication and the freedom of a person to be "deviant" (behave differently than the norm). For example, in a hunting society, a substantial percentage of a tribe can choose to dissociate itself and form a new tribe with different mores without endangering the technological base of the civilization. In agricultural societies, a much smaller percentage of dissidents can be tolerated. Fields and irrigation ditches are vulnerable enough to disruption that social unrest must be strictly controlled or a famine could be brought about by the actions of a minority (hence, feudal society.) In addition, private ownership of the vital technical resources (land and water rights) precludes solving disputes via creation of a separate, deviant society.

Industrial societies have an even more severe limit on the percentage of deviants needed to threaten the technological base. Disruption of its transportation system or power grids will shut down almost any industry. A single worker can sabotage a manufacturing plant so thoroughly in five minutes that the damage will take months to repair.

Furthermore, the stability of industrial economies requires predictable consumer buying patterns that must be maintained if the society is to survive.

Our incipient postindustrial society can tolerate still less deviance; a single person trained in the arts of modern warfare can ravage a city with nuclear or biochemical weapons. The employees at one key plant can, by refusing to work, force an entire industry (such as the automotive industry) to capitulate or risk plunging the economy into a depression. One person can shut off a valve in a major natural gas line, and heat will be lost in thousands of homes for days while each and every pilot light is relit by gas company employees so the gas can be turned back on. Our seamless web of national and international services and industries is completely vulnerable to a single break in a single strand of commerce. Small wonder that such emphasis is placed on adherence to certain types of conformity; small wonder that even a small group of terrorists is greatly feared.

If we attempt to climb "the cliff" with technology, opponents of our present policy argue, even greater suppression of deviance will be required, especially during the crucial period while the "quantum leap" to a high technology is taking place. This vulnerability to deviance is likely either to result in a collapse brought about by terrorism, or to necessitate a "friendly fascism" so profound that our emergence at the top of the cliff will hardly presage entrance to a Garden of Eden (Harman, 1974, p. 220). Hence, those who favor a change in technological policy see a technological attack on "the cliff" as a dead end.

A second argument advanced against the "tiger-by-the-tail" concept of technological expansion is the idea that a multiplicity of low-probability "disaster" futures can add up to a high-risk situation. For example, suppose that 400 future branches on the "tree" are technological disasters—destruction of the ozone layer, ignition of the earth's atmosphere by fusion, accidental release of a recombinant strain of deadly bacteria, triggering a "greenhouse effect" by increasing the percentage of carbon dioxide in the atmosphere, pollution of the oceans until the oxygen-producing plant life dies, and so forth. Each of these particular future branches may have a very low probability, say one chance in a thousand (although our estimating skills are not precise and a best guess as to the chances of each of the examples listed above is between one in a hundred and one in a million). Four hundred future catastrophes, each with a probability of one in a thousand—or forty with a chance of one in a hundred, or ten with a chance of one in twenty-five (e.g., total nuclear war)—add up to a 40 percent overall chance of a highly undesirable future. The low-probability branches that technology adds to the "tree" can cumulatively be deadly.

Proponents of technology maintain that this argument is fallacious because scientists can anticipate when their work is becoming dangerous and then can observe the precautions necessary to avoid a catastrophe. Certainly, for example, steps have been taken to reduce the likelihood of damage to the ozone layer long before the damage would have become dangerous in the absence of controls. The majority of case studies, however, support the opponents of present technological policy who argue that our safeguards are inadequate.

Primack and von Hippel, in *Advice and Dissent* (1974), document instance after instance in which a technological threat has been ignored both by its scientific perpetrators and by the government agencies charged with monitoring the safety of new scientific advances. Recent instances include the suppression of information about the possible teratogenic consequences of exposure to certain defoliants (notably "2, 4, 5-T"), the FDA refusal to reclassify cyclamates despite evidence that these substances are no longer "Generally Recognized As Safe," the withholding of knowledge on the Army's transport plans for the obsolete nerve gases stored in the Denver Arsenal, and the Atomic Energy Commission coverup of concerns about nuclear reactor safety. So far, we have been fortunate that no catastrophe has engulfed the entire society, although the losses to individuals have been quite high. These case studies provide a warning of how inadequate our safeguards are to protect against the dangerous consequences of an unforeseen side-effect in a pervasively used technology.

A similar concern expressed by those who favor revising our attitude toward technology is that eventually our society may develop a set of technologies that produce *retrogressive* change. That development of a few key technologies may completely alter a civilization for the better is a familiar theme; the agricultural and industrial revolutions are examples. Mutations, however, are not always for the better; in fact, 90 percent of all mutations are lethal. Similarly a technology that strikes at the weak points of a civilization might result in profound short-term retrogressive change, followed by stagnation after the science necessary to maintain the "lethal" technology has been lost.

Several historical examples exist of technologies that caused societal retrogression. For instance, Lauriston Sharp (1954) documents an Australian tribe in which as seemingly innocuous a change as the substitution of steel axes for stone axes caused a rapid and irreversible deterioration of the entire culture. The notion that an "advanced" technology can adversely affect a "primitive" people is not new, but how far beyond the primitive we have come and whether we are not now capable of developing a technology too advanced for our own good are matters certainly open to question.

Such a destructive technology might well not appear dangerous at first; in fact, a potential "steel ax" may initially seem beneficial. We have not yet developed sufficient skill in technological assessment to predict accurately what the secondary and tertiary effects of a technology will be. When the automobile was introduced, for example, it was primarily envisioned as a more efficient, less expensive, and less polluting form of transportation. Who then foresaw the tertiary effects of changes in sexual mores produced by the availability of a "portable bedroom," or the problems of decay of the central cities as a result of the city/suburb urban pattern made possible (perhaps inevitable) by automotive technology, or the development by automobile manufacturers of economically destabilizing vertical monopolies untouchable under current antitrust laws?

Similarly, one can hypothesize new technologies that our society would likely embrace with open arms and yet might well result in severe retrogressive change (just as some conceive the legalization of heroin might do). For example, imagine a drug to improve memory that, when taken, allows future voluntary total recall on all senses of the events that took place during the four hours while the drug was active. On close inspection, this seemingly beneficial technology has a host of dangerous secondary and tertiary effects associated with it which could well act as a "steel ax" for society. (The proof is left as an exercise in technology assessment for the reader.)

Overall, then, the opponents of our present technological policy have advanced a series of arguments that illustrate how dangerous a technological assault on "the cliff" might be. The proponents of technology, on the other hand, point to the "tiger" we have by the tail and ask what alternative strategy would be less risky. Thus, the outcome of the cleavage concepts presented thus far is to paint a picture of a present torn by crisis, with the proven problem-solving method containing many risks and no alternative method readily discernible.

In the past several years, some evidence has accumulated that a well-articulated alternative approach to technological policy is slowly being developed, piecemeal, by researchers in various parts of the world. This new approach, which combines technological and social invention, would in theory offer a chance of solving the problems discussed above. While the strands of this new paradigm are not yet sufficiently developed to allow presentation of a definite model, the directions of research which to date appear most fruitful can be elaborated.

One such direction is the notion of a "superrationality" that Pirsig discusses in *Zen and the Art of Motorcycle Maintenance*. One of the disturbing cultural blind spots we have developed is that we use the words "rational" and "logical" as if they meant "correct." In fact, a rational and logical decision may very well be wrong; logic and rationality are simply tools used to deduce consequences from an initial set of assumptions. If these initial assumptions are true, then the rational decision is likely to be correct; however, if the initial assumptions are false, then a rational decision is almost certain to be wrong. An arational, intuitive strategy may well be more effective in any situation in which the assumptions being made are highly uncertain; yet, we worship rationality and cling to logical decision-making processes, regardless of the actual circumstances. In fact, we do not comprehend how the concept of "rationality" functions in relation to paradigmatic assumptions. (Space prohibits further elaboration of this topic; the interested reader may wish to consult Lakatos and Musgrave [1970] for further discussion.)

This false emphasis on the preeminence of rationality leads to the "irrational logic" of situations such as the arms race. Many individual decisions to develop new weaponry are ultimately rational, based on the perceived intentions and capabilities of the opponent. Cumulatively, however, these decisions lead to a disastrous spiral in which the equivalent of 100 tons of TNT per person on the globe is deemed an insufficient retaliatory force. Discrete rational decisions breed an aggregate irrational policy, either because of inaccuracies in the overall assumptions being used or because of some fundamental, as yet undiscovered, flaw in the nature of logic itself.

The "Prisoner's Dilemma" from game theory provides an analogous, less complex situation (Rapaport, 1971). Two opponents can, by cooperating, each achieve a positive outcome. Rationally, however, the strategy of inducing the other to cooperate, then backstabbing to accumulate a relative advantage, seems best. However, if both opponents pursue this "best" strategy (as rationally both should), then each accumulates an increasingly negative outcome. The "Dilemma" has been solved mathematically by the development of a "superrationality," in which a different type of reasoning is used to argue for the cooperative strategy from an alternate set of initial assumptions.

Similarly, if we could substitute a superrational approach for our present purely rational technological policy, we could avoid "irrational logic" spirals and conceivably solve some of our current crises. This superrational approach would definitely require a paradigm shift, as science is intensely rational. In addition, superrationality potentially involves combining ethical considerations with pragmatic assumptions in decision-making. Harman (1974), Ferkiss (1974), and Brown (1972) have each suggested possible strategies for such a synthesis.

Pirsig discusses this need for the inclusion of ethics with superrationality in his description of "quality," a hypothesized shared "sixth sense" which acts as the source of values (1974, p. 182). The debate in futures research on the future of technology has centered on pragmatic considerations rather than "quality"; the "tiger," the "cliff," the "steel ax," and the "uniqueness of the present" are all concepts that illumine our chances for survival, but do not discuss the nature of "the good." Obviously, survival is essential to attain "the good," but Pirsig provides a different framework in emphasizing values, for what is "best" becomes the central issue and survival is then defined within that context. For example, Meadows, despite his opposition to present technological policy, basically shares the same value base as Kahn and Bell; he agrees that a high technology world would be wonderful, disagreeing only on whether we will survive to reach that future if our present policy continues. Pirsig, on the other hand, questions whether we want a high technology world, and thus he changes the perceived problem from "how do we safely climb the cliff?" to "should we walk in a different direction and avoid the cliff altogether?"

This shift in perspective is far more profound than "solving" a problem by substituting a different problem. Pirsig's approach corresponds more to the metaperspective used in formulating a new type of reasoning for the "Prisoner's Dilemma." Harman's concept of "friendly fascism" provides a way of illustrating this point; "friendly fascism" might well work in solving all our crises, yet when we see this future depicted (1974, p. 220), we realize that this whole class of solutions results from a faulty definition of the original problem.

These ideas suggest that we may be in a position analogous to that of the person who has built a career around perceived goals of accumulating power, respect, and wealth, only to find after succeeding that these were all actually means to attaining the true goal of affection—which in fact has not been reached, since power, wealth, and respect are isolating factors. Our ultimate goal is not technological power to affect ourselves and the environment, or even affluence, but happiness (c.f. Aristotle). To reformulate the question in these terms undercuts many of the arguments used to justify technological expansionism.

Roszak, in *Where the Wasteland Ends,* carries this approach one step further: if trees, once seen as the residence of gods, are now perceived as mere accumulations of atoms locked in a mechanistic mode of growth and decay, how long will it be before other people (and ourselves) are perceived in an equally reductionist framework—and then where is our purpose for life? "Idolatry" is the substitution of worship of an inanimate object for worship of God; has rationality led us to an idolatry so profound that all that now exists are inanimate objects activated by the laws of physics? If rationality ultimately leads to dehumanization and meaninglessness—which are antithetical to happiness—then some perspective transcending rationality is needed.

Ethical considerations cannot be easily combined with pragmatic assumptions, as those who have attempted to define social indicators have learned. Thus, the development of a superrationality will not be an easy task—but then no scientific revolution is. As with all paradigm shifts, the end product will build on what has previously been successful; superrationality will contain all the elements of rationality and logic and use them where appropriate. Logic will be a subunit of super-rationality, just as Newtonian physics is a subunit of Einstein's Theory of Relativity (Kuhn, 1970, p. 144ff.) The successful parts of present technology policy will be retained, but will be seen as limited tools to be applied within a larger framework based on a new value system. Ferkiss (1974) presents one such rough model, and Schumacher (1973) another.

A second strand within the new paradigm deals with strategies for containing the psychological damage caused by the responsibility often concomitant with technological innovation. For example, in the past, people with total kidney failure would invariably die; no conceivable treatment existed, and no ethical problems or responsibilities were involved. Now, many hospitals have "God committees" to decide which few of the many kidney patients in residence will be allowed life through treatment on the dialysis machines. The ethical responsibilities and psychological burdens of choice are staggering, as McFaul discusses in his chapter in this Handbook; science has removed an evil (involuntary death) but has substituted a major moral dilemma.

This Faustian problem recurs repeatedly in the history of technology; an innovation gives more control over an undesirable situation, but only at the cost of extreme personal and social stress. The psychological pressures involved are similar to those discussed in Toffler's *Future Shock* but are far more fundamental. As Toffler's critics have observed, the decisions consumers face in choosing among thirty-seven varieties of bread are hardly staggering when all types taste like whipped plastic. The decisions a "God committee" must make *are* staggering and create the "work-a-few-years-and-then-burn-out" career styles seen in many of the emerging human service professions.

Any attempt to define a nontechnological approach to issues such as "the cliff" involves enormous ethical decisions which will result in great psychological stress. To ignore these moral choices or to make them in a dehumanized manner would be disastrous, but to cope with the responsibilities inherent in arguing that we should "let go of the tiger's tail," those involved will need some set of psychological tools (perhaps similar to those utilized by successful therapists) to protect their sanity. The occupational hazard of technological reform is otherwise likely to be suicide.

A third strand that may become a part of this new model for controlling technology centers on the concept that our democracy may gradually be slipping into a technocracy, a governing system run by specialists in technology which increasingly is accountable only to its own "experts." The 100-year trends discussed earlier have created a nation so large and technologically complex as to seemingly require a host of bureaucrats advised by myriads of scientists on how to keep our productivity at a high level. The decisions now routinely made on science policy seem too complicated for even an intelligent and well-informed layperson to understand—the SST, the B1 bomber, the ABM, auto emissions standards deadlines, the relative safety of food additives, recombinant DNA research, public health and pesticides, and so on. Often, the public is not resolving these issues directly in its collective mind but is electing whoever promises most plausibly that his experts understand these issues and will make the correct decisions.

Few of us genuinely wish to be governed by "experts"; we want to retain a feeling of control over our lives and to understand what risks we are taking in pursuit of our goals. However, the amount of technical sophistication required to understand the current science policy issues is very great, and the reading and thought necessary would consume more time than most of us have available. The educational system, no matter how well constructed, can no longer convey the knowledge one needs to be an intelligent citizen for the fifty-odd years of voting he has after graduation.

The solutions proposed to keep at least a flavor of democracy in our increasingly technocratic society vary greatly in terms of the amount of change required from the present status quo. On one end of the continuum, antitechnologists such as Roszak have argued that the entire industrial base of society should be simplified to the point that the average citizen can again completely understand the working of government. At the opposite extreme, proponents of technology such as Primack and von Hippel feel that nothing more major than a shift in the responsibilities of the scientific advisory system from subservience to bureaucrats to accountability to the public interest is required.

Neither extreme position seems very satisfactory. We are too dependent on technology for the production of necessities for Roszak's simplified economic base to seem attractive, and the very case studies Primack and von Hippel cite in arguing for their position make their proposal look unrealistic—no matter how responsive and trustworthy public interest scientists may attempt to be, they still will be cast in the position of an elite whom the masses follow by faith alone. Some of the middle-ground solutions proposed are more promising, however, and may contain the social inventions required for a new paradigm.

For example, Etzioni (1973) discusses institutionalizing a series of Health-Ethics Commissions to formulate policy on new technologies in the biomedical sciences. (The recently formed HEW Human Subjects Committee is one step in this direction.) These commissions would be staffed largely by intelligent laypersons representative of the constellation of values within American society. The function of the commissions would be technology assessment, with the power to requisition any specialized advice deemed necessary, followed by internal determination via democratic processes of whether the proposed new technology would be, on balance, more beneficial than harmful. On reaching this decision, the commission would release its findings as a policy recommendation to the existing legislative system. This microcosm-of-democracy approach is not likely to solve the problem of cur drift into technocracy, but its relative successes and failures may provide clues as to the next type of social invention to try.

As another possibility, Ferkiss (1974) postulates an "ecological humanism" emerging in society which would redefine the relationships between science and government. This new philosophic perspective would be based on the convictions that man "must live in a conscious ecological relationship with nature and other men, and that the ecological perspective on the natural order provides a necessary analogue for the social order" (Ferkiss, 1974, p. 206). The emergence of this new approach is seen as arising out of a radical transformation of social structures brought about by highly educated persons within technological society itself.

A third alternative seems to be developing from recent work in biomedicine. Brody (1976) discusses a systematic way of applying a consequentialist approach to ethics in making medical decisions when an ethical dilemma exists. Several of his strategies apply in situations characterized by incomplete information and might be adapted to resolving some of our parallel societal predicaments. Such a cognitive approach, when coupled with the ethical assumptions discussed by McFaul in his article, might provide the basis of a new scientific/legislature paradigm.

All of these nontechnocratic models seem promising. The ultimate manner in which these strands of research in progress may be components of a new paradigm can be glimpsed. The Health-Ethics Commission (or its equivalent) will utilize superrationality as a tool for evolving policy while minimizing the psychological strains involved with advanced affective techniques similar to those that protect therapists. Whether the final model which emerges will resemble this rough description is questionable, but these isolated types of research do give promise of eventually combining into some form of concrete alternative to present technological policy. Compiled with a common societal ethical base (such as that hypothesized by Harman in *Changing Images of Man*), these ideas could constitute a wave of social innovation that would control our technological advances of the past century.

Whether such a set of social inventions, once defined, would be implemented as an alternative to present technological policy is problematic. History documents that a new approach to societal problem-solving is only implemented when the previous method has drastically and publicly failed. The difficulty we face is that a collapse of present technology would leave no option of implementing an alternative policy; rather, we would be faced with the task of rebuilding civilization from the ashes. Unlike previous crises, the unique danger of our present situation is that we must make the correct choice not at the moment of crisis, but far in advance. Human nature being what it is, a decision made in advance of crisis is apt to be to choose the status quo, no matter how theoretically convincing the arguments for an alternate course of action.

This choice between predominantly technological or predominantly social inventions to control science may well be the single most crucial decision within our lifetimes. The "tree," the uniqueness of the present, the "tiger-by-the-tail," the "cliff," "disaster" futures, "friendly fascism," the "steel ax," "superrationality," the microcosm-of-democracy, and ethical overchoice stresses are all metaphorical attempts to understand a situation ultimately too complex for any single person to grasp completely. Science has mastered phenomena which exemplify "organized simplicity"; given billiard balls on a pool table, we can predict their movements with total accuracy. We also have conquered "unorganized complexity"; the movements of individual molecules in an enclosed gas may be too complex for prediction, but the statistical behavior of the aggregate gas can readily be analyzed and controlled. But phenomena illustrating "organized complexity" still elude our theoretical tools; scientists are still baffled by the hydrodynamics of liquids, let along the far more changeable dynamics of a complex post-industrial society.

The work we do in futures research to reduce this uncertainty—to define more accurately our future options with regard to technology and to assess what decisions we should be making now—may well be the most vital intellectual endeavor now occurring in any area of knowledge. For better or for worse, our achievements have given us the Faustian responsibility. As the ancient Chinese curse goes, "May you live in exciting times."

## REFERENCES

Bell, Daniel. 1973. *The Coming of Post-Industrial Society.* New York: Basic Books.

Bowman, Jim, and John Pulliam 1974. *Educational Futurism.* Norman: University of Oklahoma Press.

Brody, Howard. 1976. *Ethical Decisions in Medicine.* Boston: Little, Brown and Co.

Brown, Lester. 1972. *World Without Borders.* New York: Random House.

Dede, Christopher. 1973. "Futuristics and the Structure of Knowledge." *Massachusetts Educational Forum,* Volume 1, Number 1 (April), p. 3–5.

Etzioni, Amitai. 1973. *Genetic Fix.* New York: Macmillan Co.

Ferkiss, Victor. 1974. *The Future of Technological Civilization.* New York: George Braziller.

Fowles, Jib. 1976. "Hands Off the Future." *World Future Society Bulletin,* Volume 10, Number 4 (July/Autust), 7–11.

Fuller, Buckminster. 1969. *Operating Manual for Spaceship Earth.* Carbondale, Ill.: Southern Illinois University Press.

Harman, Willis, et al. 1974. *Changing Images of Man.* Menlo Park, Calif.: Stanford Research Institute.

Kahn, Herman, and B. Bruce-Briggs. 1972. *Things to Come.* New York: Macmillan Co.

Kuhn, Thomas. 1970. *The Structure of Scientific Revolutions.* Chicago: University of Chicago Press.

Lakatos, Imre, and Alan Musgrave (eds.). 1970. *Criticism and the Growth of Knowledge.* Cambridge: Cambridge University Press.

Meadows, Donella, Dennis Meadows, et al. 1972. *The Limits to Growth.* New York: Universe Books.

Mesarovic, Mihajlo, and Eduard Pestel. 1974. *Mankind at the Turning Point.* New York: E. P. Dutton.

Mumford, Lewis. 1967. *Technics and Human Development.* New York: Harcourt Brace Jovanovich.

Pirsig, Robert. 1974. *Zen and the Art of Motorcycle Maintenance.* New York: Bantam Books.

Platt, John. 1969. "What We Must Do." *Science,* Volume 166 (November 28), 1115–1121.

Primack, Joel, and Frank von Hippel. 1974. *Advice and Dissent.* New York: Basic Books.

Rapaport, Anatol. 1971. "Escape from Paradox." *Scientific American,* Volume 225, Number 4 (October), 30–56.

Schumacher, E. F. 1973. *Small Is Beautiful: Economics as If People Mattered* New York: Harper and Row.

Sharp, Lauriston. 1954. "Steel Axes for Stone Age Australians." *Human Problems in Technological Change.* In E. Spicer (ed.), New York: Russell Sage Foundation.

Theobald, Robert. 1972. *Habit and Habitat.* Englewood Cliffs, N.J.: Prentice-Hall.

WILLIAM L. RENFRO
and MARVIN KORNBLUH

# Futures in the Political Process

*The sense of the future is behind*
*all good politics. Unless we have*
*it, we can give nothing either wise*
*or decent to the world.*
  *C. P. Snow*

From the basic concepts expressed in the U.S. Constitution 200 years ago to the growing interest in political futurism today, our political institutions have been based on a process that looks to the future. The Preamble to our Constitution sets out our goals and outlines a planning process for achieving them. The Constitution itself is a bold statement about the future. Our evolving political and governmental institutions are implicitly both an expression of these stated goals and the embodiment of the process for achieving them. However, the new interest and activities of futurism in the political process suggest that the process of looking to the future should be made more explicit and systematic.

This need for political futurism has grown from many diverse sources. The increased importance of technological and social forecasting have encouraged the use and development of forecasting in political and governmental processes. The value of forecasting and futurism was demonstrated by such early applications as the transition from a wartime to peacetime economy, including the GI Bill of Rights conceived by President Roosevelt's National Planning Board and the work of the RAND Corporation in the defense area. Later, as large businesses and entire industries began to use forecasting and futures research, the concepts gained additional credibility and acceptance, setting the stage for futurism in the political process.

The continuing economic growth following World War II produced an economy whose size alone became a problem. At $1.5 trillion, the economy and its social institutions have a momentum that both seeks its own course in the immediate future and requires longer range forecasting and policy planning. The time required by the political process to develop new policies and respond effectively to problems seems unduly long compared with the time required for new problems to arise—such as foreign energy dependence, stagflation, and environmental pollution. It may take four to six years to build the national consensus so vital to Congress in developing major new policies. While it seems impossible to shorten this response time, Congress is developing new procedural rules and new resources to identify problems sooner and to gain insight into potential future problems through forecasting and futures research. With the development and implementation of these rules and the use of new resources outlined here, Congress is becoming active in using and developing political futurism. As citizens develop a new role in identifying long-term goals, the roles of our political institutions are changing. Congress is exploring ways and means to increase the participation of its constituents in shaping the future. While the many congressional developments serve as examples of new rules, roles, and resources in political futurism, equally significant are future developments evolving in other branches and levels of government.

## RULES

The need for an early identification of problems having strong political overtones is obvious; problems that require years to resolve need to be anticipated years in advance. Congress recognized this need in the early 1970s and began to explore how it could improve its ability to identify potential problems and issues well before they reached the crisis stage.

In 1973, the House of Representatives established a Select Committee which invited prominent futurists to suggest possible changes (U.S. House of Representatives, 1973). Though many ideas on how to speed up the legislative process became available, the Select Committee found them all to have drawbacks. However, the essential idea of an early warning system that would allow the process to start sooner was accepted. Hopefully, if this first step could be expedited, then so could the many subsequent steps, including defining and understanding the problem; deciding what kind of action is needed; developing and evaluating legislative proposals; considering the interests of all those potentially affected by legislation; coordinating policy development with the president; resolving differences between House and Senate proposals; and overseeing the implementation of the legislation.

Since the House uses its committees in undertaking most of the early steps in the legislative process, the Select Committee on Committees recommended that the House amend its rules and assign the task of looking to the future to its committees. Known as the House foresight provision, this amendment to the House rules of procedure assigns three responsibilities to each of the twenty-two committees (except for Budget and Appropriations, which has its own foresight activities):

First, ". . . , each (standing committee other than Budget and Appropriations) shall review and study any conditions or circumstances which may indicate the necessity or desirability of enacting new or additional legislation within the jurisdiction of that committee (whether or not any bill or resolution has been introduced with respect thereto), . . ."

second, ". . . , and shall on a continuing basis undertake futures research and forecasting on matters within the jurisdiction of that committee."

and third, "Each standing committee of the House shall have the function of reviewing and studying on a continuing basis the impact or probable impact of tax policies affecting subjects within its jurisdiction . . ." (Brown, 1976).

The House foresight provision was adopted along with other recommendations on October 8, 1974. In presenting its recommendations, the Select Committee elaborated on the foresight provision:

The recommendation of the select committee also includes a "foresight" responsibility for each standing committee, which will probably be assigned to the oversight subcommittees. That is, these legislative units would have the additional responsibility of identifying and assessing conditions and trends that might require future legislative action. More specifically, this would provide a locus for the systematic, long-range, and integrated study of our principal future national problems. Such studies would include forecasting so that, to some degree, relevant circumstances could be foreseen and the relevant decisions anticipated. They would also make probabilistic estimates that certain events would occur by certain times or within specified time periods. In addition, by means of futures research, future options and times could be identified; and the costs, benefits, and effects of the various options, including present programs, could be assessed and compared.

In this way, it is hoped, the House may become more responsive to national needs, anticipating problems before they become crises.

The proposed "foresight" function should provide a better basis for substantive legislation as well as oversight. It should also assist in setting national priorities and making budget allocations (U.S. House of Representatives, 1974).

In addition to early warning, this language suggests two other aspects of foresight: first, the use of futures research and forecasting in drafting and developing legislation on issues and problems already identified and presented to the committee and the House; and second, the listing of the assumptions used in developing the legislation and the expected effect of the legislation. This information might be useful in the future to guide the implementation of the legislation along the lines intended (Renfro, 1977).

The House committees are working to implement the foresight rules. The House Committee on International Relations, for example, established the first foresight subcommittee specifically charged with meeting the committee's foresight responsibilities. Others have used the new futures resources outlined below. Congressman Charles Rose has suggested that committees hold "foresight" hearings as part of implementing the foresight rules. Even though the foresight rules are still evolving, the commitment of the House to change its procedures may, if successful, represent a major development in political futurism.

The Senate has also been considering a change in its procedural rules. An expanded role for forecasting and futures research has been recommended to the Seante by the Commission on the Operation of the Senate. In its final report, the commission recommended that the Senate:

Establish in or through the majority and minority policy committees responsibility for foresight—early identification and analysis of major policy problems. These committees should:

   —Stimulate inquiry by appropriate standing committees of emerging problems before they become matters of public concern and hasty legislative action.
   —Insure that legislation coming to the floor is accompanied by sufficient analysis to illuminate all relevant considerations (U.S. Senate, 1975).

The recommendations are supported by the work of a special committee Congress created to study the policy-making process. In *Forging America's Future,* the Advisory Committee on National Growth Policy Processes reported its recommendations to the National Commission on Supplies and Shortages on December 22, 1976. The Advisory Committee recommended that:

Congress take steps to improve its ability to react to cross-cutting and longer-range problems which cannot be easily dealt with by the present narrowly organized Congressional structure.
The Congressional committee report accompanying each bill includes an outline of the bill's foreseeable indirect and middle-to-long-range effects, as well as a concise statement of the general goals and specific objectives to which the bill is directed (U.S. Senate, 1976).

These recommendations are now being studied by several senators, and proposals to incorporate them in the rules of Senate procedure may be introduced during the 95th Congress.

In addition to these specific rules focusing on foresight and futurism in the political process, Congress has adopted other procedural rules that require its committees to study the future. The House and Senate adopted the Legislative Reorganization Act of 1970 which, among other things, requires that the reports accompanying each proposed piece of legislation reported to the floor of the House and Senate contain estimates or forecasts of the expected costs of the legislation for the next five fiscal years (in Legislative Reorganization Act of 1970, as Amended, Section 252 [a] [1]). The House has expanded this responsibility, requiring its committees to report on the likely inflationary impact of all legislation reported to the floor. The number of rules and proposals for additional rules indicates the Congressional interest in and commitment to futurism in the political process.

The concepts of futurism have continued to grow in the executive and judicial branches. Many of the executive departments and agencies have formal forecasting and long-range planning functions such as those in the Departments of Agriculture, Commerce, Defense, and Interior (Comptroller General of the United States, 1976). A broad range of futures research has been sponsored by other government agencies such as the Environmental Protection Agency, the National Science Foundation, and National Institute of Mental Health. These efforts are supported by the many monitoring and forecasting activities of groups such as the Bureau of Labor Statistics, Federal Reserve Board, and Bureau of the Census. President Carter has promised that he "will press every government agency to pursue futures research and technology assessment to help them make wiser decisions" (Hitchcock, 1976, p. 2). In the judiciary, Chief Justice Burger has called for "systematic anticipation" to guide the evolution of "the basically sound mechanisms of our system of laws to new conditions" (Burger, 1976).

At the state level, political futurism is manifested by the new role of citizen participation in establishing goals. In over a third of the states, these projects have been used to identify long-range goals, priorities, and outlines of the future of the state (Bea and Huston, 1976). Typical of these was the Goals for Georgia Project that Jimmy Carter launched as governor. After a year-long effort to identify goals and alternative responses using citizen hearings across the state, the governor organized the Office of Planning and Budget to guide implementation (Congressional Clearinghouse on the Future, 1977, p. 1). Perhaps the most advanced exercise in state political futurism is Minnesota's Horizons project. For the new General Assembly in 1975, over the course of three days Minnesota Horizons presented a detailed image of the future of the state, its population, labor force, economy, resources, and so on. These presentations were broadcast live over the public radio network and were summarized for evening TV broadcast on public television. This program is being repeated for the 1977 General Assembly (Minnesota State Legislature, 1975). Some states have organized regional projects such as the Southern Growth Policies Board, located in Research Triangle Park, North Carolina. Some metropolitan areas and large cities have goal-oriented projects such as Atlanta 2000.

These wide-ranging developments—from the new House rules, to technology assessment, to citizen participation projects—are all aspects of political futurism. Though by no means complete, the evolution of these rules, methods, and developments is beginning to suggest new roles for our political institutions.

## ROLES

A central aspect of political futurism is identifying and defining long-range goals. In spite of its importance, the goals process remains largely undefined and unstructured. While there is often broad consensus on the general nature of our national goals, these too appear to be largely unarticulated and vague. Nevertheless, differing concepts of our national goals often lie behind issues of public policy. One of the methods of addressing national goals is the public election and campaign process. This process of looking into the future involves complex interactions and communications between citizens, public institutions (social, business-economic, academic, and the like), and the political institutions. The growing complexity of the election process in identifying goals has encouraged the search for new roles for existing institutions as well as for entirely new institutions.

Some of the problems of identifying goals can be seen in the process of electing a president. The 1976 campaign involved many major substantive issues relating to our national goals. While most of the candidates struggled to articulate the issues and their positions, only on rare occasions did they explicitly interrelate these issues with each other or with national goals. The subject of goals, however, was implicit in much of the political debate.

As communications resources expand, the candidates are able to communicate directly *to* the voter more information and detail on more issues with more complex positions. Unfortunately, the voters are increasingly finding themselves flooded with incoming information. The candidates, of course, do gather communications *from* the voters through polls; however, these are indirect communications from sample voters amounting to less than 1 percent of all voters. The only direct communication from the voting citizen is the ballot. With this instrument that can carry only one bit of information in the presidential election—"for Candidate X"—the voter communicates back *to* the candidates, and ultimately the government, his opinions on the issues and, implicitly, on national goals. A voter's opinions on nuclear power, national health insurance, busing, unemployment, defense spending, abortion, energy dependence, detente, amnesty, and all the other issues and implied statements of goals are reduced to "for Candidate X" (for expansion, see Wills, 1970, pp. 499–575; and Pateman, 1970, pp. 1–44). Efforts to increase the information carried by the ballot have not been of much success. The idea of public referenda through the ballot seems to be able to work effectively only for one or two major issues at a time. Ballots that include a half-dozen or more detailed propositions are too often confusing to the voter, especially where there has not been sufficient public discussion. This leaves most voters without an effective means of communicating their opinions to the candidates and their government.

The communication dilemma of the voter is the information problem for the successful candidate who may not know which of his positions, policies, objectives, and implied goals the voters support—beyond those few which dominated the campaign. Recognizing the limits of the representative process and the responsibility of those elected to use their judgment in representing the citizens, a movement seems to be developing to expand and increase citizen participation in the political process, particularly in policy-making at the highest level—determining national goals.

Citizens have been participating in the political process but at a different level. Citizen participation in the civil rights, antiwar, environmental, and other movements has demonstrated the interests and effectiveness of citizens in defining and shaping national goals. These citizen participation efforts have worked from the bottom up, attacking already established policies and goals at their lowest operating level— the segregated lunch counter, the draft card, the polluting facility, and so forth. From this participation by veto, citizen participation is evolving a new role that seeks not only to resolve problems and other undesirable developments, but also to search out opportunities for positive goals that might not otherwise be realized.

This new role for the citizen in the goal-establishing process can evolve through traditional political institutions. Several members of Congress are now using citizen questionnaires designed to solicit the opinions of their constituents on the future and what they would like to see develop—their goals. The citizen hearings used in the Goals for Georgia Project provided an important input in developing goals and planning programs to achieve them (State of Georgia, no date). In December 1976, Jimmy Carter asked the people to write him and suggest how they thought they could better participate in government.

Within a month, more than 10,000 responses had been received. This call for suggestions matches Carter's pledge in October to seek greater citizen participation in the decision-making process (Hitchcock, 1976).

As citizen participation in defining goals expands, citizens will play a more direct role in shaping their future. This tends to provide Congress with a new role as it becomes the center for these activities. As Congress addresses more clearly articulated citizen goals, it inevitably will find conflicts, difficult trade-offs, and unexpected side-effects and interconnections. Before communicating these problems to the citizens, it will need to know as much as possible about alternative futures and the options available for achieving them. In fact, the development and effective communication of these alternative futures can serve as a conflict resolution mechanism. For example, where environmental goals conflict with energy goals, Congress can use forecasts of energy needs and technologies to guide it and the citizens in developing an optimal path for the future. While this is no panacea, Congress's role in the use of futures information may serve as a less adversary mechanism, increasing the involvement and understanding of citizens and diverse groups in the policy-making processes. A key element of this process is efficiently organizing and applying information resources concerning the future.

## RESOURCES

The process of shaping the future through the political process involves several major steps. It begins at the broadest level with the question, where is the nation now? This is the basic process of monitoring key descriptors, indicators, and measures of the status quo. The importance of this monitoring was recognized by the framers of the Constitution who built in several aspects of this process: the complete census to be taken every ten years; and the report to Congress by the president on the State of the Union. Naturally, today we need much more information and have many resources to provide it.

In addition to knowing where the nation is, we need to know where it is going. This is the basic task of forecasting likely developments or the expected future. This forecasting task involves futures research, technology assessments, an early warning system, the development of models, analysis of the expected impact of current policies and programs in a changing world, and all of the associated supporting activities.

Through the political process, Congress, the president, the courts, and other levels of government integrate the assessment of where we are and where we are going with ideas about our goals as expressed by citizens—the "where do we want to be?" question. This integration is not a passive process. The idealism of our goals must be tempered by the realism of where we are and where we are likely to be. In developing policies, programs, and plans, government needs a wide range of organizational and informational resources.

One of these resources is the Office of Technology Assessment (OTA) which works for and reports only to Congress. The basic function of OTA as specified in the Technology Assessment Act of 1972 is "to provide early indications of the probable beneficial and adverse impacts of the applications of technology and to develop other coordinate information which may assist the Congress."

In carrying out this function, OTA has conducted assessments on a broad range of issues, identifying policy options, evaluating alternative programs, and comparing the effects of alternative technologies or technological programs (Office of Technology Assessment, 1976).

Another resource available to Congress is the General Accounting Office (GAO). In a role which has evolved from accounting to program evaluation, GAO is beginning to evaluate legislative programs before they are enacted. These anticipatory evaluations are designed to help Congress understand the expected or likely consequences of alternative legislative proposals before they become law. One of the major evaluations now under way is focused on forecasting the likely impact of five key national health insurance proposals.

To facilitate the use and distribution of information and other resources about the future, ten members of Congress formed the Congressional Clearinghouse on the Future in the spring of 1976. The Clearinghouse has sponsored a number of seminars and programs for members and prominent futurists. The news of developments in political futurism is presented in the Clearinghouse newsletter, *What's Next?* which is published periodically and distributed to senators, members, and committee staffs.

The goals of the Clearinghouse are:

First, to assist Members as they become aware of the ways in which the future is affected by today's decisions.

Second, to help committee members implement the foresight provision by holding foresight hearings as well as oversight hearings by identifying witnesses, suggesting questions, helping to organize meetings.

Third, help Members foresee the impact of legislation on State and local governments so that legislation will have foresight.

Fourth, let Members know what citizens groups are eager to work in the planning process of government and give Members new methods of citizen involvement to use with their constituents (Bedell, 1976).

Congressman Bedell outlined the plans of the Clearinghouse, which include:

bimonthly seminars, presentations to delegation meetings about State and local citizen activity, and addresses by distinguished guests on issues related to the future of the country and the world. An index of futures-related information found in the Record will be added to our monthly newsletter as well (Bedell, 1976).

The Clearinghouse on the Future has become an important component of Congress's resources for information on the future.

At the Library of Congress, the Congressional Research Service (CRS) was developed from its predecessor, the Legislative Reference Service. CRS has the general responsibility of analyzing, appraising, and evaluating legislative proposals and estimating the probable results of these proposals and their alternatives (Legislative Reorganization Act of 1970). To meet its broad responsibility of serving the Congress, CRS established the Futures Research Group which works with other CRS groups in helping the committees meet their foresight responsibilities. From its beginning in January 1975, this group has offered three new services to Congress: first, futures research and analysis in response to requests from members, committees, and their staffs; second, seminars, workshops, and other training programs for CRS and congressional staff; and third, a growing futures-oriented information system that is providing a wide range of information resources and services.

Obviously, many more organizational resources are available to government. Some of the major ones include the Office of Management and Budget, the Council of Economic Advisors, Federal Advisory Council on Regional Economic Development, Council on Wage and Price Stability, the Domestic Council, the Federal Judicial Center, and, as already noted, the groups in eleven executive departments and more than fifty agencies. Also to be included are the special boards, committees, and commissions such as the National Commission on Electronic Funds Transfer (EFT) which is involved in a technology assessment of electronic banking. Available from the private sector are resources of more than fifty think-tanks and futures-oriented consulting firms (Guarisco, 1976).

In spite of this apparent wealth of resources, there are many proposals for more. The Advisory Committee on National Growth Policy Processes, which recommended the creation of a central monitoring function in a Center for Statistical Policy and Analysis, also recommended the creation of an independent and permanent Growth and Development Commisssion. It would have a broad mandate to study the future and report to the president, Congress, and the people (U.S. Senate, 1976).

One of the major proposals for expanding the organizational resources on the future is presented in the Balanced Economic Growth and Planning Act of 1976 (S. 1795, 94th Congress) sponsored by Senator Humphrey. This act traces some of its concepts back through a chain of proposed legislation:

> The Balanced National Growth and Development Act of 1974 (S. 3050, 93rd Congress, Sponsored by Senators Humphrey and Javits)
>
> Balanced National Growth and Development Act (H.R. 16585, companion to S. 3050, sponsored by Congressman George Brown)
>
> National Growth Policy Planning Act of 1973 (S. 1286, sponsored by Senator Hartke)
>
> Full Opportunity and National Goals and Priorities Act of 1973 (S. 5, sponsored by Senator Mondale)

These various acts have proposed many new resources for forecasting and planning, including:

> An Agency for Population and Demographic Analysis
>
> The Office of Balanced National Growth and Development
>
> Congressional Office of Policy Planning
>
> Foundation on the American Future
>
> Economic Planning Board
>
> Division of Economic Information
>
> National Citizens Council on the American Future

Not all of the proposals have been focused on the legislative and executive branches. In a recent issue of the *American Bar Association Journal,* Professor Maurice Rosenberg of Columbia Law School called for a "government depository or information resource (to) be established to provide courts with the necessary social and technical data" (Rosenberg, 1976).

Although the merits of these proposals vary tremendously, the fact that so many ideas are being presented from such a range of proponents suggests that a broad need exists for greater resources for information about the future. At the same time, the wealth of information from all of the public and private sources seems more than sufficient to supply all of government's needs. This apparent paradox suggests that perhaps before each and every department, agency, and subagency creates its own specialized organization and resources, all of the currently available resources need to be surveyed and organized to provide a clear picture of what information about the future already exists and is in the public domain. This does not lead to a new resource, but rather to an information system that provides access to existing organizations and the information they produce. Depending on the nature of the available organizational and informational resources, as well as government's needs for information about the future, the capabilities and requirements of any new resources can be identified.

Two different aspects of an information system are involved in determining what is available and what is needed. The availability issue is a broad one, including the kinds, costs, and access-time of information, futures-oriented materials, services, and methods, as well as biographical information on the individuals and organizations producing these services. These might be grouped in five main categories:

1. *Reporting services,* including commercial and government services which regularly report forecasts, trends, historical data, projections and survey results. These services may be offered through a computer link or publications.
2. *Periodicals, journals, and newsletters,* presenting information on social and technological developments which may contain forecasts or other information about the future.
3. *Organizations* regularly publishing research reports and other futures-oriented documents.
4. *Books and handbooks,* containing directory-type information, futures research, forecasts, scenarios, or other futures-oriented information.
5. *Data services,* including data bases, programs, modeling, and other software services.

While all of this information on availability has not been compiled, some important steps have been taken. The GAO has surveyed seven government agencies and the CRS of the Library of Congress has compiled information on more than fifty think-tanks (Comptroller General of the United States, 1976 and Guarisco, 1976). In addition, the Futures Research Group of CRS is exploring ways to organize and possibly automate the futures information available to the Library of Congress.

An information system, of course, does not need to contain all the information available, but only the part that is needed. Some screening or admission/retention criteria are necessary. Factors such as information relevancy, quality, timeliness, and cost might be used in formulating criteria. These might be developed in conjunction with the needs of users as determined by surveys, use patterns, and the like.

An analysis of user needs might contribute to the design of the system itself. This could include access modes, formatting and display patterns, and organization of the data files. Based on the informational needs that have already surfaced, at least six files can be identified:

1. *Bibliographic file:* The items in this file would include references to published documents containing futures-oriented information and otherwise satisfying system content criteria. Standard bibliographic information might be supplemented by annotations, summaries, and so forth. These reference documents might include books, articles from popular and professional journals, publications by the U.S. Government Printing Office, the Congressional Budget Office (CBO), OTA, GAO, as well as executive agencies and departments.

*Forecasts file:* This file would include forecasts and projections about the future obtained from the available literature. Assumptions used in developing the forecast might be included, along with information about the method(s) employed. Several different formats might be used. For specific events, the file might contain a statement of the event and information about its probability of occurrence by various given years—e.g., 35 percent probability of occurring by 1985. For projections of trends, graphic displays might be used. These forecasts might be organized using several of the popular taxonomies by which historical information is now available.

3. *Issue Impacts and Assessments file:* For major or current issues, the information available through the system might be organized and compiled for rapid access. This might include relevant forecasts; expected impacts of events; related issues/forecasts; proposed responses/solutions; and sources for more information.

This file might be updated as resources and developments permit.

4. *Directories file:* This file would contain basic directory-like information on individuals in futures research; organizations; professional societies; futures-oriented legislation; automated data bases; public grants, studies, research; and futures projects in progress.

5. *Technical file:* This file would contain information on methods of futures research and a glossary of terms and procedures. It might also include information on new or emerging technologies similar to the issue impacts file.

6. *Interactive file:* Through this file, the user could access computer routines such as curve fitting and statistical packages as well as simulation models. This would allow the user to test ideas, assumptions, and policies in an interactive mode, thereby enabling the user to develop his own forecasts using the data and models in the system.

This information system with its various files and interactive programs must be viewed as a first step in developing information and organizational resources about the future. These resources need to be developed in a manner that assures their availability, use, and effectiveness to the various levels and branches of government. As government uses information about the future, it will be defining and organizing its role and responsibilities for addressing the future. Eventually, like Congress, other parts of the government may adopt procedural rules to formalize their responsibilities. As this is accomplished, the various levels and branches of government will be able to better identify their needs for information about the future and the organizations best able to satisfy them. To assure effective citizen participation, the informational and organizational resources available to government must be available to responsible citizen groups contributing to the goal-setting and policy-making process.

The evolution of future-oriented information resources and their role in government will be slow and will involve many complex issues. How can a centralized information system be organized to serve the three branches of government without raising the issue of separation of powers? How can government information resources be made available to citizen groups without competing with the various private resources? How can government effectively monitor all of the needed social and economic variables without raising the issues of right of privacy, business trade secrets, and the like?

The development of these resources, however difficult, is essential to determining in detail the constitutionally mandated state of the union and its possible futures. As these resources become available, they must be used in the political process by government and the citizens to determine national goals. The roles of Congress, the president, and other political institutions should be developed in concert with emerging roles of citizen participation to define futures in politics. As Lincoln put it: "If we could first know where we are and whither we are tending, we could better judge what to do and how to do it."

## REFERENCES

Bea, Keith A., and Cynthia E. Huston. 1976. *Citizen Futures Organizations: Group Profiles.* Library of Congress, Congressional Research Service. Washington, D.C.: Government Printing Office. Multilith Number 76–260 SP.

Bedell, Congressman Berkely. 1976. "Congressional Clearinghouse on the Future." *Congressional Record* (Daily Edition), Volume 122 (August 26), H–9160.

Brown, William H. 1976. "Rules of the House of Representatives." Washington, D.C.: U.S. Government Printing Office.

Burger, Chief Justice Warren. 1976. "Agenda for 2000 A.D.—Need for Systematic Anticipation." Keynote Address, National Conference on the Causes of Popular Dissatisfaction with the Administration of Justice, St. Paul, Minn. (April 7).

Comptroller General of the United States. 1976. *Long-Range Analysis Activities in Seven Federal Agencies.* Washington, D.C.: U.S. Government Printing Office, (PAD-77-18).

Congressional Clearinghouse on the Future. 1977. "President Carter Supports Foresight/Planning." *What's Next?,* Number 7 (January), 1.

Guarisco, Elizabeth J. 1976. *Think Tanks—What Are They and What Do They Do?* Library of Congress, Congressional Research Service. Washington, D.C.: U.S. Government Printing Office. Multilith Number 76-183 SP.

Hitchcock, Henry. 1976. "Candidates Answer ISTA Querry." *TA Update,* the Newsletter of the International Society for Technology Assessment, Volume 3, Number 5 (October), 1-7.

Kornbluh, Marvin, and Dennis Little. 1976. "The Nature of a Computer Simulation Model." *Technological Forecasting and Social Change,* Volume 9, Numbers 1/2, 3-26.

Legislative Reorganization Act of 1970, Public Law 91-510, 84 Stat. 1140, October 26, 1970.

Minnesota State Legislature. Minnesota State Planning Agency and Commission on Minnesota's Future. 1975. "Minnesota Horizons: A Legislative Symposium." St. Paul, Minn.

Office of Technology Assessment. 1976. *Annual Report to Congress.* Washington, D.C.: U.S. Government Printing Office.

Pateman, Carole. 1970. *Participation and Democratic Theory.* London: Cambridge University Press.

Renfro, William L. 1977. *Foresight: Congress Looks to the Future.* Library of Congress, Congressional Research Service. Washington, D.C.: U.S. Government Printing Office.

Rosenberg, Maurice. 1976. "Anything Legislatures Can Do Courts Can Do Better." *American Bar Association Journal,* Volume 62 (May), 587-590.

State of Georgia. Office of the Governor, Office of Planning and Budget. *Blue Print for Action: Goals for Georgia in the Seventies.* Atlanta, Ga.

U.S. Congress. The Joint Economic Committee. 1975. *Toward a National Growth Policy: Federal and State Developments in 1974.* Library of Congress, Congressional Research Service. Washington, D.C.: U.S. Government Printing Office.

U.S. House of Representatives, 93d Congress. House Select Committee on Committees. 1973. *Panel Discussions.* Washington, D.C.: U.S. Government Printing Office.

———. 1974. *Committee Reform Amendments of 1974.* Report 93-916. Washington, D.C.: U.S. Government Printing Office.

———94th Congress. Committee on Merchant Marine and Fisheries, Subcommittee on Fisheries and Wildlife Conservation and the Environment. 1975. *Computer Simulation Methods to Aid National Growth Policy.* Washington, D.C.: U.S. Government Printing Office.

———. Committee on Science and Technology, Subcommittee on the Envi-

ronment and the Atmosphere. 1976. *Long Range Planning.* Washington, D.C.:
U.S. Government Printing Office.

    U.S. Senate, 94th Congress. Commission on Operation of the Senate. 1975.
*Toward a Modern Senate.* Washington, D.C.: U.S. Government Printing Office.

    ————. Advisory Committee on National Growth Policy Processes to the
National Commission on Supplies and Shortages. 1976. *Forging America's
Future: Strategies for National Growth and Development.* Washington, D.C.:
U.S. Government Printing Office.

    Wills, Gary. 1970. *Nixon Agonistes: The Crisis of the Self-Made Man.* Boston:
Houghton Mifflin Co.

HAROLD G. SHANE
and ROY A. WEAVER

# Futures in Education

Many classrooms, both in the United States and overseas, have changed relatively little since the 1930s. There have been numerous small-scale innovations but virtually no major developments. In short, in terms of methods and materials a 1930s-style teacher would not feel totally out of place in a 1978 or 1980 classroom. The so-called New Math and New Science, emphasis on linguistics in language instruction, Operation Headstart for the disadvantaged child, the Right to Read program, and career education are representative of programs that reflected efforts to refine educational practice rather than to introduce profound changes.

As we contemplate educational futures for the next twenty-five years, however, potentially revolutionary developments seem to be on the horizon. Widespread use of chemicals for inducing intelligence or for lengthening retention, breakthroughs in subcellular research, and application of psychosurgical techniques such as electrode implantation to control brain functions might well anticipate the day when educators, in cooperation with scientists, will be able to manipulate the intellectual capacity of learners even before birth as well as in the early years of life. Mass-marketed computerized calculators, environments simulated through the use of holography, mind-reading machines, and other technological inventions may appreciably alter instructional processes.[1]

Other developments that may have an impact on teaching and learning can be readily identified. They include the prospects for increased leisure, demands for greater participatory democracy, extended family "affinity groups," growing dissatisfaction by the "underemployed," and entangling global politico-corporate alliances. Their potential impact on learning systems underscores the fact that schooling may emerge tomorrow in a form radically different from what it is today, and with many aspects of education taking place outside the walls of today's schools.

The interrelationship between education and societal change was stressed by one of the writers who identified nine critical problem-issues in education and urged action to alter the process of educating learners so as "to contain and then to end the 50 year crisis of transition that was created as we moved from yesterday to tomorrow" (Shane, 1973a). Making a less optimistic appeal for restructuring schooling and reordering educational priorities, B. B. Johnson argued that "with changes coming at us with increasing speed the task [of educating children and youth to inhabit a world of tomorrow we cannot predict with certainty] seems both more urgent and more hopeless" (1973). The rapid breakdown of conventional perceptions of a future mirroring the present with its problems removed was most aptly described by Toffler as "the dizzying disorientation brought on by the premature arrival of the future" (1965).

As social decisions lead to new policies both in America and in countries overseas, education probably will have an increasingly important contribution to make. Mankind's desire to imagine, consider, select, shape, and foster more desirable tomorrows even now has prompted an increasing interest in applying futures research methodologies to educational problems and has begun to encourage the conceptualizing of lifelong education in contexts that truly will alter traditional concepts of both the learning process and of the classroom.

## FUTURES PLANNING IN EDUCATION

For the most part, futures planning techniques such as mathematical modeling, simulation and gaming, scenario-writing, Delphi, and cross-impact analysis have emerged from private institutions that are often involved in military or corporate research. Among them, the RAND Corporation, the Hudson Institute, The Futures Group, the Institute for the Future and, in the late 1960s, the U.S. Office of Education (USOE) policy research centers established at Stanford and Syracuse Universities have been the leaders in developing futures methodologies. The most comprehensive discussion of these techniques, as applied to education, can be found *Futurism in Education: Methodologies* (Hencley and Yates, 1974).

Since most of the futures research techniques are explored in detail in other articles in the Handbook, we shall not attempt to examine how they work but rather how some of them have been used in educational planning. At the national planning level, futures projections are an integral part of the data that are reported. For example, such estimations and projections as "Population of the United States in Selected Age Groups, by Sex: 1960 to 2000" in *Current Population Reports* provide numerical descriptions of educational level attainment by age, race, sex, income, and occupation (U.S. Department of Commerce, 1974).

A more comprehensive examination of data compiled by the National Center for Education Statistics in *The Condition of Education* focuses on "Students and School," "Outcomes of Schooling," "Concerns of Elementary and Secondary Education," and other selected topics (National Center for Education Statistics, 1976). These and other data have been beneficial in defining a quality of education factor. Social indicators reports by Johnson and others examine the level of achievement in "basic education and the opportunity for higher and continuing education . . . [as] the two major social concerns" related to education (Statistical Policy Division, 1973).

When we extrapolate data on changes in percentage of the population age sixty-five or older, it becomes apparent how valuable future projections can be in educational planning. Proportionate increases in that segment of the population—3 to 4 million per decade, or approximately 300,000 to 400,000 per year—have far-reaching implications for change in education. Based on these data, Buchen concludes that more education will be needed, whether for occupational retraining or for exploring avocational activities (1974, p. 109). Such an interpretation carries greater weight if we forecast a lowered retirement age coupled with a reduced work week. Federal policies aimed at meeting this significant age shift in the population could encourage investment of more federal and state monies over the next decades and more extensive postsecondary program planning to meet the needs and interests of this group. Conversely, higher retirement ages, quite possibly resulting from meeting the increasing cost of Social Security payments, and longer work weeks and "moonlighting" could demand quite different policies, but regardless of developments, education and reeducation seem certain to be involved.

While the problem of how best to prepare an educational policy conducive to nurturing this expanding human resource rather than exploiting it is far more complex than considered herein, this issue provides one of a myriad number having an impact on choices in the present which, in time, will affect our future.[2]

At the state level, the New Jersey State Department of Education Futures Project serves to illustrate the application of futures planning to statewide programs (Weber, 1973). The initial stage of this project focused on assembling a futures study group whose purpose was to explore the domain of futures literature. As a result, a continuing bibliography has been assembled for dissemination. Another component of the project was in-service training for the staff and assistants in the Office of the Commissioner of Education.

Through a Delphi study alternative, scenarios were created to explore cultural lag, demographic change, and comparable issues. Implementation of this exploration took the form of curricular programs for grades 9 through 12. Increasingly, other states have followed suit in anticipating the interrelationship of forces impinging on education so as to create intervention strategies for managing the future of education within their geographic borders.

Chase and Clark have noted the importance of planning at the district school level (1974). They indicate that, with a variety of pressures from "budgetary limitations [to] innovations in the technology of education," school districts must more consciously and systematically explore emerging alternatives. The structure of the planning process includes (1) a statement of objectives for the district at the conclusion of five years, (2) the role of subsystems in meeting these objectives, (3) alternative plans for meeting system demands, (4) plans for each subsystem, and (5) "monitoring and shifting procedures" to change the system on the basis of unexpected or altered events.

While a number of futures planning studies have been undertaken at the local school district level, the Dallas Public School Skyline Wide Educational Plan (SWEP) probably is the most notable and comprehensive to date (Burns, 1973). Having brought in prominent futures-oriented consultants to describe potential future events and having explored alternative scenarios for the district, the Dallas Independent Administration developed an extensive report. This report noted such matters as the implications of demographic shifts on personnel hiring, curriculum structure, budgetary demands, and related problems. Scenarios also were created, complete with accompanying contingency plans, for meeting alternative future needs.

In sum, futures planning has become a more and more widely accepted procedure ranging from national to school district educational offices. By identifying some of the possible forms of tomorrow's society, educational planners have stressed the capacity of various educational agencies to respond to problems that must be anticipated in order to assure an excellent system of education for all learners.

## FUTURES STUDIES IN THE CLASSROOM

A second way in which futures research has had an impact on education is mirrored in the curriculum practices found in schools and universities. Rojas and Eldredge provide a partial but useful description of sources of information on educational futures, sample curricula, and the scope and nature of futures studies programs in North America (1974).

In a later survey of futures courses at the university level Eldredge noted approximately a 50 percent increase every two years in the number of offerings. He warned, however, that the study of the future was developing a "poor intellectual image" and, as a result, he called for "rigorous standards and sophisticated Ph.D. programs" (1975). Examples of university programs which have received the most publicity include (1) Futures Lab, an affiliate of Earthrise, Inc., which emphasizes a highly personalized approach, (2) the M.A. and Ph.D. programs in Social and Educational Futures at the University of Minnesota, (3) the USOE-funded program in Global-Survival Studies at the University of Massachusetts, and (4) the recently established M.S. in Studies of the Future at the University of Houston at Clear Lake City.[3]

Programs that emphasize a futures perspective have infiltrated the public elementary and secondary schools as well. Griffith (1974) provides a detailed description of the Melbourne High School experience; Damlo (1974) reports the outcomes of Futuristics: Theory and Application, a course taught at Burnsville High School in Minnesota; Glenn and Guy (1974) discuss work with ten year olds in New Hampshire; and McCallough et al. (1974) report on the array of experiences offered in the Palo Alto schools. Because of the influx of futures courses in the schools, it is important to stress that those mentioned herein provide an extremely limited listing of current developments.

## THE EVOLUTION OF FUTURES STUDIES CONTENT IN THE CLASSROOM

Perhaps as much as any other publication, *Learning for Tomorrow: The Role of the Future in Education* (1974), edited by Alvin Toffler, was instrumental in providing a comprehensive overview of how the study of the future could be made an integral part of the disciplines or could provide a framework for interdisciplinary learning in the schools. The growth of futures courses has now reached a point which justifies a discussion of possible changes both in *content areas* and in *methods* designed to encourage students to think about the future. A selected review of the literature in this realm illustrates the growing influence of futurism in the subject areas.

Focusing on the social studies, McDanield (1974) described a project initiated by the Center for Adaptive Learning, Inc., in May 1971, which was planned so as to create a theoretical basis for a futures studies curriculum in grades 10 through 12 and to translate theory into useful learning materials. Criticizing the "old" social studies, Vonk (1973) disclaimed the fact that "the dead issues of the distant, cold past are marched in and out of the classroom like so many obedient tin soldiers," and he urged that formal instruction in history and geography focus on "priorities essential to survival." Johnson (1974) and Klee (1975) provided a rationale for study of the future in geography. They also identified issues they deemed important and called for skill development aimed at anticipating, shaping, and coping with the future.

With the rapid development of technologies that threaten the future of humans unless they are wisely used, and with the exploding dimensions of knowledge in science, the science curriculum, like the social studies curriculum, calls for the study of possible futures. In "Educating Scientists for Tomorrow," J. Wren-Lewis contended that "science education is fatally incomplete if it does not include . . . some explicit training in how to think about the kinds of futures that may be in store for [humankind]" (1974). He also urged that the training of scientists and technologists not be devoid of valuing, of sensitivity, and of emotion since the "scientist's work touches on human issues outside the range of his [or her] strict professional discipline" (1974, p. 171).

In an article emphasizing the utility of studying futures in science, Cornish noted the motivation that is intrinsic in examining unresolved problems for which answers often lie in the domain of science—particularly developments related to the laws of motion, ocean and space colonization, artificial food, weather control, energy, and the like (1969).

While futurism has been explored with reference to a variety of areas—from counseling to music[4]—the language arts including futuristic literature have for decades been an especially promising avenue for surveying the future (see Farrell, 1971; Franks and Howard, 1974). Initially, such writings as More's *Utopia* and Bellamy's *Looking Backward,* and, later, such works as Orwell's *1984* (*Intellect,* p. 352) and Huxley's *Brave New World* and *Brave New World Revisited* stimulated thoughts as to whether the human race faced utopian or dystopian futures. More recently, the science fiction of such notables as Asimov, Bradbury, Clarke, and Heinlein has provided a source of prophetic thinking and shrewd conjectures about future worlds both on our planet and elsewhere. Livingston indicates that while science fiction literature has been available for some time, educators have been reluctant to incorporate it into the conventional curriculum. He points out that in the past it has been viewed as "detrimental to students' future mental stability, [thus] promoting the subversion of prevailing values" (1974).

Calkins and McGhan's synopsis of 200 science fiction novels and anthologies by Hollister, McNelly and Stevens, and others demonstrate the wide reaches of science fiction literature.[5] Because it is spread over such a huge, imaginative canvas, science fiction transcends the language arts and stimulates thought and discussion in other areas as well. Emphasizing this fact, Friend points to the way science fiction has permeated such fields as ecology, history, religion, and medicine. She states that the genre "presents many shelters from which we can preview expected changes and possibly alter the fates we wish to avoid" (1972).

Feature-length films such as *The Planet of the Apes, 2001: A Space Odyssey, Soylent Green,* or *Embryo,* the long-running television series "Star Trek," "Space 1999," and newer ones such as the "Six Million Dollar Man" and "Bionic Woman" have presented a popularized examination of the future.[6] Even imaginative versions of future worlds, however, may tend to stereotype or to oversimplify tomorrow's world. In his comprehensive survey of futures films, K. R. Miller identifies and describes the nature of over seventy films from the technical to the purely speculative and imaginative. Declaring that the "greatest single challenge in futures education is to liberate the imagination [and] . . . to take the incredible seriously," Miller observes that film archives are loaded with potentially useful "abstract fantasies" to meet the challenge (1974).

Utilizing film as a way of organizing the futures studies curriculum, Howard and Franks, co-directors of the Futuristics Curriculum Development Project in the greater Cleveland, Ohio, area, have created a mini-course guide covering (1) an introduction to futuristics, (2) the contemporary biological revolution, and (3) such themes as the interrelatedness of systems and of the dangers potentially impinging on Spaceship Earth.[7]

In recent years, a number of interesting filmstrips have been developed as instructional aids for studying futurism. *Newsweek*'s *2000 A.D. Program* focuses on the central theme "Growth: How Much More?" by examining (1) the positive and negative effects of growth, (2) the food and population crisis, (3) the governmental influence, (4) the impact of technology, (5) the debate over nuclear power, and (6) the accelerated growth in urban centers.[8]

A comprehensive collection of twenty futures-oriented sound filmstrips has been compiled by Doubleday Multimedia in four kits: *Change Here for Tomorrow, Dimensions of Change, Econonics and the Future,* and *The Population Debate.*[9]

While the preceding résumé suggests the availability of futures-oriented materials, it should be borne in mind that the development of these rather recent materials remains in a formative stage and that a variety of improved packaged kits probably are forthcoming.

*INSTRUCTIONAL PROCESSES*

As print and nonprint materials rapidly have flooded the education market, increasing discussion of processes for involving learners in futures-thinking has ensued. For the most part, these activities emphasize simulated activities since the future cannot be experienced in any depth within conventional views of the present. As much as any publications to date, Kauffman's *Teaching the Future* (1976) and a volume edited by Stirewalt, *Teaching Futures* (1974), provide an overview of instructional approaches to studying the future in the classroom.

Torrance describes a rationale for simulated experiences for envisioning alternative worlds. He emphasizes the need for "creative problem solving to keep us from letting the future take us too much by surprise." He also cites stages for creating an appropriate environment, and he identifies and describes the use of the soliloquy, projection, mirroring, role reversal, and other useful techniques (1975). Utilizing a similar approach, Hollister describes a three-pronged examination of a personal level future view. In "The Future Is Me," "The Future Is Us," and "The Future Is Me—And Us," he asks participants to probe serious questions with respect to their own lives projected into the future (1974). A number of more complex simulation games have been created, games ranging from computerized models of future worlds with intervention strategies and their consequences to social decision-making experiences. In "Simulating Alternative Futures in Education" (SAFE), Debenham has created a planning game focusing on twelve major social events coupled with twenty potential intervening events (1974). Planning decisions are made for each of five ten-year periods. Participants in the game are encouraged "to mathematically optimize their decisions [through analysis of] public relations and cost-benefit." The computer is used to evaluate and rank the long-range consequences of selected choices. The purpose of the game is to model decisions which educators may make "with respect to possible social, educational, and technological developments from 1975 to 2024."

Two interesting simulations, *Cope* and *Utopia,* have been marketed by Interact. Their purposes are to explore adaptation to change and to anticipate the future which this adaptation suggests; and to construct "an ideal society in the latter."[10] *Cope* encourages participants to examine what civilization would gain or lose, during a time span from 2000 to 2040, by following alternative routes in communications, language, transportation, production, entertainment, general life quality, and innovative technology. *Utopia* stimulates learners to work cooperatively to organize a society based on the consensus of participants. Through exploration of alternative conceptions of politics, technology, economics, and morality, learners create personal views of the "ideal" future for discussion, synthesis, and final agreement as to the nature of the ultimate society. While a number of other useful simulations exist, the preceding discussion has attempted to provide an overview of the nature of such activities and their utility for classroom futuring.

A closing word of caution seems appropriate insofar as gaming and simulation approaches are concerned. At least some of them fail realistically to recognize cost factors, national cleavages, and the perversity of some humans who, as Bertrand Russell once pointed out, may be motivated by acquisitiveness, rivalry, greed, vanity, and the love of power (1950). It would be faulty judgment to simulate with youth worlds that are too unrealistic!

## EDUCATIONAL ISSUES FOR THE THIRD MILLENNIUM

Neither extensive futures planning nor an abundance of programs and materials can assure that youth can share effectively in shaping a desirable future. Futurism in education must move beyond its present level, escape being a passing fad, and become a responsive and decisive action-oriented movement.[11] If it is to have an influence on the *creation* rather than *imposition* of tomorrow's society, then a broadly based program should be implemented—a program designed effectively to confront six critical dimensions of education. Let us now examine several issues in the field of education which seem likely to be the objects of lively discussion and disagreement during the coming decade.

### INSURING OPTIMUM HUMAN DEVELOPMENT

While the issue of insuring fulfillment of human potential is a complex one, education in the future must contribute to its fruition in whatever ways it can. Such a decision demands that many of the traditional and conventional responsibilities assigned to educational agencies be reordered so as to provide an environment conducive to self-growth. Beginning with conception, education broadly construed must strive through therapy, instruction, and prescription to help the young achieve well-coordinated physiological, emotional, and intellectual development. Emphasis is placed on pre- and postnatal care because of the potential brain damage and physical problems that can result from malnourishment of an unborn child (Mayer, 1973).

A second requirement to insure human development is the creation of varied and stimulating experiences for learners—experiences that provide the qualities which, in part, create what later is measured and labeled "intelligence." When a formal environment cannot provide such experiences, then an appropriate intervention strategy must be promoted in order to minimize the extent to which noninstitutional variables—socioeconomic status, restricted verbal interaction, socialization constraints, or inadequate nutrition—impede or impair human development.

As learners reach maturity and move through educational settings, rich opportunities for personal decision-making must ensue. As Theobald notes, "It is surely extraordinarily arrogant to believe that anyone can make better decisions for another individual than that individual can make for him- or herself. It is surely extraordinarily naive to believe that any process developed by one person can maximize the potential of another individual" (1976, p. 43). The loosening of the rules and intellectual impositions of the school of the future does not, however, imply anarchy or disregard for the welfare of one's associates. A sharp line must be drawn between responsible and irresponsible decision-making. The child and youth is free *to* create, learn, develop. They are not free *from* the obligation to become better, more effective human beings. The school of the future, therefore, is not without discipline and rules to live by. But the rules are seen as less arbitrary and, as quickly as possible, the discipline becomes inner discipline rather than imposed behavior control.

An integral part of personalizing learning lies in the self-perceptions individuals maintain. Careful efforts must be made to assist each person in identifying and building on strengths rather than comparing one's capabilities to group norms. Accordingly, extending positive self-concepts in future time horizons may encourage striving toward greater self-fulfillment. As Singer (1974) and Shane have noted, this concept of a "future-focused role-image" promotes seeking options "toward a life-role that brings satisfactions and promises self-respect and dignity" (Shane 1936, p. 63).

### EXPLORING ALTERNATIVE VALUING MODES

As information overload has intensified the sorting, filtering, and integrating of knowledge, so too has the stress of making value choices in a change-oriented society been intensified. Noting the crippling effects of overchoice, Toffler criticizes contemporary education by declaring that, "the more crucial the question of values becomes, the less willing our present schools are to grapple with it." He concludes: "It is no wonder that millions of young people face erratic pathways into the future" (1970, p. 417).

Elaborating on Toffler's indictment, Kirschenbaum and Simon assert that "in a world in which the future bore a close resemblance to the past, moralizing was a relatively effective means of transmitting or 'teaching' values" (1974, p. 259). Agreement between educators and parents as to the appropriate values to be instilled, however, produced one-dimensional schools. Then, with the explosion of value choices brought on by the civil rights movement, international warfare, student dissent, drugs, political scandal, sensitivity training groups, and comparable events, what was "moral" and "good," what was "right" and "wrong," became badly obscured as permissiveness and convention collided.

Today, children and youth continue to be bombarded by conflicting value positions. Furthermore, the impact of one's actions has been extended from the neighborhood and a small circle of friends to encompass a global world inhabited by billions who are influenced by the consequences of those actions. The resultant confusion as to what one should value may be traumatic (Vickers, 1970). Education in the future clearly should become more effective in helping learners select a set of congruent values that serve the individual in a general welfare context.

### STRUCTURING KNOWLEDGE

With respect to the transmission of knowledge, Kenneth Boulding has noted that "the whole stock of human knowledge is lost by death at least every seventy years and this has to be replaced by transferring the knowledge structure from decaying old minds into decaying young ones" (1975, p. 69). As the vast stores of knowledge have been taxed by explosive information generation, the rate at which knowledge is transmitted becomes increasingly critical.

Today, as many learners move through conventional schooling from which they extract fragmented understandings, it has become apparent that many traditional modes for transmitting data are no longer suitable. As complexity and change increase their momentum, the process of filtering data into young minds aggravates the problem. Unless the system can increase the speed at which learning occurs, perhaps through electronic technology, learners will be condemned to onerous repetition.

One possible answer lies in selection processes. For the most part, selection of information for learning has not relied on a continuous rethinking of either that which may be essential for creating a desirable future or that which may facilitate a match between the learner's interests and needs and appropriate data. Immediate accessibility to and availability of information, selected either individually or through counsel with others, may very well become an integral part of educational systems of the future (Chase, 1974).

The task of helping learners to cope with new or changing information and with its impact on the roles in which they see themselves is increasingly significant. For example, in a rapidly changing society, requisite information necessary for vocational training or "preparation for life" may become obsolete as occupational slots change or even disappear as the nature of life itself changes. The extent to which persons heretofore have been trapped by their inflexible tactics for confronting and managing change often determines the undesirable effects change has upon them. The ability to make wholesome, rapid, and insightful adjustments to change can appreciably improve the mental and social health of many Americans.

## RESPONDING TO SOCIETAL PROBLEMS

Historically, schools have been viewed as mirrors of the society; that is, events that occur in the society may be reflected in schools, but schools have had little or no power in modifying or effecting change in society. In recent years, a number of writers have decried the fact that the schools have been so passive.[12]

Those who would have education assume a more assertive role in confronting and dealing with societal problems insist that such a role is essential because mankind stands at a critical juncture in its history. From this point of view, unless the process of education encourages positive self-growth and renewal, opens societal issues to active and continuous analyses, provides learners with survival skills for a myriad number of potential tomorrows, and empowers individuals to be insightful and action-oriented, prospects for a desirable future seem increasingly slim.

## CREATING LEARNING ENVIRONMENTS

The responsibility for developing facilitating educational environments cannot easily be assigned. The schools have a decreasing monopoly on schooling, and other agencies, in direct proportion, are assuming greater responsibility for learning opportunities. Out-of-school experiences for young people have increased in both scope and legitimacy in the past fifteen years. The prospects are good that alternative and nonschool forms of education will flourish in the future (Hipple, 1975, p. 125). In speculations and specifications for "Alternative Educational Designs for the 1980's," Research for Better Schools, Inc., has encouraged discussions of a variety of learning approaches.[13] Behind such planning is the hope that it will be feasible to guarantee an environment conducive to learning for any prospective client of the schools at any age.

Beyond alternative learning approaches, school facility design—how to create superior schools—has emerged as an area of speculation. After a systematic and comprehensive analysis of mobile, interlocking learning units, Gage surmises that structures conceivably could be assembled and disassembled much like tinker toys (1972). Depending on the purpose of the learning and the instructional design, he argues that such an architectural concept could open space and place consideration to the educational planner's imagination.

Criticizing the "school fortress" concept, Passantino envisions increasing use of "nonspecialized environments—the marketplace, the workshop, the farm, the home"—and recognizes the usefulness of the interplay of school and community, in facility design (1975). Gores builds on the idea of synergistic interagency use of facilities and observes that events in the realms of technology, energy, politics, economics, and citizen participation will force a revolutionary view of the schoolhouse (1975).

Mead perceives the schools as educational geometry contingent on human resources (1965). In other words, learning is based on human interaction, and as a result, the development of a shared learning concept should replace more conventional views of institutionalized learning. Experience becomes an organizational structure for learning. The creation of learning exchanges in which persons negotiate mutually satisfactory skill-sharing or service for skill, or service for service in an informal setting, illustrates the application of culture-sharing.

In sum, a changing perception of in-school and out-of-school learning environments promises to broaden the choices available to educational planners in the future. Rethinking of conventional formats for schooling also seems likely to energize the perceptions of both teachers and parents as to the nature of appropriate places for learning.

## PROMPTING EDUCATIONAL COMPONENTS

As we contemplate the stage for educational change in the future, attention must be focused on the training of educators who can function in changing environments. A recent Yearbook of the National Society for the Study of Education (NSSE) states that the concept of a lifelong, open exit-entry-exit-reentry type of education may speed changes in teacher preparation, with emphasis on helping them to understand and to relate effectively to a wide variety of age groups and to culturally different learners. It also seems likely that tomorrow's teachers will concentrate on a more narrowly delimited field of study in addition to broad preparation in elementary or secondary education

(Shane, 1975). To meet the complexity of demands on instructional personnel, Corrigan contends "that teachers and other educational personnel will [be asked to] perform a broad range of human services" and that many of these services will require highly specialized training (1974). Both Shane, writing in the NSSE Yearbook, and Corrigan consider transformed institutional teaming approaches—from "partnerships" to differentiated staffing—to be productive strategies for developing increased competence. The ramifications of these proposals for the preparation of educational personnel are far-reaching.

## NOTES

1. See, for example, Fuller (1973); Ellul (1964); Longmore (1973). For a useful bibliography of futures literature, see Marien (1970, 1971, 1972).

2. Futures planning in education is not a North American phenomenon. For example, the following studies are but a few from many ventures in other countries: Organization for Economic Co-operation and Development (1972); Worth et al. (1972); Information Department of the Ministry of Education and Science (1975); Borghi et al. (1974).

3. For information on Futures Lab, write Thomas Carleton, Director, Futures Lab, P.O. Box 120, Annex Station, Providence, Rhode Island 02901. Regarding other programing, see Harkins (1973); Schimmel (1973); Fowles (1975); H. C. Eurich (1968, 1970); and Weaver (1975).

4. See Morgan, (1974) for a discussion of the role of an action-oriented perspective on school counseling in the future. See also K. R. Miller (1974) and Benner (1975). Both authors envision a coming revolution in entertainment brought on by the interaction of a variety of media and development of more sophisticated visual and sound equipment.

5. Calkins and McGhan (1972); also Hollister (1974a); and McNelly and Stoves (1972). Recent Vintage and Ballantine listings are given in "Futuristics: Fact and Fiction," a brochure available from Random House. Useful teachers' guides to both science fiction and futures studies can be obtained from Bantam Books, 666 Fifth Avenue, New York, New York 10019.

6. Earlier films, such as *Metropolis, Modern Times, Things to Come, Flash Gordon, Buck Rogers,* and the classic radio production "War of the Worlds," while often forgotten in discussions of futures media, should not be ignored for their contributions to futures-thinking.

7. Available from McGraw-Hill Films, Dept. BF, 1221 Avenue of the Americas, New York, New York 10020. The guide contains summaries of eight films— "Future Shock," "Stranger than Science Fiction," "Man-Made Man," "Miracle of the Mind," "The Weird World of Robots," "The Four Day Week, "Cities of the Future," "The Food Revolution," along with objectives and activities.

8. Available from Newsweek, Inc., 444 Madison Avenue, New York, New York 10022. Program materials include two teachers' guides: *Technology: Matching Machine to Man* and *2000 A.D.,* both of which contain duplicating masters and visuals for transparencies.

9. Available from Doubleday Multimedia, Box 11607, 1371 Reynolds Avenue, Santa Ana, California 92705. The total package contains twenty filmstrips along with records or cassettes and teachers' guides. Each guide covers objectives and activities.

10. *Cope*, developed by J. K. Ward, and *Utopia*, created by J. Hildebrand, are available from Interact, P.O. Box 262, Lakeside, California 92040. B. B. Franks, *Future Decisions: The I.Q. Game* is available from SAGA Publications, 4833 Greentree Road, Lebanon, Ohio 45036. For an analysis of the game, see Franks and Howard (1974). *Global Futures Game,* which explores various dimensions of worldwide problems—population, food, technology, education, and the need for international cooperation for resolving these problems, is available from Earthrise, Inc., P.O. Box 120, Annex Station, Providence, Rhode Island 02901. Cf. See Plummer (1974).

11. For a discussion of this problem, see Strudler (1974). For a comprehensive international analysis, see "The Future as an Academic Discipline," Shane (1973c).

12. For example, see Irvine (1972) and Johnson (1973). Both writers describe a number of activities aimed at consciously examining what learners "should be able to do in order to live at all in our shrinking planet" (p. 518).

13. For information, write Research for Better Schools, Inc., Suite 1700, 1700 Market Street, Philadelphia, Pennsylvania 19103. Also see Barnes (1972); Dow (1974); Martin and McCartney (1976).

## REFERENCES

Baier, K., and N. Rescher (eds.). 1969. *Values and the Future.* New York: Free Press.

Barnes, R. 1972. *Learning Systems for the Future.* Bloomington, Inc.: Phi Delta Kappa.

Benner, C. H. 1975. "Music Education in a Changing Society." *Music Educators Journal,* (May) 33–36.

Borghi, L., et al. 1974. *Perspectives on Primary Education.* Project I Series, *Educating Man for the 21st Century, Plan Europe 2000,* Volume 7. The Hague: Martinus Nijhoff.

Boulding, K. 1975. "Predictive Reliability and the Future: The Need for Uncertainty." In Louis Rubin (ed.), *The Future of Education: Perspectives on Tomorrow's Schooling.* Philadelphia: Research for Better Schools, 57–74.

Brickman, W. W. 1975. "Futurology in Education." *Intellect* (November) 188–190.

Buchen, J. H. 1974. "Social Trends, 1959–2020." *Intellect* (November), 109.

———. 1975. "Science Fiction Futures." *Intellect* (April), 459.

Burns, R. J. 1973. *Evaluation Design for Skyline Wide Educational Plan.* Research Design Number 73–215. Department of Research and Evaluation, Dallas Independent School District.

Calkins, E., and B. McGhan. 1972. *Teaching Tomorrow: A Handbook of Science Fiction for Teachers.* Dayton, Ohio: Pflaum Publishers.

Carnegie Commission of Higher Education. 1973. *A Mood, the Future of Higher Education.* New York: McGraw-Hill.

Chase, C. W. 1974. "Educational Research and Development Priorities to Create the Future." In C. W. Chase and Paul A. Olson (eds.), *The Future: Create or Inherit.* Lincoln, Neb.: Study Commission on Undergraduate Education and the Education of Teachers.

Chase, R. B., and D. C. Clark. 1974. "Long Range Planning in School Districts." *Educational Technology* (October), 32–36.

Cornish, E. 1969. "The Science Teacher as a Futurist." *The Science Teacher* (January), 21–24.

———. 1974. "Everyperson's Genesis II." *The Science Teacher* (May), 29–36.

Corrigan, D. C. 1974. "The Future: Implications for the Preparation of Educational Personnel." *Journal of Teacher Education* (Summer), 100–107.

Cyphert, F. R., and W. L. Gant. 1971. "The Delphi Technique: A Case Study." *Phi Delta Kappan* (January), 267–273.

Damlo, P. 1974. "Futuristics Cures 'Doomsday Syndrome'." *The Futurist* (August), 183–184.

Debenham, J. 1974. "A Computerized Simulation Game for Studying the Future of American Education." *Educational Technology* (February), 14–19.

Doussaint, A. F. In press. "The Black Child's Image of the Future." *Journal of Negro Education.*

Dow, J. A. 1974. "Alternative Futures for Education: Trends and Implications." *Journal of Teacher Education* (Summer), 138–140.

Dror, Yehezkel. 1975. "Some Fundamental Philosophical, Psychological and Intellectual Assumptions of Futures Studies." In C. H. Waddington, *The Future as an Academic Discipline.* Amsterdam: Elsevier-Excerpta Medica-North Holland, 145–154.

Dyoli, O. E., T. Langan, and T. Liao. 1975a *Designing for the Future.* Middletown, Conn.: Xerox Corp.

———. 1975b. *Fitting Machine to Man.* Middletown, Conn.: Xerox Corp.

Elardo, P., and B. Caldwell. 1974. "The Kramer Adventure: A School for the Future?" *Childhood Education* (January), 143–152.

Eldredge, H. W. 1972a. "Courses in Futuristics Grow in Number and Variety." *The Futurist* (August), 158–160.

———. 1972b. "Teaching the Future at North American Universities." *The Futurist* (December), 250–252.

———. 1975. "University Education in Futures Studies." *The Futurist* (April), 98–102.

Ellul, J. 1964. *The Technological Society.* New York: Random House.

Eurich, H. C. (ed.). 1968. *Campus 1980.* New York: Delta.

———. 1970. *High School 1980.* New York: Pitman.

Farrell, E. J. 1971. *Deciding the Future: A Forecast of Responsibilities of Secondary Teachers of English, 1970–2000 A.D.* Urbana, Ill.: National Council of Teachers of English.

Fowles, J. 1975. "University of Houston Offers Master's Degree in Futures Studies." *The Futurist* (August), 100–101.

Franks, B. B., and M. K. Howard, 1974a. "Thinking Futures: A Cure for Disease." *Media and Methods* (November) 29+.

———. 1974b. "Tomorrow's Curriculum Today." *English Journal* (April), 80–82.

Friend, B. 1974. "Reaching the Future Through Paperback Fiction." *Media and Methods* (November), 35–36+.

Fuller, W. (ed.). 1973. *The Biological Revolution.* New York: Doubleday.

Gage, G. J. 1972. "A Design Process for a School Facility, Year 2001." Ph.D. dissertation, University of California at Los Angeles.

Glenn, J., and C. Guy, 1974. "Easy Ways to Help Children Think About the Future." *The Futurist* (August), 186–188.

Gores, H. B. 1975. "The Future File: Schoolhouse 2000." *Phi Delta Kappan* (January), 310–312.

Gresham, R. L., et al. 1970. *The Albuquerque Story: Future Schools Study Project.* New Mexico: Albuquerque Public Schools.

Griffith, P. 1974. "Teaching the Twenty-First Century in a Twentieth Century High School." In A. Toffler (ed.), *Learning for Tomorrow.* New York: Random House, 197–216.

Harkins, A. 1973. "Futurizing a University," *The Futurist* (August), 172–174.

Heinmiller, J. L. 1976. "Contemporary Forecasting Methodologies: An Evaluation Review with Some Conceptual Prescriptions." Ph.D. dissertation, Bloomington, Indiana. Indiana University.

Hencley, P., and R. Yates. 1974. *Futurism in Education: Methodologies.* Berkeley, Calif.: McCutchan Publishing Corp.

Hipple, T. W. 1975. "Some (Specific and Not-So-Specific) Notions About the (Distant and Not-So-Distant) Future of Education." In T. W. Hipple (ed.), The *Future of Education: 1975–2000.* Pacific Palisades, Calif.: Goodyear Publishing Co., 119–135.

Hogan, J. F. 1974. "The Influence of School Organizational Properties on the Development of Future-Focused Role-Image." Ph.D. dissertation, Indiana University, Bloomington.

Hollister, B. 1974a. *Another Tomorrow: A Science Fiction Anthology.* Dayton, Ohio: Pflaum Publishers.

———. 1974b. "Tracking the Future: A Personal Approach," *Media and Methods* (November), 26–27+.

Hostrop, R. W. (ed.). 1973. *Foundations of Futurology in Education.* Palm Springs, Calif.: ETC Publications.

Information Department of the Ministry of Education and Science. 1975. *Contours of a Future Education System in the Netherlands.* Amsterdam, The Netherlands.

*Intellect.* 1972. "Orwell's Futuristic Realism." (March), 352.

Irvine, D. J. 1972. "Specifications for an Educational System of the Future" *Phi Delta Kappan* (February), 362–364.

Johnson, B. B. 1973. "Practical Preparation for the 21st Century." *Phi Delta Kappan* (April), 518–521.

Johnson, W. H. 1974. "The Future as a Learning Exercise in Geography." *Journal of Geography* (December), 59–63.

Johnstone, J. N. 1974. "Mathematical Models for Use in Educational Planning." *Review of Educational Research* (Spring), 177–201.

Kauffman, D. L., Jr. 1976. *Teaching the Future.* Palm Springs, Calif.: ETC Publications.

Kirschenbaum, H., and S. B. Simon. 1975. "Values and the Futures Movement in Education." in A. Toffler (ed.), *Learing for Tomorrow.* New York: Random House, 257–270.

Klee, G. A. 1975. "Future Studies and Geography." *Journal of Geography* (October), 430–435.

Livingston, D. 1974. "Science Fiction as an Educational Tool." in A. Toffler (ed.), *Learning for Tomorrow.* New York: Random House, 234–256.

Longmore, D. 1973. *Machines in Medicine.* New York: Doubleday.

*Los Angeles Times.* 1976. "17 Percent in U.S. to be 65 or Older by 2030." June 1, 1.

McCallough, T., O. W. Markley, and M. Moses. 1974. *Futuring.* Santa Clara Component, Research Report 14. San Jose, California.

McDanield, R. 1974. "Tomorrow's Curriculum Today." In A. Toffler (ed.), *Learning for Tomorrow.* New York: Random House, 103–137.

McInnis, N. F. 1972. "Social Education Asks: 'What Can Social Studies Teachers Do to Help Prepare Their Students for the Future?' " *Social Education* (March), 243–246.

McNelly, W., and L. Stoves (eds.). 1972. *Above the Human Landscape: An Anthology of Social Science Fiction.* Pacific Palisades: Goodyear Publishing Co.

Marien, M. 1970. *Essential Reading for the Future.* Syracuse, N.Y.: Educational Policy Research Center.

————. 1971. *Alternative Futures for Learning; An Annotated Bibliography.* Syracuse, N.Y.: Syracuse University Research Corp.

————. 1972. *The Hot List Delphi: An Exploratory Survey of Essential Reading for the Future.* Syracuse, N.Y.: Educational Policy Research Center, Syracuse University.

Martin, R., and R. J. McCartney. 1976. "The Future Revisited: Education's Big Boom Is Ending, But Studies to Get More Diverse." *Wall Street Journal,* April 8, 15.

Mayer, J. (ed.). 1973. *U.S. Nutrition Policies in the Seventies.* San Francisco: W. H. Freeman.

Mead, M. 1965. "The Future as the Basis for Establishing a Shared Culture." *Daedalus* (Winter), 135–155.

Miller, D. C. 1972. "Futures on Films." Two-72, Extension Media Center, University of California, 2223 Fulton Street, Berkeley, California, California 94720. Pp. 1–3, 15–18.

————. 1974. "16mm Measures the Future: Futures Film Update." One-74, Extension Media Center, University of California, 2223 Fulton Street, Berkeley, California 94720. Pp. 14–17.

————. 1975. "Target: The Impossible—." One-75, Extension Media Center, University of California, 2223 Fulton Street, Berkeley, California 94720. Pp. 13–14.

Miller, K. R. 1974. "Life A.D. 2000 Music Education." *Music Educators Journal* (December), 61.

Mitzel, H. E. 1974. "Computer Technology: Its Future Role in Basic Education." *Journal of Teacher Education* (Summer), 124–129.

Morgan, L. B. 1974. "Counseling for Future Shock." *Personnel and Guidance Journal* (January), 283–287.

National Center for Education Statistics. 1976. *The Condition of Education.* Washington D.C.: U.S. Government Printing Office.

Organisation for Economic Co-operation and Development. 1972. *Alternative Educational Futures in the United States and Europe: Methods, Issues and Policy Relevance.* Paris: Centre for Educational Research and Innovation.

Passantino, R. J. 1975. "Community/School Facilities: The Schoolhouse of the Future." *Phi Delta Kappan* (January), 306–309.

Plummer, C. 1975. " 'Future Shock' Is Modification of Traditional (Less Shocking) Starpower." *Simulation Gaming News* Volume 2, Number 6 (November), 11–12.

———. (ed.). 1976. "Dynamic Modeling of Alternative Futures Through Simulation/Gaming." *Viewpoints* Volume 52, Number 2 (March), 135 pp.

Rasp, A. Jr. 1973. "Delphi: A Decision-Maker's Dream." *Nations Schools* (July), 29–32.

Rojas, B., and H. W. Eldredge. 1974. "Status Report: Sample Syllabi and Directory of Futures Studies." In A. Toffler (ed.), *Learning for Tomorrow.* New York: Random House, 345–396.

Russell, Bertrand. 1950. "The Springs of Human Action." (Speech made when he received the Nobel Prize in Literature.) Stockholm, Sweden.

Scanlon, R. G. 1974. "A Curriculum for Personalized Education." *Journal of Teacher Education* (Summer), 119–123.

Schimmel, D. 1973. "A Curriculum for Today and Tomorrow." *Changing Education* (Summer), 6–9.

Schwartz, P. "Some Instructive Science Fiction Feature Films." One-74, Extension Media Center, University of California, 2223 Fulton Street, Berkeley, California 94720.

Shane, H. G. 1967. "Future Shock and the Curriculum." *Phi Delta Kappan* (October), 67–70.

———. 1971. "Future Planning as a Means of Shaping Educational Change." In *The Curriculum: Retrospect and Prospect*, Seventieth Yearbook of the National Society for the Study of Education. Chicago: University of Chicago Press, 201–217.

———. 1973a. "Looking to the Future: A Reassessment of Educational Issues of the 1970's." *Phi Delta Kappan* (January), 326–337.

———. 1973b. *The Educational Significance of the Future.* Bloomington, Ind.: Phi Delta Kappa, 1–13.

———. 1973c. "The Future as an Academic Discipline." In *The Educational Significance of the Future*, 35–38.

———. 1975. "Possible Changes in Teacher Preparation: 1975–85." In *Teacher Education*, 1975 Yearbook of the National Society for the Study of Education. Chicago: University of Chicago Press, 321–325.

———, and R. A. Weaver. 1975a. "Education as a Lifelong Process." *Vital Issues* (June), 1–4.

————. 1975b. "Educational Developments Anticipating the 21st Century and the Future of Clinical Supervision." *Journal of Research and Development in Education* (Winter), 90–98.

Sidwell, R. 1974. "Education and Future Shock." *Media and Methods* (November), 25.

Singer, B. 1974. "The Future-Focused Role-Image." In A. Toffler (ed.), *Learning for Tomorrow.* New York: Random House, 19–32.

Smith, N. B. 1975. "Child Nutrition in a Changing World." *Childhood Education* (January), 142–145.

Statistical Policy Division, Office of Management and Budget. 1973. *Social Indicators, 1973.* Washington, D.C.: U.S. Government Printing Office. (*Social Indicators, 1976,* in press.)

Stirewalt, J. N. (ed.). 1974. *Teaching Futures.* Washington, D.C.: The World Future Society.

Strudler, H. L. 1974. "Educational Futurism: Perspective or Discipline." In A. Toffler (ed.), *Learning for Tomorrow.* New York: Random House, 173–180.

Swanson, A. D., and R. E. Lamithe. 1971. "Project 1990: Educational Planning at the Metropolitan Level." *Socio-Economic Planning Sciences*, Volume 5, 535–545.

Theobald, R. 1976. *Beyond Despair: Directions for America's Third Century.* Washington D.C.: New Republic Book Co.

Toffler, A. 1965. "The Future as a Way of Life." *Horizons* (Summer), 109–115.

————. 1970. *Future Shock.* New York: Random House.

Toffler, A. (ed.). 1974. *Learning for Tomorrow: The Role of the Future in Education.* New York: Random House.

Torrance, E. P. 1975. "Sociodrama as a Creative Problem-Solving Approach to Studying the Future." *Journal of Creative Behavior* (3d Quarter), 182–195.

U.S. Department of Commerce, Social and Economic Statistics Administration. 1972. "Demographic Projections for the United States." *Current Population Reports: Population Estimates and Projections.* Series P-25, Number 476. Washington, D.C.: U.S. Government Printing Office.

————. 1974. "Educational Attainment in the United States: March, 1973 and 1974." *Current Population Reports: Population Characteristics.* Series P-20, Number 274. Washington, D.C.: U.S. Government Printing Office.

Vickers, G. 1970. *Freedom in a Rocking Boat: Changing Values in an Unstable Society.* Baltimore, Md.: Penguin Books.

Vonk, H. G. 1973. "Education and the 27-Year Countdown." *Phi Delta Kappan* (April), 514–517.

Weaver, R. A. 1975. "The Futurists Gather in Washington." *Phi Delta Kappan* (September), 49–50.

————. In press. "Schooling and Black Children's Future-Focused Role-Image." *Journal of Negro Education.*

Weaver, W. T. 1971. "The Delphi Forecasting Method: Newest Crystal Ball for Educators." *Phi Delta Kappan* (January), 267–271.

Weber, R. E. 1973. "Human Potential and the Year 2000: The Futures Project of the New Jersey Department of Education." *Journal of Creative Behavior* (2d Quarter), 133–151.

Welty, G. 1973. "Some Problems of Selecting Delphi Experts for Educational Planning and Forecasting Exercises." *California Journal of Educational Research* (May), 129–134.

Werdell, P. 1974. "Futurism and the Reform of Higher Education." In A. Toffler (ed.), *Learning for Tomorrow.* New York: Random House, 272–311.

Williams, C., and C. Nusberg, 1973. *Anticipating Educational Issues Over the Next Two Decades: An Overview Report of Trends Analysis.* Research Memorandum Number 18. Menlo Park, Calif.: Educational Policy Research Center.

Worth, W. H., et al. 1972. *A Choice of Futures.* Edmonton, Alberta, Canada: Alberta Commission on Educational Planning.

Wren-Lewis, J. 1974. "Educating Scientists for Tomorrow." In A. Toffler (ed.), *Learning for Tomorrow.* New York: Random House, 157–172.

Young, D. P. 1974. "Futuribles Marathon." *The Futurist* (August), 184–186.

ERVIN LASZLO

# Global Futures

Confronted with the question of global futures, the first objection that comes to mind is whether one can say anything meaningful about such a vast topic. On second thought, however, it becomes evident that there is nothing inherently meaningless about questioning the future of mankind as a whole, i.e., global futures. It is but an extension to a broader scale of questions concerning the future of an individual, a community, state, nation, or culture. Nothing we can say about the future of any human being or group is certain, but all reasonable forecasts of possible futures are meaningful—and they may be most important ones.

Today, the importance of debating global futures has become crucial. Social scientists note the function of images of the future as practical guides to social planning and behavior (Polak, 1973; Boulding, 1956). Polak points out that "never before in the history of human civilization, as far as we know, has there been a period without any kind of positive image of the future." Yet, today positive images of the human future are displaced by increasing pessimism about the fate of our species altogether. Gone is "a cheerful confidence in things to come" (Wordsworth), and emerging instead is the view unintentionally expressed by a high school girl who wrote, "man is descended from the apes, and he has been descending ever since."

On the other hand, we can note the emergence of concern with global futures as a topic of general discussion, not only in academia but also in business, government, and the public media. Whereas the automatic assurance that things will get better and better is missing, the blindness associated with such an assurance is likewise gone. As may be expected, humanity has obtained its newer visions through an experience of shock. Economic growth curves have flattened, expectations have been exposed to disappointment, and crises of various kinds—environmental, energy, food, security, population—have mushroomed.

The work of several futurists has contributed to the new visions of doom. These visions were first catalyzed by the computer scenarios of Forrester (1971) and Meadows et al. (1972). The magic of a giant computer, unable to find solutions to interconnected crises except through measures that appear unrealistic even to the utopian mind, shocked the public into an awareness of long-range global issues. The age of global futures consciousness has begun—and on an extremely pessimistic note.

Criticism of the first computer scenarios of humanity's future has led to improved simulation models. The most discussed models are these in Mesarovic and Pestel (1974). They do not model doomsday explicitly, for in their view the problems are not mainly the result of such physical factors as depletion of nonrenewable resources and pollution, as in the Forrester and Meadows models. Widening gaps between the world's rich and poor occupy centerstage and augur the rise of tensions well before population soars to unsustainable heights and resource reserves sink to uneconomical depths. Mesarovic and Pestel argue that the transfer of capital and resources must begin immediately, for delays can be deadly for all concerned. Since such large-scale and farsighted thinking is unlikely to dominate the minds of contemporary politicians, bankers, and corporate executives, the sense of acute doom projected by the earlier scenarios has merely been transformed into a duller sense of gloom.

By the mid-1970s, most observers realized that the critical factors in determining global futures were not directly such physical limits as were first modeled, but rather the socioeconomic and sociocultural limits associated with the foresight with which individuals and societies have managed the resources and environment in which they function. Technological optimists, such as Kahn (Kahn, Brown, and Martel, 1976), now argue that the depletion of resources is not a real problem as long as technologies are available for mining the earth and the seabed, recycling wastes, synthesizing low-grade elements to constitute high-grade raw materials, and evolving substitutes for the few minerals that are truly in short supply.

But the bloom forecast by technological optimists fails to disperse the gloom that succeeded the doom seen in the early 1970s. It has failed mainly because demands for equitable access to the fruits of science and technology are increasing and because pressures for a redistribution of global wealth are reaching the boiling point. The world today is beset by tensions caused by perceived imbalances. To be sure, imbalances have always existed, but in the past they were masked by low levels of interaction over vast distances and the slow speed of communication. Thus colonial peoples living in equatorial Africa or the highlands of Southeast Asia were not only physically but also psychologically removed from the city dwellers of European colonizing powers. Demands and expectations remained highly divergent. Today, however, the world is rocked by the "revolution of rising expectations" which brings close the demands of developing populations to those of the industrialized countries. Almost all of the world's four billion humans demand an adequate diet, decent housing and clothing, paid jobs or other forms of remunerative work, access to health services, some form of social security, and a basic education. The people whose demands in these respects fail to be met satisfactorily encompass most of the peoples of developing countries—some 70 percent of the world population. These vast masses of humanity continue to grow both in absolute numbers and in share of the total population, until by the middle of the next century as much as 90 percent of mankind may live in the presently underdeveloped countries. The miracles wrought by modern technology would be quickly assimilated by such a rise in population, if indeed the growing masses of poor countries could ever find access to its benefits.

Contemporary pessimism about global futures is motivated not only by injustices and gaps, but also by a number of interconnected factors. Pessimism is associated with the international arms race: the world's arsenals contain enough explosives to kill the entire human population not once but nineteen times over, and nuclear weapons are proliferating to as many as thirty countries by the mid-1980s, while highly sophisticated conventional arms are pouring into such trouble spots as the Middle East and Southeast Asia.

Pessimism is also associated with the world food situation. Whereas world food production has more than kept pace with world food demand over the past twenty years, the Green Revolution, which was largely responsible for increases in food production, is running into serious trouble. Its technologies are for the most part energy-intensive, and energy is becoming prohibitively expensive for poorer countries. The technologies also call for high levels of irrigation and fertilizer use, factors that likewise price them out of reach of a growing number of countries. In addition, they favor the large landowner over the small farmer who falls further and further behind in practicing subsistence farming. Grave problems are associated with the choice of crops and the use to which they are put: instead of growing grains for human consumption, world food production is oriented to growing cash crops for immediate profit and to feeding grains to animals who convert it to expensive meat at the wasteful rate of seven pounds of feed for one pound of beef and three pounds of grain for one pound of poultry meat. Other problems beset the food marketing, storage, and transportation system, with the result that some 40 percent of the world population suffers from undernourishment—notwithstanding the fact that, equally distributed, the current food crop could nourish all people.

Long-term energy prospects also give rise to serious concern. Conventional fossil fuels will sooner or later be used up (though optimists maintain that vast new reserves will be discovered in the near future), and alternative energy sources will have to be at hand. The major alternative source today is nuclear fission which, as conservationists and worried students of the international scene point out, is highly hazardous. Such hazards are not uniquely associated with engineering problems but involve the human factor: vulnerability to misuse by governments as well as by bands of terrorists. Safe renewable energy sources do exist—nuclear fusion, energy from the sun, wind, ocean tides, and any thermal differential that can be harnessed to bring a working liquid to boil and cool it again. For the present, however, they are not economically competitive. It is entirely conceivable that mankind, using short-term economic logic, is making a Faustian bargain with high-risk technologies, selling future safety to satisfy its current energy needs.

The resource picture, while rosier than a few years ago, is likewise not a cause for jubilation. Prospecting constantly adds to the known reserves of nonrenewable resources, but usage rates now surpass the enlargement of known reserves for such critical resources as natural gas and several industrially important metals. Mining the seabed and extracting secondary deposits are theoretically and even often technologically feasible, but they raise enormous ecological and political problems. Will mankind disregard environmental costs and sacrifice the tenuous principles of fair competition in the race for new resources? The vast amounts of energies required for the large-scale processing of lower grade materials could not be indefinitely won from fossil fuels but call for nuclear technologies, of which the fission components are available but risky, and the fusion components, while safe, are not yet developed.

Finally, the applications of science and technology are serious grounds for pessimism. Technologies are used to generate wealth and power, and serve conceptions of individual and collective prestige. "Appropriate" technologies are much discussed but little used. If for Schumacher "small is beautiful" (1973), for industrial and governmental leaders size and profit correspond to desirability. One consequence of such choices is a decreasing quality of life in industrialized countries, manifested by such signs as a growing sense of alienation, invasion of privacy, impersonal and indifferent bureaucracies, professional pressures, alcoholism, drug abuse, crime, suicides, and divorces. Another consequence is unjust as well as wasteful development in nonindustrialized countries where a small elite often invests in high-profit and high-prestige technologies, regardless of the urgent needs of the large but inarticulate masses.

Faced with such interconnected problems, and the inability of the international free market system to overcome them, the wealthy and powerful seek ways to maintain and further increase their wealth and power, while the poor and powerless search for strategies to modify the behavior of the international system in their own favor. Numerous leaders among the advanced industrialized countries attempt to consolidate their economic and political position by making themselves independent of the resources controlled by the Third World. They also seek greater collective power through functional economic cooperation not only among the countries of the OECD and among the blocs formed by the industrial giants of West and East (the United States and the U.S.S.R.), but also through "trilateralism": a still closer cooperation between the United States, the European Community, and Japan. At the same time, many of the more active and militant leaders of the Third World attempt to consolidate the developing countries of Latin America, Africa, and Asia under the banner of Third World solidarity. The leaders exert joint pressure on the developed world, using as leverage their possession of indigenous natural resources such as oil and, to a lesser extent, bauxite, copper, phosphate, and other metals and minerals. Confronting the system-preserving forces massed behind the existing economic order in the industrialized world are the system-changing forces gathering in support of a new international order in the Third World. The example of OPEC has encouraged the Third World to use natural resources as a force in the coming battle and has led to smaller scale but significant victories. For example, Rabat could triple the price of phosphate for export to the industrialized world without causing repercussions, and Tehran could double the price of natural gas sold to the Soviet Union. On the other hand, the rich countries are suffering from a bad conscience with respect to waging systematic economic warfare against the poor. Moreover, leaders such as former U.S. Secretary of Agriculture Earl Butz, who claimed that "food is a weapon," are slowly disappearing from the political scene. Tanzanian President Julius Nyerere expressed a view frequently heard in the speeches of Third World leaders when he said that the rich countries are on the same planet as the poor and if they keep getting richer at the latter's expense the poor must demand change, as the industrial proletariat did in the past. "As far as we are concerned, the only question at issue is whether the change comes by *dialogue or confrontation*" (Nyerere, 1976).

Despite such farsighted policies as the granting of preferential terms of trade to over 100 developing countries by the European Community, the dialogue between "North" and "South" threatens to degenerate into confrontation. Clashes occurred in the United Nations, where the Third World bloc managed to pressure acceptance of a Declaration and

Programme of Action on the New International Economic Order introduced by Algeria, and of a Charter of Economic Rights and Duties of States proposed by Mexico. Should tensions mount, however, the confrontation will spill over from the diplomatic into the economic, and possibly the military, areas. Other resource cartels may attempt to follow OPEC's example; governments could nationalize industries extracting natural resources on their territories, and declared warfare could be combined with undeclared guerrilla action and acts of terrorism to force acceptance of Third World demands. In the military area, the possession of high explosives and large military establishments does not guarantee victory, as the United States learned in Vietnam. If the North-South dialogue breaks down, the international waters ahead could be choppy for all concerned.

The phenomenal growth of industrial economies creates rifts that have their own ideological bases, rooted in the perceived morality of using all means to relieve suffering on the one side and the perceived duty to preserve the free market system (or the system of socialism) through continued growth and prosperity on the other. These rifts now join the traditional ideological rift between free market democracy and centrally planned socialism, and may come to dominate the international scene. The postwar East-West confrontation is mitigated by strategic declarations of detente and the underlying commonality of basic economic interests. It is gradually overshadowed by the prospect of hundreds of millions of unemployed and undernourished masses emerging in the Third World, and the determination of their leaders not to join one camp or the other but to form an economic and political bloc of their own. Thus, current issues in the world system are as much moral and ideological as they are economic and physical. The frames of reference are given by the distribution of physical resources, but the arena of action is provided by the expectations and demands made by actors small and large, governmental and corporate, concerning their share of the wealth and power, and their ability to sustain their people with improved conditions of existence.

The shift of concern from outer to inner limits, and from local to global futures, calls for rethinking traditional priorities within enlarged spatial and temporal horizons. The interdependence of the world's economies, political systems, and environments renders the isolation of any nation or bloc of nations from the rest all but impossible. Imbalances in the distribution of production capacities, wealth, natural resources, and population, together with long lead-times between the research, development, and application of new technologies, and even longer delays between the institution of social policies concerned with population control and institutional reform, and their anticipated or unanticipated effects, make imperative a time horizon of several decades. The ultimate test for mankind, and the crucial issue in the determination of the global future, may be whether people, businesses, and governments are capable of operating with expanded horizons, or whether they remain wedded to the perspectives of monthly household budgets, annual corporate accounting, and four- or five-year governmental programs and platforms.

Long-term global thinking is in its infancy, but even at this early stage it raises basic conceptual issues. Can we reasonably expect that a centralized or a decentralized world system will evolve? Would the future world constitute a hierarchically organized system, or one of equal participation by all actors? Since mankind has no experience with global social orders other than temporary military conquests (by Alexander, Caesar, etc.) and the mercantilism-reinforced conquests of the seventeenth- and eighteenth-century European powers, mental models for thinking about the future world need to rely on experience with other types of systems. Perhaps the most obvious candidate is the model of the modern nation-state. This system is a relatively centralized and hierarchical one, although these factors vary from participatory democracy on the one hand to military or ideological dictatorships on the other. World federalists and advocates of world government perceive in the nation-state a necessary, though in detail modifiable, model for a global society.

It is also evident, however, that modern nation-states are increasingly unable to operate efficiently even in the more limited context of national populations, resources, and territories. Bureaucracies tend to become perpetuated and outlive their usefulness. Patterns of organization resist change, with the result that, while some tasks are duplicated by several agencies, others are not carried out by any. Linked to administrative inefficiency is the problem of assuring the allegiance of diverse cultures and subcultures to a single, often ethnically and geographically removed, central administration. Among the world's nearly 150 nation-states, only a handful of European nations constitute relatively unified entities, and even they suffer from internal strife and dissension. Examples are the Flamand versus French populations of Belgium, the Basque and Catalan populations of Spain, the Swedish and Finnish segments of Finland, the four different subcultures of Switzerland, and so on. Other federated nations manifest signs of acute internal tension; among these are Canada with separatist movements in Quebec and, to a lesser extent, in Alberta and Labrador, the Soviet Union with the "nationality problem" encountered in the Ukraine, in White Russia as well as in several of the republics (other than the Russian Republic), and even the United States, where regionalization is

only those who engage in socially conscious science fiction, such as Arthur C. Clarke, but also respected social scientists such as John Platt (1966), Kenneth Boulding (1956), Willis Harman (1974, 1976), Erich Jantsch (1975), and William Irwin Thompson (1976). While they differ in the details of their visions and recommendations, they are united in their perception of fundamental changes coming about in the near future, amounting to a complete transformation of the patterns of human life. Rather than be controlled by technocrats and systems engineers (a feature of a more conservative variety of transformational image propounded by Bell in the "postindustrial society" concept (1973), people and societies would attune themselves to mutual cooperation within a new institutional and technical framework. While many such views have a distinctly utopian ring, they do provide images for the future that could capture the popular imagination. It is well to recall Oscar Wilde's admonition: "A map of the world that does not include Utopia is not worth even glancing at, for it leaves out the one country at which Humanity is always landing."

Images of totally centralized future world systems may be as far from the mark as concepts of totally decentralized systems. Neither the organism, with its central nervous system, nor the ecosystem, with its genetically evolved coordination of populations, is a suitable model for human societies. Whereas smaller scale social systems, including nation-states, could emulate the organic concept with moderate success in producing a central coordinating system in the form of national governments, such a large and heterogeneous system as the system of all nations and peoples cannot be subjected to centralized control except through the exercise of highly coercive power. Global futures may involve catastrophes, but if mankind survives them, the shape of a sustainable and humane world order is not likely to be either fully centralized or fully decentralized but may combine elements of both. There may well have to be central coordination in such critical areas of global concern as security, energy, nonrenewable resource use, oceans, space, the distribution of capital, technology, and the division of labor. There may also have to be appropriate changes in values and beliefs, and therewith in individual life-styles and social institutions. Long-term thinking may have to prevail, and long-term policies may need to be harmonized. To achieve this, mankind would need both new social and institutional structures—some on regional and others on world levels—and new transformation in values and beliefs, including a growing sense of mutual solidarity.

It therefore appears that a question even more basic than that of centralization or decentralization may be continuity versus discontinuity. Will the future world be continuous with the past, in the sense that so-called linear projections of past trends would properly describe it? Or would it be discontinuous, manifesting a "step-function," a "nonlinearity," or a "system-break"? Plans and policies produced by current establishment institutions, such as major corporations, governments, and military complexes, implicitly assume a continuous future. They rely on linear projections of past trends and attempt to eliminate factors that would change the growth curves. The frequent use of terms such as *crisis-management* and *managing the future* mask an underlying belief in the irreplaceability of the status quo, and the resulting need to counteract trends that threaten it. Such views are represented in the numerous books and policy papers of the Hudson Institute which, contrasted with the Club of Rome, perceives no problems that could not be overcome through technological expertise and the determined exercise of power by the currently dominant elites. But even the Club of Rome, perhaps the world's most influential consciousness-raiser about global futures, began with a basically static orientation. The first report to this group, the already cited work by Meadows et al., embodied a strong suggestion of status quo in the concept of the equilibrium state, even if that state presumes lower rates of fertility and more conservation of resources and the environment. On the other hand, later reports to the Club, including the previously cited works by Tinbergen et al. and Laszlo et al., manifest a definite belief in the feasibility, and indeed the necessity, of basic transformations in the international order.

Forecasts of static or dynamic, centralized or decentralized, doomsday or rosy futures are not predictions, but expressions of possibilities perceived by analysts grappling with the complexities of contemporary issues. The discussion of global futures is no longer in the province of politics or economics, and it would be wrongly shifted into that of engineering. The issues transcend disciplinary boundaries, just as they transcend geographic ones. Their principal elements include physical factors associated with the finiteness of the planetary environment; socioeconomic factors concerned with the way in which the resources of this finite environment are extracted, processed, distributed, used, and discarded; and sociocultural factors centered on the choices of people and institutions with respect to basic goals and policies. The tenor of human life is not uniquely determined by physical constraints, nor is it solely commanded by goals and policies. Human values, beliefs, and the resulting behaviors interact with a complex preexisting structure of institutions and technologies. The resulting dynamic interplay is often dominated by the possibilities inherent in the institutions and the technologies, at the expense of human needs and fundamental values. The reversal of Kant's moral imperative "ought implies can" into the technological imperative "can implies ought," subjugates human values and needs to the force of technological and institutional possibilities. Those who see in human cultures a new force capable of mastering the technological and institutional imperatives are the true optimists of our species. They believe in something far greater and miraculous than the engineer's "technological fix": they believe in a "cultural transformation"—not a temporary repair but a step to a new plateau of human existence.

In the welter of contemporary forecasts and expectations, the extreme positions are increasingly unwarranted. The long-term global future is not likely to remain like the past, and it is not likely to move smoothly from the chaos of some 150 nation-states with shifting alliances and short-term interests, to a functionally coordinated world system either through central management or distributed cultural change. The intervening steps are likely to be numerous and may include multinational regionalism, following the example of the European Community. In Latin America, Africa, as well as Asia, regional organizations already exist, and their role could grow in importance. More effective authority could be transferred to them through the selective surrender of the rights of sovereignty by member nations, in areas where regional cooperation serves each member's long-term interest (for example, in collective security, health care programs, research and development, information networks, trade, extraction and processing of resources, and energy production). Such intervening steps would eventually strengthen global cooperation coordinated by the existing world body, the United Nations. If the steps are taken in time, collective self-reliance could become a reality for the international community. Inasmuch as human rights are now universally accepted as attaching to all individuals and requiring guarantees by nation-states, collective self-reliance could become accepted as a norm governing the formation of multinational regions and the relations among such regions.

Current imbalances are not likely to be redressed by the independent coexistence of some 150 nation-states, including giants and midgets. To create a balanced distribution of wealth, power, skills, and capacities for development, the powerless and poor nations may have to form lasting alliances with other states in their geographic and cultural region. Larger socioeconomic, sociocultural, and political blocs in Latin America, the Middle East, sub-Saharan Africa, and South and Southeast Asia could create viable conditions for their populations and release member states from the bondage of continued dependence on charity aid. Thus, the scenario which harbors perhaps the greatest promise for an equitable and sustainable future for mankind is one that includes many incremental steps leading beyond present imbalances, transcends the fiction of the unconditional sovereignty of already interdependent nation-states, and conduces toward a new social and international order as different from the present as the present world order is different from the world of the Middle Ages.

Whatever the scenario, a new and humane world order is not likely to emerge without serious birth pangs. King argues that we should insure at least a holding position for humanity, to give ourselves a little more time to evolve a strategy in the face of multiple uncertainties (in press). On the other hand, mankind confronts the "deadly delays" described by Mesarovic and Pestel (1974) which make holding actions costly both in socioeconomic and in human terms. Thus, we are caught on the horns of a dilemma: it may be unwise to act now, with imperfect knowledge and uncertain outcomes, and it may be deadly to wait much longer.

The resolution of this dilemma can take multiple forms. It may be resolved by too small and too careful steps that pass up opportunities and lead to more serious problems. It may be resolved by the ostrich posture of telling ourselves that all is well until the crises are wringing our necks out of the sand. And it may be (but is unlikely to be) resolved by bold and imaginative action that creates conditions for the organic growth of the human community toward multiregional balance and collective self-reliance.

In the final analysis, it is very likely that some tenable organization of human affairs will crystallize on this planet in the last decades of this century or the beginning of the next. What is unclear is the cost this organization will entail. The most pessimistic of doomsday scenarios must yet allow for the survival of mankind and must acknowledge changed circumstances following the apocalypse. Even a thermonuclear World War III is unlikely to wipe out the entire human population, for the total annihilation of human life does not serve any power's perceived interest. Other apocalypses associated with massive starvation, the spread of epidemics, violence in the wake of widespread economic breakdown, chemical and thermal pollution, violent competition for wealth and resources, and the proliferation of nuclear arms among governments and bands of terrorists also allow a much decimated population to survive to reorder its priorities and reorganize its social structures. But we need not go as far as visions of apocalypse to perceive high costs associated with the emergence of a new order. Some 40 percent of the world population is presently undernourished, whereas 50 percent is under fifteen years of age. If those living today survive to the age of fertility and reproduce (even in smaller numbers), the world population will double in thirty to forty years. To maintain eight billion people with a modicum of human dignity, mankind will need to create and develop more than twice the current amounts of jobs, housing, clothing, basic consumer goods, services, and food. By the time our institutions and power structures adapt to such phenomenal increases in human demands, many people are likely to die, and many more to suffer from hunger and deprivation.

To work for the smoothest and most efficient transition to an order capable of sustaining the world population, in conditions satisfying at least its minimum non-negotiable demands, is not only a matter of long-term rationality but also of basic morality. Ultimately, the study of global futures moves from the area of physical-technological constraints, to social-economic processes, to the heart of the matter: the investigation of perceptions of human interest and the advocacy of genuine morality among fellow-passengers on a small, crowded, and fragile planet Earth.

## REFERENCES

Bell, Daniel. 1973. *The Coming of Post-Industrial Society.* New York: Basic Books.

Boulding, Kenneth. 1956. *The Image.* Ann Arbor: University of Michigan Press.

Falk, Richard. 1976. *Future Worlds.* New York: Foreign Policy Association.

Forrester, Jay. 1971. *World Dynamics.* Boston: Wright-Allen Press.

Harman, Willis. 1974. "Humanistic Capitalism: Another Alternative." *Journal of Humanistic Psychology* (Winter), 5–32.

———. 1976. "Business and Society in Transformation." *Planning Review*, Volume 4, Number 3 (May 3,), 1, 4–7, 28.

Jantsch, Erich. 1975. *Design for Evolution.* New York: George Braziller.

Kahn, Herman, William Brown, and Leon Martel. 1976. *The Next 200 Years.* New York: William Morrow.

King, Alexander. In press. *Some Reflections on the State of the Planet.*

Laszlo, Ervin. 1974. *A Strategy for the Future.* New York: George Braziller.

———, et al. 1977. *Goals for Mankind.* New York: E. P. Dutton.

Meadows, Donella, Dennis Meadows, et al. 1972. *The Limits to Growth.* New York: Universe Books.

Mesarovic, Mihajlo, and Eduard Pestel. 1974. *Mankind at the Turning Point.* New York: E. P. Dutton.

Nyerere, Julius. 1976. "The Economic Challenge: Dialogue or Confrontation?" *International Development Review*, Volume 18, Number 1, 2–8.

Platt, John. 1966. *The Step to Man.* New York: John Wiley and Sons.

Polak, Fred. 1973. *The Image of the Future.* San Francisco: Jossey-Bass.

Schumacher, E. 1973. *Small Is Beautiful: Economics As If People Mattered.* New York: Harper and Row.

Thompson, William Irwin. 1976. *Evil and World Order.* New York: Harper and Row.

Tinbergen, Jan, et al. 1976. *Reshaping the International Order.* New York: E. P. Dutton.

MAGOROH MARUYAMA

# Settlements in Space

The technological feasibility of large, spacious extraterrestrial communities accommodating several thousand to a few million inhabitants each has been established (O'Neill, 1977). Such communities will be highly habitable, with Earth-like landscapes including farms, hills, trees, grass, and animals. They will run on solar energy and will be constructed with materials mostly from the moon and other astronomical bodies. They will be financially self-supporting and will export solar energy to Earth. Once the first extraterrestrial community is built, the construction of the subsequent communities becomes easier, using the first communities as the base.

With the advent of the era of extraterrestrial communities, we will have to think in terms of hitherto unknown cultural options. In extraterrestrial communities, many of the constraints of life on Earth will be removed. Temperature, humidity, seasons, length of day, weather, artificial gravity, and atmospheric pressure will be set at will, and new types of cultures, social organization, and social philosophies will become possible. The thinking required will be far more than technological and economic; more basically, it will be cultural and philosophical. We will be in a position first to invent new cultural patterns and new social philosophies, and then to choose material conditions and community design to fit the desired cultural goals and philosophies.

This new vista, suddenly open, changes our entire outlook on the future, not only for those who eventually want to live in extraterrestrial communities but also for those who want to remain on Earth. In the future, Earth might be considered an uncomfortable and inconvenient place to live compared to the extraterrestrial communities. Within a century or two, most of humanity—with ecologically needed animals and plants—will be living outside Earth. The meaning, purpose, and patterns of life on Earth will also be considerably altered. Earth might be regarded as a historical museum, a biological preserve, a place that has harsh climate and uncontrolled weather for those who love physical adventure, or a primitive and primeval place for tourism. This cultural transition may be comparable to the transitions in the biological evolution when our aquatic ancestors moved onto land or when our quadrupedal ancestors became bipedal and bimanual.

We now need anthropological, psychological, and philosophical thinking to guide technology. We must examine as many possibilities as can be imagined, both desirable and undesirable, long before they might, can, or will happen. We must choose our goals among many alternatives, and we must gear our technology toward these goals.

If we look several centuries ahead, there are possibilities that *Homo sapiens* will have branched off biologically into several different species spread over different parts of the universe. Biological changes can occur rapidly with the advancement of our knowledge on genetic codes. We therefore need to consider the intercultural relations not only within the same species of *Homo sapiens* but also between many post-*Homo* species.

This article discusses philosophical, psychological, and anthropological considerations needed as we enter the era of extraterrestrial human and posthuman civilizations. It should be pointed out that (1) the basic principle of biological, social, and even some physical processes is the increase of heterogeneity and symbiotization; (2) diversity has a survival value for several reasons; and (3) diversity contributes to a higher rate of cultural evolution.

## THE HETEROGENISTIC PRINCIPLE

For three decades, a paradigmatic shift has been occurring in science. Advances in the study of *reciprocal* causal processes are making it increasingly clear that the basic principle of biological and social, and even some physical processes, is increase of heterogeneity, differentiation, and symbiotization (Maruyama, 1963, 1974; Buckley, 1968). Consequently, the heterogenistic view of the universe has become more scientific than the homogenistic view.

Heterogeneity is the very source of growth, enrichment, resource diversification, evolution, symbiotization, and survival. Traditional Western (European and American) logic preached the ideology of unity by similarity and regarded differences as sources of conflicts. But the new scientific logic is "symbosis thanks to diversity." For example, the animals convert oxygen into carbon dioxide while the plants do exactly the opposite, and in so doing, they help each other. "The survival of the fittest" does not mean "the survival of the strongest." On the contrary, it means "*the survival of the most symbiotic.*" The "strongest" individual or species who destroys others and the environment cannot survive at all.

Heterogeneity also allows for diversification of supplies as well as demands. The richness of life in a tropical rain forest or coral reef results from the heterogeneity of species: if all animals ate the same food, there would be a food shortage; and if not all animals are eaten, there will be waste. Even solar energy is used maximally if different organisms employ different means to absorb it.

Obviously, heterogeneity increases the probability of survival in unforeseen catastrophes. More importantly, interaction between heterogeneous subpopulations or subcultures increases the speed of biological or cultural evolution (Wright, 1931; Maruyama, 1963). Therefore, the design of extraterrestrial communities must be heterogenistic. Different communities can be constructed in different forms, suitable for different cultural, social, and biological patterns. Each community must incorporate heterogeneity, variety, changeability, and flexibility.

## DIFFERENT LOGICS

The design of extraterrestrial communities can be based on different systems of logic. Let us therefore discuss some contrasting logics. Many Americans know only one type, the Aristotelian deductive logic, and believe it to be "the" logic. However, there are many other types.

One of the drawbacks of deductive logic is that it prohibits "circular reasoning." Until recently, the deductive logical order was often confused with the causal order in physical, biological, and social processes. As a result of this confusion, the concept of mutual causality (A and B cause each other: many things cause one another) was tabooed in spite of the fact that mutual causal relations are abundant in biological, social, and some physical processes. As mentioned earlier, mutual causal processes can increase differentiation, heterogeneity, and complexity, and can make evolution and growth possible.

Another drawback of deductive logic is that it leads to hierarchical social structure, dictatorship, aristocracy, elitocracy, technocracy, bureaucracy, and the like. Deductive logic cannot see any alternative order of society. The only alternative conceivable within its logical limitation is anarchy or numerocracy (majority rule, domination by quantity). However, once we recognize other types of logics, other alternatives become possible. For example, the mutual causal logic enables us to conceptualize a network system of mutual interaction.

Interestingly, philosophies of some American Indian tribes, some West Africans (but not North Africans), some Far East Asians, and Eskimos are based on mutual causal logic (Maruyama, 1974; Camara, 1975). However, Islamic, Hindu, and Chinese philosophies, which Westerners often refer to as "Eastern" philosophies, are much closer to the Western philosophies.

One of the most serious faults of deductive logic is that it fosters homogenistic thinking, belief that differences create conflicts, belief in the existence of one truth, one ultimate God, and so on. As these are very basic problems, let me comment on them one by one.

The logic of the Mandenka tribe who live in West Africa is hetero-genistic (Camara, 1975). According to this logic, homogeneity, not heterogeneity, creates conflicts. They say: "If you force individuals to be similar, the only way left to them to be different is to get on top of one another." There is a great deal of wisdom in this saying. Furthermore, the individual in this tribe goes through different phases of tasks and functions in the society: adolescents are assigned certain specific tasks; those between thirty and thirty-five perform the administrative and caretaker functions of the tribe; those older are given less de-manding tasks, and so on. By going through these different phases, the individual learns to see the same situation from different points of view and to understand individuals in different situations. The individual becomes heterogeneous in himself and becomes capable of poly-ocular vision. They are skeptical of Westernization mainly because the system of specialization brought by the Westerners will lock each individual into one task, and he will become incapable of seeing other persons' points of view.

Likewise, the Japanese think in polyocular vision. Americans, who believe in the existence of one truth, will inevitably ask: If you have different views, which one is right? But consider the following: In the binocular vision it is irrelevant to raise the question as to which eye is correct and which is wrong. Binocular vision works, not because two eyes see different sides of the same object, but because the *differential* between the two images enables the brain to compute the invisible dimension. When there are different points of view, Americans tend to say: "Let's ignore the parts on which we differ and work on the parts on which we agree." But if you cut down the binocular vision to parts on which two eyes agree, what is left is much less than the monocular vision. For the same reason, insistence on the "objective" parts on which everybody agrees impoverishes our vision tremendously, even though many people would consider this approach to be "scientific" thinking. We can say that the "objective" parts are the most in-significant parts of our thinking. The Japanese do not even bother to discover "objectivity" because they can go much further with cross-subjectivity.

## DIFFERENT CULTURES

The word "culture" is used here in the sense of philosophy and pattern of life shared by a number of interacting individuals. It does not mean fine arts, music, and literature as is the case in many European countries, nor entertainment facilities and restaurants as is the case among urban planners in America. "Culture" includes life-style, but it goes much deeper. It also goes further than what is commonly called "social value system," which consists of the preferential order in which the community members rank various physical, psychological, ethical, and aesthetic qualities. More basically, "culture" means the cognitive and behavioral structure through which a person interacts with others and interprets the universe. It is more like "philosophy of life" or "paradigm of life." Some examples may be helpful.

> *Example A:* Life is a cut-throat competition. The stronger takes advantage of the weaker. Success depends on efforts. If someone is unsuccessful, it is his fault because he is not making the necessary effort. Outdo others or you will be a loser. People who are equal to you are your competitors. People who are different are your enemies. Life is a zero-sum game: what someone gains is what someone else loses. Life is a constant competition.

Another example is:

> *Example B:* Life is a harmony of mutual relations. Life is a non-zero-sum game. People can help one another and gain from one another without anybody necessarily losing. Different people can contribute different talents to one another. Some people are born and live under disadvantaged conditions, and they should be helped.

"Culture" is not a geographic concept. Within the same community, the same office, or even the same family, one can find people belonging to different cultures. This is obvious in the case of the generation gap. *Example A* stems from hierarchical, competitive logic, while *Example B* is based on mutualistic logic. There are many other paradigms of life stemming from other different logics:

> *Example C:* Everybody should earn his living. He can work as much as he wants or as little as he wants. But he must be self-sufficient. He must save for his rainy days. He does not need to help others. Do your own thing. Everybody minds his own business.

This individualistic, isolationistic paradigm is closely related to the logic of probabilistic independent events (Maruyama, 1974). It is different both from hierarchism and mutualism. There may also be several different paradigms based on one logic. An example is the following, which stems from the hierarchical logic but is different from *Example A*.

*Example D:* Life is exploitation. I have been exploited. I am a victim. It is not my fault. Rich people should give me what they owe me. I will go begging for a dime on the street, not because I am starving, but because I am entitled to the dime.

An example of a paradigm based on mutualistic logic but slightly different from *Example B* is:

*Example E:* I tend to have a surplus. There is no need to save for rainy days because when I am in need, someone will help me. So I keep giving away my surplus.

It is interesting to note that seemingly similar or identical behavior may be governed by different paradigms stemming from different logics. Compare the following with the preceding example:

*Example F:* I keep giving thing to others because I want to have power over others. Others, who want to receive things from me, would have to obey me. I keep showing off my ability to give because those who have not yet received anything from me would obey me in the hope of getting something from me.
*Example G:* I give things to others because I want to be famous for being generous. I do not expect anything in return. I just want to be a generous man. I am a good guy and a do-gooder. I am superior to others.

Both examples are based on hierarchical logic, even though the behavior may appear to be identical to that in *Example E* which is based on mutualistic logic. As these examples show, culture cannot be identified from or defined by behavior and other observable manifestations only. Both the paradigm underlying the behavior and the logic underlying the paradigm must be understood.

The design of extraterrestrial communities does not have to be based on the paradigm and logic with which we are familiar. We need to examine a wide range of paradigms and logics for their possible use in extraterrestrial communities.

## PRINCIPLES OF COMMUNITY STRUCTURE

There are, and can be, many different principles of community structure. We give here three principles as examples: *hierarchical, individualistic*, and *mutualistic*. Theoretically, it is possible for each of the three to be either *homogenistic* or *heterogenistic*. A hierarchical community is heterogeneous in the sense of vertical stratification, but philosophically it tends to be homogenistic for the reason that hierarchism is related to deductive logic. A mutualistic community has no vertical stratification and allows for horizontal heterogenity. Mutual causal processes are more capable of producing heterogenity than the process of random independent events (Maruyama, 1974). It is also useful to discuss the distinction between *Gesellschaft structure* and *Gemeinschaft structure* in terms of horizontal mobility as they are relevant to heterogenization and homogenization. Also related are two different textures of heterogeneity called *localization* and *interweaving.*

First, let us explain the notion of hierarchy. This word is used with different meanings in different fields of specialization. In physical sciences, the word is often used in the sense of unit of organization. For example, atoms make a molecule; molecules make a biological cell; cells make a tissue; tissues make an organ; organs make a body, and so on. This type of ordering is called "hierarchy."

On the other hand, in social sciences the word "hierarchy" is used in the sense of power structure: who has power over whom. A hierarchical society has a vertical power structure: somebody is at the top, and some people are at the bottom; in between, there are chains of command.

We must also distinguish between homogen*eous* and homogen*istic*, and between heterogen*eous* and heterogen*istic.* For example, American society has been heterogeneous in its population, but ideologically it has been homogenistic with its concepts of melting pot, assimilation, and standardization. Canada has been much more heterogenistic than the United States, with its official recognition of at least two cultural groups and two languages. Recently, heterogenism began to emerge in the United States, especially in the form of ethnic and counterculture movements, but some aspects of the ethnic movement and much of the women's liberation movement are aiming toward homogenization of the entire society.

Here it is important to distinguish two opposite concepts of social integration: one is homogenistic, and the other is heterogenistic. A nonwhite person who wants to move into a white neighborhood in order to behave like a white persom is aiming at homogenistic integration. On the other hand, a Japanese who wants to move into a white neighborhood and build a Japanese house is aiming at heterogenistic integration. This distinction is relevant to the design of extraterrestrial communities.

It is also important to consider two different principles of heterogenization: *localization* and *interweaving.* In localization, each of the heterogeneous elements separates itself and settles in one locality. Chinatown in San Francisco is an example. In localization, heterogeneity increases between different localities, but each locality becomes homogeneous. On the other hand, in interweaving, each of the heterogeneous elements is not localized, but is interwoven with others.

In this system, the accessibility to different elements increases. This system creates no great differences between localities, but within each locality there is great diversity. In an interwoven system, it becomes easier for the individual to *heterogenize* himself or to become something other than what he was. For example, a white person may eat Chinese food on Sunday and Italian food on Friday, learn Judo on Wednesday, and so on. All these activities involve the concept of *Gesellshaft.*

The German sociologist Tönnies made an important distinction between two types of social systems: *Gesellshaft* and *Gemeinshaft.* There are many differences between the two, but the one that concerns us here is that it is easy to move in and out of a *Gesellshaft,* but difficult to do so with a *Gemeinschaft. Gesellschaften* allow for horizontal mobility of people between them. For example, one can relatively easily change jobs between companies or agencies in the United States, while it is more difficult to do so in Germany or in Japan. In this respect, American companies and agencies are more like *Gesellschaften,* and German and Japanese companies are more like *Gemeinschaften.* One characteristic of a *Gesellschaft* is that it can amplify its eccentricity: those who do not like it will leave, and those who like it will join and stay. It can also easily eliminate nonconformists. Thus, homogeneity tends to increase within a *Gesellschaft,* although heterogeneity may increase between *Gesellschaften.* At the same time, a *Gesellschaft* may become very intolerant of nonconformists.

There is an interesting relationship between the fact that the United States began as a colony of voluntary immigrants and the fact that its past philosophy and ideology has been homogenistic. The United States simply began as a *Gesellschaft* with a slogan: "If you like our ideology, you are welcome. But if you do not like our ideology, go back to where you came from." Thus began the policy of assimilation, and immigrants were eager to become "standard Americans."

A *Gemeinschaft,* on the other hand, must deal with nonconformists differently. It must either suppress or accept them. Thus, it may become either homogenistically totalitarian or heterogenistic, depending on its policy and philosophy. These considerations are very important in the design of extraterrestrial communities. The degree to which the extraterrestrial communities are *Gesellschaft*-like or *Gemeinschaft*-like makes a great difference in the degree of homogeneity or heterogeneity they attain. As discussed earlier, there must be heterogeneity between communities as well as within each community.

## THE MATCHING PROBLEM

Needless to say, individuals vary in their tastes, abilities, and optimal rates of communication. No culture is "healthy" or "unhealthy" for everybody. Each culture is healthy for those whose tastes, abilities, and rates of communication match with it, and unhealthy for others (Maruyama, 1959, 1961; Hendin, 1964). High-communication individuals will suffer in a low-communication community, and low-communication individuals will suffer in a high-communication community. The same holds for the matching of individuals to jobs, or individuals to individuals.

Successful matching requires availability of variety, which in turn depends on the number of different types of communities as well as the degree of heterogeneity within a community. Also, certain types of facilities require a certain size of population. For example, a symphony orchestra cannot exist in a small town.

There is also the problem of size versus number. For example, many areas of the American Midwest have a large number of small colleges, each with 1,000 or 2,000 students. They all have libraries with more or less the same basic books. In a way, this large number of small colleges creates heterogeneity, but in another sense, a small number of large universities can create more heterogeneity, especially in the variety of library books or in the variety of departmental subjects.

The same problem will be encountered in planning extraterrestrial communities. Certain types of heterogeneity can be maximized by having a large number of small communities, and other types by making a small number of large communities.

Also involved is the problem of horizontal mobility (migration between communities) of individuals in order to increase matching. Then there will be the problem of the *Gesellschaft* syndrome of localized homogeneity and intolerance.

## THE DECISION PROCESS AND ADMINISTRATION

The principle of American democracy involves two logical fallacies: first, it is based on majority rule, which amounts to domination by the larger group and the imposition of homogeneity, and the disregard of and discrimination against minorities; second, it is based on "voting for your own interest," encouraging the individual to disregard the interests of others. Such a system promotes noncontextual thinking, competitiveness, and partisan-mindedness.

Most Americans propose the consensus system as an alternative to the majority system. However, the consensus system also tends to be homogenistic if it assumes that everybody should do the same thing.

Another system is that of eliminating hardships on any single individual. This system is practiced by Navajos. Sitting in a circle, each person expresses his point of view, and alternative solutions are explored until a way is found which does not cause hardship on any individual and at the same time allows for individual diversity for all persons.

Let me illustrate how the three systems produce three different solutions for the same problem. Suppose we have to decide whether to build a bridge over a river. If people disagree, we cannot build just half a bridge; we must build either the whole bridge or none at all. The majority system will count the votes, take the majority decision, and forget about the minorities. This is considered democratic. The consensus system will listen to the minorities and will work hard until a unanimous decision is reached. The hardship-on-nobody system will be concerned not so much with whether to build the bridge, but rather with what to do for those who will suffer any hardship, whichever way the decision goes: i.e., if the bridge is to be built, some people may suffer from it. Then a way to alleviate the hardship must be found. If the bridge is not to be built, some other people may suffer. Then a way to alleviate their hardship must be found.

With the first two systems people will be happy as soon as the decision is reached either to build the bridge or not. They do not have to be concerned about eliminating the negative consequences of the decision. The third system is concerned more with eliminating the negative consequences of the decision than with the direction of the decision per se. The third system has more respect for each individual than the first two systems.

In a large society, consensus is difficult to reach, even with the help of computers and communications technology. The third system, on the other hand, is less difficult and should be feasible with the communications and computer technology currently available. Nevertheless, I suspect that the voting system would continue for a while until the hardship-on-nobody system became established. If the voting system is to continue, the majority has the responsibility of taking the minorities' points of view into consideration when they vote. The so-called minority problems are really the majority problems as long as the voting system continues. It is no longer permissible to "vote for your own interest" only. The majority has the duty to understand the minorities' situations. In the long run, this will require more communication, education, and information than the replacement of the voting system by the hardship-on-nobody system.

## PSYCHOLOGICAL DIFFICULTIES

Several geometrical forms for the physical shape of the extra-terrestrial communities have been studied. Among them are a cylinder a few kilometers in diameter; a torus a few kilometers in diameter and several tens of meters in cross-section; a bundle of more narrow parallel tori; a necklace shape consisting of small spheres; and a pair of large spheres, each of which has a diameter of several kilometers. They have been examined from the points of view of volume, mass, rotational speed, shielding needed, construction costs, and the like. There are also some psychological considerations which affect the mental health of the inhabitants. Different geometrical forms of the communities may also influence the types of social interactions and social organization that take place in them.

Some environments are conducive to the state of mind in which everything appears to be a dream, not real. This state of mind occurs, for example, in the arctic winter when it is night twenty-four hours a day. It is also known to occur in some of the youths who have been brought up on television as a reality substitute.

Solipsism, a theory which states that the self is the only reality, is interesting as a philosophical theory because it is internally consistent and therefore cannot be disproved. As a psychological state, however, it is highly uncomfortable. Just try to force yourself to think for one hour that nothing exists outside your brain, that your whole life is a long dream from which you can never wake up. You are trapped in a nightmare. Even your friends are not real—they are part of your dream. You feel very lonely and detached, and eventually you become apathetic and indifferent.

I lived in Sweden for four years, in the small town of Lund. During the winter, there were six hours of daylight and eighteen hours of night. I spent most of my life under artificial light. In such an environment, my life acquired a special quality. When I went outdoors, rather than landscapes all I saw were street corners lit by lamps; these street corners looked like theater stages, detached from one another. As a result, it appeared that there was no connectedness or depth in the universe. As with theater stages, the universe took on a counterfeit quality. (Ingmar Bergman's film *Wild Strawberries* expresses this quality very well.)

This state of mind can easily be produced in an environment where everything is artificial, where everything is like a theater stage, where every wish can be fulfilled by a push-button, and where there is nothing beyond the theater stage and beyond your control.

Solipsism in extraterrestrial communities can be alleviated by several means:

1. A design which enables one to see far beyond the "theater stage" vicinity. Something must exist physically at a distance and must be overwhelmingly visible.
2. Something must exist beyond man's manipulation. One learns to cope with reality precisely because the reality is different

from one's imagination. If the reality is the same as the imagination, one cannot avoid falling into solipsism. In extraterrestrial communities, everything will be controlled. However, some amount of "unpredictability" can be built in within the controllable range, partly by generating artificial unpredictability by means of a table of random numbers and partly by allowing animals and plants a degree of freedom and independence from human planning. Both types of unpredictability must have a high visibility in order to be effective. This high visibility is easier to achieve in a macro-geometry which allows a longer line of sight.

3. Something must exist which *grows.* It is important to feel that the universe is not static or thermodynamically and informationally decaying, but instead is self-generating and morphogenetic. Interactive processes generate new patterns which cannot be inferred from the information contained in the old state. This is not the result of randomness but rather of differentiation-amplifying mutual causal loops (Maruyama, 1963). It is important to feel that one can personally contribute to something which grows, that in order to do so he must learn reality principles, that the reality often goes in a direction different from one's expectation, and finally that which is taken care of (one's child, for example) may possess more wisdom than oneself and may grow into something beyond himself. From this point of view, it is important for parents to raise their children themselves.

4. It is also important to have "something beyond the horizon" which gives one the feeling that the world is larger than what can be seen.

Five forms of macrogeometry can be compared on the basis of the four criteria discussed above:

| | cylinder | sphere | circular torus | bundle torus | necklace |
|---|---|---|---|---|---|
| (1) | excellent | excellent | medium | poor | very poor |
| (2) | excellent | excellent | medium | poor | very poor |
| (3) | excellent | excellent | medium | poor | very poor |
| (4) | very poor | very poor | excellent | medium | medium |

The cylinder and spherical forms provide no horizon at all. In the torus forms, the "horizon" is really the ceiling which hides the "place behind," instead of the floor or the ground as in the case on Earth. The circular torus with a cross-section diameter of several tens of meters will allow several hundred meters of line of sight. The bundle torus consists of much narrower tori and the line of sight is much shorter.

Another difficulty is what I call *shimanagashi* syndrome. During the feudal period in Japan, political offenders were often sent away and confined on small islands. This form of punishment was called *shimanagashi*. Many American prisons today have isolation units or segregation units where inmates considered to be troublemakers are confined for a length of time.

To a smaller degree, the "mainlanders" who spend a few years in Hawaii share the prisoner's sense of isolation. Announcements of conferences, manuscript deadlines, and the like often arrive in Hawaii long after the conferences have taken place or the deadlines have passed. Although physically life in Hawaii is very comfortable, mentally the newcomer at least suffers from the *shimanagashi* syndrome. For many people, Alaska holds more challenge and excitement than Hawaii. Daily life in Alaska often consists of emergencies that test man's resourcefulness and ability to cooperate with others. Furthermore, Hawaii is a group of small islands and so does not allow travel beyond the shoreline. In contrast, in Alaska travel possibilities are unlimited because the snow on land and ice on the ocean serve as unending highways for sleds and skis.

Would immigrants to extraterrestrial communities suffer from the *shimanagashi* syndrome? Technologists assure us that journals and books will be transmitted electronically between Earth and extraterrestrial communities. Therefore, extraterrestrial communities will not be isolated in terms of communication. However, in terms of physical travel they will be, at least between Earth and these communities, because Earth is at the bottom of a deep gravity hole. But when numerous extraterrestrial communities have been constructed, travel between them will be quite inexpensive because of the lack of gravity.

## INTERNATIONAL PARTICIPATION

Some extraterrestrial communities will probably belong to different nations on Earth, some will be international, and others may even form new independent extraterrestrial nations.

It cannot be assumed that the first extraterrestrial communities will be purely American for by the time the first extraterrestrial community materializes the United States may no longer be a major world power or a major technological center. And even if the United States remains a major world power, many nations, including non-Western nations, will be highly technological by then. It will therefore be a waste of human resources if we do not internationalize the first extraterrestrial community.

a movement of growing importance. In most of sub-Saharan Africa and Southeast Asia, nation-states represent arbitrary inheritances of colonial powers. Boundaries cross ethnic lines and unite different subcultures while often dividing members of a single clan or extended family. Since nation-states are at best inefficient and at worst arbitrary and inhuman, they constitute poor models for a global society. Not only is a large bureaucratic presence on the world level dangerous because of its centralization of power and responsibility, but it is also unrealistic in view of current trends that question nation-state legitimacy even in a more local dimension.

In the past years, a number of theorists, perceiving the need for global coordination but finding the concept of world government undesirable and impracticable, advocated the creation of international organizations of a strictly functional character (see Falk's "central steering system" [1976]; and Laszlo's "World Homeostat System" [1974]). Such organizations would operate like a vastly improved and more powerful United Nations but would stop short of constituting a world government. Their mandate would be to monitor and regulate global trends in areas such as the environment, population, security, energy, resources, trade, and the "global commons" (the oceans, polar regions, and space), leaving governments to control domestic affairs in all areas that do not have a direct impact on the global future. More recently, similar recommendations were made by an international team coordinated by Tinbergen (1976). This group set forth proposals for international decision-making in ten functional areas: the international monetary system; income redistribution and financing of development; food production; industrialization, trade, and international division of labor; energy, ores, and minerals; the human environment; transnational enterprises; scientific research and technological development; arms reduction; and ocean management. Still more recently, another international team, led by Laszlo (1977), called for international organizations and centralized management only in the areas of security, food, energy, and resources. This group maintains that other issues can be adequately handled on national, regional, and subnational levels, provided that long-range planning is practiced, that plans are exchanged among the policy-makers prior to implementation, and that conflicts are ironed out through negotiation.

At the opposite end of the spectrum of current recommendations for a future world order from that of world governmentalists and federalists, we find those of more revolutionary policy advocates. These reject all attempts at centralization and hierarchical management as arbitrary and coercive, instead they seek spontaneous transformations in basic values, behaviors, and institutions. Among such advocates we find not

Hendin, H. 1964. *Suicide and Scandinavia*. New York: Grune and Stratton.

Kawagley, D. 1975. *Yupik Stories*. Anchorage: AMU Press.

Maruyama, M. 1959. "A Critique of Some Widely Held Assumptions on the Relationship Between Culture and Mental Health." *Revue de Psychologie des Peuples*, Volume 14, 273–276.

———. 1961. "The Multilateral Mutual Causal Relationships Among the Modes of Communication, Sociometric Pattern and Intellectual Orientation in the Danish Culture." *Phylon*, Volume 22, 41–58.

———. 1963. "The Second Cybernetics: Deviation-amplifying Mutual Causal Processes." *American Scientist*, Volume 51, 164–179, 250–256.

———. 1974. "Paradigmatology and Its Application to Cross-disciplinary, Cross-professional and Cross-cultural Communication." *Cybernetica*, Volume 17, 136–156, 237–281.

Michaud, M. 1976. "The Consequences of Space Colonization." Paper presented at the meeting of the American Anthropological Association.

O'Neill, Gerard. 1977. *The High Frontier*. New York: William Morrow.

Wright, S. 1931. "Evolution in Mendelian Population." *Genetics*, Volume 16, 97–159.

# Part V

## The Challenges for Futures Research

What lies ahead for this new field of activity? The authors of these final chapters believe that futures research is just beginning to get under way. These are likely people to deal with the question of the prospects for futures research because they were present at the beginning; in fact, each in his own way helped to get futures research started. They have well-defined, if different, notions about where the field has come from and where it should be going.

Olaf Helmer, who more than any other single person has been responsible for the methodological underpinnings of the field, lists twenty-one concerns that should be investigated if the more scientific aspects of the field are to progress. Futures research, he says, "calls for an immense amount of basic research effort in order to bring it to full fruition."

Not all futurists would agree with Helmer that methodological concerns should be paramount or that activism should be avoided. One who takes issue with him is Frank Snowden Hopkins, vice-president of the World Future Society, which he helped found in 1966. Hopkins' agenda for futures research calls for a heightened awareness of where mankind is straying and a willingness to intervene in behalf of a more successful future. For all the differences between them, Hopkins is as forthright as Helmer.

These two perspectives on futures research are combined in the chapter by Willis Harman and Peter Schwartz. Although long involved in the operations of think-tanks, they are sympathetic to the most deeply felt concerns of futurists. They state that certain attributes of the field will become more conspicious as it matures, and that certain problems can be identified now whose solutions are not yet apparent.

On this temperate note, we conclude.

Although we may stop, saying that is all our particular mosaic of futures research reveals at this point, the field moves on, picking up and sloughing practitioners, opening and closing lines of investigation, ever growing. We can be certain that the body of practices and data will expand. It is in the nature of the societies that sustain futures research, as well as their institutions and organizations, that there can be no reduction in the need to anticipate and plan. This is because, like it or not, modern societies are traveling where *Homo sapiens* has never been before; the upshot can only be greater uncertainty and greater demand for an uninjurious future. It appears that increased knowledge and control of the future are our destiny.

OLAF HELMER

# The Research Tasks Before Us

Futures research, as an organized activity, is still in its adolescence. It was in the early 1960s that the Futuribles group, under Bertrand de Jouvenel, began to carry out future-directed social and political studies; that Daniel Bell formed the Commission on the Year 2000; that Dennis Gabor wrote *Inventing the Future*; and that the first major technological forecasting study was carried out at RAND by Theodore Gordon and myself.

True, there were earlier, precursory developments, such as the work of the Prospective group in France led by Gaston Berger and my own invention of the Delphi technique in the early 1950s in conjunction with Norman Dalkey. Another, more philosophically oriented contribution might be seen in the essay "On the Epistemology of the Inexact Sciences," in which I collaborated with Nicholas Rescher in the late 1950s (Helmer and Rescher, 1959). But these were just signs in the wind, and it was not until the mid-1960s that the efforts particularly of the Futuribles and the RAND-sponsored futures groups began to be emulated throughout the world. These efforts have resulted in a full-fledged futures movement, with institutes, journals, professional societies, and such governmentally supported offspring as the Educational Policy Research Centers and the Office of Technology Assessment.

This proliferation of futures studies, while gratifying in some respects, has had some decided drawbacks. The reason for the explosive adoption around the world of Delphi-type explorations of the future, of simulation techniques for long-range planning, and of other futures-oriented methods was not merely the quality of the original, prototype studies. A more important impetus was the recognition of the crucial need for the social sciences to begin to catch up with the physical sciences in their ability to cope with the problems of the real

SOURCE: Presented at the Conference on Research Needs in Futures Research, January 10–11, 1974, conducted by The Futures Group under National Science Foundation Grant GI-37178; to be published in Wayne I. Boucher (ed.), *The Study of the Future; An Agenda for Research* (forthcoming).

world—a need made more urgent by the growing complexity and the accelerated pace of change in our operating environment. The widely felt requirement for better long-range planning in the areas of social and political institutions, of the physical environment, and of international relations has caused too many people to place too great hopes in the benefits to be derived from the new discipline of futures research. Its failure to live up to these expectations has begun to produce a backlash, in that some new doubts have been raised as to whether futures research is altogether an activity worth pursuing.

Many people forget that a decade or so is a very short time period in the development of any intellectual movement. First, there has been insufficient time to place the discipline of futures research on a solid conceptual foundation. Second, the pursuit of this desideratum—though well recognized as such by some—has been encumbered simply because demands for pragmatic results have had priority over solidifying the foundation and because, of necessity, along with serious researchers, some charlatans and incompetents have joined the increasing number of practitioners.

The time has come, therefore, to reflect on the content of futures research, the genuine promise it offers, measures to improve its intellectual basis, and the priorities that should be assigned to its applications.

The function of futures research is to provide decision-makers with operationally meaningful assistance in the form of information and analysis that can facilitate better decision-making. Operations research, its parent, originated in World War II and proved to be of immense help in the conduct of wartime military operations. Most of its later applications to problems of the civilian sector of government and to problems of commerce and industry, while different in subject matter, were similar in purpose. They concerned management decisions affecting either the daily operations of an agency or firm, or its relatively short-range planning activity—short-range in the sense that the operating environment at the time the plans were to be implemented could be expected to be essentially the same as that at the time the planning decisions were being made.

The main characteristic differentiating futures research from standard operations research is that its objective is to improve decision-making in the case of long-range plans. Here "long-range," in contrast to "short-range," clearly means that the operational conditions at the time of implementation are expected to differ substantially from those prevailing at the time of planning.

We note in passing that more and more of the important decisions are moving from the short-range into the long-range category. There are two reasons for this shift: first, many of our decisions concern increasingly complex situations, where the time horizon is farther in the future, as illustrated by our attempts to solve the energy crisis, to plan a new city, or to develop an underdeveloped country. Second, as we all know, we live in an age of ubiquitous future shock, in which changes in our living environment occur with ever-increasing rapidity, due primarily as a result of technological advances and their societal implications. These two trends, by mutual reinforcement, have given futures research the premature prominence that we observe today.

Because of the pragmatic nature of futures research, its function is primarily predictive rather than explanatory. By forecasting the future environment and the consequences of alternative plans for coping with the environment, it attempts to improve the decision-making process. Often its findings may merely be based on observed correlations between phenomena or on the intuitive, pre-theoretical judgment of experts, falling far short of a causal explanation for the expected consequences of proposed actions. While a fuller understanding of the underlying causes would surely always be welcomed, the success of futures research has to be measured in terms of the quality of the decisions it makes possible rather than of its explanatory force.

Therefore, futures research is pre-scientific in nature. The urgency of the task—whether it be the conduct of military operations, the management of the energy crisis, or the search for cures for our sick society—is so great that we do not have the time to construct neat scientific theories which would permit us to identify the optimal plan of action to be followed. Instead, in the tradition of operations research, the futures researcher constructs ad hoc models as best he can, well knowing that they may be imperfect and will have to be corrected and improved as more data are obtained and more experience is accumulated.

No claim is made that such imperfect models produce perfect foresight. That the resulting decisions are often non-optimal should be no reason to reject the futures research effort. Its aim is to produce the best practically attainable decisions, even if not necessarily the theoretically best decisions. Considering the often enormous payoff attached to decisions regarding the long-range future, even a small improvement in the quality of such decisions may yield very appreciable returns.

Next, it seems to me, that the following observation ought to be made. A rigorous scientific approach involves three interactive elements: theory construction, empirical-data collection, and controlled experimentation. I have already pointed out that the model-building endeavor of futures research falls short of the rigor demanded of scientific theory construction. Not only are its models comparatively "soft" but so too, at times, are its data and its experimental procedures. There are no hard data about the future, and the futures analyst must instead rely on soft, judgmental data. That is, he must use probabilistic pronouncements by experts about the future operating environment as a substitute for firm, observational data. Real experimentation is often replaced by pseudo-experimentation. A simulation model is used in which players, acting the parts of real world decision-makers, test the implications of alternative decisions in the model, in the hope that the simulation has sufficient verisimilitude to permit a transfer of the model results to the real world.

Thus, reliance on the intuitive judgment of experts is not just a temporary expedient but a necessary ingredient of futures research, for they are needed in all phases of the effort. They are called upon (1) to supply judgmental data about the future, based on their intuitive, though often theoretically unstructured, insights into real world phenomena; (2) to construct ad hoc models or to judge the suitability of existing models; (3) to apply their expertise as role players in simulation games, and in addition, they are often required (4) to use their imagination and inventiveness to design the instrumentalities and long-range strategies that result in appropriate action programs.

Despite its relative softness and, in particular, its inevitable reliance on expert judgment, futures research aspires to be objective. At first glance, this statement appears to be a contradiction in terms, since objectivity of a discipline can almost be defined as "the intersubjectivity of its findings independent of any one person's intuitive judgment" (Helmer and Rescher, 1959). To preserve the claim to objectivity, the futures researcher must dissociate himself logically from the experts. That is, he must regard himself as an experimenter who uses the experts as measuring instruments of reality, taking their pronouncements about the future world in the same spirit as, say, the readings on a measuring device are taken as an indication of some property of the present world. The experts are thus viewed as black boxes which receive questions as inputs and produce answers as outputs. Different experimenters, using different but comparable sets of such "black boxes," should be expected to arrive at comparable results. This places a special obligation on the discipline of futures research to devise suitable measures for the degree of reliability of these instruments and to seek ways of improving their quality (i.e., of helping the experts increase the reliability of their performance).

Another point to be made is that, since futures research is concerned with the planning of human activities, it is, of necessity, multi-disciplinary. Even if the planning objective itself is unidisciplinary (which is seldom the case), attention must be given to the technological, socioeconomic, cultural, and physical environmental circumstances, in consideration of which plans have to be made, as well as to the psychology of the decision-makers. Usually, the more important a planning decision is, the more complex is the area to be surveyed, and the more intricately interwoven are the considerations that different disciplines have to contribute. In planning a transportation system, or a reform of the educational or the health-care delivery systems, or a new city, there is hardly a single discipline that will not be required to supply specialized inputs to the planning process in the form of assessments by experts of probable future developments. Therefore, futures analysis has to develop effective and efficient means of facilitating cross-disciplinary cooperation toward common planning objectives.

Finally, to fulfill its purpose of improving the decision-making process regarding long-range plans, futures research has to address itself explicitly to the criteria problem. First it must identify the planning criteria, that is, the payoff function or functions or the utility vector to be maximized. This problem involves several extremely difficult sub-problems—specifically, those of exchange ratios in the case of multi-dimensional utiliities, relative weights in the case of a multiplicity of beneficiaries who need to be satisified; and changing values systems, which may cause future criteria of optimization to be different from present criteria. Second, given a set of criteria, there is a question of determining the comparative degree to which alternative action programs can be expected to satisfy these criteria. All of these tasks are analytical in nature, require cost-effectiveness and systems analysis, and must be clearly distinguished from the normative problems of what ought to be done about the future. A large faction among futures researchers wants to emphasize this normative aspect of their work. In contradistinction to futures analysis, this segment of futures research, which is devoted to what is sometimes called "normative forecasting," might perhaps best be described as "futures synthesis." To date, this segment, which covers the spectrum from abstract utopian writing to belligerent demagogic activism, is poorly organized and badly in need of conceptual systematization.)

These, then, are some of the features of futures research as seen by one of its practitioners. It is a methodological approach for which there is a great pragmatic need in our society. It has a great deal of promise and calls for an immense amount of basic research effort in order to bring it to full fruition. This constellation of urgency, of great potentialities, and of wide-open opportunities for original research ought to attract the participation of some of our best intellects and the support of our public and private funding sources.

Let me now attempt to outline an agenda for some of the specific research tasks that lie ahead, as suggested by the above analysis of the purpose and present status of futures research. This agenda is organized under the following headings: data collection; model construction; experimentation; systems analysis; substantive applications: exploratory; and substantive applications: normative. In each of these categories I will list some of the areas that seem to me to be particularly in need of research.

## DATA COLLECTION

All our knowledge about the future is ultimately derived by some form of extrapolation, however subtle, from the past. The kind of empirical data on which such extrapolations might be based are no different from the data that provide us with whatever insight into our present world we have. Leaving aside whatever standard difficulties there may be in amassing such basic empirical information, the analysis of the future, as I pointed out before, requires as inputs another kind of quasi-data in the form of judgmental estimates about future operating conditions. While these judgments are formed by experts through some implicit process of extrapolation from the past, this process is rarely based on a well-articulated theoretical procedure but more often is intuitive and pre-theoretical in nature. Epistemologically, their function is comparable to that of measuring instruments.

This whole area of judgmental data collection is in considerable need of further exploration. This suggests the following specific research items:

1. *Rating and improving the performance of individual experts as forecasters:* How can the performance of an expert be calibrated? How do self- and peer ratings compare with one another and with other, more "objective" rating systems? How can an expert's performance be enhanced? What data, data processing facilities, models, simulations, or communication devices would be most helpful to him?
2. *Utilization of groups of experts:* If two or more experts supply probability distributions over time for the occurrence of some potential future event, what is the appropriate mode of combining their individual estimates into a joint probability distribution? What use can be made here of any available performance calibrations or information about systematic bias of the experts? How can the judgments of experts belonging to different fields of specialization best be combined into an interdisciplinary estimate? How do the anonymity and feedback

features of Delphi compare with other modes of using experts, such as polling, face-to-face discussion, or other conventional conference procedures?

3. *Improvements in the Delphi technique:* What degree of anonymity is most helpful to the performance of a Delphi panel? What influence does the wording of questions have? How should the entire questioning process be structured? If the subject of inquiry is multidisciplinary and if differential calibrations of the experts with regard to each discipline are available, how can the best use be made of this information? How does a hierarchical panel structure compare with a homogeneous one? How stable is a panel's judgment over time? What is the optimal panel size? Is a panel of two or three top-notch experts preferable to a panel of a dozen reasonably good experts?

All of these questions call for extensive experimentation. There is an obvious obstacle to carrying out such experiments, because good experts are too rare a commodity and their time is too precious for them to be readily available as experimental laboratory subjects. Some of the indicated experiments have indeed been carried out, notably by Norman Dalkey, but using graduate students as surrogate experts. There remains a gnawing doubt whether all of the results obtained in this manner carry over to the case of real experts, and at least some careful experimentation is mandatory to establish this crucial point. (Parenthetically, the kind of spectacular convergence of opinions obtained by Dalkey and myself in our first Delphi experiment in connection with a military problem has rarely been repeated in subsequent applications [Dalkey and Helmer, 1963]. My intuition tells me that the technique was successful in this regard at the time because of a fortunate combination of circumstances, namely, the discriminate use of specialists in several relevant disciplines and the availability of at least a crude model structure that facilitated interaction of the panelists' inputs. In contrast, many of the later applications and experimental explorations of Delphi have been much more simplistic, prohibiting the subtle kind of interplay that contributed to the success of that first Delphi study. A return to a more sophisticated approach may well be worthwhile.)

## MODEL CONSTRUCTION

Futures-analytical models, as I indicated before, tend to be more tentative than rigorous scientific models are. Because of their soft, ad hoc character, their quality—like that of soft data—depends greatly on the good sense of their constructors. The question arises whether, as in the case of judgmental data collection, a group effort might be superior to an individual effort in selecting or inventing a model. This suggests the following, fourth, research area:

4. *Application of Delphi to model construction:* How should a Delphi inquiry be structured, if its aim is to produce a model for a specific forecasting or decision-making purpose? In particular, how can the facility of a remote-conferencing network best be used toward this end?

The construction of models of any kind is not an easy undertaking when they are intended to cope with a subject matter within the general domain of the social sciences, and hardly any futures-analytical topics are devoid of social science aspects. In this context, it would be helpful to have a simple, general-purpose model kit that would permit the construction of at least a rudimentary model, no matter what the subject matter. One such kit, however inadequate in some respects, in fact exists in the form of the cross-impact approach. Its prescription is very simple: If your concern is with the future of Topic X, make a list of potential future developments whose occurrence or non-occurrence would either make a decisive difference to the future of X or would be a significant indicator of X's future status. Make probability estimates for the occurrence of these developments. Then look at them in pairs and estimate how much the occurrence of each would affect the probability of occurrence of the other. Finally, use a Monte Carlo process to decide for each development whether it does or does not occur, making prescribed adjustments in the probabilities of the others as you go along. The result, in effect, is a modeling process that produces scenarios of the future, incorporating all important aspects relevant to the phenomena that were intended to be explored.

There are numerous problems in connection with this tool for the future-oriented social scientist, some of which I am about to list. Yet, its promise seems far from negligible, and a pursuit of improvements in this technique seems worthwhile. Specifically, this suggests the following, fifth item of study:

5. *Basic cross-impact concept:* How can double accounting in a cross-impact matrix be properly avoided? That is, if Event A has a direct impact on Event C but also has an indirect impact on it via another event, B, how can we make sure that this indirect impact is not also reflected in the direct impact of A on C, and thus counted twice? How can multidimensional aspects

be handled, where two or more occurrences jointly affect the probability of another event?

Since the cross-impact approach attempts to deal with causal rather than merely correlative effects, the traditional case distinction for two attributes A and B into

$$A.B, \; A.\bar{B}, \; \bar{A}.B, \; \bar{A}.\bar{B}$$

needs to be replaced, in the case of two events A and B, by

$$A.B, \; B.A, \; A.\bar{B}, \; \bar{A}.B, \; \bar{A}.\bar{B},$$

where the first two instances differ in that either the occurrence of A precedes that of B, or vice versa. Hence the following item:

6. *Causal probabilities:* Is there a need for a special "causal probability" calculus, or is the traditional, correlational probability calculus adequate for causal cross-impact applications?

The original approach to cross impact, which Theodore Gordon and I introduced in 1965, dealt with events only, that is, with occurrences at specific points in time. In considering potential future developments, however, it is important to give some attention also to trends, that is, to gradual fluctuations over time. In fact, most of the traditional econometric models, and similarly the systems dynamics approach utilized in the *Limits to Growth* study, go in just the opposite direction by examining interrelations between trends only and neglecting point events altogether. In the cross-impact approach, it is conceptually easy (though troublesome in detail) to adjoin the consideration of trends to that of events. In the case of a trend, the equivalent of an "event," for cross-impact purposes, is a deviation of the trend value from its anticipated course. Some of the problems arising in this context are the following:

7. *Trend-enriched cross-impact concept:* Since the impact of a trend, T (on either an event or another trend), depends on the amount, $\Delta T$, by which it deviates from its anticipated value, should the effect be considered a linear function of $\Delta T$, or what other functional form is appropriate? Does an impact on a trend cause a persistent shift in its future course, or a gradually declining shift, or merely a momentary blip? How does one decide which of these, in a particular case, is the most appropriate form of the impact? Can the separate, independent impacts caused by two or more developments be considered additive?

8. *Production of cross-impact inputs:* What efficient procedures

are there for eliciting large numbers of entries into a cross-impact matrix from a panel of experts? How can this process be expedited with the help of a network of computer terminals?

9. *Continuous cross impacts:* How can the present discrete cross-impact format, where an occurrence in one time period has an effect in the next or some later time period, be made continuous, so that occurrences can take place at any time and their impacts be registered at any time thereafter?

## EXPERIMENTATION

In the absence of a time machine, true experimentation about the future is a logical impossibility. Data obtained from an experiment always are data about the past, and statements about the future can only be derived from them by extrapolation. Hence, we have to resort to pseudo-experimentation, which means the construction of a simulation model about the future and experimentation within that model, in the hope that results thus obtained carry over to the real world of the future. There are some obvious questions in this connection:

10. *Validity of pseudo-experimentation:* How can the validity of results obtained by pseudo-experimentation be checked or measured? By what means can at least the relative validity be enhanced? How can the effectiveness of simulation gaming as an aid to the forecasting performance of an expert be increased?

Let me now turn to a particular form of simulation gaming, namely, cross-impact gaming. Just as the basic cross-impact approach is a (perhaps somewhat simplistic) general-purpose type of modeling, so cross-impact gaming is a general-purpose mode of simulation. A cross-impact model of the future of Topic X is turned into a simulation game by introducing one or more players into the model and giving them the option of intervening in the normal course of developments by interjecting an action program. The effects of such actions are handled in the model just as those of any other events are in that their impacts on the events and trends represented in the model are estimated and superimposed on the cross impacts already present in the model. Perhaps the most important application of this idea is to planning situations, where a single player, the planner, intervenes in the normal course of events by trying out alternative action programs. But there is no reason why the simulation model cannot also be used by several players, representing different interests, who can use the model to study the interactions of their separate interventions. Some of the questions to be answered in this context are summarized in the following item:

11. *Cross-impact gaming:* How can the realism of cross-impact gaming be increased? How can it best be used to aid the forecasting and planning performance of the participating players? Can it be an effective stimulant to the invention of new strategies for meeting future contingencies? Can the simulation be used, by having the players observe the intuitive acceptability of the results of their actions, to correct and thereby improve the probability and cross-impact estimates on which the cross-impact model is based? What would be the legitimacy of such a self-correcting procedure? In the multiplayer case, can effective use be made of a network of computer terminals for processing the interactions of the various players' interventions?

## SYSTEMS ANALYSIS

The application of futures research to long-range planning involves the choice of policies and the design of action programs. These, in turn, if they are intended to be rational and practical rather than mere exercises of the imagination, have to take into account both the resource constraints on the actions and the expected payoff in terms of improved conditions at some future time. Thus, cost-effectiveness considerations enter into the picture and, with them, all the problems of systems analysis:

12. *Systems costs:* How can nonmonetary social costs be appropriately related to monetary costs so that overall systems costs can be meaningfully estimated? How can future costs be reliably estimated? What discount rate is appropriate, considering present interest rates, uncertainties regarding future costs and benefits, and our diminishing concern over the future as a function of the time horizon? Hence, how should future costs be compared to present costs? How should expenditures in the private sector be compared with public sector expenditures? How should outright expenditures be compared with investments made in the expectation of future repayment? Since future costs depend on future contingencies, is it possible to design a cost cross-impact model, in which the impacts of events and trend changes on costs are systematically analyzed?
13. *Systems benefits:* Given a topic X, for the future of which

plans are to be made, what is an appropriate set of social or other indicators in terms of which a future condition of X can be described and different future conditions can be compared? What are the interest groups whose differential desires regarding the future condition of X must be considered? What rational methods are there for assigning weights to different interest groups? What are the dimensions of satisfaction in terms of which gratification with the future condition of X can be measured? How can such multidimensional utilities be combined, and what are their exchange ratios? What is the appropriate discount rate for future benefits, again considering increasing uncertainties of, and decreasing concern over, the future as the time horizon recedes? In the absence of a single payoff function, how can the overall degree be measured to which a given action program can be expected to comply with a variety of goal criteria? Can the kind of cost cross-impact model mentioned under the preceding item ("Systems costs") be extended to include benefit cross impacts, reflecting diminished or enhanced benefits associated with substitutabilities and complementarities among proposed actions?

14. *Representative scenarios:* Considering the usually vast number of possible scenarios of the future, no specific one of which has a more than negligible chance of occurring, is it possible to single out a small, manageable set of "representative" scenarios, in the sense that any scenario is sufficiently similar, for planning purposes, to one of the representative scenarios? Can a planner then confine himself to planning on action program against the contingencies depicted in the representative scenarios and still be confident that his program will stand up to every possible contingency? How can the scenario-generating mechanism of the cross-impact approach best be utilized in this context?

## SUBSTANTIVE APPLICATIONS: EXPLORATORY

The research agenda outlined thus far has been concerned with methodology. Turning now to substantive applications, one might cite virtually all the woes of our society as suitable subject areas for futures research. However, I will confine myself to listing only some of those areas that seem to be of outstanding importance and to have a specific requirement for the long-range aspects of futures research (in the sense that the operating environment at the time when the effects of any reform plans might be felt are expected to differ substantially from present operating conditions). Thus, for example, the subject of a reform of our criminal justice and our health-care delivery systems, while of unquestioned importance, will not be listed. Changes in technology and in our value systems, which may indeed affect these societal institutions, will do so in only a very minor way, considering the very major deficiencies that are already in evidence.

The listing is broken down into four subcategories:

15. *Public sector applications:* How should the educational system at all levels be reformed, utilizing new technologies now available or on the horizon, so that to those being educated the results will be meaningful during the rest of their lifetimes—much of which may be in the first half of the twenty-first century? What should be done to regulate and to preclude mismanagement of our anticipated ability to intervene in the human genetic structure through molecular engineering? In what direction should we concentrate our efforts to open up new sources of energy? What economic controls should be applied to cushion our society against the effects of a severe crisis in the supply of energy and other resources, and, conversely, against the effects of an eventual abundant supply of such resources? What provisions should be made through the planning of new cities for an increase in the U.S. population by another 50 million within the next generation? What measures should be taken to reduce all forms of pollution in the long run to acceptable or even comfortable levels? What transportation and communication networks should be planned for the future? How can governmental inefficiencies be reduced without endangering our democratic institutions?

16. *Private sector applications:* What major research and development efforts should be supported? What power plants should be built? In what direction should the automobile industry move? What forms of collaboration with the public sector should be sought to facilitate the building of new cities and of new transportation networks? What are the potentialities of the still exploding communication and computer industries? What will be the potentialities of space exploration, if and when it is resumed on a full scale?

17. *Technology assessment:* What will be the direct and, particularly, the indirect effects on our society of anticipated developments in the communications area, such as the general availability of portable telephones and the ability to dial any-

one in the world at negligible cost, the installation of auto-mated libraries and of national data banks, the availability in most homes of two-way TV terminals, and the introduction of a national computer utility? What will be the societal con-sequences of possible technology-induced crises, such as a severe energy or raw materials shortage, the necessity to ban automobiles from the central cities, or a radioactive or biolog-ical-warfare mishap that kills more than a million people? What would be the indirect and unexpected implications of certain social-engineering measures, such as the in-troduction of a negative income tax, of major penal reforms, or the abandonment of the Congressional seniority system? What would be the social consequences of certain major technological breakthroughs, such as genetic intervention, fusion power generators, artificial protein, or the commercial feasibility of transmuting chemical elements into one an-other?

18. *International applications:* What are the global prospects re-garding energy and raw materials resources (the Club of Rome problem), and what can be done to avert a catastrophic crisis? What reasonable international agreements can be made to reduce the pollution of the oceans? Similarly, what reasonable international agreements can be made to extend national control to larger areas of the oceans than is presently the case? What would be the implications of adopting a single world currency? What can be done to effect an orderly devel-opment of the underdeveloped countries? What is the future of arms control and disarmament? What would be the impli-cations of a large-scale joint effort at space exploration? What would be the long-run effect of the introduction of an international social welare system? What are the exchange ratios, in terms of expected long-term benefits to the United States, of federal expenditures in areas related to foreign affairs, such as defense, espionage, diplomacy, international development, cultural exchange, and joint ventures?

## SUBSTANTIVE APPLICATIONS: NORMATIVE

Some members of the futures movement consider social reform the overriding objective of futures research. While I thoroughly sympathize with their motivations, there is a deplorable and self-defeating right-eousness about their position, which seems to imply a resentment against any attempts at an objective exploration of what the future has to offer.

Futures research can well make a profound contribution to social reform, and indeed it may rightly be considered to have an obligation to do so. But as a research activity it has to remain as objective as possible, drawing a clear line between analytical exploration and political activism. In fact, if a political activist wishes to be constructive rather than merely destructive, he will derive all the more guidance and support from futures research, the more objectively such research clarifies the distinction between real potentialities and merely wishful thinking.

In addition to activist reformers, there are the utopians and anti-utopians, who describe fictitious future states of the world that they regard as desirable or detestable, and the inventors, who use their imagination to design specific social innovations intended to change our society for the better. Futures research is very relevant to their interests, as it is to those of the activist social reformers. Specifically, the following topics bear upon the normative aspects of exploring the future:

19. *Critique of present conditions:* What are the dimensions of the quality of life (the "satisfaction indices") in terms of which satisfactions and dissatisfactions with the state of the world can be measured? With regard to which of these dimensions are dissatisfactions particularly strong, and among which segments of the public? What are the great issues of our time, and what are the anticipated issues of the future? What proposals for their resolution have been made, how feasible are these, and what would be their side-effects? What social inventions are needed to help resolve some of these issues?

20. *Criteria for social reform:* What planning criteria in the form of ethical standards, political platforms, social goals, societal movements, and utopian ideals have been proposed? How internally consistent and technologically feasible are they? What priorities and exchange ratios do they imply among the quality of life components? How would the attainment of such goals differentially affect different segments of the public?

21. *Scenarios and utopias:* Given a utopian description and interpreting it as a fictitious future state of the world that can be approximated but never fully attained, what realistic, or at least plausible, scenarios are there that could lead constructively from the present state of the world to an increasingly closer approximation of the utopian state? What are the relative satisfactions felt by different segments of the public during the transitional stages presented by such a scenario? What implementation strategies and social inventions are re-

quired to bring such a scenario about? In other words, what are its political and socio-technological prerequisites?

These, then, are some of the questions to which futures research might address itself. The list is incomplete, and others may place the emphases differently. It is hoped, however, that this compendium illustrates the large variety of topics that need and deserve to be probed and with which researchers in this field might profitably concern themselves.

## REFERENCES

Dalkey, Norman, and Olaf Helmer. 1963. "An Experimental Application of the Delphi Method to the Use of Experts." *Management Science,* Volume 9, Number 3 (April), 458–467.

Helmer, Olaf, and Nicholas Rescher. 1959. "On the Epistemology of the Inexact Sciences." *Management Sciences,* Volume 6, Number 1, 25–52.

FRANK SNOWDEN HOPKINS

# The Planning Mission Before Us

## THE QUESTION OF PURPOSE

The time has come in futures research to engage in some very tough thinking about what it is that futurists should be trying to do. Why futures research?

Such a question can be answered only in the light of one's personal philosophy and historical expectations. Presumably an optimist would answer it one way, a pessimist another. A businessman, for example, oriented toward the pursuit of profit, might say that he wants to understand and foresee the future in order to take advantage of new investment opportunities in an ever-expanding economy. As a short-range outlook, that makes a certain amount of sense, for the world economy and that of the United States doubtless will continue to expand for a while longer.

Suppose, however, that one is not oriented toward short-run economic goals but rather is worried about the great macroproblems of our planetary society—such problems as overpopulation, food shortages, economic disparities, resource depletion, the world energy crisis, environmental pollution, and the threat of nuclear warfare. What then? Does one simply want to foresee the march of events? For while it is extremely pleasant to contemplate the joys of future peace and prosperity, it is not at all pleasant to contemplate grave global problems.

We need futures research urgently, but we do not need it primarily to take advantage of the opportunities the future has to offer. Rather, we need it as a guard against unfavorable developments and as a means of understanding where we are heading and what is likely to happen to us—not in order to drift along with trends, but to halt some and moderate others. We must study the future so that we can change and improve it. It is not enough to engage in futures research just to foresee what will happen if we drift passively. Unless we intend to be activists and to play a positive role in shaping future history, acquiring foreknowledge is a luxury without much pragmatic long-range purpose.

## FORECASTING VERSUS PLANNING

Every field of human endeavor undergoes a series of stages as it develops and gathers momentum. In the futures study field, the early emphasis has been on forecasting. This made sense in the past when the dangers to world civilization were not as well understood or as worrisome to futurists as they are today. As long as the outlook seemed rich in promise, what every futurist wanted to know, and what he tried to analyze for the benefit of others was: Where are we heading? What can we expect? What lies in store for us?

These questions were of particular concern to the field of technological forecasting. Here in a relatively few years, much brilliant work has been done which has cast light on the discoveries and developments that lie ahead, assuming favorable social, economic, and political conditions. In general, technological forecasters have indeed made these assumptions, for all of us in futures research tend to concentrate on the areas in which we have expertise. Implicitly, we assume that our own aspect of the future will develop dynamically, while all other aspects will remain stable. We almost always focus on subsystems, rarely on a complete system.

In all fairness, all we can expect from experts is that they be knowledgeable in their own fields. No one can consider every possible variable; if we did not assume some stability in our lives, we could never make it through an ordinary work day. It therefore makes little sense to ask researchers in nuclear fusion what they think about peace prospects in the Middle East, or virologists working on cancer cells where our future supply of industrial energy is to come from. We are best off if every one focuses on his own area of expertise.

But forecasting is clearly not an end in itself. It is the beginning of a process that leads to planning, decision, and creative action—the first step in preparing for the future. Olaf Helmer has said that the purpose of futures research is to provide meaningful assistance "in the form of information and analysis" to the maker of decisions, so that better decision-making will ensue; and that the distinguishing feature of futures research is that it requres us to foresee conditions at the time of implementation different from those prevailing at the time of planning. (See previous chapter.)

This is fair enough, as far as it goes. In every field, we engage in forecasting future trends and developments so that we can make more useful and fruitful decisions. These decisions are all part of planning for the future. When implemented, this planning will lead to further decisions, which will be carried out at some future time when conditions will be quite different from those we now know. All the time we are planning, we are preparing, consciously or not, for some hypothetical future that may or may not be realized in fact. In the course of preparation, we are increasing our capabilities for dealing with whatever eventually does happen.

Futures research, then, is a necessary and indispensable part of the planning process. We cannot plan intelligently without information—even conjectural or hypothetical information—on what lies ahead. We need the research to obtain the understanding required for formulating meaningful goals and for making plans for progressing toward these goals.

The early emphasis on forecasting was justified only for so long as we could accept the forecast future as satisfactory. I propose that the emphasis is now shifting from forecasting to planning and pragmatic implementation. This shift is taking place because, in more and more fields, the forecast future is not satisfactory. If the future, as foreseen and predicted, is not satisfactory, then action is required to plan a better future—one that will be more in accord with realities and will have a better chance of preserving our civilization in an acceptable manner.

If I am correct in this analysis, then the future of futures resarch is evolving into the future of futures planning. Forecasting will, of course, remain important, but the future of futures research will consist of increased emphasis on the planning process. The more planning takes place in the future, the more research will be needed to give it assistance and support.

## THE NEED FOR PLANNING

When I think about the future, I become apprehensive. While it appears that our world problems are still manageable, providing enough intelligence and political cooperation are applied, there are not yet many signs that we are going to plan our planetary future in a rational manner. Our accomplishments in technological and economic fields have been impressive, but our skills in social management have not kept pace. Hence, problems have accumulated which threaten the global future—and along with it even the national futures of such fortunate countries as the United States.

Am I being too pessimistic when I focus more on our problems than on our accomplishments? I think not, for there are obviously limits to the number of people our planet can support, the amount of food we can produce, the quantities of minerals we can mine and smelt at acceptable levels of energy expenditure, the amount of energy we can generate at acceptable costs, and the burdens and abuses which

Earth's biosphere can tolerate. There are also social and psychological limits to the inequalities our world community will permit without breaking down in disorder. We shall learn more about these limits when our global population enters into an era of acute shortages of food and other necessities while our planet simultaneously provides high standards of living for its more privileged peoples.

The dangers visible on the horizons of the future are not at this stage a reason for panic. But if I were charged with planning mankind's future, I would want to exercise a reasonable degree of prudent foresight in all my actions and decisions. As Kenneth Watt has written in *The Titanic Effect* (1974), we should all keep in mind the importance of planning for disasters. The S.S. *Titanic* sank in 1912 with great loss of life because no one exercised ordinary prudence in equipping and operating this ill-fated ship. But when we prepare for disasters, Watt points out, at least we can minimize their effects. Even if the *Titanic* had to sink, it would have still been possible to greatly reduce the loss of life if sufficient lifeboats had been provided for passengers and crew.

The contemporary world community has the capabiltiy of so organizing the nations of mankind that we can protect and preserve our civilization. If we are going to plan man's future, however, then we have a long way to go in public education. Futures research has a tremendous job to do and a tremendous responsibility to discharge. We need to analyze and evaluate possibilities and probabilities, and, as I shall discuss later, we need to get deeply into the whole question of plans and their implementation—what to do, how to do it, and with what goals in mind.

My point, of course, is that our problems tend to be planetary in scope. Futurists must therefore be concerned not only with local, regional, and national futures but also with the entire global future. The world community in the late twentieth century is beginning to encounter limitations to the indefinite quantitative expansion of modern civilization. If civilization is to be preserved, this quantitative expansion has to be transformed into qualitative improvement. That is, the great technological society spawned by Western culture cannot develop for much longer in an unplanned and unrestrained manner. The only acceptable and viable future for mankind must be a planned one.

## THE "TWO FUTURES" APPROACH

The great issue that must necessarily concern every person contemplating mankind's destiny is the contrast between the future that our civilization appears to be drifting into and a much better future that lies within the planning capabilities of the human race. This contrast is sharp and most disturbing.

I am convinced that a planned future is infinitely to be preferred to an unplanned one. With an unplanned future human desires would have full sway. Generally, the Western world has been operating with an unplanned future in recent centuries, especially since the Industrial Revolution. As long as planetary resources were abundant and large areas of the world remained open to human settlement, human appetites for material gain led to steady economic expansion.

Now we face a different situation. With our world fully populated and our industries drawing heavily upon our planetary resources, we no longer need the motivation of individual desire for economic improvement. Instead of economic expansion, our problem is to make better use of our space and resources and to create societies in which men can live together in reasonable equity and amity. From now on, material human appetites will be a disadvantage, and the motivations of mankind will have to be rational, subdued, and disciplined. Only through a planned future can our society be kept balanced and viable, with the desires of individuals subordinated to the welfare of society.

There are "two futures" that we should consider for planning purposes: (1) the future that we might reasonably expect if we drift passively, letting events take their natural, unplanned course—unplanned, that is, from the standpoint of society; and (2) the future we might hope to achieve by planned effort. I call the first the postulated future, and the second, the invented future.

The postulated future is a generalized concept. While I attempt to make it as realistic as I can, I claim no accuracy or predictive value for it. The test of my model is not its accuracy, but its usefulness in enabling realistic and creative thinking about the kind of world one wants to plan and strive for. The model must not be too optimistic (as the Hudson Institute models tend to be) because optimism encourages complacency and inaction. Nor must one be too pessimistic, as in the books of Robert Heilbroner and others, because too much pessimism breeds despair. Without faith that we can in fact shape the future by our human efforts, we lack the incentive to make the attempt.

What the postulated future says, in effect, is that a number of most worrisome trends are operating in the final quarter of the twentieth century, which if allowed to continue unabated will undermine our civilization and precipitate its collapse in the foreseeable future. The postulated future does not assume that every dangerous or harmful trend will continue unabated, but that in general the world community will fail to act on the necessary scale; that some solutions will be attempted, but not fully achieved; and that some ameliorations will be effected, but not enough to alter a generally downward trend in the worldwide quality of life. The postulated future is not a disastrous future because I cannot realistically imagine that major countries will fail to act to ward off disaster. It is an inadequate future, however, and it most certainly contains some disastrous possibilities.

If the future I postulate for planning purposes is inadequate and unsatisfactory, then the next step is to invent a much better one. I call this much better future the invented future, a term taken from Dennis Gabor's famous statement that the future cannot be predicted, but that futures (plural) can be invented; and that the job of the inventor is to work backwards from the goal he has in mind and forwards from the means at his disposal, until he can find a way to get from one to the other (1964).

The invented future is a world in which some of the most dangerous present trends have been halted and favorably modified; a world in which desirable options for future generations are still open; a world which is functionally and politically viable, with a good chance to keep going for a further indefinite period of years.

Even though life in the invented future might lack some of the enjoyments of 1976, it will be far preferable to the unplanned postulated future, or indeed to any unplanned future into which the human race may drift. For the invented future will be one in which there will be enough social and political order to insure survival. For example, the rate of demographic growth in the invented future would be slowed to the point at which the growth would be socially manageable. In worldwide terms, this would be a world population in 2001 of around 6 billion people, which is approaching stability because of dropping birthrates. In the food realm, production would be increased and distribution improved to the point that 6 billion human beings could be fed at minimal basic levels, avoiding famines and starvation. In economic development, I would strive in the invented future for a shift away from capital-intensive technologies toward those making more use of human labor, thus employing more people and using less machinery and less electrical and mechanical power. In the use of mineral resources, I would visualize rationed mining and smelting, a great deal of recycling of scrap materials, and shifts away from the scarcest metals (like copper) toward more abundant substitutes. The minerals situation would be helped, of course, if new sources of energy could be developed. However, by 2001, it would seem more likely that we would be in a real energy crunch with our diminishing fossil fuels, while not yet ready to exploit new energy sources on a massive scale.

In the environmental field, by 2001 I would strive for much more complete protection of all arable soils, of all waters in lakes, rivers, and coastal bays and estuaries, and of the atmospheres of all industrial areas. This protection would involve increases in the production expenses of industry; the cost would have to be paid by producers and consumers and not shunted off to be borne by Earth's biosphere. Industry would have to proceed on a pay-as-you-go basis, for pollution is a form of borrowing from social capital, often without the possibility of restoring to capital what has been taken away.

My most important requirements for an invented future would lie in the field of political, economic, and social management. Neither in the postulated future nor in the invented one can I visualize the possibility of a freely expanding private enerprise economy, for it seems apparent that scarcer raw materials, more expensive energy, rising social and administrative costs, and other factors will have greatly slowed economic expansion by 2001. An expanding system of corporate capitalism can finance itself through earnings and new investment, but a static system would be quite a different situation.

## THE ECONOMIC OUTLOOK

To get a better idea of what the problems will be in a static or very slowly expanding economy, readers should consult a paper by Hazel Henderson, presented at the "Limits to Growth, '75" conference in Texas and subsequently published in *Technological Forecasting and Social Change* (1976). One basic problem with modern industrial economies, Henderson states, is the declining productivity of capital. That is, it takes more capital to accomplish the same result as resources become scarcer and more expensive. Social and environmental costs also increase. Social costs increase not only because labor insists on high wages, but also because a high-technology, capital-intensive economy produces human casualties, especially among the unemployed as these become a permanently higher proportion of the work force. Among these casualties are the people who cannot adjust to society and instead become educational dropouts, drug addicts, criminals, and generally alienated persons. As Henderson puts it "the maximizing of profits stretches the social fabric in many costly ways; for example, excessive mobility demanded of corporate employees can result in less stable communities, less committed voters and citizens, alcoholic wives and disturbed children and schools."

Among the environmental costs Henderson lists are problems with the pollution of air, water, and other assets once regarded by economists as "free goods" and "externalities." Neither the social nor the environmental costs of corporate industrialism can be regarded in the future as external to the productive process, for in one way or another society will have to pay for them—if not through higher costs to producers and consumers, then in higher taxes on everyone.

Henderson also points out that in energy extraction processes, more and more of "society's activities, wealth, and income must be diverted into getting the energy to get the energy. The GNP continues to climb and we work harder, but our money simply becomes worth less in real terms, and the multiplier effect is felt in manufacturing and throughout the economy as inflation."

Henderson also focuses on some of the structural tendencies of our economy which she considers harmful. One is that corporations tend to overinvest in further growth, and the government encourages this over-investment by its tax policies, as well as by coming to the aid of large corporations when they get into financial difficulties. Another harmful structural tendency is to seek efficiency through substitution of machin-ery for human labor, even though there is an historical trend toward more plentiful labor and less plentiful capital, not only in the United States but throughout the world economy. Thus, we are in danger of creating a top-heavy economic structure and will have some painful readjustments in the transitional period to slower growth which obvi-ously lies ahead.

Turning now from Hazel Henderson's ideas, it seems that over the next twenty-three years an invented future would have to involve a great deal of government planning and control over the American economy as an essential ingredient in the operation of a balanced economic system meeting the needs of all the people. This process has already progressed much further in most European countries than here. I see no hope of maintaining an uncontrolled private enterprise economy for much longer in any country of the world, or an economy run primarily for the benefit of corporations and investors. That will not be the case in any probable future which a reasonable futurist can postulate, and it cannot be the case in any improved future which one seeks to invent and to bring to realization through planned effort.

## PLANNING FOR A STEADY FUTURE

In early 1976, the *Bulletin of the Atomic Scientists* ran a series of articles on the general theme "The Coming Age of Shortages," ad-dressed to the question of how mankind can plan to continue civ-ilization indefinitely into the future. These articles were written by Emile Benoit, an economist who is senior research associate and professor emeritus at Columbia University, where he taught in the graduate schools of business and of international affairs. Dr. Benoit contends that there are feasible alternatives to a policy of unrestricted growth, and he outlines what he calls "a dynamic equilibrium economy" which he says would make possible rising living standards, even in an age of scarcities.

Benoit starts from the conviction that mankind and its economy have grown so fast in recent decades that they have now passed a critical point. As some of the limits to growth have come into view, he writes, some of the owners of scarce resources have begun to act like monopolists, converting long-term into short-term scarcities. Meanwhile, he says, our civilization is gravely threatened by environmental pollution and the accumulation of waste. Benoit does not believe that pollution can be controlled by devoting 2 or 3 percent of GNP to environmental remedies. "If the volume of world industry and its by-products increased by a really large factor, then we would find that hundreds of thousands of substances, now naturally recycled, would have passed the certain critical levels and emerged as new pollutants—which we would have to identify, evaluate, and control." Even the developing countries, because they resist anti-pollution measures in order to attract more industry, may be heading for trouble.

Benoit rejects the thesis that technological progress will be able to solve most of the upcoming problems, such as "averting famine by increasing plant yields, finding adequate substitutes for scarce energies and raw materials, and providing new and more ingenious equipment for pollution control and recycling." Technology, he says, is no miraculous escape hatch, "nor would its exponential growth guarantee that it could solve the problems created by the exponential growth of everything else." After discussing the various problems involved in trying to induce industrial producers all over the world to act for the general welfare of mankind, Benoit comes to the conclusion that only governments can plan and administer economies in the coming era of scarcities where each man's drive to maximize his own wealth is a force to reduce the welfare of other men.

So what is Benoit's proposed solution? His "dynamic equilibrium" consists essentially of maintaining an equilibrium between the whole world economy and the whole natural environment, an equilibrium so planned that the environment can sustain the economy far into the indefinite future. The first of three essential policies would be to conserve resources by simplifying consumption. This he would do by eliminating all forms of waste and wasteful consumption (such as, for example, consumption for status display purposes), and by turning man's attention away from the consumption of goods toward the greater use of services, adopting a life-style oriented toward low-cost pleasurable activities and the creative use of leisure. This policy, he argues, would reduce consumption of material goods to a sustainable level, and yet actually raise living standards by teaching populations to appreciate intangible pleasures.

Benoit's second policy proposal to achieve dynamic equilibrium would be a greatly increased effort in science and technology. No other form of investment yields as high a return, he argues, as research and development focusing on building up our scientific and technological resources to the maximum extent. Technology need not be used for economic growth, in his view, but for any purpose to which we choose to apply it. His idea would be to apply it to living as well as possible without waste, without conspicuous consumption for status display purposes, and within the resources available to us on a steady-state basis. He would also have the nations of the world shift their priorities away from military weapons and away from the kind of technology that involves substituting scarce and expensive resources for readily available human labor. He gives a long list of examples of the new priorities we need, focusing on conserving energy and materials, developing nonpolluting processes, producing products with maximum durability and requiring minimum repairs, recycling of materials, and so on.

What this new emphasis on science and technology would do for us, Benoit argues, "would be to help us achieve the highest living standards that are compatible with minimal environmental polluton and depletion, and ultimately reducing environmental damage to minimal proportions. They would help enable us to maintain and raise these living standards without the unemployment and inflation we now encounter."

The third policy proposal of this thoughtful futurist has to do with reducing the planet's human population. This goal should be accomplished by reducing birthrates, not by waiting until there is an unavoidable rise in the mortality rate, resulting from overcrowding, undernutrition, and other problems of overpopulation in relation to space and resources. Negative population growth (decrease instead of increase) would raise per capita wealth and incomes because most countries already have populations that are larger than optimum. There is a limit to which negative population growth should be carried, and Benoit proposes that research be undertaken to establish just what population levels would be best for each geographic area. He grants that limiting birthrates and reducing population in this way is an extremely difficult undertaking, which to most people appears quite impossible. But "once we recognize reducing population size is essential to survival, we have the technology to make it happen—and in a way conducive to human happiness, albeit at some sacrifice of parental inclinations," he argues.

Benoit's conclusion is that if population were sufficiently reduced, if technological development were properly focused and sufficently rapid, and if all forms of wasteful consumption could be eliminated, then a situation could be reached in which man's civilization would truly be in equilibrium with the natural environment. When people ask how large a population our planet could support, they are asking the wrong question—one he regards as misguided and trivial.

What we really want to know is how large a population can be supported at a high and rising standard of living for an indefinite period of time into the future. *That* is the really crucial question, and it is a question about which we know extremely little as yet. The second main question is, how can we induce mankind to make whatever changes are necessary in its numbers and institutions so that a condition of Dynamic Equilibrium can be attained and maintained.

He then asserts that while we are spending billions of dollars on education and on R and D, "there is hardly anything being spent on research directly focused on issues that could be crucial to human survival."

## SOME CONCLUDING THOUGHTS

I have discussed the ideas of Hazel Henderson about our increasing economic difficulties and those of Emile Benoit about planning a completely different type of world society and economy in order to illuminate the whole question of what futures studies is all about. Henderson and Benoit help us realize that any unplanned future that one can reasonably postulate as realistic will be seriously inadequate—and that, consequently, we had better put a lot of emphasis on inventing a better future for our planet and our country.

Futures research is a broad field, offering a variety of opportunities. One can engage in futures research on a modest scale, focusing on short-term objectives and seeking mainly to provide decision-makers with better information and better analysis so that they will decide more intelligently. This kind of futures research makes good sense if one believes that the overall prospect for our civilization is satisfactory, that ongoing trends are not threatening, and that our principal responsibility is to see that the promise of a highly attractive technological society is realized.

Most professional futurists very likely think in such terms. It is very likely, too, that organizations such as the World Future Society have so much appeal because most Americans are optimists, thinking more in terms of near-term opportunities than of future difficulties. This society has now grown to nearly 25,000 members and subscribers, and close to 3,000 attended its Second General Assembly in Washington in 1975. I believe that the real job of the society is not to sell the public on the exciting possibilities of the future, but rather to stimulate greater awareness of the difficulties and dangers ahead and of the need to engage in imaginative and constructive planning. The kind of future we want—any kind of future that any of us wants—will not come about automatically in the natural course of events.

It is clear that all futurists face a truly colossal challenge. They all need to think about our present civilization and where it is heading, and to come up with some models for planning purposes. They also must think about the goals of an invented future, one that is realistic enough to inspire us to hopeful effort and continuous striving. Most of all, however, it seems that people engaged in futures research need to think about what must be done if mankind is to break out of the present disturbing patterns of values, life-styles, and social activity. It is not just a question of setting new goals, based on better and sounder human values. The really vital question is, how do we get from here to there?

## REFERENCES

Benoit, Emile. 1976. "The Coming Age of Shortages." *Bulletin of the Atomic Scientists,* Volume 32, Number 1 (January), 6–16.

———. 1976b. "A Dynamic Equilibrium Economy." *Bulletin of the Atomic Scientists,* Volume 32, Number 2 (February), 47–55.

———. 1976c. "First Steps to Survival." *Bulletin of the Atomic Scientists,* Volume 32, Number 3 (March), 41–48.

Gabor, Dennis. 1964. *Inventing the Future.* New York: Alfred A. Knopf.

Henderson, Hazel. 1976. "The Coming Economic Transition." *Technological Forecasting and Social Change,* Volume 8, Number 4, 337–352.

Watt, Kenneth. 1974. *The Titanic Effect: Planning for the Unthinkable.* Stamford, Conn.: Sinauer Associates.

WILLIS W. HARMAN
and PETER SCHWARTZ

# Changes and Challenges for Futures Research

Futures research examines the future to help guide present actions. Thus, we learn something about present options if we ask about the future of futures research:

1. What will futures research be used for?
2. What will be the significant characteristics of futures research?
3. Who will use it?
4. What will be the main methodological and substantive issues and problems?

## THE FUTURE CONTEXT OF FUTURES RESEARCH

How useful has futures research been in the past? Perhaps not too useful if one judges by the extent of incorporation into formal decision-making procedures. On the other hand specific research outputs, such as *The Limits to Growth* and Herman Kahn's sanguine prognostications, have been extremely influential in sharpening the debate about our future course as a society. The concept of "alternative futures" has probably been almost as formative in present thought as the concept of "spaceship Earth." The identification of possible future consequences of alternative actions has been institutionalized in the Environmental Impact Statement, the Office of Technology Assessment, and the Congressional "foresight" provision for new legislation. Thus, in looking to the future of futures research we need to keep in mind both formal and informal uses, both direct and indirect effects.

It seems useful to distinguish two main uses for the delineation of alternative futures. One is to be better able to *respond* to the unknown future environment; the other is to be *responsible* for helping shape the future. The first we might term "anticipatory response planning," and the second, "intervention assessment."

The first is by far the simplest context for futures resarch. In anticipatory response planning, the research is embedded in or supports a planning activity wherein the aim is to compare available options in the context of an environment on which one can have negligible influence. Much private sector planning is of this sort, for example, In deciding whether to introduce a new product or service, or to risk a particular investment, the implicit assumption about the future environment is typically that it cannot be appreciably modified—only forecast. The planning objective is to be in a position to take advantage of, or to respond to, or to avoid adverse consequences of, certain characteristics of the contingent future.

The second context for futures research involves assessing a contemplated major intervention that may affect the future environment. The intervention might be a piece of legislation, a major agency policy decision, or a large public works project. The objective of the assessment might be to identify what interventions could lead toward a desired future state or help in avoiding an undesirable one, or to assess the long-term impact of a particular intervention on the likelihood of attaining a desired future state. (We postpone for the moment discussion of just who is doing this desiring.)

The nation does not have even at the federal government level where it is most obviously needed, institutionalization of such a process for guiding society by systematically planned intervention. (Lest this sentence conjure up the specter of centralized state planning, let us hasten to note that we are referring to "choosing the future" in a democratic society. The fact that similarly rational logic might be used to plan a totalitarian state is no reason for eschewing rational logic.) The essential elements of this process are suggested in Figure 1. In essence, they amount to perceiving accessible alternative futures; selecting among these the desired state on a normative basis; designing and implementing an intervention to influence toward the desired state; monitoring the resulting change; and repeating the process on a systematic iterative basis. The accompanying box delineates these steps in slightly more detail.

It is immediately apparent that *who* makes the normative decisions regarding desired future states is a central issue. There is a simplistic model of meritocratic democracy in which the public decides what future state is to be aimed for, and then the expert futures researchers and policy analysts tell them how to get there. If that model ever fit, most certainly it no longer does. As will be discussed more fully below, we can probably look forward to the public being more involved in all stages of intervention assessment and implementation.

We have been arguing that one probable future characteristic of futures research is that increasingly it will be carried out embedded in more focused efforts, in order to improve the ability either to respond to an uncertain future or to affect the future in desired ways.

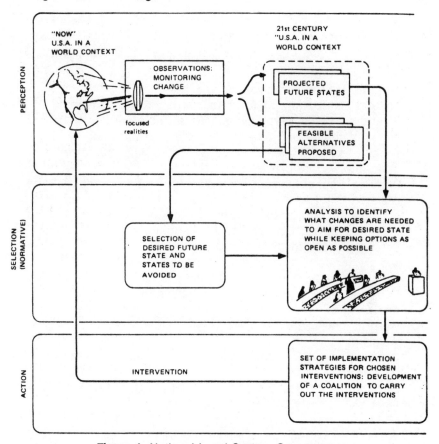

**Figure 1.** National-Level System Governance

## FURTHER EMERGENT CHARACTERISTICS OF FUTURES RESEARCH

Several other emergent characteristics of futures research are worth noting. Namely, it will be more utility-oriented, more holistic, more explicitly normative, more participative, and more explicitly a part of the change process. That is, it will be more of these *if* it is responsive to the challenges ahead.

*It will be increasingly utility-oriented.* Two concepts of futures research have tended to dominate much of the past work: (1) futures research as a new scientific discipline, and (2) futures research as an early warning system. In some sense both of these concepts will tend to yield the center stage to yet another concept (3) futures research as a

---

### STEPS IN NATIONAL-LEVEL SYSTEM GOVERNANCE

- Observing and arriving at a perception of the overall system—the United States in a world context—and of whatever sub-systems are the particular focus of attention (e.g., energy supply and distribution; welfare; housing and transportation).
- Extending those perceptions into a set of projected future states of the system (e.g., future energy shortages in the absence of successful interventions; food riots in the absence of adequate welfare provisions).
- Deriving a set of feasible alternative future states that could be reached via identified and plausible interventions (e.g., incentives to implement a rational energy policy, guaranteed income legislation, mass transit subsidies).
- Selecting those feasible future states which the consensus of the electorate finds desirable, or (much more likely) which it is assumed the body politic would find desirable if it were suitably informed; similarly, with states to be avoided.
- Analyzing the set of changes needed to move the system toward the desired state, while keeping options as open as possible.
- Devising a set of implementation strategies for the chosen interventions.
- Developing, through a coalition of stakeholder groups, the political will to carry out the interventions.
- Monitoring the system to ascertain the effects of the interventions in changing the perceived state of the system, thus closing the loop to form a continuous process.

---

planning tool, employed to assist in capitalizing on opportunities and ameliorating problems.

Some of the early enthusiasm for futures research as a scientific discipline has dimmed as it has become more apparent that this concept arose from a misunderstanding of the nature of the activity. History and archaeology bear some similarities to futures research, except that they look backward in time instead of forward. Although they may make very sophisticated use of scientific tools such as radiocarbon dating and microchemical analysis, they are in fact essentially art rather than science. The central historical or archaeological skill is intuitive pattern recognition. Similarly, however much use futures research may make of computer models and elaborate matrices, it is essentially a task of forward-looking pattern recognition employing intuitive synthesizing ability and imaginative judgment. Futures research is a skill that can be learned, but not a set of instructions that can be taught. Thus, we may anticipate that the future of futures research is probably a matter of its viewpoints informing, enriching, and becoming an integral part of other disciplines and areas such as ecology, law, engineering, management, and education.

Futures research has indeed played a significant role thus far as a general early-warning activity. It has helped bring awareness of the historical significance of the present time. On the one hand, industrialized society has developed the power to modify to an indeterminate extent the physical, social, and psychological environment; the plant and animal population of the biosphere; the physical, mental, and emotional characteristics of individual human beings; and the evolutionary development of the human race. On the other hand, pursuit of these industrial-era goals has brought a "new scarcity" of energy and mineral resources; of fresh water, arable land, and habitable space; of the waste-absorbing capacity of the natural environment; and of the resilience of the planet's life-supporting ecosystems. Under the strain of such a fundamental challenge as is posed by these newfound capabilities and limits, the free enterprise democratic system shows serious signs of stress and possible disintegration. Few persons today remain unconvinced that the near-term future is fraught with hazards and ordeals. The key task now is to find how together we can make it through this time of troubles to a tolerable—may be even a splendid—future.

*It will be increasingly holistic and global.* This statement may seem almost a banality, so accustomed are we by now to hearing the refrain "everything is connected to everything else." Yet, if we reflect on its ramifications, we see that we have hardly begun to appreciate the implications.

Comparison with health care may be helpful. Undoubtedly, one of the great inventions of medicine, so old that its origins are lost in history, is the concept of disease. The directly observable facts of disease are symptoms—and a part of medicine has always been the treating of symptoms. But a momentous advance was made through the recognition that symptoms occur in patterns and that these disease patterns tend to have certain behaviors through time, so that prognostications can be made, alternative futures forecast, and interventions designed. However, the whole picture takes on a still different case when it is recognized that only a fraction of mental activity is conscious, and that unconscious processes contribute to susceptibility to disease and even create disease—so that illness has a large and not easily determinable psychosomatic component. The conceptualization changes yet again with the recognition that it is the *whole organism* that has the disease. Disease susceptibility, resilience, and recoverability are consequences of the individual's whole life-style, including attitudes, beliefs, and values.

We appear to be in the process of recognizing similar attributes of societies. They have symptoms—urban decay, air and water pollution, a Vietnam War, a Watergate—and our first response is to treat the symptoms. Then we begin to find the complex interconnections between energy, environment, and state of the economy; between water pollution and agricultural methods; and between alientation, drug use, and crime. We then realize that whole patterns may have to be treated. Finally, against powerful psychological resistance, the realization begins to dawn that the whole life-style of industrialized society needs to be reexamined if we are to understand our predicament.

There are several important corollaries to this proposition. For one thing, it implies that we have to pay much more attention to the "soft" descriptors of the state of society—culture, value change, attitudes, moral commitments, hints of collective unconscious processes. It suggests that one task in futures work is to purge the research of bias toward those aspects of the social description that are more easily quantified and hence seem easier to deal with. It shows the need for a new understanding of social change and for a clearer distinction between those aspects of society that are appropriately modeled in some sort of computer-based simulation (e.g., physical quantities, economic variables) and those aspects, equally important and not to be neglected, that need to be systematically handled in some quite different way, external to the model.

*It will be more explicitly normative.* As noted earlier, futures research is not an objective science—nor should it try to become one. Even natural science has grown up strongly influenced by the industrial-era values of prediction and control. The health sciences and agricultural sciences are much more explicitly normative, with their predilection for favoring life over death. Economics too is overtly normative, with implicit valuing of system stability, employment, and (at least in some versions) economic growth. Futures research is intrinsically concerned with preferred outcomes. It needs to be self-consciously normative.

Now that, of course, does not mean that futures research can allow itself to be attitudinally, ideologically, or culturally biased, in the sense that it obscures that which it was intended to reveal. The optimistic bias that conceals trouble ahead, or the pessimistic bias that neglects real opportunities, or the ideological bias that screens out future developments which conflict with dogmatic premises, are all to be assiduously avoided.

Thus far, futures research has often tended to be biased by its penchant for forecasting quantifiably measurable variables, which leads to neglect of nonquantifiable aspects. This is most apparent in attempts to set up indicators of quality of life; the many measures available, from number of toilets per family to per capita GNP, still reveal rather little about whether people are enjoying life more.

A pessimistic bias has probably also afflicted much of futures research, reflecting a general loss of the visionary pull in the culture. This century, particularly the last third of it, has been far richer in dystopias than in utopias. As psychologist Kenneth Kenniston notes in *The Uncommited*,

Our visions of the future have shifted from images of hope to vistas of despair . . . Huxley's *Brave New World,* Orwell's *1984* and *Animal Farm,* Young's *The Rise of the Meritocracy,* and ironically even Skinner's *Walden Two*—the vast majority of our serious visions of the future are negative visions, extensions of the most pernicious trends of the present.

A notable exception is Ursula Le Guin's novel *The Dispossessed.* Perhaps futures research needs to be guided more by the ancient dictum: "Where there is no vision, the people perish."

If futures research is to be explicitly normative, however, our culture's general confusion about values poses a problem. It is, of course, not true that there is complete lack of value consensus, although the erosion of traditional bases for value assumptions left a serious vacuum that is slowly being filled. Perhaps futures research will in time develop a set of guiding value propositions something like the following:

1. Futures tend to be desirable if they lead toward system adaptability and resilience, and hence toward survivability. Scientists of living system, such as C. S. Holling and Roy Rappoport, have long emphasized the high value position, in system terms, of adaptability and resilience (as contrasted with rigid stability and even reliability in the usual sense). The self-healing, learning, evolving system survives through transforming experiences and even traumatic change.

2. Futures tend to be desirable if they lead toward fruition of the perennial values of human civilization—individual freedom with equal justice under law; democratic liberation from oppression by institutions; intellectual, moral, and spiritual evolution; reverence for and oneness with Nature; community and the brotherhood of man.

3. Futures tend to be desirable if their social structure is compatible with whatever can be discovered to be man's most fundamental nature. (Many today, for example, are insistent that *homo economicus* is not man's most fundamental nature. On the other hand, some sort of

rediscovery of man's spiritual side and revaluing of inner experience seems to be taking place.)

*It will be increasingly participative.* Several indicators that made their appearance in the 1960s were forerunners of the new participative attitudes to be expected to predominate in futures research. The first signs that appeared were of public disenchantment with science and technology—both in the awareness that the social costs of some technological applications might outweigh the benefits and in a distrust of Big Science and its involvement with the "military-industrial complex." There were the fluoridation battles, and the freeway battles, and the SST and the ABM—and then the instances followed so rapidly that they became a torrent. Citizens without formal scientific training refused to accept expert decisions on highly complex technical matters such as nuclear safety and preservation of the ozone layer. The principle was established that major scientific and technological decisions are *political* decisions, not to be made for the electorate by an elite of technical experts. This principle became institutionalized when the National Environmental Protection Act of 1970 required that a public Environmental Impact Statement precede major technological innovations which could have a significant impact on the environment. Developments in the consumer and women's liberation movements made clear the future position—that major scientific and technological decisions are too important to be left to the experts. At the 1975 World Future Society meeting in Washington, D.C., women and minority groups made it abundantly clear that if futures research was going to have power to affect the future, they were going to have a piece of the action.

Thus, not only are there powerful arguments against developing elite futurist-managers; that outcome is unlikely to be permitted. Instead, ways will be found to engage the participation of affected populations and parties-at-interest in futuristic activities. The Alternatives for Washington (state) process is a fairly successful experiment in achieving this sort of participation. In an alternative futures exercise for the state of Washington, it has involved tens of thousands of those citizens whose future will be affected, the legislators who will be implementing the choices, and the agencies who will be carrying out the legislative mandates.

*It will be more explicitly part of the change process.* The very act of observing is itself an intervention. Futures research, which is observing and drawing out implications, is even more so.

Seers and oracles have been around since the days of Delphi and before. The function of the oracle was to tell you what would come to pass—what was fated. There was not much to be done about it but accept it.

The explicit consideration of alternative futures resulting in part from nondeterministic choices is quite a different matter. It is assumed that interventions can change the future. The most fundamental intervention of all is this assumption of responsibility for the future society of ourselves and our progeny.

But if this is not fatalistic, neither is it at the other extreme of hubris. In recent years, we have become much more humble about the extent to which man, with his rational mind and his technology, can manipulate a desired future into being. Powerful psychological currents, such as characterized the Nazi phenomenon in Germany and events in the United States in the 1960s, are evidence that the future is not shaped by rational planning alone. The possibility of major climatic change with consequent disastrous effects on world food production has reminded us of our total dependence on the natural environment. Limits to growth of diverse sorts have had a sobering influence on the "technological imperative."

Rather than man the helmsman steering his ship of destiny confidently with the aid of radar, sonar, and loran, the more appropriate metaphor appears to be that of a cell in an organism, inexorably going where the larger body goes and yet in some small way affecting its course. Futures research is the attempt to illuminate the effecting of that small change.

## METHODOLOGICAL PROBLEMS AND ISSUES

It is apparent from the above that futures research needs a better model of social change. Major change does not come about as a consequence of an historic intervention brought into being by a powerful decision-maker. Perhaps it can be considered to be the consequence of a pattern of interventions initiated and supported by a multitude of decision-makers. But if indeed "everything is connected to everything else," those decision-makers are in turn acted on by forces, and it is the total flow of all these forces we must somehow deal with. Furthermore, since we know that the actions of individuals are partly, or even largely, in response to unconscious processes, it follows that it is not only the visible part of this flow that must be perceived but the invisible part, the unconscious processes of the collective, that must be taken in as well.

This is not to deny that decision analysis, computer simulations, system dynamics models, cross-impact matrices, and the like have their place, especially as conceptual frameworks in communication. It does suggest, however, the need for much more humility with regard to what can be accomplished with them, and much more respect for those mysterious intuitive processes with which we grasp such complexities as the richness of a personality or the significance of a death or the beauty of a mountain peak. The pattern perceptions in the past that have demonstrated power to forecast represent this kind of intuitive leap. For example, Condorcet perceiving the implications of the twin forces of scientific rationality and the new value of equality, de Tocqueville exploring the future of democratic society, and Tawney identifying the institutionalization of acquisitiveness as a key flaw in capitalism.

Observations of recent events reveal numerous hints regarding the future. There are trends that may grow and others that cannot continue; social movements that may peter out and others that may precipitate traumatic change; dilemmas that cannot be evaded and attempts at resolution that will affect the future; value and attitude shifts that may be fads or may persist. To futures research falls the task of identifying patterns in this sea of data which will be fruitful for insight into the future.

If we now refer back to Figure 1, we see that it still fits except the actors are changed. Persons throughout the society are perceiving patterns that make sense to them and that they use to interpret the probable future and plausible alternatives. Persons throughout the society are making their selections of future states to be desired and others to be avoided. Persons throughout the society are making microdecisions that add up to macrodecisions that intervene and alter the state of society. The most significant task of futures research is to guide this organic process.

But now comes the rub. People do not perceive the same reality. They see different realities; this is literally true. The fact that different persons see different patterns of facts and issues, different pictures of social reality, is evident in the public debates over vital ecological and economic issues. The complication introduced by this fact is of extreme importance to democratic decision-making.

Everyone is familiar with the type of visual illusion in which the observer sees, alternatively, a particular pattern as "figure" against the remainder of the display as "ground," or else the reverse. One observer may see a particular pattern or Gestalt, while another may see a wholly different configuration. Something like this clearly happens in human affairs, where observers with the same data at their disposal perceive situations quite differently. The paranoid person who sees in his environment pervasive threat and malevolent persecutors is an obvious, if exaggerated, example.

An excellent example in the field of management is provided by Douglas McGregor's "Theory X" and "Theory Y," as described in *The Human Side of Enterprise* (1957). At a time when American management was divided in its opinions as to what kinds of incentives would make for the most viable organizational structure, two theories of human motivation held sway—one based essentially on fear and other negative emotions, and the other on self-fulfillment. Clearly, different observers were looking at the same behaviors and perceiving quite different implied motivations.

Futurists observing present U.S. society have much the same data available, and yet they see vastly different patterns. Some see signs of breakdown and disintegration of the present form of capitalist industrialized society. Others see different signs—e.g., the revolution in self-determination, rise of an "ecological ethic," movement toward "appropriate technology," widespread search for transcendental meanings—of the rise of some sort of "trans-industrial" society in which economic incentives will be tempered far more by humane values. Some see neither of these sets of signs as having a major effect in causing departure from past trends. And some see the two sets together as presaging an imminent and traumatic transformation. Persons who perceive these four different pictures of reality (four patterns of relevant data) will come to four quite different conclusions as to what interventions are called for.

Thus, we see that *pattern-uncertainty* is characteristic of planning the future. This is very different from data-uncertainty, which we have recognized ways of resolving—e.g., scientific research. Furthermore, the society does not have adequate ways of dealing with conflict centering around contradictory pattern perceptions. The adversary procedure, as institutionalized in the courts, is adapted to settling disputes in an equitable manner; it is not suited to providing the kind of neutral forum that would foster collaborative exploration to establish which Gestalt fits better.

Probably the first essential step is to *legitimate* different perceptions of reality. This is precisely what was not done in the religious wars of the past and in what was once termed the "warfare between science and religion." Perhaps, just perhaps, we are coming to a fuller understanding of human psychology which will make this legitimating possible.

In this somewhat speculative essay, we have attempted to indicate some characteristics of futures research of the future and to suggest some of the unmet challenges. Two of the unmet challenges stand out in particular—the need for a more adequate model of social change and the need for better ways to handle alternative perceptions of reality.

# APPENDIX

## Journals, Periodic Reports, Graduate Programs, and Organizations in Futures Research

### A. JOURNALS

*Futures: The Journal of Forecasting and Planning.* Publishes scholarly articles by European and American futures researchers. Bimonthly; 90 pages; $65 per year. IPC Press, 32 High Street, Guildford, Surrey, England, GU1 3EW.

*Futurics.* As well as reviews and announcements, contains researched articles on alternatives for the future. Quarterly; 60 pages; $15 per year. Futurics, Science Museum of Minnesota, 30 East 10th Street, St. Paul, Minnesota 55101.

*The Futurist.* Magazine of the World Future Society, designed for a general audience. Articles touch on a wide variety of possibilities for the future. Bimonthly; 56 pages; $15 per year. The World Future Society, 4916 St. Elmo Avenue (Bethesda), Washington, D.C. 20014.

*Journal of the International Society for Technology Assessment.* Carries scholarly articles on the potential impact of technologies. Quarterly; 60 pages; $30 per year. Science and Technology Publishers, P.O. Box 4926, Cleveland Park Station, Washington, D.C., 20006.

*Long Range Planning.* Focuses on concepts and techniques of planning that may prove useful in business and government. Bimonthly; 112 pages; $66 per year. Pergamon Press, Maxwell House, Fairview Park, Elmsford, New York, 10523.

*Planning Review.* For corporate planners; contains articles on various aspects of planning and forecasting. Bimonthly; 36 pages; $30 per year. Crane, Russak and Co., 347 Madison Avenue, New York, New York, 10017.

*Technological Forecasting and Social Change.* Publishes scholarly, often technical articles on various aspects of forecasting. Quarterly; 100 pages; $33 per year. American Elsevier Co., 52 Vanderbilt Avenue, New York, New York, 10017.

*World Future Society Bulletin.* Publishes articles of interest to professional futures researchers. Bimonthly; 32 pages; $27 (includes subscription to *The Futurist*). The World Future Society, 4916 St. Elmo Avenue (Bethesda), Washington, D.C. 20014.

## B. PERIODIC REPORTS

*Center for Futures Research Newsletter.* Update of the Center's activities. Bimonthly; 2 pages; free. Center for Futures Research, University of Southern California, Los Angeles, California, 90007.

*Footnotes to the Future.* Summarizes significant trends as reported in current periodicals. Reports on meeting, courses, books. Monthly; 4 pages; $15 per year. Futuremics, Inc., 2850 Connecticut Avenue N.W., Washington, D.C., 20008.

*Future-Abstracts.* Abstracts futures-related publications on 5-by-8 inch cards. Monthly; 48 abstracts per issue; $110 per year. Futuremics, Inc., 2850 Connecticut Avenue N.W., Washington, D.C., 20008.

*Future Report.* Covers predictions, plans, patents, and other indicators of things to come. Monthly; 6 pages; $48 per year. Foundation for the Future, Box 2001, Newburyport, Massachusetts, 01950.

*The Scout Index.* Abstracts forecasts from a wide range of periodical literature. Monthly; 100 pages; $375 per year. The Futures Group, 124 Hebron Avenue, Glastonbury, Connecticut, 06033.

*Social Indicators Newsletter.* Covers research on social indicators. Quarterly; 8 pages; free. Social Science Research Council, Center for Coordination of Research on Social Indicators, 1755 Massachusetts Avenue N.W., Washington, D.C., 20036.

*TA/Update.* Newsletter of the International Society for Technology Assessment. Included with subscriptions to the *Journal of the International Society for Technology Assessment.*

*What's Next?* Describes aspects of futures research activity likely to be of interest to U.S. Congress. Monthly; 8 pages; free. Congressional Clearinghouse on the Future, 722 House Annex No. 1, Washington, D.C., 20515.

## C. DEGREE-GRANTING GRADUATE PROGRAMS IN AMERICAN HIGHER EDUCATION

Cybernetic System Program; San Jose State University; San Jose, California 95192. Norman O. Gunderson, Director, M.S. in Cynernetic Systems with a concentration in futures studies.

Future Studies; University of Massachusetts; Amherst, Massachusetts 01002. Peter Wagschal, Faculty Director. M.Ed. and Ed.D. in Education with a concentration in future studies.

Futures Planning, Forecasting and Assessment; Fairleigh Dickinson University; Madison, New Jersey 07940. Irving H. Buchen, Director. M.A. in Futures Planning, Forecasting, and Assessment.

Program in Alternative Social and Educational Futures; University of Minnesota; Minneapolis, Minnesota 55409. Arthur M. Harkins, Director. M.A. and Ph.D. in Education with a concentration in alternative social and educational futures.

Studies of the Future; University of Houston at Clear Lake City; Houston, Texas 77058. Jib Fowles, Chairman. M.S. in Studies of the Future.

System Dynamics; Massachusetts Institute of Technology; Cambridge, Massachusetts 02139. Jay W. Forrester, Director. B.S., M.S., and Ph.D. in Management with a concentration in system dynamics.

Systems Science Doctoral Program; Portland State University; Portland, Oregon 97207. Harold A. Linstone, Director. Ph.D. in Systems Science with a concentration in forecasting and planning.

## D. ORGANIZATIONS

Center for Futures Research, University of Southern California, Graduate School of Business Administration, Los Angeles, California 90007. Burt Nanus, Director. Conducts multidisciplinary policy analysis and forecasting studies in economic, business, technological, and social areas.

Center for Integrative Studies, University of Houston, Houston, Texas 77004. John McHale, Director. Studies and projects major consequences of ongoing global trends. Analyses available in publications and occasional conferences.

Center for the Study of Social Policy, Stanford Research Institute, Menlo Park, California 94025. Thomas C. Thomas, Director. For government and industry, conducts policy and planning studies in the interest of the public good.

The Club of Rome, 163 Via Giorgione, 00147 Rome, Italy. Aurelio Peccei, Organizer. Supports reports and conferences on the future of mankind.

The Committee for the Future, 2325 Porter Street, Washington, D.C. 20008. Barbara Marx Hubbard, Chairperson. Provides information on major issues for the future through conferences and other communications activities.

Congressional Clearinghouse on the Future, 722 House Annex No. 1, Washington, D.C. 20515. Anne W. Cheatham, Director. Organizes seminars and circulates information on futures research to members of Congress and their staff.

The Futures Group, Inc., 124 Hebron Avenue, Glastonbury, Connecticut 06033. Theodore J. Gordon, President. Conducts policy analysis and forecasting studies to assist corporations and institutions in the management of change. Maintains extensive data bank.

The Futures Research Group, Congressional Research Service, Library of Congress, Washington, D.C., 20540. A research and information service for the U.S. Congress.

Hudson Institute, Croton-on-Hudson, New York 10520. Rudy L. Ruggles, Jr., President. Conducts policy studies on long-range alternatives for business and government.

Institute for the Future, 2740 Sand Hill Road, Menlo Park, California 94025. Roy Amara, President. Executes forecasting and planning studies for public and private sectors.

International Institute for Applied Systems Analysis, Schloss Platz 1, Laxenburg, A-2361 Austria. Brings together scientists of different nationalities and disciplines to work on questions of mankind's future.

International Society for Technology Assessment, Box 4926, Cleveland Park Station, Washington, D.C. 20008. Vary T. Coates, President. Professional society for those concerned with assessment of technology.

Mankind 2000, 1 rue aux Laines, 1000 Brussels, Belgium. Supports conferences and projects concerned with humanistic development of mankind.

North American Society for Corporate Planning, 147 Laird Drive, Toronto, Ontario, Canada M4G 3W1. Richard J. Allio, President. Professional organization for corporate forecasters and planners.

Planning Executives Institute, P.O. Box 70, Oxford, Ohio 45056. James D. Thompson, Executive Director. Association of corporate planners.

The Rand Corporation, 1700 Main Street, Santa Monica, California 90406. Donald B. Rice, President. Conducts research and analysis on aspects of national security and public welfare.

Resources for the Future, Inc., 1755 Massachusetts Avenue, N.W., Washington, D.C. 20036. Charles J. Hitch, President. Conducts research into the future for natural resources and the environment. Holds conferences and issues reports.

Science Policy Research Unit, University of Sussex, Mantell Building, Falmer, Brighton, Sussex BN1 9RF, England. Conducts research into various aspects of the long-term forecasting of social change. Examines both methodological and substantive issues.

World Future Society, 4916 St. Elmo Avenue, Washington, D.C. 20014. Edward S. Cornish, President. General organization for all interested in the study of the future. Has divisions and local chapters as well.

Worldwatch Institute, 1776 Massachusetts Avenue N.W., Washington, D.C. 20036. Lester R. Brown, President. Identifies and reports on emerging global issues.

# Glossary

*Alternative futures.* It is a tenet of futures research that there is little that is inevitable about the future. The future is best described as a cluster of possibilities, known as alternative futures. The alternative that becomes the reality can be the result of choices and plans made now.

*Cross impact analysis.* This forecasting technique analyzes the interactions of specified trends and events. See the chapter "Cross-Impact Analysis" by John G. Stover and Theodore J. Gordon.

*Delphi technique (or method).* This frequently employed forecasting procedure is used to obtain a consensus of opinion from a panel of experts through a series of questionnaires. Between question rounds, the panel members are informed of the group's previous distribution of opinion. See the chapter "The Delphi Technique" by Harold A. Linstone.

*Discontinuity.* An abrupt change in enduring features or trends of human life. The energy crises portends a discontinuity, for instance.

*Extrapolation.* The projection of trend data into the future. See the chapter "Trend Extrapolation" by Kim Quaile Hill.

*Future shock.* As described in Alvin Toffler's book of this title, future shock is the disorientation brought on by rapid social change.

*Futurible.* An alternative future. The term was fashioned by the French futurist Bertrand de Jouvenel.

*Images of the future.* Visions of ideal conditions that could become realities in the forseeable future. Images of the future are thought to elicit interest in working for an improved future. See the chapter "Images of the Future" by Bettina J. Huber.

*Gaming.* See Simulation gaming.

*Modeling.* See Simulation modeling.

*Neo-Malthusian.* A term used to refer to those holding the belief, like the early nineteenth-century thinker Thomas Malthus, that population growth will outstrip the supply of food and other essentials.

*Postindustrial society.* The next stage in societal evolution, according to Daniel Bell. The primary activity will be the production of knowledge, and the majority of the labor force will be in the service sector of the economy. See the chapter "The Post-industrial Economy" by Daniel Bell.

*Scenario.* A narrative sketch of a hypothetical sequence of future events. Herman Kahn, to whom this device is credited, emphasizes that a scenario is constructed for the purpose of focusing attention on causal processes and decision points. See the chapter "Scenarios" by Ian H. Wilson.

*Simulation gaming.* A projective activity in which players imitate the components of real-world systems, and act out in the course of a game various alternative futures and their consequences. See the chapter "Simulation Gaming" by Richard D. Duke.

*Simulation modeling.* A forecasting method that, usually with the aid of a computer, attempts to replicate the behavior of a system and to trace its changes through time. See the chapter "Simulation Modeling" by J. Michael McLean.

*Social indicator.* A data series that measures social features of normative interest, such as educational trends, housing, and quality of life. See the chapter "Social Indicators and Social Forecasting" by Denis F. Johnston.

*Spaceship Earth.* An image suggested by Buckminster Fuller to indicate the unity and fragility of the world as it moves through the universe.

*Technology assessment.* The examination, often by means of quantitative methods, of the potential impacts of a problematic technology. See the chapter "Technology Assessment" by Joseph F. Coates.

*Technological (or technology) forecasting.* The quantitative prediction of advances in a particular technology. See the chapter "Technological Forecasting" by Joseph P. Martino.

# Index

# Notes on Contributors

**ROY AMARA** is the president of the Institute for the Future, a consulting and research firm headquartered in Menlo Park, California. Previously he was vice-president of Stanford Research Institute. The topics of his many published papers include control systems, communications networks, systems engineering, societal forecasting, and futures research.

**DANIEL BELL,** professor of sociology at Harvard University, is the author of *The End of Ideology* and *The Cultural Contradictions of Capitalism.* His *The Coming of Post-Industrial Society,* translated into seven languages, has earned him worldwide fame.

**LESTER R. BROWN** is president of Worldwatch Institute. Formerly a senior fellow at the Overseas Development Council and administrator of the International Agricultural Development Service of the U.S. Department of Agriculture, he is the author of *Seeds of Change, World Without Borders,* and *By Bread Alone.*

**WILLIAM M. BROWN** was a senior scientist at the RAND Corporation before joining the Hudson Institute as the director of Technological Studies. Co-author with Herman Kahn of *The Next 200 Years,* Dr. Brown is currently involved in energy, resource, and space technology research.

**ARTHUR C. CLARKE**, the writer of scores of popular science fiction works, was co-author of the book and movie, *2001: A Space Odyssey.* The concept of communications satellites is credited to him. He now lives and works in the nation of Sri Lanka.

**JOSEPH F. COATES**, formerly a senior staff member of the Institute for Defense Analyses, and program manager for technology assessment at the National Science Foundation, is now assistant to the director of the Congressional Office of Technology Assessment. His numerous speeches and articles cover various aspects of forecasting and planning.

**BARRY COMMONER**'s *The Closing Circle* has had a profound effect upon the reading public's understanding of threats to the natural environment. Director of the Center for the Biology of Natural Systems at Washington University, Dr. Commoner is also the author of *Science and Survival* and *The Poverty of Power.*

**CHRISTOPHER DEDE**, co-founder of the first doctoral program in futures studies (at the University of Massachusetts), publishes articles in the areas of educational futures and technological futures. President of the Educational Division of the World Future Society, Dr. Dede teaches in the Studies of the Future program at the University of Houston at Clear Lake City.

The more technologically advanced nations do not necessarily have an advantage, for their technology is "Earth-bound" in addition to being culture-bound. They may first have to *unlearn* the forms, assumptions, and habits of Earth-bound technology before they can learn the new forms and assumptions useful in extraterrestrial communities.

More important than Earth-boundness is the question of culture-boundness. A number of new types of cultures can be developed in extraterrestrial communities; these will be free of physical constraints such as climate and gravity. The way of life in these communities may be based on epistemologies and logics different from those now prevailing in European and American cultures. Many so-called underdeveloped nations have an advantage because they have undergone what may be called "trans-epistemological processes," i.e., exposure to several epistemologies; therefore, they know what is meant by different epistemologies, while most Americans do not.

In fifteen or twenty years, the first extraterrestrial community will be completed, during which time those who will migrate can prepare themselves. They will need not only technological training but also much broader education, including different logics and epistemologies. Since we have no educational system for this training, we must begin from scratch. If we begin now, in fifteen or twenty years all nations will have produced potential immigrants to the first extraterrestrial community.

## CONCLUSION

Our cultural transition into the extraterrestrial era is comparable to that experienced by our aquatic ancestors when they moved onto land or by our quadrupedal ancestors when they became bipedal and bimanual. For the first time in the history of man, we will be in a position to invent new cultural patterns and to choose the design of the material and organic environment to fit the desired cultural goals and philosophies. We will have to invent new systems of logic and to set up new cultural and philosophical guidelines. Finally, we will have to become accustomed to long-range thinking in formulating our goals.

## REFERENCES

Buckley, W. 1968. *Modern Systems Research for the Behavioral Scientist.* Chicago: Aldine Publishing.

Camara, S. 1975. "The Concept of Heterogeneity and Change among the Mandenka." *Technological Forecasting and Social Change*, Volume 7, 273–284.

**RICHARD D. DUKE** is chairman of the Urban Planning Program at the University of Michigan. His publications include *Gaming: The Future's Language* and *Gaming/Simulation: Rationale, Design and Applications.*

**H. WENTWORTH ELDREDGE**, professor of sociology at Dartmouth College, is a long-time contributor to futures studies. Among his books are *Taming Megalopolis* and *World Capitals: Toward Guided Urbanization.*

**VICTOR FERKISS** is professor of government at Georgetown University. *Technological Man* and *The Future of Technological Civilization* are the most widely known of his numerous publications.

**JAY W. FORRESTER** made significant contributions to the development of digital computer technology before becoming professor of management at the Massachusetts Institute of Technology. He went on to devise the computerized modeling technique called Systems Dynamics, which has been the basis of his books—*Industrial Dynamics, Urban Dynamics, World Dynamics,* and *Principles of Systems.*

**JIB FOWLES**, chairman of the graduate program in Studies of the Future at the University of Houston at Clear Lake City, is the author of *Mass Advertising as Social Forecast.* His articles have appeared in periodicals concerned with social forecasting and social change.

**TOMAS FREJKA**, an economist-demographer, is on the staff of the Center for Policy Studies of the Population Council. Earlier, he worked at the Czechoslovak Academy of Sciences in Prague, the Office of Population Research at Princeton University, and the United Nations Demographic Center for Latin America. He is the author of *The Future of Population Growth.*

**THEODORE J. GORDON** is president of The Futures Group, a research organization devoted to long-range forecasting and policy analysis. He has contributed substantially to the development of forecasting and policy analysis methodology, and has written many articles and books, among them *The Future* and (with H. Harrison) *Ahead of Time.*

**WILLIS W. HARMAN** is associate director of the Center for the Study of Social Policy at the Stanford Research Institute and professor of Engineering Economic Systems at Stanford University. His long association with futures research has culminated in a recently published book, *An Incomplete Guide to the Future.*

**YUJIRO HAYASHI** is a professor at the Tokyo Institute of Technology and president, Tokyo Institute of Future Technology. He has served as the chairman of the Japan Society of Futurology.

**OLAF HELMER**, after many years with the RAND Corporation, was appointed Quinton Professor of Futures Research at the Center for

Futures Research of the University of Southern California. His many publications include *Social Technology* and the monograph, *On the Future State of the Union.* He has been responsible for devising several widely used forecasting methods.

**HAZEL HENDERSON** is co-director of the Princeton Center for Alternative Futures. A lecturer and civic activist, her writings have appeared in many journals and anthologies. She is the co-author of the forthcoming *Managing the Decline of Industrialization.*

**RICHARD L. HENSHEL** teaches sociology at the University of Western Ontario and is a contributor to sociological journals. The author of two textbooks (*Reacting to Social Problems* and *Perspectives on Social Problems*), he has also published the monograph, *On the Future of Social Prediction.*

**KIM QUAILE HILL** teaches courses in forecasting techniques and research methodology in the program in Studies of the Future, University of Houston at Clear Lake City. A political scientist, Dr. Hill's published articles reflect his interests in public policy, comparative politics, and research methods.

**IDA R. HOOS**, a research sociologist at the Space Sciences Laboratory of the University of California, Berkeley, has as her general scholarly concern the utilization and assessment of technology; her special interest is in methodological aspects. Her writings on the subject include many journal articles as well as the book, *Systems Analysis in Public Policy.*

**FRANK SNOWDEN HOPKINS** is vice-president of the World Future Society, which he helped to start in 1966 and which he has served in a variety of administrative roles ever since. After a long career in the Foreign Service, he retired from the Policy Planning Council in 1968.

**BETTINA J. HUBER** teaches sociology at the University of California at Santa Barbara. She is the compiler of a highly regarded bibliography of futures research, "Studies of the Future: A Selected and Annotated Bibliography," in W. Bell and J. A. Mau, *The Sociology of the Future.* Her continuing research on images of the future has lately centered on South African leaders and American college students.

**DENIS F. JOHNSTON** is director of the Social Indicators Project of the executive branch's Office of Management and Budget. His publications include *Social Indicators 1976.*

**HERMAN KAHN** is a founder and director of the Hudson Institute, a policy research organization. Among his books are *On Thermonuclear War, The Year 2000,* and most recently, *The Next 200 Years.*

**MARVIN KORNBLUH,** long involved in public policy analysis and operations research, has written on simulation modeling, information systems development, and the application of futures research techniques to issues in energy, climate, and transportation. Currently, he is a futures research analyst in the Congressional Research Service of the Library of Congress.

**ERVIN LASZLO** is on the faculty of the program in Studies of the Future, University of Houston at Clear Lake City. Dr. Laszlo is the author or editor of over twenty books, including *A Strategy for the Future* and the fourth Club of Rome report, *Goals for Mankind.*

**HAROLD A. LINSTONE**, editor of the journal *Technological Forecasting and Social Change,* is also director of the Futures Research Institute at Portland State University. He has co-edited *The Delphi Method: Techniques and Applications, Technological Substitution,* and, most recently *Futures Research: New Directions.*

**DENNIS LIVINGSTON** is a political scientist at Rensselaer Polytechnic Institute, where he teaches courses in alternative world futures and the social science aspects of science fiction. His publications range across the fields of international environmental affairs, world order, science fiction, technology and public policy, and appropriate technology. *Futures* carries his regular column, "Science Fiction Survey."

**THOMAS R. MCFAUL,** a sociologist, writes on the interrelationships of society, religion, and science. He teaches courses on religion and social change, and on biomedical futures, in the Studies of the Future program at the University of Houston at Clear Lake City.

**JOHN MCHALE,** director of the Center for Integrative Studies at the University of Houston, has published extensively on resources, technology, mass communications, and the future. His recent books include *The Changing Information Environment, The Futures Directory, World Facts and Trends, The Ecological Context,* and *The Future of the Future.* Dr. McHale is also known as an artist and designer.

**J. MICHAEL MCLEAN** is a research fellow with the Science Policy Research Unit of the University of Sussex, England. He has served as a computing consultant to the United Kingdom Department of Health and Social Security, UNESCO, and ILO. He has published over twenty articles on modeling methods.

**JOSEPH P. MARTINO** held numerous assignments concerned with technological forecasting and research and development planning during his career with the Air Force. Now at the University of Dayton Research Institute, he continues his research into technological forecasting, technology assessment, and technology planning. Dr. Martino has edited four books on forecasting and planning, and has authored *Technological Forecasting for Decision Making.* He is an associate editor of the journal *Technological Forecasting and Social Change.*

**MAGOROH MARUYAMA** is an anthropologist currently at the Center for Advanced Study of the University of Illinois. He has contributed numerous articles to futures journals and has edited *Cultures Beyond the Earth* and *Cultures of the Future.*

**ELEONORA BARBIERI MASINI** was for several years responsible for compiling the directory *Social and Human Forecasting* for the Institute for Futures Research and Education in Rome. She is now secretary-general of the World Future Studies Federation.

**JAY S. MENDELL** is professor of business and public administration at Florida Atlantic University. During his ten years in the aircraft industry, Dr. Mendell devised one of the first early-warning systems for social and technological change. He is a member of the editorial advisory board of several futures journals, including *The Futurist* and *Technological Forecasting and Social Change.*

**IAN MILES,** a social psychologist by training, is a fellow at the Science Policy Research Unit of the University of Sussex, England, where he contributes to their extensive research and publication program. His books include *The Poverty of Prediction* and the co-authored *World Futures: The Great Debate.*

**JAMES O'TOOLE,** a specialist in public policy, is senior research associate at the Center for Futures Research, University of Southern California. He is the principal author of *Work in America* and the author of two recent books, *Energy and Social Change,* and *Work, Learning and the American Future.*

**INDIRA RAJARAMAN** teaches at the Indian Institute of Management in Bangalore, India. She was previously attached to the Department of Economic and Social Affairs of the United Nations.

**WILLIAM L. RENFRO,** who has degrees in physics, law, and nuclear engineering, has worked as a futurist in management consulting. Presently he is an analyst in Futures Research with the Congressional Research Service of the Library of Congress.

**PETER SCHWARTZ** joined the Center for the Study of Social Policy at Stanford Research Institute after teaching futures research at San Jose State University. He is currently leading a project for the Office of Science and Technology Policy to assess future national and international problems.

**HAROLD G. SHANE** is University Professor of Education at Indiana University. He has authored or co-authored more than 300 articles and over 100 books, among them *The Educational Significance of the Future.*

**JOHN G. STOVER** is a member of the senior staff of The Futures Group. He has worked extensively on the development of forecasting techniques and their application to policy analysis, and is now setting up an interactive computerized forecasting system.

**ROY A. WEAVER** teaches graduate courses in curriculum and instruction, and in futures studies, at the School of Education, University of Southern California. He is the author of the forthcoming *Beyond Identity: Education and the Role of Black Americans in the Future.*

**IAN H. WILSON** conducts policy research for the General Electric Company, where he helped establish one of the first futures research offices, Business Environment Studies. He is the co-author of *Business Environment of the Seventies* and *Corporate Environments of the Future: Planning for Major Change.*